W9-APY-560

THE COMPLETE STUDY GUIDE FOR SCORING HIGH

HOW TO PASS Employment Tests

By Arthur Liebers

- Vital Help in Passing High on All Types of Employment Tests Given by Private Industry.
- Analysis, Complete Study Material, Practice Questions and Answers For All the Most Important Tests and Subjects.
- The Inside Story on Interview Rating Forms and Personality Tests.
- Essential for Anyone Seeking Career Employment or Promotion in His Present Job.

arco 219 Park Avenue South
New York, N.Y. 10003

Sixth Edition B-3306

Published by ARCO PUBLISHING COMPANY, INC.
219 Park Avenue South, New York, N.Y. 10003

Library of Congress Catalog
Card Number 75-37088

Arco Catalog Number 668-00715-X

Printed in the United States of America

CONTENTS

HOW TO USE THIS INDEX
Slightly bend the right-hand edge of the book. This will expose the corresponding Parts which match the index, below.

PART

1

2

3

4

5

...continued on next page

CONTENTS continued

PART

1

2

3

4

5

PART THREE
STUDYING FOR ADVANCEMENT TO SUPERVISORY POSITIONS

CONTENTS continued

PART

1

2

3

4

5

PART FOUR
INTENSIVE STUDY COVERING THE RANGE OF QUESTIONS PUT BY EMPLOYERS

...continued on next page

CONTENTS continued

PART

1

2

3

4

5

PART FIVE
ABILITY TO REASON AND PERCEIVE SPATIAL RELATIONS

OVERCOMING EMPLOYMENT TESTS

Please read this book studiously. It required a great deal of research and took a long time to write. Although its careful organization and style will enable you to finish it easily, it deserves more than a casual skimming. You owe yourself the advantage of giving it all the time it demands. Thorough study will be well rewarded.

IN principle, these examinations are designed to measure the aptitudes, skills, and experience needed to perform acceptably the duties of the position that is to be filled. The idea behind the examination is not only to distinguish between applicants who have the required abilities and those who do not, but also to select those who are best qualified in a lesser degree. The applicants who receive the highest scores on the pre-employment tests have the best opportunity for appointment.

In practice it has been noted that the same questions recur on many different tests, and that the same types of questions appear on test after test. By studying the type of tests which are given for the type of job which he is seeking, the user of this book can improve his chances of making a test grade that will get him the job.

Types of Examinations

SOME tests measure *aptitude*—the ability to learn to perform the duties of a position. These tests are used for positions that do not require previous specialized training or experience. Aptitude tests select the persons who have the characteristics that are known to be related to success on the job. A good example is the dexterity test in which the applicants copy a pattern of dots in squares by pricking pinholes in smaller squares. The ability to do this extremely delicate work accurately and well is valuable in jobs that require the assembling of fine mechanical equipment; it is also related to success in training for draftsmen positions.

Examples of other aptitude tests are: (1) The checking test used for clerical positions; (2) tests of reasoning ability, used in combination with other tests for positions requiring alert mental processes and the use of good judgment; and (3) tests on the understanding of mechanical movements—an ability needed in various trades.

Other tests *measure achievement* in certain fields, such as physics or other sciences, and others measure *skills*, for example skill in shorthand.

Sometimes an examination consists of several short tests of different kinds. Such an examination is given when a certain combination of abilities has been found necessary to perform the duties of a position successfully.

Sometimes more weight is given to certain parts of a test if these parts have been found to measure the abilities most important to the successful performance of the duties of the position. Test papers are scored, with any weighting that is needed, so that the persons who earn the highest scores are the ones who have to the highest degree the abilities and skills necessary for success on the job.

Timing of Tests

TESTS are timed for two reasons. To set a limit on the time for answering the questions, and to conduct the examination in a uniform way for all applicants for the same job. Limits may be set to allow competitors a generous time to work on difficult questions. The limit of this type of test, called a *power test,* allows everyone who has a good grasp of the subject to finish within the prescribed time. A *speed test,* on the other hand, has a short time limit because it is designed to rank the applicants on their speed and accuracy in the performance of a large number of repetitive tasks. Older people sometimes object to this type of test, which they feel handicaps them; but if speed is important on the job, it must be considered in selecting people for the job.

Examples of tests that combine speed and a specific ability are the clerical checking tests, the dexterity tests and the measuring gage test. In each of these tests more questions are given than any applicant is expected to finish. The number of correct answers determines the score.

It surprises most people to find that "slow but sure" is not generally true. Years ago, experiments were made to find whether mail clerks who were slow in sorting made up for the smaller amount of work done by making fewer errors. The work of the fastest 25% of a large number of clerks was compared with the slowest 25%. It was found that only an insignificant number of errors was made, but of these, the slow group accounted for nearly three times as many as the fast group. At the same time, the employer's dollar was buying more than twice as much work from the fast group of sorters. After selection procedures were revised to include a speed test, nearly all the new clerks appointed were better workers than the average clerk selected by the old style examination.

The speed test in an examination is generally given for 15 minutes or less, during which everyone is working at top speed. On the job, the fastest clerks find it no great effort to work at a fairly good rate all day. If an applicant who failed the speed test were to try the same job, he would be putting in more effort and doing less than half as much work.

Test Research

AS you will see in later chapters, there is considerable criticism of the widespread use of these written tests in selecting and promoting employees. However, as long as they are being so widely used by private industry and in government, the job-seeker and worker must meet the situation by trying to do his best on the tests that he will face while hunting for a job or searching for a better job.

The psychologists who prepare these tests say that they are constantly aiming to improve the examinations. When a new test is developed for a special aptitude, or for an acquired skill or knowledge, it is usually tried out on a number of persons known to possess that characteristic. If the persons known to possess the skill, aptitude or knowledge in a high degree get high scores on a test, and those known to possess it in a lower degree get low scores, the test is considered to be valid.

However, preparation of these tests has been refined to such a point that getting a too-high score on part of a test may actually count against you, because the job or promotion may call for a low score on a certain test or part of a test. (See the Section "How to Cheat on Personality Tests" for more on that phase of beating the test-makers at their own game.)

When the psychologists feel that the important elements necessary for success in a certain type of work can be measured by suitable tests, an examination containing the essential tests is prepared and is used for employee selection.

Sometimes, as one of the forms of research by which the psychologists "prove" their tests, they make a follow-up study of the job performance of those hired after testing. The purpose of test research is to develop tests that are practical, fair to all applicants and appropriate for the jobs to be filled.

Using This Book

ON the first 35 pages of this book you will find samples of many of the tests given persons who apply for employment. In most cases, correct answers are shown as they appear if marked on the standard answer sheet.

All the types of questions that are likely to be encountered in pre-employment tests have been included, and additional material, to enable you to practice answering such questions, appears on later pages. Other types of questions may be encountered as new tests are developed in the future, but the main principle—making a choice from among several suggested answers will be the same in most cases.

None of the questions in this section may appear on the actual job test you take, although some of them may be used as practice questions. Practice questions are given to competitors in most examinations before they begin work on the actual examinations. They are allowed time to work them and set down the answers, but the answer sheet is not counted in the score. In this way, each competitor can better understand what he is expected to do. Sometimes, most often in government job tests, the applicant will be sent sample questions when he applies for the job, so that he can study them before reporting for an examination.

It is fairly obvious that just memorizing the questions and answers will prove of little help. What you should try to do is understand the way in which the answers must be recorded. If you feel that practice with some of the tests will help you, you can make your own practice material for a good many of them. For example, copy a list of names, copy it again with some changes, and then time yourself as you try to spot the differences. Copy telephone numbers and use them to practice addition. Use your own dictionary for spelling and vocabulary practice. Find your old grade school books for arithmetic problems. In addition, use the study material in back of this book for your job test and for tests for related jobs which may cover the same field.

Written examinations when they are used as the chief means of selection are naturally intended to be difficult enough to eliminate those who could not perform the duties of the position. The samples on the following 35 pages do not, for the most part, represent the material covered in any one specific test, nor do they always indicate the difficulty of the test. For the more difficult jobs, more difficult questions are asked. However the questions in the following sections are closer in content and in difficulty to the actual test questions.

If certain kinds of questions seem hard to you, do not worry about it. People have different aptitudes. For example, a person who has a great deal of difficulty checking names and numbers may be far ahead of others in ability to understand mechanical problems.

Many examinations make use of an answer sheet that is scored by machine. In such cases you will be given a special pencil that must be used in order to have the scoring machine count properly. Whenever a machine-scored examination is used, you will be given a few sample questions so that you can practice recording the answers. There are many examples of machine-scored question and answer sheet sections in this section.

SCORING HIGH ON EMPLOYMENT TESTS

WHAT THIS BOOK WILL DO FOR YOU

To get the greatest help from this book, please understand that it has been carefully organized. You must, therefore, plan to use it accordingly. Study this concise, readable book earnestly and your way will be clear. You will progress directly to your goal. You will not be led off into blind alleys and useless fields of study.

Arco Publishing Company has followed testing trends and methods ever since the firm was founded in 1937. We have specialized in books that prepare people for tests. Based on this experience it is our modest boast that you probably have in your hands the best book that could be prepared to help *you* score high. Now, if you'll take a little advice on using it properly, we can assure you that you will do well.

To write this book we carefully analyzed every detail surrounding the forthcoming examination . . .

* the job itself
* official and unofficial announcements concerning the examination
* all the available previous examinations
* many related examinations
* technical literature that explains and forecasts the examination.

As a result of all this (which you, happily, have not had to do) we've been able to create the "climate" of your test, and to give you a fairly accurate picture of what's involved. Some of this material, digested and simplified, actually appears in print here, if it was deemed useful and suitable in helping you score high.

But more important than any other benefit derived from this research is our certainty that the study material, the text and the practice questions are right for you.

The practice questions you will study have been judiciously selected from hundreds of thousands of previous test questions on file here at Arco. But they haven't just been thrown at you pell mell. They've been organized into the subjects that you can expect to find on your test. As you answer the questions, these subjects will take on greater meaning for you. At the same time you will be getting valuable practice in answering test questions. You will proceed with a sure step toward a worthwhile goal: high test marks.

Studying in this manner, you will get the feel of the entire examination. You will learn by "insight," by seeing through a problem as a result of experiencing *previous similar situations.* This is true learning according to many psychologists.

In short, what you get from this book will help you operate at top efficiency . . . make you give the best possible account of yourself on the actual examination.

CAN YOU PREPARE YOURSELF FOR YOUR TEST?

We believe, most certainly, that you *can* with the aid of this "self-tutor!"

It's not a "pony." It's not a complete college education. It's not a "crib sheet," and it's no HOW TO SUCCEED ON TESTS WITHOUT REALLY TRYING. There's nothing in it that will give you a higher score than you really deserve.

It's just a top quality course which you can readily review in less than twenty hours . . . a digest of material which you might easily have written yourself after about five thousand hours of laborious digging.

To really prepare for your test you must motivate yourself . . . get into the right frame of mind for learning from your "self-tutor." You'll have to urge *yourself* to learn and that's the only way people ever learn. Your efforts to score high on the test will be greatly aided by the fact that you will have to do this job on your own . . . perhaps without a teacher. Psychologists have demonstrated that studies undertaken for a clear goal . . . which you initiate yourself and actively pursue . . . are the most successful. You, yourself, want to pass this test. That's why you bought this book and embarked on this program. Nobody forced you to do it, and there may be nobody to lead you through the course. Your self-activity is going to be the key to your success in the forthcoming weeks.

Used correctly, your "self-tutor" will show you what to expect and will give you a speedy brush-up on the subjects peculiar to your exam. Some of these are subjects not taught in schools at all. Even if your study time is very limited, you should:

- Become familiar with the type of examination you will meet.
- Improve your general examination-taking skill.
- Improve your skill in analyzing and answering questions involving reasoning, judgment, comparison, and evaluation.
- Improve your speed and skill in reading and understanding what you read—an important part of your ability to learn and an important part of most tests.
- Prepare yourself in the particular fields which measure your learning—

  Vocabulary
  Problem solving

This book will tell you exactly what to study by presenting in full every type of question you will get on the actual test. You'll do better merely by familiarizing yourself with them.

This book will help you find your weaknesses and find them fast. Once you know where you're weak you can get right to work (before the test) and concentrate your efforts on those soft spots. This is the kind of selective study which yields maximum test results for every hour spent.

This book will give you the *feel* of the exam. Almost all our sample and practice questions are taken from actual previous exams. Since previous exams are not always available for inspection by the public, these sample test questions are quite important for you. The day you take your exam you'll see how closely this book follows the format of the real test.

This book will give you confidence *now*, while you are preparing for the test. It will build your self-confidence as you proceed. It will beat those dreaded before-test jitters that have hurt so many other test-takers.

This book stresses the modern, multiple-choice type of question because that's the kind you'll undoubtedly get on your test. In answering these questions you will add to your knowledge by learning the correct answers, naturally. However, you will not be satisfied with merely the correct choice for each question. You will want to find out why the other choices are incorrect. This will jog your memory . . . help you remember much you thought you had forgotten. You'll be preparing and enriching yourself for the exam to come.

Of course, the great advantage in all this lies in narrowing your study to just those fields in which you're most likely to be quizzed. Answer enough questions in those fields and the chances are very good that you'll meet a few of them again on the actual test. After all, the number of questions an examiner can draw upon in these fields is rather limited. Examiners frequently employ the same questions on different tests for this very reason.

Probably the most important element of tests which you can learn is vocabulary. Most testers consider your vocabulary range an important indication of what you have learned in your life, and therefore, an important measuring rod of your learning ability. With some concentration and systematic study, you can increase your vocabulary substantially and thus increase your score on most tests.

After testing yourself, you may find that your reading ability is poor. It may be wise to take the proper remedial measures now.

If you find that your reasoning ability or your ability to handle mathematical problems is weak, there are ways of improving your skill in these fields.

There are other things which you should know and which various sections of this book will help you learn. Most important, not only for this examination but for all the examinations to come in your life, is learning how to take a test and how to prepare for it.

JOB OPPORTUNITIES

Young people in an ever growing and changing society are faced with the difficult task of choosing sound career plans from among the thousands of alternatives. As the economy continues to expand, creating more and different kinds of jobs, this planning process becomes more difficult. Making career plans calls for an evaluation of an individual's interests and abilities, as well as for specific information on occupations.

Several questions are of major importance to young persons as they view the variety of occupational choices open to them. Among these questions are: What fields look especially promising for employment opportunities? What competition can be expected from other workers? What type and how much training and education are required in order to enter particular jobs? How do earnings in certain occupations compare with earnings in other occupations requiring similar training? What types of employers provide which kinds of jobs? What are the typical working conditions associated with particular occupations?

Of importance in evaluating information that answers these and related questions is knowledge of the dynamic changes that are continually occurring in our economy—the trends in the Nation's work force and in its business, industrial, and occupational development. New ways of making goods, new products, and changes in living standards are constantly changing the types of jobs that become available. To throw light on the changing characteristics of occupations and to provide background for understanding the outlook in specific occupations, this chapter focuses on overall patterns of change in the country's industrial and occupational composition. It also discusses the implications of these changes for education and training in relation to occupational choice.

No one can forecast the future. Nevertheless, by using the wealth of information available, extensive economic and statistical analyses, and the best judgment of informed experts, the work future can be described in broad terms. Of course, some aspects of the future can be predicted more accurately than others. For example, the number of 18-year-olds in 1985 can be estimated with a very high degree of accuracy because individuals 5 years old in 1972 are accounted for in our vital statistics, and the death rate of children between 5 and 18 is extremely low and stays about the same from year to year. On the other hand, forecasting employment requirements for automobile assemblers in 1985 is extremely difficult. Employment of these workers can be affected by the changing demand for American-made automobiles, shifts in buyers' preference (toward the compact car, for example), changes in the ways cars are made (more automation or the use of new types of engines), and unpredictable economic developments outside of the automobile industry.

To project the demand for all workers in the economy, specific assumptions have to be made about general economic movements and broad national policy. The picture of the future employment outlook is based on the following fundamental assumptions:

1. Maintenance of high levels of employment and of utilization of available manpower in 1985;

2. that no major event such as long-duration or widespread energy shortages will alter substantially the rate of economic growth. (Although energy shortages are being experienced in the economy no conclusive assessments can be made at this time of the magnitude or duration of the shortages or their long-run effect on employment either as a factor stimulating or restricting employment opportunities in specific industries or occupations.)

3. that economic, social, and educational trends will continue to change according to patterns of the recent past;

4. that scientific-technological advancement will continue at about the same rate as in recent years;

5. that the United States will not be at war, but that there will be no substantial reduction in the defense budget beyond that already in effect.

This assessment of the 1985 industrial and occupational outlook assumes a projected total labor force of 107.7 million in 1985, all-volunteer Armed Forces of 2.0

million, and a resulting civilian labor force of 105.7 million.

Knowledge of specific industries is necessary because employers seek a wide variety of skills; for example, many different industries employ engineers, salesmen, and secretaries. Employment patterns have shifted considerably over the years and are expected to continue to do so. These changes greatly affect employment opportunities and occupational choices.

Industrial employment and occupational requirements change as a result of many factors. A new machine or a newly automated process may require different occupational skills or may even create an entirely new occupation; a change in product demand may affect the number of workers needed; an invention may all but eliminate an industry or create a new one.

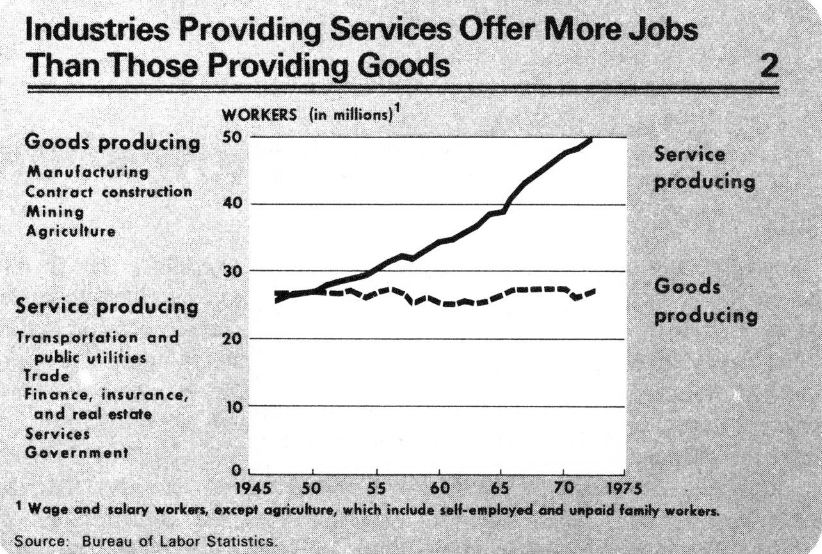

Industrial Profile

To help understand the Nation's industrial composition, industries may be viewed as either goods-producing or service-producing. They may further be grouped into nine major divisions according to product or service. (See chart 1.)

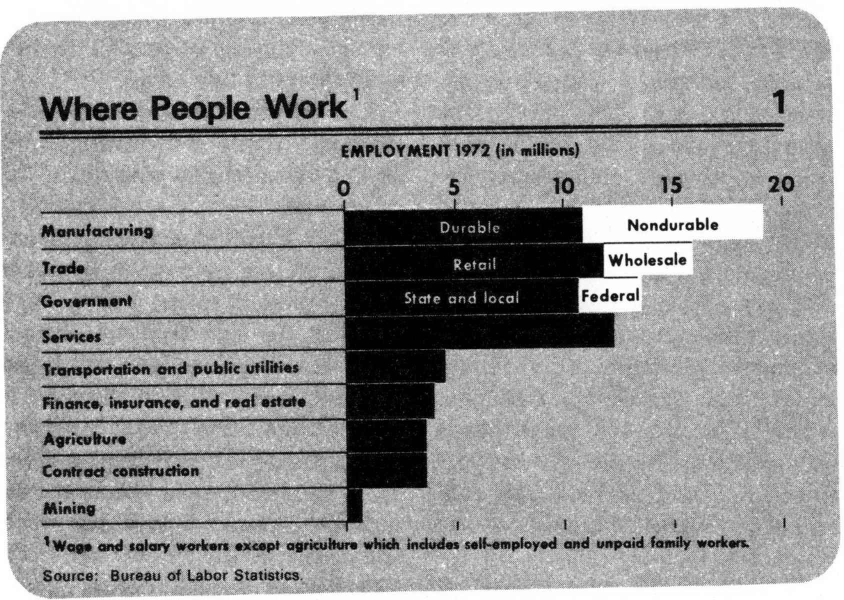

Most of the Nation's workers are in industries that produce services, in activities such as education, health care, trade, repair and maintenance, and in government, transportation, and banking and insurance service. The production of goods—raising food crops, building, extracting minerals, and manufacturing of goods—has required less than half of the country's work force since the late 1940's. (See chart 2.) In general, job growth through the 1970's is expected to continue to be faster in the service-producing industries than in the goods-producing industries. However, among industry divisions within both the goods-producing and service-producing sectors, the growth pattern will continue to vary. (See chart 3.)

Service-producing industries. In 1972, about 49.7 million workers were on the payrolls of service-producing industries—trade; Government; services and miscellaneous; transportation and other utilities; and finance, insurance, and real estate—about 15.9 million greater than the number employed in 1960. The major factors underlying the rapid growth of the 1960's have been (1) population growth; (2) increasing urbanization with its accompanying need for more city services; and (3) rising income and living standards accompanying demand for improved services, such as health, education, and security. These factors are expected to continue to result in rapid growth of service industries as a group, and they are expected to help employ (8.7 million by 1985, an increase of about 38 percent over the 1972 level.

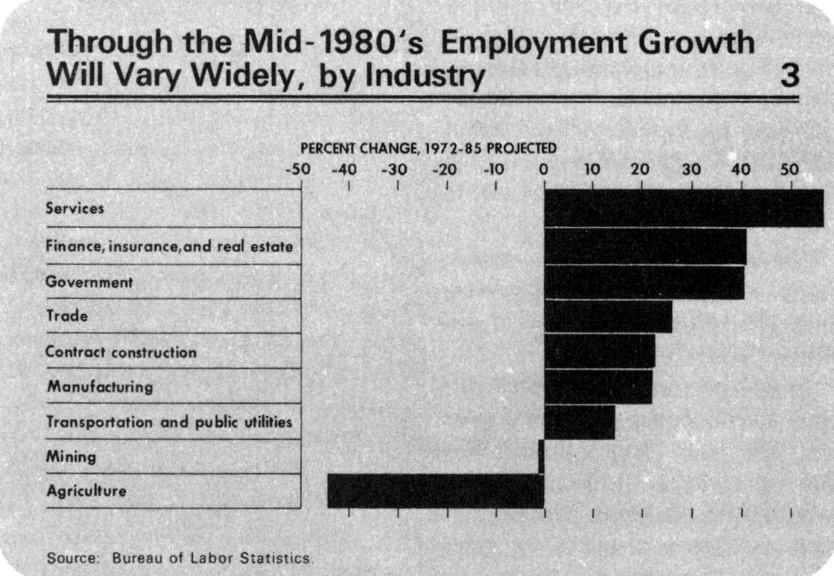

Trade, the largest division within the service-producing industries, has expanded sharply since 1960. Wholesale and retail outlets have multiplied in large and small cities to satisfy the need of an increasingly urban society. Employment in trade was about 15.7 million in 1972, about 38 percent above the 1960 level.

Employment in trade is expected to grow by about 26 percent between 1972 and 1985. Although an ever-increasing volume of merchandise will be distributed as a result of increases in population and consumer expenditures, the rate of increase in manpower needs will be slowed by laborsaving technology, such as the greater use of electronic data processing equipment and automated warehousing equipment, growth in the number of self-service stores, and the growing use of vending machines.

Government employment has grown faster than any other industry division, and has increased by almost three-fifths, from 8.4 million to 13.3 million, between 1960 and 1972. Growth has been mostly at the State and local levels, which together expanded by more than two-thirds. Employment growth has been greatest in agencies providing education, health, sanitation, welfare, and protective services. Federal Government employment increased about 21 percent between 1960 and 1972.

Government will continue to be a major source of new jobs through the mid-1980's. By the mid-1980's employment in Government may be as much as 42 percent higher than in 1972. Most of the growth will be in State and local governments, in which employment needs may rise by 1985 to 16.0 million, about 50 percent higher than the 10.6 million employed in 1972. Federal Government employment is expected to rise slowly to about 2.8 million in 1985, 150,000 or about 6 percent above the 1972 level of 2.7 million.

Service and miscellaneous industries employment has increased rapidly since World War II as a result of the growing need for maintenance and repair, advertising, domestic, and health care services. From 1960 to 1972, total employment in this industry division rose by about two-thirds, from 7.4 million to about 12.3 million.

Service and miscellaneous industries will continue to be among the fastest-growing industries through the mid-1980's. More than half again as many workers are expected to be employed in this industry division in 1985 as in 1972. Manpower requirements in health services are expected to grow rapidly due to population growth and the increasing ability of persons to pay for health care. Business services, including accounting, data processing, and maintenance, also are expected to grow very rapidly.

Transportation and public utility employment in 1972 at 4.5 million was only slightly more than one-tenth higher than in 1960. Different parts of this industry, however, have experienced different growth trends. For example, air travel employment increased rapidly but the railroad industry declined.

The number of jobs in transportation, and in public utilities as a whole, is expected to continue to increase slowly to 1985, and widely differing employment trends will continue to be experienced among individual industries within the division. Rapid increases in employment are expected in air transportation, and a decline is expected to continue in railroad employment, and little or no change is expected in water transportation. Overall employment in this industry division is expected to increase to almost 5.2 million in 1985, 15 percent above the 1972 level.

Finance, insurance, and real estate, the smallest of the service-producing industry divisions, has grown about 47 percent since 1960 to more than 3.9 million in 1972. Employment has grown especially rapidly in banks; in credit agencies; and among security and commodity brokers, dealers, exchanges, and services.

Job growth in finance, insurance, and real estate will keep in step with the overall employment increases of nonfarm employment through the mid-1980's. Finance, insurance, and real estate employment is expected to expand to nearly 5.6 million by 1985, about 42 percent above 1972 levels.

Goods-Producing Industries. Employment in the goods-producing industries—agriculture, manufacturing, construction, and mining—more than 26.5 million in 1972—has increased slowly in recent years. Significant gains in productivity resulting from automation and other technological developments as well as the growing skills of the work force have permitted large increases in output without corresponding increases in employment. Employment in goods-producing industries is expected to increase to about 30 million in 1985, 13 percent above the 1972 level. However, widely different patterns of employment changes have occurred and will continue among the industry divisions in the goods-producing sector.

Agriculture (farming), which until the late 1800's employed more than half of all workers in the economy, employed only 4 percent, or 3.5 million workers, in 1972. Increases in the average size of farms, rapid mechanization, and improved fertilizers, feeds, and pesticides have created large increases in output at the same time that employment has fallen sharply.

Farming is facing a continuing decline in manpower needs. Factors resulting in past declines will continue, and the outlook is for a 1985 farm work force 45 percent lower than in 1972.

Mining employment, at about 607,000 workers in 1972, has declined by nearly 15 percent since 1960, primarily because of labor-saving technological changes. This trend is likely to continue, and mining is the only nonagricultural industry division that is not expected to increase between 1972 and 1985.

Contract construction employment, at more than 3.5 million in 1972, has increased more than one-fifth since 1960. The Nation's growing need for homes, offices, stores, highways, bridges, dams, and other physical facilities resulted in this increase in employment.

Between 1972 and 1985, employment in contract construction is expected to grow by more than one-fifth to about 4.3 million.

Manufacturing, the largest division within the goods-producing sector that had about 18.9 million workers in 1972, increased about 13 percent in employment between 1960 and 1972. New products for industrial and consumer markets and the rapid growth of the defense-space market have spearheaded the post World War II growth.

Manufacturing employment is expected to increase about 23 percent through the mid-1980's and to reach about 3.2 million in 1985. Employment in durable goods manufacturing is projected to increase slightly faster, and nondurable goods somewhat more slowly than the total. However, the rate of growth will vary among the individual manufacturing industries.

Occupational Profile

As American industries continue to grow larger, more complex, and more mechanized, basic changes will take place in the Nation's occupational structure. Furthermore, occupations will become more complex and specialized. Thus, an imposing and confusing number of occupational choices is provided to individuals who are planning their careers. An individual, in examining the vast number of choices, should first look at broad groupings of jobs that have similar characteristics such as entrance requirements. (See chart 4.)

Among the most significant changes in the Nation's occupational structure has been the shift toward white-collar jobs. In 1956, for the first time in the Nation's history, white-collar workers—professional, managerial, clerical, and sales—outnumbered blue-collar workers—craftsmen, operatives, and laborers. (See chart 5.)

Through the 1970's, we can expect a continuation of the rapid growth of white-collar occupations, a slower-than-average growth of blue-collar occupations, a faster-than-average growth among service workers, and a

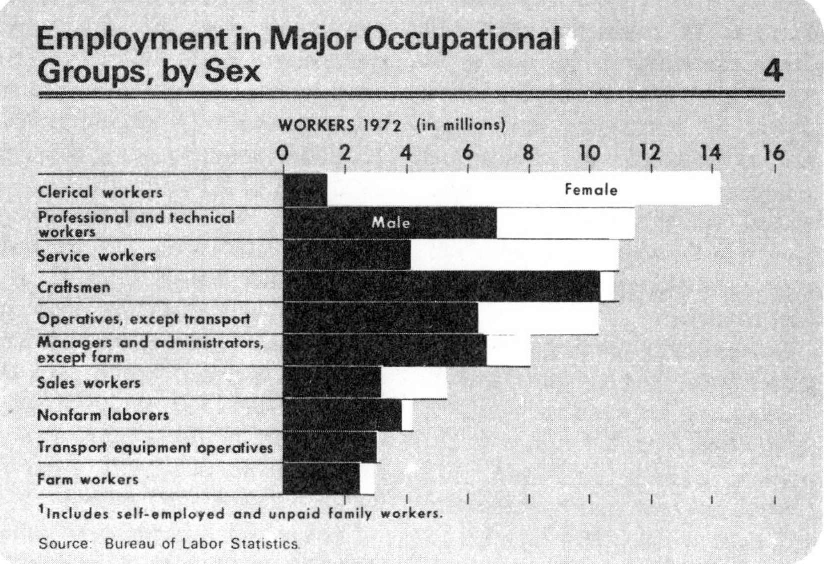

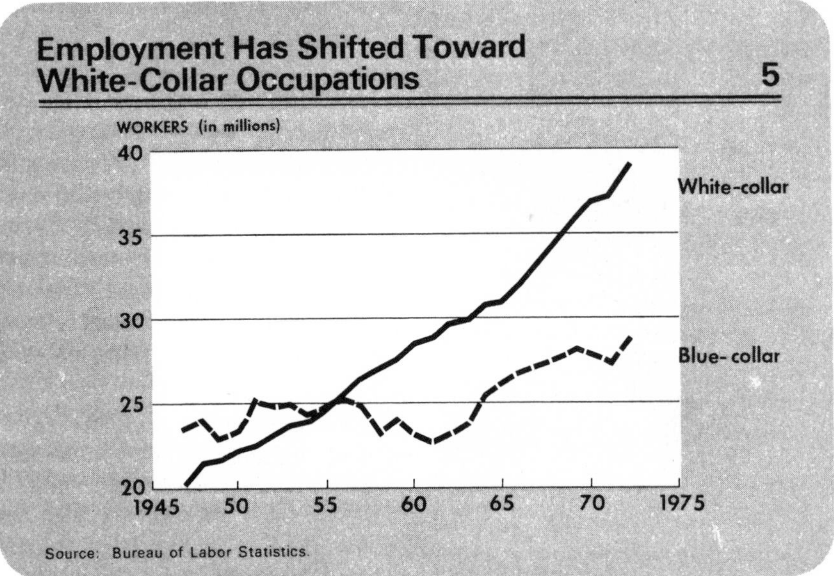

further decline of farm workers. Total employment is expected to increase about 24 percent between 1972 and 1985. In comparison, an increase of about 37 percent is expected for white-collar jobs, and only about 15 percent for blue-collar occupations. By 1985, white-collar jobs will account for more than one-half of all employed workers compared with about 48 percent in 1972. The rapid growth expected for white-collar workers and service workers reflects continuous expansion of the service-producing industries, which employ a relatively large proportion of these workers. The growing demand for workers to perform research and development, to provide education and health services, and to process the increasing amount of paperwork throughout all types of enterprises, also will be significant in the growth of white-collar jobs. The slower-than-average growth of blue-collar and farm workers reflects the expanding use of labor-saving equipment in our Nation's industries and the relatively slow growth of the goods-producing industries that employ large proportions of blue-collar workers. (See chart 6.)

The following section describes in greater detail the changes that are expected to occur among the broad occupational groups through the mid-1980's.

Professional and technical workers, the third largest occupational group in 1972, number about 11.5 million, and include such highly trained personnel as teachers, engineers, dentists, accountants, and clergymen.

Professional occupations will be the fastest-growing occupations from 1972-85. (See chart 7.) Workers in this area will be in great demand as the Nation makes greater efforts toward the country's socio-economic progress, urban renewal, transportation, harnessing the ocean, and enhancing the beauty of the land. The quest for scientific and technical knowledge is bound to grow, and to raise the demand for workers in scientific and technical specialties. The late 1970's and early 1980's will see a continuing emphasis on the social sciences and medical services. By 1985, the requirements for professional, technical, and kindred workers may be almost one-half greater than 1972 employment.

Managers, officials and proprietors totaled about 8.0 million in 1972. As a group they will increase about 30 percent between 1972 and 1985. As in the past, requirements for salaried managers are likely to continue to increase rapidly because of the increasing dependence of business organizations and government agencies on management specialists. On the other hand, the number of self-employed managers is expected to continue to decline as larger businesses continue to restrict growth of the total number of firms,

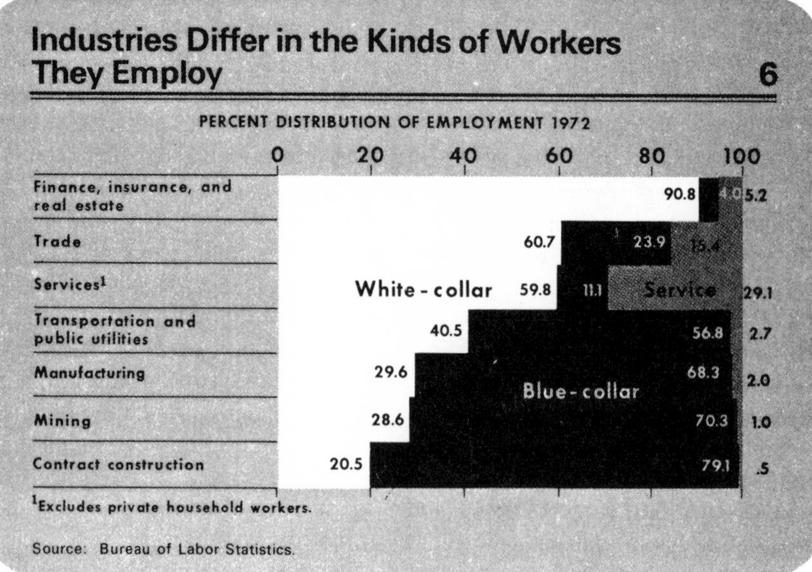

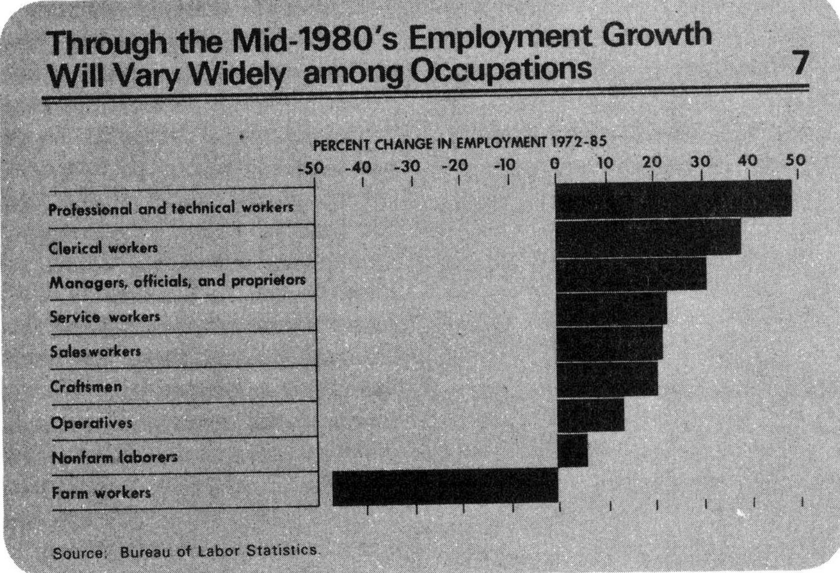

and as supermarkets continue to replace small groceries and general stores.

Clerical workers, numbering 14.2 million in 1972, include workers who operate computers and office machines, keep records, take dictation, and type. Clerical workers made up the largest group of workers in 1972. Many new clerical positions are expected to open up as industries employing large numbers of clerical workers continue to expand. The trend in retail stores toward transferring to clerical workers functions that were performed by salespersons also will tend to increase employment needs of clerical workers. The demand also will be strong for those qualified to handle jobs created by electronic data processing operations. The need for clerical workers as a group is expected to increase by almost two-fifths between 1972 and 1985.

Sales workers, accounting for about 5.4 million workers in 1972, are found primarily in retail stores, wholesale firms, insurance companies, real estate agencies, as well as offering goods door-to-door. Sales workers are expected to increase more than one-fifth between 1972 and 1985.

Increasing sales of many new products resulting from rapid population growth, new product development, business expansion, and rising business levels will be the major reason for increasing employment of sales workers.

Craftsmen, numbering about 10.8 million in 1972, include carpenters, tool and die makers, instrument makers, all-round machinists, electricians, and typesetters. Industrial growth and increasing business activity are the major factors expected to spur the growth of craft occupations through the mid 1980's. However, technological developments will tend to limit the expansion of this group. Craftsmen are expected to increase by about one-fifth, somewhat slower growth than the average for all occupations.

Semiskilled workers (operatives) made up the second largest major occupational group in 1972 with about 13.5 million workers engaged in assembling goods in factories; driving trucks, buses and taxis; and operating machinery.

Employment of semiskilled workers is expected to increase about 13 percent above the 1972 level, despite continued technological advances that will reduce employment for some types of semiskilled occupations. Increases in production generated by rising population and rapid economic growth, as well as the increasing trend toward motor truck transportation of freight, are expected to be major factors contributing to the increasing employment.

Laborers (excluding those in farming and mining), who numbered nearly 4.2 million workers in 1972, for the most part move, lift, and carry materials and tools in the Nation's workplaces. Employment of laborers is expected to increase slightly between 1972 and 1985 in spite of the rises in manufacturing and construction, which employ most laborers. Increased demand is expected to be offset by rising productivity resulting from continued substitution of mechanical equipment for manual labor.

Service workers, including men and women who maintain law and order, assist professional nurses in hospitals, give haircuts and beauty treatments, serve food, and clean and care for our homes, totaled about 11.0 million in 1972. This diverse group will increase about 22 percent between 1972 and 1985. Some of the main factors that are expected to increase requirements for these occupations are the rising demand for hospital and other medical care; the greater need for protective services as urbanization continues and cities become more crowded; and the more frequent use of restaurants, beauty parlors, and other services as income levels rise and as an increasing number of housewives take jobs outside the home.

Farm workers—including farmers, farm managers, laborers, and foremen—numbered nearly 3.1

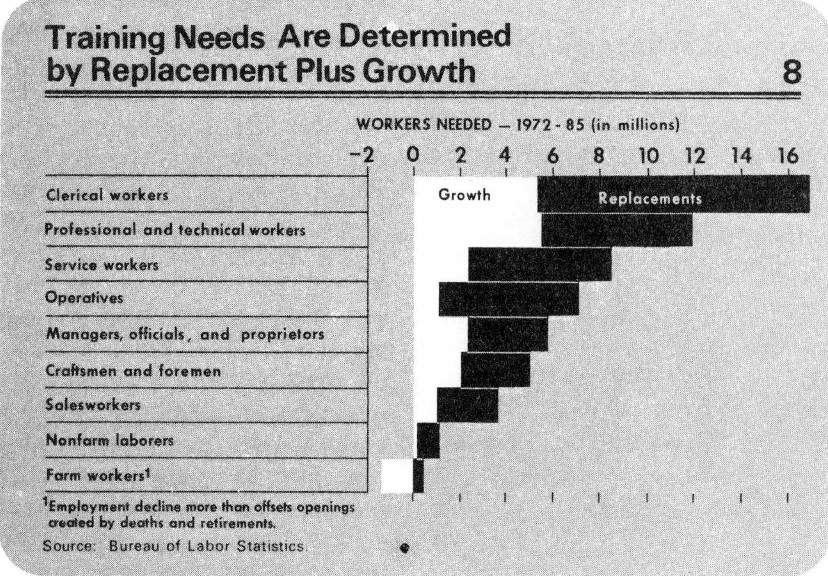

million in 1972. Employment requirements for farm workers are expected to decline to about 1.6 million in 1985. This decrease is anticipated, in part, because of continued improvement in farm technology.

Job Openings

In considering careers, young people should not eliminate occupations just because their preferences will not be among the most rapidly growing. Although growth is a key indicator of future job outlook, more jobs will be created between 1972-85 from deaths, retirements, and other labor force separations than from employment growth. (See chart 8.) Replacement needs will be particularly significant in occupations which have a large proportion of older workers and women. Furthermore, large occupations that have little growth may offer more openings than a fast-growing, small one. For example, among the major occupational groups, openings for operatives resulting from growth and replacement combined will be greater than for craftsmen, although the rate of growth in the employment of craftsmen will be considerably more rapid than the rate of growth for operatives.

Outlook and Education

Numerous opportunities for employment will be available for job-seekers during the years ahead. Employers are seeking people who have higher levels of education because many jobs are more complex and require greater skill. Furthermore, employment growth generally will be fastest in those occupations requiring the most education and training. For example, professional occupations requiring the most education will show the fastest growth through the mid-1980's. (See chart 7.)

A high school education has become a standard for American workers. Thus, because of personnel practices in American industries, a high school graduate is in a better competitive position in the job market than a nongraduate.

Although training beyond high school has been the standard for some time for many professional occupations, many other areas of work require more than just a high school diploma. As new, automated equipment is introduced on a wider scale in offices, banks, insurance companies, and government operations, skill requirements are rising for clerical and other jobs. Employers increasingly are demanding better-trained workers to operate complicated machinery. In many areas of sales work, new developments in machine design, use of new materials, and the complexity of

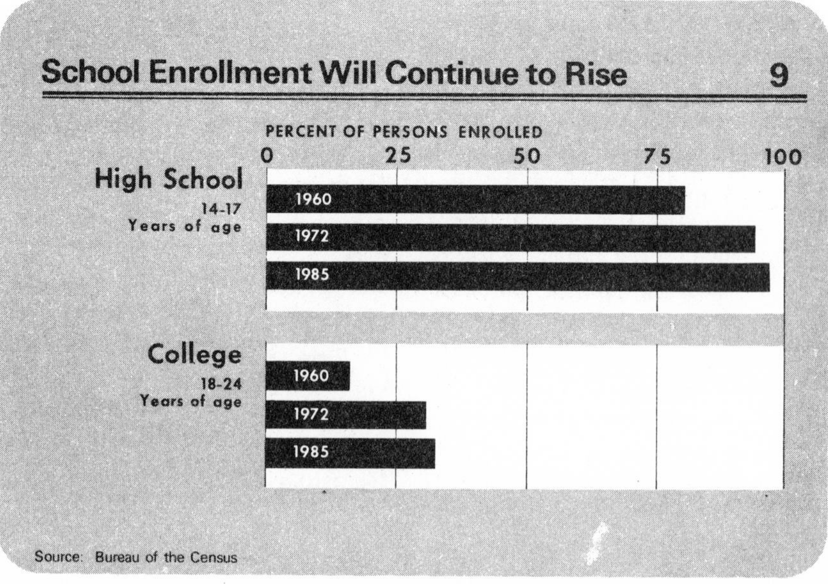

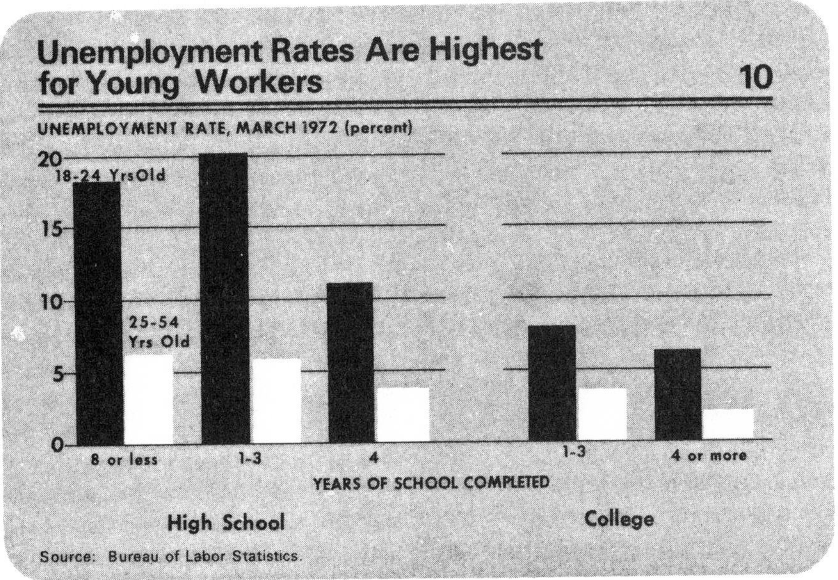

equipment are making greater technical knowledge a requirement for demonstrators; and repairmen must become familiar with even more complicated machines. Because many occupations are becoming increasingly complex and technical, specific occupational training such as that obtained through apprenticeship, junior and community colleges, and post-high school vocational education courses is becoming more and more important to young people preparing for successful careers.

As part of the demand for greater education, the proportion of youth in high school has increased, and an even larger proportion of high school graduates pursue higher education. (See chart 9.) This trend is expected to continue through the mid-1980's.

With so much competition from young people who have higher levels of education, the boy or girl who does not get good preparation for work will find the going more difficult in the years ahead. Employers will be more likely to hire workers who have at least a high school diploma. Furthermore, present experience shows that the less education and training a worker has, the less chance he has for a steady job, because unemployment falls most heavily on the worker who has the least education. (See chart 10.)

In addition to its importance in competing for jobs, education is highly valued in the determination of income. According to the most recently available data, men who had college degrees could expect to earn more than $600,000 in their lifetimes, or nearly three times the $214,000 likely to be earned by workers who had less than 8 years of schooling, nearly twice that earned by workers who had 1 to 3 years of high school, and nearly one and two-thirds as much as high school graduates. Clearly the completion of high school pays a dividend. A worker who had only 1 to 3 years of high school could expect to earn only about $31,000 more than workers who had an elementary school education, but a high school graduate could look forward to a $94,000 lifetime income advantage over an individual completing elementary school. (See chart 11.)

In summary, young people who have acquired skills or good basic education will have a better chance for interesting work, good wages, and steady employment. Getting as much education and training as one's abilities and circumstance permit should therefore be a top priority for today's youth.

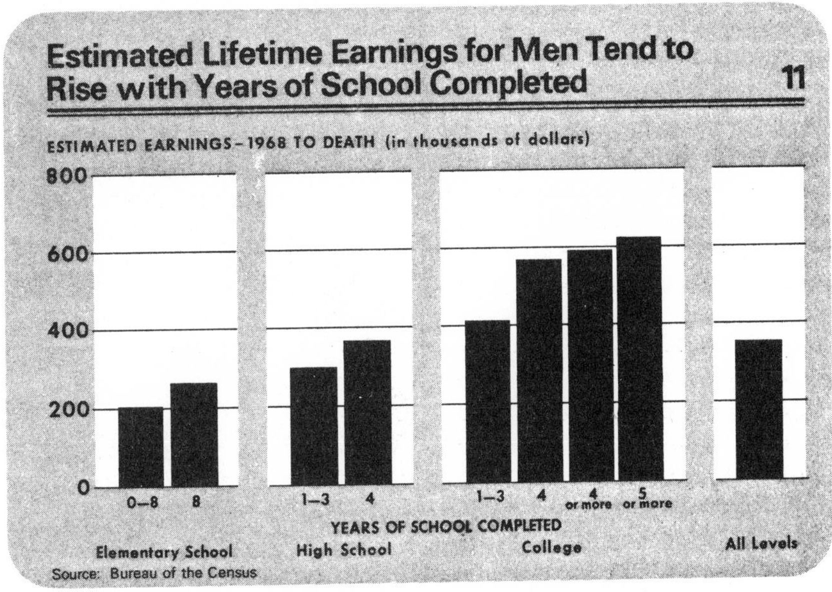

PART 1

Questions That Forecast Your Tests

What the Tests Mean

IT costs a company money to give a test. So when you are asked to take a test it generally means that the interviewer or the person who read your application form was favorably enough impressed to invest the company's time and money in checking your ability to perform the job. However, there are some exceptions to this general rule that you should keep in mind when job-hunting.

A number of fly-by-night sales operations use a sales aptitude test as a "gimmick" to lend respectability to their operations and to set an atmosphere in which they can induce people to work for them on a commission or percentage basis.

Some few companies use the "test" as an excuse to avoid hiring members of minority groups or to discourage annoyingly persistent job-seekers.

In general, however, the pre-employment test is just that, and a satisfactory score is usually the key to a place on the company's payroll.

Keep in mind that reputable employers use tests for the following six purposes:

1. To select employees who are qualified for employment—and not too highly qualified for the jobs which are open.

2. To insure the most effective employment of job applicants.

3. To eliminate floaters and job-skippers.

4. To discover "promotable" employees.

5. To check on the value of training programs.

6. And to check on employees' job interest, morale, and company loyalty.

I. EXAMINATION FORECAST

Sample Questions That Forecast the Test

If you want a preview of your exam, look these questions over carefully. We did . . . as we compiled them from official announcements and various other sources. A good part of this book is based on these prophetic questions. Practice and study material is geared closely to them. The time and effort you devote to the different parts of this book should be determined by the facility with which you answer the following questions.

A look at the following questions is the easiest, quickest, most important help you can get from this book. These predictive questions give you foresight by providing an "overview" with which to direct your study. They are actual samples of the question types you may expect on your test.

Before you're finished with this book you'll get plenty of practice with the best methods of answering each of these question types. However, you're going to do a little work yourself. You're going to plan your study to make sure that each available hour is used most effectively. You're going to concentrate where it will do you the most good. And you'll take it easy where you have no trouble.

In other words, discover what you're going to face on the test and make plans to pace yourself accordingly.

More and more positions in industry are being filled through examinations. Employment officers depend on tests such as those in this book to test the ability of job-applicants to do the work—as demonstrated by their performance on the test. Some of the larger companies prepare their own pre-employment tests. Others buy tests from different testing organizations and use them; still others call in outside testing organizations to do the job of qualifying or rejecting job applicants.

ANSWER SHEETS AND CORRECT ANSWERS APPEAR AFTER EACH TEST

Directory of Pre-Employment Tests

THE directory below lists some of the jobs for which more and more employers are using pre-employment tests as part of the hiring procedure. If you will turn to the pages indicated, you will find samples of the kinds of questions that are being used on these job tests. By studying them, you will have some idea of the questions used in an actual examination for the job in which you are interested. You should understand, however, that the actual examination may not include all the kinds of questions for which samples are given and it may include other kinds.

CLASSES OF TESTS

Practice Using Answer Sheets

Alter numbers to match the practice and drill questions in each part of the book.
Make only ONE mark for each answer. Additional and stray marks may be counted as mistakes.
In making corrections, erase errors COMPLETELY. Make glossy black marks.

1 A B C D E	1 A B C D E	1 A B C D E	1 A B C D E	1 A B C D E
2 A B C D E	2 A B C D E	2 A B C D E	2 A B C D E	2 A B C D E
3 A B C D E	3 A B C D E	3 A B C D E	3 A B C D E	3 A B C D E
4 A B C D E	4 A B C D E	4 A B C D E	4 A B C D E	4 A B C D E
5 A B C D E	5 A B C D E	5 A B C D E	5 A B C D E	5 A B C D E
6 A B C D E	6 A B C D E	6 A B C D E	6 A B C D E	6 A B C D E
7 A B C D E	7 A B C D E	7 A B C D E	7 A B C D E	7 A B C D E
8 A B C D E	8 A B C D E	8 A B C D E	8 A B C D E	8 A B C D E
9 A B C D E	9 A B C D E	9 A B C D E	9 A B C D E	9 A B C D E
0 A B C D E	0 A B C D E	0 A B C D E	0 A B C D E	0 A B C D E

1 A B C D E	1 A B C D E	1 A B C D E	1 A B C D E	1 A B C D E
2 A B C D E	2 A B C D E	2 A B C D E	2 A B C D E	2 A B C D E
3 A B C D E	3 A B C D E	3 A B C D E	3 A B C D E	3 A B C D E
4 A B C D E	4 A B C D E	4 A B C D E	4 A B C D E	4 A B C D E
5 A B C D E	5 A B C D E	5 A B C D E	5 A B C D E	5 A B C D E
6 A B C D E	6 A B C D E	6 A B C D E	6 A B C D E	6 A B C D E
7 A B C D E	7 A B C D E	7 A B C D E	7 A B C D E	7 A B C D E
8 A B C D E	8 A B C D E	8 A B C D E	8 A B C D E	8 A B C D E
9 A B C D E	9 A B C D E	9 A B C D E	9 A B C D E	9 A B C D E
0 A B C D E	0 A B C D E	0 A B C D E	0 A B C D E	0 A B C D E

1 A B C D E	7 A B C D E	13 A B C D E	19 A B C D E	25 A B C D E
2 A B C D E	8 A B C D E	14 A B C D E	20 A B C D E	26 A B C D E
3 A B C D E	9 A B C D E	15 A B C D E	21 A B C D E	27 A B C D E
4 A B C D E	10 A B C D E	16 A B C D E	22 A B C D E	28 A B C D E
5 A B C D E	11 A B C D E	17 A B C D E	23 A B C D E	29 A B C D E
6 A B C D E	12 A B C D E	18 A B C D E	24 A B C D E	30 A B C D E

TEAR OUT ALONG THIS LINE AND MARK YOUR ANSWERS AS INSTRUCTED IN THE TEXT

Clerical and Stenographic Tests

Various kinds of checking and computation questions are given to test aptitude for clerical jobs. Many of the tests are machine-scored, and some use a simple code which itself is part of a test of aptitude.

Name and Number Comparison

In each line across the page there are three names or numbers which are much alike. Compare the three names or numbers and decide which ones are exactly alike. On the Answer Sheet, blacken the space lettered

A if ALL THREE names or numbers are exactly ALIKE
B if only the FIRST and SECOND names or numbers are exactly ALIKE
C if only the FIRST and THIRD names or numbers are exactly ALIKE
D if only the SECOND and THIRD names or numbers are exactly ALIKE
E if ALL THREE names or numbers are DIFFERENT

1. Davis Hazen	David Hozen	David Hazen
2. Lois Appel	Lois Appel	Lois Apfel
3. June Allen	Jane Allan	Jane Allan
4. Jno. M. Dea	Jno. M. Dea	Jno. M. Dea
5. Ann K. Dove	Ann H. Dove	Ann K. Dove
6. 21107	21017	21117
7. 34212	34212	34112
8. 10235	10235	10235
9. 32614	32164	32614
10. 23544	25344	25344

Explanation: In question 1 all three names are different; therefore the space under E is blackened. In question 3 only the second and third names are exactly alike; therefore the space under D is blackened. Check your answers with the correct answers properly marked in the lower right corner of this page.

Alphabetizing

In each of the following questions there is a name enclosed in a box and a series of four other names in proper alphabetic order. The names are printed between spaces lettered A, B, C, D, and E. Decide in which space the boxed name belongs in that series. Then blacken the proper space on the answer sheet.

11. Jones, Jane
A)→
Goodyear, G. L.
B)→
Haddon, Mary
C)→
Jackson, Harry
D)→
Jenkins, William
E)→

12. Robeson, Carl
A)→
Robey, Clarke
B)→
Robinette, Claude
C)→
Robinson, Claude
D)→
Robinton, Chas.
E)→

13. Kessler, Neilson
A)→
Kessel, Oscar
B)→
Kessinger, D. J.
C)→
Kessler, Karl
D)→
Kessner, Lewis
E)→

14. Olsen, C. C.
A)→
Olsen, C. A.
B)→
Olsen, C. D.
C)→
Olsen, Charles
D)→
Olsen, Christopher
E)→

Explanation: In question 11 the name in the box follows "Jenkins, William" when all five names are in alphabetic order; therefore the space under E is blackened. In question 13 the name in the box follows "Kessler, Karl" when all five names are in alphabetic order; therefore the space under D is blackened.

Compare your answers with the correct answers, properly marked at the right.

	A	B	C	D	E
1					▮
2		▮			
3				▮	
4	▮				
5			▮		
6					▮
7		▮			
8	▮				
9			▮		
10				▮	
11					▮
12	▮				
13				▮	
14		▮			

CLERICAL AND STENOGRAPHIC

Arithmetic

If you take an aptitude test which includes arithmetic, some of the questions in the test may be of the nature of checking short computations rather than completely working out the answer. The time allowed for the test may be rather short, in order to show whether you can answer the questions quickly as well as correctly.

For the multiplication problems, blacken the space under A if the answer is CORRECT; blacken the space under B if the answer is WRONG. For the addition problems, you will use the same answer sheet, but mark D if the sum is CORRECT, and E if it is WRONG. Work as quickly as you can.

MULTIPLICATION

1.	2.	3.
16	69	27
4	8	3
64	552	71

4.	5.	6.
46	79	58
5	2	4
51	158	222

ADDITION

1.	2.	3.	4.	5.	6.
68	44	37	24	20	48
30	57	63	43	59	42
46	60	12	72	66	77
52	32	78	57	81	16
206	193	190	197	236	184

Accounting and Auditing clerks and trainees need to be able to understand the rules and laws that apply to their work; for example, tax laws and leave regulations.

Questions 7 and 8 are based on the following regulation: Employees of the XYZ Corporation earn 1½ days of emergency leave each month, which is credited to them on the first day of the month and may be taken at any time during that month or at any time thereafter. (For the purposes of this regulation, 1 day equals 8 hours.)

The table below gives the leave records of two employees for the calendar year 1950. For each question, determine the amount of emergency leave to the credit of the employee at the end of December 1950. If the correct answer is in column A, B, C, or D, mark the proper space on the answer sheet. If the correct answer is not given in one of these columns, blacken the space under E.

Employee	Accumulated leave on 12/31/49	Emergency leave used in 1950	Balance of Accumulated Leave 12/31/50				
			A	B	C	D	E
	Days–Hr.	Days–Hr.	Days–Hr.	Days–Hr.	Days–Hr.	Days–Hr.	
7. No. 1	4 5	20 1	2 4	2 7	4 4	7 4	None of these
8. No. 2	20 2	16 5	3 4	20 5	21 5	21 7	

Question 9 is based on the following portion of a withholding tax table:
If the payroll period with respect to an employee is MONTHLY:

And wages are—		And number of withholding exemptions claimed is—				
At least	But less than	0	1	2	3	4
		The amount of income tax to be withheld shall be—				
$172	$176	$31.30	$21.30	$11.30	$1.30	$0
176	180	32.00	22.00	12.00	2.00	0
180	184	32.80	22.80	12.80	2.80	0

9. K received a monthly wage of $176.40 the first 3 months of the year and $182.50 the remaining 9 months. He claimed 3 exemptions for the first 4 months and 4 for the remaining 8 months. What was the total income tax withheld during the year?

A) $0.00
B) $6.00
C) $8.80
D) $11.20
E) none of these

1	A	E	C	D	E
2	A	B	C	D	E
3	A	B	C	D	E
4	A	B	C	D	E
5	A	B	C	D	E
6	A	B	C	D	E
7	A	B	C	D	E
8	A	B	C	D	E
9	A	B	C	D	E

Copying from Plain Copy (Typewriting)

The sample given below shows the kind of material that competitors must copy. See whether you can copy it twice in 10 minutes and how many errors your copies contain. Competitors will be required to meet a certain minimum in accuracy as well as in speed. Above the minimum speed and accuracy requirements, accuracy counts twice as much as speed in determining whether the competitor is eligible on Copying from Plain Copy.

Space, paragraph, spell, punctuate, capitalize, and begin and end each line precisely as shown in the exercise. There is no penalty for a neat erasure other than the loss of time for making the erasure.

In the examination you will have 10 minutes in which to make copies of the test exercise, keeping in mind that your eligibility will depend upon accuracy as well as speed. Each time you complete the exercise, simply double space once and begin again. Use both sides of the paper.

A paper will be rated only to a point at which it earns a rating of eligible, or a point at which it contains so many errors that it cannot earn a rating of eligible. If you do not have veteran preference, your typing must go a little over halfway through a second copy of the exercise to make you eligible in speed. With that minimum speed, your paper must not have more than 9 errors. The number of errors permitted increases with the amount typed, up to the end of the first paragraph in the third copy. When you finish the first paragraph in your third copy of the exercise, further typing will not affect your eligibility; stop typing. If you have more time, you should correct any errors you find you have made.

```
     This practice exercise is similar in length and diffi-
culty to the one that you will be required to typewrite for
the Plain Copy Test.  You are to space, capitalize, punctu-
ate, spell, and begin and end each line precisely as in the
copy.  The use of an eraser is permitted and erasures will
not be penalized if they are neat.  Make no other changes,
omissions, or insertions in this test.  Practice typewriting
this material on scratch paper until the examiner tells you
to stop, remembering that for this examination it is more
important to typewrite accurately than to typewrite rapidly.

     There are several ways in which a typist can prepare
herself to be an efficient worker in a business office.
First of all, she should know her typewriter thoroughly, the
location of all the keys, even those used infrequently, and
the use of the marginal stops and extra devices furnished
on modern typewriters.  In addition to being completely
familiar with the typewriter, she should be equipped with
knowledge of the correct spellings and correct use of a
large number of words.  Although a letter has been type-
written neatly, without omissions or insertions, it will
still be considered unsatisfactory if it contains any mis-
spellings whatsoever.
```

Qualifying for Stenographer and Typist Positions

Typists will be required to take the typing test described above, and a general abilities test containing questions on word meaning, interpretation of paragraphs, grammar and English usage, and spelling. (See pages 9–12 for examples.) To qualify, you must pass both of these tests.

Stenographers will be required to take the stenography test in addition to these two tests. The stenography test will not be rated unless you qualify as a typist.

Stenographic Dictation

A practice exercise and a dictation exercise will be dictated to competitors for stenographic positions. Any system of taking notes is acceptable, provided that the notes are given to the examiner at the end of the examination. The use of shorthand machines is allowed, but the use of a typewriter for taking notes is not permitted because the noise would interfere with the dictation.

Instead of making a complete transcript of the notes, you will compare your notes with a Transcript Sheet containing the same material except that many of the words have been left out. Decide what word or group of words belongs in each blank, and look at the ALPHABETIC WORD LIST to see what letter is printed beside it. Fill in that letter in the blank on the Transcript Sheet. If the *exact* word or group of words is not in the word list, write E in the blank.

A sample dictation exercise begins:
"In recent years there has been a great increase in the need for capable stenographers, not only in business offices but also in public service agencies, both governmental and private. The high schools and business schools in many parts of the country have tried to meet this need by offering complete commercial courses."

The transcript sheet contains this list of words for these sentences:

ALPHABETIC WORD LIST
Write E if the answer is NOT listed.

advertising—A	many—D
agencies—D	marked—A
almost—C	met—A
also—C	most—C
and—D	need—D
business—B	offering—D
but—A	only—B
claimed—B	opening—A
colleges—C	parts—A
complete—B	private—C
country—A	schools—D
demand—B	sections—B
especially—D	the need—A
even—B	their—D
government—B	there—C
great—C	to complete—C
has been—D	to meet—C
high schools—A	to offer—B
in—C	trained—C
in government—A	tried—A

TRANSCRIPT:

In recent years C (1) D (2) a C (3) increase C (4) A (5) for E (6) stenographers, not B (7) C (8) B (9) offices A (10) C (11) in public E (12) D (13), both E (14) and C (15). The A (16) and business D (17) in D (18) A (19) E (20) A (21) have A (22) C (23) this need by D (24) B (25) commercial courses. . . .

The blanks in the transcript sheet have been filled in with the letters corresponding to the words and phrases that would appear in correct shorthand notes. In the examination, after the time for the transcript had expired, you would transfer these answers to a machine-scored answer sheet. You would still be permitted to use your notes after you had begun working on the answer sheet, to verify answers or to complete any part of the transcript you had not finished.

In the examination, another word list would be furnished for the next few sentences of the dictation exercise.

Tests of Verbal Abilities

Tests of verbal abilities (often referred to in employment testing as "general tests") are designed to test a wide range of abilities, including the ability to understand words, interpret the meaning of sentences and paragraphs, and recognize and apply the rules of grammar and spelling. There are many kinds of questions which could be used for this purpose; the ones most commonly used are shown on this page and the next three.

Vocabulary

These words are not limited only to words actually used on the job. Vocabulary questions are a good measure of a competitor's general ability, as well as his aptitude for work requiring skill with words.

There is no printed list of all words whose meanings are tested in civil service examinations. No study of a selected list of words is likely to help in preparing for an examination. The general improvement of your vocabulary will help, however, and you will find that this improvement will make other kinds of questions more understandable also.

Directions: In each of the following questions you are to find which one of five words or phrases offered as choices has most nearly the same meaning as the word or phrase in CAPITAL LETTERS or *italics*. On the answer sheet mark the letter of the suggested answer which you think is the best.

1. If a report is VERIFIED it is
   A) changed
   B) confirmed
   C) replaced
   D) discarded
   E) corrected

Since "confirmed," lettered B, means most nearly the same as "verified," the space under B is marked on the answer sheet for question 1.

2. A clerk who shows FORBEARANCE TOWARD THE OPINION OF OTHERS shows
   A) severity
   B) hypercriticism
   C) tolerance
   D) quietness
   E) thankfulness

3. *A controversy* between two persons is
   A) an agreement
   B) a dispute
   C) a partnership
   D) a plot
   E) an understanding

4. To say that a condition is *generally or extensively existing* means that it is
   A) artificial
   B) prevalent
   C) recurrent
   D) timely
   E) transient

5. *Authentic* means most nearly
   A) detailed
   B) reliable
   C) valuable
   D) technical
   E) practical

6. *The two farms lie close to each other, but are not in actual contact.* This sentence means most nearly that the two farms are
   A) adjoining
   B) abutting
   C) touching
   D) adjacent
   E) united

The space under D is marked for this question because "adjacent" best describes the meaning of the sentence in italics. The other choices all indicate that the farms are in contact in some degree or are touching each other.

Word Relations

In each of the following questions the first two words in capital letters go together in some way. Find how they are related. Then select from the last five words the one that goes with the third word in capital letters in the same way that the second word in capital letters goes with the first. The answer sheet is marked to show the correct choice of answers for these two questions.

7. FOOD is to HUNGER as SLEEP is to
   A) night
   B) dream
   C) weariness
   D) health
   E) rest

Food relieves hunger and sleep relieves weariness. Therefore, C, the letter before "weariness," is marked on the answer sheet for this question.

8. SPEEDOMETER is related to POINTER as WATCH is related to
   A) case
   B) hands
   C) dial
   D) spring
   E) numerals

On the answer sheet the space under B has been blackened to show that *watch* and *hands* are related in most nearly the same way as *speedometer* and *pointer*.

	A	B	C	D	E
1		▮			
2			▮		
3		▮			
4		▮			
5		▮			
6				▮	
7			▮		
8		▮			

VERBAL ABILITIES

Interpretation of Paragraphs

Each question consists of a quotation followed by a series of five statements. Among the five statements there is only one that *must* be true if the quotation is true. Other statements among the five may or may not be true, but they are not necessary conclusions from the quotation. You are to select the *one* statement which is *best supported* by the quotation.

1. (*Reading*) "The application of the steam engine to the sawmill changed the whole lumber industry. Formerly the mills remained near the streams; now they follow the timber. Formerly the logs were floated downstream to their destination; now they are carried by the railroads."

   What besides the method of transportation does the quotation indicate has changed in the lumber industry?

   A) speed of cutting timber
   B) location of market
   C) type of timber sold
   D) route of railroads
   E) source of power

The quotation says nothing about the speed of steam-powered sawmills, location of the market for lumber, the type of timber sold, or the route of railroads. It does, however, mention "the application of the steam engine to the sawmill"—which gave a new source of power for sawmill operations. E is therefore the answer, and the space under E is blackened for question 1.

2. (*Reading*) "More patents have been issued for inventions relating to transportation than for those in any other line of human activity. These inventions have resulted in a great financial saving to the people and have made possible a civilization that could not have existed without them."

   Select the alternative that is best supported by the quotation. Transportation

   A) would be impossible without inventions
   B) is an important factor in our civilization
   C) is still to be much improved
   D) is more important than any other activity
   E) is carried on through the Patent Office

The space on the Answer Sheet under B is marked for question 2 because the statement lettered B is implied in the quotation. A is not strictly true, since manpower without inventions could supply transportation of a sort; C is probably true but is not in the quotation; D is exaggerated; E is not implied in the information given.

3. (*Reading*) "There exists a false but popular idea that a clue is some mysterious fact which most people overlook, but which some very keen investigator easily discovers and recognizes as having, in itself, a remarkable meaning. The clue is most often an ordinary fact which an observant person picks up—something which gains its significance when, after a long series of careful investigations, it is connected with a network of other clues."

   According to the quotation, to be of value, clues must be

   A) discovered by skilled investigators
   B) found under mysterious circumstances
   C) discovered soon after the crime
   D) observed many times
   E) connected with other facts

The quotation does not say that the clue must be (A) discovered by an investigator in order to make it of value; it does not mention (B) the circumstances under which a clue must be found; nothing in the paragraph implies that the value of a clue depends upon the (C) time of its discovery, nor upon the (D) number of times it is observed. E is the answer, because the quotation does say that a clue gains its significance, or value, when *connected with other clues or facts.*

4. (*Reading*) "Just as the procedure of a collection department must be clear-cut and definite, the steps being taken with the sureness of a skilled chess player, so the various paragraphs of a collection letter must show clear organization, giving evidence of a mind that, from the beginning, has had a specific end in view."

   The quotation best supports the statement that a collection letter should always

   A) show a spirit of sportsmanship
   B) be divided into several paragraphs
   C) express confidence in the debtor
   D) be brief, but courteous
   E) be carefully planned

	A	B	C	D	E
1	⁞	⁞	⁞	⁞	▌
2	⁞	▌	⁞	⁞	⁞
3	⁞	⁞	⁞	⁞	▌
4	⁞	⁞	⁞	⁞	▌

Proverbs

These questions test ability to understand meanings and apply generalizations. The answer is the sentence which means the same thing as the saying quoted.

1. The saying "Many hands make light work" means most nearly
   A) Most people prefer easy jobs.
   B) When several work together, each finds his task easy.
   C) Much light work can be done by hand.
   D) There are often too many to help.
   E) One does his best work when working alone.

2. The saying "To know the road, ask of those who have traveled it" means most nearly
   A) Know your destination before you start.
   B) Seek counsel of experienced persons.
   C) When in doubt, stop.
   D) The traveled road is the easiest route.
   E) If you would advance, profit by your past.

The statement lettered B means most nearly the same as "Many hands make light work." Therefore the space under B is blackened for question 1.

Judgment

These questions are based on a variety of facts, sometimes on facts with which the candidate would be expected to be familiar, sometimes on facts explained in the question itself. The questions are of various degrees of difficulty. In some cases judgment items may pertain to a particular field of subject-matter, knowledge of which is necessary for the job.

3. Hospital beds are usually higher than beds in private homes. Which of the following is the BEST reason for this fact?
   A) Hospital beds are in use all day, instead of at night only.
   B) Many hospital patients are children.
   C) Private homes seldom have space enough for high beds.
   D) The care of patients is less difficult when the beds are high.
   E) The danger of falling out of bed is greater where there are no nurses.

The suggestion lettered D is the answer and is marked on the answer sheet. Of all the suggestions given as possible reasons why hospital beds are higher than other kinds, the one lettered D is clearly the most reasonable and best.

4. Objects are visible because
   A) they are opaque
   B) they are partially in shadow
   C) they absorb light from the sun
   D) light falls on them and is reflected to the eye
   E) light rays penetrate their surfaces

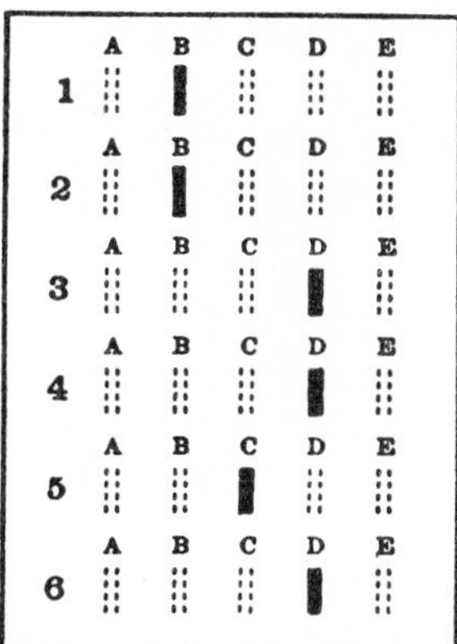

On the section of the answer sheet at the right, the space under D is marked for question 4 because the statement lettered D is the only one that explains why objects are visible. The other statements may be true, but they do not account for the visibility of objects.

5. In starting a load, a horse has to pull harder than he does to keep it moving, because
   A) the load weighs less when it is moving
   B) there is no friction after the load is moving
   C) the horse has to overcome the tendency of the wagon to remain at rest
   D) the wheels stick to the axles
   E) the horse becomes accustomed to pulling the load

6. Which of the following would be the *surest* indication that a druggist may have violated the legal requirement that narcotic drugs be dispensed only on a physician's prescription?
   A) A number of people known to have purchased other drugs from him are believed to possess narcotics, but no prescriptions issued to these persons are in the druggist's file.
   B) He is himself an addict.
   C) His wholesaler refuses to sell him narcotics.
   D) The total of his present narcotics stock and the amount legally accounted for is much less than his purchases.
   E) The supply of narcotics in stock is less than the amount which he recently reported.

The facts related in A do not indicate that these customers have secured their narcotics from this druggist—the narcotics may have been obtained from some other druggist on a proper prescription; B is no indication that prescriptions did not cover all the narcotics he has dispensed, either for his own use or for other people; C might be true for many reasons—for example, his credit may be bad; and E could be explained by legal sales made since his last report. The answer is D, because violation of the requirement mentioned is a likely explanation of the large difference; therefore D is marked on the answer sheet.

VERBAL ABILITIES

Grammar and English Usage

In each of questions 1 and 2, select the sentence that is preferable with respect to grammar and good usage in a formal letter or report.

1. A) They do not ordinarily present these kind of reports in detail like this.
   B) Reports like this is not generally given in such great detail.
   C) A report of this kind is not hardly ever given in such detail as this one.
   D) This report is more detailed than what such reports ordinarily are.
   E) A report of this kind is not ordinarily presented in such detail as this one.

2. A) Although that statement is true, I did not leave it influence my decision.
   B) My decision is not effected by that statement, even though it is true.
   C) Although true, I have not let that statement influence my decision.
   D) That statement is true, but it does not affect my decision.
   E) Because that statement is true does not have any effect on my decision.

In questions 3 and 4, four words or phrases have been underlined and lettered A, B, C, and D. If there is an error in usage in one of the underlined words or phrases, mark on the answer sheet the letter of the one in which the error occurs. If there is no error, mark the E space.

3. The gasoline tank bust [A] and escaping [B] gasoline became [C] ignited in an unknown manner. [D]

4. The truck was [A] in good mechanical [B] condition when examined [C] ten hours before [D] the accident occurred.

Spelling

5. Select the one misspelled word.
   A) reliable
   B) detailed
   C) different
   D) accurrate
   E) sanctioned

In questions like the following, find the correct spelling of the word and blacken the proper space on your answer sheet. If none of the suggested spellings is correct, blacken space D on your answer sheet.

6. A) occassion
   B) occasion
   C) ocassion
   D) none of these

The correct spelling of the word is *occasion*. Since the B spelling is correct, the space under B is marked for this question.

Look at each word in the following list and decide whether the spelling is *all right* or *bad*. On the answer sheet blacken space

A if the spelling is ALL RIGHT
B if the spelling is BAD

7. running
8. indien
9. skool

	A	B	C	D	E
1					■
2				■	
3	■				
4					■
5				■	
6		■			
7	■				
8		■			
9		■			
10			■		

In questions like 10, a sentence is given in which one word, which is underlined, is spelled as it is pronounced. Write the correct spelling of the word in the blank. Then decide which one of the suggested answers, A, B, C, or D, is the correct answer to the question. (Sometimes the question will refer to one letter in the word, sometimes to a combination of letters.)

10. The new treasurer uses the same system that his pred-eh-sess′-urr did.
    In the correct spelling, ..., what is the tenth letter?
    A) s
    B) e
    C) o
    D) none of these

The correct spelling of the underlined word is *predecessor*. Since the tenth letter is "o," which is given as answer C, the space under C has been blackened.

Tests of Reasoning

In some jobs, it is necessary to understand, interpret, and apply rules and principles. In others, it is necessary also to discover principles from available data or information. These types of reasoning ability can be tested by different kinds of tests—for example, questions on the relationship of words, understanding of paragraphs, or solving of numerical problems.

Other types of questions that have been found useful in testing reasoning abilities are illustrated on these two pages. Here the competitor is asked to find relationships between elements (numbers, letters, or patterns), to find the rule by which they are bound together in groups or arranged in a certain order, and to select or arrange other elements according to that rule.

Number Series

Each of these three questions gives a series of six numbers. Each series of numbers is made up according to a certain rule or order. You are to find what the next number in the series should be; then blacken the space on the answer sheet that is lettered the same as the correct suggested answer.

1. 2 4 6 8 10 12
   A) 14
   B) 16
   C) 18
   D) 20
   E) none of these

In question 1, the rule is to add 2 to each number (2+2=4; 4+2=6; etc.). The next number in the series is 14 (12+2=14). Since *14* is lettered A among the suggested answers, the space lettered A is blackened on the answer sheet for question 1.

2. 7 8 6 7 5 6
   A) 2
   B) 3
   C) 4
   D) 5
   E) none of these

In question 2, the rule is to add 1 to the first number, subtract 2 from the next, add 1, subtract 2, and so on. The next number in the series is 4. On the answer sheet, the letter C should be blackened for question 2.

3. 3 6 9 12 15 18
   A) 39
   B) 40
   C) 45
   D) 59
   E) none of these

In question 3, the rule is to add 3, making 21 the next number in the series. The correct answer to question 3 is *none of these*, since 39, 40, 45, and 59 are all incorrect answers; therefore E is marked on the answer sheet.

The next two questions are more difficult. In these, the arrangement is more complicated, and the answer is chosen from groups of two numbers, of which one group gives the next two numbers in the series.

4. 1 1 2 1 3 1 4 1
   A) 1 5
   B) 4 1
   C) 5 1
   D) 5 5
   E) 6 1

The series consists of 1's alternating with numbers in ascending numerical order. The next two numbers would be 5 and 1; therefore C is the correct answer.

5. 2 8 3 7 5 6 8 5
   A) 10 6
   B) 11 3
   C) 11 4
   D) 12 4
   E) 12 6

This series consists of a subseries for which the rule is to add 1, add 2, add 3, add 4, alternating with another subseries in descending numerical order. The next number in the first subseries would be 8+4, or 12; and the next number in the descending series would be 4. Therefore D is the correct choice.

Letter Series

In each of these questions there is a series of letters which follow some definite order, and at the right there are five sets of two letters each. Look at the letters in the series and determine what the order is; then from the suggested answers at the right, select the set that gives the next two letters in the series in their correct order. Mark the space that has the same letter as the set you have chosen.

6. X C X D X E X A) **F X** B) **F G** C) **X F** D) **E F** E) **X G**

The series consists of X's alternating with letters in alphabetical order. The next two letters would be F and X; therefore, A is the correct answer.

7. A B D C E F H A) **G H** B) **I G** C) **G I** D) **K L** E) **I H**

If you compare this series with the alphabet, you will find that it goes along in pairs, the first pair in their usual order and the next pair in reverse order. The last letter given in the series is the second letter of the pair G—H, which is in reverse order. The first missing letter must, therefore, be G. The next pair of letters would be I—J, in that order; the second of the missing letters is I. The alternative you look for, then, is G I, which is lettered C.

	A	B	C	D	E
1	▮	⁞	⁞	⁞	⁞
2	⁞	⁞	▮	⁞	⁞
3	⁞	⁞	⁞	⁞	▮
4	⁞	⁞	▮	⁞	⁞
5	⁞	⁞	⁞	▮	⁞
6	▮	⁞	⁞	⁞	⁞
7	⁞	⁞	▮	⁞	⁞

REASONING

Symbol Series

Questions 1 and 2 consist of a series of five symbols at the left and five other symbols labeled A, B, C, D, and E at the right.

In each question, first study the series of symbols at the left; then from the symbols at the right, labeled A, B, C, D, and E, select the one which continues the series most completely. Next to the question number on the answer sheet blacken the space lettered the same as the symbol which you have chosen.

1.

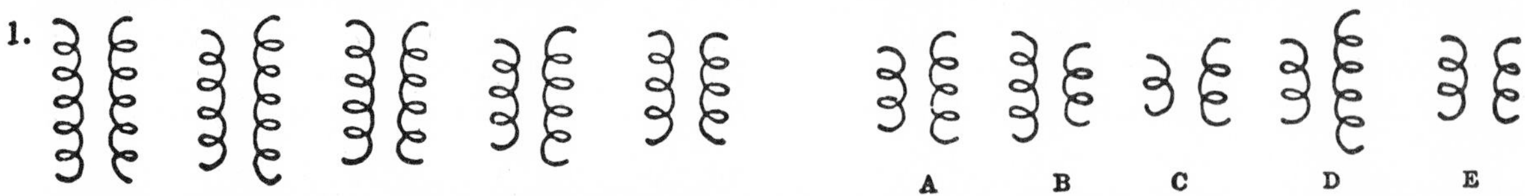

Each symbol in the series at the left has two coils. The symbols differ from one another in the number of loops that each coil has. In the first symbol, each coil has five loops; in the second, the left-hand one has four and the right-hand one has five; in the third, each coil has four. In this series, first the left-hand coil loses a loop and then the right-hand coil loses one.

Since the fifth symbol has three loops in each coil, the next symbol in this series must have two loops in the left-hand coil and three in the right-hand coil. Since symbol A is the only one which has two loops in the left-hand coil and three in the right-hand coil, A is the answer, and you should blacken space A for question 1 on the answer sheet.

2.

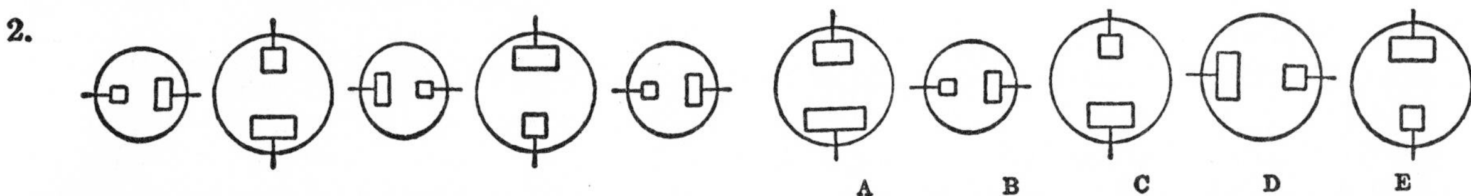

Question 2 is harder. The first five symbols show an alternation from small to large to small; and a quarter-turn in a counterclockwise direction each time. The answer should be a large circle, therefore (which eliminates B from the alternatives), with the larger rectangle at the bottom of the circle (which eliminates D and E). A second look at A shows that the rectangles within it are larger than any of the rectangles in the other circles; this change has no basis in the series. Thus C is left as the correct answer.

Symbol Classification

Each of the next two questions has two boxes at the left. The first box has three symbols, and the second box has two symbols with one missing symbol represented by a question mark. There is always some difference between the symbols in the first box and the symbols in the second box. You are to decide what the difference between the symbols in the first box and the symbols in the second box is, and choose the symbol lettered A, B, C, D, or E, which can best take the place of the missing symbol in the second box.

(NOTE.—Do not confuse this type of question with the type above. The symbols in each box are simply a *group* and not a series with a definite progression.)

In question 3 all the symbols in the first box are curved, while the symbols in the second box are straight. Of the lettered symbols in the third box, only B is straight, so B has been marked on the answer sheet. (Note that although one symbol in the second box is made of dashes, the other is not. The type of line, therefore, is not the feature that distinguishes the second box from the first.)

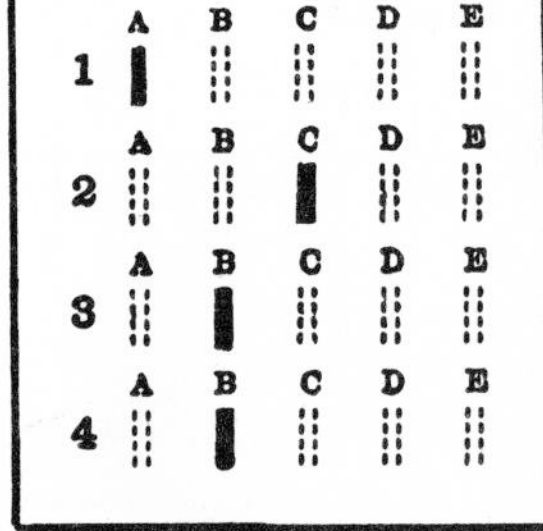

In question 4 the given symbols consist of two lines making an angle. There are curved lines and straight lines in each box; therefore the difference that must be found cannot be the difference between curved and straight. The angles formed in the first box are *obtuse*; those in the second box are *acute*. Now a check of the alternatives shows that only one of them consists of lines making an acute angle; the correct answer B is therefore marked.

Tests for mail and shipping room workers

THE general character of the examination is indicated by the material on these pages. Study it carefully and answer each question. Be sure that you understand how to answer all the different kinds of questions, and how to mark your answers. Mark all the questions in this folder, so that when you take the examination you will remember how to do the tests.

This page is a sample of the test in which you will be given addresses to compare.

Mark each answer on the Sample Answer Sheet in the row that has the same number as the number of the question.

For Part I of the test, mark the space on your answer sheet under A if the two addresses are exactly *alike* in every way. Mark the space under B if they are *NOT alike* in every way.

For Part II, go back to number 1 on the answer sheet, but this time mark the space under D if the two addresses are exactly *alike* in every way and mark the space under E if they are *NOT alike* in every way.

When you have finished the test, you should have marks in columns A and B for Part I and in columns D and E for Part II. There should be no marks in column C.

Mark your answers to these sample questions on the Sample Answer Sheet at the right.

PART I

1. 2134 S 20th St — 2134 S 20th St

   Since the first two addresses are exactly alike, mark A on the Sample Answer Sheet.

2.	4608 N Warnock St	4806 N Warnock St
3.	1202 W Girard Dr	1202 W Girard Rd
4.	3120 S Harcourt St	3120 S Harcourt St
5.	4618 W Addison St	4618 E Addison St
6.	39–B Parkway Rd	39–D Parkway Rd
7.	6425 N Delancey	6425 N Delancey
8.	5407 Columbia Rd	5407 Columbia Rd
9.	2106 Southern Ave	2106 Southern Ave
10.	Highfalls N C	Highlands N C
11.	2873 Pershing Dr	2873 Pershing Dr
12.	1329 N H Ave NW	1329 N J Ave NW
13.	1316 N Quinn St Arl	1316 N Quinn St Alex
14.	7507 Wyngate Dr	7505 Wyngate Dr
15.	2918 Colesville Rd	2918 Colesville Rd
16.	2071 Belvedere Dr	2071 Belvedere Dr
17.	Palmer Wash	Palmer Mich
18.	2106 16th St SW	2106 16th St SW

PART II

1.	2207 Markland Ave	2207 Markham Ave
2.	5345 16th St NW	5345 16th St NE
3.	239 Summit Pl	239 Summit Pl
4.	152 Continental Bldg	152 Continental Blvd
5.	8092 13th Rd S Aberdeen	8029 13th Rd S Aberdeen
6.	3906 Queensbury Rd	3906 Queensbury Rd
7.	4719 Linnean Ave NW	4719 Linnean Ave NW
8.	Bradford Me	Bradley Me
9.	Parrott Ga	Parrott Va
10.	K–42 Lowell House	K–42 Lowell House
11.	6929 W 135 Place	6929 W 135 Plaza
12.	5143 Somerset Cir	5143 Somerset Cir
13.	8501 Kennedy St	8501 Kennedy St
14.	2164 W McLean Ave	2164 W McLean Ave
15.	7186 E St NW	7186 F St NW
16.	2121 Beechcrest Rd	2121 Beechcroft Rd
17.	3609 E Montrose St	3609 E Montrose St
18.	324 S Alvadero St	324 S Alverado St

Now compare your answers with the Correct Answers for Sample Questions. If your answers are not the same, go back and study the questions to see where you made a mistake.

SAMPLE ANSWER SHEET

	A	B	C	D	E
1					
2					
3					
4					
5					
6					
7					
8					
9					
10					
11					
12					
13					
14					
15					
16					
17					
18					

CORRECT ANSWERS FOR SAMPLE QUESTIONS

	A	B	C	D	E
1	█				█
2		█			█
3		█		█	
4	█				█
5		█			█
6		█		█	
7	█			█	
8	█				█
9	█				█
10		█		█	
11	█				█
12		█		█	
13		█		█	
14		█		█	
15	█				█
16	█				█
17		█		█	
18	█				█

FOLLOWING INSTRUCTIONS—SAMPLE TEST

Directions: Read carefully.

Follow the directions in this sample carefully so that when you take the examination you will remember *how* to do the test.

Finding train numbers:

Below is a SORTING SCHEME and KEY. In the SORTING SCHEME is a list of post offices. Each post office is followed by a letter. (For example, after "Guilford" is the letter "F." This "F" refers to the KEY at the right which reads "F Atlantic 6." Mail for Guilford is sent by way of Atlantic on Train 6.) Always begin with a post office in the SORTING SCHEME and find the train number in the KEY.

SORTING SCHEME

Atlantic	F	Melfa	G	Shields	J
Bloxam	T	Nandua	M	Silva	O
Greta	O	Nelson	F	Tangier	J
Groton	K	Oak Hill	H	Tasley	G
Guilford	F	Onley	S	Withams	P
Hopeton	K	Painter	I		
Hopkins	I	Parksley	S		
Kane	G	Paulson	H		
Keller	J	Quimby	U		
Mears	U	Sanford	S		

Do not make any marks in this SORTING SCHEME or KEY before you read the directions below.

KEY

Mail sent by way of—

F	Atlantic	6
G	Melfa	2
H	Oak Hill	7
I	Hopkins	3
J	Tangier	8
K	Hopeton	5
M	Painter	
O	Greta	9
P	Keller	
S	Sanford	4
T	Groton	
U	Parksley	

BEGIN HERE. Do not skip any part of these directions. Work with a pencil so that if you want more practice you can erase the work.

Completing the KEY:

Look at "Painter" in the KEY. It is not followed by a number. Write after it the letter which you find after Painter in the SORTING SCHEME. Your KEY should now read "M Painter I." Find the letters after Keller, Groton, and Parksley in the SORTING SCHEME and write them after those offices in the KEY.

Recording Answers:

In each question below a post office name is followed by five train numbers. Use the SORTING SCHEME and KEY to find the correct train number. Then see what column (A, B, C, D, E) the correct train number is in, and mark this letter on your Sample Answer Sheet on the next page.

For Example.—For the first post office below, Painter, you are to find the correct train number. In the SORTING SCHEME, Painter is followed by the letter "I." This tells you to look at "I" in the KEY, which reads "Hopkins 3," and means that mail for Painter is routed by way of Hopkins on Train 3. The number 3 after Painter, below, is in column B, so, to mark your answer, you should blacken the space under B for question 1 on the Sample Answer Sheet.

Question No.	*Post Office*	A	B	C	D	E	*(Sample Answer Sheet columns)*
1	Painter	2	3	5	7	9	*(Train numbers)*
2	Paulson	3	4	5	7	8	
3	Mears	2	3	4	5	7	
4	Kane	2	3	4	5	6	

Mail for Mears is sent by way of U Parksley S through S Sanford on Train 4, which is in column C, so you should blacken the space under C on the Sample Answer Sheet for question 3.

Making Changes in the SORTING SCHEME and KEY:

Never put numbers in the SORTING SCHEME. Make changes from the Bulletins *exactly* as they direct you to.

Never cross out names in the SORTING SCHEME.

Bulletin No. 1:

CHANGES IN ROUTING

(When changing SORTING SCHEME change KEY, too, if the name is in KEY. Note that the names in the SORTING SCHEME are in alphabetical order, but those in the KEY are not.)

Silva by way of I.
Shields by way of O.
Guilford by way of P.

Painter by way of K.
Change KEY G to read: G Train 10.
Melfa by way of H.

To make the change for Silva, cross out the "O" after Silva in the SORTING SCHEME and write "*I.*" Now your SORTING SCHEME for Silva should read "Silva Ø *I.*" This means that mail for Silva is now sent by way of I, that is, through Hopkins on Train 3.

To make the change for Painter, cross out the I after Painter in the SORTING SCHEME and write "*K.*" Then find Painter in the KEY and change the I after it to K. Mail for Painter will now go through K, that is, through Hopeton on Train 5. To change KEY G, cross out "Melfa 2" and write "*Train 10.*" Make the other changes ordered.

Mark on your Sample Answer Sheet the space for the letter showing the train on which you should put mail for:

Question No.		A	B	C	D	E
5	Tasley	2	3	7	8	10
6	Nandua	2	3	5	8	9
7	Withams	4	6	8	9	10

In answering question 6 for Nandua, did you start to mark C for *question* 5 because you were thinking of *Train* 5? Be sure to mark the right question on the answer sheet.

Bulletin No. 2:

OFFICES ESTABLISHED
(Add to SORTING SCHEME)

Saxis by way of F.
Talbot by way of H.

CHANGES IN ROUTING

(When changing SORTING SCHEME change KEY, too, if the name is in KEY.)

Paulson by way of G.
Parksley by way of O.
Change KEY J to read: J Tangier 2.

To add Saxis to the SORTING SCHEME, write "*Saxis F*" on the first line at the end of the SORTING SCHEME. To change KEY J, cross out 8 after J Tangier and write "*2.*"

Make the other changes ordered.

Mark on your Sample Answer Sheet the space for the letter showing the train on which you should put mail for:

Question No.		A	B	C	D	E
8	Mears	4	5	7	9	10
9	Silva	2	3	5	7	9
10	Guilford	2	6	8	9	10
11	Painter	2	3	4	5	6
12	Parksley	3	4	5	7	9
13	Shields	2	3	5	7	9
14	Talbot	3	4	7	9	10
15	Melfa	2	3	5	7	10

NOTE.—If you have chosen 4 for Mears, you have not made the change for Parksley in both SORTING SCHEME and KEY. Mail for Mears should be sent through U Parksley O by way of O Greta on Train 9.

Bulletin No. 3:

OFFICES ESTABLISHED (Add to SORTING SCHEME)	CHANGES IN ROUTING (When changing SORTING SCHEME change KEY, too, if the name is in KEY.)
Somerset by way of G. Elkton by way of W.	Oak Hill by way of W. (Be sure to change Oak Hill in the KEY.) Add to KEY: W Train 12. Parksley by way of K. Change KEY F to read: F Atlantic 3.

To make the addition to the KEY, write "*W Train 12*" on the first line at the end of the KEY.

Mark on your Sample Answer Sheet the space for the letter showing the train on which you should put mail for:

Question No.		A	B	C	D	E
16	Parksley	4	5	7	8	9
17	Talbot	3	6	7	10	12
18	Somerset	2	4	8	10	12
19	Saxis	3	4	5	6	8
20	Paulson	2	4	7	10	12
21	Elkton	2	4	7	10	12

Bulletin No. 4:

CHANGES IN ROUTING

(When changing SORTING SCHEME change KEY, too, if the name is in KEY.)

Painter by way of O. Hopkins by way of J. Kane by way of P.	Change KEY S to read: S Melfa. (Cross out Sanford 4 in the KEY.) Sanford by way of H.

To complete the change for KEY S, you must refer to the SORTING SCHEME to find the letter which should be written after Melfa.

Mark on your Sample Answer Sheet the space for the letter showing the train on which you should put mail for:

Question No.		A	B	C	D	E
22	Sanford	2	4	7	10	12
23	Nandua	3	5	8	9	10
24	Hopkins	2	3	4	6	8
25	Kane	2	4	6	8	10

NOTE.—If you have chosen Train 5 for Nandua, you have not made the change for Painter in both SORTING SCHEME and KEY.

When you have completed the sample questions, check your work with the completed SORTING SCHEME and KEY, and Correct Answers to Sample Questions.

SORTING SCHEME

Atlantic	F	Melfa	~~G~~ H	Shields	~~Y~~ O
Bloxam	T	Nandua	M	Silva	~~G~~ I
Greta	O	Nelson	F	Tangier	J
Groton	K	Oak Hill	~~H~~ W	Tasley	G
Guilford	~~F~~ P	Onley	S	Withams	P
Hopeton	K	Painter	~~I~~ ~~K~~ O	Saxis	F
Hopkins	~~I~~ J	Parksley	~~S~~ ~~O~~ K	Talbot	H
Kane	~~G~~ P	Paulson	~~H~~ G	Somerset	G
Keller	J	Quimby	U	Elkton	W
Mears	U	Sanford	~~S~~ H		

KEY

Mail sent by way of—

F	Atlantic	~~5~~ 3
G	~~Melfa~~	~~2~~ Train 10
H	Oak Hill	~~7~~ W
I	Hopkins	~~3~~ J
J	Tangier	~~8~~ 2
K	Hopeton	5
M	Painter	~~I~~ ~~H~~ O
O	Greta	9
P	Keller	J
S	~~Sanford~~	~~4~~ Melfa H
T	Groton	K
U	Parksley	~~S~~ ~~O~~ K
W	Train 12	

SAMPLE ANSWER SHEET

	A	B	C	D	E
1					
2					
3					
4					
5					
6					
7					
8					
9					
10					
11					
12					
13					
14					
15					
16					
17					
18					
19					
20					
21					
22					
23					
24					
25					

CORRECT ANSWERS TO SAMPLE QUESTIONS

	A	B	C	D	E
1		■			
2				■	
3			■		
4	■				
5					■
6			■		
7			■		
8				■	
9		■			
10	■				
11				■	
12					■
13					■
14			■		
15				■	
16		■			
17					■
18				■	
19	■				
20				■	
21					■
22					■
23				■	
24	■				
25	■				

Knowledge Tests for Professional and Semiprofessional Positions

Supervision

1. In general, the most important advantage of good employee morale is that it results in
   A) high production
   B) decreased work for the supervisor
   C) increased ease in rating workers' efficiency
   D) high standing for the supervisor with management
   E) less desire for wage increases among employees

Since A is the best answer, the space under A is marked on the sample answer sheet.

2. Which one of the following types of information would be most useful to a supervisor in determining which employee should lose his job in case lay-offs are necessary?
   A) length of service with the supervisor
   B) marital status
   C) education
   D) age
   E) job performance rating

Since E is the best answer, the space under E is marked on the sample answer sheet.

Administration

3. A number of national organizations require the approval of the headquarters office on all actions originating in the field offices, instead of following the alternate procedure of delegating authority for such actions. This requirement of headquarters' review and approval is frequently unsatisfactory to the headquarters office itself. In general, the most frequent reason for the *dissatisfaction* in the headquarters office is that
   A) headquarters may lack the information necessary for approving these cases
   B) field offices resent the review
   C) the review causes delay
   D) it is felt that authority should be commensurate with responsibility
   E) clearance through a large number of divisions is required in most headquarters offices

Since A is the best answer to question 3, the space under A is marked on the sample answer sheet.

Occupational Analysis

4. In the machine shop of a manufacturing firm, a job with the title of Foreman has the following duties: "Installs cutting tools in various types of semiautomatic machinery. Adjusts the guides, stops, working tables of machines, and other controls to handle the size of stock to be machined. Operates and adjusts machine until accurate production (based on blueprint specifications, patterns, or templates) has been achieved. Checks production with precision gages, often to tolerances of 0.0005 inch. Turns machine over to regular operator when it is producing satisfactorily."

Which of the following would be the most descriptive title for this job?
   A) cutting-machine mechanic
   B) dimensional checker
   C) job setter
   D) machinist
   E) tool and die maker

Since C is the best answer to question 4, the space under C is marked on the sample answer sheet.

Public Affairs

5. The most important way in which geographic factors influence rural community structure is by
   A) influencing the size of the farms and thus the density of the population
   B) influencing the birth rate
   C) dictating the habits of the people
   D) influencing the temperament of the people in such a way as to make them cooperative or noncooperative
   E) being the most important determinants of community boundaries

Since A is the best answer to question 5, the space under A is marked on the sample answer sheet.

6. The following table indicates the distribution, by type of economic activity, of those employed in a country. Which of the following five countries most probably has the occupational distribution indicated in this table?

Employment by Activity

Activity	Number
Agriculture and Fishing	655, 190
Mining	51, 449
Manufacturing	926, 997
Construction	257, 466
Transport and Communications	296, 737
Commerce, Banking, Insurance	447, 242
Domestic Service	243, 555
Total Employment	3, 185, 816

   A) Bulgaria
   B) Hungary
   C) Netherlands
   D) Portugal
   E) Turkey

Since C is the best answer to question 6, the space under C is marked on the sample answer sheet.

	A	B	C	D	E
1	█	::	::	::	::
2	::	::	::	::	█
3	█	::	::	::	::
4	::	::	█	::	::
5	█	::	::	::	::
6	::	::	█	::	::

Engineering and Other Physical Sciences

Engineers and scientists hired by their employers at the lower professional grades are sometimes given a written test covering their branch of science, as well as the aptitude tests appropriate for the type of work. The written test nearly always requires a knowledge of whatever branch of mathematics is involved in the scientific field.

1. A plane figure consists of a square 10 inches on a side and an isosceles triangle whose base is the left edge of the square and whose altitude dropped from the vertex opposite the 10-inch base of the triangle common to the square is 6 inches. Approximately how far in inches from the left side of the square is the center of gravity of the whole figure located?
   A) 2.92 D) 3.75
   B) 3.15 E) 4.28
   C) 3.38

   In the Sample of the Answer Sheet, the space under C has been marked for Sample 1, as 3.38 is the correct answer.

2. The stiffness of a rectangular beam varies
   A) as the depth
   B) inversely as the depth
   C) as the square of the depth
   D) as the cube of the depth
   E) inversely as the cube of the depth

3. At atmospheric pressure, steam at 100° C. is passed into 400 grams of water at 10° C. until the temperature of the water rises to 40° C. It is then found that the weight of the water has increased to 420 grams due to the condensing steam. The heat of vaporization of steam in calories per gram at 100° C. is
   A) 60 D) 600
   B) 300 E) none of these
   C) 540

4. The addition of HCl to a solution of sodium acetate causes
   A) the precipitation of sodium chloride
   B) a decrease in the concentration of acetate ion
   C) an increase in the concentration of sodium ion
   D) an increase in the concentration of hydroxide ion
   E) no change in the concentration of hydroxide ion

Psychology

5. In experiments on the localization of sound in space, the sounds which can be most accurately located by the hearer are those sounds originating at points
   A) in the plane equidistant from the two ears of the hearer
   B) in front of the hearer
   C) above and below the hearer
   D) to the left and to the right of the hearer
   E) behind the hearer

6. In the field of measurement of interests, the Preference Record is associated with the name of
   A) Remmers D) Viteles
   B) Kuder E) Bell
   C) Bingham

	A	B	C	D	E		A	B	C	D	E
1			▮			6		▮			
2				▮		7	▮				
3			▮			8			▮		
4		▮				9			▮		
5				▮		10					▮

Statistics

7. If 4 is added to every observation in a sample, the mean is
   A) increased by 4
   B) increased by 4 times the number of observations
   C) increased by 4 divided by the number of observations
   D) decreased by 4
   E) not affected

8. A distribution for which one of the following variables would constitute a discrete series?
   A) weight of eighth-grade pupils
   B) width of the visual field
   C) "items right" score on a history test
   D) auditory reaction time
   E) age at marriage of 850 charwomen

   Since C is the best answer to the question, the space under C has been marked.

9. Of the following measures, which one is the most stable under conditions of random sampling?
   A) mode D) harmonic mean
   B) median E) geometric mean
   C) arithmetic mean

10. The standard deviation is a measure of which one of the following characteristics of a population
    A) skewness D) randomness
    B) symmetry E) variability
    C) normality

KNOWLEDGE TESTS

Accounting

An accounting position in many types of industry may involve one or more of the following activities, with varying degrees of responsibility: Cost accounting, tax accounting, auditing, bookkeeping, analysis and interpretation of financial statements, constructive accounting, and fund or governmental accounting. Very few positions require a specialized knowledge of governmental accounting; most positions require experience or training in commercial accounting principles and practices.

Examinations may be announced for accountants or for accountants and auditors in general; the test in such cases will be based on principles generally applicable to all accounting activities. Occasionally, an examination for a specialized position will test the accounting principles more directly applicable to the duties of that position.

1. An operating mining company properly charged $1,200 to expense to reflect the wear and tear on its equipment. The corresponding credit should have been made to
   A) reserve for contingent liability
   B) reserve for depletion
   C) reserve for depreciation
   D) surplus reserve
   E) earned surplus

2. The Jones Company had a merchandise inventory of $24,625 on January 1, 1950. During the year the company purchased $60,000 worth of goods, sales were $85,065, and the cost of goods sold was $28,060. The inventory on December 31, 1950, was
   A) $25,065.00
   B) $28,500.00
   C) $49,690.00
   D) $57,005.00
   E) none of these

   The answer to question 2 is $56,565, which is not given as A, B, C, or D. The answer sheet is marked under E, therefore.

Weather Forecasting

Weather forecasting is an increasingly important science, which uses many skilled workers, both professional and subprofessional. Ordinarily the persons selected for trainee jobs are given aptitude tests containing mechanical and physical problems. A knowledge of algebra and physics is sometimes required. Professional tests contain questions in the science of weather, or meteorology.

3. Particles of dust, smoke, or microbes often cause the air to be
   A) hazy
   B) clear
   C) humid
   D) dry
   E) cold

4. Helium, neon, krypton, and xenon are
   A) never found in the atmosphere
   B) found in place of hydrogen in the upper atmosphere
   C) found in the atmosphere in very small quantities
   D) found in the Arctic region in largest proportion
   E) found only over the ocean

5. The air is warmed to the greatest extent by
   A) the sun's rays directly
   B) only conduction from the earth
   C) hot vapors
   D) dust particles
   E) both convection and conduction from the earth

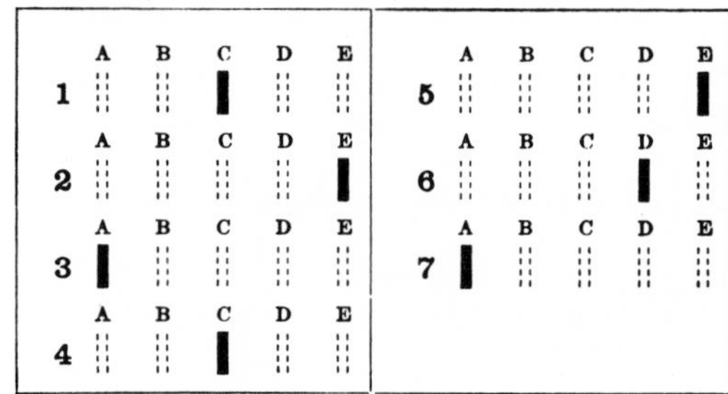

Safety

Examinations for the position of safety inspector or foreman in dangerous occupations, such as mining, stress knowledge of safety devices, rules, and precautions. The correct answers for the two following questions are marked on the section of the Answer Sheet.

6. An electrical detonator is
   A) an instrument used to measure electrical energy
   B) a part of an electrical signaling apparatus
   C) a device used for detecting sound
   D) a device used to fire explosives
   E) a part of an electric-light bulb

7. Most authorities in the field of safety planning agree that the ultimate success of any safety program depends on the
   A) individual worker
   B) foreman
   C) management
   D) state government
   E) safety instructor

Aircraft Mechanics

1. A propeller that has blades which may be modified in flight to get the most advantageous blade angle is called a
   A) controllable pitch propeller
   B) feathered propeller
   C) variable speed propeller
   D) counter-rotating propeller

2. A hinged section of an airplane wing that is used to reduce airspeed for landing is called
   A) a rudder
   B) an elevator
   C) a flap
   D) a rib

Radio Maintenance

3. The symbol at the right represents a
   A) fixed resistance
   B) rheostat
   C) rectifier tube
   D) variable condenser

4. The symbol at the right represents
   A) current
   B) an amplifier
   C) a battery
   D) a transformer

5. A device used for point to point analysis of either voltage or resistance is known as a
   A) volt-ohm-milliammeter
   B) ballistic galvanometer
   C) chanalyst
   D) vacuum tube voltmeter with external probe
   E) megger

Mathematics

In some positions, even at the trainee level, a working knowledge of algebra or geometry is needed to perform the duties of the job or to complete the training course. For Junior Scientist and Engineer positions, candidates are tested on their ability to work out formulas from information supplied. Mathematicians are given more difficult material, including trigonometry, differential equations, and other branches.

6. The product of $(3m-n)$ and $3m$ is
   A) $9m^2-3mn$
   B) $9m^2-mn$
   C) $9m-3n$
   D) $9m^2-n^2$
   E) $3m^2-3mn$

   Since $9m^2-3mn$ is the answer, the Sample Answer Sheet at the right has been marked to show that A is the answer to question 6.

7. The length l of a spiral spring supporting a pan is increased c centimeters for x grams of weight placed on the pan. What is the length of the spring if w grams are placed on the pan?
   A) $lc+\frac{x}{w}$
   B) $l+\frac{w}{cx}$
   C) $l+\frac{cw}{x}$
   D) $\frac{l+cw}{x}$
   E) $\frac{l+cx}{w}$

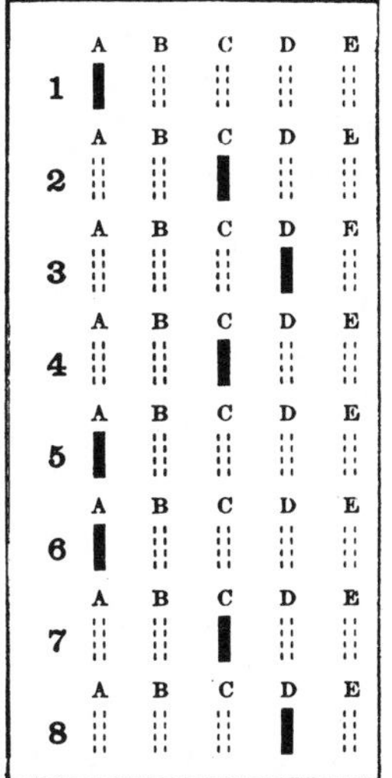

	A	B	C	D	E
1					
2					
3					
4					
5					
6					
7					
8					

8. Find the total differential of $(x^2+y^2)^{\frac{1}{2}}$.
   A) $x(x^2+y^2)-\frac{1}{2}$
   B) $y(x^2+y^2)-\frac{1}{2}$
   C) $xdx+ydy$
   D) $\frac{xdx}{\sqrt{x^2+y^2}}+\frac{ydy}{\sqrt{x^2+y^2}}$
   E) $xdx-ydy$

Sometimes the use of a slide rule is permitted in examinations which contain problems that could be worked with its aid. If there is a statement in the announcement of examination, or in the card of admission to the examination room, that the use of a slide rule, protractor, scale, or any other device is permitted, the applicant must furnish the instrument himself if he wishes to use it. If any instrument or device is *required* to be furnished by the applicant, the announcement or admission card will say so. If it is not required but simply permitted, it is up to the applicant to decide whether he will use it or not.

Mechanical and Nonverbal Tests

As used in this booklet, "nonverbal" describes tests that do not depend on knowledge of language or understanding of words, so much as on the ability to work with numbers, diagrams, and other symbols.

Shop Arithmetic

In each of the following machine-scored problems, five different answers are suggested. Sometimes the last one is "none of these." In question 9, none of the figures given is the correct answer; hence the proper letter to choose is E, which is the letter preceding the answer "none of these."

1. When 100, 125, 75, and 20 are added the answer is
(A)220 (B)270 (C)325 (D)320 (E)420
The sum of these numbers is 320. Look at the choices given and you will find the number 320 after the letter (D). Therefore, to answer question 1, the space under the letter D on the answer sheet should be blackened.

2.
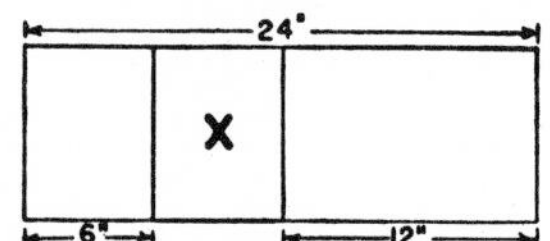

X is what part of the whole sheet?
(A)1/6 (B)1/3 (C)1/4 (D)1/5
(E) none of these

3.
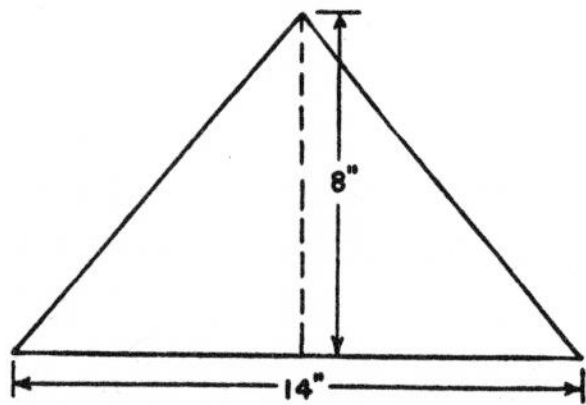

The area of the triangle in square inches is
(A)56 (B)112 (C)122 (D)22 (E)448

4.
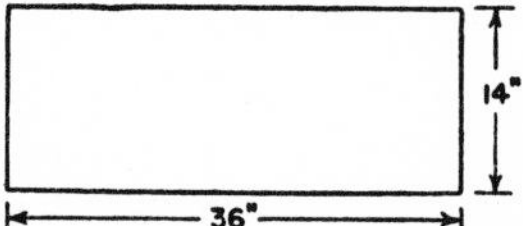

What is the greatest number of pieces 9″ x 2″ that could be cut from the given sheet of metal?
(A)18 (B)21 (C)26 (D)80 (E)28

5.
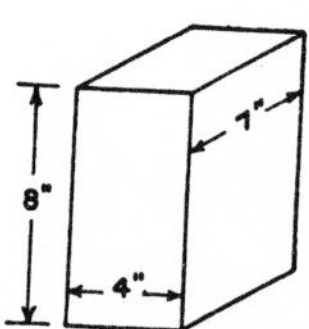

The volume of the rectangular solid in cubic inches is
(A)224 (B)28 (C)896 (D)56 (E)32

6. ½ of ¼ is
(A)1/12 (B)1/8 (C)½ (D)¼ (E)8

7. A circular saw cuts 8 boards per minute. If there are 1,440 boards to be cut, the number of *hours* required to cut these boards is
(A)2⅓ (B)2⅔ (C)4 (D)3⅔ (E)3

8. A drawing of a certain building is 10 inches by 15 inches. On this drawing 1 inch represents 5 feet. If the same drawing had been made 20 inches by 30 inches, 1 inch on the drawing would represent
(A)7½ feet (B)5 feet (C)10 feet
(D)3⅓ feet (E)2½ feet

9. During his first 8-hour day, an apprentice earned 40 percent as much as a master mechanic. If the master mechanic earned $28.00, what was the apprentice's average *hourly* earning?
(A)$1.60 (B)$2.40 (C)$1.68
(D)$1.12 (E) none of these

10. An opening 6 yards long and 3 feet wide is to be covered by sheathing. Enough lumber is available to cover two-thirds of the area of the opening. How many square feet will remain uncovered?
(A)2 (B)4 (C)6 (D)12
(E) none of these

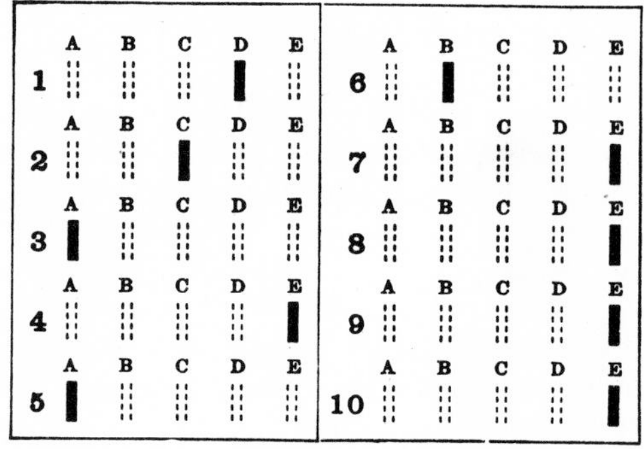

Sometimes questions testing knowledge of mechanical facts are included in tests for mechanical positions. Often, however, such positions, particularly those at the apprentice level, require aptitude rather than knowledge. Many types of questions, some measuring aptitude, others measuring knowledge and ability, are likely to be found in mechanical tests. Illustrations are given on this page and on pages 25 through 35.

Tools and Mechanical Principles

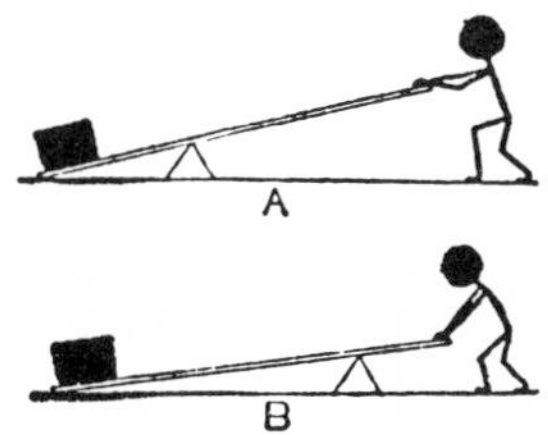

1. In which, if either, of the figures shown above can the man lift more weight?
   A) A
   B) B
   C) The men in figures A and B can lift equal weights.
   D) The man who can lift more weight cannot be determined.

The position of the fulcrum gives the man in figure A a greater mechanical advantage so space A is blackened for question 1.

2. In the gears shown above, as gear X turns in a counterclockwise direction, gear Y turns
   A) clockwise at the same speed
   B) clockwise at a faster speed
   C) counterclockwise at a slower speed
   D) counterclockwise at the same speed

3. In order to smooth and standardize a straight or tapered hole, the best of the following tools to use is a
   A) reamer
   B) drill
   C) tap
   D) cold chisel
   E) compass saw

4. The tool illustrated above is a
   A) counterbore
   B) tap
   C) center punch
   D) rose countersink
   E) pin punch

Information and Judgment

5. Which one of the following frequencies is most commonly used in the United States in alternating-current lighting circuits?
   A) 10 cycles
   B) 25 cycles
   C) 40 cycles
   D) 60 cycles
   E) 110 cycles

6. The device used to mix the air and the fuel in a gasoline engine is called the
   A) carburetor
   B) cylinder
   C) distributor
   D) manifold
   E) valve

7. Which one of the following would cause excessive backlash in the rear axle assembly?
   A) bent rear axle shaft
   B) chipped differential gears
   C) improper lubrication
   D) worn differential gears and thrust washers
   E) ring gear adjusted too close to pinion

8. As a driver brought his truck into a long curve to the left at 40 miles per hour, he made a moderate application of his air brakes, and at that point he felt a pull to the right on the steering wheel. Which one of the following could *not* have caused that pull?
   A) sudden loss of air from right front tire
   B) lack of superelevation on curve
   C) lack of adequate tread on front tires
   D) unbalanced adjustment of brakes

	A	B	C	D	E		A	B	C	D	E
1	▌	⁞	⁞	⁞	⁞	5	⁞	⁞	⁞	▌	⁞
2	▌	⁞	⁞	⁞	⁞	6	▌	⁞	⁞	⁞	⁞
3	▌	⁞	⁞	⁞	⁞	7	⁞	⁞	⁞	▌	⁞
4	⁞	⁞	▌	⁞	⁞	8	⁞	⁞	▌	⁞	⁞

MECHANICAL AND NONVERBAL

Messenger and Guard

A medical and physical examination may be more important to the person applying for a Messenger or Guard position than the written test. However, the written test, when given, is based on the duties which the job applicant will be required to perform.

A test of word meaning (see p. 9) is given in addition to the test described below.

Each box below contains several names. You will be given a few minutes to memorize the arrangement, and then you will be given a list of names. For each name, you will mark on the answer sheet the letter of the box in which the name appears. For example, question 1 is Gaynor. Gaynor is in box C, so the answer sheet is marked to show that C is the answer to question 1.

A	B	C	D	E
Reed	Bliss	Ryder	Mead	Stroud
Molton	Case	Gaynor	Hook	Barry
Robbins	Osmer	Richmond	Blum	Cole
Sheldon	Harris	Bruce	Hortmer	Rakow

1. Gaynor
2. Stroud
3. Sheldon
4. Bruce
5. Molton
6. Case
7. Mead
8. Osmer

	A	B	C	D	E
1			▌		
2					▌
3	▌				
4			▌		
5	▌				
6		▌			
7				▌	
8		▌			
9	▌				
10					▌
11			▌		
12	▌				

Warehousing

Suppose that a stockroom is divided into three sections, each containing several bins. Each bin contains one type of stock item which is numbered the same as the bin.

LOCATION PLAN

Section	*Bin and Item Numbers*
West	1–10
Central	11–20
East	21–30

Each question consists of a list of stock numbers making up an order. Mark the answer sheet

A) if the order is filled from only ONE section
B) if the order is filled from the WEST and CENTRAL sections only
C) if the order is filled from the WEST and EAST sections only
D) if the order is filled from the CENTRAL and EAST sections only
E) if the order is filled from ALL THREE sections

9. 26, 28, 29.
The answer to question 9 is A, because all three items in this order are found in only ONE section.

10. 2, 12, 25, 29.
The answer is E, because items must be taken from ALL THREE sections to fill this order.
From time to time, bins and the items they hold will be moved from one section to another. Also, items may become unavailable and other items will be substituted for them. Write the location plan out and make the changes in the plan.

Change 1. Bins 11 and 12 are moved from Central to West.
Bin 21 is moved from East to Central.
Item 15 is discontinued and is replaced by item 25.
Item 27 is discontinued and is replaced by item 3.

Your location plan should now look like this:

Section	Bin and Item Numbers		
West	~~1–10~~	1–12	
Central	~~11–20~~	13–21	For 15 use 25
East	~~21–30~~	22–30	For 27 use 3

11. 2, 11, 22, 23.
After the changes this order is filled from the WEST and EAST sections, so the answer is C.

12. 15, 24, 29.
Item 25 is now used for 15, and the order is filled from only ONE section; the answer is A.

Identical Forms

In each question there are five drawings lettered A, B, C, D, and E. Four of the drawings are alike in every way. Find the one that differs from the rest, and mark the answer sheet under the letter of that drawing.

1.

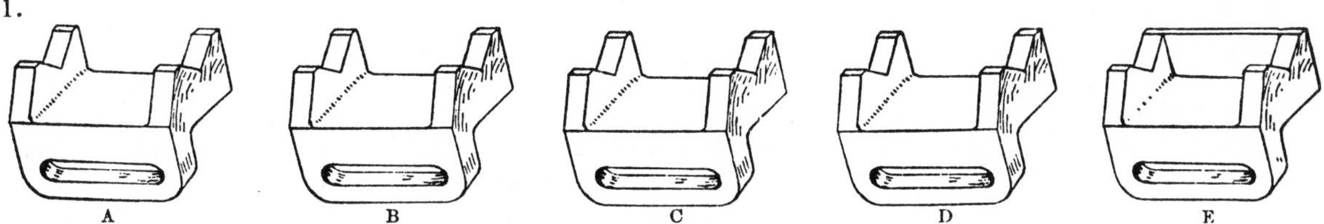

In question 1 the object in drawing E has a wall across the back of the shelf-like space. All the other objects are open at the back. The answer sheet is marked E for question 1.

2.

3.

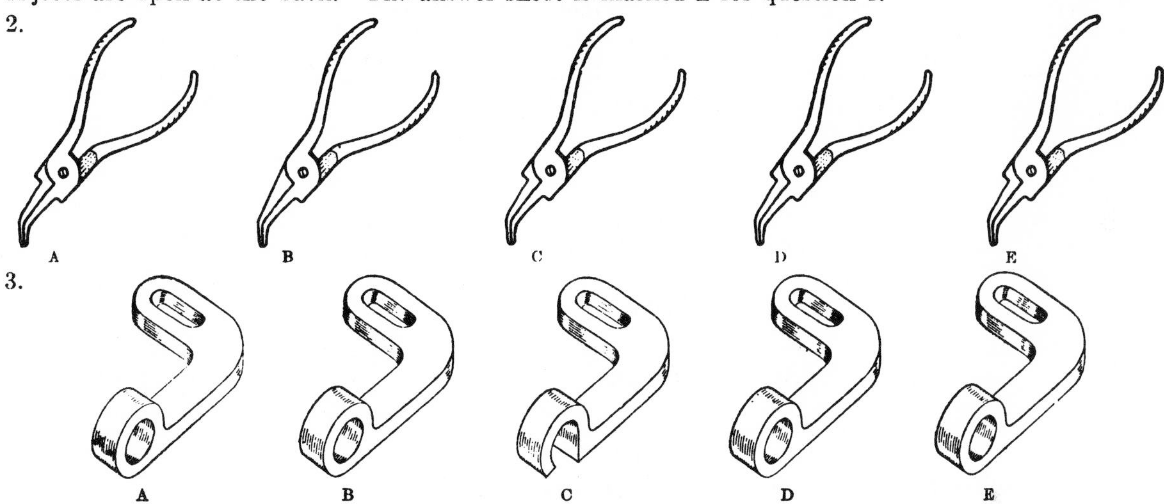

Touching Cubes

Questions 4 and 5 are based on one group of touching cubes, and questions 6 and 7 on another group. All the cubes are exactly the same size, and there are only enough hidden cubes to support the ones you can see. The question number is on a cube in the group. You are to find how many cubes in that group touch the numbered cube. A cube is considered to touch the numbered cube if any part, even an edge or a corner, touches. Then mark the Sample Answer Sheet to show how many cubes touch the numbered cube by blackening space—

A if the answer is 1 or 6 or 11 cubes
B if the answer is 2 or 7 or 12 cubes
C if the answer is 3 or 8 or 13 cubes
D if the answer is 4 or 9 or 14 cubes
E if the answer is 5 or 10 or 15 cubes

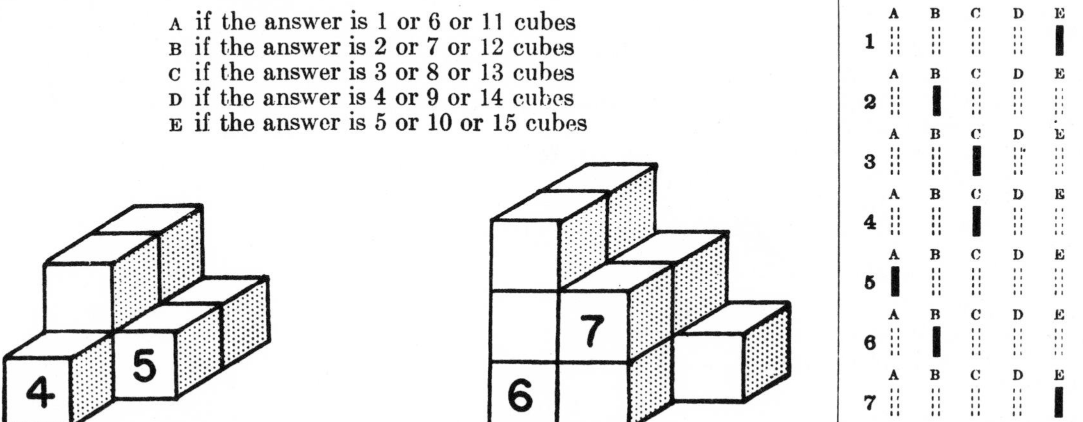

In question 4, there are three cubes that touch the cube marked 4—the one right behind it which you cannot see, the one on top of that, and the one marked 5. Because the answer is three cubes, the space marked C should be blackened.

MECHANICAL AND NONVERBAL

Graph Reading

Many jobs require ability to read graphs and charts, or to make graphs and charts from collected information so that others can find the information there.

The following questions can be answered by reading the bar graph at the right.

OUTPUT OF RADIO SETS AND TELEVISION SETS BY FACTORY "K"
1947—1951

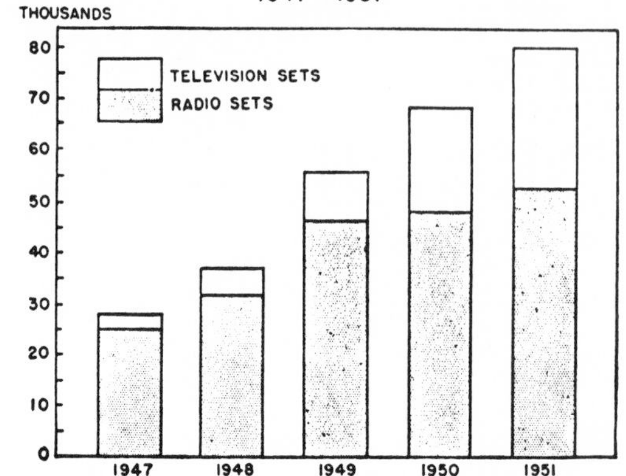

1. In the year in which the total output of the factory was the least, the percentage of that output which consisted of television sets was approximately
   A) 10%
   B) 20%
   C) 25%
   D) 30%
   E) 40%

2. In which year did the production of television sets total approximately 20,000?
   A) 1947
   B) 1948
   C) 1949
   D) 1950
   E) 1951

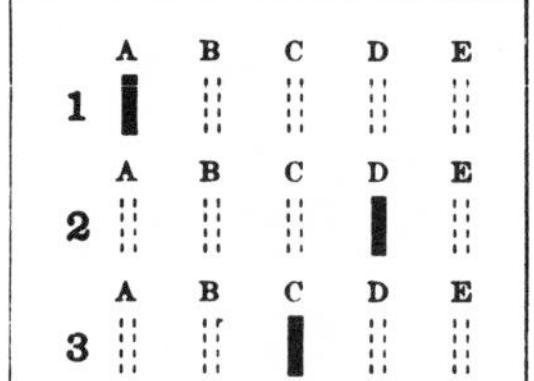

Meter Reading

3. The position of the pointer on the meter scale is nearest to
   (A)2.6 (B)3.1 (C)3.2 (D)3.3

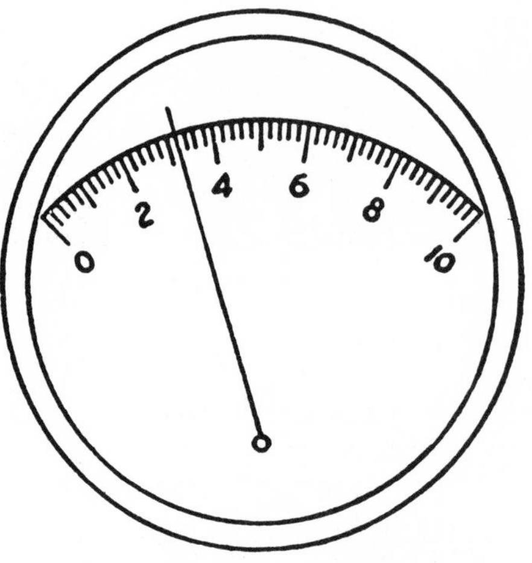

An examination of the meter scale shows, first, that only the even numbers are given on the dial. Between each pair of numbers are 10 small subdivisions. The position of the odd numbers is indicated by the slightly longer subdivision mark. Since there are five subdivisions between the positions of two successive whole numbers, each subdivision indicates ⅕ or .2.

The pointer in the example is closest to one subdivision beyond 3; the correct reading of the meter would be 3 + ⅕, or 3.2.

For a reading of 3.1, the pointer would be midway between the mark corresponding to 3 and the mark corresponding to 3.2.

Matching Parts and Figures

These questions test understanding of spatial relations. They also present problems found in making templates and patterns. The first two questions show, at the left side, two or more flat pieces. In each question select the arrangement lettered A, B, C, or D that shows how these pieces can be fitted together without gaps or overlapping. The pieces may be *turned around* or *turned over* in any way to make them fit together. On the answer sheet you should blacken the space lettered the same as the figure that you have selected.

From these pieces *which one of these arrangements can you make?*

1. 

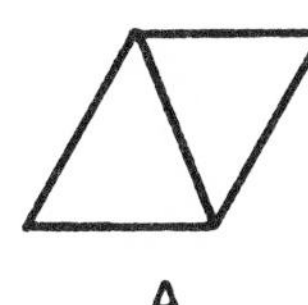
A

B

C

D

In sample question 1, for instance, only the arrangement lettered D could be formed by fitting together the pieces on the left. Note that the pieces are turned around to make D. None of the other arrangements shows pieces of the given size and shape.

From these pieces *which one of these arrangements can you make?*

2. 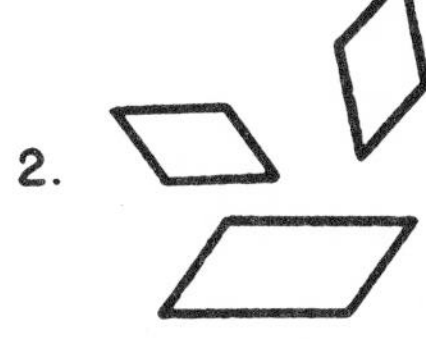

A

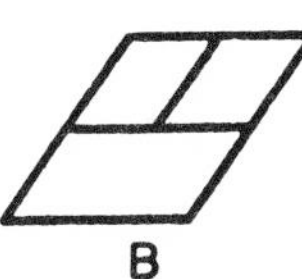
B

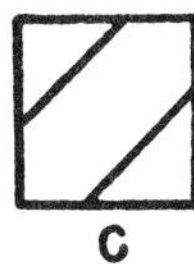
C

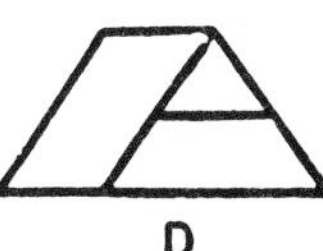
D

The next questions are based on the four solid patterns shown below.

Each of the questions shows *one* of these four patterns cut up into pieces. For each question, decide which one of the four patterns could be made by fitting *all of the pieces* together without having any edges overlap and without leaving any space between pieces. Some of the pieces may need to be *turned around* or *turned over* to make them fit. The pattern must be made in its exact size and shape.

A

B

C

D

Look at sample question 3. If the two pieces were fitted together they would make pattern D. The piece on the left fits at the bottom of pattern D, and the piece at the right is turned around and over to make the top of the pattern.

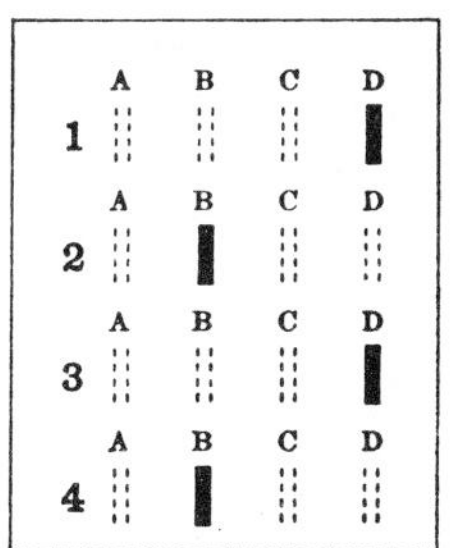

MECHANICAL AND NONVERBAL

Perception of Form

Look at the rows of drawings below. In each row, the design at the left is contained in *one or more* of the more complex drawings. A drawing is to be marked as an answer if it contains the exact design in the same position. The designs in the drawings need not be alined with the original design, but they are not to be *turned*. The designs and drawings are two-dimensional. In some rows more than one drawing contains the exact design in the correct position. In these cases, you should mark more than one answer on your answer sheet.

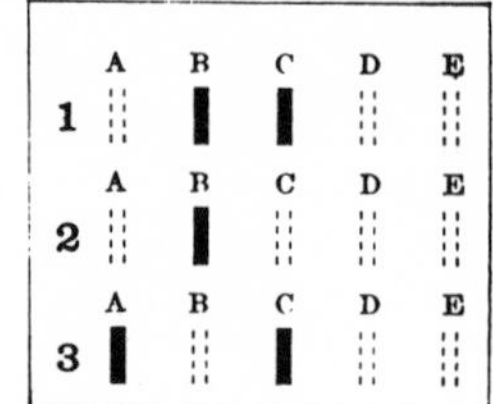

Look at question 1. The design at the left is contained in the more complex drawings B and C, so these are marked as answers for question 1. The design is also in drawing D, but not in the correct position, so this is not an answer.

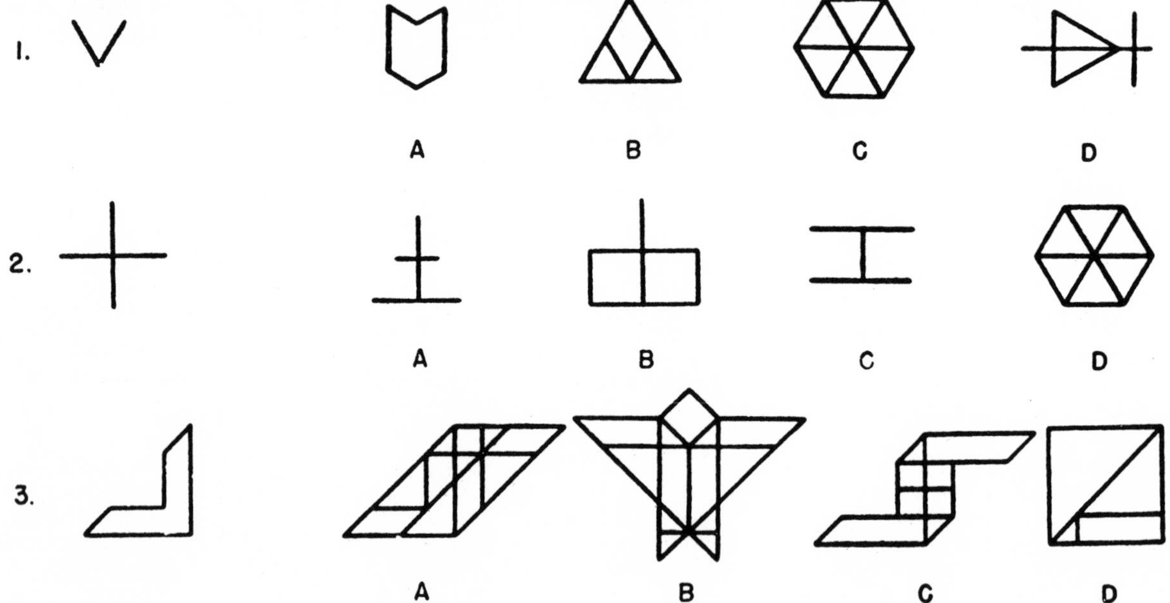

Matching Solid Figures and Parts

In each question the object pictured at the left is a combination of two pieces. One *set* of the five sets of pieces at the right can be combined to make the object at the left. Watch both the sizes and shapes of the pieces. The section of answer sheet at the right is blackened under the letter for the correct set of pieces in each question.

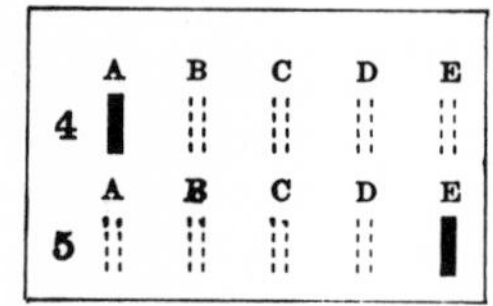

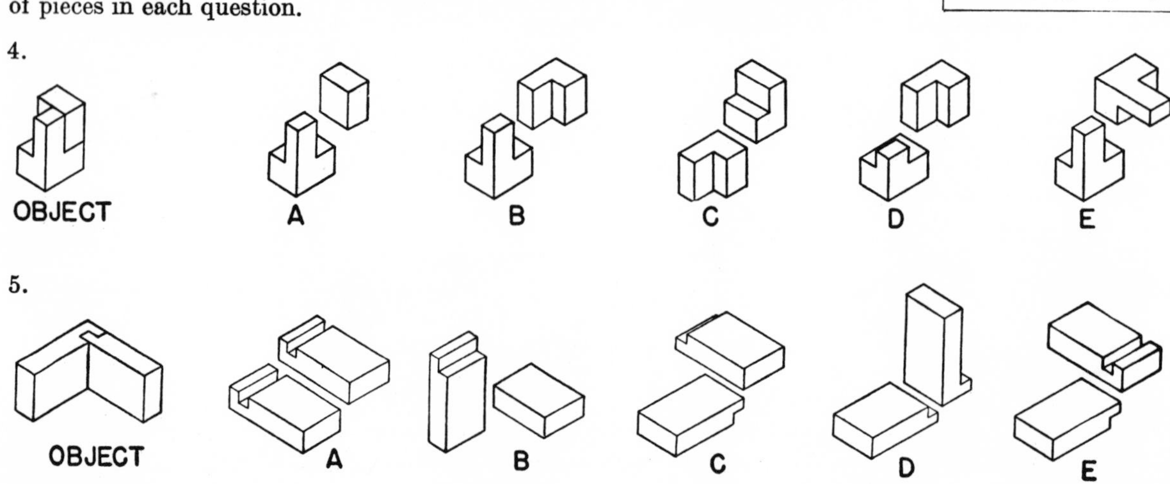

Cube Turning

The drawing at the left in each of the two following sample questions represents a cube. There is a different design on each of the six faces of the cube. Four other drawings of cubes are lettered A, B, C, and D.

You are asked to show, by marking the correct space on your Answer Sheet, which *one* of the four could possibly be the cube on the left turned to a different position. (The cube at the left may have been turned *over*, it may have been turned *around*, or it may have been turned *both* over and around, and faces not seen in the drawing on the left may become visible.)

1. 

A

B

C

D

In sample question 1 you will notice that only B could be the same cube as that shown on the left. Study the sample carefully and be sure you understand why B is the cube on the left turned to a different position. Also, be sure you understand why A, C, and D could *not* be the same cube. For instance, A is wrong because when the block is turned with the square on the right and the cross in front, the triangle would be on top, but it would point toward the cross instead of away from it.

If the cube were turned upside down, the cross and triangle would appear as they do in C, but the square would be on the bottom and would not show; the former bottom, now the top, would have a different design, since no two faces are alike. Or if the original cube were given a quarter-turn clockwise, the square would still be on top and the cross would be in front as in C but again a new face would show, which could not be a triangle. D is not the answer either, since the triangle ought to point toward the cross, and in D it points toward a circle.

2. 

A

B

C

D

Pattern Folding

In questions like No. 3, you are to select the *one* object, A, B, C, or D, that could be made from the flat piece shown at the left, if this flat piece were folded on the dotted lines shown in the drawing, or rolled so that the edges meet.

3. 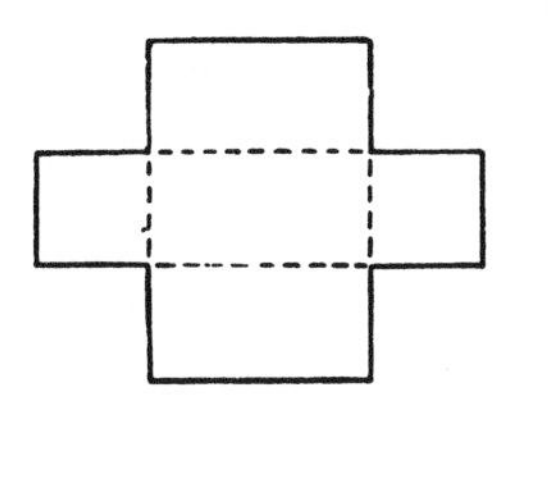

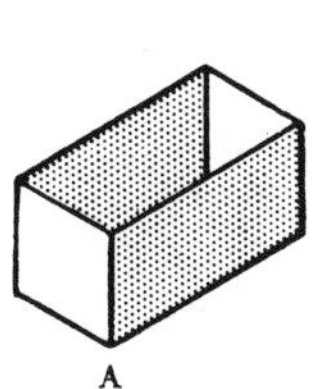
A

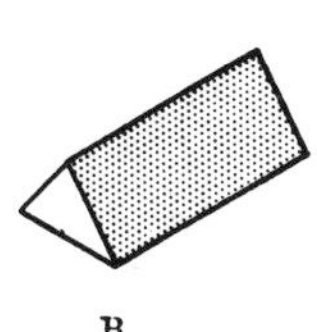
B

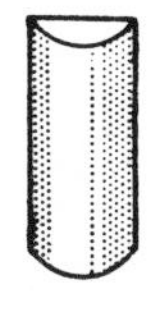
C

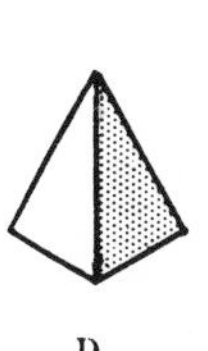
D

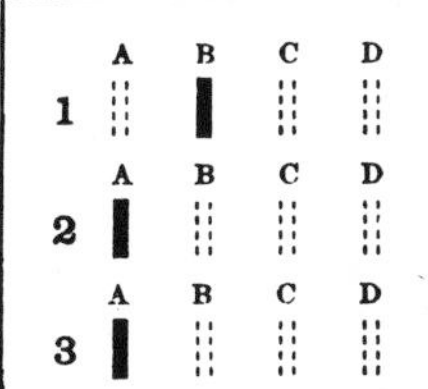

MECHANICAL AND NONVERBAL

Elevations and Perspective

An elevation is a drawing of one side of an object. Think of an object inside a glass box. The tracing of the object's shape on the top of the box would be a "top elevation" or "top view." Tracings can be made from any side. In mechanical drawing, usually three views are given.

Directions: In the following questions you are given a top view, a front view, and a view of the right side of a solid object. The problem is to find the *one* of the four objects lettered A, B, C, and D that would look like these views; then mark the letter of that object on the answer sheet.

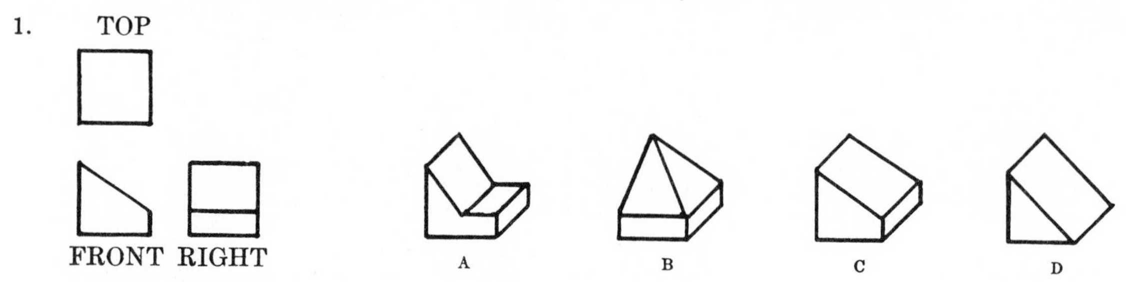

In question 1, both A and C have the correct right view; both C and D have the top view shown; but only C looks like the view marked "FRONT." C is therefore the answer to the question.

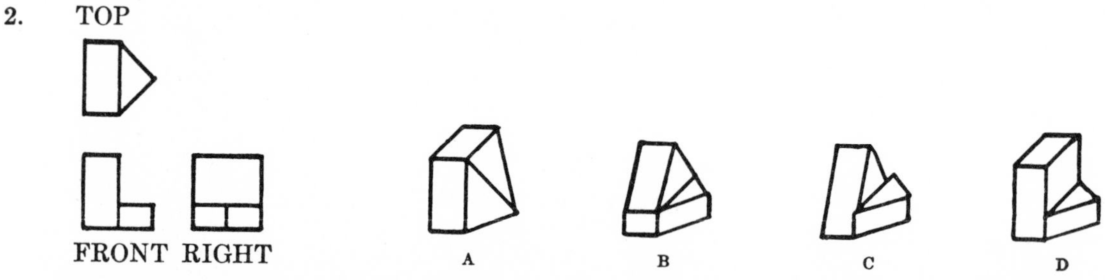

When you work these problems, you may check any one of the views first; one or more of the objects may show up as being clearly different from this view. Then compare the other views with the remaining objects. You will find that only one object finally remains which looks like all three of the given views.

In question 2, for example, beginning with the front view: A is ruled out at first glance, B has one line in the wrong place, but C and D are left. Now a check of the top view shows that C should have a line which is not in the given top view, and a final check of the right side view against D shows that D is the answer.

If you had started with the top view in question 2, you would have had A and D remaining as possibilities. Then a check of either the front or right view would have eliminated A, and D would be the correct letter to mark on the answer sheet. If you had started with the right view, you could have found the answer on the first try. There is no way to tell which order will prove to be the quickest for any given question—as you see in question 1, the front view would have given the answer at once. It is best, if you have the time, to check all views of each object so that you are sure you have found the *one* answer.

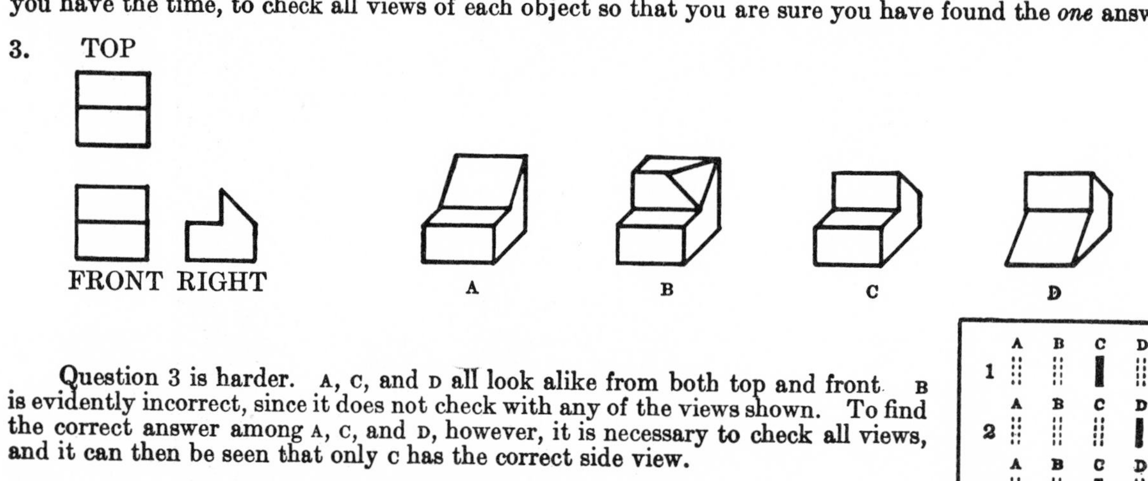

Question 3 is harder. A, C, and D all look alike from both top and front. B is evidently incorrect, since it does not check with any of the views shown. To find the correct answer among A, C, and D, however, it is necessary to check all views, and it can then be seen that only C has the correct side view.

Observation and Memory

This kind of test is used in examinations for various kinds of investigators, for example, Treasury Enforcement Agent. Read the directions under the picture.

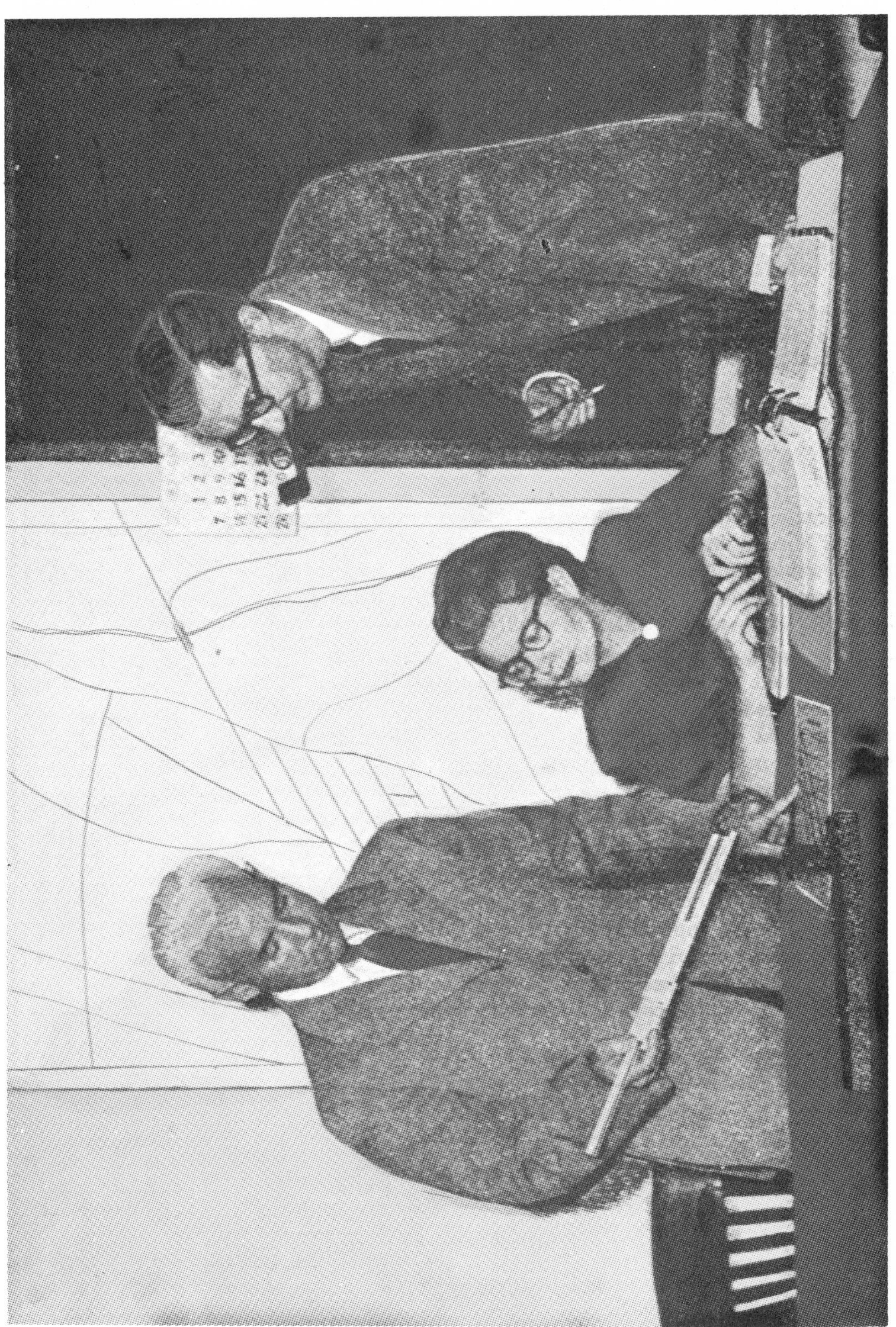

Study the picture for 5 minutes. Observe all the details of the scene—what the people are wearing, what kinds of furniture and equipment are in the room, and where each object is. Do not make any written notes.

After 5 minutes, turn the page and see if you can answer the questions at the top of the next page without looking back at the picture.

MECHANICAL AND NONVERBAL

Observation and Memory—Continued

Do not read these questions until you have studied the picture on the other side of this sheet. After you have studied the picture for 5 minutes, you must not look back at it for the answers to the questions. *After* you have answered the questions, look at the bottom line on this page.

1. Which one of these things can be seen in the picture?
   A) a telephone
   B) an initialed belt buckle
   C) a list of names on the blackboard
   D) a brief case
   E) a calendar with one date circled

2. The man in the light suit is
   A) holding a pencil in his left hand
   B) smoking a pipe
   C) holding a slide rule in his right hand
   D) pointing to the blackboard
   E) opening a loose-leaf notebook

3. The secretary in this picture
   A) wears no jewelry
   B) has a light-colored dress
   C) is writing in a loose-leaf binder
   D) wears a short-sleeved dress
   E) is looking at the blackboard

4. The man who is smoking a pipe is also
   A) pointing to a statistical chart
   B) leaning on the table
   C) wearing a bow tie
   D) writing on the map
   E) wearing rimless glasses

Test of Fine Dexterity

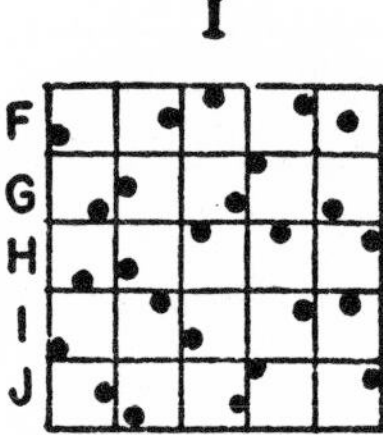

This test is used to examine competitors for a position that requires carefulness, patience, and accuracy of sight and movement. Competitors who have excessive trouble with this test would probably not qualify for work that involves the assembly of delicate timing devices (to give one example), and almost certainly would not like such work if they did manage to qualify.

Each competitor receives a diagram resembling the one on the right, a small card with a diagram like that at the left below, and a fine pin. The first part of the test is to make pin-holes in the card in the exact pattern of the dots on the printed diagram. Note that there is only one dot to each square, and that it could be in the center, at one corner, at the middle of one side, or at one side halfway between the middle and the corner.

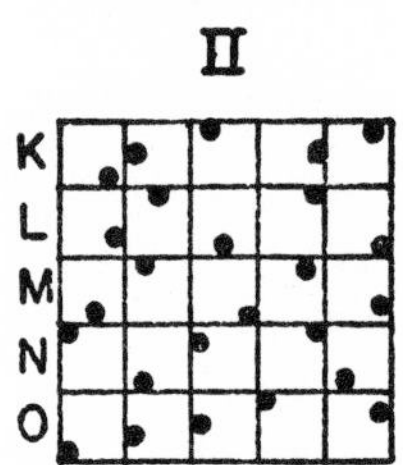

After the competitors have punched all the squares in the small diagram, the large diagram is taken away. Then for the second part of the test the competitors mark the answer sheet to show where each dot was made, according to a code that describes each possible position. This code is a large square with all possible positions of the pin-prick shown, and differently lettered. If the competitor has placed his pin-pricks in exactly the right place, he will be able to read the right letters from the code square. If he has made a pin-prick in the wrong position, he will read the wrong letter from the code and mark the wrong answer.

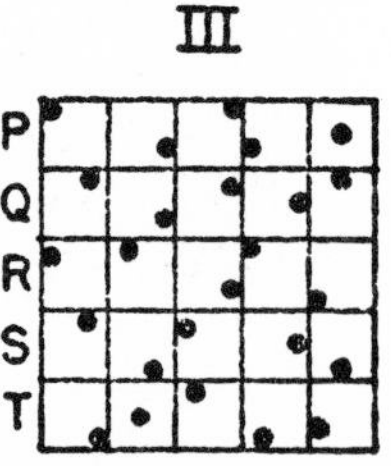

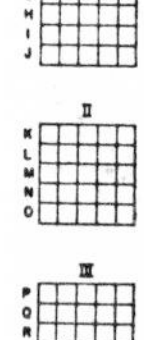

If you wish to practice this test, use a fine pin or a needle to punch the very small squares, and try to copy the position of each dot in the larger squares. Then, reading from the small squares, describe the location of each pin prick and check it with the large diagram.

For a test of dexterity that is not so hard as this, see page 35.

ANSWERS TO MEMORY TEST: 1. E; 2. C; 3. D; 4. B

Dexterity Tests

Many kinds of work require some degree of accuracy and skill with your hands. If you have the right amount of this aptitude, you can be successful on the job; if you do not, you would probably not enjoy the work, since you would find it difficult to do.

The test on this page is one of a variety of tests that measure hand skill. Cut out the gage at the right on the dotted lines, and trim it off carefully on the left-hand edge. (Save it for the questions on page 34 also.) Each question in the test has 5 rectangles lettered the same as those on the gage. Measure each one, laying the gage down so that the rectangles overlap a little and all the thin lines run the same way. Use A on the gage to measure A in the question; B to measure B, and so on. One of the five is just a little too large or too small; the letter of that rectangle is the answer to the question. These drawings show how the gage is used.

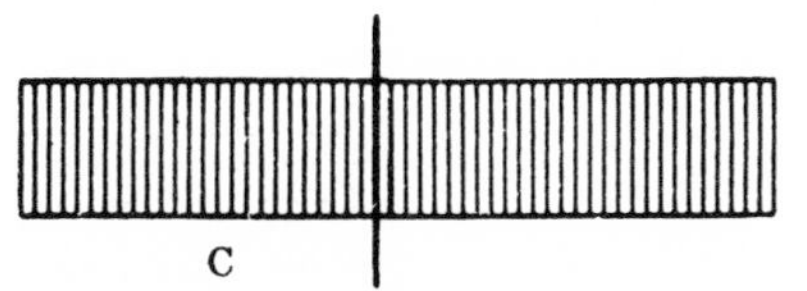

These rectangles match.

Use the gage to verify the answers to these sample questions. Remember that the letter of the *wrong* rectangle is the answer.

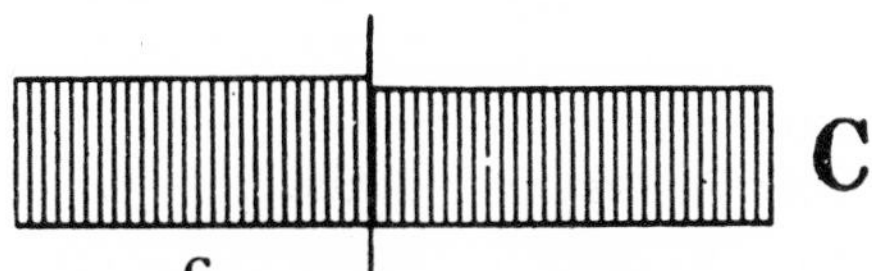

These rectangles do not match.

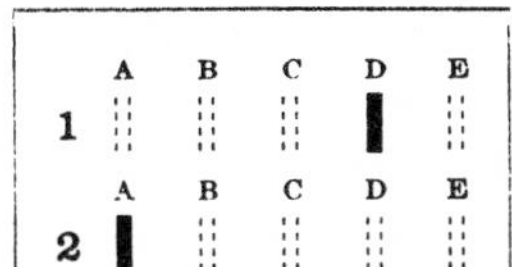

MEASURING GAGE

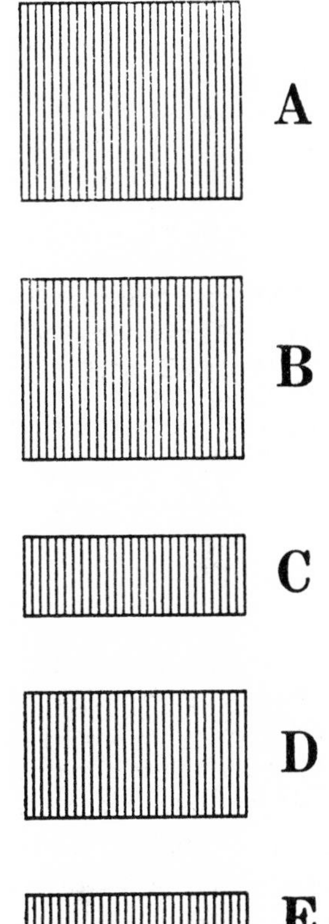

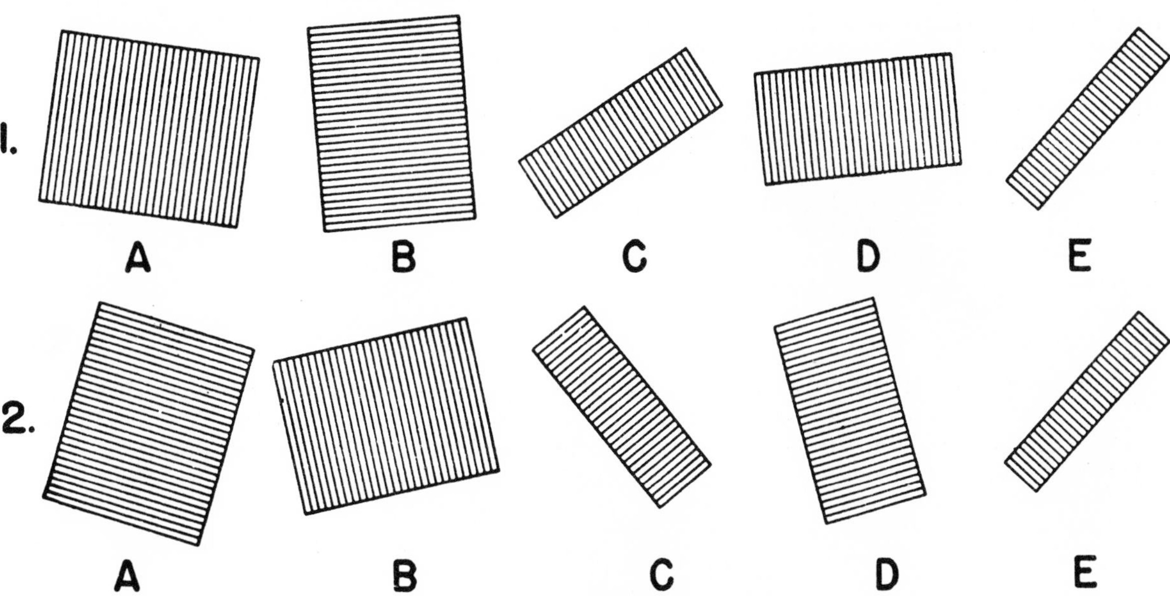

CODE FOR INSPECTION TEST

Bin A – All Right

4 4

Bin B – Bashed In

2 2

Bin C – Combination of Same

6 6

Bin D – Different Numbers

3 5

Bin E – Empty

MECHANICAL AND NONVERBAL

Inspection Tests

The ability to inspect, sort, and examine objects of many kinds can be tested by some pencil and paper tests. Two of these are described here.

The diagram at the left shows five bins into which pairs of parts are to be sorted. In each pair of parts, one part should be round and the other square; both should have the same number.

Bin A is for pairs that are ALL RIGHT.

Bin B is for pairs that have a part which is BASHED IN.

Bin C is for a COMBINATION of two round or two square parts.

Bin D is for pairs in which the parts have DIFFERENT numbers.

Bin E is for pairs in which the number spaces are EMPTY.

Look at each pair of parts below, and decide which bin they go into. The letter of that bin should be recorded on the answer sheet. (To save space, the answer sheet is not reproduced here, but the correct answers are indicated.)

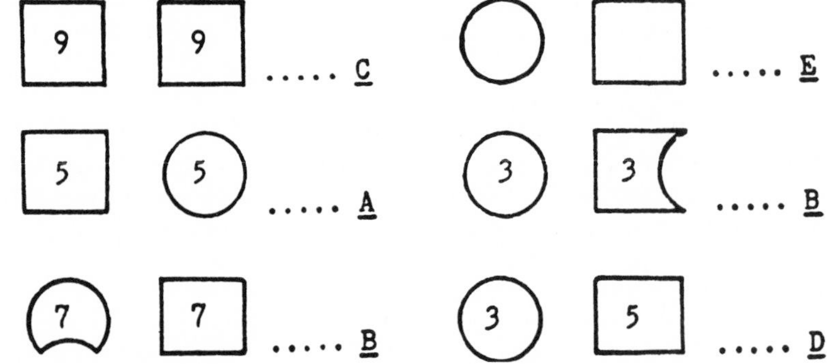

For another type of inspection test the competitor counts small objects. Each question asks for the number of x's or o's, or both, in a certain area of the diagram shown. Count the objects as directed. If an x or o falls across a line dividing one area from another, count it as being in the area in which most of it falls. Look for your answer among those suggested, and mark the answer sheet accordingly. If your answer is not listed, mark E. (To save space, the answer sheet is not printed here, but the correct answers are given below.)

1 2 3

1

2

3

1. How many x's are there in Row 1, Col. 2? A)12 B)13 C)14 D)15 E)none of these
2. How many o's in Row 1, Columns 1 and 2? A)13 B)14 C)15 D)17 E)none of these
3. How many x's in Row 2, Col. 1? A)11 B)13 C)14 D)16 E)none of these
4. How many o's in Row 3, Col. 3? A)11 B)13 C)15 D)16 E)none of these
5. How many x's and o's in Row 3, Col. 2? A)22 B)23 C)24 D)25 E)none of these
6. How many o's in Row 2, Col. 3? A) 9 B)10 C)11 D)12 E)none of these

The correct answers are: 1.B; 2.D; 3.C; 4.E; 5.A; 6.B.

Gross Dexterity Test

This is a timed test that shows how quickly and accurately you can work, by finding and filling in the spaces on the answer sheet. Look at the picture on page 4, and notice that the answer sheet has an upper and a lower section. Since there are 25 numbers in each column, the upper section has the first 10 of each group of 25—that is, numbers 1 to 10, 26 to 35, 51 to 60, 76 to 85, and 101 to 110. On this page, only the upper section is reproduced, and all the questions given here are to be marked in that section. In a real examination the questions would be scattered all over the page.

To work this test, simply go down the list and mark each space as you are directed. The first question is 26. B; blacken space B after number 26 on the answer sheet. Work as fast as you can.

26. B	77. E	8. B	7. D	60. D	55. B
57. C	81. A	104. D	106. A	4. B	107. E
31. D	105. A	6. C	108. E	83. E	79. B
9. E	53. B	80. C	51. E	102. A	35. A
110. D	106. C	34. E	78. A	29. D	27. D

Following Oral Directions

This is another test which uses only the answer sheet. In this test the examiner reads directions aloud, and the competitors mark their answer sheets as directed. You can use this material for practice by reading each sentence aloud and covering the directions while you follow them, or by copying the directions and having someone else read them to you. Try to work quickly. In the examination room the reading of each paragraph is timed carefully, so that all competitors have the same time to work. (Note: If you have worked the Gross Dexterity Test above on the answer sheet below, you do not have to erase your answers—the samples for Following Oral Directions will not interfere with them.)

"Mark E for 7, 8, 10, (slight pause) 3, and 52. (Pause.)
"Mark C for 32, 35, and 78. (Pause.)
"Mark D as in dog for 26, 35, (slight pause) 76, and 10. (Pause.)

"For the next set of questions, mark space E and also mark the letter I call, unless E is already marked. If E is already marked for that number, do not make any mark for that number.

"Mark B as in boy for 56, 3, (slight pause) 80, and 84. (Pause.)
"Mark A for 33, 29, (slight pause) 8, and 58. (Pause.)
"Mark C for 79, 52, (slight pause) and 28."

NOTE: This answer sheet provides spaces for both types of questions on this page. You do not have to erase your answers to one practice test before you work the other.

	A	B	C	D	E		A	B	C	D	E		A	B	C	D	E		A	B	C	D	E		A	B	C	D	E
1						26						51						76						101					
2						27						52						77						102					
3						28						53						78						103					
4						29						54						79						104					
5						30						55						80						105					
6						31						56						81						106					
7						32						57						82						107					
8						33						58						83						108					
9						34						59						84						109					
10						35						60						85						110					

II. HOW TO BE A MASTER TEST TAKER

It's really quite simple. Do things right . . . right from the beginning. Make successful methods a habit by practicing them on all the exercises in this book. Before you're finished you will have invested a good deal of time. Make sure you get the largest dividends from this investment.

SCORING PAPERS BY MACHINE

A typical machine-scored answer sheet is shown below, reduced from the actual size of 8¼ x 11 inches. Since it's the only one that reaches the office where papers are scored, it's important that the blanks at the top be filled in completely and correctly.

The chances are very good that you'll have to mark your answers on one of these sheets. Consequently, we've made it possible for you to practice with them throughout this book.

ANSWER SHEET

SERIES No ______ YOUR IDENTIFICATION NUMBER ______

TEST No. ______ PART ______ TITLE OF POSITION ______ (AS GIVEN IN EXAMINATION ANNOUNCEMENT - INCLUDE OPTION, IF ANY)

PLACE OF EXAMINATION ______ (CITY OR TOWN) ______ (STATE) DATE ______

RATING

IF YOU CLAIM VETERAN PREFERENCE, PUT AN "X" IN THE APPROPRIATE BOX:

☐ VETERAN ☐ DISABLED VETERAN ☐ DISABLED VET'S WIFE ☐ VET'S WIDOW ☐ VET'S MOTHER

USE THE SPECIAL PENCIL. MAKE GLOSSY BLACK MARKS.

1	A B C D E	26	A B C D E	51	A B C D E	76	A B C D E	101	A B C D E
2	A B C D E	27	A B C D E	52	A B C D E	77	A B C D E	102	A B C D E
3	A B C D E	28	A B C D E	53	A B C D E	78	A B C D E	103	A B C D E
4	A B C D E	29	A B C D E	54	A B C D E	79	A B C D E	104	A B C D E
5	A B C D E	30	A B C D E	55	A B C D E	80	A B C D E	105	A B C D E
6	A B C D E	31	A B C D E	56	A B C D E	81	A B C D E	106	A B C D E
7	A B C D E	32	A B C D E	57	A B C D E	82	A B C D E	107	A B C D E
8	A B C D E	33	A B C D E	58	A B C D E	83	A B C D E	108	A B C D E
9	A B C D E	34	A B C D E	59	A B C D E	84	A B C D E	109	A B C D E
10	A B C D E	35	A B C D E	60	A B C D E	85	A B C D E	110	A B C D E

Make only ONE mark to answer any one item. Additional and stray marks may be counted as mistakes. In making corrections, erase errors COMPLETELY.

11	A B C D E	36	A B C D E	61	A B C D E	86	A B C D E	111	A B C D E
12	A B C D E	37	A B C D E	62	A B C D E	87	A B C D E	112	A B C D E
13	A B C D E	38	A B C D E	63	A B C D E	88	A B C D E	113	A B C D E
14	A B C D E	39	A B C D E	64	A B C D E	89	A B C D E	114	A B C D E
15	A B C D E	40	A B C D E	65	A B C D E	90	A B C D E	115	A B C D E
16	A B C D E	41	A B C D E	66	A B C D E	91	A B C D E	116	A B C D E
17	A B C D E	42	A B C D E	67	A B C D E	92	A B C D E	117	A B C D E
18	A B C D E	43	A B C D E	68	A B C D E	93	A B C D E	118	A B C D E
19	A B C D E	44	A B C D E	69	A B C D E	94	A B C D E	119	A B C D E
20	A B C D E	45	A B C D E	70	A B C D E	95	A B C D E	120	A B C D E
21	A B C D E	46	A B C D E	71	A B C D E	96	A B C D E	121	A B C D E
22	A B C D E	47	A B C D E	72	A B C D E	97	A B C D E	122	A B C D E
23	A B C D E	48	A B C D E	73	A B C D E	98	A B C D E	123	A B C D E
24	A B C D E	49	A B C D E	74	A B C D E	99	A B C D E	124	A B C D E
25	A B C D E	50	A B C D E	75	A B C D E	100	A B C D E	125	A B C D E

C. S. C. FORM 3636, DECEMBER 1950 UNITED STATES CIVIL SERVICE COMMISSION IBM FORM I.T.S. 1000A 2145

FOLLOW DIRECTIONS CAREFULLY

It's an obvious rule, but more people fail for breaching it than for any other cause. By actual count there are over a hundred types of directions given on tests. You'll familiarize yourself with all of them in the course of this book. And you'll also learn not to let your guard down in reading them, listening to them, and following them. Right now, before you plunge in, we want to be sure that you have nothing to fear from the answer sheet and the way in which you must mark it; from the most important question forms and the ways in which they are to be answered.

HERE'S HOW TO MARK YOUR ANSWERS ON MACHINE-SCORED ANSWER SHEETS:

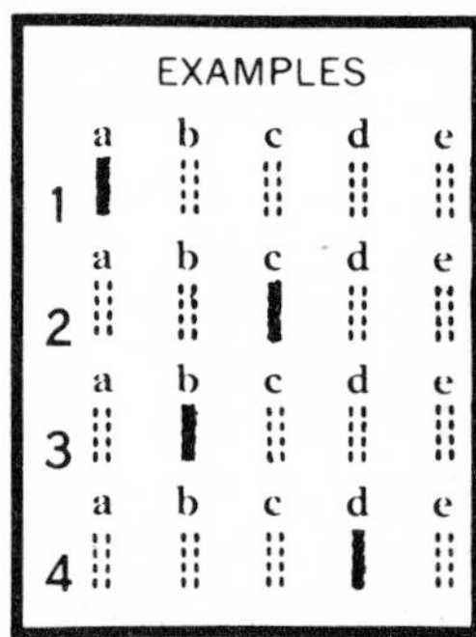

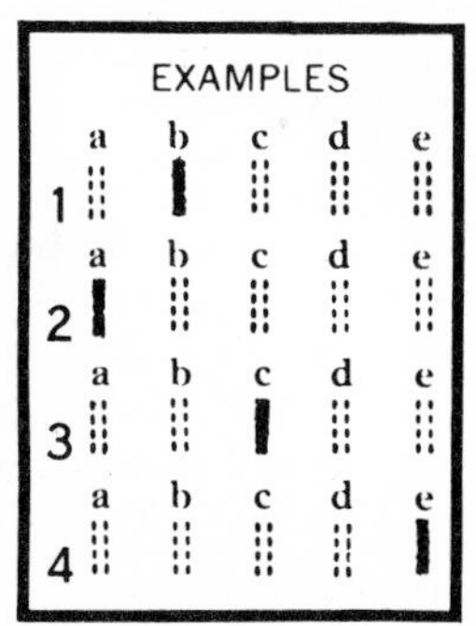

Make only ONE mark for each answer. Additional and stray marks may be counted as mistakes. In making corrections, erase errors COMPLETELY. Make glossy black marks.

(a) Each pencil mark must be heavy and black. Light marks should be retraced with the special pencil.

(b) Each mark must be in the space between the pair of dotted lines and entirely fill this space.

(c) All stray pencil marks on the paper, clearly not intended as answers, must be completely erased.

(d) Each question must have only one answer indicated. If multiple answers occur, all extraneous marks should be thoroughly erased. Otherwise, the machine will give you *no* credit for your correct answer.

MULTIPLE CHOICE METHODS

Multiple choice questions are very popular these days with examiners. The chances are good that you'll get this kind on your test. So we've arranged that you practice with them in the following pages. But first we want to give you a little help by explaining the best methods for handling this question form.

You know, of course, that these questions offer you four or five possible answers, that your job is to select *only* the *best* answer, and that even the incorrect answers are frequently *partly* correct. These partly-true choices are inserted to force you to think . . . and prove that you know the right answer.

USE THESE METHODS TO ANSWER MULTIPLE CHOICE QUESTIONS CORRECTLY:

1. Read the item closely to see what the examiner is after. Re-read it if necessary.
2. Mentally reject answers that are clearly wrong.
3. Suspect as being wrong any of the choices which contain broad statements hinging on "cue" words like

absolute
absolutely
all
always
axiomatic
categorical
completely
doubtless
entirely
extravagantly
forever
immeasurably
inalienable
incontestable
incontrovertible
indefinitely
indisputable
indubitable
inevitable
inexorable
infallible
infinite
inflexible
inordinately
irrefutable
inviolable
never
only
peculiarly
positive
quite
self-evident
sole
totally
unchallenged
unchangeable
undeniable
undoubtedly
unequivocal
unexceptionable
unimpeachable
unqualified
unquestionable
wholly
without exception

If you're unsure of the meanings of any of these words, look them up in your dictionary.

4. A well-constructed multiple choice item will avoid obviously incorrect choices. The good examiner will try to write a cluster of answers, all of which are plausible. Use the clue words to help yourself pick the *most* correct answer.
5. In the case of items where you are doubtful of the answer, you might be able to bring to bear the information you have gained from previous study. This knowledge might be sufficient to indicate that some of the suggested answers are not so plausible. Eliminate such answers from further consideration.
6. Then concentrate on the remaining suggested answers. The more you eliminate in this way, the better your chances of getting the item right.
7. If the item is in the form of an incomplete statement, it sometimes helps to try to complete the statement before you look at the suggested answers. Then see whether the way you have completed the statement corresponds with any of the answers provided. If one is found, it is likely to be the correct one.
8. Use your head! Make shrewd inferences. Sometimes with a little thought, and the information that you have, you can reason out the answer. We're suggesting a method of intelligent guessing in which you can become quite expert with a little practice. It's a useful method that may help you with some debatable answers.

NOW, LET'S TRY THESE METHODS OUT ON A SAMPLE MULTIPLE-CHOICE QUESTION.

1. Leather is considered the best material for shoes chiefly because
   (A) it is waterproof
   (B) it is quite durable
   (C) it is easily procurable
   (D) it is flexible and durable
   (E) it can be easily manufactured in various styles.

Here we see that every one of the answer statements is plausible: leather is waterproof if treated properly; it is relatively durable; it is relatively easily procurable; it bends and is shaped easily, and is, again, durable; it constantly appears in various styles of shoes and boots.

However, we must examine the question with an eye toward identifying the key phrase which is: *best* for shoes *chiefly*.

Now we can see that (A) is incorrect because leather is probably not the *best* material for shoes, simply because it is waterproof. There are far better waterproof materials available, such as plastics and rubber. In fact, leather must be treated to make it waterproof. So by analyzing the key phrase of the question we can eliminate (A).

(B) seems plausible. Leather is durable, and durability is a good quality in shoes. But the word *quite* makes it a broad statement. And we become suspicious. The original meaning of *quite* is completely, wholly, entirely. Since such is the case we must reject this choice because leather is *not completely* durable. It does wear out.

(C) Leather is comparatively easy to procure; but would that make it *best* for shoes? And would that be the *chief* reason why it is used for making shoes? Although the statement in itself is quite true, it does not fit the key phrase of the question and we must, reluctantly, eliminate it.

(D) is a double-barreled statement. One part, the durability, has been suggested in (B) above. Leather is also quite flexible, so both parts of the statement would seem to fit the question.

(E) It is true that leather can be manufactured in various styles, but so can many other materials. Again, going back to the key phrase, this could be considered one, but not the *chief* reason why it is *best* for shoes.

So, by carefully analyzing the *key* phrase of the question we have narrowed our choices down to (D). Although we rejected (B) we did recognize that durability is a good quality in shoes, but only one of several. Since flexibility is also a good quality, we have no hesitation in choosing (D) as the correct answer.

The same question, by slightly altering the answer choices, can also call for a *negative* response. Here, even more so, the identification of the key phrase becomes vital in finding the correct answer. Suppose the question and its responses were worded thus:

2. Leather is considered the best material for shoes chiefly because
   (A) it is waterproof
   (B) it is easily colored
   (C) it is easily procurable
   (D) it can easily be manufactured in various styles
   (E) none of these.

We can see that the prior partially correct answer (B) has now been changed, and the doubly-correct answer eliminated. Instead we have a new response possibility (E), "none of these."

We have analyzed three of the choices previously and have seen the reason why none of them is the *chief* reason why leather is considered the *best* material for shoes. The two new elements are (B) "easily colored," and (E) "none of these."

If you think about it, leather *can* be easily colored and often is, but this would not be the chief reason why it is considered *best*. Many other materials are just as easily dyed. So we must come to the conclusion that *none* of the choices is *completely* correct—none fit the key phrase. Therefore, the question calls for a negative response (E).

We have now seen how important it is to identify the key phrase. Equally, or perhaps even more important, is the identifying and analyzing of the key *word*—the qualifying word—in a question. This is usually, though not always, an adjective or adverb. Some of the key words to watch for are: *most, best, least, highest, lowest, always, never, sometimes, most likely, greatest, smallest, tallest, average, easiest, most nearly, maximum, minimum, chiefly, mainly, only, but* and *or*. Identifying these key words is usually half the battle in understanding and, consequently, answering all types of exam questions.

Rephrasing the Question

It is obvious, then, that by carefully analyzing a question, by identifying the key phrase and its key words, you can usually find the correct answer by logical deduction and, often, by elimination. One other way of examining, or "dissecting," a question is to restate or rephrase it with each of the suggested answer choices integrated into the question.

For example, we can take the same question and rephrase it.

(A) The chief reason why leather is considered the best material for shoes is that it is waterproof.

or

(A) Because it is waterproof, leather is considered the best material for shoes.

or

(A) Chiefly because it is waterproof, leather is considered the best material for shoes.

It will be seen from the above three new versions of the original statement and answer that the question has become less obscure because it has been, so to speak, illuminated from different angles. It becomes quite obvious also in this rephrasing that the statement (A) is incorrect, although the *original* phrasing of the question left some doubt.

The rules for understanding and analyzing the key phrase and key words in a question, and the way to identify the *one* correct answer by means of intelligent analysis of the important question-answer elements, are basic to the solution of all the problems you will face on your test.

In fact, perhaps the *main* reason for failing an examination is failure to *understand the question*. In many cases, examinees *do* know the answer to a particular problem, but they cannot answer correctly because they do not understand it.

METHODS FOR MATCHING QUESTIONS

In this question form you are actually faced with multiple questions that require multiple answers. It's a difficult form in which you are asked to pair up one set of facts with another. It can be used with any type of material . . . vocabulary, spatial relations, numbers, facts, etc.

A typical matching question might appear in this form:

Directions: Below is a set of words containing ten words numbered 1 to 10, and twenty other words divided into five groups labeled Group A to Group E. For each of the numbered words select the word in one of the five groups which is most nearly the same in meaning. The letter of that group is the answer for that numbered item.

Although this arrangement is a relatively simple one for a "matching" question, the general principle is the same for all levels of difficulty. Basically, this type of question consists of two columns. The elements of one of the columns must be matched with some or all of the elements of the second column.

1. fiscal
2. deletion
3. equivocal
4. corroboration
5. tortuous
6. predilection
7. sallow
8. virtuosity
9. scion
10. tenuous

Group A
indication ambiguous
excruciating thin

Group B
confirmation financial
phobia erasure

Group C
fiduciary similar
yellowish skill

Group D
theft winding
receive procrastination

Group E
franchise heir
hardy preference

Correct Answers

1. B	4. B	6. E	8. C
2. B	5. D	7. C	9. E
3. A			10. A

There are numerous ways in which these questions may be composed, from the simple one shown to the most difficult type of arrangement. In many cases the arrangement of the question may be so complicated that more time may be spent upon the comprehension of the instructions than on the actual question. This again, points up the importance of fully and quickly understanding the instructions before attempting to solve any problem or answer any question.

Several general principles apply, however, when solving a matching question. Work with one column at a time and match each item of that column against all the items in the second column, skipping around that second column looking for a proper match. Put a thin pencil line through items that are matched so they won't interfere with your later selections. (This is particularly important in a test that tells you to choose any item only once. The test gets real tricky, however, when you are asked to choose an item more than once.)

Match each item very carefully—don't mark it unless you are certain—because if you have to change any one, it may mean changing three or four or more, and that may get you hopelessly confused. After you have marked all your *certain* choices, go over the unmarked items again and make a *good* guess at the remaining items, if you have time.

USE CONTROLLED ASSOCIATION when you come to an item which you are not able to match. Attempt to recall any and all facts you might have concerning this item. Through the process of association, a fact recalled might provide a clue to the answer.

TRUE-FALSE TACTICS

True-false questions may appear on your test. Because they are easier to answer they are used less frequently than multiple-choice questions. However, because examiners find that they are easier to prepare, here are some suggestions to help you answer them correctly.

I. Suspect the truth of broad statements hinging on those *all or nothing* "cue" words we listed for you in discussing multiple-choice questions.

II. Watch out for "spoilers" . . . the word or phrase which negates an otherwise true statement.

Vegetation is sparse on the Sahara desert where the climate is hot and humid. T F

III. Statements containing such modifiers as *generally, usually, most,* and similar words are usually true.

IV. If the scoring formula is "Rights minus Wrongs", don't guess. If you know it's true, mark it T. If you don't know it's true, ask yourself "What have I learned that would make it false?" If you can think of nothing on either side, omit the answer. Of course, if the R-W formula is not being used it is advisable to guess if you're not sure of an answer.

V. Your first hunch is usually best. Unless you have very good reason to do so, don't change your first answer to true-false questions about which you are doubtful.

Single-Statement Question

The basic form of true-false question is the "single-statement" question; i.e., a sentence that contains a single thought, such as:

1. The Statue of Liberty is in New York T F

The same statement becomes slightly more difficult by including a negative element

2. The Statue of Liberty is not in New York T F

or, more subtly:

3. The Statue of Liberty is not in Chicago T F

or, by adding other modifiers:

4. The Statue of Liberty is sometimes in New York T F

5. The Statue of Liberty is always in New York T F

Even from these very simple and basic examples of a "single-statement" true-false question it can be seen that a *complete understanding* of the subject area as well as of the phrasing of the question is essential before you attempt to answer it. Careless or hasty reading of the statment will often make you miss the *key* word, especially if the question appears to be a very simple one.

An important point to remember when answering this type of question is that the statement must be *entirely true* to be answered as "true"; if even just a *part* of it is false, the answer must be marked "false."

Composite-Statement Question

Sometimes a true-false question will be in the form of a "composite statement," a statement that contains more than one thought, such as:

6. The Statue of Liberty is in New York, and Chicago is in Illinois T F

Some basic variations of this type of composite-statement question are these:

7. The Statue of Liberty is in New York, and Chicago is in Michigan T F
8. The Statue of Liberty is not in New York and Chicago is in Illinois T F
9. The Statue of Liberty is not in New York and Chicago is in Michigan T F

Of the four questions above, only question 6 is true. Each of the other statements (7 , 8 , 9), is false because each contains at least *one* element that is false.

It can be seen from the above that in a composite statement *both* elements, or "substatements," must be true in order for the answer to be "true." Otherwise, the answer must be "false."

This principle goes for all composite statements that are, or can be, connected by the word "and," even if the various "thoughts" of the statement seem to be entirely unrelated.

We have seen how to handle a composite statement that consists of *unrelated* substatements. Finally, we will examine a composite true-false statement which consists of *related* elements:

10. The Golden Gate Bridge is in San Francisco, which is not the capital of California. T F
11. The Golden Gate Bridge is in San Francisco, the capital of California. T F
12. The Golden Gate Bridge is not in San Francisco, the capital of California. T F
13. The Golden Gate Bridge is not in San Francisco, which is not the capital of California. T F

Again, only the first composite statement (10) is true. All the rest are false because they contain at least one false substatement.

PART 2

The Successful Job-Hunter

DIRECTIONS FOR ANSWERING QUESTIONS

DIRECTIONS: For each question read all the choices carefully. Then select that answer which you consider correct or most nearly correct. Write the letter preceding your best choice next to the question. Should you want to answer on the kind of answer sheet used on machine-scored examinations, we have provided several such facsimiles. On some machine-scored exams you are instructed to "place no marks whatever on the test booklet." In other examinations you may be instructed to mark your answers in the test booklet. In such cases you should be careful that no other marks interfere with the legibility of your answers. It is always best NOT to mark your booklet unless you are sure that it is permitted. It is most important that you learn to mark your answers clearly and in the right place.

FOR THE SAMPLE QUESTION that follows, select the appropriate letter preceding the word which is most nearly the same in meaning as the capitalized word:

1. DISSENT: (A) approve (B) depart (C) disagree (D) enjoy

DISSENT is most nearly the same as (C), disagree, so that the acceptable answer is shown thus on your answer sheet:

A B C D

Practice Using Answer Sheets

Alter numbers to match the practice and drill questions in each part of the book. Make only ONE mark for each answer. Additional and stray marks may be counted as mistakes. In making corrections, erase errors COMPLETELY. Make glossy black marks.

1	A	B	C	D	E	1	A	B	C	D	E	1	A	B	C	D	E	1	A	B	C	D	E	1	A	B	C	D	E
2	A	B	C	D	E	2	A	B	C	D	E	2	A	B	C	D	E	2	A	B	C	D	E	2	A	B	C	D	E
3	A	B	C	D	E	3	A	B	C	D	E	3	A	B	C	D	E	3	A	B	C	D	E	3	A	B	C	D	E
4	A	B	C	D	E	4	A	B	C	D	E	4	A	B	C	D	E	4	A	B	C	D	E	4	A	B	C	D	E
5	A	B	C	D	E	5	A	B	C	D	E	5	A	B	C	D	E	5	A	B	C	D	E	5	A	B	C	D	E
6	A	B	C	D	E	6	A	B	C	D	E	6	A	B	C	D	E	6	A	B	C	D	E	6	A	B	C	D	E
7	A	B	C	D	E	7	A	B	C	D	E	7	A	B	C	D	E	7	A	B	C	D	E	7	A	B	C	D	E
8	A	B	C	D	E	8	A	B	C	D	E	8	A	B	C	D	E	8	A	B	C	D	E	8	A	B	C	D	E
9	A	B	C	D	E	9	A	B	C	D	E	9	A	B	C	D	E	9	A	B	C	D	E	9	A	B	C	D	E
0	A	B	C	D	E	0	A	B	C	D	E	0	A	B	C	D	E	0	A	B	C	D	E	0	A	B	C	D	E

I. STUDYING AND USING THIS BOOK

Even though this course of study has been carefully planned to help you get in shape by the day your test comes, you'll have to do a little planning on your own to be successful. And you'll also need a few pointers proven effective for many other good students.

SURVEY AND SCHEDULE YOUR WORK

Regular mental workouts are as important as regular physical workouts in achieving maximum personal efficiency. They are absolutely essential in getting top test scores, so you'll want to plan a test-preparing schedule that fits in with your usual program. Use the Schedule on the next page. Make it out for yourself so that it really works with the actual time you have at your disposal.

There are five basic steps in scheduling this book for yourself and in studying each assignment that you schedule:

1. SCAN - the entire job at hand.
2. QUESTION - before reading.
3. READ - to find the answers to the questions you have formulated.
4. RECITE - to see how well you have learned the answers to your questions.
5. REVIEW - to check up on how well you have learned, to learn it again, and to fix it firmly in your mind.

Scan

Make a survey of this whole book before scheduling. Do this by reading our introductory statements and the table of contents. Then leaf through the entire book, paying attention to main headings, sub-headings, summaries, and topic sentences. When you have this bird's eye view of the whole, the parts take on added meaning, and you'll see how they hang together.

Question

As you scan, questions will come to your mind. Write them into the book. Later on you'll be finding the answers. For example, in scanning this book you would naturally change the headline STUDYING AND USING THIS BOOK into *What don't I know about studying? What are my good study habits? How can I improve them? How should I go about reading and using this book?* Practice the habit of formulating and writing such questions into the text.

Read

Now, by reviewing your questions you should be able to work out your schedule easily. Stick to it. And apply these five steps to each assignment you give yourself in the schedule. Your reading of each assignment should be directed to finding answers to the questions you have formulated and will continue to formulate. You'll discover that reading with a purpose will make it easier to *remember* the answers to your questions.

Recite

After you have read your assignment and found the answers to your questions, close the book and recite to yourself. For example, if your question here was "What are the five basic steps in attacking an assignment?" then your answer to yourself would be scan, question, read, recite, and review. Thus, you check up on yourself and "fix" the information in your mind. You have now seen it, read it, said it, and heard it. The more senses you use, the more you learn.

Review

Even if you recall your answers well, review them in order to "overlearn". "Overlearning" gives you a big advantage by reducing the chances of forgetting. Definitely provide time in your schedule for review. It's the clincher in getting ahead of the crowd. You'll find that "overlearning" won't take much time with this book because the text portions have been written as concisely and briefly as possible. You may be tempted to stop work when you have once gone over the work before you. This is wrong because of the ease with which memory impressions are bound to fade. Decide for yourself what is important and plan to review and overlearn those portions. Overlearning rather than last minute cramming is the best way to study.

Your Time is Limited—Schedule Your Study

SUBJECT SCHEDULE

1. SCOPE OF EXAMINATION

Test Subjects	No. of Questions	Percentage of Total (Weight)
	Total:	100 percent

2. YOUR KNOWLEDGE OF SUBJECT

Test Subjects	Poor	Fair	Good	Very Good	Excellent

3. DIVIDING YOUR STUDY TIME

Test Subjects	Total Hours	Hours Per Week
	Total:	

Total number of weeks for study ....

Hours per week ....

Total number of hours ....

The SUBJECT SCHEDULE is divided into three parts: 1. Scope of Examination; 2. Your Knowledge of Subject; and 3. Dividing Your Study Time. To use your schedule, put down in part 1 all the subjects you will face on your test, the number of questions in each subject, and the "weight," or percentage, given to each subject in the total make-up of the test.

In part 2, again fill in all the test subjects and, with a check mark, rate yourself *honestly* as to your knowledge of each subject.

At the top of part 3, put down the number of weeks you will be able to devote to your studying. Determine the number of hours you will study each week and multiply that figure by the number of weeks to give you the total hours of study.

Again fill in the subjects. Then, take the weight given to each test subject (in part 1) and average it against your knowledge of that subject (as checked in part 2) to arrive at the number of hours you should allow for study of that subject out of your total study hours. In Chapter 2, under the heading "10. Total Time Allowed For Each Subject," you will find a more detailed explanation of how to divide your study time.

After you have fixed the total number of hours to be devoted to each subject, divide them by the number of weeks of study to arrive at the total weekly hours you will study each subject.

STUDY TIMETABLE

PRELIMINARY

Key Letters	Study Subjects
A	
B	
C	
D	
E	
F	

Key Letters	Study Subjects
G	
H	
I	
J	
K	
L	

Mon.									
Tues.									
Wed.									
Thur.									
Fri.									
Sat.									
Sun.									

HOW TO USE THE STUDY TIMETABLE

At right is a sample timetable filled in for a whole week to show you how a typical schedule might be arranged. The letters *A, B, C,* etc., are keyed to your study subjects so that, for example, *A* might stand for Vocabulary, *B* for Numerical Relations, and so forth. You will note that each day is divided into nine possible study hours and each hour, in turn, is divided into four 15-minute periods.

	7 AM	12 PM		7 PM	8 PM	9 PM			
Mon.	BB	AA	B	BCC	CCEE	E GG			
		12 PM		7PM	8PM	9PM			
Tues.		FF	A	AABB	DDD	D GG			
	7AM	12PM		7PM					
Wed.	CC	BB	BB	BB					
		12PM		7PM	8PM	9PM	10PM		
Thur.		A	A	A	BBEE	E FF	HH		
	7AM		7PM	8PM					
Fri.	AA	FF	FEE	CC					
	10AM	11AM	12PM	3PM	4PM				
Sat.	DDD	AAA	A	BBB	FF				
	1 PM	2PM	3PM	4PM	8PM				
Sun.	DDD	CCC	C AA	HHH	BB				

STUDY TIMETABLE

FINAL

Key Letters	Study Subjects
A	
B	
C	
D	
E	
F	

Key Letters	Study Subjects
G	
H	
I	
J	
K	
L	

Mon.									
Tues.									
Wed.									
Thur.									
Fri.									
Sat.									
Sun.									

Plan to study difficult subjects when you can give them your greatest energy. Some people find that they can do their best work in the early morning hours. On the other hand, it has been found that forgetting is less when study is followed by sleep or recreation. Plan other study periods for those free times which might otherwise be wasted . . . for example lunch or when traveling to and from work.

Plan your schedule so that not more than 1½ or 2 hours are spent in the study of any subject at one sitting. Allow at least a half-hour for each session with your book. It takes a few minutes before you settle down to work.

You will find that there is enough time for your study and other activities if you follow a well-planned schedule. You will not only be able to find enough time for your other activities, but you will also accomplish more in the way of study and learning. A definite plan for study increases concentration. If you establish the habit of studying a subject at the same time each day, you will find that less effort is required in focusing your attention on it.

Where To Study

SELECT A ROOM THAT WILL BE AVAILABLE EACH DAY AT THE SAME TIME. THIS WILL HELP YOU CONCENTRATE.

USE A DESK OR TABLE WHICH WILL NOT BE SHARED SO THAT YOU CAN "LEAVE THINGS OUT". IT SHOULD BE BIG ENOUGH TO ACCOMMODATE ALL YOUR EQUIPMENT WITHOUT CRAMPING YOU. ELIMINATE ORNAMENTS AND OTHER DISTRACTIONS.

SELECT A ROOM WHICH HAS NO DISTRACTIONS. KEEP IT THAT WAY.

PROVIDE FOR GOOD AIR CIRCULATION IN YOUR STUDY ROOM.

KEEP THE TEMPERATURE AROUND 68°.

PROVIDE ADEQUATE LIGHTING . . . USE A DESK LAMP IN ADDITION TO OVERHEAD LIGHTS.

NOISE DISTRACTS SO KEEP RADIO AND TV TURNED OFF.

ARRANGE TO HAVE A PERMANENT KIT OF NECESSARY STUDY EQUIPMENT . . . PEN, PENCIL, RULER, SHEARS, ERASER, NOTEBOOK, CLIPS, DICTIONARY, ETC.

Study On Your Own

As a general rule you will find it more beneficial to study with this book in your room, alone. There are times, however, when two or more individuals can profit from team study. For example, if you can't figure something out for yourself, you might get help from a friend who is also studying for this test. Review situations sometimes lend themselves to team study if everyone concerned has already been over the ground by himself. Sometimes you can gain greater understanding of underlying principles as you volley ideas back and forth with other people. Watch out, though, that you don't come to lean on the others so much that you can't work things out for yourself.

PROVEN STUDY SUGGESTIONS

1. Do some work every day in preparation for the exam.
2. Budget your time—set aside a definite study period for each day during the week.
3. Study with a friend or a group occasionally—the exchange of ideas will help all of you. It's also more pleasant getting together.
4. Answer as many of the questions in this book as you can. Some of the questions that you will get on your actual test will be very much like some of the questions in this book.
5. Be physically fit. Eat the proper food—get enough sleep. You learn better and faster when you are in good health.
6. Take notes.
7. Be an active learner. Participate. Try harder.

TECHNIQUES OF EFFICIENT STUDY

DO NOT ATTEMPT SERIOUS STUDY WHILE IN TOO RELAXED A POSITION.

AVOID SERIOUS STUDY AFTER A HEAVY MEAL.

DO SOMETHING WHILE STUDYING . . . MAKE NOTES, UNDERLINE, FORMULATE QUESTIONS.

BEGIN CONCENTRATING AS SOON AS YOU SIT DOWN TO STUDY. DON'T FOOL AROUND.

MAKE TIME FOR STUDY BY ELIMINATING NEEDLESS ACTIVITIES AND OTHER DRAINS ON YOUR PRECIOUS TIME.

MAKE UP YOUR OWN ILLUSTRATIONS AND EXAMPLES TO CHECK ON YOUR UNDERSTANDING OF A TOPIC.

FIND SOME PRACTICAL APPLICATION OF YOUR NEWLY ACQUIRED KNOWLEDGE.

RELATE NEWLY ACQUIRED KNOWLEDGE TO WHAT YOU KNEW BEFORE.

CONSCIOUSLY TRY TO LEARN, TO CONCENTRATE, TO PAY ATTENTION.

LOOK UP NEW WORDS IN YOUR DICTIONARY.

Concentrating

Most students who complain that they don't know how to concentrate deserve no sympathy. Concentration is merely habit and ought to be as readily acquired as any other habit. The way to begin to study is simply to begin.

Don't wait for inspiration or for the mood to strike you, nor should you permit yourself to indulge in thoughts like, "This chapter is too long" or "I guess I could really let that go until some other time."

Such an attitude throws an extra load on your mental machinery, and by making you work against a handicap, makes it harder for you to begin.

Reading aloud is a good device for those whose minds wander while studying. Articulating "subvocally" for a few moments is another tonic for drifting thoughts. If this doesn't work, write down the point you happen to be dealing with when your mind "goes off track."

Do your studying alone, and you'll find it much easier to concentrate. If you are certain you need help on doubtful or difficult points, check these points and list them; you can go back or ask about them later. In the meantime, proceed to the next point.

A "little tenseness" is a good thing because it helps you keep alert while studying. Do without smoking, or newspapers, or magazines, or novels which may lead you into temptation. Studying in one place all the time also helps.

Boiling it all down, the greatest asset for effective studying is plain, garden variety "common sense" and will power.

Grasshoppers Never Learn

Don't be a "skipper." Jumping around from one part of your course to another may be more interesting, but it won't help you as much as steady progress from page one right through the book.

Studying and learning takes more than just reading. The "text" part of your course can be a valuable tool in test-preparation if you use it correctly. Introductions to the various sections of your book must be "studied." Re-read the paragraph that gives you trouble. Be certain that you understand it before you pass on to the next one. Many persons who have been away from school for a long time, and those people who have a habit of reading rapidly, find that it helps if they hold a piece of white paper under the paragraph they are reading, covering the rest of the page. That helps you concentrate on the facts you are absorbing. Keep a pen or pencil in your hand while reading, and underline important facts. Put a question mark after anything that isn't quite clear to you, so that you can get back to it. Summarize ideas in the margins of your book. You'll be surprised how much easier it is to remember something once you have written it down, and expressed it in your own words.

Taking Notes

Although your "self-tutor" has done a great deal for you in summarizing the information that is essential to success on the test, it's still worth your while to do some notetaking. Your notes, which can be made either in a separate notebook or in the margins of this book, will help you concentrate; are a form of self-recitation; will provide you with concise outlines for review before the test; will help you identify basic and essential materials; will help you retain what you learn, with greater accuracy for a longer period of time; and will help you learn better because they require thinking and active participation on your part.

The following suggestions will help you take the kind of notes that will be of greatest use to you on the test:

RECORD ESSENTIAL FACTS AND AVOID TOO MUCH DETAIL. JOT DOWN CLUES.

ADOPT AN ACTIVE MEANING-SEEKING ATTITUDE. STICK TO BASIC SIGNIFICANCE.

USE YOUR OWN WORDS. BUT BE BRIEF.

DON'T HURRY. WRITE READABLY AND ACCURATELY. YOU'LL BE READING THEM AGAIN.

BE NEAT. WRITE TITLES AND LABELS. DON'T BE SPARING OF PAPER.

USE A SINGLE LOOSELEAF NOTEBOOK SO THAT YOU CAN RE-ORGANIZE AND COMBINE NOTES.

TAKE NOTES IN ALL LEARNING SITUATIONS RELATING TO THIS TEST.

DON'T COPY VERBATIM.

REVIEW YOUR NOTES OF THE PREVIOUS DAY BEFORE STARTING THE CURRENT ASSIGNMENT.

USE QUESTION MARKS IN THE MARGINS OF THE BOOK FOR VAGUE OR DIFFICULT PASSAGES WHICH MAY BE CLARIFIED AS YOU READ ON. YOU MAY WANT TO COME BACK TO THEM TO BE SURE YOU UNDERSTAND THEM.

TRY TO DO SOME FOLLOW UP WORK ON UNDERLINED SECTIONS.

SOME SUGGESTED SYMBOLS FOR MAKING NOTES IN THIS BOOK.

| , ( ), [ ] A vertical line in the margin, or a bracket, or parenthesis around a sentence or group of sentences is used to indicate an important idea or ideas.

— Underlining is used to indicate especially important materials, specific points to be consulted during reviews.

O A circle around a word may be used to indicate that you are not familiar with the word, and that you will come back later to look it up in the dictionary.

√ E The letter "E" or a check mark (√) in the margin may be used to mark materials that are important and likely to be used in the examination.

1 , 2 , 3 , 4 Arabic numerals, circled or uncircled may be placed before a word or at the beginning of a sentence to indicate a series of facts, ideas, important dates, etc.

D The letter "D" may be used to indicate your disagreement with a passage or a statement.

Keep in mind that effective notetaking is vital to learning. If your notes are effective, your learning is likely to be effective.

Test Yourself Frequently

The major part of your course consists of study questions and answers prepared by experts. Try to answer every question in the book as you reach it. Each study session should end with a self-test.

Develop Careful Reading Habits

While present-day examinations seldom have "trick" questions, the men who make up examinations often frame questions so that careful reading is necessary to understand the question fully and to give the proper answer. Use this book as a personal reading-improver. Rephrase every question in your own words before you answer, to be sure that you really understand what is being asked.

Don't Try to Memorize

It is true that the same questions often reappear on examinations of the same kind, but it would not be worthwhile to try to memorize the hundreds of questions in your book. After all, the *scope* of any examination is fairly limited. Using your book as a self-tester will show you the fields in which you may be weak or strong. The questions and answers will help put you into the important examination-taking frame of mind, and give you an excellent idea of the different types of information about which you will be questioned on your test.

Be Tough With Yourself

One error made by many persons who are preparing for examinations is to give themselves too much of a break. They will peek at the book answer to a question and excuse themselves on the grounds that if they had "really" been taking a test, they would have been more careful and would have given the correct answer. Don't let yourself get away with that!

You have to be a stern teacher to get the most out of any program of self-study. When you test yourself, be as tough as if the test-taker were someone you didn't know. Don't let yourself get away with an "almost right" answer. Today there is keen competition on most tests, and the habits you develop while preparing for your test will show up on the examination in the form of earned or lost percentage points. Mark yourself rigidly. Be honest in appraising your weaknesses, and try to correct them before you sit down to take the real test.

And don't take anything for granted. Even if you find yourself scoring 100% in some area of your test, don't relax too much. When you find that you have answered a question correctly, use that as a lever for self-improvement. Ask yourself *why* your answer was correct. Try to think of other forms in which the same question could have been asked. Try to frame your own questions that are "harder" or more demanding than the ones you can answer easily.

You may find that some sections of this book are difficult, just as some portions of the test will be more difficult than others. Don't worry about it. Don't panic. Remember that the test is a competitive one . . . that your score is relative to the scores of all the oher competitors. What's hard for you will be just as hard (or harder) for them.

When the going gets rough you're on notice to study more carefully. You've discovered one of your weaknesses. You're ahead of the game because you have the opportunity of strengthening yourself. Concentrate on your weak spots and you won't be caught off balance by the test questions.

On the other hand don't permit yourself to be lulled into a false sense of security when you discover material which is very easy for you. Don't quit studying—just give the easy portions less time. Adjust your schedule and use the time you pick up in this way to work where it is most needed.

This technique of devoting as much time and thought as is required by each job (and no more) should be applied to the actual test, with one caution. The easy questions should be answered as rapidly as you can, as you come to them. But if a question appears very difficult and likely to take a lot of time to answer, defer spending too much time on it. Continue on, giving the quick, easy answers. Then go back and use the time remaining to answer the slow, hard ones.

Scissors and Glue for Review

One helpful form of review, as your examination date approaches, is this: Cut out individual questions from your book. Paste them on slips of paper, and mark the correct answers on the back of each question.

Then, whenever you have a few minutes to spare, you can shuffle the questions around and find out whether you have the correct answers in your mind. This is especially helpful in dealing with questions of the "information" type which are basically tests of how well you remember important information and facts.

Another good learning technique is to have someone read the questions and suggested answers to you. "Hearing" will serve as a memory aid after you have read and studied the material.

Analyze Your Weaknesses—And Correct Them

One purpose of this course is to familiarize you with the types of questions you will face and to prepare you for them. Perhaps its more important purpose is to help you find your own weaknesses and to correct them before the examination.

Every time you give the incorrect answer to a practice question you should ask yourself, "Why?" Be honest with yourself and you'll soon discover the subjects in which you're weak. Devote extra time to these subjects and you will have taken giant steps to test success.

We have analyzed test failures and have found time after time that many persons who are perfectly able to pass a test fail it simply because of their weakness in such basic subjects as arithmetic or vocabulary.

If you find that you have such a problem, be brave. Put in the extra effort each day.

SCORING HIGH ON EMPLOYMENT TESTS

II. WHAT EMPLOYERS WANT

While most government employment tests are given to groups of applicants at one time, many companies prefer to administer individual tests. Almost always, the tester remains in the room with the person taking the test, but he's not there to be sociable. Actually, he is keeping you under close observation, and he may be making notes on his check list while he is giving the preliminary instructions, during the test and afterwards. Even if the tester isn't in the room with you, he may be watching you through a two-way mirror or window. This is a hard thing to beat because almost everything you do during the examination can be interpreted in different ways.

The following, which is typical of the standard Examiner's Check List, will give you an idea of how every action of yours can be interpreted. Note that every "action" has several "interpretations" and it really depends on how you impress the examiner. It's the old story. If you are on time you can be rated "compulsive". If you are a few minutes late, you can be rated "resistant." If you come in early you can be called "over eager." But perhaps reading this list will give you some clues as to how to behave in the test room.

WHAT THEY LOOK FOR...

ACTIONS OF THE TEST—TAKER	INTERPRETATION
I. During the Pre-Test Instructions	
A. Looks steadily at the examiner; seems to listen intently.	☐ 1. Is actually attentive ☐ 2. Can look at a person without listening
B. Gazes around the room	☐ 1. Can give effective divided attention ☐ 2. Cannot concentrate ☐ 3. Is not interested
C. Asks questions	☐ 1. Has heard imperfectly due to poor hearing or lack of concentration ☐ 2. Has not understood ☐ 3. Is especially interested ☐ 4. Is stalling for time
D. Asks no questions	☐ 1. Is stupid ☐ 2. Understands the directions well ☐ 3. Is in a hurry to start the test
E. Approaches the test quickly	☐ 1. Is interested in the test ☐ 2. Lacks foresight ☐ 3. Comprehends quickly ☐ 4. Has an active nature

ACTIONS OF THE TEST-TAKER (Cont.)	INTERPRETATION (Cont.)
F. Approaches the test slowly	☐ 1. Is apathetic ☐ 2. Lacks interest in the test ☐ 3. Is apathetic and uninterested
G. Approaches the test hesitatingly	☐ 1. Does not understand the instructions ☐ 2. Is overcautious ☐ 3. Is indecisive or shy ☐ 4. Is unwilling to take the test
H. Talks as if the test were easy	☐ 1. The test is easy for him ☐ 2. Does not see the difficulties ☐ 3. Tends to boastfulness and conceit
I. Says he cannot do the test	☐ 1. Is aware of his limitations ☐ 2. Has an inferiority complex ☐ 3. Does not understand the test ☐ 4. Has no interest in taking the test
J. Judgment or Criticism of the Test	a. Aloud ☐ 1. Wants to cooperate ☐ 2. Tends to find fault ☐ 3. Wants to assert himself b. Through gestures ☐ 1. Indicating interest ☐ 2. Indicating dislike ☐ 3. Indicating disdain

II. During the Test

A. Deliberates at the start	☐ 1. Finds the test difficult ☐ 2. Is of a cautious nature ☐ 3. Has a tendency to reflect
B. Does not deliberate at the start	☐ 1. Understands at once ☐ 2. Cannot reflect ☐ 3. Resents the test
C. Makes repeated starts always in the same way	☐ 1. Mental inertia ☐ 2. Cannot reflect ☐ 3. Resents the test
D. Makes repeated starts always in different ways	☐ 1. Is alert to possibilities ☐ 2. Feels he should be able to do it ☐ 3. Working on sheer will power
E. While at work is attentive to the test	☐ 1. From a desire to score well ☐ 2. In order to get it over with
F. While at work attention wanders	☐ 1. Lack of interest ☐ 2. Lack of power of concentration
G. Attention is fully concentrated on the test	☐ 1. Is interested in the test ☐ 2. Is overawed by the examiner ☐ 3. Has perseverance and determination
H. Is distracted from the test	☐ 1. By interest in new surroundings ☐ 2. Lacks interest in the test ☐ 3. Lacks power of attention ☐ 4. Is apathetic
I. Bodily movements are well coordinated with the task at hand	☐ 1. Is clever and able ☐ 2. Has had good physical training ☐ 3. Is motivated to finish the test quickly
J. Bodily movements are not coordinated	☐ 1. Poor control over motor movements ☐ 2. Lacks ability to see what to do
K. Work tempo is quick	☐ 1. Has a lively disposition ☐ 2. Wants to finish an unpleasant task
L. Work tempo is slow	☐ 1. Has a phlegmatic nature ☐ 2. Is naturally lazy ☐ 3. Is indifferent to the test
M. Works systematically	☐ 1. As a result of reflection ☐ 2. Naturally orderly person
N. Works unsystematically, darting from one thing to another	☐ 1. Is active, vivacious ☐ 2. Nervous response ☐ 3. Scatterbrained response ☐ 4. Seems to be continually searching for something more interesting
O. Works regularly	☐ 1. Shows poise and foresight ☐ 2. Has a firm purpose
P. Works irregularly—at first slowly, then more and more quickly	☐ 1. He finds that a persistent attack succeeds ☐ 2. The test gradually becomes clearer and seems easier ☐ 3. Interest mounts progressively

ACTIONS OF THE TEST-TAKER (Cont.)	INTERPRETATION (Cont.)
Q. Works irregularly—at first quickly then more slowly	☐ 1. Shows loss of interest ☐ 2. Weak concentration ☐ 3. Quick fatigue
R. Works irregularly—alternating periods of fast and slow work	☐ 1. Unstable way of thinking ☐ 2. Attention fluctuates ☐ 3. Is making attempts to renew waning powers
S. Careful, neat performance	☐ 1. Has natural aptitude for correct and exact work ☐ 2. Is interested in the test
T. Careless, sloppy work	☐ 1. Is careless ☐ 2. Lacks interest ☐ 3. Unable to control temper
III. Attitude Towards His Work	
A. Notices his mistakes occasionally	☐ 1. Purely by accident ☐ 2. Applicant is a casual person
B. Notices his mistakes at the end, when he checks his work for the first time	☐ 1. Is careful, but not systematic ☐ 2. Has been completely absorbed in the test
C. Notices his mistakes during the work, always proving his work before he proceeds	☐ 1. Is systematic and cautious ☐ 2. Has been trained to be critical of his work
D. Does not correct his mistakes or check his results	☐ 1. Is convinced of his own ability ☐ 2. Has concentrated on the end result ☐ 3. Is not critical ☐ 4. Is indifferent ☐ 5. Does not care
E. Shows mild feeling	☐ 1. Indicating he is pleased ☐ 2. Indicating he is displeased
IV. Conduct After the Test	
A. Remains silent and watches quietly	☐ 1. He is shy ☐ 2. Is well trained ☐ 3. Lacks decision ☐ 4. Lacks initiative; does not know what to do
B. Expresses emotions of satisfaction	☐ 1. Is pleased at having finished ☐ 2. Feels that test has confirmed his awareness of his own ability ☐ 3. Is relieved from fear of the nature of the test
C. Expresses emotions of vexation	☐ 1. Feels his ambitions have been thwarted ☐ 2. Is disappointed ☐ 3. He anticipates family or other reproval for failure
D. Asks questions of examiner, such as "Isn't that a good paper"	☐ 1. Feels need to communicate ☐ 2. Feels uncertain, wants confirmation ☐ 3. Wants to hear himself praised
V. After the Testing is Over	
A. Leaves the desk and papers in order	☐ 1. Has a love of order ☐ 2. Is considerate of others ☐ 3. Has been well-trained
B. Leaves the desk and papers in disorder	☐ 1. Is naturally disorderly ☐ 2. Is restless ☐ 3. Is inconsiderate ☐ 4. Has no time
C. Disposes of materials in a way which indicates he is	☐ 1. Economical ☐ 2. Wasteful
D. Leaves the place of work quickly	☐ 1. Is brisk ☐ 2. Is eager to get away to something else.
E. Leaves the place of work slowly	☐ 1. Is sluggish ☐ 2. Is reluctant to leave

A summary

READING the check list above will indicate to you the pattern of behavior that the person who administers the test considers the most favorable. While you cannot predict which of the "interpretations" he will place on your acts, you can plan ahead to create the picture of the individual who rates high in the test room. Then, if you manage to get a favorable test score, you are "in." Above all, it's most important not to let the fact that you are being observed upset you to the point where you become uneasy and make mistakes on the examination paper.

III. SUCCEEDING ON THE INTERVIEW

This appendix presents samples of interview rating forms. Inspection of these forms will quickly indicate substantial differences among them in many important respects, yet it is doubtful as to whether present knowledge would indicate, on technical grounds, that any of these forms is superior or inferior in the results it will produce. It may be useful, however, to indicate the virtues of each particular approach.

1. *Selection of rating factors.*—In the selection of factors, there is need for, on the one hand, analysis of the job in order to be certain that all relevant factors are included and, on the other hand, exclusion of those factors which cannot be appraised well in an interview or are being better measured by other selection methods.

2. *Specificity of factors.*—On some forms the factors are broad and general, while on others specific words and phrases are used. The important question is not which is better but rather whether the definition of each term is sufficiently specific that each rater knows what he is rating. The language used should be appropriate for the vocabulary level of the interviewer.

3. *Rating methods.*—As will be noted from inspection of the sample rating forms, almost all possible rating methods are used from, on the one extreme, checking off descriptive statements to, on the other, general narrative statements. Narrative statements, either for each general factor or for the whole interview, seem to be a necessary precaution to help insure that the evaluation is based on sound grounds, to help eliminate the "halo" effect, and to provide an opportunity for review. Such statements are also useful as a guide in the specific placement of applicants when several different types of jobs are available. The use of other rating devices, such as rating on a scale or checking off phrases or words, helps also. They can help guide and clarify the thinking of the interviewer in preparing his narrative statement, since such statements, when well done, will often contain both favorable and unfavorable comments.

When scale rating on specific factors is done, it is unlikely that more than 3 points on the scale should be used; namely, high, satisfactory, and low. It should be noted that the terms high, satisfactory, and low for each factor are not being recommended as the most desirable way of expressing the points on the scale but as an illustration of a 3-point scale. A better method for expressing the points on a rating scale is to use a descriptive phrase or sentence which represents specific behavior on the factor being rated. For example, the 3 statements on 1 rating form under the factor "Persuasiveness" are: "Forceful, could easily persuade reluctant group" for the high statement, "Presents ideas inoffensively but not too effectually" for the middle statement, and "Irritates people he is trying to convince" for the lowest evaluation. This specificity of definitions for the points on a scale should help in obtaining consistency of judgment between one applicant and another and between interviewers. On general factors and in overall evaluation of applicants, a 5-point scale is often used. It is unlikely that interviewers could make finer distinctions than those required in sorting the applicants into 5 groups.

4. *Summarizing the ratings.*—A combination of ratings on a scale and a narrative statement are desirable methods for summarizing the total results of an interview for the same reason that such a combination was suggested for rating each factor. When the interview was conducted for a particular position, the comments should be related to the requirements of that position. It should be pointed out to the interviewer that the narrative statement should be more than an endorsement or rejection—that its detail should be such that someone reading the statement would get a full picture of the applicant's behavior and the reasoning behind the interviewer's summary rating on the scale. It is obvious that the summary may go beyond the ratings on each factor to include behaviors which were observed and are relevant but are not included in the factors because the list would have become too long. In such cases the interviewer needs to account for the discrepancy between his factor and summary ratings by his narrative comment.

AN EMPLOYER'S INTERVIEW FORM

WORK AND RATING SHEETS FOR INTERVIEW

(To be completed independently by each interviewer)

EXAMINATION TITLE:

NAME OF CANDIDATE:

PLACE OF INTERVIEW: TIME OF INTERVIEW: A. M.

DATE OF INTERVIEW: P. M.

WORK SHEET

Describe the candidate relative to each of the six rating factors, and do a preliminary rating of the elements comprising each factor. *The description on each rating factor is a requisite.* These descriptions should be word pictures of the individual characteristics of the candidate. In rating, circle the + if the candidate is strong; if he is weak, circle the —; and if he is average or indeterminate circle the O.

I. APPEARANCE, BEARING AND MANNER:

Describe:

Check these elements:

A. Appearance.. + O —
Observe: Dress, features, carriage, stature.

B. Bearing and Manner.. + O —
Observe: Dignity, politeness, self-control, affectation, distracting mannerisms.

II. ABILITY IN ORAL EXPRESSION:

Describe:

Check these elements:

A. Effectiveness.. + O —
Observe: Does he make his point? Command attention? Do justice to his thought?

B. Construction and Language.. + O —
Observe: Clarity and structure of presentation, adequacy of vocabulary, correct usage of words, questionable use of slang and colloquialisms.

C. Voice and Manner.. + O —
Observe: Defects or distractions in voice, adjustment to audience, affectation, orations, emotional appeals, salesmanship.

III. STABILITY AND SOCIAL ADJUSTMENT:

Describe:

Check these elements:

A. Stability.. + O —
Observe: Tension, repression, emotionalism, self-possession, relaxation, confidence.

B. Social Adjustment.. + O —
Observe: Interest in and understanding of others, acceptance by others, adjustment of approach to individuals, withdrawal, stiffness, discourtesy, eccentricity, ineptness.

IV. MENTAL QUALITIES OTHER THAN BASIC INTELLIGENCE:

Describe:

Check these elements:

A. Understanding and Perception.. + O —
Observe: Definition of issues, production of or inquiry for perti-

nent facts, introduction of pertinent considerations, paraphrasing or summaries of others' contributions, building upon others' thoughts.

B. Reasoning Powers .... + 0 –
Observe: Soundness of logic, statement or questioning of premises, filling gaps and finding faults in reasoning of others, coherence and structure of thought, elimination of nonpertinent considerations.

C. Objectivity .... + 0 –
Observe: Discrimination between fact and opinion, re-examination of his own position, acceptance of corrections, consideration of the thought of others, evidence of prejudices.

D. Judgment and Common Sense .... + 0 –
Observe: Expression of pros and cons, recognition and avoidance of the absurd, modification of extremes, consideration of obstacles to, limitations in, and untoward effects of proposals.

E. Constructive Thought .... + 0 –
Observe: Advancement of the thought, vision; original ideas, striking concepts.

V. INTEREST AND MOTIVATION:

Describe:

Check these elements:

A. Interest .... + 0 –
Observe: Definition of aims and purpose, positive expression of interest in any field or activity, interest in the interview proceedings, appropriateness of aims and interests to the purposes of JMA development.

B. Motivation .... + 0 –
Observe: His rationale of his aims and actions, possible revelation of motives which he does not admit or of which he is not conscious, depth and enduring nature of motivation.

C. Vitality .... + 0 –
Observe: Positiveness of viewpoint, willingness to defend ideas, attempts to persuade, physical vitality, perseverance.

VI. GROUP LEADERSHIP AND PARTICIPATION:

Describe:

Check these elements:

A. Leadership .... + 0 –
Observe: Initiating group thought, bringing order into group action, influence on group, quality of results.

B. Impact on Group Thought .... + 0 –
Observe: Advancement of group thought, clarification of thought, elimination of fallacies, pulling group back to main issues, group's acceptance of his ideas, quality of results.

I. Appearance, bearing, and manner .... + 0 –
II. Ability in oral expression .... + 0 –
III. Stability and social adjustment .... + 0 –
IV. Mental qualities other than basic intelligence .... + 0 –
V. Interest and motivation .... + 0 –
VI. Group leadership and participation .... + 0 –
Rating (circle one) .... In Out

SUMMARY: The interviewer must prepare a narrative summary to give his total impression of the whole man, and to clarify and support the rating. This summary will be used for further evaluation, placement purposes, or in answering possible appeals, and should therefore be specific and complete.

SIGNATURE OF INTERVIEWER:

AN EMPLOYER'S INTERVIEW FORM

UNITED STATES CIVIL SERVICE COMMISSION

INTERVIEW RATING FORM

INSTRUCTIONS: This work sheet is designed to assist you in analyzing the behavior of the applicant. The symbols +, O and − appear after each item. If the applicant's entire behavior in the area described in the item makes a favorable impression, circle the +. If the applicant's entire behavior in the area described in the item makes an unfavorable impression, circle the −. If his behavior is neither favorable nor unfavorable, circle the O. All the items are to be filled out in the case of the group oral, while only items 1 through 6 are to be filled out in the case of individual interviews.

1. Voice and Language:
   Observe: Clarity of voice; clarity of content; directness; affected delivery; pleasantness of voice .... + O −
2. Self-confidence:
   Observe: Relaxed; willingness to choose among alternatives; willingness to defend ideas against challenge; shy .... + O −
3. Effectiveness in dealing with others:
   Observe: Attitude toward other persons; understanding of methods of dealing effectively with others; interest in dealing with others; persuasive; domineering; tactful; cooperative; fair; won't antagonize people .... + O −
4. Effectiveness in organizing a shop or section:
   Observe: Has initiative; has high standards of efficiency; interested in administration; will get job done; planning ability .... + O −
5. Practical Intelligence:
   Observe: Responsive; takes appropriate facts into account; can hold his own in a discussion; not theoretical .... + O −
6. Energy and Vitality:
   Observe: High level of activity; posture; alertness .... + O −
7. Impact on Group Decision:
   Observe: Extent to which candidate influenced the group in reaching a decision .... + O −
8. Participation in Discussion:
   Observe: Quality of contributions; willingness to adapt to others' views; over-participation .... + O −
9. Impact on Group Discussion:
   Observe: Attempts to clarify group thinking, efforts to move discussion along, consideration of different aspects of problems; putting things in perspective .... + O −

OVERALL EVALUATION

Keeping in mind *all* of the information obtained from the interview, this candidate should be (circle the correct word):

PASSED *FAILED*

SUMMARY: The interviewer must prepare a narrative summary to give his total impression of the whole man, and to clarify and support the rating. This summary will be used for further evaluation, placement purposes, or in answering possible appeals, and should therefore be specific and complete.

Signature of Interviewer	Name of Applicant
Title	Place of Interview
Agency	Date of Interview

AN EMPLOYER'S INTERVIEW FORM

RAY-O-VAC COMPANY

PATTERNED ANALYTICAL INTERVIEW

Part II—Interviewer's judgments blank

Applicant ____________________

Date __________ Interviewer ____________________

Recommended __________ Not recommended __________

As soon as possible after the interview, the interviewer should record his judgments of the applicant by checking either a "Yes," "No," or "?" after each of the questions on the following pages.

At the end of each section there is room to record whether the final overall judgment in that section is favorable, unfavorable or uncertain.

The division marked "Serious Handicaps" is used to remind the interviewer that there are some serious handicaps which may prove to be practical "knockout" factors, despite a favorable general impression. These negatives must be taken into consideration before arriving at a final decision to employ a man.

The "Summary" brings together all the judgments on the six parts of the interview and enables the interviewer to *see* how the applicant stacks up in the final analysis.

I. Early Years and Education

	Yes	No	?
1. Is his cultural background an asset?			
2. Does his educational record indicate a satisfactory intelligence level for the job?			
3. Was he able to adjust himself readily as a boy?			
4. Are his early interests assets?			
5. Did he begin to develop work habits early in life?			
6. Did he show any evidence of capacity for leadership?			
Total number of yeses			

FINAL JUDGMENT (check one)
Favorable ________
Unfavorable ______
Uncertain ________

II. Experience

	Yes	No	?
1. Does he show ability to adjust himself to situations and people?			
2. Is his reaction to failure sound?			
3. Is he able to appraise himself with reasonable objectivity?			
4. Is he strongly motivated?			
5. Has he planned any definite satisfactory objective for the future?			
6. Is his objective within reasonable limits of his capacity?			
7. Does his previous work experience show evidence of qualities of leadership?			
Total number of yeses			

FINAL JUDGMENT (check one)
Favorable ________
Unfavorable ______
Uncertain ________

III. Clubs, Sports, and Social Activities

	Yes	No	?
1. Does he have a normal social life?			
2. Is he physically vigorous and active?			
3. Is he social-minded?			
4. Does he know how to relax?			
5. Does he show capacity for leadership?			
Total number of yeses			

FINAL JUDGMENT (check one)
Favorable ________
Unfavorable ______
Uncertain ________

IV. Health

	Yes	No	?
1. Would his health permit him to stand the rigors of the job?			
2. Does he appear to be free from tension and anxiety?			
3. Would the health of himself and family permit him to live on his income from the job?			
Total number of yeses			

FINAL JUDGMENT (check one)
Favorable ________
Unfavorable ______
Uncertain ________

V. Economic Status

	Yes	No	?
1. Does his economic status show a need to work?			
2. Has he made reasonable economic progress, considering his age and circumstances?			
3. Could he take care of himself and family until he reached the stage when he could pay his way on the job?			
4. Has he exercised good financial judgment?			
5. Are his desires and plans within the limits of his earning capacity?			
6. Would you lend him your own money (if you had it) to get him started?			
Total number of yeses			

FINAL JUDGMENT (check one)
Favorable ________
Unfavorable ______
Uncertain ________

VI. Knowledge of and Skill in Selling

	Yes	No	?
1. Has he had any formal training in selling (not on-the-job training)?			
2. Has he had any formal sales training in previous jobs?			
3. Does he do anything now to improve his knowledge of and skill in selling?			
4. Is he familiar with sound sales techniques?			
5. Does he have a healthy attitude toward selling as a career?			
Total number of yeses			

FINAL JUDGMENT (check one)
Favorable ________
Unfavorable ______
Uncertain ________

SERIOUS HANDICAPS

(Check those items which in your judgment might prove to be serious handicaps, and, consequently, the basis for failure in this job)

☐ 1. Age
☐ 2. Education
☐ 3. Apparent cultural level
☐ 4. Voice and speech
☐ 5. Personal habits
☐ 6. Appearance
☐ 7. Apparent intelligence level
☐ 8. Experience
☐ 9. Emotional instability
☐ 10. "Chronic griper"
☐ 11. Argumentative
☐ 12. "Play-boy"
☐ 13. Too aggressive and high-pressure
☐ 14. Too meek, mild and submissive
☐ 15. Too sensitive and "thin-skinned"
☐ 16. Health of self or family
☐ 17. Financial needs
☐ 18. ____________________________

Total number of serious handicaps____________

SUMMARY

	Favorable	*Unfavorable*	*Uncertain*	*Remarks*
I. Early years and education	☐	☐	☐	
II. Experience	☐	☐	☐	
III. Clubs, sports, and social activities	☐	☐	☐	
IV. Health	☐	☐	☐	
V. Economic status	☐	☐	☐	
VI. Knowledge of, and skill in selling	☐	☐	☐	

Number of serious handicaps____________________

Recommended________________________ Not recommended_______________

AN EMPLOYER'S INTERVIEW FORM

DIAGNOSTIC INTERVIEWER'S GUIDE

Name______________________________ Telephone__________________________
Address___________________________ Interviewed by______________________
City______________________________ Date______________________________

PART I.

WORK HISTORY

(Ask the applicant)

1. Please give me detailed information as to how you secured your last position; what kind of work you did; and why you left. (This question should be asked concerning the other positions held by applicant.)
2. How did your previous employers treat you?
3. (a) Have you ever been refused a recommendation by a former employer?
   (b) May we contact your former employers for references?
4. What type of criticism was most frequently made of your work by your former employers?
5. Give me some concrete examples of mistakes or failures from which you profited.
6. What experience have you had in handling people?
7. When you consider your work history, what type of work do you really enjoy most? Mechanical work?—— Detail work?—— Contact work?—— Other?——
8. What experience have you had in your previous work that prepares you for success with our company?

(Interviewer: Continue with Question No. 9, Part II, Social History.)

EVALUATION

(Ask yourself)

1. Has the applicant had the type of work history which has prepared him for the position for which he is being considered?__ Yes No ?
2. Does the applicant's work history indicate a capacity to work steadily and systematically?__________________________ Yes No ?
3. Does his work history reveal that he possesses a healthy capacity for self-criticism?__________________________________ Yes No ?
4. Does his work history indicate that he has grown in effectiveness with each change of position?______________________ Yes No ?
5. Does the applicant's work history indicate that he is persistent and aggressive?____________________________________ Yes No ?
6. Does his work history reveal attitudes of cooperativeness and good will toward the companies for whom he has worked?__ Yes No ?
7. Does his work history indicate leadership potential?_________ Yes No ?

PART II.

SOCIAL HISTORY

(Ask the applicant)

9. When you were in high school what kind of work did you hope to do when you were a man?
10. When you entered college did this ambition change? If so, how and why did it change?
11. Did your (college experience)—(work experience) cause you to change your vocational plans?

12. When in high school or college did you take part in debating, dramatics, sports, or work on the school paper?

13. When in high school or college were you ever elected an officer or leader in any social or athletic organization?

14. Have you retained to this day many friendships which were made in school?

15. (a) What courses in high school or college did you like best?
    (b) What courses did you dislike the most?
    (c) What was your high school scholastic average? College scholastic average?

16. What experience during your high school or college days stood out as meaning the most to you?

17. Did you work part-time while you were in school? If so, what kind of work did you do?

18. Have you ever contributed to the support of your family or assisted in meeting the educational expenses of brothers or sisters?

19. Did your parents encourage you and aid you in securing an education?

20. Are you active now in any social, fraternal, or civic organizations?

(Interviewer: Continue with question No. 21, Part III, Economic and Financial History.)

EVALUATION

(Ask yourself)

8. Has the applicant had the kind of educational background that has prepared him for the position for which he is being considered?	Yes	No	?
9. Has the applicant's educational history revealed a desirable level of achievement in his school work?	Yes	No	?
10. Is the kind of work for which he is applying in line with his early ambitions?	Yes	No	?
11. Has the applicant's experience been such as to make him appreciate the necessity of work?	Yes	No	?
12. Has his early history been such as to develop habits of self-reliance and independence?	Yes	No	?
13. Does his social history reveal that he has the capacity for learning new things that will prepare him for advancement?	Yes	No	?
14. Does his social history reveal a capacity for making and holding friends?	Yes	No	?
15. Do you have the impression that the applicant has matured socially and emotionally?	Yes	No	?
16. Does he seem to have the ability to express himself effectively?	Yes	No	?

PART III.

ECONOMIC AND FINANCIAL HISTORY

(Ask the applicant)

21. Do you plan your savings and expenditures by means of a budget?

22. Have you been successful in getting along without becoming involved in debt?

23. Have you been able to maintain a systematic savings program?

24. Have you ever held two jobs at one time in order to increase your income? (For instance, working full time for one company and part-time for another?)

25. (If applicant is married.) Who manages the financial affairs of your home?

26. When you compare yourself with other men of your age and experience do you believe that you have made satisfactory economic progress?

27. How much money do you want to earn 10 years from now?

28. What position do you want to hold at that time?

29. What are you going to do to obtain the position and income that you want at that time?

(Interviewer: Continue with question No. 30, Part IV, Personality Appraisal.)

EVALUATION

(Ask yourself)

17. Does the applicant's record show that he has been systematic and intelligent in planning his finances?	Yes	No	?
18. Are the applicant's economic aims in line with the opportunities offered by our company?	Yes	No	?
19. Does he have a definite vocational goal?	Yes	No	?
20. If so, does he have a definite plan in mind for realizing that goal?	Yes	No	?
21. Is the applicant well motivated for the position for which he is being considered?	Yes	No	?

PART IV.

PERSONALITY APPRAISAL

(Ask the applicant)

30. What do you consider your strongest qualities and characteristics?
31. What are your weak points; things you need to improve in?
32. When you compare yourself with other men of your age and experience, what factors in your own makeup and personal history give you a feeling of indecisiveness or inferiority?
33. Looking back over your life history: What experiences or persons have had an outstanding influence on you? Why?
34. Why do you want to work for our company? Why do you want this job?
35. In summary, what particular assets in experience, personality, or character do you have that you feel will be of greatest value to our company? In other words, why should we hire you?

(Interviewer: When you have completed this interview turn back to Part I and begin asking yourself the 29 Evaluation questions at the bottom of the pages. Circle each question YES, NO or ?. Circle a ? only if you are entirely unable to answer either YES or NO.)

EVALUATION

(Ask yourself)

22. Does the applicant appear to have the kind of personality that is needed for the position for which he is being considered?	Yes	No	?
23. Does he seem vitally eager to succeed?	Yes	No	?
24. Does he have a sound estimation of his worth to our company?	Yes	No	?
25. Does he possess the ability to be critically self-analytical?	Yes	No	?
26. Does he appear to be well-adjusted emotionally?	Yes	No	?
27. Does he create the impression of a man who has significant possibilities for growth?	Yes	No	?
28. Considering the applicant's personality, and his work, social and economic history, does he seem to be stable and dependable?	Yes	No	?
29. Is he the kind of a man that you would like to work with?	Yes	No	?

Scoring Rules—Give one point for each YES, one-half point for each ? and no points for a NO. Record total number of points in upper right hand corner of first page.

AN EMPLOYER'S INTERVIEW FORM

THE NATIONAL CASH REGISTER COMPANY

DAYTON 9, OHIO

INTERVIEWER'S GUIDE AND REPORT

Applicant's name --

Address ------------------------------------ Telephone ---------------
Street City Zone State

Interviewed by ----------------------------- Date --------------------

Branch office --

I. ABILITY TO SELL:

LEAD: "Tell me all about your employment experience—including selling and non-selling." . . . "Do you feel that you could sell our product?"

Notes: --

What is your estimate of his capacity to sell NCR products? ☐ Accounting Machines ☐ Cash Registers ☐ Adding Machines

(Base your judgment on (1) your general observation of the man; (2) his ability to sell himself to you; (3) the way he discusses his employment background; (4) your estimate of his "sales sense.")

☐ No: Would not make the grade.

☐ Marginal "might get by."

☐ Would do an adequate job.

☐ Would be a good salesman.

☐ Would be highly effective.

Summary comment: --

II. LOYALTY AND JOB SATISFACTION:

LEAD: "How was the (X) Company as a place to work? Were you always well treated? Did you have sufficient opportunity to 'progress?' "

Notes: --

Will he really and basically "accept" your job and be proud of it? Will he be enthusiastic and loyal?

(Base your judgment on his reply to the above questions, and upon your general observation of the man up to this point.)

☐ Will be quick to suspect and resent.

☐ May entertain doubts sometimes.

☐ Will be reasonably contented.

☐ Will work cheerfully.

☐ Will improve loyalty of others.

Summary comment: --

III. LEADERSHIP AND SUPERVISORY CAPACITY:

LEAD: "Have you held any positions requiring supervision of others?" . . . (Later) "What are the best ways to handle subordinates?"

Notes: --

How well can he supervise a group of subordinates and manage a department?

(Base your judgment on general observations and answers to above questions. Does he have the right ideas (stated or implied) about handling people? Does he have a personality capable of carrying out his own ideas?)

☐ Could not supervise.

☐ Would get along with difficulty.

☐ Reasonably satisfactory.

☐ Would do a good job.

☐ Excellent; his personality builds morale.

Summary comment: --

IV. EDUCATION AND CULTURAL BACKGROUND:

LEAD: "Tell me about your schooling from first grade on—including special courses taken at night, or by correspondence, or as 'on-the-job' training."

Notes: --

Is his education and cultural background appropriate for the job of selling

☐ Accounting Machines? ☐ Cash Registers? ☐ Adding Machines?

(Base your judgment on (1) amount of schooling he has had (too much or too little); (2) the vocabulary he uses (too slangy or too high-powered); (3) the appropriateness of special courses like accounting; (4) the occupational level of family and relatives; (5) his implied ambitions.)

☐ Poor: too much or too little.

☐ Fair: might do.

☐ Would fit in.

☐ Would fit in well.

☐ Highly appropriate background.

Summary comment: --

V. PERSONALITY AND SOCIAL EFFECTIVENESS:

LEAD: "Tell me about what clubs you belonged to in school (college), and since? Did you hold office in any of them? What recreation do you like most?"

Notes: --

Will he be "well taken" and liked in his territory?

(Base your judgment in part upon answers to the above leads and in part upon your overall feeling about him at this time. Does he create a good impression on you?)

☐ Poor: will create resistance.

☐ Fair: would get by.

☐ Will be accepted.

☐ Will be liked.

☐ Will be highly effective.

Summary comment: --

VI. HEALTH AND STAMINA:

LEAD: "Give me an account of the ups and downs of your health (in the past ten years)."

Notes: --

Would he be able to stand up physically in the job?

(Base your judgment on his account of his health, and his general physical appearance.)

- ☐ Too weak.
- ☐ Marginal stamina.
- ☐ Adequate vigor.
- ☐ Good physical capacity.
- ☐ Excellent health reserve.

Summary comment: --

VII. MARRIAGE SITUATION:

LEAD: "Are you single, married, divorced, separated—Children? Ages? Who carries main responsibility for discipline of the children? Do you agree on this point? What are areas of greatest disagreement?"

Notes: --

Is his present home life a helpful or harmful influence on him, or his morale?

(Base your judgment on what seems to be the "real family situation".)

- ☐ Serious worries about home life.
- ☐ Constant mild tensions over family.
- ☐ Happy home life.
- ☐ Occasional minor family worry.
- ☐ Reasonably contented home.

Summary comment: --

VIII. PERSONAL APPEARANCE:

Is his personal appearance satisfactory for meeting the customers he would contact?

(Is his appearance befitting a high-grade salesman?)

- ☐ No: too sloppy or too overdressed.
- ☐ Would get by.
- ☐ Satisfactory appearance.
- ☐ Very acceptable.
- ☐ Highly appropriate appearance.

Summary comment: --

IX. ALERTNESS AND INTELLIGENCE:

Does he seem to be mentally alert and quick to see a point?

(Base your judgment on previous observation. Does he "catch on" readily—does he follow the line of conversation without apparent effort?)

- ☐ Definitely dull.
- ☐ Somewhat slow.
- ☐ Holds his own.
- ☐ Bright: good impression.
- ☐ Very alert: "on his toes."

Summary comment: --

NOTES BASED ON REVIEW OF APPLICATION BLANK

FINAL SUMMARY COMMENTS: Write in additional impressions or judgments not covered above, such as: self-confidence, sense of humor, quality of voice, undesirable mannerisms and habits, rigidity of ideas, headstrong tendencies, etc. Any trait, characteristic or mannerism which is present to a marked degree or with striking quality should be described.

AN EMPLOYER'S INTERVIEW FORM

GENERAL ELECTRIC COMPANY

SUPERVISORY INTERVIEW RATING FORM

(For Use In Interviewing Candidates)

Name of Candidate J. Hobsell Evaluator H. Werner Date 6/8/51

A. WORK EXPERIENCE Below Average — Average ✓ — Above Average

Duties?
Number of previous jobs?
Many contacts with people?
Likes and dislikes?
How closely supervised?
Working conditions?
Hard work, long hours?
Physical demands?
Level of earnings?
Any leadership experience?
Able to organize?
Able to delegate?
Reasons for changing jobs?
Attitude toward upgrading?
Factors of job satisfaction?

- Wkd hard as child - Money needed at home.
Serv station during H.S. Nursery summers.
- Worked his way while in college.
- Low level assembly jobs before war.
- Army 42-46 Infantry - rose to Master Sgt
- Leader and Acting Supv. at Zip Piston
- Evidently an organizer
- Switched to GE because future looked better.
- Very eager to advance.
- Likes to work with people - likes to plan + organize

B. EDUCATION AND TRAINING Below Average — Average ✓ — Above Average

Too little—too much schooling?
Level of school grades?
Best—poorest subjects?
Honors—activities?
Reason for leaving school?
Any additional training?
How was education financed?

- Grad H.S. '37 "Fairly good grades - didn't work hard at studies"
- Football and basketball teams 1st 2 years, but had to quit to work (didn't make 1st teams)
- 1 yr. at M.I.T. but too much strain financially had to quit

C. EARLY HOME BACKGROUND Below Average — ✓ Average — Above Average

Fathers (Mother's) occupation?
Interests and temperament?
Socio-economic factors?
Childhood factors?
Number of brothers and sisters?
Over-protective parents?
Parental discipline, guidance?
Earliest age partially or wholly financially independent?
Motivational influences?
Moral standards?

- Father truck driver - happy go lucky
- Very happy home, but then father killed when Joe. 10 yrs old
- 2 bros. + 1 older sister supported home and mother
- Mother died 2 yrs. ago - cancer
- Had to work hard as a boy, but still seemed to have happy go lucky attitude

D. PRESENT HOME ADJUSTMENT Below Average — Average — Above Average ✓

Present interests and hobbies?
Any leadership responsibilities?
Marital status?
Present living arrangements?
Wife's attitude toward job?
Dependents (number and age)?
Financial stability?
Housing, Life insurance?

- Likes sports. spectator + participator. Softball, bowling, golf.
- Scoutmaster
- President of neighborhood improvement group. Civic minded.
- Wife a good influence - [illegible] him.

E. HEALTH AND PHYSICAL CONDITION Below Average — Average ✓ — Above Average

Unfavorable health history?
Any disabilities?
Vigor, energy, stamina?

- "Health has always been O.K."

F. MANNER AND APPEARANCE Below Average — Average — Above Average ✓

Favorable appearance?
Pleasant, friendly manner? ✓
Any unfavorable mannerisms?
Persuasive?
Tactful?

Very good.
- Persuasive - expresses himself well
- Would seem to command respect of others.

G. MOTIVATION AND INTERESTS Below Average — Average — Above Average ✓

- ⊞ Hard worker, production-minded?
- ⊞ Ambition?
- ⊞ Initiative?
- ⊞ Cost-conscious?
- ⊞ Interest in people?
- ⊞ Interest in supervisory job?
- ⊞ Interest in GE?

H. PERSONALITY QUALIFICATIONS — Below Average | Average | Above Average ✓

- Mature?
- Emotional stability, even-temper?
- Conscientious?
- Self-discipline?
- Unobtrusively aggressive?
- Persistence, determination?
- Honest and sincere?
- Self-confidence?
- Courage of convictions, firm?
- Fair, impartial?
- Social sensitivity?
- Adaptable?
- Teamworker?
- Enthusiasm?

SUMMARY OF ASSETS

- Good personality.
- Mature
- Persuasive.
- Would command respect of others.
- Has "color" - enthusiastic
- Good leadership characteristics
- Enjoys it

SUMMARY OF LIABILITIES

- Says he sometimes "flys off the handle," but forgets quickly
- a little weak in technical experience.
- Experience restricted to rather routine work for a man with some college.

OVER-ALL SUMMARY Should make a good leader of others. Very good personality and experience for this work. Should first prove his ability to acquire technical skill in order to be considered for advancement to higher supervisory levels.

OVER-ALL RATING — Poor | Below Average | Average | Above Average ✓ | Excellent

IV. THE ORGANIZATION TESTS MEN

THE DOMINANT ideological drift in organization life is toward (1) idolatry of the system and (2) the misuse of science to achieve this. I would now like to go into some detail on one manifestation of this drift: the mass testing of "personality." These curious inquisitions into the psyche are becoming a regular feature of organization life, and, before long, of U.S. life in general. And these tests are no play-things; scoff as the unbeliever may, if he has ambitions of getting ahead he would do well to develop, or simulate, the master personality matrix the tests best fit.

I hope these chapters will be instructive in this respect, and in examining the curious ways tests are scored, I will give some quite practical advice on how to beat them. But it is the underlying principles of testing that will be my main consideration. Ordinarily, The Organization's demands for conformity are so clouded in mystique that their real purport is somewhat obscured. In personality tests, however, they are abundantly evident. Here is the Social Ethic carried to the ultimate; more than any other current development, these tests dovetail the twin strands of scientism and the total integration of the individual. The testers can protest that this is not so, that really the tests are for the individual, that they encourage difference, not conformity. But the tests speak otherwise. They are not, I hope to demonstrate, objective. They do not respect individual difference. They are not science; only the illusion of it.

PERSONNEL TESTING

PERSONNEL TESTING OF ONE KIND OR ANOTHER HAS BEEN GOING ON for a long time, but the testing of personality has been a fairly recent development. Spiritually, it is not descended so much from the scientific-management movement of the twenties but rather from the later, and presumably more liberal, human-relations movement. The scientific-management people, such as Taylor, were primarily interested in getting *things* done, and their concern with the employee was with those aspects that contributed to this—such as his ability to distinguish distance, or the dexterity of his hands. The development of testing during this period was almost wholly concerned with aptitudes, and some fair success was accomplished along these lines; by having job applicants try their hand at putting wiggly blocks together and such, management was much better able to tell what kind of work a man was best suited for.

Concurrently, organizations were finding vocabulary and intelligence tests similarly useful. During World War I, psychologists had developed, in the "Alpha" tests, a very serviceable vocabulary and intelligence test, and civilian organizations were quick to see its usefulness. While these were not precise, enough people were being tested to produce rough norms that would enable an organization to tell whether a person's mental capacities were sufficient for the particular work at hand. While schools and colleges have been the primary users of such tests, industry found that with the growing complexity of certain kinds of jobs, I.Q. tests were just as valuable as physical-aptitude tests in gauging employees. By the time of World War II, the use of aptitude and intelligence tests had become so widespread that it was almost impossible for any white-collar American to come of age without having taken a battery at one time or another.

But something was eluding The Organization. With aptitude tests The Organization could only hope to measure the specific, isolated skills a man had, and as far as his subsequent performance was concerned, it could predict the future only if the man was magnificently endowed or abysmally deficient in a particular skill. Aptitude tests, in short, revealed only a small part of a man, and as more and more group-relations advocates have been saying, it is the whole man The Organization wants and not just a part of him. Is the man well adjusted? Will he remain well adjusted? A test of potential merit could not tell this; needed was a test of potential *loyalty*.

PEN AND PENCIL TESTS

For a long time applied psychologists had been experimenting with inmates of mental institutions and prisons to plumb the deeper recesses of maladjustment, and in the course of this work they had developed some ingenious pen and pencil tests. While most of these were originally designed to measure abnormality, they could not do this unless they were applied to normal people to get some sort of standard. Before long, the psychologists, spurred by the lively interest of professional educators, began applying these to ordinary groups of people. At first there were only crude indexes—chiefly of the degree people were extroverted or introverted. But the psychologists were nothing if not ingenious, and they designed tests which presumably can measure almost any aspect of a man's personality. Now in regular use are tests which tell in decimal figures a man's degree of radicalism versus conservatism, his practical judgment, his social judgment, the amount of perseverance he has, his stability, his contentment index, his hostility to society, his personal sexual behavior—and now some psychologists are tinkering with a test of a sense of humor. More elaborate yet are the projective techniques. With such devices as the Rorschach Inkblot test and the Thematic Apperception test, the subject is forced to apply his imagination to a stimulus, thereby X-raying himself for latent feelings and psychoses. Asking a normal adult to reveal himself is not the same thing as asking an inmate of a mental institution, of course, and some adults have balked at the self-revelation asked. But this recalcitrance, psychologists have advised organizations, is no great stumbling block. Testers have learned ways to attach great significance to the manner in which people respond to the fact of the tests, and if a man refuses to answer several questions, he does not escape analysis. Given such a man, many psychologists believe that they can deduce his suppressed anxieties almost as well as if he had co-operated fully.

HERE, IN SHORT, WAS JUST WHAT THE ORGANIZATION WANTED. NOT ALL organizations, to be sure, but since the war there has been a steady increase in the numbers which have taken up this tool. In 1952, one third of U.S. corporations used personality tests; since then the proportion has been climbing—of the 63 corporations I checked in 1954, some 60 per cent were already using the tests, and these include such bellwether firms as Sears, General Electric, and Westinghouse. Today, there remain some companies opposed to personality testing, but most of the large ones have joined and a fair number of smaller ones too.

The most widespread use of tests has been for the fairly mundane job of screening applicants. Even in companies which aren't yet fully sold on personality tests, it is part of standard operating procedure to add several personality tests to the battery of checks on the job applicant. If business declines, the tests may also be used to help cut down the work force. "For trimming inefficiency in the company operation," Industry Psychology Inc. advises clients, "there is no better place to direct the ax than in the worker category." And there is no better way to do this, it adds, than to run the work force through tests.

TEST USES

But the most intriguing development in personality testing lies in another direction. In about 25 per cent of the country's corporations the tests are used not merely to help screen applicants for The Organization but to check up on people already in it. And these people, significantly, are not the workers; as in so many other aspects of human relations it is the managers who are being hoist. Some companies don't bother to give personality tests to workers at all. Aside from the fact that testing can be very expensive, they feel that the limited number of psychologists available should concentrate on the more crucial questions.

Should Jones be promoted or put on the shelf? Just about the time an executive reaches fifty and begins to get butterflies in his stomach wondering what it has all added up to and whether the long-sought prize is to be his after all, the company is wondering too. Once the man's superiors would have had to thresh this out among themselves; now they can check with the psychologists to find out what the tests say. At Sears, for example, for the last ten years no one has been promoted in the upper brackets until the board chairman has consulted the tests. At Sears, as elsewhere, the formal decision is based on other factors too, but the weight now being given test reports makes it clear that for those who aspire to be an executive the most critical day they may spend in their lives will be the one they spend taking tests.

Giving them has become something of an industry itself. In the last five years the number of blank test forms sold has risen 300 per cent. The growth of psychological consulting firms has paralleled the rise. In addition to such established firms as the Psychological Corporation, literally hundreds of consultants are setting up shop. Science Research Associates of Chicago, a leading test supplier, reports that in one year seven hundred new consultants asked to be put on its approved list of customers. Colleges are also getting into the business; through research centers like Rensselaer Polytechnic's Personnel Testing Laboratory, professors in mufti have been tailoring tests for companies on a consultant basis—a kind of competition, incidentally, which annoys a good many of the frankly commercial firms.

Types of service offered vary greatly. Some firms will do the entire operation by mail—the Klein Institute for Aptitude Testing, Inc., of New York, for example, within forty-eight hours of getting the completed test back will have an analysis on its way to the company. Usually, however, the job is done on the premises. Sometimes the consultant group, like the Activity Vector Analysts, will process the entire management group at one crack. More usually the analysts will come in and study the organization in order to find the personality "profiles" best suited for particular jobs. They will then work up a battery of tests and master profiles. (Somehow, most batteries always seem to be made up of the same tests, but they are presumably just the right mix for the particular client.) The analysts may help out with the day-in, day-out machinery of testing, but the company's personnel department generally handles the rest of the job.

A dynamic would appear to be at work. The more people who are tested, the more test results there are to correlate, and the more correlations, the surer are many testers of predicting success or failure, and thus the more reason there is for more organizations to test more and more people. Some companies have already coded their executives onto IBM cards containing vital statistics, and adding test scores would seem an inevitable next step. What with the schools already doing much the same thing, with electronics making mass testing increasingly easy, there seems no barrier to the building of such personnel inventories for every organization. Since so many of the tests are standard, in time almost everyone can be followed from childhood on, as, echelon by echelon, he makes his way up the ladder of our organization society.

FANCIFUL? THERE'S NO LIMIT TO WHAT SOME PEOPLE WOULD LIKE TO see done. Several years ago, I wrote a little piece for *Fortune* satirizing current integration trends. Under the nom de plume of Otis Binet Stanford, I presented a plan for a Universal Card. The idea was to do away with the duplication of effort in which each company goes about testing independently. Instead of each company tackling the job on its own, there would be one central organization. Eventually everyone would be processed by it—from school on. One's passport to organization life would be his card. On it would be coded all pertinent information: political leanings, marital relations, credit rating, personality test scores, and, if the states co-operated, the card would also be one's operator's license and car registration. (We had a very realistic card gotten up, complete with laminated photo of a young man wearing thick horn-rimmed glasses.) With this tool, organization could get full loyalty: if a man developed hostility he could not escape by leaving an organization. His card would be revoked and that would be that. Lest readers get too excited, I made the end patently ridiculous: with the card, I said, society would be protected from people who questioned things and rocked the boat. For good measure there was a footnote indicating that the whole thing was a hoax.

To our surprise, a considerable number of people took it seriously. Some thought it was appalling. (*Punch* devoted an article to it, as one more evidence of Yankee boorishness.) Many readers wrote indignant letters, and several newspapers editorialized with great heat. All this we didn't mind; we were sorry they were mad at us but we were glad they were mad at the card.

Unfortunately, however, many who took it literally thought it was a splendid idea and the net effect of the article on them was to embolden them to action. The president of the country's largest statistical firm called in great excitement to find out if anyone had yet started the central processing organization—he said it was the sort of idea you kick yourself for not having thought of first. His firm, he suggested, was just the right outfit on which to build the central unit. When I last heard from him he was on his way to see a testing outfit he might team up with.

The idea of a card I thought so novel, it also developed, was not novel at all. After the article had appeared I came across an account of an index system Westinghouse Electric had had in operation for several years. For each management man they had a "Management Development Personnel Code Card," Westinghouse Form 24908. It is a square card containing basic data on the man, the edges of which are punched so that it can be run through the machines at central files. In fairness to Westinghouse let me point out that it does not delve and there is no personality test information on it. But it does give one ideas.

MASS TESTING

THERE IS, EVIDENTLY, NOT MUCH POINT AT THIS DATE IN BELABORING the moral implications of mass testing. Ethical considerations are paramount, to be sure, but to put the case against testing on these grounds seems to array the critic with the ancient forces of superstition against the embattled followers of science. By default, the basic claims of the testers are left unchallenged. Worse yet, the criticism that portrays testing as a black art only serves to whet the curiosity of organizations all the more.

But do the tests do what they purport to do? Let us examine the testers on their own grounds: the scientific method. As a preliminary, let me ask the reader to study the following composite test and its scoring table. To my knowledge, the printing of these guides gives the layman his first opportunity of judging for himself how sensibly prefabricated answers are scored. Until recently, testers have successfully kept such matters within the club; exposure of answers, they have maintained, would be highly unethical—it takes a trained mind to interpret scores, meaningful only to men with Ph.D.s in psychology, individual scores are the property of the organization, the layman would get the wrong idea, etc., etc.

The layman has every right in the world to have a look at the business—in particular, those "right" and "wrong" answers that are not supposed to exist. Whether or not he is unable to distinguish the scientific method from the abuse of it, I leave to the reader.

In detailing scoring methods, I have a practical purpose also. In a small way, I hope to redress the balance of power between the individual and The Organization. When an individual is commanded by an organization to reveal his innermost feelings, he has a duty to himself to give answers that serve his self-interest rather than that of The Organization. In a word, he should cheat. To put it so baldly may shock some people—I was scolded severely by several undergraduate groups for giving just such advice. But why be hypocritical? Most people instinctively cheat anyway on such tests. Why, then, do it ineptly? Usually, the dice are loaded in favor of The Organization, and the amateur, unprepared, is apt to slant his answers so badly as to get himself an even worse score than his regular maladjustments would warrant.

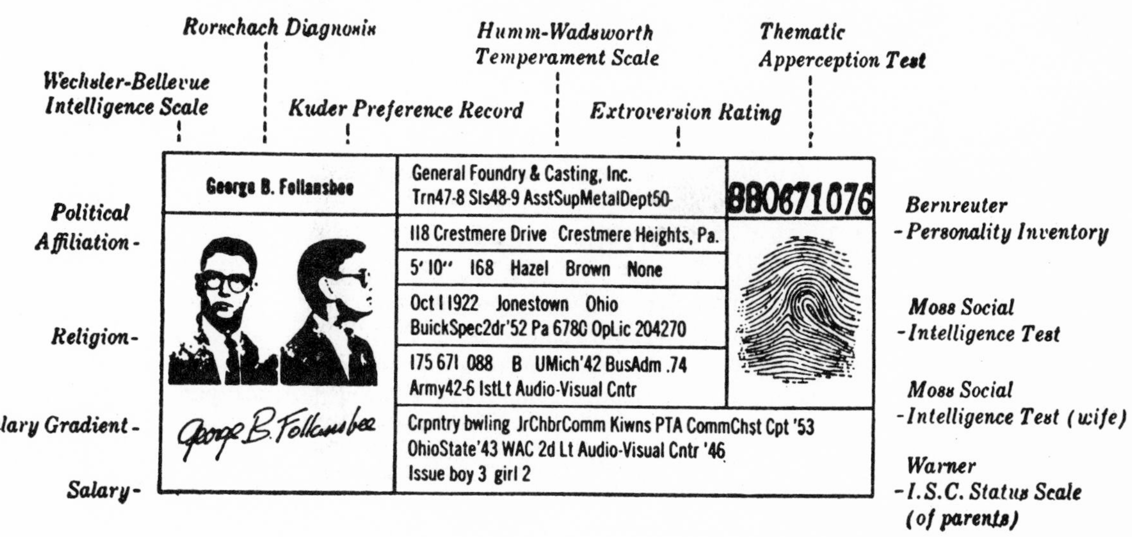

A trot is in order. In providing this service, I could not expect the individual to memorize specific questions and answers—there are scores and scores of different tests and far too many hundreds of answers for memorizing to be of any real help. What I have done is to paraphrase the essence of the different types of questions that come up most frequently, and in giving answers in the composite test I have abstracted the basic rules of the game which, once learned, will help the reader master most of the testing situations he may come across.

I suggest to the reader that, before going on to the next chapter, he pause and take the test. If he will then turn to the appendix, he will find a condensed guide on how he should have answered the questions and some tips on test-taking in general. I hope all this may be of some practical benefit, but in asking the reader to pore over these details my main purpose is to give him a chance to evaluate for himself the underlying *principles* of personality testing. To repeat, here is the voice of The Organization, and if one wishes to judge what the future would be like were we to intensify organization trends now so evident, let him ponder well what the questions are really driving at.

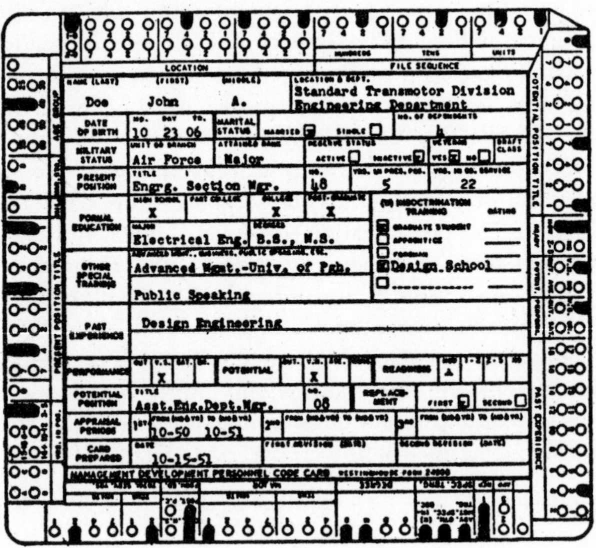

LOCATION
FILE SEQUENCE
HUNDREDS TENS UNITS
NAME (LAST) (FIRST) (MIDDLE): Doe John A.
LOCATION & DEPT.: Standard Transmotor Division Engineering Department
DATE OF BIRTH: MO. 10 DAY 23 YR. 06
MARITAL STATUS: MARRIED ☒ SINGLE ☐
NO. OF DEPENDENTS: 4
MILITARY STATUS: UNIT OR BRANCH: Air Force; ATTAINED RANK: Major; RESERVE STATUS: ACTIVE ☐ INACTIVE ☒; VETERAN: YES ☒ NO ☐; DRAFT CLASS
PRESENT POSITION: TITLE: Engrg. Section Mgr.; NO. 48; YRS. IN PRES. POS. 5; YRS. IN CO. SERVICE 22
FORMAL EDUCATION: HIGH SCHOOL X; PART COLLEGE; COLLEGE X; POST-GRADUATE X; MAJOR: Electrical Eng.; DEGREES: B.S., M.S.
INDOCTRINATION TRAINING — RATING: GRADUATE STUDENT; APPRENTICE; FOREMAN; ☒ Design School
OTHER SPECIAL TRAINING: Advanced Mgmt.-Univ. of Pgh.; Public Speaking
PAST EXPERIENCE: Design Engineering
PERFORMANCE: V.S. X
POTENTIAL: V.S. X
READINESS
POTENTIAL POSITION: TITLE: Asst.Eng.Dept.Mgr.; NO. 08; REPLACEMENT: FIRST ☒ SECOND ☐
APPRAISAL PERIODS: 1ST FROM (MO & YR) TO (MO & YR) 10-50 10-51; 2ND; 3RD
CARD PREPARED: DATE 10-15-51; FIRST REVISION (DATE); SECOND REVISION (DATE)
MANAGEMENT DEVELOPMENT PERSONNEL CODE CARD
AGE GROUP
PRESENT POSITION TITLE
POTENTIAL POSITION TITLE
PAST EXPERIENCE

COMPOSITE PERSONALITY TESTS

Self-report Questions

1) Have you enjoyed reading books as much as having company in?
2) Are you sometimes afraid of failure?
3) Do you sometimes feel self-conscious?
4) Does it annoy you to be interrupted in the middle of your work?
5) Do you prefer serious motion pictures about famous historical personalities to musical comedies?

Indicate whether you agree, disagree, or are uncertain:

6) I am going to Hell.
7) I often get pink spots all over.
8) The sex act is repulsive.
9) I like strong-minded women.
10) Strange voices speak to me.
11) My father is a tyrant.

Hypothetical Question – Dominance Type

12) You have been waiting patiently for a salesperson to wait on you. Just when she's finished with another customer, a woman walks up abruptly and demands to be waited upon before you. What would you do?
   a) Do nothing
   b) Push the woman to one side
   c) Give her a piece of your mind
   d) Comment about her behavior to the salesperson

Opinion Questions – Degree of Conservatism

Indicate whether you agree or disagree with the following questions:

13) Prostitution should be state supervised.
14) Modern art should not be allowed in churches.
15) It is worse for a woman to have extramarital relations than for a man.
16) Foreigners are dirtier than Americans.
17) "The Star-Spangled Banner" is difficult to sing properly.

Word Association Questions

Underline the word you think goes best with the word in capitals:

18) UMBRELLA (rain, prepared, cumbersome, appeasement)
19) RED (hot, color, stain, blood)
20) GRASS (green, mow, lawn, court)
21) NIGHT (dark, sleep, moon, morbid)
22) NAKED (nude, body, art, evil)
23) AUTUMN (fall, leaves, season, sad)

Hypothetical Situations–Judgment Type

24) What would you do if you saw a woman holding a baby at the window of a burning house:
   a) Call the fire department
   b) Rush into the house
   c) Fetch a ladder
   d) Try and catch the baby

25) Which do you think is the best answer for the executive to make in the following situation:

   Worker: "Why did Jones get the promotion and I didn't?"
   Executive:

   a) "You deserved it but Jones has seniority."
   b) "You've got to work harder."
   c) "Jones's uncle owns the plant."
   d) "Let's figure out how you can improve."

Opinion Questions – Policy Type

26) A worker's home life is not the concern of the company.
   Agree........ Disagree........
27) Good supervisors are born, not made.
   Agree........ Disagree........
28) It should be company policy to encourage off-hours participation by employees in company-sponsored social gatherings, clubs, and teams.
   Agree........ Disagree........

Opinion Questions – Value Type

29) When you look at a great skyscraper, do you think of:
   a) our tremendous industrial growth
   b) the simplicity and beauty of the structural design
30) Who helped mankind most?
   a) Shakespeare
   b) Sir Isaac Newton

V. DO YOU CONFORM?

IF PERSONALITY TESTS ARE THE VOICE OF THE ORGANIZATION IT IS NOT that testers mean them to be. A few are lackeys, but the great majority cherish the professional's neutrality; they try hard to be objective, and "value judgments" they shun. And this is the trouble. Not in failing to make the tests scientific enough is the error; it is, rather, in the central idea that the tests *can* be scientific.

They cannot be, and I am going into quite some detail in this chapter to document the assertion. I do so because the tests are the best illustration of the underlying fallacies of scientism—and the underlying bias. As in all applications of scientism, it is society's values that are enshrined. The tests, essentially, are loyalty tests, or rather, tests of potential loyalty. Neither in the questions nor in the evaluation of them are the tests neutral; they are loaded with values, organization values, and the result is a set of yardsticks that reward the conformist, the pedestrian, the unimaginative—at the expense of the exceptional individual without whom no society, organization or otherwise, can flourish.

What I am examining is not the use of tests as guides in clinical work with disturbed people, or their use in counseling when the individual himself seeks the counseling. Neither is it the problems of professional conduct raised by the work of some practitioners in the field, interesting as this bypath is. What I am addressing myself to is the standard use of the tests by organizations as a gauge of the "normal" individual, and the major assumptions upon which the whole mathematical edifice rests.

The first assumption is the idea that if we can measure minor variations in most human beings, we can to a large degree predict what they will do in the future. If the principle of this were true, tests of aptitude—such as vocabulary, or finger dexterity tests—should have long since proved the point. Unlike personality tests, they measure what is relatively measurable, and they have been used so long and on so many people that a vast amount of before-and-after documentation is available.

APTITUDE TESTS

Aptitude tests have proved useful in distinguishing capabilities. Once past establishing whether a person probably can or cannot meet minimum requirements, however, their predictive success is not impressive. The Army Air Force mass testing experience furnishes perhaps the largest body of evidence available. During the war the Air Force tested hundreds of thousands of men with the standardized battery of tests known as the "Stanines." Now, by going back and comparing the initial prediction with how the men actually performed, we gain a rather clear idea of their usefulness Here are the conclusions psychiatrist Lawrence Kubie has drawn from the comparison:

> The tests of aptitudes were remarkably accurate as far as they went; they selected accurately a small group at one extreme, most of whom would succeed in training, and another small group at the opposite pole, most of whom would fail. (There were exceptions to the results even at both extremes.)
>
> As was to be expected, however, the vast majority of the men tested fell into the central zone of the normal curve of distribution, while only a relatively small percentage of the tested population was placed at the two extremes. With rare exceptions, the individuals who fell into the extremes knew their own aptitudes and ineptitudes before going through any tests. From their experiences at play, in sport, in school, and on various jobs, they knew already that they were specially adept or specially maladroit with respect to certain types of activity. Indeed the representatives of the two extreme ends of the scale were usually able to describe their strong and weak points almost as precisely as these could be measured.
>
> The next important lesson of the entire experiment with the "Stanines" was that for the majority, who fall in the great middle zone of the normal curve of distribution, their minor variations in aptitudes do not determine either success or failure, happiness or unhappiness in a career. For most of us (that is, for the Average Man), a subtle balance of conscious and unconscious forces determines how effectively we use our native aptitudes, whether intellectual, emotional, sensory, neuromuscular, or any combination of these aptitudes. For most of us it is not the minor quantitative differences in the machine itself, but the influence of these conscious and unconscious emotional forces on our use of the human machine which determines our effectiveness. For me this was the ultimate lesson from the experience of the Air Force with the "Stanines"

The personality tester can reply that this merely proves his point —i.e., if a combination of aptitude tests cannot predict the future because of subtle emotional forces, why, then, all we have to do is add some tests that will measure these forces. Once again, the fatal step from science to scientism. In aptitude testing the responses are of a character that can be rated objectively—such as the correctness of the answer to 2 plus 2 or the number of triangles in a bisected rectangle. The conclusions drawn from these aptitude and intelligence scores are, furthermore, limited to the relatively modest prediction of a man's capability of doing *the same sort of thing he is asked to do on the tests.* If the tests indicate that a man has only 5,000 words in his vocabulary, it is a reasonable assumption that he won't do particularly well in a job requiring 50,000 words. If he is all thumbs when he puts wiggly blocks together, he won't be very good at a job requiring enough manual dexterity to put things like wiggly blocks together.

PERSONALITY TESTS

To jump from aptitude testing to personality testing, however, is to jump from the measurable to the immeasurable. What the personality testers are trying to do is to convert abstract traits into a concrete measure that can be placed on a linear scale, and it is on the assumption that this is a correct application of the scientific method that all else follows. But merely defining a trait is immensely difficult, let alone determining whether it can be measured as the opposite of another. Is "emotionalism," for example, the precise statistical opposite of "steadiness"? People are daily being fitted onto linear scales for such qualities, and if their dimensions don't fit they are punished, like those on Procrustes' bed, for their deviance.

BUT WHAT IS "PERSONALITY"? THE SURFACE FACETS OF A MAN—THE way he smiles, the way he talks? Obviously not, the psychologists admit. We must go much deeper. But how much deeper? Few testers would dream of claiming that one can isolate personality from the whole man, yet logic tells us that to be able statistically to predict behavior we would have to do just this. The mathematics is impeccable—and thus entrapping. Because "percentiles" and "coefficients" and "standard deviations" are of themselves neutral, the sheer methodology of using them can convince people that they are translating uncertainty into certainty, the subjective into the objective, and eliminating utterly the bugbear of value judgments. But the mathematics does not eliminate values; it only obscures them.

Let's take the interpretation of test scores. Testers argue that the human element has largely been eliminated from this process; except with "projective" tests the scoring is standardized—if you choose answer (d.) you get so many points, and what the tester may think has nothing to do with it. But you don't take just one test; you usually take several different tests, and the crux of the process comes when the tester attempts to build a composite picture out of all these different sub-scores. The more different scores there are to put together, the more a job of interpretation, not less, the tester has.

With even the most disciplined mind, it is impossible to erase the influence of one's own environment and outlook. Testers likewise, and when any have some stray neuroses themselves, their interpretations can be downright dangerous. Several years ago, a midwest executive sent a job applicant he had investigated and thought very well of to a psychological consultant for testing. The report that came back was surprisingly ominous: according to the analyst, the man was abnormally anti-authority and would have "insufficient feelings of loyalty to the organization." The executive hired the man anyway—he didn't care whether the man loved the company or not; he just wanted a job done. The man worked out fine. A year later, when a similarly ominous report came in on a similarly able man, the executive became curious. He decided to go over and chat with the analyst. "The poor guy was pathetically jealous," the executive recalls. "He was eating his heart out because men his own age that I was sending over had gone way past him. I asked him about the first man he had warned me against. Obviously unstable, he told me; the man had two kids, yet he had bought a convertible. Also, he was building an ultra-modern house."

In the case of projective tests, interpretation is even more critical. Originally, they were meant to be used only as part of an exhaustive clinical diagnosis, and the few men who are expert in them have warned against their application to selection. As they point out, the tests can sometimes be more a projection of the man who is doing the evaluation than of the man who is being evaluated.

What do symbols symbolize? David Riesman tells of a Thematic Apperception Test taken by a graduate student in history. In these tests you are shown a picture—of a man going out a doorway, for example—and asked to tell a story about it. The history student, not too surprisingly, told a story about a famous historical figure who had had a difficult choice to make. Ah-ha! said the man who interpreted the tests, maladjustment. The student had talked about people who were *dead*. This was the first thought that a historical figure had called up in the mind of the tester.

No matter what tests are used, the interview experience itself is surcharged with values. The dehumanized literature of the field gives little hint of the highly personal overtones that mark the meeting of interviewer and interviewee. Consider the situation in which a man who has reached middle age sees himself weighed in the balance by a man whom he has never seen before. Even were both impossibly "normal" the relationship would be difficult, for all the amenities of civilized discourse cannot suppress in either the consciousness that there is a conflict of interests between the two. There is no interviewee who does not have something within himself that he fears to reveal, and there are few interviewers who do not wish to find it. For professional reasons alone the interviewer wishes to probe for the bared nerve.

And sometimes for personal reasons too. I remember vividly a conversation a colleague and I had with a well-known consultant. Quite voluntarily, he bared his own nerve. In the course of explaining his technique of interviewing he referred to the OSS testing program in World War II and how candidates were submitted to a grueling series of experiences to test their reaction under shock. He spoke warmly of the "final" interview: in this the candidate was taken into a room filled with men dressed as superior officers. They told him that he had done fine and now had only one more test to pass. This was a test of binocular vision in which he was to peer into a box and by turning handles bring two objects together. Unknown to him, one of the onlookers would manipulate a knob which made it impossible to accomplish the task. While the poor devil of a candidate fumbled away, the officers would begin making disparaging remarks. On the very threshold of acceptance, he was told that he had failed. The onlookers then observed his reaction.

The consultant explained that for obvious reasons this sort of thing could not be done in an industrial situation. But the principle could be used. He explained his interview technique. "I sit down with a man with a record of the tests and his vital data in front of me. I am very friendly with him. It is a tense situation, and by increasing the stress I can get him to reveal much more of himself. For example, I will be running down the list and I will read aloud 'married: seventeen years.' Then I will read 'children: none.' I will let my eyebrows go up just a little and then pause thoughtfully. He is probably very sensitive on this point and in a few minutes he will begin to blurt out something about his wife or himself being sterile, and how maybe they have seen doctors about it. Just at this point I may ask him how his sexual relations with his wife are now. After several more minutes of stress I build him up again. Toward the end of the interview I usually smile and say, 'Well, why don't we stop while we're ahead.' That makes him relax and makes him think everything is going to work out all right. Then I shoot a really tough one at him. He is caught off guard."

I am not trying to suggest that testers are abnormal, though there would be, I am tempted to add, a certain poetic injustice in such a suggestion. When they are confronted with recalcitrance or criticism, many testers, as is so characteristic of followers of scientism, do not address themselves to the ideas in dispute but speculate, instead, on the hidden maladjustments that drove one to take a position contrary to theirs. They use sympathy like a weapon.

But turnabout would not be fair play. Most testers are fair and as normal as the next fellow, and as far as underlying hostilities of their own are concerned, they would be abnormal if they didn't have some. They would also be abnormal if they suppressed them completely. The interviewer is sorely tempted to play God—and if the difference in age or salary or background or temperament between himself and the person he is evaluating is wide, the temptation to play somebody else is strong too. This can be resisted by the man with great insight into himself as well as others, the man with wisdom, forbearance, humility. To all such men in the testing field my remarks do not apply.

QUESTION VALUE

We have been talking of how testers interpret answers; now let's turn to the questions themselves. Are they free of values? In designing the questions, testers are inevitably influenced by the customs and values of their particular world. Questions designed to find a man's degree of sociability are an example. Do you read books? The reading of a book in some groups is an unsocial act, and the person who confesses he has at times preferred books to companions might have to be quite introverted to do such a thing. But the question is relative. Applied to someone brought up in an environment where reading books is normal—indeed, an excellent subject for much social conversation—the hidden "value judgment" built into the test can give a totally unobjective result. People are not always social in the same terms. A person who would earn himself an unsocial score by saying he would prefer reading to bowling with the gang is not necessarily unsocial and he might even be a strong extrovert. It could be that he just doesn't like bowling.

If the layman gags at the phrasing of a question, testers reply, sometimes with a superior chuckle, this is merely a matter of "face validity." They concede that it is better if the questions seem to make sense, but they claim that the questions are not so important as the way large numbers of people have answered them over a period of time. To put it in another way, if a hundred contented supervisors overwhelmingly answer a particular question in a certain way, this means something, and thus no matter whether the question is nonsensical or not, it has produced a meaningful correlation coefficient.

Meaning what? This is not the place to go into a lengthy dissertation on statistics, but two points should be made about the impressive test charts and tables that so often paralyze common sense. A large proportion of the mathematics is purely internal—that is, test results are compared with other test results rather than with external evidence. Now, this internal mathematics is valuable in determining a test's "reliability"—that is, whether it is consistent in its measurements. If a group of people take Form B of a test, for example, and a mathematical correlation shows that their percentile scores rank just about as they did when they took Form A of the same test, we have an indication of the test's reliability in measuring something.

VALIDITY OF TESTS

But *what* is that something? A test's reliability tells us little about its validity. A test may give eminently consistent results, but the results are worthless unless it can be determined that the test is actually measuring the trait it is supposed to measure. Do the tests measure sociability or introversion or neurotic tendencies? Or do they merely measure the number of times an accumulation of questions about putting out fires or reading certain books will be answered certain ways?

To show a test is valid, scores must be related to subsequent behavior of the people tested. Examine the "validation" evidence for many tests, however, and you will find they consist chiefly of showing how closely the average scores for the particular test come to the average scores of somebody else's test. That there should be a correlation between test scores is hardly surprising. Test authors are forever borrowing questions from one another (some questions have been reincarnated in as many as ten or twelve different tests) and what the correlations largely prove is how incestuous tests can be.

But how much have scores been related to individual behavior? Among themselves psychologists raise the same question, and for muted savagery there is nothing to match the critiques they make of one another's tests.[1] The Bernreuter Personality Inventory is a particular case in point. This is by far the most widely used test in business (1953 sales by Stanford University Press, one of several distributors: 1,000,000 copies). Yet a reading of the professional journals shows many reports on it to have been adverse. Some psychologists checked Bernreuter scores against other, more objective, evidence of what the people tested were like and found no significant relationships, and sometimes reverse correlations. "It must be concluded," writes Cecil Patterson in the *Journal of Social Psychology* (24, 3-50), "that the results of studies using the Bernreuter Personality Inventory are almost unanimously negative as far as the finding of significant relationships with other variables is concerned. . . . It is no doubt largely due to the nature of the questionnaire approach, which appears to be a fruitless technique for the study of personality."

As top psychologists point out, a really rigorous validation would demand that a firm hire all comers for a period of time, test them, seal away the tests so the scores would not prejudice superiors, and then, several years later, unseal the scores and match them against the actual performance of the individuals involved.[2] This has rarely been so much as attempted. Dr. Robert L. Thorndike of Columbia Teachers College, certainly no fortress of anti-science, points out that most follow-up studies of personality tests known to the field

---

[1] For the flavor of this internecine kind of battle read between the lines of the following succession of papers: Peck, R. F. and Worthington, R. E., "New Technique for Personnel Assessment," *Journal of Personnel Administration and Industrial Relations,* January 1954; Clark, J. G. and Owens, W. A., "A Validation Study of the Worthington Personal History Blank," *Journal of Applied Psychology,* 1954, Vol. 38, 85-88; Peck, R. F. and Stephenson, Wm., "A Correction of the Clark-Owens Validation Study of the Worthington Personal History Technique," *Journal of Applied Psychology,* Vol. 38, No. 5, 1954; Owens, W. A., "A Reply to Drs. Peck-Stephenson," *Journal of Applied Psychology,* Vol. 38, No. 5, 1954. This sort of thing can go on for years.

The layman who wishes to delve into the field might with profit browse through *The Fourth Mental Measurements Yearbook,* edited by Oscar K. Buros (Highland Park, N. J.: Gryphen Press, 1953). This is a hefty collection of critiques, pro and con, made by psychologists of all the principal aptitude and personality tests. Another, and more readable, book is *Essentials of Psychological Testing,* by Lee J. Cronbach (New York: Harper & Brothers, 1949).

[2] In the field of projective tests, validation is skimpier yet: psychiatrist Dr. Sol W. Ginsburg, Vanderbilt Clinic, College of Physicians & Surgeons, Columbia University, says, "Rorschach never dreamed his test would be used in the way that it has been used. His most distinguished pupils have also warned against misapplying the test. It has no place in industry for selection purposes. It would be possible to test personalities of future teachers or future executives, but it would be very expensive. You would have to find competent persons to administer the test and such competent persons do not exist in any large numbers. Moreover, it would take more than a generation before one could judge whether the tests one was using were valid." (*What Makes an Executive,* Eli Ginzberg, editor. New York: Columbia University Press, 1955.)

are "contaminated." To make a genuine validation, Thorndike says, it is necessary "to apply the procedure and make the evaluation . . . to keep the results out of the hands of the operating people who can control each man's career and the appraisal of it . . . to get appraisals of job success that are entirely independent of the [original] appraisal, and then to bring together the two *independent* sets of data."

Comparisons have been made between groups that have been tested—for example, a group considered productive may be found to have had an average score on a particular test higher than that of another group less productive. The average of a group, however, tells us very little about the individuals involved. Invariably, some of the people in the "best" group will have lower test scores than some of those in the "poor" ones.

Testers evade this abyss by relying on a whole battery of tests rather than on just one or two. But no matter how many variables you add you cannot make a constant of them. If a man has a high "contentment index" and at the same time a very high "irritability index," does the one good cancel out the other bad? Frequently the tester finds himself right back where he started from. If he is a perceptive man he may pay little heed to the scores and make a very accurate prognosis; if the prognosis later turns out to be correct, however, this will be adduced as one more bit of evidence of the amazing accuracy of the tests.

As AN EXAMPLE OF HOW VALUES GET ENTWINED IN TESTING, LET'S watch as a "Worthington Personal History" is constructed. This particular technique is a "projective" one; it is so projective, as a matter of fact, that the tester doesn't even have to bother seeing the man at all. The client company has the applicant fill out what seems to be an innocuous vital-statistics blank and then mails it to Worthington Associates at Chicago. There an analyst studies it for such clues as whether the man used check marks or underlinings, how he designated his relatives, what part of his name he gives by initials, what by the full word. He is then ready to reconstruct the man.

INDIVIDUAL ANALYSIS

Let the reader match his diagnostic skill against the testers. In a hypothetical example given in the *Personnel Psychology* journal, we are told that the applicant, one Jonathan Jasper Jones, Jr writes down that he is twenty-six, that the date of his marriage was November 1951, that he has only one dependent, his wife, that her given name is Bernadine Butterfield, her age twenty-eight, and that she works as a nurse-receptionist in a doctor's office.

Enigma? Carefully, the analyst writes that these clues indicate that Jones "may not take his general obligations very seriously, may have a tendency to self-importance, wishful thinking, may be inclined to be passive-dependent—i.e., reliant on others for direction and guidance—in his general work relationships, may be inclined to take pleasure in unearned status or reflected glory."

How in the world did the analyst deduce all this? Let us peek into the laboratory. The name was the first clue. It told the analyst that Jones was narcissistic. Whenever a man writes his name out in full, the tester notes in his chart that he is "narcissistic." Two initials, last name: "hypomanic." First initial, middle and last name: "narcissistic, histrionic." Any erasure or retracing: "anxious, tense." Characteristically, the applicant gets the short end of every assumption. Even if he adopts the customary first name, middle initial, last name, he is put down as "mildly compulsive."

Deeper and deeper the analyst goes:

> Spouse's age: twenty-eight
>
> Fact: married a girl two years older than himself.
>
> Empirical observation: the majority of men marry women younger than themselves.
>
> Primary deduction: may have been influenced in marrying her by unconsciously considering her as a mother-surrogate.
>
> Tentative inference: may like to have an older woman, or people, take care of him.
>
> Provisional extension: may be inclined to be passive-dependent—i.e., reliant on others for direction and guidance—in his general work relationships.

And so on.

Analysts, of course, have just as much right to read between the lines as the next man. What makes their posture interesting is the claim that theirs is the scientific method. There are all the inevitable tables ("the biserial correlation for tenure on Worthington cutoff is 0.34") in which the accuracy of the internal mathematics is confused with the accuracy of the premises. There is the usual spurious humility: the authors caution that no single deduction is necessarily correct; it is only when all the deductions are fitted into a "formal, quantitative scoring procedure based on an organized system of psychodynamic factors" that they become correct. Add up enough wrongs, in short, and you get a right.

The analysis of J. J. Jones is a rather extreme example but it leads us to a defect characteristic of all tests. Against what specifications is the man being measured? Assuming for the moment that we are able to diagram Jonathan Jones exactly, how are we to know the kind of work the diagram indicates he is suited for? There is not much point in testing people to find out if they will make good salesmen or executives unless we know what it is that makes the good ones good.

There are, of course, some fairly simple common denominators such as energy and intelligence, but beyond these we get into very muddy waters indeed. Is the executive, as is so often assumed, one who was more attached to his father than his mother? And what, for example, of the liking for other people that is supposed to be a key executive trait? Many successful executives are very gregarious, but a great many equally successful ones are not, and some are very cold fish. Conversely, are writers, research people, and the like necessarily introverts? One writer I know rather well was advised by a testing laboratory to go into clerical work and steer clear of writing. While he scored just slightly "introverted," the laboratory still felt that his score indicated enough enjoyment of the company of other people to prove him unsuited for writing. Another laboratory tells people whether they are good at communication by determining their "ability to write freely without blocking or searching for the right word or phrase." You are given a topic and so many minutes in which to write on it. No matter how much gibberish it may be, the more words you write on this glibness test the more "creative" you are rated to be.

THE PROFILE

Testers often admit their knowledge of personality requirements is still too sketchy, but they feel this can be cleared up by more testing. And thus we come to the "profile." Testers have been busy collating in chart form the personality scores of people in different occupations to reveal how they differ with other adult groups on particular personality traits. These comparisons are generally expressed as a "percentile" rating—if the total of thirty salesclerks' scores on sociability averages somewhere around the 80th percentile, for example, this indicates that the average salesclerk is more sociable than 79 out of 100 adults. With such data a man being considered for a particular kind of job can be matched against the master profile of the group. The closer he fits the better for him.

Profiles are also worked up for work in individual companies. At Sears, Roebuck there are charts that diagram the optimum balance of qualities required. Here is the one an executive values:

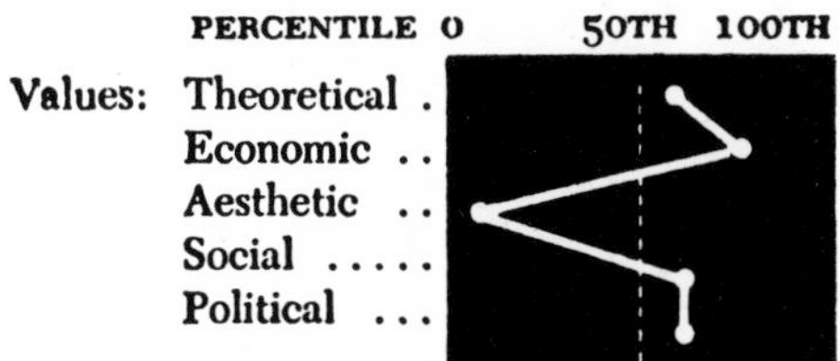

A man does not have to match this profile exactly, but it won't help him at all if his line zigs where the chart zags. Take a man who scores considerably higher than the 10th percentile on aesthetic values, for example; such people, Sears notes, "accept artistic beauty and taste as a fundamental standard of life. This is *not* a factor which makes for executive success. . . . Generally, cultural considerations are not important to Sears executives, and there is evidence that such interests are detrimental to success."

Sears has every right to de-emphasize certain qualities and emphasize others; and in hewing to this type, it should be noted, Sears has built up one of the most alert management groups in the country. But the process should not be confused with science. When tests are used as selection devices, they are not a neutral tool; *they become a large factor in the very equation they purport to measure.* For one thing, the tests tend to screen out—or repel—those who would upset the correlation. If a man can't get into the company in the first place because he isn't the company type, he can't very well get to be an executive in it and be tested in a study to find out what kind of profile subsequent executives should match. Long before personality tests were invented, of course, plenty of companies had proved that if you hire only people of a certain type, then all your successful men will be people of that type. But no one confused this with the immutable laws of science.

Bias doesn't have to be personal. Now it's institutionalized. For the profile is self-confirming; when it doesn't screen out those who fail to match it, it will mask the amount of deviance in the people who do pass. Few test takers can believe the flagrantly silly statement in the preamble to many tests that there are "no right or wrong answers." There wouldn't be much point in the company's giving the test if some answers weren't regarded as better than others. Telling the truth about yourself is difficult in any event. When someone is likely to reward you if you give answers favorable to yourself the problem of whether to tell the truth becomes more than insuperable; it becomes irrelevant. In this respect, let us give the tests their due; they may tell little about personality, but they do tell something about intelligence. "Do you daydream frequently?" In many companies a man either so honest or so stupid as to answer "yes" would be well advised to look elsewhere for employment.

Even when the man who should have looked elsewhere slips through, the profile will be self-confirming. For the profile molds as well as chooses; it is, as Sears puts it, a statement of "the kind of behavior we have found to be desirable." If he is going to get ahead, let alone survive, the man is going to have to adjust. Several years of give and take, and the organization will have smoothed him out, and thus when the psychologists do their "validating," or rechecking, later he will score near enough to the median to show them how right they were all along. At Sears psychologists retested employees about two and a half years after their first test. Of the thirteen personality factors they were investigating, nine showed a definite change. "All the factors," concluded Sears' V. C. Benz, "indicate a 'better' or more adequate psychological adjustment. . . . The individuals are better people."

Up to a point the company "type" has some virtue; any first-rate organization must have an *esprit de corps*, and this requires a certain degree of homogeneity. But the pitfalls are many, for while a self-confirming profile makes for a comfortable organization, it eventually can make for a static one. Even the largest corporations must respond to changes in the environment; a settled company may have its very existence threatened by technological advances unless it makes a bold shift to a new type of market. What, then, of the pruning and molding that adapted it so beautifully to its original environment? The dinosaur was a formidable animal.

THE PROFILE CAN BE SELF-CONFIRMING FOR THE INDIVIDUAL TOO. FOR tests intensify a mutual deception we practice on one another. Who is "normal"? All of us to some degree have a built-in urge to adjust to what we conceive as the norm, and in our search we can come to feel that in the vast ocean of normality that surrounds us only we are different. We are the victims of one another's façades.

And now, with the norm formally enshrined in figures, we are more vulnerable than ever to this tyrant. "Science" seems its ally, and thus, faulty or not, the diagnosis can provoke a sense of guilt or inadequacy; for we can forget that the norm is often the result of the instinctive striving of previous test takers to answer as they think everyone else would answer.

If the organization man escapes the danger of self-tyranny he faces another. At first superiors may scoff at the diagnosis, but if they have been putting reliance on testing they have a stake themselves in the correctness. Suspicion, unfortunately, demands proof, and sometimes it so counterbalances judgment that unconsciously a management will punish the man so that faith in the tests may be confirmed. One large midwestern company was about to promote a man when it decided to have him take a test. The report that the consultant firm mailed back to the company was freighted with warnings about the man's stability. The company was puzzled. The man had consistently done a fine job. Still. . . . The more the company mused, the more worried it became; at last it decided to tell the man the promotion he had expected so long was going to someone else. Six months later, the company reports, the man had a nervous breakdown. As in all such stories, the company says what this proves is how accurate the test was.

Are the people who don't score well necessarily the misfits? Almost by definition the dynamic person is an exception—and where aptitude tests reward, personality tests often punish him. Look at a cross section of profiles and you will see three denominators shining through: extroversion, disinterest in the arts, and a cheerful acceptance of the status quo. Test scoring keys reveal the same bias. As I note in How to Cheat on Personality Tests, if you want to get a high score you will do well to observe these two rules:

(1) When asked for word associations or comments about the world, give the most conventional, run-of-the-mill, pedestrian answer possible.

(2) When in doubt about the most beneficial answer to any question, repeat to yourself:

> I loved my father and my mother, but my
> father a little bit more.
> I like things pretty much the way
> they are.
> I never worry much about anything.
> I don't care for books or music much.
> I love my wife and children.
> I don't let them get in the way of
> company work.

If you were this kind of person you wouldn't get very far, but, unfortunately, you won't get very far unless you can seem to be this kind. Check the norms and you will find that the advice is not flippant.[3] Norms are based on group scores, and as often as not the group turns out to have been 1,000 college freshmen, 400 high-school students, or some similarly less-than-outstanding aggregation. There are norms for selected groups like executives, chemists, and the like, and there will in time be more and more. But these can be illusory too. Usually, the norms are based on the responses of people who are being tested by The Organization; in such a situation self-preservation demands a certain circumspection in answering, and the norms are more a playback of what the people taking the tests think The Organization wants to hear rather than the reality of their own selves. Daydream? Of course not.

THE EXCEPTIONAL MAN

THE SHEER MECHANICS OF THE TESTS PUNISH THE EXCEPTIONAL MAN. A test with prefabricated answers is precisely the kind of test that people with superior intelligence find hardest to answer. Writing of the using of "objective," forced-choice college examinations, Jacques Barzun says in his *Teacher in America,* "I have kept track for some ten years of the effects of such tests on the upper half of each class. The best men go down one grade and the next best go up. It is not hard to see why. The second-rate do well in school and in life because of their ability to grasp what is accepted and conventional. . . . But first-rate men are rarer and equally indispensable. . . . To them, a ready-made question is an obstacle. It paralyzes thought by cutting off all connections but one. Or else it sets them to thinking and doubting whether *in that form* any of the possible answers really fits. Their minds have finer adjustments, more imagination, which the test deliberately penalizes as encumbrances."

If the reader has taken the test in the previous chapter he has probably come to the same conclusion about personality-test questions. How big was that fire in the house with the mother and child? What about the worker who wanted a promotion? Was he any good? Maybe the office did want the boss's nephew to get the job. These are not quibbles; they are the kind of questions that occur to the intelligent mind, and the ability to see shadings, to posit alternatives, is virtually indispensable to judgment, practical or otherwise.

---

[3] Several who have followed this advice, I am glad to report, have profited well. One engineer who was asked by his company to take a battery of tests studied my trot and took the tests in the frame of mind recommended above. To his surprise, he shortly received quite a promotion. The company had found unsuspected depths of normalcy in him; as one executive later confided to him, the tests had eliminated certain doubts some had had about his personality. He has, incidentally, done very well in the new job.

How well do group averages fit the outstanding man? For a practical check my colleagues and I decided to do some testing of our own. What would happen, we wondered, if the presidents of some of our large corporations had to take the same tests their juniors do? We obtained a supply of test blanks and scoring keys for the principal tests and managed to persuade a dozen of the most well-known corporation leaders to take the tests and let us do the scoring. For good measure, we gave the same battery of tests to sixteen of the country's most brilliant scientists, and a condensed version to thirty-eight middle-management men who had been picked by their respective companies as outstanding for their age group.

When the tests were scored one thing became clear. If the tests were literally applied across the board today, tomorrow half of the most dynamic individuals in our big corporations would be out pounding the streets for a job. Here are the high lights of the test results.

(1) Not one corporation president had a profile that fell completely within the usual "acceptable" range, and two failed to meet the minimum profile for foremen. On the "How Supervise" questions, presidents on the average got only half the answers right, thus putting them well down in the lower percentiles. They did particularly badly on the questions concerning company employee-relations policies. Only three presidents answered more than half of these questions correctly.

(2) The scientists' Personal Audit profiles were more even than the presidents'—if anything, they scored as too contented, firm, and consistent. They did, however, show up as extremely misanthropic, over half falling under the 20th percentile for sociability.

(3) The middle-management executives scored well on stability and sociability, but on practical judgment only three reached the mean indicated for executive work.

(4) The range of scores was so great as to make a median figure relatively meaningless. On the Thurstone "S" score for sociability, for example, only eight of the forty-three management men fell between the 40th and the 60th percentiles, the remainder being grouped at either extreme.

(5) The scores were highly contradictory. Many of the same people who got high "steadiness" scores on the Personal Audit scored very badly for "stability" on the Thurstone test. Similarly, many who scored high on "contentment" had very low "tranquillity" scores.

One explanation for the variance between the men and the norms would be that the men in our sample were answering frankly —no job being at stake—and thus their scores could not be properly compared with the standard norms given. But if this is the case, then we would have to conclude that the norms themselves embody slanted answers. Another explanation of the men's poor showing would be that they scored low because they were in fact neurotic or maladjusted, as the tests said. But this would only leave us with a further anomaly. If people with an outstanding record of achievement show up as less well adjusted than the run of the mill, then how important a yardstick is adjustment? Our sample, of course, was small. So is the supply of outstandingly talented people.[4]

Not only do such people disturb the statistical equilibrium, they are the kind of people those of moderate ability frequently distrust. They always did, of course, but now they have a way of rationalizing the distrust; sometimes it seems almost as though they were joined together in a great League of the Mediocre against those who would confound them. The specifications for research people are a case in point. In picking those to be advanced to leadership, some management experts seem to go out of their way to pick the mediocre almost for their mediocrity, as if brilliance in a field disqualifies one for leadership. "When we're looking for a guy to be made a research director," says one consultant, "we try to find a guy who's just a fair chemist but whose test indicates potential leadership qualities. We'd sooner push him up than a guy who is a top chemist but only an average leader." Sometimes, the consultant adds, they can salvage an introvert. "When we spot a guy with a score like that, we single him out for counseling. Once in a while we're able to make the man over."

PAST PERFORMANCE

A record of achievement is no defense. What a person has actually done over a long period of time would seem to be the single most valuable indication of how he will perform in the future. But a record is not measurable; unlike a forced-choice answer, it cannot be reduced into statistical form, and thus the more anxious an organization is for certainty, the less attention does it pay to past performance. The fault here is management's, it should be noted, more than the psychologists', for management often asks them to deliver much more definite recommendations than they are willing to certify. Even the management consultants, whose chief competence is supposed to be personnel evaluation, frequently farm out the decisions about their own hiring to testing firms.

The study of a man's past performance, the gauging of him in the personal interview are uncertain guides. But they are still the key, and the need is not to displace them but to become more skilled with them. The question of who will be best in a critical situation cannot be determined scientifically before the event. No matter how much information we may amass, we must rely on judgment, on intuition, on the particulars of the situation—and the more demanding the situation the less certain can we be of prediction. It is an im-

[4] Management consultant Robert N. McMurry: "Large organizations in particular have a very specific attraction to those with an unusual need for security and so come to have a disproportionate share, a supersaturation, of the passive, dependent, and submissive. This condition would not be such a threat to the morale and organizational integrity of an enterprise if it were recognized for what it is and its implications understood. But this is rarely the case. (*Harvard Business Review*, January-February 1954)

mensely difficult task, perhaps the most difficult one that any management faces. But the question cannot be fed into a computer, nor can it be turned over by proxy for someone else to decide, and any management that so evades its most vital function needs some analysis of its own.

Finally, let us suppose that the tests could in fact reveal the innermost self. Would they even then be justified? The moral basis of testing has been tabled in this discussion, but it is the paramount issue. Were the tests truly scientific, their effectiveness would make the ultimate questions more pressing, not less. Is the individual's innermost self any business of the organization's? He has some rights too. Our society has taught him to submit to many things; thousands of civilians who went into the military meekly stood naked in long lines waiting for their numbered turn in the mass physical examinations. Many civilians who have been asked to work on government projects have submitted to being fingerprinted and to the certainty that government agents would soon be puzzling their friends and neighbors with questions about their backgrounds. But in these cases a man can console himself that there is a reason; that if he is to enjoy the benefits of collective effort he must also pay some price.

But there is a line. How much more must a man testify against himself? The Bill of Rights should not stop at organization's edge. In return for the salary that The Organization gives the individual, it can ask for superlative work from him, but it should not ask for his psyche as well. If it does, he must withhold. Sensibly—the bureaucratic way is too much with most of us that he can flatly refuse to take tests without hurt to himself. But he can cheat. He must. Let him respect himself.

VI. HOW TO CHEAT ON PERSONALITY TESTS

THE important thing to recognize is that you don't win a good score: you avoid a bad one. What a bad score would be depends upon the particular profile the company in question intends to measure you against, and this varies according to companies and according to the type of work. Your score is usually rendered in terms of your percentile rating—that is, how you answer questions in relation to how other people have answered them. Sometimes it is perfectly all right for you to score in the 80th or 90th percentile; if you are being tested, for example, to see if you would make a good chemist, a score indicating that you are likely to be more reflective than ninety out of a hundred adults might not harm you and might even do you some good.

CONVENTIONALITY

By and large, however, your safety lies in getting a score somewhere between the 40th and 60th percentiles, which is to say, you should try to answer as if you were like everybody else is supposed to be. This is not always too easy to figure out, of course, and this is one of the reasons why I will go into some detail in the following paragraphs on the principal types of questions. When in doubt, however, there are two general rules you can follow: (1) When asked for word associations or comments about the world, give the most conventional, run-of-the-mill, pedestrian answer possible. (2) To settle on the most beneficial answer to any question, repeat to yourself:

a) I loved my father and my mother, but my father a little bit more.
b) I like things pretty well the way they are.
c) I never worry much about anything.
d) I don't care for books or music much.
e) I love my wife and children.
f) I don't let them get in the way of company work.

TEST FORMAT

Now to specifics. The first five questions in the composite test are examples of the ordinary, garden variety of self-report questions.[1] Generally speaking, they are designed to reveal your degree of introversion or extroversion, your stability, and such. While it is true that in these "inventory" types of tests there is not a right or wrong answer to any *one* question, cumulatively you can get yourself into a lot of trouble if you are not wary. "Have you enjoyed reading books as much as having company in?" "Do you sometimes feel self-conscious?"—You can easily see what is being asked for here.

Stay in character. The trick is to mediate yourself a score as near the norm as possible without departing too far from your own true self. It won't necessarily hurt you, for example, to say that you have enjoyed reading books as much as having company in. It will hurt you, however, to answer every such question in that vein if you are, in fact, the kind that does enjoy books and a measure of solitude. Strive for the happy mean; on one hand, recognize that a display of too much introversion, a desire for reflection, or sensitivity is to be avoided. On the other hand, don't overcompensate. If you try too hard to deny these qualities in yourself, you'll end so far on the other end of the scale as to be rated excessively insensitive or extroverted. If you are somewhat introverted, then, don't strive to get yourself in the 70th or 80th percentile for extroversion, but merely try to get up into the 40th percentile.

---

[1] Leading Tests of this type include:
The Personality Inventory by Robert G. Bernreuter. Published by The Stanford University Press, Stanford, California. Copyright 1935 by The Board of Trustees of Leland Stanford Junior University. All rights reserved.

125 questions; measures several different things at once; scoring keys available for neurotic tendency; self-sufficiency; introversion-extroversion; dominance-submission; self-confidence; sociability.

Thurstone Temperament Schedule by L. L. Thurstone. Copyright 1949 by L. L. Thurstone. Published by Science Research Associates, Chicago, Ill. 140 questions. Measures, at once, seven areas of temperament: to wit, degree to which one is active, vigorous, impulsive, dominant, stable, sociable, reflective. "The primary aim of the Thurstone Temperament Schedule . . . is to evaluate an individual in terms of his relatively permanent temperament traits. One of the values of the schedule is that it helps provide an objective pattern, or profile, of personal traits which you can use to predict probable success or failure in a particular situation."

Minnesota T-S-E Inventory by M. Catherine Evans and T. R. McConnell. Copyright 1942 by Science Research Associates, Chicago, Illinois.
150 questions. Measures three types of introversion-extroversion—thinking, social and emotional.

The Personal Audit by Clifford R. Adams and William M. Lepley, Psycho-Educational Clinic, Pennsylvania State College. Published by Science Research Associates, Chicago, Ill. Copyright 1945 by Clifford R. Adams. All rights reserved.
450 questions. Nine parts, of 50 questions each. Each part measures "a relatively independent component of personality." Extremes of each trait listed thus: seriousness-impulsiveness; firmness-indecision; tranquillity-irritability; frankness-evasion; stability-instability; tolerance-intolerance; steadiness-emotionality; persistence-fluctuation; contentment-worry.

Since you will probably be taking not one, but a battery of tests, you must be consistent. The tester will be comparing your extroversion score on one test with, say, your sociability score on another, and if these don't correlate the way the tables say they should, suspicion will be aroused. Even when you are taking only one test, consistency is important. Many contain built-in L ("lie") scores, and woe betide you if you answer some questions as if you were a life of the party type and others as if you were an excellent follower. Another pitfall to avoid is giving yourself the benefit of the doubt on all questions in which one answer is clearly preferable to another, viz.: "Do you frequently daydream?" In some tests ways have been worked out to penalize you for this. (By the same token, occasionally you are given credit for excessive frankness. But you'd better not count on it.)

Be empathic to the values of the test maker. Question five asks: "Do you prefer serious motion pictures about famous historical personalities to musical comedies?" If you answer this question honestly you are quite likely to get a good score for the wrong reasons. If you vote for the musical comedies, you are given a credit for extroversion. It might be, of course, that you are a very thoughtful person who dislikes the kind of pretentious, self-consciously arty "prestige" pictures which Hollywood does badly, and rather enjoy the musical comedies which it does well. The point illustrated here is that, before answering such questions, you must ask yourself which of the alternatives the testmaker, not yourself, would regard as the more artistic.

Choose your neurosis. When you come across questions that are like the ones from 6 to 11—"I often get pink spots all over"—be very much on your guard. Such questions were originally a by-product of efforts to screen mentally disturbed people; they measure degrees of neurotic tendency and were meant mainly for use in mental institutions and psychiatric clinics.[2] The Organization has no business at all to throw these questions at you, but its curiosity is powerful and some companies have been adopting these tests as standard. Should you find yourself being asked about spiders, Oedipus complexes, and such, you must, even more than in the previous type of test, remain consistent and as much in character as possible—these tests almost always have lie scores built into them. A few mild neuroses conceded here and there won't give you too bad a score, and in conceding neuroses you should know that more often than not you have the best margin for error if you err on the side of being "hypermanic"—that is, too energetic and active.

Don't be too dominant. Question 12, which asks you what you would do if somebody barged in ahead of you in a store, is fairly typical of the kind of questions designed to find out how passive or dominant you may be. As always, the middle course is best. Resist the temptation to show yourself as trying to control each situation. You might think companies would prefer that characteristic to passivity, but they often regard it as a sign that you wouldn't be a permissive kind of leader. To err slightly on the side of acquiescence will rarely give you a bad score.

[2] Outstanding example is the *Minnesota Multiphasic Personality Inventory*, Revised Edition, by Starke R. Hathaway and J. Charnley McKinley. Published by The Psychological Corporation, N. Y. 495 questions. This yields scores on hypochondriasis, depression, hysteria, psychopathic deviation, masculinity and femininity, paranoia, psychoasthenia, schizophrenia, hypomania. It also yields a score on the subject's "test-taking attitude," with a score for his degree of "defensiveness-frankness." If the subject consistently gives himself the benefit of the doubt, or vice versa, the scoring reveals the fact. This is not a test for the amateur to trifle with.

Incline to conservatism. Questions 13 through 17, which ask you to comment on a variety of propositions, yield a measure of how conservative or radical your views are.[3] To go to either extreme earns you a bad score, but in most situations you should resolve any doubts you have on a particular question by deciding in favor of the accepted.

Similarly with word associations. In questions 18 through 23, each word in capitals is followed by four words, ranging from the conventional to the somewhat unusual. The trouble here is that if you are not a totally conventional person you may be somewhat puzzled as to what the conventional response is. Here is one tip: before examining any one question closely and reading it from left to right, read vertically through the whole list of questions and you may well see a definite pattern. In making up tests, testers are thinking of ease in scoring, and on some test forms the most conventional responses will be found in one column, the next most conventional in the next, and so on. All you have to do then is go down the list and pick, alternately, the most conventional, and the second most conventional. Instead of a high score for emotionalism, which you might easily get were you to proceed on your own, you earn a stability score that will indicate "normal ways of thinking."

Don't split hairs. When you come to hypothetical situations designed to test your judgment, you have come to the toughest of all questions.[4] In this kind there are correct answers, and the testers make no bones about it. Restricted as the choice is, however, determining which are the correct ones is extremely difficult, and the more intelligent you are the more difficult. One tester, indeed, states that the measurement of practical judgment is "unique and statistically independent of such factors as intelligence, and academic and social background." He has a point. Consider the question about the woman and the baby at the window of the burning house. It is impossible to decide which is the best course of action unless you know how big the fire is, whether she is on the first floor or the second, whether there is a ladder handy, how near by the fire department is, plus a number of other considerations.

On this type of question, let me confess that I can be of very little help to the reader. I have made a very thorough study of these tests, have administered them to many people of unquestioned judgment, and invariably the results have been baffling. But there does seem to be one moral: don't think too much. The searching mind is severely handicapped by such forced choices and may easily miss what is meant to be the obviously right answer. Suppress this quality in yourself by answering these questions as quickly as you possibly can, with practically no pause for reflection.

---

[3] An example of this kind of testing is the *Conservatism-Radicalism Opinionaire* by Theodore F. Lentz and Colleagues of The Attitude Research Laboratory. Published by Character Research Association, Washington University, St. Louis, Mo., Dept. of Education. Copyright 1935. 60 statements are given; the subject indicates whether he tends to agree or disagree. His score is obtained by checking the number of times he sides with the conservative statement side *vs.* the radical one.

[4] Two tests of this type are:

Test of Practical Judgment by Alfred J. Cardall, N.B.A., Ed.D. Published by Science Research Associates, Inc., Chicago, Ill. Copyright 1942, 1950 by Science Research Associates, Inc. All rights reserved. 48 Forced-choice questions "designed to measure the element of practical judgment as it operates in everyday business and social situations." How were the "best" answers chosen? "Rigorous statistical analysis was supplemented by consensus of authority. . . ."

Practical Social Judgment by Thomas N. Jenkins, Ph.D. Copyright 1947. All rights reserved. Executive Analysis Corporation, N. Y. 52 questions about hypothetical situations; subject must choose the "best" and the "poorest" of given answers.

The judgment questions from 25 through 28 are much easier to answer.[5] The right answers here are, simply, those which represent sound personnel policy, and this is not hard to figure out. Again, don't quibble. It is true enough that it is virtually impossible to tell the worker why he didn't get promoted unless you know whether he was a good worker, or a poor one, or whether Jones's uncle did in fact own the plant (in which case, candor could be eminently sensible). The mealy-mouthed answer d)—"Let's figure out how you can improve"—is the "right" answer. Similarly with questions about the worker's home life. It isn't the concern of the company, but it is modern personnel dogma that it should be, and therefore "agree" is the right answer. So with the question about whether good supervisors are born or made. To say that a good supervisor is born deprecates the whole apparatus of modern organization training, and that kind of attitude won't get you anywhere.

Know your company. Questions 29 and 30 are characteristic of the kind of test that attempts to measure the relative emphasis you attach to certain values—such as aesthetic, economic, religious, social.[6] The profile of you it produces is matched against the profile that the company thinks is desirable. To be considered as a potential executive, you will probably do best when you emphasize economic motivation the most; aesthetic and religious, the least. In question 29, accordingly, you should say the skyscraper makes you think of industrial growth. Theoretical motivation is also a good thing; if you were trying out for the research department, for example, you might wish to say that you think Sir Isaac Newton helped mankind more than Shakespeare and thereby increase your rating for theoretical learnings. Were you trying out for a public relations job, however, you might wish to vote for Shakespeare, for a somewhat higher aesthetic score would not be amiss in this case.

There are many more kinds of tests and there is no telling what surprises the testers will come up with in the future. But the principles will probably change little, and by obeying a few simple precepts and getting yourself in the right frame of mind, you have the wherewithal to adapt to any new testing situation. In all of us there is a streak of normalcy.

---

[5] An example of this kind of test is *How Supervise?* by Quentin W. File, edited by H. H. Remmers. Published by The Psychological Corporation, N.Y. Copyright 1948, by Purdue Research Foundation, Lafayette, Indiana. 100 questions on management policy and attitudes.

[6] *A Study of Values*, Revised Edition, by Gordon W. Allport, Philip E. Vernan, and Gardner Lindzey. Copyright 1951, by Gordon W. Allport, Philip E. Vernan, and Gardner Lindzey. Copyright 1931 by Gordon W. Allport and Philip E. Vernan. Published by Houghton, Mifflin Co.

45 forced-choice questions. Answers are scored to give a measure of the relative prominence of six motives in a person: theoretical, economic, aesthetic, social, political, and religious. A profile is charted to show how he varies from the norm on each of the six.

VII. HOW SALESMEN ARE HIRED

Developing a test that really indicates the applicant's probabilities of success as a salesman has been a challenge to the aptitude testers for many years. Some companies have found that a carefully prepared job application form, which they analyze for desirable features, works better for them than a test. For instance, some companies have found that men of a certain age, with certain financial responsibilities, with a certain amount of personal investments, owning their own homes usually worked out better than men without these typical backgrounds. However, even in this respect, different companies have arrived at conflicting ideas of the "ideal" type salesman.

ONE of the larger testing organizations, the Klein Institute for Aptitude Testing, in New York City, sends the prospective salesman a test which he takes at home and mails back to the institute. Then a "profile" on the salesman is mailed to the employer as a guide to hiring or not hiring the applicant. Obviously there is a chance for the person who takes this test to analyze it at leisure and get plenty of outside help in answering the questions. Studying the chapters on personality tests will help you to make a better score on a test of salesmanship aptitude.

In answering a test of this type it is important to be consistent. Keeping in mind that a salesman should be an extrovert, should like people and activities which involve other people, and shouldn't be too intellectual, will steer you on a safe course through a test of this kind.

A sample test

THE following short sales aptitude test may be a bit less involved than some of the tests which are used on prospective salesman. Many are "padded" with extraneous questions which have little bearing, but the test is basically one of attitude and personality. This test was prepared by the Psychological Corporation of New York, one of the oldest and foremost authorities in the field of vocational testing.

Directions: Which of these statements describe you? Check the box in the "Yes" or "No" column after each statement. It is to your own interest to be as fair and accurate as possible in your answers. When you have finished, match your answers with the key answers.

1. I'd rather deal with things than people.
   ☐ Yes ☐ No
2. I think chemistry is a very interesting subject.
   ☐ Yes ☐ No
3. I like talking to strangers.
   ☐ Yes ☐ No
4. I would like to be a college teacher.
   ☐ Yes ☐ No
5. People find it easy to approach me.
   ☐ Yes ☐ No
6. I would like to do research in science.
   ☐ Yes ☐ No
7. I enjoy raising money for a charity.
   ☐ Yes ☐ No

8. I would like to teach in a school.
☐ Yes ☐ No
9. I like fashionably dressed people.
☐ Yes ☐ No
10. I would like to be a watchmaker.
☐ Yes ☐ No
11. I like to attend conventions.
☐ Yes ☐ No
12. I've more than average mechanical ingenuity.
☐ Yes ☐ No
13. I dislike people who borrow things.
☐ Yes ☐ No
14. I would like to be a mechanical engineer.
☐ Yes ☐ No
15. I like blind people.
☐ Yes ☐ No
16. I like to have regular work hours.
☐ Yes ☐ No
17. I would enjoy making speeches.
☐ Yes ☐ No
18. I would like to be head of a research department.
☐ Yes ☐ No
19. I like to keep meeting new people.
☐ Yes ☐ No
20. I enjoy bargaining when I'm buying something.
☐ Yes ☐ No
21. I would like to develop some new scientific theories.
☐ Yes ☐ No
22. I like to have a definite salary.
☐ Yes ☐ No
23. I'd rather have only a few really intimate friends.
☐ Yes ☐ No
24. I'm better than average at judging values.
☐ Yes ☐ No
25. I like to play cards.
☐ Yes ☐ No

From "Your Career in Selling" published by National Sales Executives. This test is printed with the permission of the original publisher.

Key to Self Evaluation Test

Add up your answers that agree with these in order to obtain your total score. If your score is 16 or above, your chances of success in the selling field are favorable.

1.	—	N	10.	—	N	19.	Y	—
2.	—	N	11.	Y	—	20.	Y	—
3.	Y	—	12.	—	N	21.	—	N
4.	—	N	13.	Y	—	22.	—	N
5.	—	N	14.	—	N	23.	—	N
6.	—	N	15.	Y	—	24.	Y	—
7.	Y	—	16.	—	N	25.	Y	—
8.	—	N	17.	Y	—			
9.	Y	—	18.	—	N			

PART 3

Studying for Advancement to Supervisory Positions

Tests for supervisory and junior executive positions

In many large organizations, the way to supervisory and junior executive positions, and ultimately executive posts, is the examination route. While the original hiring tests are most often tests of natural aptitude, attitudes and skills, the promotion tests are likely to be designed to test the employee's knowledge of business practices and theory. The questions on many of these tests are so presented that the person with a "knack" for taking tests may do better than the person who has actually faced similar situations at work and has met them satisfactorily.

Careful study of PRINCIPLES OF SUPERVISION and PRINCIPLES OF ADMINISTRATION will help you pass high on the written tests used in industry.

PRINCIPLES OF SUPERVISION

Our analysis of previous examinations indicates that you should possess a fairly good knowledge of this subject. Here are the key points . . . the information on which they are likely to quiz you. Following the text you'll find a quiz, composed of actual previous test questions. The text should help you score high on the quiz. And our answers, which follow the quiz, should clear up any remaining doubts.

If you carefully study the following material you will get a bird's eye view of the essential elements of Personnel Supervision and Control. Most of the material is presented as an easily understood quizzer which teaches while it tests. The questions have all been culled from previous exams, and therefore are a consensus of what's most important in this field.

Though supervisors of long experience will undoubtedly be familiar with the material that is given in this section, it has been included to enable them to score high on tests. It is unfortunately true that the usual test question on administrative and supervisory subjects is very often more easily answered by the person with book knowledge than by the one who has successfully handled, in practice, the question posed on paper.

A widespread belief, which modern research has done much to correct, has it that once an individual has developed fully there is little that can be done to change him. Consequently, according to this belief, if a man has qualities which prevent him from being a good supervisor, there is little he can do to improve. The fact of the matter is that while personality improvement in maturity is much more difficult than in childhood, particular habits with respect to particular situations can be modified considerably. A man may be a grouch, but if it is brought in upon him that this seriously affects his progress, if he is shown just where he is at fault, and if he is able to recognize the necessity of improvement, it is quite possible for him to become a passably cheerful person in the office, even though his personality remains morose.

It is important to analyze the qualifications needed to become a better supervisor and to successfully answer questions on an examination. The following is a consensus of several authorities.

THE SUPERVISOR'S QUALITIES

No man possesses all these qualities completely, but the man who understands what they mean and who understands wherein he is deficient is making progress toward that goal.

1. There should be *mutual respect* between supervisor and subordinate; and the burden of fostering this mutual respect should fall upon the supervisor. He should ask himself whether he enjoys the respect of each individual under him. What is more, he should ask himself whether he has done any specific thing, by act or word, to demonstrate conclusively to each person that he respects him or her.

2. There should be *an understanding with subordinates* of what is required by the job. A good supervisor makes it her business to let each person know what he is supposed to do in order to win advancement, sits down with him at least once each year and has a sincere talk with him about his work, his opportunities and his obligations.

3. The good supervisor is *easily approachable.* He never tries to avoid the approach of a subordinate by putting on a busy air nor does he try to hurry through a talk with one of his people. Rather, he tries to make it easy for a subordinate to take up even personal matters with him by giving immediate, interested attention.

4. She maintains *an attitude of open-mindedness* in disagreements, and toward suggestions. She is glad to have subordinates come to her with their suggestions. She is not stubborn about ac-

cepting the view-point of subordinates, and listens patiently, without annoyance, when a subordinate presents an idea with which she disagrees.

5. He is *fair and impartial,* insofar as it is possible. He does not have special arrangements or dealings with individuals that could not be explained satisfactorily to others under his supervision. And he tries not to allow his personal likes or dislikes to alter his treatment of individuals.
6. *He controls himself.* He doesn't lose his temper, in fact he makes it a point never to indulge in arguments with his subordinates.
7. If he *makes promises he keeps them.* He doesn't make promises the fulfillment of which is dependent upon the approval or act of some one above him, nor does he ever make promises with the intention of finding some way out before the time for fulfillment arrives. Employees never have to remind him of unfulfilled promises.
8. *She requires patience of herself.* If new employees are slow to grasp new ideas, or if experienced employees fail to measure up to expectations, she does not become irritable.
9. *She is properly appreciative* not only of a good piece of work, but also of consistently good work over a long period of time, and she expresses this appreciation to others besides the individual doing the good work.
10. *She is consistent,* and does not ask for too much work at some times and for too little work at others. She does not grant privileges on some days which are not granted on others.
11. *He is loyal to the interests of his workers.* He accepts full responsibility for the mistakes of his department instead of laying the blame on individuals under him.
12. *He is reasonable in his demands.* Thus, in assigning tasks that he has never done himself he gives careful consideration to the amount of work a subordinate can reasonably be expected to turn out. He does not require any one to put in more overtime than he does himself.
13. *He is observant of the details of his office administration.* He knows what work each subordinate is doing each day and can write down in detail the way work is handled in his department. Infractions of the rules or of good practice are usually observed by him first, rather than called to his attention by others.
14. *She works with an aim,* sets a definite goal, expects to get out a certain volume of work, has a standard of accuracy, and plans to develop subordinates by a definite plan.

RELATION OF SUPERVISOR AND EMPLOYEE

In the foregoing, stress has been laid upon the personal qualities of the supervisor, as they relate to his or her work. We must now go forward and consider the workers in their relation to the supervisor.

The supervisor's function as a leader is to develop the individuals under him and to integrate them into a co-operative team. To accomplish this end, he must constantly have the motives and feelings of his subordinates in mind. Though no individual's motives can be reduced to a formula, the supervisor should have some insight into the reasons people have for working.

Why Workers Work

1. The most important reason is the necessity for earning money. Though some people earn money for the common necessities of life, others want it to achieve a higher standard of life, or independence. People with families want to achieve economic security, education for their children.

2. There are some who feel obligated to take part in the world's work; to do something constructive. When working, their chief desire is to feel the usefulness of their work.

3. Some people work so that they may attain a position of authority. People are affected in various degrees by this reason. Some take pleasure in directing others, while some simply like to have a sense of personal prowess.

4. Part of the pleasure in working comes from the approval and recognition which it may yield. This is inseparably related to the motives given previously. In fact all the reasons for working given here are related to each other. No person is subservient to any single motive though close observation may reveal the dominant drives. Approval and recognition are probably the most important motives that the supervisor can make use of in his dealings with people.

5. Man is essentially social; finds joy in being an accepted member of a social group. This forms one of the bases of team-work.

6. Judicious cultivation of the spirit of rivalry is a wise office policy. Most individuals wish to excel those about them.

7. People will work through loyalty to their group and their leader even though they are not interested in the work they are doing.

People will also work through fear, but this is a poor incentive in the long run because it is inhibitory in its action. Just as an animal is paralyzed by extreme fear, so, in more subtle fashion, the will and interest of the human being are deadened by constant driving through fear of discharge or displeasure.

Appeal should always be made to the positive motives in building up interest and teamwork. Since the motives mentioned early in the list are satisfied by almost any job, once a job has been obtained they are not likely to have much effect in getting the clerk to work harder than is necessary to avoid being dismissed. The motives in the latter part of the list must be called into play to secure real effectiveness.

DEVELOPING INTEREST AND CO-OPERATION

Interest and co-operation cannot be elicited from an employee if the work is not suited to the person's abilities. Thus a highly intelligent clerk may be very difficult to handle if he is forced to do a very monotonous job. If possible, previous knowledge, experience and expressed interests should be utilized in placement. While indiscriminate transfer is not advisable, the supervisor should take the initiative in shifting a worker to a job more suited to him, if that course seems calculated to arouse interest in the work.

Since interest can hardly be expected to exist where there is no understanding, the supervisor should teach each worker the reasons for what he does and the relation of his work to the work of the rest of the organization. It is frequently necessary for the supervisor to shift emphasis from one part of the work to another. An occasional change of emphasis from the volume of work, to the accuracy with which it is done, or the speed of completion, or to the cost of doing it, will help hold interest. Another aid in holding interest is the shifting of emphasis from one part of the work to another. Thus the supervisor may sometimes stress the volume of work, the accuracy with which it is done; the speed of completion or the cost of doing it.

Individual records of production stimulate the spirit of rivalry and consequently arouse interest. It is well not to suggest that the records are being kept in order to punish the poorer workers. The introduction of such an idea is a potent force in breaking down office morale. When individual records can only be kept with difficulty, it is good procedure to stimulate the group spirit by keeping a record of group production and making each member of the group feel that he is doing an essential part of the group work. If team rivalries can be stimulated, they can often be more potent than individual competitions in the organization's interests. If a group goal is set, for instance, the production of a good set of figures for the examination of some high official at some stated time, interest in the work is heightened.

When each member of the organization is interested in his work, the foundation of teamwork has been laid. In order to achieve teamwork, co-operation must be obtained from each worker, and this is the result of broadening the interest of the individual to include the whole group. In reaching this goal, the energy, and enthusiasm of the leader are all important. Achieved through many months, even years of right actions, teamwork, interest, co-operation can be easily destroyed. by causes that are easily discernible.

RULES

When interest and co-operation have been raised to a really effective level, the question of rules is of minor importance. However, the manner in which orders are given and rules laid down are one important determinant of teamwork.

The guiding principle should be "As few rules as possible." The more efficient the supervisor, the smaller his quota of rules.

Direction and routine are certainly necessary, for there is a great demand upon energies when clerks must continually direct themselves to their labors, but this direction should be given only as new circumstances arise, not continuously, persistently, captiously.

When rules have been made they should be followed. However, the supervisor should not expect blind obedience, but instead an intelligent, understanding respect for the rules which have been established. When rules are not adhered to, the supervisor should discover the reason and if the new procedure is better he should adopt it. At the same time he should make clear that teamwork demands coordination. That an apparently insignificant point is of vital importance to someone else in completing the job.

FRIENDLY RELATIONS

It is difficult to lay down a general rule regarding personal relationships of supervisor and subordinate.

One should be friendly; one should take an interest in each member of the staff; but too much intimacy should be avoided because the conditions in different places vary so widely. Organizations in small towns would naturally have different standards than those that prevail in a very large metropolitan organization employing people with widely divergent backgrounds.

Toleration of a nickname or the use of the first name may be the custom or it may denote too great familiarity. Playing practical jokes on or with his staff and failure to maintain firm and fair discipline should be avoided by the supervisor. The difficulty of being intimate with members of the staff lies in the resentment it arouses and the possible charge of favoritism.

WASTING TIME

The supervisor can usually do much to control this common fault, for it it usually caused by poor supervision or general management.

When a department is overmanned, when the flow of work is uneven, when machines or other equipment are improperly installed and where departments do not co-operate, there is almost certain to be a waste of time. All these causes serve as excuses for the time wasters;they are used to greatest advantage by those who dislike the work the most.

REPRIMAND AND PRAISE

If criticism is necessary, it should not be given in front of fellow clerks, for such a procedure violates the sense of loyalty and mutual consideration.

Praise can be given in the presence of others. It should neither be lavish nor stinted. The tendency of most supervisors seems to be to overdo a good thing; to give so much of it that it no longer has any meaning to those who are praised.

Two general methods of speeding up production are:

1. Past "good work" may be praised (not the worker). The difficulty of the present task may be admitted.

2. Reprimand in a disguised form may be employed by challenging the worker's ability to do a task at all or to do it as well as others. Challenge should be applied to the more aggressive individual while encouragement should be given to the submissive type of person.

AN APPROACH TO MANAGEMENT IMPROVEMENT

ANALYSIS		
Evaluation of the Situation	Immediate Cause	Basic Cause
Factual analysis of problem areas in relation to mission. The factors of quality and quantity of product or services are defined in the statement of mission. Most actual problems affecting the efficient accomplishment of the mission can be resolved on a cost basis, such as: 1. High costs of operations. 2. High overhead. 3. Wastes, errors, rejects, spoilage of materials. Work situations are continuously changing and evaluations should be frequent and thorough.	Exploration of immediate cause of inefficient productivity (or high costs) and identification of reasons, such as: 1. Wrong organization. 2. Poor communication. 3. Low morale. 4. High turnover. 5. Absenteeism. 6. Lack of job skills. 7. Poor methods. 8. Bad lay-out. Action should be taken immediately to eliminate these causes of inefficient operation BUT the analysis should not be stopped until the BASIC cause has been identified and corrective action taken to prevent future trouble.	Recognition that each of the immediate causes of problems stem from the failure of some PERSON: 1. To plan adequately. 2. To act effectively. This represents the area of executive or supervisory responsibility which can be strengthened, but, because of human fallibility, never reaches perfection.
ACTION		APPRAISAL
Stimulus to Change	Provision of Means	Evaluation of Results
Creation of a climate conducive to improvement—a willingness to cooperate in reducing the Basic Cause of Management Problems. The following features are essential to the creation of such a climate: 1. The stimulus emanates from the top. 2. Personal encouragement and assistance from superior officials are necessary. 3. Participation by employee or supervisory groups should be encouraged. 4. A recognition of the need for improvement must be developed.	Provision of facilities to improve management competence at all levels through development of all employees to perform assigned duties effectively. Includes: 1. Development of executives. 2. Supervisor training. 3. Orientation. 4. Job skills training. These items utilize such techniques as: —self development —special assignment —coaching on the job —participation in conferences and work meetings, informal training, in trade or professional associations. As indicated in column 2, corrective action must be taken promptly to reduce immediate causes of problems. Prevention of future difficulties comes about through means utilized to remove the basic cause.	Appraisal of the effectiveness of action taken. The inquiry is in two phases. 1. Did the action taken eliminate or reduce the causes of the trouble? 2. Is the total program for management improvement solving the fundamental operating problems described in column 1? When evaluation shows that results have not been wholly satisfactory, further analysis is needed: a new problem situation has arisen. Identification of causes and provision of corrective and preventive actions carries the process through the original cycle again.

FACTORS THAT BREAK MORALE

CAUSES	REMEDIES
Failure to delegate responsibilities.	Delegate responsibilities.
Too many outside interests.	Talk over with worker and point out effects.
Too sure of his job.	Talk over with worker and point out effects.
Partiality on part of superiors.	See that the man gets a square deal.
Man on wrong job.	Transfer to another job.
Laziness.	Hold the worker strictly responsible for what he produces.
Lack of vision by man.	Point out possibilities.
Outside job.	One job or the other.
Too monotonous.	Transfer if possible—if not, time off to look for another job.
Too much routine work.	Study routine—eliminate unnecessary. Distribute routine work.
Poor planning by foreman.	Self-analysis by supervisor.
No future.	Point out possibilities. Transfer if possible—if not, time off to look for another job.
Low wages.	Recommend raise. Point out wages are fair.
Homesickness.	Time off to go home.
Irresponsibility.	Discipline.
Too much responsibility.	Relieve him of some of his responsibility.
Too many bosses.	Definite line of authority.
Slow advancement.	Point out reasons for.
Changeable orders.	Self-analysis by supervisor.
Ill health.	Recommend medical attention.
"Passing the buck"	Do not do it, and do not tolerate it.
Too detailed supervision.	Only when necessary.
Poor teamwork.	Conference to point effects of co-operation.
Jealousy.	Find the cause and administer square deal.
No training.	Proper training.
Lack of leadership on part of superior.	Self-analysis by supervisor.
Too much overtime.	Split up the overtime.
Man has no hobbies.	Talk to man and offer suggestions.
Bad working conditions.	Study situation. Correct conditions if possible; otherwise find explanation.
Lack of recognition.	Give him credit when due.
Domestic trouble.	Recommend investigation of home conditions.
Interference by fellow workers.	Closer supervision.
Lax discipline.	Enforcement and self-analysis.

EVALUATION CHART FOR DETERMINING SUPERVISOR TRAINING NEEDS

Function/level	Outstanding	Satisfactory	Unsatisfactory
SELECTING WORKERS—matching workers' qualifications to job requirements; identifying capacity to improve in service. More important for coordinating than immediate supervisors. Does not apply when decision is made elsewhere.	Recognizes desirable qualifications; interprets test results; devises simple performance tests; interviews skillfully; employees happy and busy; work proceeds smoothly and efficiently; knows job requirements thoroughly.	Interviews applicant personally but depends largely upon personnel office; few requests for transfer to other kinds of work; skills fairly well utilized; few personality conflicts; needs help to define position requirements.	No idea of job requirements; interview lacking or useless; dissatisfied workers and very high turnover; square pegs in round holes; much lost time and many errors; accident rate frequently high; production unsatisfactory.
TRAINING WORKERS in the operation of the unit. Covers oral, written, individual, or group instruction; break-in of new and retraining of old workers. Securing assistance when needed.	Complete job analyses on hand; maintains the training schedule; repeated instructions seldom necessary; makes himself understood the first time; few errors or accidents; passes on the tricks of the trade.	Spends some time on break-in but often without adequate preparation; seldom fails to explain changes in work; answers intelligently when questioned by workers; waste, errors, accidents not excessive.	No plan for training; instructions sometimes incorrect or incomplete; constant interruptions by workers asking directions; conceals tricks of the trade; feels workers should learn "the hard way."
EVALUATING WORKERS as to job efficiency, capacities, or weaknesses. The merit rating process. Understanding aspects of the worker that affect the job—habits, attitudes, skills, disabilities, learning speed, etc.	No adverse decisions on appeals; ratings backed by factual evidence; reputation for complete impartiality; pattern of ratings explainable; studies employees without snooping or prying; keeps individual progress records.	Ratings usually supported by some substantial facts; recognizes good work; tries to be fair; judgment occasionally affected by recent events; follows rating procedure as well as he can but it is not wholly clear.	No useable records of performance; ratings largely based upon opinion influenced by current attitudes toward workers; obvious cases of favoritism; delays or avoids rating; argues with employees about grades.
EXERCISING AUTHORITY and securing cooperation. Involves meriting the respect of employees. A means of getting work done, not an end in itself. Includes leadership.	Fair, confident, and decisive: orders complete, concise, clear; prompt and willing response; never loses temper; insists on compliance but listens to reasons for failures.	Orders generally understood; seldom resented; few serious discipline cases; seldom exceeds authority; usually controls temper; morale or discipline seldom a problem.	Employees appear to be doing as they please; make fun of the boss; orders ineffectual and ignored, or unneccessarily strict and resented; little cooperation; quarrels with workers.
PLANNING WORK both long range and for the immediate future. Involves knowledge of objectives, needs, and facilities. Coordination with other units and with planning and control functions. Delegation of work.	Makes it his business to find out production plans; peaks and valleys smoothed out; no excessive backlogs; all employees busy productively; work distributed evenly; unusually steady production.	Fairly familiar with quantity and nature of work flow; seldom has to call for help; few complaints about assignments; only occasional overtime requests; usually has materials and equipment ready.	Buried in routine work or busy aimlessly; always worried about schedules; some employees overworked while others loaf; frequent bottlenecks; constantly making excuses for failure to meet deadlines or standards.
IMPROVING METHODS—recognizing poor methods and finding better ones. Involves process analysis and study; alertness to possible changes; resourcefulness and initiative; vision applied practically.	Constantly studying operations and trying sensible changes; new methods carefully worked out before use; production records show gradual increase with reduced fatigue and accident ratio.	Occasionally makes improvements; ideas not thoroughly worked out; can make job breakdown; willing to make change when better method is pointed out; glad to receive suggestions from employees.	Resents suggestions as interference; avoids making desirable changes; much unnecessary effort; workers' ideas spurned; equipment antiquated or in poor condition; production much lower than necessary.
INTERPRETING RULES AND REGULATIONS—not only knowing what has been decided as to policies and procedures but understanding the underlying purposes, explaining them intelligently, and seeing that they are observed.	Workers are following established policies and procedures with understanding; explains pertinent parts of new regulations promptly; uses good judgment in applying decisions of higher authority.	Reads most new regulations; informs employees on important points; sometimes posts directives; answers ordinary inquiries and refers some others; occasionally checks compliance as to major policies or procedures.	"Passive resistance" to all rules and regulations; confusion as to work flow in and out; frequently misinterprets directives and seldom inquires about them; many discipline problems from broken rules.
MAINTAINING RECORDS AND MAKING REPORTS—involves securing sufficient current facts that can be and are used. No dead files. Systems relatively simple. Includes both recurrent and special reports, narrative or formalized.	Maintains simple but effective record system; collects no data that is unusable; material systematized and easily accessible; has the answers when needed; reports complete, concise, correct, and on time.	Fairly satisfactory system for handling data; records seldom lost; may accumulate material seldom used; for the most part, reports are checked and submitted on time; may be difficult to understand; willing to make corrections.	Data insufficient, incorrect, or out of date so often that it is undependable; files untidy and unposted; reports not only a burden but an imposition; usually late; incorrect and of little value; revision helps little.

TEST QUESTIONS IN SUPERVISION

The questions provided are an authoritative summary of what should be known about supervision. When you answer questions of this type you will be getting valuable practice in scoring high on your test and performing well on your job.

DIRECTIONS FOR ANSWERING THESE MULTIPLE CHOICE QUESTIONS. For each question read all the choices carefully. Then select that answer which you consider correct or most nearly correct. Write the letter preceding your best choice next to the question.

You may want to answer on facsimiles of the kind of answer sheets provided on machine-scored examinations. For practice purposes we have provided several such facsimiles . . . throughout the book. Tear one out if you wish, and mark your answers on it . . . just as you would do on an actual exam.

In machine-scored examinations you should record all your answers on the answer sheet provided. Don't make the mistake of putting answers on the test booklet itself.

It is most important that you learn to mark your answers clearly and in the right place.

On some machine-scored exams you are instructed to "place no marks whatever on the test booklet." In some examinations you may be instructed to mark your answers in the test booklet. In such cases you should be careful that no other marks interfere with the legibility of your answers.

It is always best NOT to mark your booklet unless you are sure that it is permitted.

Correct answers follow each group of questions. Please try to answer the questions by yourself before comparing your answers with those we have given. Where you find that your answers differ from ours try to understand why. Re-examine the question and the several options to arrive at the principle governing the correct answer. Make appropriate notes in the book to record your findings. They will point out your weaknesses. Later on, if you have time to review, devote yourself to these questions and findings. Your review time will be shortened and you will be concentrating on those areas wherein you can achieve the greatest improvement.

SUPERVISORY REASONING

Employers have long realized that mere knowledge does not make a good supervisor. Much more important is the ability to think, to solve problems as they arise. Thus we find that in examinations for the higher grade clerical jobs there is a type of question designed to test reasoning ability. It's easy to understand what these questions are when you see them and try to answer them. You'll find fifty-seven reasoning questions in this part. Answer them and you'll probably improve your chances on the actual examination because you will have had experience with practically every type of reasoning question on the supervisory level.

1. "The first line supervisor executes policy as elsewhere formulated. He does not make policy. He is the element of the administrative structure closest to the employee group." From this point of view, it follows that a major function of the first line supervisor is to
   (A) suggest desirable changes in procedure to top management
   (B) prepare time schedules showing when his unit will complete a piece of work so that it will dovetail with the requirements of other units
   (C) humanize policy so as to respect employee needs and interests
   (D) report danger points to top management in order to forestall possible bottlenecks
   (E) discipline employees who continuously break departmental rules.

2. A new employee who has shown that she is capable of performing superior work during the first month of her employment falls far below this standard after the first month. For the supervisor to wait until the end of the probationary period and then recommend that she be discharged if her work is still unsatisfactory is
   (A) undesirable; she should have been discharged when her work became unsatisfactory
   (B) desirable; there is no place in the civil service for unsatisfactory employees
   (C) undesirable; he should immediately attempt to determine the cause of the poor performance.
   (D) desirable; the employee is entitled to an opportunity to prove herself
   (E) undesirable; the employee is obviously capable of performing good work and simply requires some guidance from the supervisor.

3. The number of subordinates that can be supervised directly by one person tends to
   (A) increase as the level of supervision progresses from the first-line supervisory level to the management level
   (B) decrease as the duties of the subordinates increase in difficulty and complexity
   (C) decrease with an increase in the knowledge and experience of the subordinates
   (D) increase as the physical distance between supervisor and subordinates, as well as between the individual subordinates, increases.

4. In order to make sure that work is completed on time, the unit supervisor should
   (A) use the linear method of delegating responsibility
   (B) pitch in and do as much of the work himself as he can
   (C) schedule the work and keep himself informed of its progress
   (D) not assign more than one person to any one task
   (E) know the capabilities of his subordinates.

5. Of the following, the statement concerning the organization of a department which is true is:
   (A) in general, no one employee should have active and constant supervision over more than ten persons
   (B) it is basically unwise to have a supervisor with only three subordinates
   (C) it is desirable that there be no personal contact between the rank and file employee and the supervisor once removed from him
   (D) there should be no more than four levels of authority between the top administrative office in a department and the rank and file employees.

6. In order to estimate properly the amount of time it will take a bureau to complete a given job, it is *least* desirable for the supervisor to
   (A) estimate the number of persons available to perform the job
   (B) estimate the time required for routine operations but to omit estimates of time required for non-routine operations
   (C) make an allowance for probable interruptions which can be foreseen
   (D) allow a certain amount of time for possible delays which cannot be foreseen, such as unanticipated absences of employees.

7. You are assigned in charge of a large division. It had been the practice in that division for the employees to slip out for breakfast about 10:00 a.m. You had been successful in stopping this practice and for one week no one had gone out for breakfast. One day a stenographer comes over to you at 10:30 a.m., appearing to be ill. She states that she doesn't feel well and that she would like to go out for a cup of tea. She asks your permission to leave the office for a few minutes. You should
   (A) telephone and have a cup of tea delivered to her
   (B) permit her to go out
   (C) refuse her permission to go out inasmuch as this would be setting a bad example
   (D) tell her she can leave for an early lunch hour.

8. Suppose that you have a provisional stenographer working for you. She is an excellent stenographer and has rendered highly satisfactory service for four months. Recently, however, when an emergency arose, she refused to remain overtime to help complete a special job. When you discussed her insubordination with her, she stated that she was willing to work very hard between the hours of 9 a.m. and 5 p.m., but that she would positively not remain overtime for any reason whatsoever. Her reasons for this attitude are not such as would entitle her to special consideration. A complicating factor is that efficient stenographers are very hard to secure during present conditions. Of the following, the best action for you to take is to
   (A) give her a chance to resign informing her

that if she does not do so, you will be forced to recommend her dismissal
(B) make her situation in the office very uncomfortable so that she will resign
(C) permit her to continue to work at her own terms
(D) recommend her dismissal immediately on the grounds of insubordination.

9. Of the following, the situation in which it is least important to discourage talking among the employees is where the work consists of
(A) difficult and concentrated clerical work
(B) meeting with the public
(C) a routine and mechanical stamping operation
(D) transcribing dictation.

10. A probationary employee is assigned to you. In his first three months of service, you feel that his work has been unsatisfactory. The method of procedure fairest to both the employee and the department is to
(A) ask the employee to resign
(B) dismiss the employee immediately
(C) speak to the employee explaining the situation to him and describing to him once again the rights of a probationer
(D) wait until the end of his probationary period and then have his services terminated

11. You are put in charge of a small office. In order to cover the office during the lunch hour, you assign Employee A to remain in the office between the hours of 12 and 1 p.m. On your return to the office at 12.25 p.m., you note that no one is in the office and that the phone is ringing. You are forced to postpone your 12:30 p.m. luncheon appointment, and to remain in the office until 12:50 p.m. when Employee A returns to the office. The best of the following actions is to
(A) ask Employee A why he left the office
(B) bring charges against Employee A for insubordination and neglect of duty
(C) ignore the matter in your conversation with Employee A so as not to embarrass him
(D) make a note to rate Employee A low on his service rating.

12. You are assigned in charge of a clerical bureau performing one single operation. All five of your subordinates do exactly the same work. A fine spirit of cooperation has developed and the employees help each other and pool their completed work so that the work of ony one employee is indistinguishable. Your office is very busy and all five clerks are doing a full day's work. However, reports come back to you from other offices that they are finding as much as 1% error in the work of your bureau. This is too high a percentage of error. Of the following, the best procedure for you to follow is to
(A) check all the work yourself
(B) have a sample of the work of each clerk checked by another clerk
(C) have all work done in your office checked by one of your clerks
(D) identify the work of each clerk in some way.

13. A serious error has been discovered by a critical superior in work carried on under your supervision. It is best to explain the situation and prevent its recurrence by
(A) claiming that you are not responsible because you do not check the work personally
(B) accepting the complaint and reporting the name of the employee responsible for the error
(C) assuring him that you hope it will not occur again
(D) assuring him that you will find out how it occurred, so that you can have the work checked with greater care in the future
(E) informing him that such errors are bound to occur with a poorly trained staff and a heavy load of work.

14. You are assigned the job of supervising the alphabetization of 500.000 cards. The names on the cards are handwritten and about 100 cards are illegible. You feel that you cannot be sure of the spelling of these names. The best of the following procedures is to
(A) rewrite the cards legibly and then destroy the originals
(B) file these cards in accordance with the most probable spelling of these names
(C) hold these cards out separately from the rest
(D) prepare duplicate cards and file one for each of the possible spellings of the names.

15. One of your duties is supervision of the store room clerk. Of the following, the least valid criterion by which you may judge whether the work of the store room is being well conducted is that
(A) as soon as material of any kind is received

in the store room, a standard "receiving slip" should be filled out
(B) no material should be issued from the store room unless a standard "requisition slip" has been filled out
(C) the material which is used most frequently should be located near the entrance of the store room
(D) material in the store room should be so arranged that, in general, the oldest of any variety is used first
(E) the more extensively an item is used, the less frequently should the supply be checked.

16. It is reported to you by one of the file clerks under your supervision that he is unable to locate the material in which you are interested because it has been removed from the files and is evidently being used by some other bureau. Of the following, the best action to take in order to prevent recurrence of an incident of this sort is to
(A) forbid other bureaus to borrow material from your files
(B) have your file clerk report to you all items borrowed by other departments
(C) have an out-of-file card filled out and substituted for each item borrowed
(D) have a duplicate file provided for the other bureaus
(E) set a time limit in which borrowed material must be returned to your files.

17. "Before transferring material from the active to the inactive files, the supervisor of the filing unit always consults the bureau heads directly concerned with the use of this material." This practice by the supervisor is
(A) desirable, chiefly because material that is no longer current for some bureaus may still be current for others
(B) undesirable, chiefly because it can only lead to disagreement among the bureau heads consulted
(C) desirable, chiefly because it is more economical to store records in transfer files than to keep them in the active files
(D) undesirable, chiefly because the filing supervisor is expected to make his own decisions.

18. An office supervisor may give either a written or oral order to his subordinates when making an assignment. Of the following, it would be most appropriate for a supervisor to issue an order in writing when
(A) a large number of two-page reports must be stapled together before the end of the day
(B) the assignment is to be completed within two hours after it is issued to his subordinates
(C) his subordinates have completed an identical assignment the day before
(D) several entries must be made on a form at varying intervals of time by different clerks.

19. You are a bureau head in a department in which there is a rigid rule that all mail to the other city departments must be signed by the secretary of the department. You have composed an important letter which should be sent to another department immediately, but the secretary has already left for the day. The purpose of the letter is to confirm an agreement informally arrived at. Of the following, the best procedure for you to follow in general is to
(A) explain the situation to the department head and ask him for permission to sign this letter yourself
(B) allow the matter to wait till the next day, when the secretary will be in
(C) sign the letter yourself and send a memorandum to the secretary explaining the need for haste in mailing the letter
(D) have his stenographer sign the secretary's name to the letter, so that it can be mailed immediately
(E) telephone the message to the other department.

20. Suppose that one of your subordinates asks you for information concerning the purposes of the American Society for Public Administration. You would reply that it is the essential objective of this organization to
(A) advance the science, processes, and art of public administration
(B) provide practical administrators with annotated citations to literature relative to particular cases confronting the administrator
(C) issue administrative case studies
(D) stimulate Pan-American exchange of administrative experiences
(E) furnish a medium for exchanges of administrative personnel among American municipalities.

21. "Some subdivision of work is imperative in large-scale operation. However, in subdividing work the supervisor should adopt the methods

that have the greatest number of advantages and the fewest disadvantages." The one of the following that is most likely to result from subdivision of work is
(A) measuring work performed by employees is made more difficult
(B) authority and responsibility for the performance of particular operations are not clearly defined
(C) standardizing work processes is made more difficult
(D) work is delayed in passing between employees and between operating units.

22. The delegation of responsibility and authority to subordinates by their superior generally does *not*
(A) facilitate a division of labor or the development of specialization
(B) permit the superior to carry out programs of work that exceed his immediate personal limits of physical energy and knowledge
(C) result in a downward transfer of work, both mental and manual
(D) involve a transfer of ultimate responsibility from superior to subordinate.

23. A study of the supervision of employees in a City agency reveals that the bureau chiefs are reluctant to delegate responsibility and authority to their assistants. This study is most likely to reveal, in addition, that
(A) the organizational structure of this agency should be centralized
(B) the bureau chiefs tend to spend too much of their time on minor aspects of their work
(C) the number of employees supervised by bureau chiefs is excessive
(D) significant deviations from planned performance are not called to the attention of the bureau chiefs.

24. In assigning work to his subordinates, a supervisor is most likely to lose the respect of his subordinates if he
(A) reviews with a new employee the main points of an oral order issued to this employee
(B) issues written orders instead of oral orders when a subordinate has repeatedly failed to carry out oral orders
(C) gives oral orders regarding a task which the subordinate has performed satisfactorily in the past
(D) gives an oral order which he feels the subordinate will not carry out.

25. Suppose you are the chief of a bureau which contains several operating units. On one occasion you observe one of your unit heads severely reprimand a subordinate for violating a staff regulation. This subordinate has a good record for observing staff regulations and you believe the severe reprimand will seriously undermine the morale of the employee. Of the following, the best action for you to take in this situation is to
(A) call both the unit head and the subordinate into your office at the same time and have each present his views on the matter to you
(B) refrain from intervening in this matter because the unit head may resent any interference
(C) take the subordinate aside, inform him that the unit head had not intended to reprimand him severely, and suggest that the matter be forgotten
(D) discuss the matter with the unit head and suggest that he make some mitigating explanation to the subordinate.

26. The maximum number of subordinates who can be effectively supervised by one administrative assistant is best considered as
(A) determined by the law of "span of control."
(B) determined by the "law" of span of attention.
(C) determined by the type of work supervised.
(D) fixed at not more than six.

Each of the following passages, numbered 27 to 36, contains one word which is not in keeping with the meaning which the passage is evidently intended to carry. On your Answer Sheet, next to the number corresponding to each passage, print the capital letter preceding the one of the five words following each passage which does most to spoil the true meaning of that passage.

27. "Because the merit system denotes a *result* rather than a means of attaining the result, it becomes possible to *incorporate* it in any organizational program, whether the civil service structure is *adopted* or not. Consequently the merit system has tended in recent years to *define* 'civil service' as the recognized objective of public personnel administration. But *even* the merit system does not go the whole way in outlining

the program which is adaptable to the needs of modern government."

(A) result (C) adopted
(B) incorporate (D) define
(E) even

28. "Inasmuch as a 'career' presupposes a lifetime of work of growing knowledge and skill, *promotion* should be limited, in the ordinary course of events, to the lowest positions within each service and to a *young* group of entrants. A *career* cannot be said to exist if top positions are generally recruited from *outside,* from men who do not understand the work, and in such a way as to create an effective bar to *advancement* from the bottom to the top of the service itself."

(A) promotion (C) career
(B) young (D) outside
(E) advancement.

29. "Retirement and *pension* systems are *essential* not only in justice to employees, but in order that *longevity* and charitable considerations may not upset the *retirement* possibilities for other members of the *career* service."

(A) pension (C) longevity
(B) essential (D) retirement
(E) career.

30. "The minimum rate for each class should be no *lower* than the *maximum* rate for the next lower class in a natural or probable line of *promotion,* in order that advances in duties and responsibilities may carry with them, under simple rules and methods of administration, *corresponding* advances in *function.*"

(A) lower (C) promotion
(B) maximum (D) corresponding
(E) function.

31. "Until recent years the *personnel* movement has crystallized around tenure as the essence of a *merit* system, but it is not difficult to perceive that tenure without wise *administration* will accomplish little more than to freeze in office an *incompetent* public service. The present emphasis of the personnel movement is on the development of methods of selection which will insure the *appointment* of personnel to whom tenure can safely be given."

(A) personnel (C) administration
(B) merit (D) incompetent
(E) appointment.

32. "Obviously, experience, if it has been *successful,* will have resulted in the acquisition of knowledge and skills and will have *demonstrated* the possession of essential aptitudes, personality and other *traits.* If these characteristics can be measured directly through the evaluation of experience rather than indirectly through *performance,* then greater *accuracy* in measurement will be secured as well as some saving in time."

(A) successful (C) traits
(B) demonstrated (D) performance
(E) accuracy.

33. "One of the greatest *stimulants* to the progress of in-service training has been the concept that training is a *specialized* function that can and should be *delegated* to some special officer or unit. Although training specialists have an *important* role to play, the *primary* responsibility for training lies with the managerial and supervisory officials of the administration.

(A) stimulants (B) specialized
(C) delegated (D) important
(E) primary

34. "Item *difficulty* is usually expressed in terms of the percentage of candidates who failed to answer the item correctly. If a large number of the items in any given test have a *very* high percentage of difficulty, it is *probably* an indication either that they are not *appropriate* and have little relation to the field being tested or that they are appropriate and related to the field but are too *general* for the level of competence desired."

(A) difficulty (C) probably
(B) very (D) appropriate
(E) general.

35. "In order to make the application of the service rating system *uniform* throughout the service, *job* analyses of ratings received are necessary. These usually take the form of a *frequency* distribution of ratings *within* each *administrative* unit of the service."

(A) uniform (C) frequency
(B) job (D) within
(E) administrative

36. "As a general rule, it is inadvisable to divorce disciplinary authority from the regular line of *command, but* it is often possible and desirable to *exercise* this authority by subjecting it to some outside checks or *controls.* The most com-

mon form of control is to provide some review or *appeal* machinery."

(A) command (C) exercise
(B) but (D) controls
(E) appeal

37. It is most important for an employee who is assigned to perform a lengthy monotonous task to
(A) perform this task before doing his other work
(B) ask another employee to assist him to dispose of the task quickly
(C) perform this task only when his other work has been completed
(D) take measures to prevent mistakes in performing this task.

38. As the supervisor of a unit in a city agency, you have just been instructed to put into effect a new procedure which you know will be disliked by your subordinates. Of the following, the *most* important reason for calling a meeting of your staff before putting the new procedure into effect is to
(A) help you to determine which workers will be reluctant to cooperate in carrying out the new procedure
(B) allow you to announce that the new procedure must be put into effect despite any objections which might be raised.
(C) enable you to explain that you don't approve of the new procedure and to give the reasons why it must nevertheless be put into effect
(D) permit you to discuss the purpose of the new procedure and to present the reasons for its adoption.

Answer question 39 on the basis of the following:
The supervisor of a large clerical and statistical division has assigned to one of the units under his supervision the preparation of a special statistical report required by the department head. The unit head accepted the assignment without comment but soon ran into considerable difficulty because no one in his unit had had any statistical training

39. If a result of this lack of training is that the report is not completed on time, although everyone has done all that could be expected, the responsibility for the failure rests with
(A) the department head
(B) the supervisor
(C) the unit head
(D) the employees in the unit
(E) no one.

40. Assume that as supervisor of a unit you are to prepare a vacation schedule for the employees in your unit. Of the following, the factor which is *least* important for you to consider in setting up this schedule is
(A) the vacation preferences of each employee in the unit
(B) the anticipated work load in the unit during the vacation period
(C) how well each employee has performed his work
(D) how essential a specific employee's services will be during the vacation period.

41. "In any public agency, the top administrative officials are concerned largely with the work of overall creative planning with respect to the anticipated progress of the agency. The first-line supervisors, on the other hand, are concerned largely with the control of current action for the execution of current jobs." On the basis of this quotation, a first-line supervisor would be chiefly responsible for
(A) increasing or decreasing the responsibilities of his unit to reflect changes in the policies of the agency
(B) modifying the work assignments of his present staff to handle a seasonal variation in the activities of the unit
(C) revising the procedure that is used for transmitting instructions from the head of the agency to the unit heads
(D) raising and lowering the production goals of his unit as often as necessary to adjust them to the abilities of his subordinates.

42. A generally accepted principle of supervision is that no individual can successfully handle more than a limited number of immediate supervisory contacts. This limit of control is principally a matter of the limits of
(A) functionalization of duties
(B) work knowledge
(C) type of the organization
(D) time and energy
(E) size of the organization

43. You find that a subordinate, in his reports to you, did not mention a series of thefts of department property occurring in his command. Upon questioning, he tells you that he has a plan for dealing with the problem and that he intended to make a complete report when the

problem was solved. Of the following, the best course for you to follow is to

(A) reprimand him for omitting the situation from his reports
(B) commend him for his initiative in attempting to solve the problem
(C) accept this explanation but review his previous reports to determine whether other situations have been concealed
(D) explain the necessity for a Chief to have complete reports on all problems within his jurisdiction
(E) warn him that he will be held responsible if his plan doesn't succeed.

44. Of the following, the one which would best qualify an employee for promotion to a supervisory position is his

(A) ability to perform his present task
(B) education and intellectual ability
(C) natural leadership ability with the other men
(D) length of service in the department.

45. A subordinate officer presents you with a long-standing problem which he has analyzed in detail. However, he states that he has no idea of its solution, nor can he make any recommendations. Under these circumstances, the most appropriate action for you to take at this time is to

(A) analyze the problem with the subordinate officer and suggest a number of alternative solutions from which he is to pick the most suitable
(B) indicate that failure to find a desirable means of solving the problem is indicative of lack of sufficient analysis
(C) refer the problem for conference review to determine the most effective approach to its solution
(D) study the problem alone and, at some later date, review your recommendations with the subordinate officer
(E) suggest that the subordinate officer review the matter and recommend actions which he thinks may solve the problem.

46. It had been the practice of a supervising officer to preface his issuing of some orders or instructions with the statement that he is giving them "for the record." In this way, indication is clearly made that observance will not be insisted upon. The major weakness of this approach is that

(A) discretionary orders will tend to replace those that are mandatory
(B) older subordinates will tend to resent orders which are not meant to be enforced
(C) requests for instructions or orders in writing will tend to increase rather than diminish
(D) subordinates are uncertain of whether or not to comply
(E) the authority of the supervising officer is undermined to the point of ineffectiveness.

47. The one of the following guiding principles to which an assistant supervisor should give most consideration when it becomes necessary to discipline a subordinate is that

(A) rules should be applied in a fixed and inflexible manner
(B) the discipline should be applied for the purpose of improving the morale of all his subordinates
(C) the main benefit to be derived from disciplining one offender is to deter other potential offenders
(D) the nature of the discipline should be such as to improve the future work of the offender.

48. A unit supervisor has a job to be done of a type usually done by a subordinate. The job is an important and recurring one, but not urgent at the moment. He knows that it would take more time to tell the subordinate how to do the job than to do it himself, and that it would take still more time to make the subordinate understand the situation, decide how to handle it, and then get the job done. In such a case, it would generally be best for the unit supervisor to

(A) assign the job to the subordinate without explaining it
(B) do the job himself
(C) explain the situation and help the subordinate to decide how to handle it
(D) tell the subordinate exactly what to do.

49. A recently appointed employee has reached the stage in learning his job where he is just beginning to be able to make decisions, although he still makes numerous mistakes and frequently does not know how to handle a situation. When the unit supervisor finds that the employee has handled a certain situation in an acceptable manner, but not in the best manner, it would be best for the supervisor to

(A) explain to the employee how he could have handled the situation better
(B) indicate approval of the way the situation

was handled and explain how it could have been handled better
(C) say nothing about the situation
(D) show dissatisfaction with the way the situation was handled and explain how it could have been handled better.

50. Both written and oral instructions are utilized in the supervision of staff. The one of the following comparisons between these two methods which is *not* generally true is that
(A) written instructions are less likely to be accepted than instructions given orally
(B) oral instructions are more suitable when it is believed that they will be temporary
(C) spoken instructions are more flexible and readily adaptable to situations involving possible unforeseen developments
(D) instructions given orally are less likely to be camouflaged as to the source
(E) written instructions result in less variability in interpretation.

51. The best of the following attitudes regarding departmental rules and regulations for an employee to take is that they
(A) are simply a means for justifying disciplinary action taken by a supervisor
(B) are to be interpreted by each employee as he sees fit
(C) must be obeyed even if they seem unreasonable in some cases
(D) should be read and studied but may be ignored whenever an employee feels it is necessary to do so.

52. Of the following, the most important reason why supervisors should give careful consideration to the techniques they utilize for assignment of employees to specific jobs is that
(A) an opportunity is thus offered the supervisor for periodic evaluation of the qualifications and work performance of all employees
(B) efficiency of employees is dependent in part on the techniques used by supervisory officers for selection of employees for assignments
(C) requests of employees for change in work assignments may indicate dissatisfaction with present conditions
(D) standardized techniques for the selection of employees for specific job assignments have not yet been developed.

53. Although accuracy and speed are both important for an employee in the performance of his work, accuracy should be considered more important mainly because
(A) most supervisors insist on accurate work
(B) much time is lost in correcting errors
(C) a rapid rate of work cannot be maintained for any length of time
(D) speedy workers are usually inaccurate.

54. Assume that your supervisor has asked you to present to him comprehensive, periodic reports on the progress that your unit is making in meeting its work goals. For you to give your superior oral reports rather than written ones is
(A) desirable; it will be easier for him to transmit your oral reports to his superiors
(B) undesirable; the oral reports will provide no permanent record to which he may refer
(C) undesirable; there will be less opportunity for you to discuss the oral reports with him than the written ones
(D) desirable; the oral reports will require little time and effort to prepare.

55. "A unit supervisor should select and develop an understudy to take cnarge of the unit in the supervisor's absence and to assist the supervisor whenever necessary." Of the following, the technique that would be *least* effective in developing an understudy is for the supervisor to
(A) permit him to exercise complete supervision over certain parts of the work
(B) assign him to work in which there is little likelihood of his making mistakes, so as to increase his self-confidence
(C) accustom him to making reports on the progress of work he is supervising
(D) give him responsibility gradually so that he will have time to absorb each new responsibility.

56. "A supervisor whose unit has a good production record is usually found to be more occupied with the functions associated with leadership than with the performance of the same functions as his subordinates." The most valid implication of this quotation is that
(A) a supervisor whose unit has a good production record usually is not as competent in performing routine tasks as are his subordinates
(B) ability to lead and competence in performing the day-to-day tasks of his subordinates are the requirements of a successful supervisor

(C) a supervisor who spends more time on planning and organizing the work of his unit than on performing the routine tasks of his subordinates will find that his unit's production record will be good

(D) a supervisor whose unit has a good production record usually places less emphasis on performing the day-to-day tasks of his subordinates than on planning the work of his unit.

57. In assigning a complicated task to a group of subordinates, Mr. Jones, a unit supervisor, neither indicates the specific steps to be followed in performing the assignment nor designates the subordinate to be responsible for seeing that the task is done on time. This supervisor's method of assigning the task is most likely to result in

(A) the loss of skills previously acquired by his subordinates

(B) assumption of authority by the most capable subordinates

(C) friction and misunderstanding among subordinates with consequent delays in work

(D) greater individual effort and self-reliance on the part of his subordinates.

Correct Answers

1. C	13. D	25. D	37. D	49. B
2. C	14. C	26. C	38. D	50. A
3. B	15. E	27. D	39. B-C	51. C
4. C	16. C	28. A	40. C	52. B
5. A	17. A	29. D	41. B	53. B
6. B	18. D	30. E	42. D	54. B
7. B	19. A	31. C	43. A	55. B
8. A	20. A	32. D	44. C	56. D
9. C	21. D	33. A	45. E	57. C
10. C	22. D	34. E	46. D	
11. A	23. B	35. B	47. D	
12. D	24. D	36. C	48. C	

DELEGATION OF AUTHORITY

1. Of the following, the information that is generally considered most essential in a departmental organization survey chart is
   (A) detailed operation of the department
   (B) lines of authority
   (C) relations of the department to other City departments
   (D) the department's responsibility to the Mayor.

2. Of the following, the most important principle in respect to delegation of authority that should guide you in your work if you are in charge of a bureau is that you should
   (A) delegate as much authority as you effectively can
   (B) make certain that all administrative details clear through your desk
   (C) have all decisions confirmed by you
   (D) discourage the practice of consulting you on matters of basic policy
   (E) keep all authority centralized in yourself

3. The one of the following which is *least* valid as a guiding principle for you, in your work in building spirit and teamwork in your bureau is that you should attempt to
   (A) convince the personnel of the bureau that public administration is a worthwhile endeavor
   (B) lead every employee to visualize the integration of his own individual function with the program of the whole bureau
   (C) develop a favorable public attitude toward the work of the bureau
   (D) express clearly all policies and procedures of a formal character to avoid misinterpretation
   (E) maintain impartiality by convenient delegation of authority in controversial matters.

4. Two of the bureau unit heads under your jurisdiction are in constant conflict in respect to the authority of one of the unit heads to consult certain records in the office of the other. Of the following, the most helpful action which may be taken immediately to eliminate this friction is to
   (A) call both unit heads into conference with yourself to explain the necessity for cooperation
   (B) ask each unit head separately to be more cooperative with the other
   (C) transfer the disputed records to a third unit head and center authority in the hands of this third person
   (D) reprimand both unit heads
   (E) define the authority of each unit head.

5. Your bureau is assigned an important task. Of the following, the function that you, as an administrative officer, can least reasonably be expected to perform under those circumstances is
   (A) division of the large job into individual tasks
   (B) establishment of "production lines" within the bureau
   (C) performance personally of a substantial share of all the work
   (D) check-up to see that the work has been well done
   (E) preparation of a report to your superior on the general outcome of the work.

6. In public administration functional allocation involves
   (A) integration and the assignment of administrative power
   (B) the assignment of a single power to a single administrative level
   (C) the distribution of a number of subsidiary responsibilities among all levels of government
   (D) decentralization of administrative responsibilities.

7. Of the following, the *least* accurate statement relating to district organization is that
   (A) a District Superintendent should be given authority commensurate with his responsibility
   (B) the same job assignments should be given to several units so that results may be cross-checked
   (C) job operations should be standardized, if possible, so that there is a common basis from which to seek improvment
   (D) tasks which are related should be grouped for possible assignment to a particular unit so that they may be performed more efficiently.

8. If the supervisor cannot readily check all the work done in his unit, he should

(A) hold up the work until he can personally check it
(B) refuse to take additional work
(C) work overtime until he can personally finish it all
(D) ask his superior to check the work
(E) delegate part of his work to a qualified subordinate.

9. Bureau X is composed of several clerical units, each supervised by a unit head accountable to the bureau chief. Assume that the bureau chief has a special task for an employee of one of the clerical units and wishes to issue instructions directly to the employee regarding this task. The *least* appropriate of the following procedures for the bureau chief to follow is to
(A) issue the instructions to the employee without notifying the employee's unit head
(B) give the instructions to the employee in the presence of the unit head
(C) ask the unit head to send the employee to him for instructions on this special task
(D) tell the employee to inform his unit head of the bureau chief's instructions.

10. Of the following factors, the one which is of *least* importance in determining the number of subordinates that an individual should be assigned to supervise is the
(A) nature of the work being supervised
(B) qualifications of the individual as a supervisor
(C) capabilities of the subordinates
(D) lines of promotion for the subordinates.

11. The administrator should know that in managing his division he should avoid
(A) assigning definite responsibilities to his immediate subordinates
(B) delegating necessary authority wherever responsibility has been assigned
(C) making a subordinate responsible to more than one supervisor
(D) keeping his employees currently informed about actions taken, new developments, and other matters affecting their work.

12. As division chief, you find that one of your new unit heads is constantly bogged down with detail work. This was not the case with his predecessors. The work load of the unit has remained unchanged. Of the following the most likely reason that this unit head is so overloaded with work is that
(A) he assigns too much important work to his subordinates
(B) he has failed to delegate some of the work to other members of this staff
(C) your division has too many unit supervisors
(D) this unit has too much detail work assigned to it.

13. Written instructions to a subordinate are of value because they
(A) can be kept up to date
(B) encourage initiative
(C) make a job seem easier
(D) are an aid in training
(E) encourage questions.

14. The one of the following functions of a supervisor which can be most successfully delegated is
(A) responsibility for accomplishing the unit's mission
(B) handling discipline
(C) checking completed work
(D) reporting to the bureau chief
(E) placing subordinates in the proper job.

15. A study of the supervision of employees in a City agency reveals that the bureau chiefs are reluctant to delegate responsibility and authority to their assistants. This study is most likely to reveal, in addition, that
(A) the organizational structure of this agency should be centralized
(B) the bureau chiefs tend to spend too much of their time on minor aspects of their work
(C) the number of employees supervised by bureau chiefs is excessive
(D) significant deviations from planned performance are not called to the attention of the bureau chiefs.

16. The delegation of responsibility and authority to subordinates by their superior generally does *not*
(A) facilitate a division of labor or the development of specialization
(B) permit the superior to carry out programs of work that exceed his immediate personal limits of physical energy and knowledge
(C) result in a downward transfer of work, both mental and manual
(D) involve a transfer of ultimate responsibility from superior to subordinate.

17. Of the following, a recognized procedure for avoiding conflicts in the delegation of authority is to
(A) delegate authority so as to preserve control by top management
(B) provide for a workable span of control
(C) review all assignments periodically
(D) assign all related work to the same control
(E) use the linear method of assignment.

18. The chief of a central files bureau which has 50 employees, customarily spends a considerable portion of his time in spot-checking the files, reviewing material being transferred from active to inactive files and similar activities. From the viewpoint of the department top management, the most pertinent evaluation which can be made on the basis of this information is that the
(A) supervisor is conscientious and hardworking
(B) bureau may need additional staff
(C) supervisior has not made a sufficient delegation of authority and responsibility
(D) bureau needs an in-service training course as the work of its employees requires an abnormal amount of review
(E) filing system employed may be inadequate.

19. "Much of the current criticism of the administration of large organizations is basically a criticism of our failure to place the same emphasis on accountability that we do on authority and responsibility." The one of the following acts which is most likely to insure accountability for the discharge of responsibilities inherent in the delegation of authority is the
(A) establishment of appropriate reports and controls
(B) organization of a methods analysis section
(C) delegation of authority so made as to support functional or homogeneous activities
(D) delegation of authority so made as to preserve unity of command
(E) decentralization of responsibility and authority.

20. Of the following administrative devices for preventing conflict within a board of examiners with respect to the extent of the authority of each of the examiners the most effective is, as far as is practicable, to
(A) assign all related work to the same examiner
(B) have the chairman of the board administratively responsible for resolving all disagreements
(C) set up a committee of senior members of the board to determine policy
(D) have the chairman of the board review examiners' assignments periodically
(E) assign work to examiners on a rotation basis.

21. A commanding officer best exemplifies leadership ability by
(A) arranging periodic staff meetings relating to professional development of subordinate officers
(B) delegating authority to subordinate officers so as to have time to plan precinct activity on a long-term basis
(C) devoting the major portion of his time to supervising subordinates so as to stimulate continuous improvement
(D) formulating a time schedule covering routine duties so as to conserve time for proper performance of his professional duties
(E) setting aside time for self-development and study in order to improve administrative techniques.

22. A principle which must be recognized by officers of superior rank is that the most constructive aspects of leadership are those which are exercised "face-to-face." The superior officer who recognizes this principle will
(A) avoid situations which will require direct control of the actions of subordinates several ranks below him
(B) emphasize coordination of the work of subordinates rather than assume direct long-distance control
(C) insist that communications from his office to members in his command be as short and direct as possible
(D) make certain that members in his command realize that orders are made upon his authorization
(E) place major responsibility for the execution of duties on the immediate superior of the men involved.

23. "An order, generally, to perform a certain service or effect a certain objective without specification of the means to be adopted or limit to govern the officer, leaves entire discretion with the officer as to the choice and application of the means but preserves the responsibility for his acts in the authority from which the order emanated."

The one of the following statements which is most in accord with the meaning of the above quotation is that

(A) orders should seldom be so specific as to eliminate the element of discretion
(B) generally, orders should specify means to be adopted and limits on the authority of the subordinate executing the order
(C) when methods to be employed are not stated in an order, all acts of a subordinate have the force of acts of the superior
(D) a subordinate officer is solely responsible for all actions taken at his own discretion in executing general orders
(E) generally, orders should specify the authority under which they are issued.

24. A supervisor of a unit may safely delegate certain of his functions to his subordinates. Of the following, the function which can most safely be delegated is the

(A) settlement of employee grievances
(B) planning and scheduling of the production of the unit
(C) improvement of production methods of the unit
(D) maintenance of records of the work output of the unit.

25. "To delegate work is one of the main functions of the supervisor. In delegating work, the supervisor should remember that even though an assignment is delegated to a subordinate, the supervisor ultimately is responsible for seeing that the work is done." The most valid implication of this quotation for a supervisor is that he should

(A) delegate as few difficult tasks as possible so as to minimize the consequences of inadequate performance by his subordinates
(B) delegate to his subordinates those tasks which he considers difficult or time consuming
(C) check the progress of delegated assignments periodically to make certain that the work is being done properly
(D) assign work to a subordinate without holding him directly accountable for carrying it out.

26. A recently developed practice in administration favors reducing the number of levels of authority in an organization, increasing the number of subordinates reporting to a superior, and also increasing the authority delegated to the subordinates. This practice would most likely result in

(A) an increase in the span of control exercised by superiors
(B) an increase in detailed information that flows to a superior from each subordinate
(C) a decrease in the responsibility exercised by the subordinates
(D) a decrease in the number of functions performed by the organization.

Correct Answers

(You'll learn more by writing your own answers before comparing them with these.)

1. B	6. C	11. C	16. D	21. B-C
2. A	7. B	12. B	17. D	22. E
3. E	8. E	13. D	18. C	23. C
4. E	9. A	14. C	19. A	24. D
5. C	10. D	15. B	20. A	25. C
		26. A		

PRACTICAL ADMINISTRATIVE PROBLEMS

1. You receive a request for information from another department. You are not certain whether the information can be collected in a few days or whether it may take several weeks. Of the following, the best course of action to follow in general is to
   (A) acknowledge the letter immediately, stating that collecting the information may take time, and send the information when gathered
   (B) wait a few days before answering the letter If it appears that collecting the information is going to take time, write a letter, stating that the request is being given careful attention, and send the information when gathered
   (C) acknowledge receipt of the letter immediately. If it appears as if collecting the information is going to take time, send a notice of progress within a few days and then send the information when gathered
   (D) send the information whenever it is completely gathered, together with a note explaining at that time those difficulties which may have caused any delay
   (E) send immediately a statement of the probable findings and then corroborate the statement when the actual results are available.

2. The one of the following practices which is most likely to lead to confusion, recrimination and jurisdictional conflict among the bureaus of a department is the failure to
   (A) make clear and unambiguous assignments
   (B) systematically subdivide the work
   (C) explain general policy to those responsible for its achievement
   (D) allocate equitably available resources
   (E) set up uniform operating procedures for all units.

3. A chief staff officer, serving as one of the immediate advisors to the department head, has demonstrated a special capacity for achieving internal agreements and for sound judgment. As a result he has been used more and more as a source of counsel and assistance by the department head. Other staff officers and line officials as well have discovered that it is wise for them to check with this colleague in advance on all problematical matters handed up to the department head. Developments such as this are
   (A) undesirable; they disrupt the normal lines for flow of work in an organization
   (B) desirable; they allow an organization to make the most of its strength wherever such strength resides
   (C) undesirable; they tend to undermine the authority of the department head and put it in the hands of a staff officer who does not have the responsibility
   (D) desirable; they tend to resolve internal ambiguities in organization
   (E) undesirable; they make for bad morale by causing "cut-throat" competition.

4. A serious procedural problem develops in your office. In your solution of this problem, the very first step to take is to
   (A) select the personnel to assist you
   (B) analyze your problem
   (C) devise the one best method of research
   (D) develop an outline of your report.

5. Assume that you have been given the responsibility for setting up a new bureau in your department. Of the following principles, the one which should be of *least* importance to you in carrying out this assignment is that
   (A) the functions of the bureau must be clearly defined
   (B) authority and responsibility must be clearly defined and allocated
   (C) adequate supervision to insure proper performance of work must be provided
   (D) all orders and instructions to subordinates must be in writing.

Questions No. 6-19 are designed to test your ability to check whether a particular form has been properly approved in accordance with a prescribed procedure. Although the question is framed about the processing of certain personnel papers, the type of thinking required is equally applicable to other clerical systems where requirements are prescribed, and the fulfillment of these requirements must be checked by a clerk.

This problem is concerned with required approvals for each of the following personnel changes: hiring, reinstating, return from leave of absence, transfer, job change, leave of absence and dismissal. A simplified chart of the organization in which the procedure is to be followed is as follows:

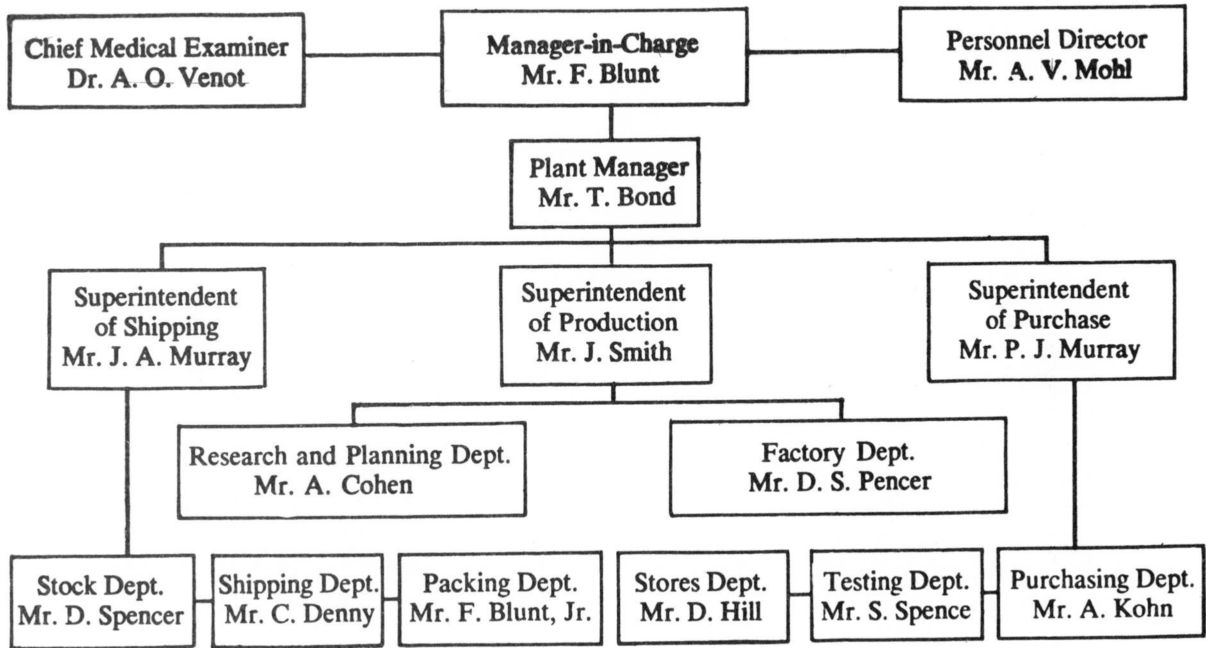

The instances in which a signature is required of the indicated official are as follows:

DEPARTMENT HEAD REQUESTING—Hire, reinstate, return from leave of absence, job change, leave of absence, and dismissal.

DEPARTMENT HEAD RELEASING—intraplant transfer.

DEPARTMENT HEAD ACCEPTING—intraplant transfer.

(Note: The terms Department Head Releasing and Department Head Accepting are used only for intraplant transfers.)

SUPERINTENDENT RELEASING — intraplant transfer, dismissal, and leave of absence.

SUPERINTENDENT ACCEPTING — hire, re-instate, return from leave of absence, intraplant transfer, job change.

PERSONNEL DIRECTOR—hire, re-instate, return from leave of absence, intraplant transfer, job change, and leave of absence.

PLANT MANAGER—hire, re-instate, intraplant transfer, job change, leave of absence, and dismissal.

MANAGER-in-CHARGE—intraplant transfer (only where a salary change is involved), job change (only where a salary change is involved), and dismissal.

The questions are the numbered forms which follow.

If you believe that the form has the required signatures of approval and no unnecessary signatures, mark an "A" alongside the appropriate number.

If one signature is missing, indicate the missing signature by the code letter given alongside the name below.

If there is substituted for one required signature, an unnecessary one, disregard the unnecessary one and merely indicate by code letter the missing required signature.

All forms which do not fall into one of the above described categories should be marked "B".

The implication of the problem is that you would not initial any form improperly signed. The signatures on the form are not necessarily in the order of importance in the organization.

The code from which you must select your answer is as follows:

(A) Has all required signatures and no unnecessary ones
(B) Lacks two or more required signatures, or contains two or more unnecessary ones (as described above)
(C) Mr. F. Blunt, Manager-in-Charge
(D) Mr. A. V. Mohl, Personnel Director
(E) Mr. T. Bond, Plant Manager
(F) Mr. J. A. Murray, Superintendent of Shipping
(G) Mr. J. Smith, Superintendent of Production
(H) Mr. P. J. Murray, Superintendent of Purchase
(K) Mr. A. Cohen, Head of Research and Planning Department
(L) Dr. A.O. Venot, Chief Medical Examiner
(M) Mr. D. S. Pencer, Head of Factory Department
(N) Mr. D. Spencer, Head of Stock Department
(O) Mr. C. Denny, Head of Shipping Department
(P) Mr. F. Blunt, Jr., Head of Packing Department
(R) Mr. D. Hill, Head of Stores Department.
(S) Mr. S. Spence, Head of Testing Department.
(T) Mr. A. Kohn, Head of Purchase Department.

Read carefully all the information given on each form below as you answer each question.

6. CERTIFICATE OF RETURN FROM LEAVE OF ABSENCE

Dept.: Factory
Name: Robert Mart
Title: Laborer
Salary: $2.50 per hour

Signatures of Approval
A. V. Mohl
T. Bond
D. S. Pencer
J. Smith

7. CERTIFICATE OF DISMISSAL

Dept.: Purchase
Name: John Snow
Title: Buyer
Salary: $10,000 p. a.

Signatures of Approval
P. J. Murray
A. V. Mohl
A. Kohn
T. Bond
F. Blunt

8. CERTIFICATE OF INTRAPLANT TRANSFER

Dept.: From Stock to Res. & Pl.
Name: Donald Stein
From: Stockkeeper at $5,000 p. a.
To: Lab. Aide at $6,420 p. a.

Signatures of Approval
J. Smith
D. Spencer
T. Bond
A. Cohen
A. V. Mohl
J. A. Murray

9. CERTIFICATE OF JOB CHANGE

Dept.: Stores
Name: Jane Forest
From: Clerk at $4,800 p. a.
To: Stock Assistant at $5,200 p. a.

Signatures of Approval
F. Blunt
D. Hill
D. S. Pencer
J. Smith
T. Bond
A. V. Mohl

10. CERTIFICATE OF HIRING

Dept.: Packing
Name: John Doe
Title: Clerk
Salary: $4,200 p. a.

Signatures of Approval
A. V. Mohl
T. Bond
P. J. Murray
F. Blunt, Jr.

11. CERTIFICATE OF REINSTATEMENT

Dept.: Shipping
Name: Joe Lovett
Title: Letterer
Salary: $2.35 per hour

Signatures of Approval
F. Blunt
T. Bond
C. Denny
J. A. Murray
A. V. Mohl

12. CERTIFICATE OF DISMISSAL

Dept.: Packing
Name: Dave Packer
Title: Laborer
Salary: $2.25 per hour

Signatures of Approval
T. Bond
J. A. Murray
F. Blunt

13. CERTIFICATE OF JOB CHANGE

Dept.: Testing
Name: Richard Roe
From: Laboratory Aide at $6,400 p. a.
To: Ass't Chemist at $7,650 p. a.

Signatures of Approval
T. Bond
S. Spence
P. J. Murray
A. V. Mohl
F. Blunt

14. CERTIFICATE OF LEAVE OF ABSENCE

Dept.: Stores
Name: Miss Florence Jones
Title: Clerk
Salary: $4,850 p. a.

Signatures of Approval
J. A. Murray
T. Bond
A. V. Mohl
D. Spencer

15. CERTIFICATE OF INTRAPLANT TRANSFER

Dept.: From Stock to Shipping
Name: C. Dennis
From Clerk at $4,620 p. a.
To: Clerk at $5,200 p. a.

Signatures of Approval
J. A. Murray
F. Blunt
A. V. Mohl
T. Bond
C. Dennis
D. Spencer

16. CERTIFICATE OF RETURN FROM LEAVE OF ABSENCE (Maternity)

Dept.: Research and Planning
Name: Mrs. Rose Pierce
Title: Statistician
Salary: $8,635 p. a.

Signatures of Approval
A. Cohen
A. O. Venot
A. V. Mohl
J. Smith

17. CERTIFICATE OF INTRAPLANT TRANSFER

Dept.: From Stores to Purchase
Name: James Dunn
From: Laborer at $2.35 per hour
To: Laborer at $2.35 per hour

Signatures of Approval
A. V. Mohl
T. Bond
P. J. Murray
A. Kohn
J. Smith
D. Hill

18. CERTIFICATE OF DISMISSAL

Dept.: Factory
Name: Anthony Riccio
Title: Electrician
Salary: $3.45 per hour

Signatures of Approval
J. Smith
F. Blunt
D. Spencer
T. Bond
A. V. Mohl

19. CERTIFICATE OF RETURN FROM LEAVE OF ABSENCE

Dept.: Stores
Name: Jack Stoll
Title: Storekeeper
Salary: $2.10 per hour

Signatures of Approval
D. Hill
A. V. Mohl
P. J. Murray

Suppose that you are assigned to duty in a hypothetical New York City Information Bureau. Questions No. 20-27 consist of communications from citizens which have been turned over to you for referral to other City departments. For each communication select the most appropriate option given on the next page and place the letter, preceding the option, alongside the number corresponding to the question number (the number given above each communication).

To refresh your memory some functions of selected City agencies are listed below. All functions are not, however, listed and your answer must be based not only on the listed duties of agencies but on any other functions that they legally perform. Your answer must be selected from the options given, even though you would prefer to refer a particular letter to a different agency. Where you would like to refer a letter to two or more agencies, you must select the best single referral. Only one answer will be accepted for each question.

Selected Functions of Some of the Departments Listed as Options Below

BOARD OF EDUCATION—Maintains and operates lunchrooms in many schools; issues employment certificates.

THE COURTS (includes any court located in New York City)—Administer justice.

MUNICIPAL CIVIL SERVICE COMMISSION—Constitutes the personnel agency of the City; conducts examinations for master and special electrician and moving picture operator.

BUREAU OF REAL ESTATE OF THE BOARD OF ESTIMATE—Rents City property to private parties.

DEPARTMENT OF FINANCE—Collects all taxes and assessments, and rents.

DEPARTMENT OF INVESTIGATION—Makes any investigation directed by the Mayor or the City Council.

DEPARTMENT OF HEALTH—Has jurisdiction to regulate all matters affecting the health of the City.

DEPARTMENT OF HOSPITALS—Maintains and operates all hospitals of the City for the care of the sick, injured, aged or infirm persons.

DEPARTMENT OF HOUSING AND BUILDINGS—Issues permits for all surface and subsurface construction.

LAW DEPARTMENT—Section 349 of the Charter states, "Except as otherwise provided by law, the corporation counsel shall be attorney and counsel for the city and every agency thereof and shall have charge and conduct of all the law business of the city and its agencies . . ."

DEPARTMENT OF LICENSES—Has control of the granting, issuing, transferring, renewing, revoking, suspending and cancelling of most licenses in the City of New York.

DEPARTMENT OF MARKETS—Operates public markets; maintains a Bureau of Consumers' Service.

PAROLE COMMISSION—Supervises prisoners released before the full expiration of their sentences.

OFFICE OF THE COMPTROLLER—Settles and adjusts all claims against the City of New York.

POLICE DEPARTMENT—Preserves the public peace, prevents crime, detects and arrests offenders, etc., maintains a Juvenile Aid Bureau.

DEPARTMENT OF PURCHASE—Does most of the purchasing of food and other items for the city.

DEPARTMENT OF WATER SUPPLY, GAS AND ELECTRICITY—Licenses master and special electricians, and moving picture operators.

DEPARTMENT OF SANITATION—Has responsibility for the removal and disposition of ashes, street sweepings, garbage, refuse, rubbish, dead animals, night soil and offal.

Options from which answers are to be selected

(A) Board of Education
(B) The Courts
(C) Municipal Civil Service Commission
(D) Bureau of Real Estate of the Board of Estimate
(E) Department of Finance
(F) Department of Investigation
(G) Department of Health
(H) Department of Hospitals
(K) Department of Housing and Buildings
(M) New York City Housing Authority
(N) Law Department
(O) Department of Licenses
(P) Department of Markets
(R) Parole Commission
(S) Office of the Comptroller
(T) Police Department
(U) Department of Purchase
(W) Department of Water Supply, Gas and Electricity
(X) Department of Sanitation

20. "I am sure that I paid that last rent bill. As a matter of fact I have a cancelled check to prove my claim. Why have I been billed again? Can't you people keep your records straight? I have no intention of paying that bill again. My factory is located in an old public building on .... Street still owned by the City."

21. "I have a house on .... Avenue in Rockaway Beach. For the past three years my water rates have been almost double those of of my neighbors on either side whose buildings are of comparable size. I believe that my water meter is not right. My gas and electric bills are comparable to those of my neighbors.

"I do not know what City department to contact on this case and will appreciate an investigation into my case."

22. "I am 15 years old. I want to work this summer, but when I apply for an errand job the boss tells me that I must get a license. How do I get a license for a job? My mother needs money badly. Please help me to be able to get a job."

23. "My husband is in the Army. I find it very difficult to take care of my child and keep my present job, in which my hours rotate. I have been told by my friends that the City departments are short of help and that, in some fields, appointments are made without examinations. If I can find myself a provisional job as a typist what rights will I have?"

24. "I worked as an electrician's helper in Minneapolis, Minnesota. I came to New York a year ago and last month I took an examination for master electrician. Yesterday I received a notice that I failed the examination. I should like to appeal my rating because I feel that an error has been made. How do I go about doing this?"

25. "I have an apartment in the .... Houses (a public housing project). Several blocks away there is a slaughter house which is kept very dirty and which smells to high heaven. My son Alexander has been very ill all summer and I am sure that the slaughter house is to blame. My wife is so worried about my son that she is suffering a nervous breakdown and is now in Bellevue Hospital. I beg you to please make the slaughter house move."

26. "The other day I saw Mr. Doe near .... Street. Now I know that 1 ½ years ago Doe was sentenced to the penitentiary for an indeterminate term not to exceed three years. He's going wrong again, and before he gets into real trouble something ought to be done about it. He's six feet tall, has a scar on his chin a little to the left, and wears a shiny brown serge suit, with a green tie. His hangout is the pool room on .... Street. I am not signing this letter for obvious reasons.

"I don't think that he has a job and how long can a fellow like that keep out of trouble if he isn't working? Please don't misunderstand me. I am not trying to squeal on him. It's just that I feel that this is the only way that I can help him."

27. "I am a soldier's wife with two children. My husband is in the Air Force. He is a sergeant and a tail gunner. I live with my widowed mother, and my only brother is in the Navy. We find it very hard to get along and would like some advice as to the best bargains in foods to buy on our limited budget during the winter.

"I think it unfair that, while my husband is fighting for this country, and while many of his friends are earning good salaries, his family should have to struggle along on such a poor allowance. This allowance should be increased."

28. You are in charge of a central file unit servicing seven bureaus. The basic file, because of the nature of the material to be filed, is a subject file. In your unit one of your assistants marks all papers for filing, and two others do all the filing. You have had continual trouble in finding filed papers. When, after exhaustive search, such papers are found, the various bureau heads maintain that the papers have been improperly marked. Under these circumstances the best procedure for you to follow is to

(A) have the various bureaus maintain their own files, and assign your file clerks on a part-time basis to each bureau
(B) reprimand your file clerks for misfiling the papers
(C) request the bureaus to mark their own papers for filing, providing them with a full description of the filing system and its subjects
(D) establish an alphabetic or numeric filing system which will make filing simpler and will reduce errors in filing.

29 An office appliance specialty machine salesman, who calls very frequently of late, is announced by the receptionist who is located at a booth in the corridor. You feel that you should see him but at the same time you are quite busy and cannot spare more than a few minutes. To make it easier to get rid of him under these circumstances, you should

(A) invite him into your office for a chat
(B) invite him into your office but act distantly and coldly toward him
(C) walk out to the corridor and speak to him there
(D) refuse to see him.

Questions No. 30 to 37 are based upon the problem described below.

Suppose that you are in charge of an office with four subordinates. Besides your own full-time work, on a certain day your office is required to turn out a job which, for purposes of efficiency, you have divided into 8 tasks. You find it necessary to order a 10 hour day in order to complete the job. Assume for purposes of this problem that you know the exact number of hours it would take each employee to perform each task. The figures given in the following table indicate the number of hours it would take each of your employees to complete each task.

Task	M	N	O	P	Q	R	S	T
Employee A	5	3	7	3	5	3	3	4
Employee B	4	7	4	4	7	5	3	6
Employee C	8	10	8	9	9	6	3	8
Employee D	9	10	9	8	10	9	8	8

Assume further the following conditions:

(A) Each employee must work at least 8 hours.
(B) No employee may work more than 10 hours.
(C) There is no question of quality of work or fatigue involved in this problem.
(D) Each task must be handled in its entirety by one person only.

In Questions 30 to 37, for each task indicated in Column I, select the one employee in Column II to whom it must be assigned under the conditions of the problem described above. In order to arrive at the correct answers, it is necessary to decide to which employee each of the eight tasks is to be assigned.

Column I	Column II
30. Task M	(A) Employee A
31. Task N	(B) Employee B
32. Task O	(C) Employee C
33. Task P	(D) Employee D
34. Task Q	
35. Task R	
36. Task S	
37. Task T	

38. Suppose that it is the practice in your department for each bureau head to keep general departmental orders, which are numbered according to date of issuance, in a special order book. The administrative head wishes to request the bureau heads in your department to reread carefully the contents of six detailed general orders, concerning routine matters of organization, which have been distributed at intervals during the preceding year. Of the following, the *most* desirable procedure for him to follow is to
(A) call a special staff conference and read each of the six orders aloud
(B) call a special staff conference and read the numbers of the orders concerned
(C) mimeograph and distribute, together with the reason therefor, a request to read these six orders, referring to them by number
(D) reissue the six orders, being careful to mark them "duplicate"
(E) notify each bureau head personally that it would be desirable for him to reread carefully the orders in his order book.

39. In administering the activities of a personnel office with a staff of fifteen employees, including seven personnel technicians, the personnel officer should
(A) delegate full authority and responsibility to each staff member and discharge those who do not meet his standards
(B) endeavor to keep tab on the work of each individual on his staff
(C) make sure each job is being done properly or do it himself
(D) plan work programs, make assignments, and check on performance
(E) concern himself only with major policies and expect subordinates to carry out actual functions.

Questions 40 through 54 should be answered by one of the following five choices. Solely on the basis of the data presented in the items, mark the appropriate answer on your answer sheet to indicate the best of the five classifications suggested for each fact given in combination with a question.

(A) Tends to prove that the answer is negative, though additional data are necessary for conclusive proof
(B) Proves conclusively that the answer is negative
(C) Tends to prove that the answer is positive, though additional data are necessary for conclusive proof
(D) Proves conclusively that the answer is positive
(E) Offers no evidence to indicate that the answer is either positive or negative.

40. *Question:* Should the regular monthly report of your bureau's activities during October be submitted on November 8 instead of November 1? *Fact:* The regular monthly report for October is due on November 1. Nothing very important has occurred during October. Your bureau is currently engaged on a project, due to be completed by November 8, in which you are certain your superior will be greatly interested.

41. *Question:* Should a formal letter of apology be written to Mr. C.? *Fact:* You have received a letter from Mr. C., who is of coordinate rank with you in your department, requesting the date on which certain information will be available. The letter which you have dictated in reply to Mr. C.'s question has been mailed by your secretary without your handwritten signature, although your name has been typewritten in the appropriate space. In mailing the unsigned letter to Mr. C, your secretary did not act on the basis of a specific instruction from you to the effect that the letter was to be sent without your signature.

42. *Question:* Should you continue holding regular conferences with supervisors under your jurisdiction? *Fact:* Only one conference of the five held thus far has produced extraordinarily significant procedural improvements.

43. *Question:* Should employee A be allowed to leave at 2 P. M. on Tuesdays in order to attend a graduate course at one of the local universities? *Fact:* Employee A is willing to make up the time lost by working 3 additional hours on another day. The course will increase employee A's value to the service.

44. *Question:* Should a note be sent to the bureau head calling attention to the nature of the typographical error? *Fact:* You have transmitted to a bureau head in your department a 12 page report. In referring to a carbon copy four days after the report has been transmitted, you discover a typographical error on page 7, line 16. The word "informational" has been substituted for "influential." This substitution affects strongly the meaning of a fundamental point.

45. *Question.* Should employee A, rather than B, be placed in charge of gathering information on which to base a report concerning payroll procedure in your department? *Fact:* Employee A has generally been more industrious and capable in the performance of his duties than employee B.

46. *Question:* Should Mr. Smith rather than Miss Jones be assigned to a particular important confidential task? *Fact:* Mr. Smith is 24 years old, ranked first on the eligible list from which he was appointed, and has completed two years of graduate work at one of the local universities. Miss Jones is 26 years old.

47. *Question:* Are mailing costs excessive? *Fact:* Mailing costs for a six months period in 1940 are 22% higher than for the comparable period in 1939.

48. *Question:* Should Mr. Black be suspended preliminary to investigation? *Fact:* You receive an anonymous letter stating that Mr. Black, an employee under your jurisdiction, has performed an act somewhat deleterious to the welfare of your department

49. *Question:* Should further action on this matter consist entirely of clipping the item and sending it to your superior? *Fact:* A letter is published in the "Letters from the Readers" column of one of the large daily newspapers. This letter praises the work of your department and makes specific reference to the fact that a specific employee, not named by the author of the letter, was most courteous and helpful on a stated occasion involving activity by one of the bureaus under your jurisdiction.

50. *Question:* On the basis of methods of computation employed in the New York City Retirement System, are the payroll deductions for pension purposes of Mr. R greater than those of Mr. S?
Fact: Mr. R is older than Mr. S. Also, Mr. R earns a greater per annum salary than Mr. S.

51. *Question:* Should a time clock be installed for the employees in your department?
Fact: Within the past week 5% of the employees in your department have arrived for work more than 15 minutes late.

52. *Question:* Should corrective action, such as reprimand, be taken against Mr. Brown?
Fact: You have called a conference for 10 A.M. A notice to this effect was sent to Mr. Brown three days in advance. Mr. Brown appears at 10:45 A. M.

53. *Question:* Should there be reexamination of the departmental policy in respect to balancing overtime with compensating time-off?
Fact: It is a policy of your department to accord to your employees an amount of time off equal to the amount of overtime completed. This time off must be taken within 90 days of the overtime.

54. *Question:* Should there be a reexamination of the procedures utilized in responding to queries from other departments?
Fact: On the average, your office takes six days in which to mail replies to queries from other departments.

55. All mimeograph work of Department X is performed by the Duplicating Unit. The stencils required for this duplicating work are cut by the Transcribing Unit. Both of these units are in the department's General Service Bureau. A schedule for cutting and running off the stencils for several long reports was recently set up by the chief of the bureau after consultation with the heads of the two units concerned. The Transcribing Unit has been unable to adhere to the established schedule. As a consequence, the Duplicating Unit is also falling behind schedule. The most appropriate of the following actions for the head of the Duplicating Unit to take is to
(A) do nothing since he cannot be criticized for not running off stencils he doesn't have
(B) notify the head of the Transcribing Unit that continued failure to adhere to the schedule will be reported to the bureau chief
(C) advise the head of the Transcribing Unit to have his staff work overtime to cut the scheduled number of stencils
(D) discuss with the head of the Transcribing Unit the advisability of having the schedule modified by the bureau chief.

56. In your work you would find the New York City Administrative Code most helpful in locating material which
(A) is helpful as a guide to the literature in public administration
(B) is helpful as a manual analyzing the advantages and disadvantages of alternative operating procedures
(C) is informative with regard to Federal, State and Municipal relationships
(D) is in harmony with and supplemental to the New York City Charter
(E) deals with annual summaries of municipal departmental activities.

57. Suppose that an administrator wishes to learn employees opinion concerning a major specific problem. Of the following, the method which is *least* likely to yield an accurate reflection of such opinion is to
(A) poll the entire staff
(B) interview personally each of the bureau heads
(C) determine employee opinion by means of an attitude questionnaire
(D) interview a random sample of the employees
(E) have a careful study made of relevant employee behavior.

58. Assume that there is an administrative regulation in your department to the effect that all outgoing letters prepared by bureau heads under the jurisdiction of the secretary's office must be signed by the secretary. Of the following, the best administrative practice to suggest in connection with this regulation is in general to
(A) include in each letter a reference to the individual to whose attention the reply should be brought
(B) assign an intelligent clerk to read all incoming letters and route them to the appropriate bureau heads
(C) maintain in the secretary's office a record of all outgoing mail and an indication of the bureau heads to whom replies should be referred
(D) have a representative of each bureau head call at regular intervals at the secretary's office for the bureau's mail
(E) place the name of the appropriate bureau head above the return address on the envelope.

59. You find that a probationary employee under your supervision is consistently below a reasonable standard of performance for the job he is assigned to do. Of the following, the most appropriate action for you to take first is to
   (A) give him an easier job to do
   (B) advise him to transfer to another department
   (C) recommend to your superior that he be discharged at the end of his probationary period
   (D) investigate the desirability of reducing the standard
   (E) determine whether the cause for his below standard performance is readily remedied.

60. Suppose that you are a bureau head with considerable correspondence to dictate daily. Of the following, the practice which should be most helpful in facilitating this dictation is to
   (A) call the stenographer a few minutes before you are ready, so that she will be available when you wish to begin
   (B) dictate terse replies to all letters
   (C) count the number of letters in advance, so that you can indicate, the amount of work for the stenographer
   (D) prepare in advance brief notes, so that you will have a guide in dictating
   (E) dictate in several sessions, calling the stenographer whenever there is a let-up in your other work.

61. A brief questionnaire from a governmental agency in another city has been referred to you in your capacity as a junior administrative assistant. Some of the questions are not quite clear. You should
   (A) answer with an explanation of the basis for your reply
   (B) use your own judgment and answer as best you can
   (C) write a letter asking for additional information
   (D) return the inquiry with the statement that you cannot understand the questions
   (E) refer the problem to a subordinate employee.

62. A personnel officer checking the turnover rate in his department found that, over a period of five years, the rate at which engineers left the organization was exactly the same as the rate at which junior clerks left the department. This information tends to indicate
   (A) that something may be amiss with the organization; the rate for engineers under ordinary circumstances should be higher than for clerks
   (B) that the organization is in good shape; neither the technical nor clerical aspects are being over-emphasized
   (C) nothing which would be of value in determining the state of the organization
   (D) that the organization is in good shape; working conditions, in general, are equivalent for all employees
   (E) that something may be amiss with the organization; the turnover rate for engineers under ordinary circumstances should be lower than for clerks.

63. A District Superintendent received a report from a Section Foreman in his district indicating that the performance of a Sanitation Man was not up to departmental standards. The Superintendent, after reading the report, transferred the man to another section in the district. This action of the District Superintendent was
   (A) proper; reports should be acted on promptly or they become dated and meaningless
   (B) not proper; unsatisfactory employees should be dismissed and not transferred
   (C) proper; a man who does poorly in one assignment may do better in another
   (D) not proper; the Superintendent should have investigated the cause of the poor performance first

64. The one of the following which is *not* a major purpose of an employee suggestion plan is to
   (A) provide an additional method by means of which an employee's work performance can be evaluated
   (B) increase employee interest in the work of the organization
   (C) provide an additional channel of communication between the employee and top management
   (D) utilize to the greatest extent possible the ideas and proposals of employees
   (E) provide a formal method for rewarding the occasional valuable idea.

65. Assume that you have received a letter requesting certain information. You know that the time required to obtain this information may extend from several days to several weeks. You may take either of two courses of action in replying to this letter. You may withhold your reply until

the requested information has been obtained, or you may acknowledge immediately the receipt of the letter and send the information when it has been obtained. For you to take the first rather than the second course of action would be
(A) desirable; you will thus reduce the amount of correspondence
(B) undesirable; a person requesting information should be informed as soon as possible that his request has been received and that it will be attended to
(C) desirable; if the information should be obtained within a few days, it would appear wasteful and ridiculous to have sent two letters in so short a period of time
(D) undesirable; some letters do not require any response at all.

66. A letter to your superior from Mr. A, an important official in City R, requesting detailed information concerning the advantages of using statistical machine X, is referred to you by your superior. Attached to the letter is a carbon copy of a note of acknowledgment from your superior to Mr. A stating that his letter has been referred to you for more detailed information. You do not employ machine X in your work, but have always used machine Y instead, for a purpose similar to that for which Mr. A wishes to use machine X. Under the circumstances, the most appropriate course of action to follow is to
(A) refer Mr. A's letter back to your superior stating that you cannot supply the information requested because you use machine Y
(B) write a brief note to Mr. A, stating that you do not use machine X but machine Y
(C) write a brief note to Mr. A, stating that unfortunately you are not able to supply the information he has requested, and send a carbon copy of your letter to your superior
(D) write a letter, several paragraphs in length, explaining that you do not use machine X, and suggest that Mr. A get in touch with the manufacturers of machine X
(E) write a letter at least a page in length, explaining that machine Y is used instead of machine X, and describe in some detail the advantages and disadvantages of machine Y.

67. You have been asked to answer a letter from the dean of a nearby school of education requesting certain information. After giving the request careful consideration, you find that it cannot be granted. Of the following ways of beginning your answering letter, the best is to begin by
(A) discussing the problem of releasing confidential information
(B) explaining in detail why the request cannot be granted
(C) indicating, if possible, that the information may be available from some other source
(D) quoting the laws which prohibit the dissemination of information of the type requested
(E) saying that you are sorry that the request cannot be granted.

Correct Answers For The Foregoing Questions

(Please make every effort to answer the questions on your own before looking at these answers. You'll make faster progress by following this rule.)

1.A	10.F	19.A	28.C	36.C	44.D	52.C	60.D
2.A	11.B	20.E	29.C	37.A	45.C	53.E	61.A
3.B	12.P	21.W	30.B	38.C	46.E	54.D	62.E
4.B	13.A	22.A	31.A	39.D	47.C	55.D	63.D
5.D	14.B	23.C	32.B	40.B	48.B	56.D	64.A
6.B	15.O	24.C	33.A	41.B	49.B	57.B	65.B
7.B	16.A	25.G	34.D	42.D	50.C	58.A	66.E
8.C	17.B	26.R	35.C	43.C	51.E	59.E	67.E
9.B	18.B	27.P					

II. PRINCIPLES OF MANAGEMENT

Our analysis of previous examinations indicates that you should possess a fairly good knowledge of this subject. Here are the key points . . . the information on which they are likely to quiz you. Following the text you'll find a quiz, composed of actual previous test questions. The text should help you score high on the quiz. And our answers, which follow the quiz, should clear up any remaining doubts.

The word "management" is sometimes confusing because it is used in two senses. The first use refers to the way things get done in an enterprise. More specifically, management, in this sense, means the effective use of people, funds, equipment, materials, and methods to accomplish a specified objective. This is the generally accepted meaning and the way the word is used here. The other way it is used is to designate the people who manage, as "middle management," "top management," and just "management."

RELATION TO ADMINISTRATION

The word "administration" is often used to mean exactly the same as "management." Recently there has been a tendency to restrict its usage to the functions performed at the very top level of an organization. Here is where the primary objectives and purposes of the whole enterprise are formulated, where broad policies are established, and where decisions are made as to financing, basic organization structure, and similar fundamental considerations.

Once these decisions have been made, they have to be carried out by executives—operating heads—line officials—at the lower levels. Their major responsibility is to get effective action that will result in accomplishment of the objectives economically within the limitations of the policies that have been established. It is this group that has heavy responsibilities for planning how to get the job done, determining who will do each part, issuing clear orders and instructions, setting quality and quantity standards, and checking on accomplishment—all part of work management.

RELATION TO SUPERVISION

Another term that is used somewhat loosely is the word "supervision." More and more this is coming to mean the job relationships that exist between an employee and those who report directly to him.

Naturally the amount of supervision that has to be exercised is far less at the top than at the bottom of an organization. More experienced employees usually need—and receive—less supervision. The first-level supervisor spends practically all of his time directing his subordinates in their work assignments.

Thus every official who directs the work activities of subordinates has definite supervisory responsibilities, but ordinarily they are *called* supervisors only at the lower levels. This is because analysis of duties and responsibilities of these jobs shows that as we go upward in the organization, more and more time has to be spent on planning, making decisions, getting plans implemented, and checking up to find out how well they have been carried out. As will be mentioned later, those are management processes and are of a somewhat different nature from the requirements for directing effectively the work of subordinates on a person-to-person basis.

THE FIVE PRIMARY PROCESSES

Management has to do with the effective use of men, money, materials, and methods to achieve a definite purpose. When we specialize on *employee* problems we are in the area of personnel management. If we emphasize the *fiscal* aspects of the operation we are concentrating on financial management. *Work* management usually stresses the use of materials and methods.

Of course, we must recognize that all jobs, all work, and all accomplishments are brought about through the efforts of people, and that it is impossible to make a division between the personal elements and the impersonal elements in supervision or work management. There appears to be no good reason to try to erect artificial and arbitrary barriers between these two aspects, but for the purposes of this study the usual practice of minimizing the human elements and factors and emphasizing the work management elements and factors will be followed.

Out of experiences of groups of people working to accomplish common purposes, we are relatively certain that some aspects of work management are very soundly established. There are a number of ways in which these actions may be grouped or identified for purposes of study. Many students of management refer to these groups as *processes of management*. This word *process* is used in about the same sense as "activity." Therefore, an analysis of work management includes such activities as planning, organization, methods, and the manipulation of things, rather than personal relationships.

Those things that management officials and supervisors do which are related more specifically to work management may be placed in a very simple classification. They are as follows:

1. Thinking about the job to be done, what is needed to do it, equipment, supplies, and space, and coming up with orderly plans and decisions as to how the job may best be accomplished: the *planning* process.
2. Formalizing the thinking and the planning into an organized structure so that we have a more or less stable grouping of activities and equipment, and so that our plans can be realized: the *organizing* process.
3. Furnishing directions, giving instructions, and all those like activities which set the organization in motion and keep it moving toward getting the mission accomplished: the *directing* process.
4. Timing and scheduling the work of the whole organization and gearing it into the efforts and programs of other organizational segments (and individuals) in order to assure proper work flow, to synchronize the activities of the unit, and to make best use of all efforts directed toward the same or related purposes: the *coordinating* process.
5. Checking progress against plans, setting up standards and checking against those standards, and by other means making certain that the mission is being accomplished as planned: the *control* process.

These five groups cover fairly well what an administrator or manager does (administrative management at any level), regardless of whether he is the director of a big corporation or the Secretary of a Government Department. They would represent what he, as a top management official, would be concerned with. On the other hand, at the lowest supervisory level, a straw boss with four or five workers and a relatively small number of simple tasks to perform would need to be concerned with similar elements. Of course there will be vast difference as to the scope and importance in these two cases, but fundamentally these areas will describe the administrative management or work management responsibilities. In all the intermediate levels of management, these same five groups of activities or processes are present to some degree.

It should be emphasized that while each of these five processes has to be performed in the management of an enterprise, they do not necessarily take place separately one from the other. There is much overlapping. An executive may be *planning* a *reorganization* of his department in order to secure better *control*: he can give *directions* and instructions to his people for the purpose of achieving smoother *coordination*. Planning cannot all be done at one time. The manager is continually planning and replanning aspects of the operation. Nor does he set aside 2 hours on Tuesday to do his coordinating for the week. Actually executives utilize these processes as the mechanic uses his tools—when they are needed—selecting the proper one for the task at hand.

THE MANAGEMENT CYCLE

There is recognizable, however, a certain sequence or phasing of the managerial processes. Certainly no one would dare plunge into an important activity without first thinking through what was involved. Not only would *planning* be required, but firm decisions would have to be made as to what was to be done. When it becomes necessary to find a solution to a problem, either immediate or foreseen, the manager starts to plan for the appropriate action to follow.

Often the situation is one requiring immediate action. The executive, then, has to start his subordinate employees to carrying out the decision. To accomplish this second phase—*executive action*—requires several things. There must be an effective *organization* through which the desired results can be effected. *Directions* and instructions must be furnished to everyone concerned. The various aspects of the action must be *coordinated* so that the whole operation can proceed harmoniously. If the plan is for the future—when and if the expected situation occurs—the same actions must be taken.

Finally, there must be real assurance that the action has produced the results desired. This means exercising sufficient *control* over the operation to prevent errors during the process and to insure a successful conclusion. Sometimes plans do not work out exactly as contemplated. Important facts may have been missing or some of the information may have been incorrect. Possibly the executive was not at top form when he used his judgment in making the decision. When he has seen the plan in action and has found that certain changes would be desirable, he has additional facts to work on and is in a position to think through and replan to secure more effective action. Thus the cycle of planning, executive action, and control starts over. In chart form, it could be represented by the diagram in figure 1.

This way of viewing management combines the five primary processes into three basic phases. Subsequent sections will describe more fully the way these aspects of a manager's work are carried out.

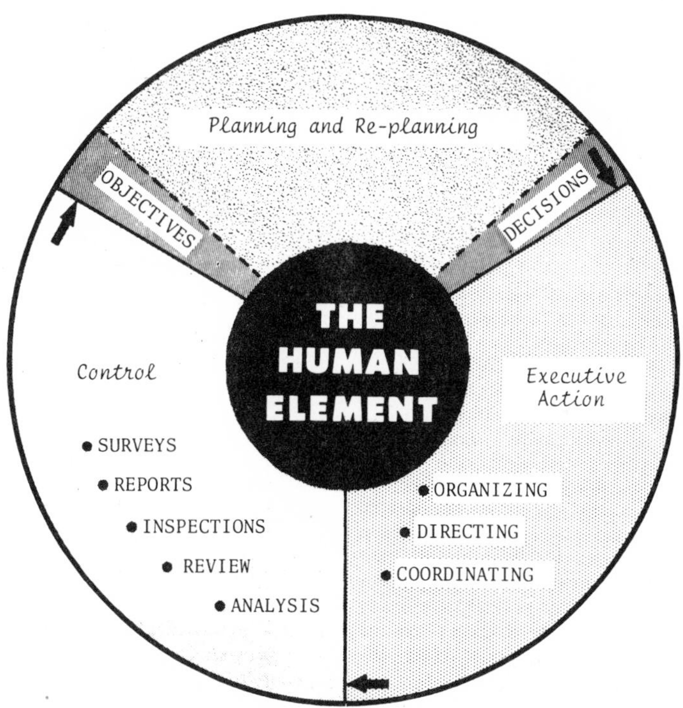

THE MANAGEMENT CYCLE

Figure 1.

MANAGEMENT FROM ABOVE

Up to this point the discussion has described in very broad strokes how one goes about managing a job. But management is not only what we *do* in relation to the work and the workers under our direction; it is also what we *receive* from higher levels of the organization.

In our day-to-day work, then, each of us is being "managed," in the sense that we receive orders, directions, instructions; policy and procedural statements; rules and regulations; work standards, specifications and deadlines; quotas, ceilings, and fund limitations. Every one of these hits us with an impact because they tell us what to do; they restrict our own freedom to operate as we please. It is not surprising, therefore, that executives sometimes resent and even resist these limitations on their jobs and on their initiative to operate as they wish.

Such attitudes are never helpful and usually are harmful. They disclose ignorance of the nature of management, particularly with respect to how authority and responsibility are delegated downward.

Few people like change unless they initiate it themselves. It is understandable that officials working at high pressure may be momentarily disturbed by a management directive that makes a change necessary. The wise man will conceal any such annoyance, understanding that there is a good reason for the decision based on the judgment of persons higher in the organization than himself. In fact, it is common management practice today to set forth the reasons for any change, preferably before or at the time of the announcement, but in any event soon thereafter. If, by inadvertence, a supervisor receives a management directive without explanation, he should make it his business to find out the reason for it.

DEVELOPMENT OF COMPETENCE

MANAGEMENT MUST BE LEARNED

From what has been said already about management, it should be evident that there is a complex system of skills, knowledges, and attitudes involved. The planning process alone requires a high order of thinking, sound judgment, and emotional stability. It is clear that no one is born with such attributes: they are to a large degree acquired and developed as we mature. Up until recently, people had to gain management competence the hard way—by trial and error or by imitation of others. Today fortunately opportunities are available in schools, professional associations, books, periodicals, and in the training program of many installations, by which learning can be greatly speeded up.

VARIATIONS IN APTITUDE TO MANAGE

There are however some practical aspects of executive development that should be kept in mind. One of these has to do with normal variations between different individuals in their *aptitudes to manage*. While everyone has to *learn* how to manage well, each of us possesses different characteristics and attributes that can hamper or facilitate our development. The man with a bad temper (one which he has not yet learned to control) will be handicapped to this extent in making correct decisions in some cases: the individual who readily sees matters in their true relations will tend to build an efficient organization. Each person varies in such attributes, habits, and feelings. Each has his own quota of strengths and of weaknesses. There are no *perfect* people and thus no perfect executives.

One special variation of aptitude to manage merits special attention. This is the tendency of an executive to delegate—or not to delegate—authority to his subordinates. The second condition is by far the more common; the hesitancy to release any authority; the insistence that everything be brought to his personal attention. Equally undesirable is the opposite extreme where a manager tries to delegate everything—including his responsibilities—to his employees. Most successful managers possess an aptitude to delegate wisely, that is to the maximum extent possible without loss of control.

APPRAISING MANAGEMENT PERFORMANCE

It is possible to appraise an executive's performance against the requirements of his job and estimate fairly well how he is doing. When we know the directions in which we are managing most effectively, we can use these strengths to better advantage. When we discover where our soft spots are, we can take steps to build them up. While it is true that anyone can develop his competence in any of the processes of management, progress will be slower and more difficult in those areas where we have less natural aptitude.

KNOWLEDGE, SKILLS, AND ATTITUDES

It does not take much research to secure evidence that the performance of most people in executive positions can be substantially improved. There are three main areas in which such improvements may be possible.

1. Knowledge: Some persons lack an understanding of what modern management really means. They have had little opportunity to review the developments that have taken place in the last few decades. They do not understand the principles on which scientific management is based.

2. Skills: Others may have read widely and kept themselves informed theoretically as to the doctrines of management, but have failed to apply the teaching of their daily work. They find it too difficult to change their habitual way of operating. They lack the skills and techniques necessary for doing a better job.

3. Attitudes: With some, the trouble is mainly one of attitude. They cannot seem to get rid of feelings and prejudices that are reducing their efficiency and precluding their development as executives. They lack motivation to change.

While we must give adequate attention to skills and knowledge, psychologists tell us that our emotions are the triggers that setoff our actions. We are moved to act in a certain way by our interests, desires, fears, or dislikes. We behave (or misbehave) in response to our feelings. If this is even partly true, our attitudes may be the key to the direction, the speed and the distance we will travel in improving our competence as managers.

Regardless of how effective our attitudes may be, without knowledge as a basis on which to act, our behavior as managers is not likely to improve. It has been said that "What we are up on, we are not down on." Familiarity with the doctrine as a result of participating in a training program, often creates interest and provides the incentives to change. Practice of the techniques also may bring about motivation to improve. Conversely, an appeal from someone at a higher level may arouse the desire to learn how to manage more competently. For most people, pride in superior accomplishment plus self-interest in their own growth will provide the incentives needed.

III. MAJOR QUALITIES OF LEADERSHIP

All of us probably have noticed that whenever two or more people get together, one individual usually seems to take the lead in what is said or done. It is a perfectly natural thing for leadership to show itself in this way and it points out that leadership is not something possessed by only a few people, but is inherent in all of us.

This points up the fact that each of us really has leadership qualities which can be developed for use with our work force. As supervisors, we know that in the long run we get more results from our employees when we lead them than when we drive them. Like everyone else, they accomplish more when they follow directions willingly than when they are motivated by fear of reprisals or loss of their jobs. What is important, then, is to identify these abilities and characteristics so that we can strengthen them.

We are not concerned with what makes great political, spiritual, or military leaders. We are interested in what will help us to become outstanding leaders of our employees. Let us see if we can identify some of the more important abilities and personal qualities useful in this situation. Think for a moment of a person you have worked for or with who, in your opinion, was a good leader.

ACTIONS TO IMPROVE LEADERSHIP

ABILITIES	PERSONAL QUALITIES
To see the goal	Resourcefulness
To plan work	Integrity
To delegate duties	Patience
To make decisions	Courtesy
To train workers	Loyalty

These qualities and abilities seem to be highly significant. Now the question arises as to what we can do to strengthen ourselves in these particulars. Shall we take a few of them and see if we can agree upon some direct ways to improve our leadership in those respects?

1. Seeing Goals

A good leader quickly senses what is to be done. This is the "I-know-where-we're-going" part of leadership. It can be developed *if* we—

- Listen or read attentively when missions are presented.
- Ask pertinent questions as to what is expected.
- Restate intelligibly to the group the part they need to know.
- Prepare plans to have them carried out.
- Include attention to safety, economy, and possible streamlining for greater efficiency.

2. Planning Work

This is the "I-plan-to-do-it-this-way" part of your job. This can be done better *if* each supervisor—

- Develops a "master plan." If feasible, gets employees to help.
- Explains this to workers so they will understand it. Lets them know where he plans to go.
- Keeps this plan constantly in mind. Sets immediate goals, intermediate goals, final goals, and reasonable time expectancy to reach each goal. Then GOES!

- Sees to it that work is properly distributed.
- Sees to it that his time is properly allocated to all operations.

3. Delegating Duties

This is the "will-you-do-this-for-me" part of the job. Each supervisor can do this better *if* he–

- Analyzes his own job to see how much of it he can delegate.
- Does not delegate all at once; begins with simpler things.
- Guides those to whom he has delegated responsibility so they may succeed in the performance of it.
- Remembers delegation does not relieve a supervisor of ultimate responsibility; therefore he must delegate carefully and wisely.

4. Making Decisions

This is the "I-have-decided" part of the job. Each supervisor can make better decisions *if* he–

- Profits by experience.
- Constantly evaluates previous decisions against their results.
- Consciously follows through on results of each decision.
- Sticks to his decision once made, if right, and plans for carrying it through.
- Develops the habit of making decisions promptly.
- Accepts full responsibility for each decision, once it is made.

5. Training Workers

This is the "here, let-me-show-you" part of the job. This can be done better *if* each supervisor–

- Understands all parts of each job so that he can concentrate on the "tough spots" and assist new workers or those on the job to master all parts of the job with equal skill.
- Sets up a training plan for each job, being careful not to attempt to instruct in more elements of the job than can be absorbed by the worker at any given time.

6. Being Resourceful

This is the "I'll-find-a-way-to-do-it" part of the job. A supervisor can be sure of finding a way *if* he–

- Keeps improving his own skill.
- Knows fully the abilities as well as the limitations of his men.
- Keeps constantly on the alert to find better and quicker ways of doing the job.
- Consults frequently about all parts of his job with others who may have good ideas too.

7. Displaying Integrity

This is the "count-on-me" part of the job. Other people will count on a supervisor *if* he–

- Makes honesty a practice in small ways as well as big ways.
- Deals absolutely fairly and squarely with all his men.
- Has no favorites.
- Makes a habit of consistency in administering corrective discipline.
- Doesn't overlook faults in one person and correct another for the same thing.
- Keeps promises to subordinates as well as superiors.

8. Being Patient

This is the "I-understand-now-let's-try-it-again" part of the job. Patience will become a habit *if* the supervisor–

- Recognizes the differences among people–that they are not all equally competent.
- Doesn't jump to conclusions.
- Gives each man a chance to explain.
- Takes time enough to be sure each man understands what he tells him–gives him a chance to ask questions.
- Remembers "haste makes waste." "Slow down to a run." He will accomplish more by not losing his head.

9. Showing Courtesy

This is the "please" and "thank you" part of the job. Courtesy becomes a habit *if* each supervisor–

- Follows the golden rule.
- Remembers the other fellow has feelings too; respects them.
- Follows the rule that courtesy begets courtesy.
- Realizes that there is always time to be a gentleman.

10. Being Loyal

This is the "I've-got-a-fine-group-working-with-me" part of the job. Each supervisor can do this part better *if* he –

– Looks for the good in each.
– Concentrates on the good points instead of the faults.
– Realizes that how his men perform is largely up to him.
– Stands by them and shows his faith in them.
– Defends them; he is at the same time defending himself.
– Refuses to listen to petty gossip about any one of them.
– Doesn't criticize unless he has a reason, and then speaks only to the man himself.

Now, push forward! Test yourself and practice for your test with the carefully constructed quizzes that follow. Each one presents the kind of question you may expect on your test. And each question is at just the level of difficulty that may be expected. Don't try to take all the tests at one time. Rather, schedule yourself so that you take a few at each session, and spend approximately the same time on them at each session. Score yourself honestly, and date each test. You should be able to detect improvement in your performance on successive sessions.

LEADERSHIP TEST

DIRECTIONS: For each of the following questions, select the choice which best answers the question or completes the statement.

Correct key answers to all these test questions will be found at the end of the test.

1. One of the important leadership functions of a supervisor is to develop a feeling of belonging in those whom he supervises. In developing this feeling which of the following is the *least* important?

   (A) encouraging participation by asking for advice and help on problems pertaining to work and production
   (B) refraining from excessive interference and over-supervision
   (C) providing plans and material for a steady workload
   (D) keeping the group informed on progress of work
   (E) discovering the political, religious, and economic background of his subordinates so as to better understand them.

2. If a supervisor rarely has actual problems or difficulties reported to him or discussed with him by his men, it is mostly likely that

   (A) the men are unusually competent
   (B) he is fortunate in having a group so self-sufficient
   (C) he is unapproachable or not respected
   (D) he is a very competent supervisor
   (E) the men are hiding their own shortcomings.

3. Which of the following devices for motivating personnel is most likely to have undesirable by-products? An appeal to:

   (A) values related to the learning objective
   (B) the desire for social approval
   (C) the desire to fulfill existing standards and ideals
   (D) a sense of competition and rivalry between individuals

4. It is generally accepted that the two most important psychological needs of men are:

   (A) comfort and discipline
   (B) discipline and recognition
   (C) recognition and security
   (D) security and comfort

5. Understanding of human behavior is primarily a matter of understanding the ________ accounting for that behavior. The word or phrase which best fills the blank in the above sentence is:

   (A) environment
   (B) instinct
   (C) motives
   (D) physiological needs
   (E) mores.

6. One of the factors making it difficult to introduce new methods which will alter procedures that have been in existence for some time is the nearly universal tendency of people to:

   (A) like something old merely because it is old
   (B) distrust management
   (C) dislike change
   (D) change rapidly in their likes and dislikes
   (E) dislike something new merely because it is new.

7. Three mechanics are needed to complete a repair job in half the time required by one mechanic. This situation most aptly illustrates the operation of law of:

   (A) supply and demand
   (B) diminishing returns
   (C) cause and effect
   (D) regression toward the mean
   (E) fractional utility

8. Studies of driving ability (involvement in accidents) and various psychophysical characteristics (depth perception reaction time, etc.) generally show a relationship which is:

   (A) direct (B) inverse (C) insignificant

9. In assigning work to his subordinates, a supervisor is most likely to lose the respect of his subordinates if he:

   (A) reviews with a new employee the main points of an oral order issued to this employee
   (B) issues written orders instead of oral orders when a subordinate has repeatedly failed to carry out oral orders
   (C) gives oral orders regarding a task which the subordinate has performed satisfactorily in the past
   (D) gives an oral order which he feels the subordinate will not carry out.

10. If you find that one of your subordinates is becoming apathetic towards his work, you should:

    (A) prefer charges against him
    (B) warn him if his work does not improve you will report him to the head of the department
    (C) request his transfer
    (D) advise him to take a medical examination

11. You are in charge of several small units, each of which has its own supervisor. A brilliant young college graduate has been appointed as a clerk and assigned to one of these units. He proves to be difficult to control, does not get along well with his fellow employees and shows little respect for his supervisor, whom he chooses to ignore on every occasion possible. One morning you receive a note from him suggesting a minor improvement in the work of his unit. You believe the idea to be a good one. The best of the following procedures is to first:

    (A) call in the supervisor, discuss the idea with him and then put it into effect
    (B) call in this employee and explain the need for definite lines of authority; give the letter back to him and ask him to discuss his idea with his supervisor
    (C) put the idea into effect
    (D) send the letter to the immediate supervisor for suggestions.

12. "In the clinical approach to disciplinary problems, attention is focused on the basic causes of which the overt reactions are merely symptomatic rather than on the specific violations which have brought the employee unfavorable notice." The most accurate implication of of this quotation is that the clinical approach:

    (A) places emphasis on the actual violation rather than on the cause of the violation
    (B) attempts to promote greater insight into the underlying factors which have led to the infractions
    (C) does not evaluate the justness and utility of applying a specific penalty in a given situation
    (D) avoids the necessity for disciplinary action.

13. As division head, you learn, through a direct appeal from an individual, that one of the supervisors in your command has made an apparently unwise decision. In such a situation, it would be best for you to:

    (A) countermand the order, explaining to the supervisor your reasons
    (B) refuse to interfere in a matter within the jurisdiction of your supervisor
    (C) discuss the matter privately with your supervisor, allowing him to execute whatever changes are necessary
    (D) support the decision of your supervisor in order to preserve his prestige and authority
    (E) present the matter to the complainant from the point of view of your supervisor.

14. A supervisor may make assignments to his subordinates in the form of a command, a request, or a call for volunteers. It is *least* desirable for a supervisor to make an assignment in the form of a command when:

    (A) a serious emergency has risen
    (B) an employee objects to carrying out an assignment
    (C) the assignment must be completed immediately
    (D) the assignment is an unpleasant one.

15. "It has come to be realized that from the standpoint of control, the certainty of punishment for a breach of duty is more important than the severity of punishment." From this statement, it follows that:

    (A) disciplinary action for errors or violations should be administered without exception
    (B) dismissal is an admission of failure to supervise a subordinate effectively
    (C) it is less important to impress an offender with his guilt than with the inevitability of punishment
    (D) more emphasis should be placed on the punishment aspect as the offenses increase in seriousness
    (E) the repetition of an offense requires greater or stricter disciplinary action.

16. When a supervisor learns that a subordinate has "gone over his head," the supervisor should:

    (A) insist that the subordinate follow regular administrative channels
    (B) ignore the complaint
    (C) use some other situation to show the subordinate how important it is for authority to be recognized
    (D) submerge his personal feelings and make as objective a study of the complaint as possible
    (E) fully investigate the possibility of violation of the rules by the subordinate.

17. A unit supervisor becomes aware that one of his subordinates has a personal problem which is causing the subordinate considerable concern and is beginning to affect his work. Of the following, the action which it would generally be best for the unit supervisor to take is to:

    (A) ignore the mater, but, if the subordinate brings the matter up, politely tell him that it is not proper for a unit supervisor to discuss personal problems of subordinates
    (B) make the subordinate aware that he may discuss personal problems with his unit supervisor who will offer whatever assistance he can, compatible with the duties of his job
    (C) refer the matter to his own supervisor
    (D) indicate that he would like to help solve the problem and insist that the subordinate provide full details.

18. An experienced subordinate complains to his unit supervisor that the latter's continual very close supervision of his work is unnecessary and annoying. The unit supervisor is a recently appointed assistant supervisor. In this case, it would generally be best for the unit supervisor to:

    (A) ask the subordinate to explain his complaint further, telling him that it will receive consideration, and then re-evaluate his supervisory practices, seeking advice from his own supervisor if necessary
    (B) assure the subordinate that there had been no intention of singling him out, but that, as a subordinate, he will have to get used to new supervisory methods employed by new, wide-awake supervisors
    (C) explain to the subordinate that it is the job of the unit supervisor to supervise him and that he should understand his role and be able to overcome his annoyance
    (D) promise the subordinate that the annoying supervisory methods will be discontinued, but remind him that the unit supervisor must be respected and looked to for assistance, training, and supervision.

19. When subordinates in a particular unit are guilty of infractions, it is the practice of the unit supervisor to give necessary warnings or reprimands in a jocular manner. This practice is generally:

    (A) unwise, because humorous or jocular aspects should be kept from relationships between assistant supervisors and subordinates
    (B) unwise, because it leaves the subordinate unsure of the true intent or extent of the discipline
    (C) wise, because it makes the subordinate realize that there is no personal animosity involved
    (D) wise, because it reduces the severity of the warning or reprimand.

20. A unit supervisor notices one of his subordinates reading a novel at his desk during working hours. This is the first time that this has happened. This investigator is an experienced employee who does above average work. For the unit supervisor to ignore the situation is:
   (A) wise, since it is never desirable to penalize a good employee because of any single incident
   (B) unwise, since it may be interpreted by the staff as condoning inattention to work
   (C) wise, since democratic supervision allows employees leeway to apportion their work day as they see fit
   (D) unwise, since it is necessary to take strong action at the first sign of insubordination.

21. In order to improve the work of an experienced employee who usually does average work, the one of the following actions which it would generally be best for the supervisor to take is to:
   (A) allow the employee to be self-directed and unsupervised except where there is a large outlay of money involved
   (B) apply strict discipline to any signs of laxness or inattention to duty
   (C) carefully list and document every error made by the employee and inform him of them
   (D) use praise as a device to motivate the employee to do better work.

Answer Sheet

1	A	B	C	D	E	2	A	B	C	D	E	3	A	B	C	D	E	4	A	B	C	D	E
5	A	B	C	D	E	6	A	B	C	D	E	7	A	B	C	D	E	8	A	B	C	D	E
9	A	B	C	D	E	10	A	B	C	D	E	11	A	B	C	D	E	12	A	B	C	D	E
13	A	B	C	D	E	14	A	B	C	D	E	15	A	B	C	D	E	16	A	B	C	D	E
17	A	B	C	D	E	18	A	B	C	D	E	19	A	B	C	D	E	20	A	B	C	D	E
21	A	B	C	D	E																		

Correct Answers For The Foregoing Questions

To assist you in scoring yourself we have provided Correct Answers alongside your Answer Sheet. May we therefore suggest that while you are doing the test you cover the Correct Answers with a sheet of white paper.....to avoid temptation and to arrive at an accurate estimate of your ability and progress.

SCORE 1

.... %

NO. CORRECT

NO. OF QUESTIONS ON THIS TEST

1. E	7. B	13. C	19. B
2. C	8. C	14. D	20. B
3. D	9. D	15. A	21. D
4. C	10. B	16. D	
5. C	11. B	17. B	
6. C	12. B	18. A	

SCORE 2

.... %

NO. CORRECT

NO. OF QUESTIONS ON THIS TEST

MANAGING EMPLOYEES

DIRECTIONS: For each of the following questions, select the choice which best answers the question or completes the statement.

Correct key answers to all these test questions will be found at the end of the test.

1. It has been the practice of a supervising officer to preface his issuing of some orders or instructions with the statement that he is giving them "for the record." In this way, indication is clearly made that observance will not be insisted upon. The major weakness of this approach is that:

   (A) older subordinates will tend to resent orders which are not meant to be enforced
   (B) the authority of the supervising officer is undermined to the point of ineffectiveness
   (C) requests for instructions or orders in writing will tend to increase rather than diminish
   (D) subordinates are uncertain whether or not to comply
   (E) discretionary orders will tend to replace those that are mandatory.

2. A generally accepted principle of supervision is that no individual can successfully handle more than a limited number of immediate supervisory contacts. This limit of control is principally a matter of the limits of:

   (A) functionalization of duties
   (B) work knowledge
   (C) type of the organization
   (D) time and energy
   (E) size of the organization.

3. "Probably the most important part of supervision is to stimulate subordinates to want to do the required work and to prepare themselves to perform more and better work." The one of the following which is the most important part of this type of supervision is:

   (A) rewarding superior work
   (B) carefully planning all work
   (C) satisfying the needs of subordinates
   (D) conducting training courses
   (E) delegating all responsibility.

4. A problem that confronts a new supervisor in relationship to his subordinates and which requires the exercise of an unusual degree of skill and diplomacy is:

   (A) selection of competent personnel
   (B) planning the work of each employee
   (C) changing established ideas
   (D) choosing personal friends.

5. Successful administration requires the exercise of good judgment on the part of each supervisor. One method by which an executive may evaluate this factor in those supervisors within his jurisdiction is:

   (A) to determine the character of the employee morale within each unit from reports required of the supervisors
   (B) by the general physical appearance of the organizational unit
   (C) to note the supervisors' appreciation of the relative importance of current and impending work
   (D) to compare departmental expense with supervisors' salaries.

6. Good supervision is essentially a matter of:

   (A) patience in training workers
   (B) care in selecting workers
   (C) skill in human relations
   (D) fairness in maintaining discipline.

7. The one of the following functions which should always be considered as being within the scope of supervisory responsibilities is the:

(A) recruitment of well-qualified personnel
(B) evaluation of employee's performance
(C) classification of positions
(D) reclassification of well qualified employees
(E) decision as to relative seniority rights.

8. Among the following indications of the effectiveness of the work of a higher-level supervisor, the most important is the extent to which:

(A) his influence and policies are operative even though he has little direct contact with most of his subordinates
(B) he is familiar with the personality traits of all subordinate employees under his jurisdiction
(C) improvement has taken place in the portion of the agency under his jurisdiction
(D) he is in touch with actual procedures or operations in the part of the agency under his jurisdiction.

9. Supervision is so essential to effective operation as to justify the rule that every subordinate at the level of execution should be under the __________ supervision of a supervisor. The word which best fills the blank in the above sentence is:

(A) constant
(B) functional
(C) implied
(D) direct
(E) general.

10. "__________ consists of a study of a problem and the presentation of a solution in such form that all which remains to be done on the part of a supervisor is to indicate approval or disapproval of the recommended solution." The blank in the above quotation is best filled by:

(A) a field audit
(B) the scientific method
(C) completed staff work
(D) operations research
(E) factor analysis.

11. Generally speaking, the most neglected phase of first-line supervision is probably:

(A) carrying out orders
(B) laying out the work
(C) training new employees
(D) disciplining employees
(E) communicating employees' attitudes to management.

12. A realistic approach to effective supervision is to consider the importance of the individual: chiefly because

(A) any group of workers, regardless of size, is composed of individuals
(B) individuals of a crew all have different backgrounds
(C) injustices can be guarded against by using this approach
(D) it is the modern approach to achieving maximum production
(E) by appreciating individual differences a smoothly operating crew can be built.

13. The chief reason it is important for a supervisor to take prompt action upon requests and suggestions from subordinates is that:

(A) the supervisor will be unable to organize his own work effectively if he accumulates a backlog of employee requests and suggestions
(B) the liklihood of favorable action is greater when a decision is promptly made
(C) such action maintains the good morale of his subordinates
(D) the department will suffer economic loss from delayed adoption of suggestions.

14. In order to assure effective supervision in an organization it is important for a supervisor, beginning his job, to know:

(A) the history and progress of the organization
(B) the progress of other agencies doing similar work
(C) the nature and scope of his authority in each field in which he functions
(D) the policy of promotion for the employees of the organization.

15. The standards required of the supervisor should be higher than those expected of his subordinates in regard to:
    - (A) punctuality
    - (B) physical strength
    - (C) skill in one phase of the work
    - (D) ability to instruct men.

16. Although the methods and immediate aims of supervision should vary with the level and the nature of each employee's function the primary purpose is the same in most instances and can be said to be:
    - (A) improvement of employee performance
    - (B) development of promotion material at all levels
    - (C) attainment by each employee of his full capacity for self direction
    - (D) channeling of information through administrative lines.

Answer Sheet

1	A	B	C	D	E	2	A	B	C	D	E	3	A	B	C	D	E	4	A	B	C	D	E
5	A	B	C	D	E	6	A	B	C	D	E	7	A	B	C	D	E	8	A	B	C	D	E
9	A	B	C	D	E	10	A	B	C	D	E	11	A	B	C	D	E	12	A	B	C	D	E
13	A	B	C	D	E	14	A	B	C	D	E	15	A	B	C	D	E	16	A	B	C	D	E

Correct Answers For The Foregoing Questions

To assist you in scoring yourself we have provided Correct Answers alongside your Answer Sheet. May we therefore suggest that while you are doing the test you cover the Correct Answers with a sheet of white paper.....to avoid temptation and to arrive at an accurate estimate of your ability and progress.

SCORE 4

.... %

NO. CORRECT

NO. OF QUESTIONS ON THIS TEST

1. D	5. C	9. D	13. C
2. D	6. C	10. C	14. C
3. A	7. B	11. E	15. D
4. C	8. A	12. E	16. A

SCORE 3

.... %

NO. CORRECT

NO. OF QUESTIONS ON THIS TEST

Practice Using Answer Sheets

DIRECTIONS:

Read each question and its lettered answers. When you have decided which answer is correct, blacken the corresponding space on this sheet with a No. 2 pencil. Make your mark as long as the pair of lines, and completely fill the area between the pair of lines. If you change your mind, erase your first mark COMPLETELY. Make no stray marks; they may count against you.

SAMPLE

I. CHICAGO is
I-1 a country
I-2 a mountain
I-3 an island
I-4 a city
I-5 a state

I 1 2 3 4 5 (space 4 blackened)

SCORES

1______ 5______
2______ 6______
3______ 7______
4______ 8______

T F	T F	T F	T F
1 a b c d e	2 a b c d e	3 a b c d e	4 a b c d e
5 a b c d e	6 a b c d e	7 a b c d e	8 a b c d e
9 a b c d e	10 a b c d e	11 a b c d e	12 a b c d e
13 a b c d e	14 a b c d e	15 a b c d e	16 a b c d e
17 a b c d e	18 a b c d e	19 a b c d e	20 a b c d e
21 a b c d e	22 a b c d e	23 a b c d e	24 a b c d e
25 a b c d e	26 a b c d e	27 a b c d e	28 a b c d e
29 a b c d e	30 a b c d e	31 a b c d e	32 a b c d e
33 a b c d e	34 a b c d e	35 a b c d e	36 a b c d e
37 a b c d e	38 a b c d e	39 a b c d e	40 a b c d e
41 a b c d e	42 a b c d e	43 a b c d e	44 a b c d e
45 a b c d e	46 a b c d e	47 a b c d e	48 a b c d e
49 a b c d e	50 a b c d e	51 a b c d e	52 a b c d e
53 a b c d e	54 a b c d e	55 a b c d e	56 a b c d e
57 a b c d e	58 a b c d e	59 a b c d e	60 a b c d e
61 a b c d e	62 a b c d e	63 a b c d e	64 a b c d e
65 a b c d e	66 a b c d e	67 a b c d e	68 a b c d e
69 a b c d e	70 a b c d e	71 a b c d e	72 a b c d e
73 a b c d e	74 a b c d e	75 a b c d e	76 a b c d e
77 a b c d e	78 a b c d e	79 a b c d e	80 a b c d e
81 a b c d e	82 a b c d e	83 a b c d e	84 a b c d e
85 a b c d e	86 a b c d e	87 a b c d e	88 a b c d e
89 a b c d e	90 a b c d e	91 a b c d e	92 a b c d e
93 a b c d e	94 a b c d e	95 a b c d e	96 a b c d e
97 a b c d e	98 a b c d e	99 a b c d e	100 a b c d e
101 a b c d e	102 a b c d e	103 a b c d e	104 a b c d e
105 a b c d e	106 a b c d e	107 a b c d e	108 a b c d e
109 a b c d e	110 a b c d e	111 a b c d e	112 a b c d e
113 a b c d e	114 a b c d e	115 a b c d e	116 a b c d e
117 a b c d e	118 a b c d e	119 a b c d e	120 a b c d e
121 a b c d e	122 a b c d e	123 a b c d e	124 a b c d e
125 a b c d e	126 a b c d e	127 a b c d e	128 a b c d e
129 a b c d e	130 a b c d e	131 a b c d e	132 a b c d e
133 a b c d e	134 a b c d e	135 a b c d e	136 a b c d e
137 a b c d e	138 a b c d e	139 a b c d e	140 a b c d e
141 a b c d e	142 a b c d e	143 a b c d e	144 a b c d e
145 a b c d e	146 a b c d e	147 a b c d e	148 a b c d e
149 a b c d e	150 a b c d e		

IV. QUIZZES THAT TEACH

This selection of questions is particularly important and relevant in preparing you for the exam. The questions come from many previous exams. In selecting them we discovered and eliminated a good number of duplicate and repetitive questions. So, what you have here is a concise presentation of those points in this field which examiners consider to be significant. Study and answer them carefully. Correct answers appear at the end of the set.

Most questions of this type are "situation" questions in which some more-or-less practical shop situation is depicted in a few sentences and the candidate is asked to select the one of a number of suggested responses which is the best. Many can be answered on the basis of the most logical common sense solution.

The questions on the following pages have been selected from a number of foreman-selection tests in different types of organizations.

Keep in mind when answering these questions that your answers should show the following qualities:

1. Forcefulness
2. Ability to command respect
3. Impartiality
4. Self-control
5. Personal interest in the men under you
6. Ability to train men
7. Ability to give clear and detailed instructions
8. Ability to follow up and see that instructions are carried out
9. Ability to make proper use of suggestions from subordinates
10. Ability to inspire teamwork
11. Ability to praise wisely and reprimand effectively
12. Ability to create a spirit of accomplishment
13. Self-confidence
14. Ability to build self-confidence, especially in new employees
15. Ability to develop enthusiasm among your crew of workers.

Now, push forward! Test yourself and practice for your test with the carefully constructed quizzes that follow. Each one presents the kind of question you may expect on your test. And each question is at just the level of difficulty that may be expected. Don't try to take all the tests at one time. Rather, schedule yourself so that you take a few at each session, and spend approximately the same time on them at each session. Score yourself honestly, and date each test. You should be able to detect improvement in your performance on successive sessions.

A portion of the standard answer sheet is provided after each test for marking your answers in the way you'll be required to do on the actual exam. At the right of this answer sheet, to make the scoring job simpler (after you have derived your own answers), you'll find our correct answers.

TEST ONE

ORGANIZING THE WORK

DIRECTIONS: For each of the following questions, select the choice which best answers the question or completes the statement.

Correct key answers to all these test questions will be found at the end of the test.

1. The main reason for keeping records on labor and material on each job handled in the shop is to
   (A) permit evaluation of past performance and to indicate the future policy and future operation of the shop
   (B) prevent theft by the mechanics on the job
   (C) eliminate all the "dead wood" from the shop personnel
   (D) provide work for the foreman.
   (E) It is part of the "red tape" that is found in most large organizations.
2. A new helper, with no previous experience, is assigned to your gang. Normally, the man should *first* be
   (A) made familiar with the layout of the entire power station
   (B) informed of the safety and other rules immediately applicable to him
   (C) given a copy of the operating instructions
   (D) taught to perform the simplest routine procedures.
3. It is correct to state that manpower is generally wasted by
   (A) rotating job assignments
   (B) lack of planning
   (C) expending time in training programs
   (D) having helpers to assist maintainers.
4. Assume that you are appointed as a foreman and are assigned to a section with which you are not familiar. Of the following, the best procedure for you to follow first is to
   (A) reorganize the routine work of the section so that it is more nearly like what you have been accustomed to in your former section
   (B) enforce stricter discipline in order to demonstrate your authority
   (C) acquaint yourself with the existing methods of work in this section
   (D) disregard minor violations by the men in order to gain their friendship and good will
   (E) request an increase in personnel so that the work will be done more quickly.

5. A properly operated stock room should contain
   (A) all replacement parts for all the types of vehicles used in the department, so as to make it possible to replace any part in any vehicle immediately
   (B) only those replacement parts which are usually difficult to obtain quickly. Parts frequently used but easily obtained should be requisitioned for purchase as needed for each job
   (C) only those parts which are not carried or accounted for in the budget
   (D) an adequate stock of those parts which past experience indicates will be needed for maintenance and repair in the near future.

6. In case of illness, a foreman may be absent from work for several days. Of the following, the best action a foreman can take to insure that the work of his gang will proceed normally would be to
   (A) make an agreement with a foreman of a nearby gang to watch the men when he is away
   (B) prepare a schedule of advance work assignments which is always readily available
   (C) tell the men to perform any fill-in job they can think of whenever you are absent
   (D) call up one of his competent men at the shop and assign him to supervise the gang.

7. Waste of materials may be most effectively reduced by
   (A) keeping records of material usage
   (B) never drawing out more than one day's supply of materials
   (C) posting general conservation notices
   (D) docking the employees' pay for any wasted material.

8. A newly appointed foreman becomes so involved trying to maintain certain office records initiated by the previous foreman that he finds he has insufficient time to devote to his regular duties. The best action would be to
   (A) inform his assistant supervisor of the problem to ascertain if any of these records may be discontinued
   (B) appoint a senior maintainer to take over part of his duties as foreman
   (C) ignore these records and devote his time to his regular duties
   (D) work on his own time to keep these records up to date.

9. Waste of materials and supplies can most effectively be reduced by a foreman if he
   (A) constantly prods his men on this topic
   (B) periodically posts conservation notices
   (C) indirectly threatens to dock those who are found wasting supplies
   (D) never draws any more supplies than he feels are needed.

10. As a foreman, it is necessary for you to know that your men are learning the work properly. A good practical method for a foreman to use in determining this in the case of a new helper is to
    (A) assume that if he asks no questions he knows the work
    (B) ask the other men how this man is making out
    (C) follow-up and inspect the work which is assigned to him
    (D) question him directly on methods.

11. If a foreman insists on perfection in each job performed by his men, the probable result would be
    (A) fast output of excellent quality work
    (B) that the men would insist on perfection in the foreman
    (C) resentment and reduced output
    (D) to increase individual initiative.

12. After you have shown a man how to do a new job, the best follow up step to take is to
    (A) watch him carefully whenever he does this job
    (B) ask him from time to time how he is getting along
    (C) check from time to time on the performance of this job
    (D) ask another experienced man to check the man's work frequently.

13. One important advantage of standardizing work procedures is that it
    (A) provides an incentive for good work
    (B) makes the work less monotonous
    (C) develops all around skills
    (D) enables the work to be done with less supervision.

Correct Answers

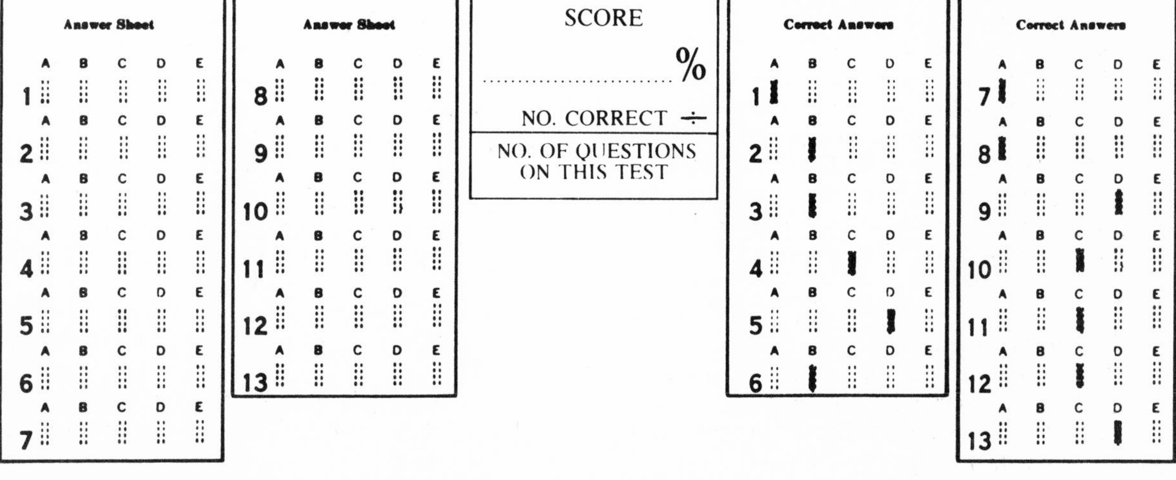

TEST TWO

GIVING INSTRUCTIONS

DIRECTIONS: Below each of the following passages, you will find questions or incomplete statements about the passage. Each statement or question is followed by lettered words or expressions. Select the word or expression that most satisfactorily completes each statement or answers each question in accordance with the meaning of the passage. Write the letter of that word or expression on your answer paper.

Correct key answers to all these test questions will be found at the end of the test.

1. As a foreman, it is necessary for you to know that your men are learning the work properly. A good practical method to use in determining this in the case of a new helper is to
   (A) question him directly on details of the work
   (B) ask the other men how this man is making out
   (C) inspect and follow-up the work which is assigned to him
   (D) assume that if he asks no questions, he knows the work.
2. In connection with the use of tools by his men, a foreman should give the most attention to
   (A) their proper use
   (B) recommendations for improvement in design
   (C) prevention of their loss by theft
   (D) their proper cleanliness after use.
3. Suppose a foreman finds that many jobs under his supervision are often delayed in completion because the men must wait for him to make decisions on the work. This situation would most likely be due to
   (A) lack of encouragement from the foreman
   (B) the fact that the foreman's orders lack clarity and completeness
   (C) not setting a time limit on each job
   (D) the fact the foreman is too easy-going with the men.
4. Assume that a recently appointed man is assigned to your gang and that this man has very little experience on the type of work performed by your gang. This man would be best broken in by
   (A) giving him your individual personal attention until he becomes proficient
   (B) having him read books on the work
   (C) immediately assigning him his full duties and allow him to learn by doing
   (D) assigning him to work with an experienced man who will help him along.
5. One of the new helpers in your gang complains to you, his foreman, that he is continually being sent on "fool errands" because he is green on shop terminology. In this case, you should
   (A) tell him he shouldn't mind because he will have his chance to do the same with any new helpers who come in after him
   (B) tell him to use similar tactics on those who are making a fool of him
   (C) warn the entire gang that such practical jokes must stop
   (D) search out the offenders and bring them up on charges.
6. If a foreman does *not* insist on perfection for every job performed by his men, the probable result would be that
   (A) the men would never turn out a perfect job
   (B) good work would still be turned out
   (C) the general attitude would be to always turn out careless work
   (D) the work output would be small.
7. A supervisory practice which is very likely to lead to confusion in a gang of men is for the foreman to

(A) issue detailed orders only in writing
(B) directly transmit simple orders verbally
(C) relay his orders to the men through their co-workers
(D) follow up his orders after issuing them.

8. A good principle to follow, after teaching a procedure to one of your new men, is to
(A) tell him you expect he will make many mistakes at first
(B) assume he knows the procedure if he has no questions to ask
(C) have him write out the procedure from memory
(D) observe his subsequent procedure and point out any errors he makes.

Correct Answers For The Foregoing Questions

To assist you in scoring yourself we have provided Correct Answers alongside your Answer Sheet. May we therefore suggest that while you are doing the test you cover the Correct Answers with a sheet of white paper.....to avoid temptation and to arrive at an accurate estimate of your ability and progress.

Answer Sheet

	A	B	C	D	E
1					
2					
3					
4					
5					
6					
7					
8					

SCORE

.... %

NO. CORRECT ÷

NO. OF QUESTIONS ON THIS TEST

Correct Answers

	A	B	C	D	E
1			▮		
2	▮				
3		▮			
4				▮	
5			▮		
6		▮			
7			▮		
8				▮	

TEST THREE

GETTING ALONG WITH THE BOSSES

The following carefully selected, actual, previous examination questions cover key points of a topic likely to be brought up on your examination. This has appeared before, often. Therefore, we're certain you'll benefit from the concise summary provided by this quizzer. Write your own answers then check with the correct answers which will appear after the last question in this series.

Correct key answers to all these test questions will be found at the end of the test.

1. As a foreman, one of the best ways of cooperating with your superior would be to
   (A) constantly bring him new ideas for him to determine the advantages and disadvantages
   (B) ask him to decide all problems which may arise
   (C) accept full responsibility for the work assigned to your men
   (D) constantly bring him all the details of the work.

2. As a foreman you receive a written order which you know will be unpopular with the men and will be difficult to carry out, it would be good policy for you to
   (A) issue the order to your men but disregard any failure on their part to comply with the order
   (B) first explain to your superior the difficulties you foresee and ask if the order can be modified
   (C) ask the men to prepare a petition signed by all the men affected by the order
   (D) issue the order, enforce it rigidly and tell the men to go to the union with any complaints.

3. Suppose your superior has given orders for a change in some of the work schedules of your crew. Your men complain to you about these changes. The proper thing to do is to
   (A) tell the men to complain to your superior, not to you
   (B) advise the men that nothing can be done, even if the complaints are correct
   (C) inform the men that the changes were not good and that you did not like them
   (D) tell the men that you will take up their complaints with your superior.

4. A foreman who finds that some of his senior workers have a better technical knowledge of the work of his gang than he has, should
   (A) ask for reassignment as foreman to another gang
   (B) make arrangements to be helped by his assistant supervisor
   (C) pick up the necessary knowledge by study and by close observation of the work
   (D) ask his men to teach him the work.

5. If you are advised that your superior has decided to make an on the spot time study of a certain job which is performed by your men, it would be advisable for you to
   (A) ask your supervisor why he is discriminating against you
   (B) request your men to work faster than usual on this job
   (C) profess ignorance of the proposal, if your men ask questions about it
   (D) briefly mention it to your men, requesting that they do this work at normal speed.

6. If an error is detected in an order issued by a superior, the foreman should
   (A) endeavor to carry out the order as is, because that is his duty
   (B) inform the superior of the error, as it probably is an oversight

(C) correct the error himself and carry out the corrected order since this is a foreman's prerogative
(D) not carry out the order, but put it aside and wait until the superior finds out for himself that he has made an error.

7. Your superior verbally orders you to perform a specific job and subsequently you realize that some of the details are not clear to you. As foreman you should
   (A) seek the advice of another foreman
   (B) carry out the directive to the best of your ability as this is all that can be expected of an ambiguous order
   (C) request that the order be put in writing because otherwise you have no recourse in the event of trouble
   (D) ask your superior to clarify the order.

8. Assume that you have been given a special assignment for several months. This necessitated the placing of a temporary foreman in your place. Upon your return you observe that the men do not seem to have the same interest in their work. The best course for you to follow would be to
   (A) follow your usual procedures, until you determine the underlying causes
   (B) prefer charges against the temporary foreman
   (C) argue this matter with the temporary foreman, until you are quite certain why the morale is low
   (D) call the men together and tell them the holiday is over.

9. Because of unusual circumstances, your gang is assigned a special job in addition to their regular assignments, and your superior informs you no additional help is available and no overtime will be permitted. To satisfy your superior, it would be best for you to
   (A) tell the men they must work at a faster rate
   (B) sacrifice quality in order to get the additional work done
   (C) personally help out your gang in order to complete the work
   (D) proceed as usual, and when the special job is not completed in the allotted time, your superior will find out for himself that he was wrong in making such a request.

10. Another foreman comes to you and states that his gang is complaining about their work-load as compared with the apparent work-load of your gang. In this case, it would be best for you to
   (A) tell this foreman his problems are his own worry and that your men are doing a day's work
   (B) immediately reprimand your men for their behavior
   (C) tell this foreman to take the matter up with the supervisor
   (D) show that your men do a full day's work pointing out any conditions which make it appear otherwise.

Correct Answers

(First write your own answers. Then compare them with these answers.)

Answer Sheet

	A	B	C	D	E
1					
2					
3					
4					
5					
6					
7					
8					
9					
10					

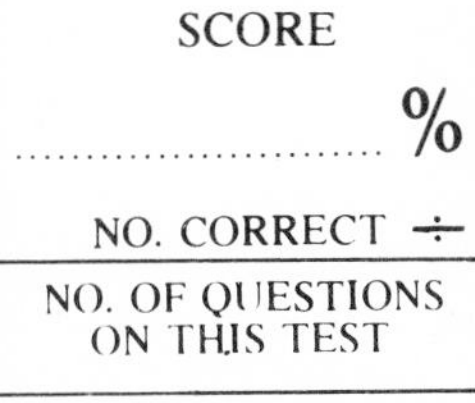
SCORE

.... %

NO. CORRECT ÷

NO. OF QUESTIONS ON THIS TEST

Correct Answers

	A	B	C	D	E
1			■		
2		■			
3				■	
4			■		
5				■	
6		■			
7				■	
8	■				
9			■		
10				■	

TEST FOUR

EMPLOYEE RELATIONS

DIRECTIONS: Below each of the following passages you will find one or more incomplete statements about the passage. Select the words or expressions that most satisfactorily complete each statement in accordance with the meaning of the paragraph.

Correct key answers to all these test questions will be found at the end of the test.

1. Occasionally some of the men in a gang will indulge in active horseplay. This should be
   (A) encouraged because it promotes good fellowship
   (B) permitted as it is a form of relaxation
   (C) discouraged because some of the men might not like it
   (D) stopped immediately because it is likely to cause accidents.
2. Assume that you have been appointed foreman of a group which includes, among others, some of your close friends. Some of the other men in the group have falsely accused you of favoritism. You should handle this situation by
   (A) asking for specific instances and disprove the charge
   (B) reporting the accusations to your superior
   (C) proving lack of favoritism by giving your friends all the undesirable jobs
   (D) telling your accusers that you are certain of the capabilities of your friends.
3. A good way of obtaining high quality work from the men is for the foreman to
   (A) give his men unusual privileges
   (B) compliment the men after each job
   (C) maintain a vigorous interest in each job
   (D) individually assist the men on every job.
4. You notice that one of your crew stops work an hour before "quitting" time although he produces as much work as his fellow workers. As foreman you should
   (A) assign him to more interesting work than he is doing at present
   (B) assign him more work than he can possibly handle
   (C) inform the man that you expect him to work until "quitting" time
   (D) report him to the assistant supervisor.
5. On returning from your vacation and resuming your assignment, you learn that the replacement foreman has changed some of your methods and procedures on his own authority. A good way to handle this situation is to
   (A) tell the replacement foreman that he had no authority to make any changes
   (B) automatically reinstate your previous methods and procedures
   (C) compare the merits of the replacement foreman's methods and procedures with yours and then make a choice
   (D) report the matter to your superior for his decision.
6. When it is necessary for a foreman to have some men work overtime, the best approach to the men is to
   (A) apologize for the necessity of having them work overtime
   (B) advise them that they were selected only because they are considered better workers
   (C) tell them that the order came from your superior and was not your fault
   (D) explain why overtime was necessary at this time.
7. Assume you are in charge of a gang of men who are continually manufacturing grievances. As foreman you should
   (A) prefer charges against the one you believe to be the ring leader
   (B) consult with your assistant supervisor on the appropriate action to take
   (C) inform the union delegate that it is his responsibility to see that these obstructive tactics cease
   (D) disregard the action of these men because they will change in due time.

8. It would be poor supervisory policy for a foreman to engage in a discussion with his men on
   (A) improvement of shop procedures
   (B) the labor activities of the various unions
   (C) improvement of shop working conditions
   (D) methods of securing good housekeeping.
9. If a foreman has a man working for him who is a fast worker but at times does poor quality work, the foreman should
   (A) do nothing to affect the speed of this worker
   (B) endeavor to give him work assignments that would require a minimum of skill and high output
   (C) compliment him for his high output
   (D) tell him that you are going to bring him up on charges.
10. If a foreman has a worker who is over confident and "cocky" in his attitude towards all work assignments, the foreman should
   (A) criticize all his work severely to hurt his pride
   (B) assign him repetitive work in order to correct this condition
   (C) give him a very forceful pep talk
   (D) give him some difficult assignments in order to attempt to correct this attitude.
11. Assume that you have a man in your gang who is very conscientious and does more and better work than anyone else. In this case, as his foreman, you should
   (A) grant him unusual privileges
   (B) persuade him to slow down because others resent a speed-up
   (C) make every effort to show him that his efforts are appreciated
   (D) assign him less work as a reward for his services.
12. If a foreman has a man in his gang who shows very little interest in the work assigned to him, it would be a good policy for the foreman to
   (A) give him work assignments which may stimulate his interest
   (B) hurt the man's pride by openly criticizing his attitude
   (C) always give him menial jobs since he probably is not qualified for any other kind of work
   (D) ignore the situation, since this is none of the foreman's business.
13. With respect to assigning work to men in his gang, a foreman should be guided mainly by
   (A) the likes and dislikes of his assistant supervisor
   (B) the aptitudes of his men
   (C) the speed with which a man performs his assignments
   (D) making certain menial jobs are not given to men who dislike them.
14. A newly appointed man in your gang makes blunders apparently regardless of the type of assignments given to him. You should
   (A) recommend his dismissal
   (B) refuse to give him further work assignments until he agrees to be more careful
   (C) ignore the condition since it will ultimately cure itself
   (D) try to determine the cause for the man's poor work before taking further action.
15. The best thing for a foreman to do if he finds himself definitely disliked by his men is to
   (A) ask a supervisor to talk to his men
   (B) take stock of himself to determine if he is at fault
   (C) supervise his men more rigidly
   (D) loosen up on his discipline of the men.
16. Assume you have a new man in your gang who is not yet an efficient worker. If this man makes a special request,
   (A) you should deny such requests until he fully earns his pay
   (B) base your decision on the merits of the request
   (C) tell him you have no right to grant any special requests
   (D) act favorably because you have no right to show partiality.
17. Suggestions on improving methods of doing work when submitted by a new employee should be
   (A) disregarded because he is too unfamiliar with the work to submit any worthwhile ideas
   (B) examined only for the purpose of judging the new man
   (C) ignored because it would make the old employees resentful
   (D) examined for possible merit because the new man may have a fresh viewpoint.
18. A good way for a foreman to retain the confidence of his men is to
   (A) say as little as possible
   (B) make infrequent checks on the work
   (C) make no promises unless they will be fulfilled
   (D) never hesitate in giving an answer to any question.
19. The job interest of the employees in your gang is best secured by
   (A) requesting their advice on all important matters
   (B) constantly bringing up new matters
   (C) creating in each man a sense of his individual importance to the job as a whole
   (D) the strictest impartiality.

20. If a foreman establishes a social relationship with his men, the result is most likely to be
   (A) loss of discipline
   (B) fewer accidents
   (C) increased respect from the men
   (D) greatly increased work output.

21. If a foreman has a man working for him who is lacking in self-confidence but is otherwise capable, the foreman should
   (A) give the man a forceful pep talk
   (B) criticize his work severely to hurt his pride
   (C) find out if the condition is caused by home problems
   (D) compliment the man's work whenever possible.

22. As a foreman, it is advisable for you to keep records of your jobs for future reference. Assume that in reviewing your records you find that whenever a certain worker has been one of the men assigned to a job, the job has taken appreciably longer than other similar jobs. In this case, you would do best to
   (A) warn the man against deliberate slowness so that he knows you are aware of the situation
   (B) take this fact into consideration when making up service rating reports
   (C) give closer supervision to future jobs to which this man is assigned
   (D) consult your assistant supervisor on the appropriate disciplinary action to be taken.

Correct Answers For The Foregoing Questions

To assist you in scoring yourself we have provided Correct Answers alongside your Answer Sheet. May we therefore suggest that while you are doing the test you cover the Correct Answers with a sheet of white paper.....to avoid temptation and to arrive at an accurate estimate of your ability and progress.

Answer Sheet

	A	B	C	D	E
1					
2					
3					
4					
5					
6					
7					
8					
9					
10					
11					
12					
13					
14					
15					
16					
17					
18					
19					
20					
21					
22					

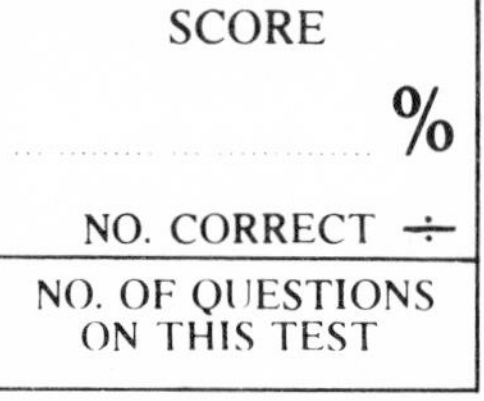
SCORE

%

NO. CORRECT ÷

NO. OF QUESTIONS ON THIS TEST

Correct Answers

	Answer
1	D
2	A
3	C
4	C
5	C
6	D
7	B
8	B
9	B
10	D
11	C
12	A
13	B
14	D
15	B
16	B
17	D
18	C
19	C
20	A
21	D
22	C

TEST FIVE

DISCIPLINE AND MORALE

DIRECTIONS: Below each of the following passages, you will find questions or incomplete statements about the passage. Each statement or question is followed by lettered words or expressions. Select the word or expression that most satisfactorily completes each statement or answers each question in accordance with the meaning of the passage. Write the letter of that word or expression on your answer paper.

Correct key answers to all these test questions will be found at the end of the test.

1. A newly appointed helper has made a blunder which has resulted in injury to an employee. As a foreman you should certainly
   (A) recommend the dismissal of the new helper
   (B) ignore the incident unless it recurs
   (C) study the accident for remedial action
   (D) reprimand his co-worker for not properly instructing the helper.
2. If the man assigned to an unpleasant routine job is not doing the job satisfactorily, you should immediately
   (A) reassign the job to another man
   (B) prefer charges against the man
   (C) reprimand the man in private
   (D) investigate the cause of poor performance.
3. A worker under your supervision is very talkative and often slows down the work of the gang by getting involved in long discussions and arguments on matters not connected with the work. A good way of handling this man would be to
   (A) Give him an assignment requiring contact with the least number of other employees
   (B) report him to your superior for slowing down the work
   (C) arrange for his transfer to another gang as soon as possible
   (D) allow the practice to continue as discussions are good for keeping up morale of the gang.
4. Effective discipline is best maintained by
   (A) never giving an inch
   (B) firmness in important matters
   (C) bringing all violators up on charges
   (D) watching the men constantly.
5. If a foreman has criticized one of his men for making a mistake, the foreman should
   (A) remind the man of his error from time to time in order to keep the man on his toes
   (B) overlook further errors which this man may make, otherwise this man may feel he is a victim of discrimination
   (C) impress this man with the fact that all his work will be closely checked from then on
   (D) forget the incident and give the man an opportunity to redeem himself.
6. A foreman will most likely secure the respect of his men if he
   (A) overlooks some of the rules and regulations
   (B) is very chummy with the men
   (C) pushes them constantly
   (D) knows his job thoroughly.
7. With respect to occasional minor infractions of working rules, the foreman's action should be guided by the practical consideration that
   (A) all violations must be punished
   (B) most violations are deliberate
   (C) the aim is to discourage violations
   (D) some violations are unintentional.
8. In administering discipline it is not a good rule for you, the foreman, to
   (A) reprimand the employee in private
   (B) reprimand an employee long after an error was committed

(C) allow the employee a chance to reply to your criticism
(D) be specific in criticizing an employee for his error.

9. Two of your best workers do not get along well with one another. You have spoken to each, but to no avail. It would probably be best to
   (A) fire them both to maintain discipline
   (B) have one of them transferred to another location
   (C) watch them carefully
   (D) fine one of them, as an example.

10. One of the mechanics in the shop is absent from work frequently enough to be disturbing to the regular routine of the shop. If you were the foreman, you would first

   (A) speak to the mechanic in an effort to determine the causes of absence and try to remedy the situation
   (B) write a report to the executive office indicating that the man is upsetting the routine of the shop
   (C) write a memorandum to your superior indicating that the man is upsetting the routine of the shop.

Correct Answers For The Foregoing Questions

To assist you in scoring yourself we have provided Correct Answers alongside your Answer Sheet. May we therefore suggest that while you are doing the test you cover the Correct Answers with a sheet of white paper.....to avoid temptation and to arrive at an accurate estimate of your ability and progress.

Answer Sheet

	A	B	C	D	E
1	⁞	⁞	⁞	⁞	⁞
2	⁞	⁞	⁞	⁞	⁞
3	⁞	⁞	⁞	⁞	⁞
4	⁞	⁞	⁞	⁞	⁞
5	⁞	⁞	⁞	⁞	⁞

Answer Sheet

	A	B	C	D	E
6	⁞	⁞	⁞	⁞	⁞
7	⁞	⁞	⁞	⁞	⁞
8	⁞	⁞	⁞	⁞	⁞
9	⁞	⁞	⁞	⁞	⁞
10	⁞	⁞	⁞	⁞	⁞

SCORE

.... %

NO. CORRECT ÷

NO. OF QUESTIONS ON THIS TEST

Correct Answers

	A	B	C	D	E
1	⁞	⁞	▮	⁞	⁞
2	⁞	⁞	⁞	▮	⁞
3	▮	⁞	⁞	⁞	⁞
4	⁞	▮	⁞	⁞	⁞
5	⁞	⁞	⁞	▮	⁞

Correct Answers

	A	B	C	D	E
6	⁞	⁞	⁞	▮	⁞
7	⁞	⁞	▮	⁞	⁞
8	⁞	▮	⁞	⁞	⁞
9	⁞	▮	⁞	⁞	⁞
10	▮	⁞	⁞	⁞	⁞

TEST SIX

RELATIONS AMONG EMPLOYEES

DIRECTIONS: For each of the following questions, select the choice which best answers the question or completes the statement.

Correct key answers to all these test questions will be found at the end of the test.

1. Assume that some of the older employees are discouraging newly appointed helpers assigned to your crew by grossly exaggerating the difficulties of the job. You should handle this situation by
   (A) segregating the older employees from the new helpers
   (B) ordering new helpers not to talk to the older employees
   (C) preferring charges against the older employees
   (D) emphasizing the good features to the helpers before assigning them.

2. An exceptionally capable man in your gang requests a transfer to another gang, apparently because of personal prejudice against some of the men in the gang. It would be good policy in this case for you to
   (A) recommend that the man be transferred
   (B) recommend the transfer of the men whom the man dislikes
   (C) refuse the request
   (D) reprimand him for his inability to get along with fellow workmen and transfer him.

3. One of the men in your gang complains to you that someone in the gang is continually playing practical jokes on him. He does not know the particular man responsible but he does want the joking stopped. The best thing for you, as foreman, to do is to
   (A) explain to the man that the practical joking should continue as it promotes good fellowship in the gang
   (B) tell the man to retaliate by playing practical jokes on the other members of the gang
   (C) warn the entire gang that all practical jokes must stop at once
   (D) have the complaining man transferred to another gang as soon as possible.

4. You are informed unofficially by another foreman that some of your men, who have been assigned to work by themselves, are loafing on the job. You should handle this situation by
   (A) telling the foreman that it is none of his business as they are not his men
   (B) calling the men together to your office and reprimanding them
   (C) changing the man's assignment so that they work under your direct supervision at all times
   (D) arranging to visit the men on the job at more frequent intervals.

5. Before attempting to settle a group grievance as compared with an individual case, the foreman should
   (A) check the record of previous complaints of each man in the group
   (B) clear his decision with a superior
   (C) check with each man to be sure his decision will be satisfactory
   (D) defer decision as long as possible to give the group a chance to forget the grievance.

6. Suppose that you observe one of your men spending a considerable amount of his working time talking to his co-workers, and yet at the end of the day he has turned out a nominal days output. As foreman, you should
   (A) give him more work so he has less time to talk
   (B) ignore his actions as long as his output is up to standard
   (C) tell him that you will bring him up on charges
   (D) tell the other workers to steer clear of him.

7. If it is apparent that two workers in your gang can not get along well together, the first thing you should do is to
   (A) assign them work, if possible, which will not bring them into close contact with each other
   (B) get the opinion of the other men on why these two don't get along
   (C) call this condition to the attention of a superior
   (D) have them both transferred out of your gang.

8. Two of your workers started to fight with one another. The procedure you should probably first follow is to
   (A) have them both fired
   (B) stop the fight
   (C) let the men fight it out
   (D) call the Police.

Correct Answers For The Foregoing Questions

To assist you in scoring yourself we have provided Correct Answers alongside your Answer Sheet. May we therefore suggest that while you are doing the test you cover the Correct Answers with a sheet of white paper.....to avoid temptation and to arrive at an accurate estimate of your ability and progress.

Answer Sheet

	A	B	C	D	E
1					
2					
3					
4					

Answer Sheet

	A	B	C	D	E
5					
6					
7					
8					

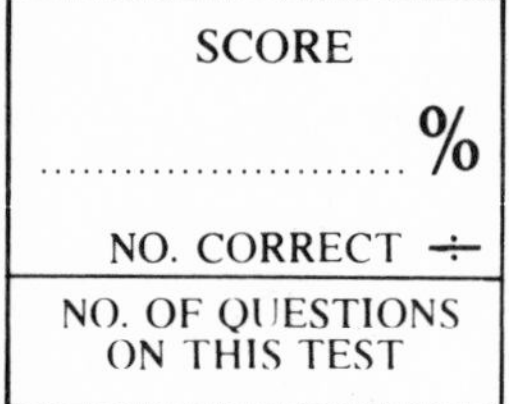
SCORE

.... %

NO. CORRECT ÷

NO. OF QUESTIONS ON THIS TEST

Correct Answers

	A	B	C	D	E
1				▮	
2			▮		
3			▮		
4				▮	

Correct Answers

	A	B	C	D	E
5		▮			
6	▮				
7	▮				
8		▮			

PART 4

Intensive Study Covering The Range Of Questions Put By Employers

THE WIDE WORLD OF JOB TESTS

Improve your vocabulary and you will improve yourself.

There is much evidence to show the close relationship between success and a good vocabulary. There are studies which show that the only common characteristic of successful people is an exceptionally good grasp of word meanings. The best executives, whether well educated or not, invariably score highest on word tests.

It would appear, then, that if you build up your word knowledge, you're going to help yourself get ahead for the simple reason that words are the tools of thought which can help you grasp the thoughts of others, and communicate your own ideas clearly to other people with whom you deal.

Twenty one pages of help and study for this vital subject are presented in TOP SCORES ON VOCABULARY TESTS and VOCABULARY TEST QUESTIONS FOR PRACTICE.

NAME AND NUMBER COMPARISONS tests are used in industry to test accuracy and speed.

Spatial relations tests such as MATCHING PARTS AND FIGURES, CUBE TURNING, TOUCHING CUBES, CUBE COUNTING, SOLID FIGURE TURNING and SIMILARITIES AND DIFFERENCES BETWEEN OBJECTS are used in a wide variety of tests leading to jobs. These are tests that do not depend on knowledge of language or understanding of words, so much as on the ability to work with diagrams and nonverbal symbols. They are frequently used in testing for jobs of a mechanical nature, as well as for ability to perform office and executive work.

TOOL RECOGNITION TESTS and MECHANICAL INSIGHT TESTS are given to applicants for mechanical type work and are used for promotion tests to foremen and plant executives. These chapters may not give you the actual questions you will have on your test, but they will familiarize you with the type of questions you are likely to encounter when adapted to your own trade.

With careful study of these practice questions, you will gain assurance and lose your fear of test questions of most types and you will be better able to understand exactly what is expected of you when you come to take your test.

Your study will be well *repaid*.

I. TOP SCORES ON READING TESTS

In the following pages you'll find every proven technique for succeeding with the reading comprehension question, the pitfall of many a test-taker. These methods have worked beautifully for thousands of ambitious people and they are certain to help you. They are well worth all the time you can afford to devote to them.

Students must be able to read the paragraphs quickly, and still be able to answer questions correctly. The more correct answers you can give, the better your score will be. But if there are twenty paragraphs, and you are able to finish only ten because you read slowly, obviously, you are going to get a score of 50 percent, even if you answer all the questions correctly. On the other hand, if you finish all the paragraphs but can only answer half of the questions correctly, you will still get only 50 percent. Your goal, then, is to build up enough speed to finish all the paragraphs, and at the same time give as many correct answers as possible.

Our goal is to help you reach your goal—and then some. We want you to get the best score possible on any test of reading comprehension; and we also want you to be able to read with enough speed and understanding so that your studying time is cut in half, and your pleasure reading time is multiplied.

You *can* upgrade your reading ability—but you must have a plan—a procedure—a method. First, let us understand that there are two aspects of success in reading interpretation:

1. READING SPEED

and

2. UNDERSTANDING WHAT YOU READ.

But these two aspects are not separate. As a matter of fact, they are totally dependent on each other. You can improve your speed by improving your comprehension—and then your comprehension will improve further because you have improved your speed. What you are improving, therefore, is your *speed of comprehension*. Your eyes and your mind must work together. As your mind begins to look for ideas rather than words, your eyes will begin to obey your mind. Your eyes will start to skim over words, looking for the ideas your mind is telling them to search for. Good reading is good thinking—and a good thinker will be a good reader. Speed and comprehension work together.

For convenience, however, let us divide our discussion into two parts—increasing reading speed and improving reading comprehension.

Increasing Reading Speed

A great many people read very slowly and with little comprehension, yet are completely unaware of just how badly they do read. Some people pronounce the words to themselves as they read, saying each word almost as distinctly as though reading aloud; or they think each one separately.

The reason for this is that many people have not gone quite far enough in their "learning to read" process. When you were first taught to read, you learned the sounds of each letter. Then you learned that if you put the letters together, they would make words. But that is where many people stop. Reading, to them, is reading words. But try reading a sentence out loud, saying each word as though it were a separate unit. How does it sound? Pretty meaningless! A more mature reader will put words together to make phrases. And the most mature reader will put phrases together to make ideas. A writer uses words to state ideas—and that is what a good reader looks for—those ideas. This will affect the way his eyes work. Let's see how.

HOW YOUR EYES WORK IN READING

As you learn to read phrases and thoughts, you will find that your eyes are increasing their *span*. This means that your eyes are seeing several words

at a time as you are reading, not just one.

Your eyes work as a camera does. When you want to take a picture, you hold the camera still and snap the shutter. If you move the camera, the picture will blur. When you read, your eyes take pictures of words—and, like a camera, when they are "photographing," they are standing still. Each time your eyes "picture" words in a line of print, they stop—and each stop is called a *fixation*. Watch someone read, and you will see how his eyes make very quick stops across the line. You know he has finished a line when you see his eyes sweep back to the beginning of the next line.

EYE SPAN AND FIXATION

The more words your eyes take in with one fixation, the larger the eye span. And the larger the eye span, the fewer stops your eyes will have to make across the line. Thus, you will be reading faster.

For example, let's divide a sentence the way a slow, word-by-word reader would:

You/ will/ find/ that/ you/ can/ read/ faster/ if/ you/ per/ mit/ your/ eyes/ to/ see/ large/ thought/ units/.

The reader's eyes have made at least nine stops on each line.

This is the way a fast reader would divide the same sentence:

You will find that/ you can read faster/ if/ you permit/ your eyes to see/ large thought/ units.

This reader's eyes have stopped only three times on each line, so of course he will be able to read much faster. Also, reading thought units will enable him to grasp the meaning more effectively. Now here are some exercises to help you increase your eye span.

EXERCISES FOR INCREASING EYE-SPAN

1.

0.................0.................0.................0
0.................0.................0.................0
0.................0.................0.................0
0.................0.................0.................0
0.................0.................0.................0
0.................0.................0.................0

In the above "paragraph," the dots stand for letters and each 0 is one eye fixation. "Read" a line, forcing your eyes to shift from 0 to 0. When you finish the first line, let your eyes swing back to the next line. Try to get an even rhythm. Now you can feel what your eyes should be doing as they read a line in four fixations. Is this different from the way they usually feel when you read? Keep practicing this "paragraph" until it feels comfortable, and then try to read a line of print in the same way. You can make up your own "paragraph" with only three fixations and practice.

2. Here is a list of three-word phrases, with a line drawn down the center. Focus your eyes on the line, and look at the three words at once. Remember, only *one* fixation. Do not read each word separately. If you have trouble at first, read the phrases through once in your usual way, and then practice the one fixation.

at the store
day and night
box of candy
come with me
in the house
bring my paper
time to finish
make every effort
all the questions
read very fast

3. Choose a newspaper column on a subject that interests you, and read it through. Then draw two vertical lines equally distant from each other down the center. Reread the column fixating on first one vertical line, then the next—two fixations per line. When you get very good at this, try drawing just one line down the center and fixating once. You can practice this daily.

VOCALIZING CAN SLOW YOU DOWN

Some readers move their lips or whisper while they read "silently." This habit is called vocalizing. It is caused by the fact that your earliest reading was done aloud, and the habit of hearing each word as you read it, persists.

It would be physically impossible for you to speak at the rate of speed at which a good reader can read—say 350 words per minute. And if you could, no one could understand you. If you read only as fast as you can talk, you will never be a fast reader.

Obviously, then, you must **stop vocalizing**. Your

lips and vocal cords must not be permitted to interfere in the exchange of ideas between eyes and mind. Even if you are not obviously vocalizing, you may be subvocalizing. Your lips are not moving, your vocal cords are not involved, but you are hearing each word as you read it. This is as much a deterrent to reading speed as actual vocalizing. Most people *do* subvocalize.

HOW TO STOP VOCALIZING

1. Put your fingers on your lips. Make sure your lips do not move as you read. If they do, put a pencil or a rubber eraser between your teeth. Then read. If you start to vocalize, the pencil will drop out. If you are reading in public you might be embarrassed to appear with a pencil in your mouth. In that case, just clench your teeth hard—and keep reading.

2. Only *you* will know if you are subvocalizing—and be honest with yourself. If you are subvocalizing (and you probably are) try this exercise. Before you start to read, repeat these nonsense syllables to yourself for 30 seconds: da-rum, da-rum, da-rum, da-rum, etc. Now begin to read and continue to repeat da-rum as you read. If you are doing this, then you cannot subvocalize what you are reading. At first you will find this extremely difficult to do, but if you keep practicing, soon you will find that there is a direct connection between written word and thought—with no intervening vocalizing.

VARY YOUR READING SPEED

One should adjust his reading speed to what he is reading. Some paragraphs will be easier for you than others, possibly because you are more interested in the subject matter, or know something about it. Other paragraphs, particularly those that deal with factual or technical material, may have to be read more slowly.

Flexibility should be employed so that the reader will change his speed from paragraph to paragraph—even from sentence to sentence, just as a driver would vary his driving speed depending on where he is driving. Some passages are open highways while others are crowded city thoroughfares.

For example, read the following passage:

> It was a sunny Sunday afternoon in December. Some people were at the movies; some were out walking; and some were at home listening to the radio. Suddenly an announcement was broadcast—and the United States was plunged into war.
>
> On December 7, 1941, the Japanese Air Force attacked Pearl Harbor, destroying battleships, aircraft carriers, planes, and a strategic military base, leaving the United States without the military arsenals needed for anti-aircraft activity and civilian protecton.

Which of these paragraphs is the "highway"? Which is the crowded city thoroughfare? Where can you breeze through? Where will you need to slow down to absorb every detail. You're right! The first paragraph is a simple introduction. A glance should suffice. The second paragraph is fact-packed, so you will need to slow down.

OTHER PHYSICAL FACTORS

Don't neglect the obvious reading aids. Good eyesight is essential. When was your last eye check-up? If glasses were prescribed, are you using them? Make sure that you are physically comfortable, sitting erect wlth head slightly inclined. You should have good direct and indirect light, with the direct light coming from behind you and slightly above your shoulder. Hold your reading matter at your own best reading distance so that you don't have to stoop or squint.

FORCE YOURSELF TO FASTER READING

Now that you know the elements that make for fast reading, you must continue to force yourself to read as quickly as you can. Use a stop-watch to time yourself. You can figure your rate of speed by dividing the number of words on a page into the number of seconds it took you to read it, and then multiplying by 60. This will give you your rate in words-per-minute. Since no one rate of speed is possible for all reading material, your rate will vary. But an average reading speed of 350 words-per-minute should be possible for uncomplicated, interesting, straightforward material. If you are already reading that fast, then try for 500 words-per-minute. You should be able to answer correctly at least 80 per cent of the questions following a reading passage.

Practice reading quickly. Move your eyes rapidly across the line of type, skimming it. Don't permit your eyes to stop for individual words. Proceed quickly through the paragraph without backtracking. If you think you don't understand what you are reading, then reread two or three times—but always read quickly. You will be amazed to discover how much you actually do understand.

Improving Reading Comprehension

Many readers are afraid of not understanding what they read quickly. But the old idea that slow readers make up for their slowness by better comprehension of what they read has been proven untrue. Your ability to comprehend what you read will keep pace with your increase in speed. You will absorb as many ideas per page as before, and get many more ideas per unit of reading time.

It has been demonstrated that those who read quickly also read best. This is probably due to the fact that heavier concentration is required for rapid reading; and concentration is what enables a reader to grasp important ideas contained in the reading material.

GETTING THE MAIN IDEA

A good paragraph generally has one central thought—and that thought is usually stated in one sentence. That sentence, the *topic sentence,* is often the first sentence of the paragraph, but it is sometimes buried in the middle, or it can be at the end. Your main task is to locate that sentence and absorb the thought it contains while reading the paragraph. The correct interpretation of the paragraph is based on that thought *as it is stated,* and not on your personal opinion, prejudice, or preference about that thought.

Here are several examples of paragraphs. Read them quickly and see if you can pick out the topic sentence. It is the key sentence. The rest of the paragraph either supports or illustrates it. The answers follow the paragraphs.

1. Pigeon fanciers are firmly convinced that modern inventions can never replace the carrier pigeon. "A pigeon gets through when everything else fails," they say. In World War II, one pigeon flew twenty miles in twenty minutes to cancel the bombing of a town. Radios may get out of order and telephone lines may get fouled up, but the pigeon is always ready to take off with a message.
2. When a piece of paper burns, it is completely changed. The ash that is left behind does not look like the original piece of paper. When dull-red rust appears on a piece of tinware, it is quite different from the gleaming tin. The tarnish that forms on silverware is a new substance unlike the silver itself. Animal tissue is unlike the vegetable substance from which it is made. A change in which the original substance is turned into a different substance is called a chemical change.
3. A child who stays up too late is often too tired to be successful in school. A child who is allowed to eat anything he wishes may have bad teeth and even suffer from malnutrition. Children who are rude and disorderly often suffer pangs of guilt. Children who are disciplined are happy children. They blossom in an atmosphere where they know exactly what is expected of them. This provides them with a sense of order, a feeling of security.

Answers: In paragraph 1, the first sentence is the topic sentence. In paragraph 2, the last sentence is the topic sentence. In paragraph 3, it is the fourth sentence—"Children who are disciplined. . . . ".

If a selection consists of two or more paragraphs, the correct interpretation is based on the central idea of the entire passage. The ability to grasp the central idea of a passage can be acquired by practice—practice that will also increase the speed with which you read.

Reading for a Purpose—The Survey Method

Many readers don't know what they are looking for when they read. They plunge into a page full of words, and often that is what they end up with —just words. It's like walking into a supermarket without having made a list of what you want to buy. You wander aimlessly up and down the aisles and end up with a basketful of cookies and fruit and pickles—and nothing for a main dish.

It is extremely important to have a purpose in mind *before* you start to read—to make a "list" before you start shopping. Good readers use the *survey* method. By "survey" we mean a quick over-view of what you are going to read before you actually start reading. It is like looking at a road map before you start on a trip. If you know in what direction you are going, you are apt to get there sooner, and more efficiently. This is what you do.

1. Read the title. Think about what the selection will probably be about. What kind of information can you expect to obtain? Gear your mind to look for the central thought.

2. Think about the kind of vocabulary you will meet. Will it be technical? Are you familiar with the subject, or will you have to prepare yourself to meet many new words? After a quick glance, you may decide to skip this selection and go back to it later. (Remember, on a timed reading test you want to give yourself a chance to sample *all* the selections. The one at the end may be easier for you than the one in the middle, but you won't know if you never get to the end.) The difficulty of the vocabulary may be the deciding factor.

3. If there are subheadings, read them. They can provide a skeleton outline of the selection.

4. Read the first sentence of each paragraph. It usually contains the most important ideas in the selection. The topic sentence is more often found in the beginning of a paragraph than in any other position.

5. READ THE QUESTIONS BASED ON THE SELECTION. The questions are there to test whether or not you understand the most important ideas in the selection. If you read them first, they will steer you through your reading in the most effective way possible. Now you really know what to look for! In any kind of reading, whether on test or in texts, always look at the questions first (unless you are directed not to do so).

The survey method can be applied to all kinds of reading, particularly textbook reading. In addition to the above, you should include the following in your textbook survey:

(a) Read the preface quickly. It states the author's purpose in writing the book.

(b) Look at the publication date (on the copyright page). This can tell you if the information is up-to-date.

(c) Look through the table of contents. See what the author has included, and the order in which it appears. Some tables of contents can serve as an outline for the book.

(d) If there are chapter or part summaries, read through them quickly. They'll give you a forecast of what's to come.

(e) Look at illustrations, maps, graphs, etc. These are meant to help you visualize essential information. Remember, one picture can be worth a thousand words.

Increase Your Vocabulary

In order to understand what you are reading, you must know the meaning of the words that are used. Very often you can guess at the meaning from the rest of the sentence, but that method is not completely reliable. The sentence itself is important for determining which of the word's several meanings is intended, but you usually have to have some idea of the word itself.

How can you build a larger vocabulary? You could sit down with a long list of words and try to memorize it, or perhaps go through the dictionary page by page. This would be very time consuming—and very boring! Memorizing words is probably the *least* successful way of building a vocabulary.

Words are best remembered when they are understood and used, when they are part of your own experience. Here are some ways in which you can do this.

1. Learn a little etymology. You already know a lot, because approximately 70 per cent of the words we use consist of roots and prefixes de-

rived from Latin and Greek. There are 84 roots and 44 prefixes that are the mainstay of our language. If you learn those you will have a clue to the meaning of thousands of words. For example, the Latin root *voc* (meaning "to call") appears in the words advocate, vocation, irrevocable, vociferous, etc. The root *port* (meaning "to carry") is found in the words report, export, support, porter, etc.

Learn to look for the roots of words, and for familiar parts of words you meet.

2. Read—everything, anything. Even signs and posters sometimes have new words in them. Try to find at least one new word every day.

3. Use the dictionary—frequently and extensively. Look up the meaning of a word you don't know, and see if you can identify its root.

4. Play word games—like Anagrams, Scrabble. And do Crossword Puzzles.

5. Listen to people who speak well. Don't be afraid to ask them the meaning of a word they use that is unfamiliar to you. They'll be flattered.

6. Make a personal word list of your new words. Make it on index cards so that you can play a "flash-card" game with yourself.

7. Look for special word meanings in special subject areas. Since most reading comprehension passages deal with science, literature, or social studies, a weakness in the vocabulary used in these subjects can put you at a great disadvantage. Be sure you know the meaning of the terms that are frequently used.

8. Use the new words you learn each day. Don't save them for a rainy day—by then they may be lost. When you talk or write, try to use as many new words as you can. A word used is a word remembered!

Cues and Clues For Readers

Examination points may be unnecessarily lost by ignoring the author's hints as to what *he* thinks is most important. Be on the lookout for such phrases as "Note that . . ." "Of importance is . . ." "Don't overlook . . ." These give clues to what the writer is stressing. Beware of negatives and all-inclusive statements. They are often put in to trip you up. Words like *always, never, all, only, every, absolutely, completely, none, entirely, no,* can sometimes turn a reasonable statement into an untrue statement. For example look at the following sentence:

When you get caught in the rain, you catch cold.

True? Of course. Now look at this sentence:

When you get caught in the rain, you *always* catch cold.

Different, isn't it? Not *always* true.

PUNCTUATION

Other hints which you should also watch for are those given by punctuation. Here are a few points to keep in mind:

1. QUOTATION MARKS—When a statement is quoted, it may not necessarily represent the author's opinion, or the main thought of the passage. Be sure you make this distinction if it is called for.

2. EXCLAMATION POINT—This mark is often used to indicate an *emphatic* or *ironical* comment. It's the author's way of saying, "This is important!"

3. COMMAS—Watch those commas. They can change the meaning of a sentence. For example:

As I left the room, in order to go to school John called me.

As I left the room in order to go to school, John called me.

In each sentence, a different person is going to school.

4. PARENTHESES—These are often used to set off a part of the sentence that is not absolutely necessary to the sentence. But don't ignore them in reading comprehension tests. Sometimes they give vital information. For example:

Shakespeare (whose life spanned the sixteenth and seventeenth centuries) was a great dramatist.

5. COLON—Often used to emphasize a sequence in thought between two independent sentences. For example:

Science plays an important role in our civilization: thus we should all study physics, chemistry, and biology.

6. ELLIPSES—Three dots often found in quoted material which indicates that there has been an omission of material from the original quotation. Often the material omitted is not important, but a good, critical reader should be aware of the omission.

A Systematic Plan

You can't sit down the night before a test in reading comprehension and "cram" for it. The only way you can build up your reading skill is to practice systematically. The gains you make will show up not only in an increased score on a reading comprehension test, but also in your reading for study and pleasure.

Trying to change reading habits that you have had for a long time can be difficult and discouraging. Do not attempt to apply *all* of the suggestions we have given to *all* your reading *all* at once. Try to follow a program like the one below.

1. Set aside 15 minutes a day to practice new reading techniques.

2. Start off with a short, easy-to-read article for a magazine or newspaper—and time yourself. At the end of your practice session, time yourself on another short article, and keep a record of both times.

3. Select a news story. Read it first, and then practice an eye-span exercise. Work towards reducing your eye fixations to no more than two for a line, the width of a newspaper column.

4. Read an editorial, book review, or movie or drama review in a literate magazine or newspaper. This type of article always expresses the author's (or the paper's) point of view and is therefore good practice for searching out the main idea. After you read, see whether you can write a good title for the article and jot down in one sentence the author's main idea. Also, you can try making up a question based on the article with five alternate answers (the kind you find on reading comprehension tests). This is excellent practice for determining main ideas, and you can use the questions to test your friends.

5. Find one new word and write the sentence in which it appears. Guess at its meaning from the context. Then look up the definition in a dictionary and try to make up a sentence of your own, using the word. Then try to use the word in your conversation at least twice the following day.

If you follow this program daily, you will soon find that you can extend to more and more reading the skills you are building, and your reading comprehension test score will show the great gains you have made.

Sample Questions Analyzed

Here is a sample question followed by an analysis. Try to understand the process of arriving at the correct answer.

(Reading Passage)

"Too often, indeed, have scurrilous and offensive allegations by underworld creatures been sufficient to blast the career of irreproachable and incorruptible executives who, because of their efforts to serve the people honestly and faithfully, incurred the enmity of powerful political forces and lost their positions."

Judging from the contents of the preceding paragraph, you might best conclude that

(A) the larger majority of executives are irreproachable and incorruptible

(B) criminals blast executives with machine guns and kill their careers

(C) political forces are always clashing with government executives

(D) underworld creatures make scurrilous and offensive allegations against incorruptible executives

(E) false statements by criminals sometimes cause honest officials the loss of their positions or the ruin of their careers.

Analysis of Choices

(A) This statement is probably true, and you may agree with it—*but* it is not stated in the paragraph. Remember, no personal opinions. Just deal with the facts.

(B) This is ridiculous and far-fetched.

(C) This choice is not stated in the paragraph at all. The catch-word "always" makes this choice entirely invalid.

(D) This is stated in the paragraph, and is true. However, in the paragraph the qualifying words "too often" are used, which limit the scope of the statement. Also, this choice does not quite summarize the entire central thought of the passage—it is too narrow. We must look further.

(E) This choice is open to no exceptions and accurately sums up the entire central thought of the paragraph. It is the best conclusion that could be drawn in the light of the five choices given.

STEPS TO BETTER READING COMPREHENSION SCORES

Here are five success steps to use when working out any reading comprehension question. If you apply them calmly, you should come up with the right answer most of the time.

1. Survey Selection

Read the entire selection quickly to get the general sense and main idea.

2. Survey Stems

Read the stem of each question (Don't look at the five possible choices of answers yet).

3. Reread Selectively

Reread the selection, concentrating on the parts which seem to be related to the questions.

4. Concentrate on Each Question

Now look at the first question with its five possible answers and eliminate any answer which is far-fetched, ridiculous, irrelevant, false, or impossible. Cross out the answers you have eliminated. You should be left with two or three answers that seem possible.

5. Shuttle Back to Selection

Reread only the part of the selection that applies to the question, and make your decision as to the correct choice based on these considerations:

(a) A choice must be based on fact actually given or definitely understood (and not on your personal opinion or prejudice.) Some questions require making a judgment—and this judgment also must be based on the facts as given.

(b) In questions involving the central thought of the passage (for example: "The best title for this selection . . .") the choice must accurately reflect the entire thought—not too narrow, and not too general.

(c) Remember, some choices have trick expressions or catch-words in them which sometimes destroy the validity of a seemingly acceptable answer. These include expressions like *under all circumstances, at all times, never, always, under no conditions, absolutely, completely, entirely, every, no.* Watch for these carefully.

USING "SUCCESS STEPS" ON A PRACTICE QUESTION

Now let us take an actual exam-type question and apply the five success steps as well as our question analysis skills for a demonstration analysis.

(Reading Passage)

Vacations were once the prerogative of the privileged few, even as late as the 19th century. Now they are considered the right of all, except for such unfortunate masses as, for example, the bulk of China's and India's population, for whom life, save for sleep and brief periods of rest, is uninterrupted toil.

They are more necessary now than once because the average life is less well-rounded and has become increasingly departmentalized. I suppose the idea of vacations, as we conceive it, must be incomprehensible to primitive peoples. Rest of some kind has of course always been a part of the rhythm of human life, but earlier ages did not find it necessary to organize it in the way that modern man has done. Holidays, feast days, were sufficient.

With modern man's increasing tensions, with the stultifying quality of so much of his work, this break in the year's routine became steadily more necessary. Vacations became mandatory for the purpose of renewal and repair. And so it came about that in the United States, the most self-indulgent of nations, the tensest and most departmentalized, vacations have come to take a predominant place in domestic conversation.

1. The title below that best expresses the ideas of this passage is:
   A. Vacation Preferences
   B. Vacations: the Topic of Conversation
   C. Vacations in Perspective
   D. The Well-Organized Vacation
   E. Renewal, Refreshment and Repair

2. We need vacations now more than ever before because we have
   A. a more carefree nature
   B. much more free time
   C. little diversity in our work
   D. no emotional stability
   E. a higher standard of living

3. It is implied in the passage that the lives of Americans are very
   A. habitual C. patriotic
   B. ennobling D. varied
   E. independent

4. As used in the passage, the word "prerogative" (line 1) most nearly means
   A. habit C. request
   B. distinction D. demand
   E. hope

STEP-BY-STEP EXPLANATIONS

STEP 1—We read the selection through quickly to get the general sense.

STEP 2—*We read the stem of each question.*

STEP 3—*We reread the passage selectively* and note that the answer to Question 1 involves the entire selection; the answer to Question 2 is in the first sentence of paragraph 2; the answer to Question 3 lies in paragraph 3; and the answer to Question 4 is in the beginning of paragraph 1.

STEP 4—*Concentrate on each question.* We now consider Question 1 and the five answer choices. We bear in mind that the selection has to do with vacations and man's growing need for them, so that the title we select must reflect that idea. We can eliminate Choice A—the selection does not deal with vacation preferences. Choice B—vacations as a topic of conversation—should also be eliminated as this is a lesser detail and not the whole main idea. Choice C looks like a possibility, but there may be a better choice, so we will look further. Choice D is completely irrelevant, for the passage does not in any way deal with the organization of a vacation. Choice E, while reflecting part of the idea of the passage, does not encompass the historical scope. Therefore, we go back to Choice C, which is direct and all-inclusive, and the best of the five possible choices.

Explanation of Question

We concentrate on Question 2 and its five possible answers. We remember that first reading indicated that the answer to this question is in the beginning of paragraph 2, so we reread just that part of the selection, which deals with the necessity or need of vacations. Choice A is irrelevant and ridiculous, and we eliminate it. Choice B may be a true statement, but it does not pertain to the *need* for vacations. Choice C looks like a good possibility, because a less well-rounded life that is increasingly departmentalized indicates little diversity—but better to check further. We eliminate Choice D immediately because of the word "no," one of our trick expressions. Choice E, like Choice B, does not refer to need. So we return to Choice C as the best possible answer.

Explanation of Question

We concentrate on Question 3 with its five possible answers, remembering that the answer is to be found in paragraph 3—so we go directly to that paragraph. The word "implied" in the stem of the question tells us that we may not find a direct answer but will have to do some thinking. The paragraph tells us that much work is stultifying, that there is much routine, and that vacations are necessary for renewal and repair. We can conclude, then, that life is pretty dull and we will look at the choices to find a word that is synonymous with "dull." Choice A is certainly a possibility, but we look quickly at the remaining choices just to be sure, and discover that there is no other possible choice; B, C, and E are irrelevant, and D is the exact opposite. Choice A is our answer.

Explanation of Question

Concentrating on Question 4 we find that it calls for the definition of a word which is located in line 1, so we go to that portion of the paragraph. Word definitions can often be answered by a careful reading of the sentence in which the word appears, and often the following sentence as well. If we read the sentence in which "prerogative" appears and look at the five possible answers, any one of them might be correct. However, if we read the first part of the second sentence in paragraph 1, we see the clue word *now*. In other words, at this time, as contrasted with the past, vacations are the right of all instead of the right of a few. We can thus conclude that the word "prerogative" is synonymous with the word "right." We look at the five possible choices in this light. We can eliminate A and E immediately since they are in no way synonymous with "right."

Choice C, while a possible synonym, is really too mild a word if we substitute it in the sentence. Choices B and D are possible, with Choice D seeming to be the most likely. But if we substitute it in the sentence for the word prerogative, it does not make as much sense as does Choice B, for vacations were not actually a demand of the privileged few—but more a distinction. Since the stem of our question asks for the nearest meaning, we can be most comfortable in choosing B.

STEP 5—*Shuttle back to the selection.* We check to see that we have answered each question and marked the answer in accordance with the directions specified at the beginning of the examination.

If you follow the outlined procedure for answering reading comprehension questions, you will find that you are answering questions correctly and quickly. Most passages will require at least two readings—one for general sense and one for answering the questions. The important thing is to know where to spot the answers, and to remain calm and collected when examining the possible choices. Don't panic—you can be pretty sure that if a question is hard for you it will be hard for everyone else, too.

INTERPRETATION OF VARIED READING PASSAGES

Skill with reading interpretation questions is an important knack for master test-takers. This chapter provides plenty of practice with the kind of reading questions you are likely to face. Although the questions cover a variety of topics, you won't have to memorize any information to select the correct answer. Clear thinking is the key to success in interpreting each passage correctly. Practice now and profit later.

Concentration, speed, retentiveness, ability to associate the ideas you read...these are the hallmarks of the master test-taker. It doesn't matter what they give you to read, these capabilities will help you score high. That's why this chapter tests your reading in a variety of fields. It asks that you flex your mental muscles and acquire competence through flexibility.

These varied reading passages question you in several ways. Can you quickly grasp the main idea? Can you remember and associate specific details? Can you judge the truth or falsity of what you read? Can you make reasonable inferences from your reading?

If you bear in mind that a good piece of writing usually has a central thought, and that each paragraph in that piece has its own important idea, the following suggestions should help you.

1. Read the paragraph through quickly to get the general sense.
2. Reread the paragraph, concentrating on the central idea, and try to picture it as a unit.
3. Examine the various choices carefully but rapidly, *eliminating immediately* those which are far-fetched or irrelevant.
4. Be sure to consider only the facts given in the paragraph to which the choice refers!
5. **Be especially careful of trick expressions or "catch-words" which** sometimes destroy the validity of a seemingly true statement. These include the expressions: "under all circumstances," "at all times," "never," "always," "under no circumstances," "absolutely," "completely," and "entirely."

6. In this sort of question you may correctly infer an answer from the information given, even if it's not actually stated.

In questions that test your ability to single out details and facts, answer *solely* on the basis of the information given.

In questions that test your ability to judge truth or falsity, your answer should also be based *solely* on the information given. If you must make inferences, infer cautiously, because these questions test your ability to spot precisely what *is* and what *is not* stated.

In most reading questions, a paragraph is followed by one or more statements based upon the paragraph. Each statement is in turn followed by several choices that will complete the statement. You may never have seen the paragraph before, but you must now read it carefully so that you understand it.

Then read the statements and choices. Choose the one that is most correct. Try to pick the one that is most complete, most accurate... the one that is best supported by and necessarily flows from the paragraph. *Be sure* that it contains nothing false so far as the paragraph itself is concerned. When you've answered all the questions, score yourself faithfully by checking with our answers that follow the last question. But please don't look at those answers until you've written your own. You just won't be helping yourself if you do that. Besides you'll have ample opportunity to do the questions again, and to check with our answers, in the event that your first try results in a low score.

TEST I. BUSINESS READINGS

TIME: 25 minutes

This reading comprehension test consists of a number of different passages. One or more questions are based on each passage. The questions are composed of incomplete statements about the passage. Each incomplete statement is followed by five choices lettered (A) (B) (C) (D) (E). Mark your answer sheet with the letter of that choice which best completes the statement, and which best conveys the meaning of the passage.

Correct key answers to these sample questions are given at the conclusion of the test. Please don't peek at our key answers until you've answered all the questions on your own.

Reading Passage

Unfortunately, specialization in industry creates workers who lack versatility. When a laborer is trained to perform only one task, he is almost entirely dependent for employment upon the demand for that particular skill. If anything happens to interrupt that demand he is unemployed.

1. This paragraph indicates that
   (A) the unemployment problem is a direct result of specialization in industry
   (B) the demand for labor of a particular type is constantly changing
   (C) the average laborer is not capable of learning more than one task at a time
   (D) some cases of unemployment are due to laborers' lack of versatility
   (E) too much specialization is as dangerous as too little

Reading Passage

Good management is needed now more than ever. The essential characteristic of management is organization. An organization must be capable of handling responsibility and authority. It must also be able to maintain the balance and perspective necessary to make the weighty decisions thrust upon it today.

2. The above paragraph is a plea for

   (A) better business
   (B) adequately controlled responsibility
   (C) well-regulated authority
   (D) better management through organization
   (E) less perspective and more balance

Reading Passage

The increasing size of business organizations has resulted in less personal contact between superior and subordinate. Consequently, business executives today depend more upon records and reports to secure information and exercise control over the operations of various departments.

3. According to this paragraph, the increasing size of business organizations

   (A) has caused a complete cleavage between employer and employee
   (B) has resulted in less personal contact between superior and subordinate
   (C) has tended toward class distinctions in large organizations
   (D) has resulted in a more indirect means of controlling the operations of various departments
   (E) has made evaluation of the work of the employee more objective

Reading Passage

Lacking a flair for positive administration, the mediocre executive attempts to insure efficiency by implanting job anxiety in his subordinates. This safe, unimaginative method secures the barest minimum of efficiency.

4. Of the following, the most accurate statement according to this quotation is that

   (A) implanting anxiety about job retention is a method usually employed by the mediocre executive to improve the efficiency of his organization
   (B) an organization will operate with at least some efficiency if employees realize that unsatisfactory work performance may subject them to dismissal
   (C) successful executives with a flair for positive administration relieve their subordinates of any concern for their job security
   (D) the implantation of anxiety about job security in subordinates should not be used as a method of improving efficiency
   (E) anxiety in executives tends to make them think that it is present in employees also

Reading Passage

In large organizations some standardized, simple, inexpensive method of giving employees information about company policies and rules, as well as specific instructions regarding their duties, is practically essential. This is the purpose of all office manuals of whatever type.

5. The above selection notes that office manuals

   (A) are all about the same
   (B) should be simple enough for the average employee to understand
   (C) are necessary to large organizations
   (D) act as constant reminders to the employee of his duties
   (E) are the only means by which the executive of a large organization can reach his subordinates

Reading Passage

The ability to do a particular job and performance on the job do not always go hand in hand. People with great potential abilities sometimes fall down on the job because of laziness or lack of interest, while people with mediocre talents achieve excellent results through industry and loyalty to the interests of their employers. The final test of any employee is his performance on the job.

6. The most accurate of the following statements, on the basis of the above paragraph, is that

   (A) employees who lack ability are usually not industrious
   (B) an employee's attitudes are more important than his abilities
   (C) mediocre employees who are interested in their work are preferable to employees who possess great ability
   (D) superior capacity for performance should be supplemented with proper attitudes

7. On the basis of the above paragraph, the employee of most value to his employer is *not* necessarily the one who

   (A) best understands the significance of his duties
   (B) achieves excellent results
   (C) possesses the greatest talents
   (D) produces the greatest amount of work

8. According to the above paragraph, an employee's efficiency is best determined by an

   (A) appraisal of his interest in his work
   (B) evaluation of the work performed by him
   (C) appraisal of his loyalty to his employer
   (D) evaluation of his potential ability to perform his work

Reading Passage

Interest is essentially an attitude of continuing attentiveness, found where activity is satisfactorily self-expressive. Whenever work is so circumscribed that the chance for self-expression or development is denied, monotony is present.

9. On the basis of this selection, it is most accurate to state that

   (A) tasks which are repetitive in nature do not permit self-expression and therefore create monotony
   (B) interest in one's work is increased by financial and non-financial incentives
   (C) jobs which are monotonous can be made self-expressive by substituting satisfactory working conditions
   (D) workers whose tasks afford them no opportunity for self-expression find such tasks to be monotonous
   (E) work is monotonous unless there is activity which satisfies the worker

Reading Passage

During the past few years business has made rapid strides in applying to the field of office management the same fundamental principles of procedure and method that have been in successful use for years in production work. Present-day competition, resulting in smaller margins of profit, has made it essential to give careful attention to the efficient organization and management of internal administrative affairs so that individual productivity may be increased and unit costs reduced.

10. According to the above paragraph
    - (A) office management always lags behind production work
    - (B) present day competition has increased individual productivity
    - (C) efficient office management seeks to reduce gross costs
    - (D) the margin of profits widens as individual productivity is increased
    - (E) similar principles have met with equal success in the fields of office management and production work

Reading Passage

Direct lighting is the least satisfactory lighting arrangement. The desk or ceiling light with a reflector which diffuses all the rays downward is sure to cause glare on the working surface.

11. The above paragraph indicates that direct lighting is least satisfactory as a method of lighting chiefly because
    - (A) the light is diffused causing eye strain
    - (B) the shade on the individual desk lamp is not constructed along scientific lines
    - (C) the working surface is usually obscured by the glare
    - (D) the ordinary reflector causes the rays to fall perpendicularly
    - (E) direct lighting is injurious to the eyes

Reading Passage

The principal advantage of wood over steel office equipment lies, surprisingly, in the greater safety afforded papers in a fire. While the wooden exterior of a file cabinet may burn somewhat, the papers will not be charred as quickly as they would in a steel cabinet. This is because wood burns slowly and does not transmit heat, while steel, although it does not burn, is a conductor of heat. So, under similar circumstances, papers would be charred more quickly in a steel cabinet.

12. Judging from this information alone, the principal advantage of wood over steel office equipment is

    (A) in case of fire, papers will not be destroyed in a wooden cabinet
    (B) wooden equipment is cheaper to replace
    (C) steel does not resist fire as well as wood
    (D) steel equipment is heavy and cannot be moved about very easily
    (E) wood is a poor conductor of heat

Reading Passage

Forms are printed sheets of paper on which information is to be entered. While what is printed on the form is most important, the kind of paper used in making the form is also important. The kind of paper should be selected with regard to the use to which the form will be subjected. Printing a form on an unnecessarily expensive grade of paper is wasteful. On the other hand, using too cheap or flimsy a form can materially interfere with satisfactory performance of the work the form is being planned to do. Thus a form printed on both sides normally requires a heavier paper than a form printed only on one side. Forms to be used as permanent records, or which are expected to have a very long life in files, require a quality of paper which will not disintegrate or discolor with age. A form which will go through a great deal of handling requires a strong tough paper, while thinness is a necessary qualification where the making of several carbon copies of a form will be required.

13. According to this paragraph, the type of paper used for making forms

    (A) should be chosen in accordance with the use to which the form will be put
    (B) should be chosen before the type of printing to be used has been decided upon
    (C) is as important as the information which is printed on it
    (D) should be strong enough to be used for any purpose

14. According to this paragraph, forms that are

    (A) printed on both sides are usually economical and desirable
    (B) to be filed permanently should not deteriorate as time goes on
    (C) expected to last for a long time should be handled carefully
    (D) to be filed should not be printed on inexpensive paper

Reading Passage

The equipment in a mail room may include a mail metering machine. This machine simultaneously stamps, postmarks, seals, and counts letters as fast as the operator can feed them. It can also print the proper postage directly on a gummed strip to be affixed to bulky items. It is equipped with a meter which is removed from the machine and sent to the post office to be set for a given number of stampings of any denomination. The setting of the meter must be paid for in advance. One of the advantages of metered mail is that it by-passes the cancellation operation and thereby facilitates handling by the post office. Mail metering also makes the pilfering of stamps impossible, but does not prevent the passage of personal mail in company envelopes through the meters unless there is established a rigid control or censorship over outgoing mail.

15. According to this selection, the post office

    (A) is responsible for training new clerks in the use of mail metering machines
    (B) usually recommends that both large and small firms adopt the use of mail metering machines
    (C) is responsible for setting the meter to print a fixed number of stampings
    (D) examines the mail metering machines to see that they are properly installed in the mail room

16. According to the above, the use of mail metering machines

    (A) requires the employment of more clerks in a mail room than does the use of postage stamps
    (B) interferes with the handling of large quantities of outgoing mail
    (C) does not prevent employees from sending their personal letters at company expense
    (D) usually involves smaller expenditures for mail room equipment than does the use of postage stamps

17. On the basis of this paragraph, it is most accurate to state that
    (A) mail metering machines are often used for opening envelopes
    (B) postage stamps are generally used when bulky packages are to be mailed
    (C) the use of metered mail tends to interfere with rapid mail handling by the post office
    (D) mail metering machines can seal and count letters at the same time

CONSOLIDATE YOUR KEY ANSWERS HERE

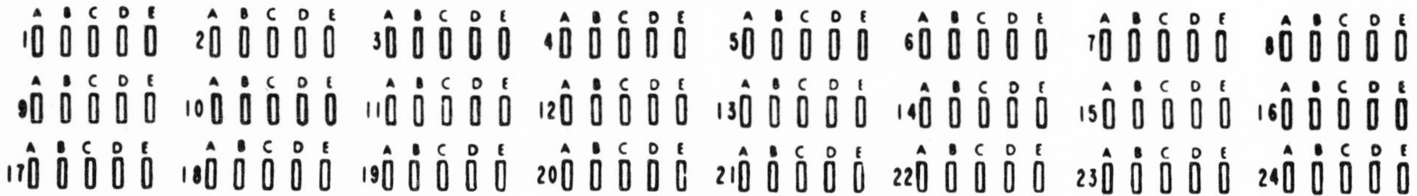

CORRECT KEY ANSWERS: BUSINESS READINGS

(Please try to answer the questions on your own before looking at our answers. You'll do much better on your test if you follow this rule.)

1.D	4.B	7.C	10.D	13.A	16.C
2.D	5.C	8.B	11.D	14.B	17.D
3.D	6.D	9.D	12.E	15.C	

TEST 11. READINGS IN SOCIAL WORK

TIME: 10 minutes

This reading comprehension test consists of a number of different passages. One or more questions are based on each passage. The questions are composed of incomplete statements about the passage. Each incomplete statement is followed by five choices lettered (A) (B) (C) (D) (E). Mark your answer sheet with the letter of that choice which best completes the statement, and which best conveys the meaning of the passage.

Reading Passage

Too often we retire people who are willing and able to work. Chronological age is no longer an effective criterion in determining whether or not an individual is capable of working. The Second World War proved this point when it became necessary to hire older experienced people to handle positions in business and industry vacated by personnel called to serve their country. As shown by production records set during the war period, the employment of older people helped us continue, and even better, our high level of production.

Life expectancy is increasing and the over-65 group will reach twenty million in 1975. A good many of these people are capable of producing and have a desire to work, but are kept from gainful employment by shortsightedness on the part of many employers who believe that young people alone can give them adequate service. It is true that the young person has greater agility and speed to offer, but on the other hand there is much to be gained from the experience, steadfastness, and maturity of judgment of the elderly worker.

1. The title below that best expresses the idea of this passage is

   (A) Increased efficiency of elderly workers
   (B) Misjudging elderly workers
   (C) Lengthening the span of life
   (D) New jobs for the aged
   (E) Production during World War II

2. The writer believes that

   (A) most people over 65 no longer desire to work
   (B) elderly people are crowding younger workers out of jobs
   (C) business and industry today demand older, experienced workers
   (D) the number of people over 65 will increase
   (E) elderly workers are shortsighted about jobs

3. According to this article, the experience of the Second World War showed that

   (A) production increased after elderly workers were employed
   (B) production slowed up after elderly workers were employed
   (C) production maintained the same level after elderly workers were employed
   (D) employers were unwilling to retire the elderly workers when the war was over
   (E) elderly workers proved as agile as the younger ones

Reading Passage

Old age insurance, under which benefits are paid as a right and not on the basis of need to upwards of thirty millions of workers, is the one feature of the Social Security Act that is wholly administered by the federal government.

4. This paragraph indicates most nearly that

   (A) under the Social Security Act, the federal government administers old age insurance to any who deserve it
   (B) the States have no part in administering Social Security old age insurance
   (C) thirty million workers are eligible for old age insurance
   (D) the Social Security Act is administered by the federal government
   (E) every year thirty million workers receive old age insurance

Reading Passage

Statutes to prevent and penalize adulteration of foods, and to provide for sanitation in their preparation, are in force in every state. Such legislation has been upheld as proper under the police power of the state, as it is obviously designed to promote the health and general welfare of the people.

5. It is reasonable to conclude from the above paragraph that

   (A) the state provides for drastic measures to deal with offenders of the pure food laws
   (B) to make laws for the purpose of promoting the general health and general welfare of the people is a proper function of the state
   (C) adulterated food is an outstanding menace to public health
   (D) every state has adequately provided for the prevention of adulteration of foods by enforcement of suitable legislation
   (E) the right of the state to penalize adulteration of foods has never been questioned

Reading Passage

Many industrial processes are dangerous to the health of workers and give rise to occupational disease. The state, as the guardian of public health and welfare, has a legitimate interest in conserving the vitality of industrial workers and may, to this end, make appropriate laws, and give to boards or departments authority to make regulations to carry out the law. Such laws and rules may prohibit dangerous conditions, regulate the plant or the person, or compensate for injuries received.

6. It can best be inferred from the preceding paragraph that

   (A) workmen's compensation laws are in force in practically all states
   (B) the state makes laws that prohibit industrial processes that it considers dangerous to the health of the worker
   (C) government regulation of industry is highly desirable
   (D) the state is interested in lessening the occurrence of occupational disease
   (E) the state compensates the worker for injuries received while carrying out the duties of his occupation

CONSOLIDATE YOUR KEY ANSWERS HERE

	A	B	C	D	E
1	▯	▯	▯	▯	▯
2	▯	▯	▯	▯	▯
3	▯	▯	▯	▯	▯
4	▯	▯	▯	▯	▯
5	▯	▯	▯	▯	▯
6	▯	▯	▯	▯	▯

CORRECT KEY ANSWERS: READINGS IN SOCIAL WORK

(Please make every effort to answer the questions on your own before looking at these answers. You'll make faster progress by following this rule.)

1.B 2.D 3.A 4.B 5.B 6.D

Practice Using Answer Sheets

Alter numbers to match the practice and drill questions in each part of the book.
Make only ONE mark for each answer. Additional and stray marks may be counted as mistakes.
In making corrections, erase errors COMPLETELY. Make glossy black marks.

1	A B C D E	1	A B C D E	1	A B C D E	1	A B C D E	1	A B C D E
2	A B C D E	2	A B C D E	2	A B C D E	2	A B C D E	2	A B C D E
3	A B C D E	3	A B C D E	3	A B C D E	3	A B C D E	3	A B C D E
4	A B C D E	4	A B C D E	4	A B C D E	4	A B C D E	4	A B C D E
5	A B C D E	5	A B C D E	5	A B C D E	5	A B C D E	5	A B C D E
6	A B C D E	6	A B C D E	6	A B C D E	6	A B C D E	6	A B C D E
7	A B C D E	7	A B C D E	7	A B C D E	7	A B C D E	7	A B C D E
8	A B C D E	8	A B C D E	8	A B C D E	8	A B C D E	8	A B C D E
9	A B C D E	9	A B C D E	9	A B C D E	9	A B C D E	9	A B C D E
0	A B C D E	0	A B C D E	0	A B C D E	0	A B C D E	0	A B C D E

1	A B C D E	1	A B C D E	1	A B C D E	1	A B C D E	1	A B C D E
2	A B C D E	2	A B C D E	2	A B C D E	2	A B C D E	2	A B C D E
3	A B C D E	3	A B C D E	3	A B C D E	3	A B C D E	3	A B C D E
4	A B C D E	4	A B C D E	4	A B C D E	4	A B C D E	4	A B C D E
5	A B C D E	5	A B C D E	5	A B C D E	5	A B C D E	5	A B C D E
6	A B C D E	6	A B C D E	6	A B C D E	6	A B C D E	6	A B C D E
7	A B C D E	7	A B C D E	7	A B C D E	7	A B C D E	7	A B C D E
8	A B C D E	8	A B C D E	8	A B C D E	8	A B C D E	8	A B C D E
9	A B C D E	9	A B C D E	9	A B C D E	9	A B C D E	9	A B C D E
0	A B C D E	0	A B C D E	0	A B C D E	0	A B C D E	0	A B C D E

1	A B C D E	7	A B C D E	13	A B C D E	19	A B C D E	25	A B C D E
2	A B C D E	8	A B C D E	14	A B C D E	20	A B C D E	26	A B C D E
3	A B C D E	9	A B C D E	15	A B C D E	21	A B C D E	27	A B C D E
4	A B C D E	10	A B C D E	16	A B C D E	22	A B C D E	28	A B C D E
5	A B C D E	11	A B C D E	17	A B C D E	23	A B C D E	29	A B C D E
6	A B C D E	12	A B C D E	18	A B C D E	24	A B C D E	30	A B C D E

TEAR OUT ALONG THIS LINE AND MARK YOUR ANSWERS AS INSTRUCTED IN THE TEXT

TOP SCORES ON VOCABULARY TESTS

Although questions on vocabulary may not actually appear on your test, it is advisable to practice with the kind of material you have in this chapter. Words and their meanings are quite important in pushing up your score on tests of reading, comprehension, effective writing and correct usage. By broadening your vocabulary, you will definitely improve your marks in these and similar subjects.

INCREASE YOUR VOCABULARY

How is your vocabulary? Do you know the meanings of just about every word you come upon in your reading—or do you find several words that stump you? You must increase your vocabulary if you want to read with understanding. Following are six steps that you can take in order to build up your word power:

(a) Read as much as you have the time for. Don't confine yourself to one type of reading either. Read all kinds of newspapers, magazines, books. Seek variety in what you read—different newspapers, several types of magazines, all types of books (novels, poetry, essays, plays, etc.). If you get into the habit of reading widely, your vocabulary will grow by leaps and bounds. You'll learn the meanings of words *by context.* That means that, very often, even though you may not know the meaning of a certain word in a sentence, the other words that you are familiar with will help you get the meaning of the hard word.

(b) Take vocabulary tests. There are many practice books which have word tests. We suggest one of these: *2300 Steps to Word Power* — (Arco Publishing Co.). These tests are fun to take—and they will build up your vocabulary fast.

(c) Listen to lectures, discussions, and talks by people who speak well. There are some worthwhile TV programs that have excellent speakers. Listen to these people—you'll learn a great many words.

(d) Use a dictionary. Whenever you don't know the meaning of a word, make a note of it. Then, when you get to a dictionary, look up the meaning of the word. Keep your own little notebook—call it "New Words." In a month or two, you will have added a great many words to your vocabulary. If you do not have a dictionary at home, you should buy one. A good dictionary is not expensive. Any one of the following is highly recommended:

Standard College Dictionary (Funk and Wagnalls)

Seventh New Collegiate Dictionary (Merriam-Webster)

American College Dictionary (Random House)

You'll never regret buying a good dictionary for your home.

(e) Play word games. Have you ever played Anagrams or Scrabble? They're really interesting. Buy one of these at a stationery store. They are quite inexpensive but effective in building up your vocabulary. Crossword puzzles will teach you new words also. Practically every daily newspaper has a crossword puzzle.

(f) Learn stems, prefixes, and suffixes.

BASIC LETTER COMBINATIONS

One of the most efficient ways in which you can build up your vocabulary is by a systematic study of the basic word and letter combinations which make up the greater part of the English language.

Etymology is the science of the formation of words, and this somewhat frightening-sounding science can be of great help to you in learning new words and identifying words which may be unfamiliar to you. You will also find that the progress you make in studying the following pages will help to improve your spelling.

A great many of the words which we use every day have come into our language from the Latin and Greek. In the process of being absorbed into English, they appear as parts of words, many of which are related in meaning to each other.

For your convenience, this material is presented in easy-to-study form. Latin and Greek syllables and letter-combinations have been categorized into three groups:

1. *Prefixes:* letter combinations which appear at the beginning of a word.
2. *Suffixes:* letter combinations which appear at the end of a word.
3. *Roots or stems:* which carry the basic meaning and are combined with each other and with prefixes and suffixes to create other words with related meanings.

With the prefixes and suffixes, which you should study first, we have given examples of word formation with meanings, and additional examples. If you find any unfamiliar words among the samples, consult your dictionary to look up their meanings.

The list of roots or stems is accompanied by words in which the letter combinations appear. Here again, use the dictionary to look up any words which are not clear in your mind.

Remember that this section is not meant for easy reading. It is a guide to a program of study that will prove invaluable if you do your part. Do not try to swallow too much at one time. If you can put in a half-hour every day, your study will yield better results.

After you have done your preliminary work and have gotten a better idea of how words are formed in English, schedule the various vocabulary tests and quizzes we have provided in this chapter. They cover a wide variety of the vocabulary questions commonly encountered on examinations. They are short quizzes, not meant to be taken all at one time. Space them out. Adhere closely to the directions which differ for the different test types. Keep an honest record of your scores. Study your mistakes. Look them up in your dictionary. Concentrate closely on each quiz . . . and watch your scores improve.

ETYMOLOGY - A KEY TO WORD RECOGNITION

PREFIXES

PREFIX	MEANING	EXAMPLE
ab, a	away from	absent, amoral
ad, ac, ag, at	to	advent, accrue, aggressive, attract
an	without	anarchy
ante	before	antedate
anti	against	antipathy
bene	well	beneficent
bi	two	bicameral
circum	around	circumspect
com, con, col	together	commit confound, collate
contra	against	contraband
de	from, down	descend
dis, di	apart	distract, divert
ex, e	out	exit, emit
extra	beyond	extracurricular
in, im, il, ir, un	not	inept, impossible, illicit
inter	between	interpose
intra, intro, in	within	intramural, introspective

PREFIX	MEANING	EXAMPLE
mal	bad	malcontent
mis	wrong	misnomer
non	not	nonentity
ob	against	obstacle
per	through	permeate
peri	around	periscope
poly	many	polytheism
post	after	post-mortem
pre	before	premonition
pro	forward	propose
re	again	review
se	apart	seduce
semi	half	semicircle
sub	under	subvert
super	above	superimpose
sui	self	suicide
trans	across	transpose
vice	instead of	vice-president

SUFFIXES

SUFFIX	MEANING	EXAMPLE
able, ible	capable of being	capable, reversible
age	state of	storage
ance	relating to	reliance
ary	relating to	dictionary
ate	act	confiscate
ation	action	radiation
cy	quality	democracy

SUFFIX	MEANING	EXAMPLE
ence	relating to	confidence
er	one who	adviser
ic	pertaining to	democratic
ious	full of	rebellious
ize	to make like	harmonize
ment	result	filament
ty	condition	sanity

LATIN AND GREEK STEMS

STEM	MEANING	EXAMPLE
ag, ac	do	agenda, action
agr	farm	agriculture
aqua	water	aqueous
cad, cas	fall	cadence, casual
cant	sing	chant
cap, cep	take	captive, accept
capit	head	capital
cede	go	precede
celer	speed	celerity
cide, cis	kill, cut	suicide, incision
clud, clus	close	include, inclusion
cur, curs	run	incur, incursion
dict	say	diction
duct	lead	induce
fact, fect	make	factory, perfect
fer, lat	carry	refer, dilate
fring, fract	break	infringe, fracture
frater	brother	fraternal
fund, fus	pour	refund, confuse
greg	group	gregarious
gress, grad	move forward	progress, degrade
homo	man	homicide
ject	throw	reject
jud	right	judicial
junct	join	conjunction
lect, leg	read, choose	collect, legend
loq, loc	speak	loquacious, interlocutory
manu	hand	manuscript
mand	order	remand
mar	sea	maritime
mater	mother	maternal
med	middle	intermediary
min	lessen	diminution
mis, mit	send	remit, dismiss
mort	death	mortician
mote, mov	move	remote, remove
naut	sailor	astronaut
nom	name	nomenclature
pater	father	paternity
ped, pod	foot	pedal, podiatrist
pend	hang	depend
plic	fold	implicate
port	carry	portable
pos, pon	put	depose, component
reg, rect	rule	regicide, direct
rupt	break	eruption
scrib, scrip	write	inscribe, conscription
anthrop	man	anthropology

STEM	MEANING	EXAMPLE
arch	chief, rule	archbishop
astron	star	astronomy
auto	self	automatic
biblio	book	bibliophile
bio	life	biology
chrome	color	chromosome
chron	time	chronology
cosmo	world	cosmic
crat	rule	autocrat
dent, dont	tooth	dental, indent
eu	well, happy	eugenics
gamos	marriage	monogamous
ge	earth	geology
gen	origin, people	progenitor
graph	write	graphic
gyn	women	gynecologist
homo	same	homogeneous
hydr	water	dehydrate
logy	study of	psychology
meter	measure	thermometer
micro	small	microscope
mono	one	monotony
onomy	science	astronomy
onym	name	synonym
pathos	feeling	pathology
philo	love	philosophy
phobia	fear	hydrophobia
phone	sound	telephone
pseudo	false	pseudonym
psych	mind	psychic
scope	see	telescope
soph	wisdom	sophomore
tele	far off	telepathic
theo	god	theology
thermo	heat	thermostat
sec	cut	dissect
sed	remain	sedentary
sequ	follow	sequential
spect	look	inspect
spir	breathe	conspire
stat	stand	status
tact, tang	touch	tactile, tangible
ten	hold	retentive
term	end	terminal
vent	come	prevent
vict	conquer	evict
vid, vis	see	video, revise
voc	call	convocation
volv	roll	devolve

IV. VOCABULARY TEST QUESTIONS FOR PRACTICE

The following questions have been selected to give you as broad a sampling as possible of words which have appeared on previous tests. The ease or difficulty with which you answer these questions will indicate whether or not your word power is adequate for the test you are about to take.

YOU will find these questions divided into separate sub-tests of ten questions each. This division has been made for two reasons: (1) the average number of vocabulary questions on tests of this grade is ten: (2) by doing each sub-test separately, you are enabled to see your progress as you proceed from one test to the next.

You will note that following each test, space is provided for recording the time you took to do the test, and for recording the number of correct answers. By comparing the second test with the first, the third with the second, etc., you will be able to see whether or not you are improving your word power as you study. Successful study should result in speedier time on each successive test, accompanied by increasing accuracy. If this is not the case when you have completed all the tests, then you had better begin again until the desired results are obtained.

These tests, as you will see, take several forms. In general, they are multiple-choice type asking for a word's definition or its opposite. Some questions ask whether a word is used correctly or not, and require you to answer "True" if it is, and "False" if it isn't. You will find, however, that a majority of questions are of the former type. The number of questions in any one form reflects its frequency on actual exams.

Use a watch or clock to keep an accurate record of the time consumed by each test. Read the instructions which precede each test carefully. You may check your accuracy by referring to the answers at the end of the chapter. Do not refer to these answers until you have completed each test.

Sample Test Question Analyzed

The questions may appear in one of several forms, but one of the most numerous is that of choosing a word which is most nearly the same in meaning as the question word. The example below has been chosen because it will help to illustrate the way in which vocabulary questions are answered.

Blacken the appropriate space for the letter preceding the word which is most nearly the same in meaning as the *italicized* word in the sentence.

Sample Question. One who is *garrulous* in his relations with others is, most nearly:

(A) complaining
(B) careless
(C) overly talkative
(D) defensive (E) dishonest.

Notice that the instructions ask for the selection of the choice which is *most nearly* the same in meaning as the italicized word.

First, examine the italicized word. If you know its meaning, your task is fairly simple. But suppose you do not know what *garrulous* means. Perhaps we can eliminate some of the choices by analyzing them.

(A) Complaining: Does *complaining* have anything to do with *garrulous*? It might. However, a synonym for *complaining* is querulous. In this case, it is best to avoid *complaining* as a possibility, since it is probably there to confuse you.

(B) Careless: Most people know what careless means. Here again is a word which only sounds like the question word. You would not use *garrulous* to describe a neglectful person.

(C) Overly Talkative: There is nothing to indicate that this phrase is not a synonym for *garrulous*. Do not eliminate it as a possibility.

(D) Defensive: You can think of synonyms for this one, like protective, safe-guarding, and maybe even fortress and garrison may come to mind. In general, any word that sounds like the question word should be avoided. You would do well to eliminate *defensive* as a possibility.

(E) Dishonest: There is not much to indicate that this is not a synonym for *garrulous*, and none of the synonyms for *dishonest* sounds like the question word. It cannot be eliminated entirely.

The choice is now between (C) and (E); *overly talkative* and *dishonest*. If you have no idea at all regarding the meaning of *garrulous*, then you must guess. Since three of the choices have already been eliminated, you have a much better chance to guess correctly.

Garrulous: The dictionary defines *garrulous* as: "given to continual and tedious talking," "habitually loquacious," "chattering," "verbose." Therefore, (C) "overly talkative" is the correct answer.

TEST-TYPE QUIZZES FOR PRACTICE

DIRECTIONS: For each question read all the choices carefully. Then select that answer which you consider correct or most nearly correct. Write the letter preceding your best choice next to the question. Should you want to answer on the kind of answer sheet used on machine-scored examinations, we have provided several such facsimiles. On some machine-scored exams you are instructed to "place no marks whatever on the test booklet." In other examinations you may be instructed to mark your answers in the test booklet. In such cases you should be careful that no other marks interfere with the legibility of your answers. It is always best NOT to mark your booklet unless you are sure that it is permitted. It is most important that you learn to mark your answers clearly and in the right place.

FOR THE SAMPLE QUESTION that follows, select the appropriate letter preceding the word which is most nearly the same in meaning as the capitalized word:

1. DISSENT: (A) approve (B) depart (C) disagree (D) enjoy

DISSENT is most nearly the same as (C), disagree, so that the acceptable answer is shown thus on your answer sheet:

A B C D

ANSWER SHEETS AND CORRECT ANSWERS APPEAR AFTER EACH TEST

SYNONYMS TEST ONE

DIRECTIONS: For each of the following questions, select the choice which best answers the question or completes the statement.

Correct key answers to all these test questions will be found at the end of the test.

1. An amendment is a
(A) civic center (B) charter
(C) penalty (D) change.

2. A quorum is a
(A) minority (B) committee
(C) majority (D) bicameral system.

3. Clearance refers to a
(A) weight (B) hoistway
(C) distance (D) cleaning process.

4. Pasteurized milk is milk that has been
(A) watered (B) condemned
(C) embargoed (D) purified.

5. Antitoxin is used in cases of
(A) corrupt governmental officials
(B) sanitary inspection
(C) disease
(D) elevator construction.

6. Libel refers to the
(A) process of incurring financial liability
(B) publication of a false statement which injures others
(C) deportation of aliens
(D) necessity for compulsory schooling.

7. Naturalization refers to the process of
(A) becoming a civil service employee
(B) being summoned to court
(C) becoming a citizen
(D) pledging allegiance to the American flag.

8. To comply with a rule means to
(A) abide by a rule (B) abrogate a rule
(C) dislike a rule (D) ignore a rule.

9. A budget is a
(A) financial statement
(B) method for training operators
(C) device for insuring courtesy
(D) means for selecting judges

10. A fulcrum is part of a
(A) typewriter (B) lever
(C) radio (D) lamp.

Correct Answers

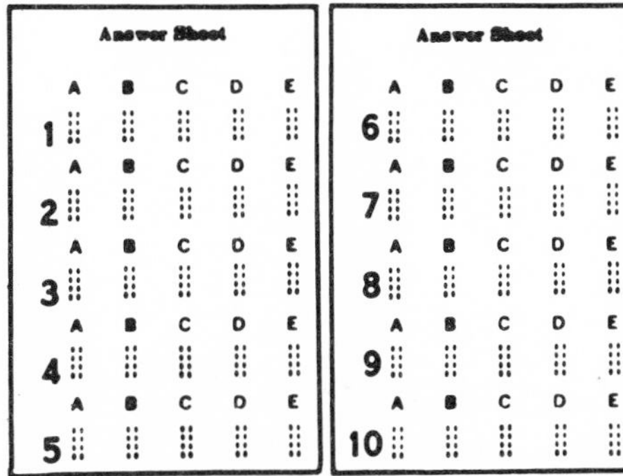

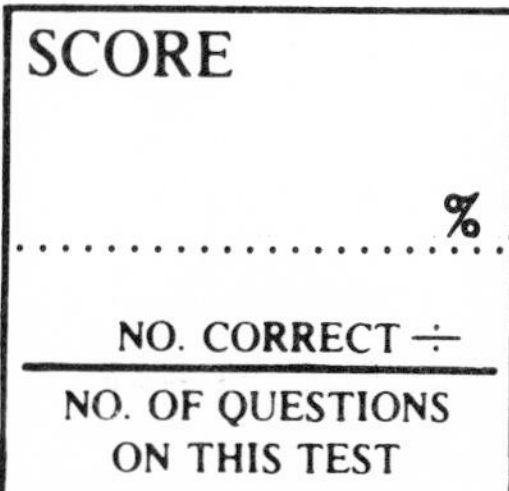

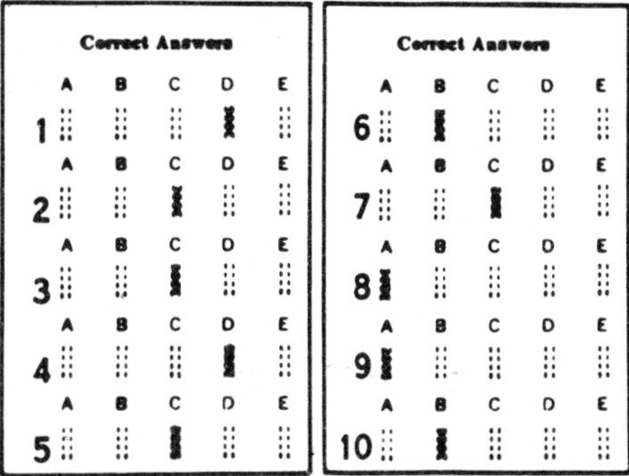

SYNONYMS TEST TWO

DIRECTIONS: Each of the questions in this test is numbered and consists of pairs of words. Each pair of words is preceded by a letter. For each question, select the one pair of words wherein both words are synonymous. Mark the letter, A, B, C, D, or E, preceding that pair on your answer sheet.

Correct key answers to all these test questions will be found at the end of the test.

1. (A) transitory-permanent (B) prohibit-allow (C) beautiful-ugly (D) broken-disunited (E) ferocious-mild.
2. (A) elucidate-clarify (B) recent-ancient (C) enthusiasm-apathy (D) equivocal-indubitable (E) evade-acknowledge.
3. (A) extricate-imprison (B) concur-endorse (C) intimidate-assure (D) lucid-obscure (E) molest-comfort.
4. (A) abandon-hold (B) awkward-skillful (C) consistent-varying (D) constrain-beseech (E) tedious-tiresome.
5. (A) deficient-ample (B) waste-conserve (C) compromise-quarrel (D) sanguine-optimistic (E) desist-persevere.
6. (A) monotony-variety (B) remote-near (C) propitiate-appease (D) many-few (E) veracity-deception.
7. (A) fraud-honesty (B) important-significant (C) mollify-vex (D) abate-maintain (E) authorize-forbid.
8. (A) eradicate-destroy (B) barbarous-humane (C) compulsion-freedom (D) concur-differ (E) incite-quell.
9. (A) morose-cheerful (B) munificent-penurious (C) censorious-fault-finding (D) predominate-subordinate (E) extricate-bind.
10. (A) gratify-displease (B) grudge-good will (C) interpose-withdraw (D) irresponsible-accountable (E) augment-increase.

Correct Answers For The Foregoing Questions

To assist you in scoring yourself we have provided Correct Answers alongside your Answer Sheet. May we therefore suggest that while you are doing the test you cover the Correct Answers with a sheet of white paper.....to avoid temptation and to arrive at an accurate estimate of your ability and progress.

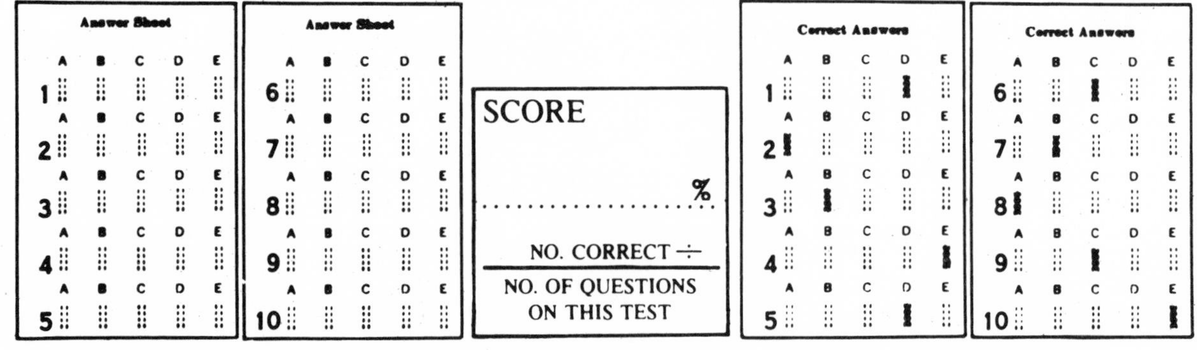

SYNONYMS TEST THREE

Although vocabulary questions may not actually appear on your test, it is advisable to try to improve your vocabulary. Words and their meanings are quite important on reading, writing and correct usage tests. By broadening your vocabulary, you will definitely improve your marks in these and similar subjects.

DIRECTIONS: For each of the following statements, mark T if the statement is True, and F if it is False.

1. A *competent* employee is one who is slow and inefficient. T F
2. A person who commits *perjury* does not tell the truth. T F
3. The *prosecutor* in a criminal case is the lawyer who presents evidence against the defendant. T F
4. A *destitute* person has a large amount of money. T F
5. A person with a *florid* complexion has a pale face. T F
6. A noise that is *audible* is capable of being heard. T F
7. Anyone who is *agile* is quick and nimble. T F
8. An employee who gives information in a *curt* manner is sympathetic and courteous. T F
9. A person who is *prudent* is careless in his attention to duty. T F
10. If a person pays an *exorbitant* amount of money for an article, he is paying a fair price. T F

Now, push forward! Test yourself and practice for your test with the carefully constructed quizzes that follow. Each one presents the kind of question you may expect on your test. And each question is at just the level of difficulty that may be expected. Don't try to take all the tests at one time. Rather, schedule yourself so that you take a few at each session, and spend approximately the same time on them at each session. Score yourself honestly, and date each test. You should be able to detect improvement in your performance on successive sessions.

A portion of the standard answer sheet is provided after each test for marking your answers in the way you'll be required to do on the actual exam. At the right of this answer sheet, to make the scoring job simpler (after you have derived your own answers), you'll find our correct answers.

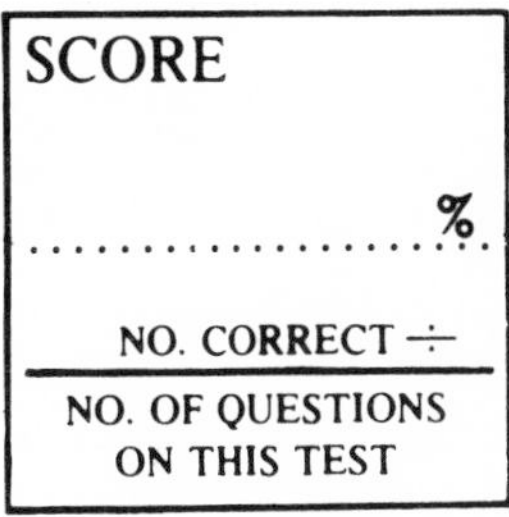

Correct Answers

(You'll learn more by writing your own answers before comparing them with these.)

1. F	6. T
2. T	7. T
3. T	8. F
4. F	9. F
5. F	10. F

SYNONYMS TEST FOUR

DIRECTIONS: This test contains a list of numbered words, and other words divided into five groups—Group A, Group B, Group C, Group D and Group E. For each of the numbered words, select that word in one of the five groups which is most nearly the same in meaning. The letter of that group is the answer for that item. Your answer sheet and our correct answers follow the last question.

Correct key answers to all these test questions will be found at the end of the test.

Group A

indication ambiguous excruciating thin

Group B

confirmation financial phobia erasure

Group C

fiduciary similar yellowish skill

Group D

theft winding receive procrastination

Group E

franchise heir hardy preference

1. fiscal
2. deletion
3. equivocal
4. corroboration
5. tortuous
6. predilection
7. sallow
8. virtuosity
9. scion
10. tenuous

Correct Answers For The Foregoing Questions

To assist you in scoring yourself we have provided Correct Answers alongside your Answer Sheet. May we therefore suggest that while you are doing the test you cover the Correct Answers with a sheet of white paper.....to avoid temptation and to arrive at an accurate estimate of your ability and progress.

Answer Sheet

	A	B	C	D	E
1					
2					
3					
4					
5					
6					
7					
8					
9					
10					

SCORE

.....................%

NO. CORRECT ÷
NO. OF QUESTIONS ON THIS TEST

Correct Answers

	A	B	C	D	E
1		■			
2		■			
3	■				
4		■			
5				■	
6					■
7			■		
8			■		
9					■
10	■				

V. LETTER-SYMBOL PRACTICE

This type of test, which is also known as a substitution test, requires the association of symbols and involves speed and accuracy in performance. It also involves visual memory.

In one form or another, it is found on the Wechsler Adult Intelligence Scale and on employment and classification tests.

DIRECTIONS FOR LETTER-SYMBOL PRACTICE

This practice consists of 100 items, all of which are based on the Letter-Symbol Code shown below.

The Letter-Symbol Code consists of ten divided rectangles. In the upper half of each rectangle there is a letter. In the lower half there is a symbol. This Code is followed by 100 rectangles divided into three parts. The upper third is the item number. The middle third contains a symbol (one of the ten symbols which form the Letter-Symbol Code). The bottom third, entitled *Letter-Answer,* is where you will record your answers by inserting the corresponding letter. You are to insert for each item the appropriate letter for the symbols shown. The first ten items are answered correctly so that you can be absolutely sure of the procedure.

Work quickly but accurately. Keep forcing yourself because in that way you will acquire skill in this type of test. Allow yourself only five minutes. You should be able to complete 75 items in that time on your first try.

The complete set of correct answers follows Item 100. Compare your answers with these correct answers and derive your score. You should have no more than two errors.

LETTER-SYMBOL CODE FOR ITEMS 1 TO 100.

LETTER	A	B	C	D	E	F	G	H	I	J
SYMBOL										

ITEMS 1 TO 100. THE FIRST TEN ARE SAMPLES, ANSWERED CORRECTLY.

ITEM NUMBER	1	2	3	4	5	6	7	8	9	10
SYMBOL										
LETTER ANSWER	F	H	I	J	C	G	D	A	E	B
ITEM NUMBER	11	12	13	14	15	16	17	18	19	20
SYMBOL										
LETTER ANSWER										
ITEM NUMBER	21	22	23	24	25	26	27	28	29	30
SYMBOL										
LETTER ANSWER										

ITEM NUMBER	31	32	33	34	35	36	37	38	39	40
SYMBOL										
LETTER ANSWER										
ITEM NUMBER	41	42	43	44	45	46	47	48	49	50
SYMBOL										
LETTER ANSWER										
ITEM NUMBER	51	52	53	54	55	56	57	58	59	60
SYMBOL										
LETTER ANSWER										
ITEM NUMBER	61	62	63	64	65	66	67	68	69	70
SYMBOL										
LETTER ANSWER										
ITEM NUMBER	71	72	73	74	75	76	77	78	79	80
SYMBOL										
LETTER ANSWER										
ITEM NUMBER	81	82	83	84	85	86	87	88	89	90
SYMBOL										
LETTER ANSWER										
ITEM NUMBER	91	92	93	94	95	96	97	98	99	100
SYMBOL										
LETTER ANSWER										

Correct Answers For The Foregoing Questions

1. F
2. H
3. I
4. J
5. C
6. G
7. D
8. A
9. E
10. B
11. G
12. E
13. D
14. H
15. I
16. F
17. C
18. J
19. B
20. A
21. A
22. J
23. H
24. G
25. B
26. C
27. E
28. F
29. D
30. I
31. C
32. I
33. F
34. E
35. J
36. H
37. G
38. A
39. B
40. D
41. D
42. G
43. A
44. B
45. F
46. I
47. H
48. C
49. E
50. J
51. E
52. F
53. J
54. I
55. C
56. H
57. A
58. D
59. G
60. B
61. A
62. D
63. H
64. F
65. G
66. B
67. I
68. J
69. C
70. E
71. B
72. E
73. I
74. C
75. A
76. J
77. H
78. G
79. D
80. F
81. I
82. C
83. G
84. J
85. D
86. E
87. B
88. A
89. F
90. H
91. J
92. D
93. E
94. I
95. B
96. A
97. F
98. C
99. H
100. G

VI. EYE-HAND COORDINATION

Speed and accuracy tests of this type are designed to show how well your eyes and hand work together. As such, they are used to test gross dexterity.

You will be given a list like the one below and an answer sheet. The list consists of several columns of numbers with letters. The numbers in the list refer to the numbers on the answer sheet. The letters refer to the answer positions, A, B, C, D and E. For each number and letter in the list find the same number on the answer sheet and mark the space for the letter.

The first question in the list below is 1B and if you will examine the Correct Answers following, you will see that answer 1 is marked in space B to show you how an answer should be marked. The next question is 2D, so find 2 on your answer sheet and mark space D.

The first 125 numbers on the list run in order from 1 to 125. After item 125 the numbers do not run in numerical order. Thus, after you have finished the first 125 items, and have marked 125 E according to the list, you will find that the next item is marked 51 E. Find item number 51 on the answer sheet and mark the E space for number 51. Then continue with the remaining items in the list in the same way. When you finish the test you will have more than one letter marked for many items on your answer sheet.

You may then compare your answer sheet with the correct answer sheet for this test on the following page.

Note the time it took you to do this first test. Compare it with the time you take on the following two tests of this type.

SPEED AND ACCURACY TEST NUMBER I

1.B	26.B	50.A	74.A	98.B	122.A	9.E	112.D	121.A	50.E
2.D	27.E	51.D	75.B	99.A	123.D	42.A	44.A	99.D	37.B
3.A	28.C	52.A	76.D	100.C	124.A	109.D	72.C	100.B	73.A
4.E	29.B	53.D	77.B	101.A	125.E	60.B	49.B	2.A	83.A
5.D	30.C	54.A	78.E	102.E	51.E	51.C	85.D	21.E	30.D
6.B	31.A	55.E	79.C	103.C	4.A	37.D	33.E	107.A	101.C
7.E	32.D	56.B	80.E	104.A	33.D	77.E	122.C	39.B	98.D
8.B	33.C	57.D	81.A	105.D	64.C	123.C	26.A	105.E	109.E
9.D	34.D	58.C	82.E	106.B	5.B	65.C	12.B	74.D	71.B
10.A	35.D	59.D	83.C	107.D	114.A	4.B	90.E	111.A	35.C
11.A	36.E	60.C	84.A	108.C	94.B	94.E	53.C	59.B	26.D
12.D	37.A	61.C	85.A	109.A	8.D	3.B	20.A	83.E	59.E
13.E	38.C	62.B	86.E	110.B	101.E	9.C	114.C	102.A	110.C
14.C	39.E	63.C	87.D	111.D	10.C	70.D	47.C	36.B	52.C
15.B	40.E	64.E	88.E	112.B	72.B	62.C	9.A	40.C	68.D
16.D	41.C	65.C	89.B	113.E	123.E	79.D	43.E	14.D	104.C
17.C	42.D	66.B	90.D	114.B	16.A	53.B	25.C	107.B	47.A
18.A	43.B	67.D	91.D	115.D	42.C	76.C	113.B	44.E	115.B
19.C	44.D	68.B	92.C	116.C	15.D	75.A	73.D	72.D	7.A
20.E	45.A	69.D	93.A	117.E	61.B	89.D	37.C	45.B	38.D
21.B	46.B	70.A	94.C	118.C	76.A	26.E	3.D	87.A	104.D
22.C	47.E	71.E	95.B	119.B	49.D	59.C	95.A	93.B	82.A
23.A	48.D	72.A	96.A	120.E	91.E	6.E	16.E	19.B	21.D
24.E	49.C	73.E	97.B	121.C	68.E	80.B	11.D	68.A	99.C
25.B									55.B

Time:______

TEST____________________ PART____________________

DATE____________________

RATING

(Slightly reduced from standard size used with many tests)

USE THE SPECIAL PENCIL. MAKE GLOSSY BLACK MARKS.

1 A B C D E	26 A B C D E	51 A B C D E	76 A B C D E	101 A B C D E
2 A B C D E	27 A B C D E	52 A B C D E	77 A B C D E	102 A B C D E
3 A B C D E	28 A B C D E	53 A B C D E	78 A B C D E	103 A B C D E
4 A B C D E	29 A B C D E	54 A B C D E	79 A B C D E	104 A B C D E
5 A B C D E	30 A B C D E	55 A B C D E	80 A B C D E	105 A B C D E
6 A B C D E	31 A B C D E	56 A B C D E	81 A B C D E	106 A B C D E
7 A B C D E	32 A B C D E	57 A B C D E	82 A B C D E	107 A B C D E
8 A B C D E	33 A B C D E	58 A B C D E	83 A B C D E	108 A B C D E
9 A B C D E	34 A B C D E	59 A B C D E	84 A B C D E	109 A B C D E
10 A B C D E	35 A B C D E	60 A B C D E	85 A B C D E	110 A B C D E

Make only ONE mark for each answer. Additional and stray marks may be counted as mistakes. In making corrections, erase errors COMPLETELY.

11 A B C D E	36 A B C D E	61 A B C D E	86 A B C D E	111 A B C D E
12 A B C D E	37 A B C D E	62 A B C D E	87 A B C D E	112 A B C D E
13 A B C D E	38 A B C D E	63 A B C D E	88 A B C D E	113 A B C D E
14 A B C D E	39 A B C D E	64 A B C D E	89 A B C D E	114 A B C D E
15 A B C D E	40 A B C D E	65 A B C D E	90 A B C D E	115 A B C D E
16 A B C D E	41 A B C D E	66 A B C D E	91 A B C D E	116 A B C D E
17 A B C D E	42 A B C D E	67 A B C D E	92 A B C D E	117 A B C D E
18 A B C D E	43 A B C D E	68 A B C D E	93 A B C D E	118 A B C D E
19 A B C D E	44 A B C D E	69 A B C D E	94 A B C D E	119 A B C D E
20 A B C D E	45 A B C D E	70 A B C D E	95 A B C D E	120 A B C D E
21 A B C D E	46 A B C D E	71 A B C D E	96 A B C D E	121 A B C D E
22 A B C D E	47 A B C D E	72 A B C D E	97 A B C D E	122 A B C D E
23 A B C D E	48 A B C D E	73 A B C D E	98 A B C D E	123 A B C D E
24 A B C D E	49 A B C D E	74 A B C D E	99 A B C D E	124 A B C D E
25 A B C D E	50 A B C D E	75 A B C D E	100 A B C D E	125 A B C D E

CORRECT ANSWERS—TEST NUMBER I

This is the way your answers should appear if you have answered all the questions correctly.

Time:________

RATING

USE THE SPECIAL PENCIL. MAKE GLOSSY BLACK MARKS.

No.	Answer	No.	Answer	No.	Answer	No.	Answer	No.	Answer
1	B	26	A B D E	51	C D E	76	A C D	101	A C E
2	A D	27	E	52	A C	77	B E	102	A E
3	A B D	28	C	53	B C D	78	E	103	C
4	A B E	29	B	54	A	79	C D	104	A C D
5	B D	30	C D	55	B E	80	B E	105	D E
6	B E	31	A	56	B	81	A	106	B
7	A E	32	D	57	D	82	A E	107	A B D
8	B D	33	C D E	58	C	83	A C E	108	C
9	A C D E	34	D	59	B C D E	84	A	109	A D E
10	A C	35	C D	60	B C	85	A D	110	B C

Make only ONE mark for each answer. Additional and stray marks may be counted as mistakes. In making corrections, erase errors COMPLETELY.

No.	Answer	No.	Answer	No.	Answer	No.	Answer	No.	Answer
11	A D	36	B E	61	B C	86	E	111	A D
12	B D	37	A B C D	62	B C	87	A D	112	B D
13	E	38	C D	63	C	88	E	113	B E
14	C D	39	B E	64	C E	89	B D	114	A B C
15	B D	40	C E	65	C D	90	D E	115	B D
16	A D E	41	C	66	B	91	D E	116	C
17	C	42	A C D	67	D	92	C	117	E
18	A	43	B E	68	A B D E	93	A B	118	C
19	B C	44	A D E	69	D	94	B C E	119	B
20	A E	45	A B	70	A D	95	A B	120	E
21	B D E	46	B	71	B E	96	A	121	A C
22	C	47	A C E	72	A B C D	97	B	122	A C
23	A	48	D	73	A D E	98	B D	123	D E
24	E	49	B C D	74	A D	99	A C D	124	A
25	B C	50	A E	75	A B	100	B C	125	E

SPEED AND ACCURACY TEST NUMBER II

COMPLETE the answer sheet following the same instructions as for Test I. Record the length of time it takes to finish this test.

Work as fast as you can without making errors. Do not waste time going over the lines you draw. Once over is enough as long as the line is clear.

(Hints: In the first part, you may find that you can work faster if you hold several numbers and letters in your mind at a time. For the second part, notice that the answer sheet has 5 columns, with 25 numbers in each column. Notice also that there are 10 numbers in the top part of each column and 15 numbers in the bottom part of each column.)

1.D	37.E	73.C	109.E	20.E	68.C	73.B
2.B	38.A	74.E	110.D	114.A	9.C	27.A
3.E	39.C	75.D	111.B	47.A	42.E	3.B
4.C	40.C	76.B	112.D	9.E	109.B	95.E
5.B	41.A	77.D	113.C	43.C	60.D	16.C
6.D	42.B	78.C	114.D	25.A	51.A	11.B
7.C	43.D	79.A	115.B	113.D	37.B	121.E
8.D	44.B	80.C	116.A	37.D	77.C	99.B
9.B	45.E	81.E	117.C	73.E	123.A	100.D
10.E	46.D	82.C	118.A	83.E	65.B	2.E
11.E	47.C	83.A	119.D	30.B	4.D	21.C
12.B	48.B	84.E	120.C	101.A	94.C	107.E
13.C	49.A	85.E	121.A	98.B	3.D	39.D
14.A	50.E	86.C	122.E	109.C	9.A	105.C
15.D	51.B	87.B	123.B	71.D	70.B	74.B
16.B	52.E	88.C	124.E	35.A	62.A	111.E
17.A	53.B	89.D	125.C	26.B	79.B	59.D
18.E	54.E	90.B	51.C	59.C	53.D	83.C
19.A	55.C	91.B	4.E	102.E	76.A	110.A
20.C	56.D	92.A	33.B	36.D	75.E	52.A
21.D	57.B	93.E	64.A	40.A	89.B	68.B
22.A	58.A	94.A	5.D	14.B	26.C	104.A
23.E	59.B	95.D	114.E	107.D	59.A	47.E
24.C	60.A	96.E	94.D	44.C	6.C	115.C
25.D	61.A	97.D	8.B	72.B	80.D	7.E
26.D	62.C	98.D	101.C	45.D	112.B	38.B
27.C	63.A	99.E	10.A	87.E	44.E	61.C
28.A	64.C	100.A	72.D	93.D	72.A	2.A
29.D	65.A	101.E	123.C	19.D	49.D	120.B
30.A	66.D	102.C	16.E	68.E	85.B	48.E
31.E	67.B	103.A	42.A	50.C	33.C	91.D
32.B	68.D	104.E	15.B	104.B	122.A	54.A
33.A	69.B	105.B	61.D	82.E	26.E	1.C
34.B	70.E	106.D	76.E	21.B	12.D	125.D
35.B	71.C	107.B	49.B	99.A	90.C	57.E
36.C	72.E	108.A	91.C	55.D	53.A	24.A

Time:______

TEST____ PART____________________

DATE____________________

RATING

(Slightly reduced from standard size used with many tests)

USE THE SPECIAL PENCIL. MAKE GLOSSY BLACK MARKS.

1 A B C D E	26 A B C D E	51 A B C D E	76 A B C D E	101 A B C D E
2 A B C D E	27 A B C D E	52 A B C D E	77 A B C D E	102 A B C D E
3 A B C D E	28 A B C D E	53 A B C D E	78 A B C D E	103 A B C D E
4 A B C D E	29 A B C D E	54 A B C D E	79 A B C D E	104 A B C D E
5 A B C D E	30 A B C D E	55 A B C D E	80 A B C D E	105 A B C D E
6 A B C D E	31 A B C D E	56 A B C D E	81 A B C D E	106 A B C D E
7 A B C D E	32 A B C D E	57 A B C D E	82 A B C D E	107 A B C D E
8 A B C D E	33 A B C D E	58 A B C D E	83 A B C D E	108 A B C D E
9 A B C D E	34 A B C D E	59 A B C D E	84 A B C D E	109 A B C D E
10 A B C D E	35 A B C D E	60 A B C D E	85 A B C D E	110 A B C D E

Make only ONE mark for each answer. Additional and stray marks may be counted as mistakes. In making corrections, erase errors COMPLETELY.

11 A B C D E	36 A B C D E	61 A B C D E	86 A B C D E	111 A B C D E
12 A B C D E	37 A B C D E	62 A B C D E	87 A B C D E	112 A B C D E
13 A B C D E	38 A B C D E	63 A B C D E	88 A B C D E	113 A B C D E
14 A B C D E	39 A B C D E	64 A B C D E	89 A B C D E	114 A B C D E
15 A B C D E	40 A B C D E	65 A B C D E	90 A B C D E	115 A B C D E
16 A B C D E	41 A B C D E	66 A B C D E	91 A B C D E	116 A B C D E
17 A B C D E	42 A B C D E	67 A B C D E	92 A B C D E	117 A B C D E
18 A B C D E	43 A B C D E	68 A B C D E	93 A B C D E	118 A B C D E
19 A B C D E	44 A B C D E	69 A B C D E	94 A B C D E	119 A B C D E
20 A B C D E	45 A B C D E	70 A B C D E	95 A B C D E	120 A B C D E
21 A B C D E	46 A B C D E	71 A B C D E	96 A B C D E	121 A B C D E
22 A B C D E	47 A B C D E	72 A B C D E	97 A B C D E	122 A B C D E
23 A B C D E	48 A B C D E	73 A B C D E	98 A B C D E	123 A B C D E
24 A B C D E	49 A B C D E	74 A B C D E	99 A B C D E	124 A B C D E
25 A B C D E	50 A B C D E	75 A B C D E	100 A B C D E	125 A B C D E

CORRECT ANSWERS—TEST NUMBER II

Time: ______

RATING

USE THE SPECIAL PENCIL. MAKE GLOSSY BLACK MARKS.

No.	Answer	No.	Answer	No.	Answer	No.	Answer	No.	Answer
1	C D	26	B C D E	51	A B C	76	A B E	101	A C E
2	A B E	27	A C	52	A E	77	C D	102	C E
3	B D E	28	A	53	A B D	78	C	103	A
4	C D E	29	D	54	A E	79	A B	104	A B E
5	B D	30	A B	55	C D	80	C D	105	B C
6	C D	31	E	56	D	81	E	106	D
7	C E	32	B	57	B E	82	C E	107	B D E
8	B D	33	A B C	58	A	83	A C E	108	A
9	A B C E	34	B	59	A B C D	84	E	109	B C E
10	A E	35	A B	60	A D	85	B E	110	A D

Make only ONE mark for each answer. Additional and stray marks may be counted as mistakes. In making corrections, erase errors COMPLETELY.

No.	Answer	No.	Answer	No.	Answer	No.	Answer	No.	Answer
11	B E	36	C D	61	A C D	86	C	111	B E
12	B D	37	B D E	62	A C	87	B E	112	B D
13	C	38	A B	63	A	88	C	113	C D
14	A B	39	C D	64	A C	89	B D	114	A D E
15	B D	40	A C	65	A B	90	B C	115	B C
16	B C E	41	A	66	D	91	B C D	116	A
17	A	42	A B E	67	B	92	A	117	C
18	E	43	C D	68	B C D E	93	D E	118	A
19	A D	44	B C	69	B	94	A C D	119	D
20	C E	45	D E	70	B E	95	D E	120	B C
21	B C D	46	D	71	C D	96	E	121	A E
22	A	47	A C E	72	A B D E	97	D	122	A E
23	E	48	B E	73	B C E	98	B D	123	A B C
24	A C	49	A B D	74	B E	99	A B E	124	E
25	A D	50	C E	75	D E	100	A D	125	C D

SPEED AND ACCURACY TEST NUMBER III

Test Number Three is longer than Test Number Two, but if you have followed the instructions carefully up to now, and if you make good use of what you have learned, you should be able to complete it in about the same amount of time.

1.C	31.A	61.C	91.D	121.C	8.B	38.C	122.E
11.C	32.D	62.E	92.C	122.A	9.D	39.E	101.D
18.E	33.C	63.C	93.A	123.D	10.A	40.E	58.A
50.D	34.D	64.E	94.C	124.A	11.A	41.C	27.A
41.E	35.D	65.C	95.B	125.E	12.D	42.D	90.B
28.A	36.E	66.B	96.A	20.A	13.E	43.B	73.E
52.E	88.B	67.D	97.B	114.C	14.C	44.D	74.A
63.E	78.A	68.B	98.B	47.C	15.B	45.A	75.B
75.D	102.C	69.D	99.A	9.A	16.D	46.B	76.D
100.A	111.B	70.A	100.C	43.E	17.C	47.E	77.B
58.E	118.A	71.E	101.A	25.C	18.A	48.D	78.E
30.A	98.E	72.A	102.E	113.B	68.E	49.C	79.C
102.A	92.A	74.E	103.C	37.B	9.E	50.A	80.E
36.B	84.E	48.C	104.A	73.A	109.D	51.D	81.A
40.C	56.E	40.A	105.D	83.A	108.D	52.A	82.E
14.D	62.A	32.B	106.B	30.D	60.B	53.D	83.C
107.B	5.C	6.D	107.D	101.C	51.C	54.A	84.A
44.E	34.B	14.A	108.C	98.D	37.D	73.D	85.A
72.D	76.C	23.D	97.D	109.E	77.E	27.C	86.E
45.B	75.A	103.D	93.E	71.B	123.C	95.A	37.C
87.A	89.D	113.A	82.C	35.C	65.D	97.A	88.E
93.B	26.E	116.B	54.E	26.D	4.B	16.E	89.B
19.B	59.C	10.D	64.B	59.E	94.E	11.D	90.D
68.A	6.E	35.E	65.E	108.A	3.B	121.A	51.E
50.E	80.B	110.C	46.A	125.D	9.C	99.D	4.A
104.D	112.D	52.C	81.E	69.C	70.D	100.B	64.C
82.A	44.A	68.D	105.C	22.E	62.C	2.A	34.C
21.D	72.C	104.C	7.D	106.E	79.D	21.E	5.B
99.C	49.B	47.A	17.B	39.D	53.B	107.A	114.A
55.B	85.D	115.B	38.A	71.C	110.E	39.B	94.B
19.C	33.E	7.A	109.A	45.E	70.C	105.E	8.D
20.E	122.C	38.D	110.B	15.A	29.E	74.D	101.E
21.B	26.A	61.E	111.D	79.A	8.A	111.A	10.C
22.C	12.B	2.C	112.B	20.D	13.D	59.B	72.B
23.A	90.E	120.D	113.E	77.D	67.A	83.E	123.E
24.B	53.C	48.A	114.B	1.B	57.C	119.E	16.A
25.B	55.E	91.B	115.D	2.D	85.E	124.B	42.C
26.B	56.B	54.C	116.C	3.A	112.A	66.D	15.D
27.E	57.D	1.E	117.E	4.E	120.B	33.A	61.B
28.C	58.C	125.B	118.C	5.D	25.E	43.A	76.A
29.B	59.D	57.A	119.B	6.B	80.A	12.C	49.D
30.C	60.C	24.C	120.E	7.E	37.A	55.D	91.E

TEST____PART____________________

DATE____________________

RATING

(Slightly reduced from standard size used with many tests)

USE THE SPECIAL PENCIL. MAKE GLOSSY BLACK MARKS.

1 A B C D E	26 A B C D E	51 A B C D E	76 A B C D E	101 A B C D E
2 A B C D E	27 A B C D E	52 A B C D E	77 A B C D E	102 A B C D E
3 A B C D E	28 A B C D E	53 A B C D E	78 A B C D E	103 A B C D E
4 A B C D E	29 A B C D E	54 A B C D E	79 A B C D E	104 A B C D E
5 A B C D E	30 A B C D E	55 A B C D E	80 A B C D E	105 A B C D E
6 A B C D E	31 A B C D E	56 A B C D E	81 A B C D E	106 A B C D E
7 A B C D E	32 A B C D E	57 A B C D E	82 A B C D E	107 A B C D E
8 A B C D E	33 A B C D E	58 A B C D E	83 A B C D E	108 A B C D E
9 A B C D E	34 A B C D E	59 A B C D E	84 A B C D E	109 A B C D E
10 A B C D E	35 A B C D E	60 A B C D E	85 A B C D E	110 A B C D E

Make only ONE mark for each answer. Additional and stray marks may be counted as mistakes. In making corrections, erase errors COMPLETELY.

11 A B C D E	36 A B C D E	61 A B C D E	86 A B C D E	111 A B C D E
12 A B C D E	37 A B C D E	62 A B C D E	87 A B C D E	112 A B C D E
13 A B C D E	38 A B C D E	63 A B C D E	88 A B C D E	113 A B C D E
14 A B C D E	39 A B C D E	64 A B C D E	89 A B C D E	114 A B C D E
15 A B C D E	40 A B C D E	65 A B C D E	90 A B C D E	115 A B C D E
16 A B C D E	41 A B C D E	66 A B C D E	91 A B C D E	116 A B C D E
17 A B C D E	42 A B C D E	67 A B C D E	92 A B C D E	117 A B C D E
18 A B C D E	43 A B C D E	68 A B C D E	93 A B C D E	118 A B C D E
19 A B C D E	44 A B C D E	69 A B C D E	94 A B C D E	119 A B C D E
20 A B C D E	45 A B C D E	70 A B C D E	95 A B C D E	120 A B C D E
21 A B C D E	46 A B C D E	71 A B C D E	96 A B C D E	121 A B C D E
22 A B C D E	47 A B C D E	72 A B C D E	97 A B C D E	122 A B C D E
23 A B C D E	48 A B C D E	73 A B C D E	98 A B C D E	123 A B C D E
24 A B C D E	49 A B C D E	74 A B C D E	99 A B C D E	124 A B C D E
25 A B C D E	50 A B C D E	75 A B C D E	100 A B C D E	125 A B C D E

CORRECT ANSWERS—TEST NUMBER III

After checking your answers and carefully noting your time, if you have not noticed a significant improvement in your score, do each test over again. Be sure that you have followed all of the directions.

Time:______

RATING

USE THE SPECIAL PENCIL. MAKE GLOSSY BLACK MARKS.

Make only ONE mark for each answer. Additional and stray marks may be counted as mistakes. In making corrections, erase errors COMPLETELY.

VII. INSPECTION TESTS

Counting Crosses and Zeros

In this type of test each question asks for the number of X's or O's or both in a certain area of the diagram shown. Count the X's as directed. If an X or an O falls across a line dividing one area from another, count it as being in the area in which most of it falls. Look for your answer among those suggested and mark the answer column accordingly. If your answer is not listed, mark E.

	COLUMN A	COLUMN B	COLUMN C	COLUMN D	COLUMN E
ROW 1	X X X X X X O O X O OO O O O X O X X X X O X O O O O O O X	O X X O X O X O O X O O O X X X X X X O O O X O O X XX OX	X O X O O X X X O X X O O X O O OX X O X OXO O X X X O X	O O O OX X X X X O XX X X X X OO O O O O OO O O O OOO	X X X X O O O O X X X O X O O O XX O X OX O OO X X X O O XO
ROW 2	O X O X O O X X X O X O O O O O O O X X X X X O O O X X X O	X O O O X O O X X X O X X X X X X X X O O O O X O X O	X O X O X O X O X O X X X O O O O O X X X X X X O	X O X O O O X O O X X O O O X O X X X O X O X O O	X O O O O O X X X O X O O O X X O O X O X X O O O
ROW 3	X O O O X O O X X X O X X O O O X O O O O O OX X X X X X X	X X X X O O O O X X X X X O O O O O X X X X X X OO	X O O X O O O X X OXO X X O O OX O O X X X O X X O X	X O O O O O X X X X O X X X X X O O O X O X O X O	X X X X X O O O O X X X X X X O O O O O X O O O XO
ROW 4	O O O O O O X X X O X O O X O X O X X O O X O O O O X X O	O O X X X X X OX X O O O O X O O X O X X X X X X	X X X O OX O O O X X X X O O XO O O X X O X X OOO	X O O X X X O O O O O X O X O X X O X O X O X X O	O X X O XO X X X O XO O O O O X X X X X O O X X X O

1. How many X's are there in Row 1, Column B?
   (A) 14 (B) 16 (C) 17 (D) 18 (E) None of these
2. How many O's in Row 1, Columns A and B?
   (A) 30 (B) 31 (C) 33 (D) 34 (E) None of these
3. How many X's in Row 2, Column A?
   (A) 10 (B) 11 (C) 12 (D) 14 (E) None of these
4. How many O's in Row 3, Column C?
   (A) 12 (B) 13 (C) 15 (D) 16 (E) None of these
5. How many X's and O's in Row 3, Column B?
   (A) 25 (B) 26 (C) 27 (D) 29 (E) None of these
6. How many X's in Row 4, Column A?
   (A) 13 (B) 14 (C) 16 (D) 17 (E) None of these
7. How many X's in Row 2, Column D?
   (A) 11 (B) 12 (C) 14 (D) 15 (E) None of these

8. **How many O's in Row 2, Column C?**
(A) 10 (B) 11 (C) 12 (D) 14 (E) None of these

9. How many X's and O's in Row 3, Column E?
(A) 24 (B) 25 (C) 26 (D) 22 (E) None of these

10. How many O's in Row 3, Column E?
(A) 10 (B) 11 (C) 12 (D) 13 (E) None of these

11. How many X's in Row 1, Column E?
(A) 16 (B) 17 (C) 19 (D) 20 (E) None of these

12. How many O's in Row 4, Col. D?
(A) 11 (B) 12 (C) 14 (D) 15 (E) None of these

13. How many O's in Rows 2 and 3, Column B?
(A) 22 (B) 23 (C) 24 (D) 25 (E) None of these

14. How many X's in Row 4, Columns D and E?
(A) 25 (B) 26 (C) 27 (D) 28 (E) None of these

15. How many X's and O's in Row 2, Column C?
(A) 25 (B) 26 (C) 27 (D) 28 (E) None of these

16. How many O's in Row 2, Column E?
(A) 13 (B) 14 (C) 15 (D) 16 (E) None of these

17. How many O's in Row 4, Column A?
(A) 17 (B) 18 (C) 20 (D) 21 (E) None of these

18. How many X's in Rows 2 and 3, Column C?
(A) 27 (B) 28 (C) 29 (D) 31 (E) None of these

19. How many O's in Row 4, Columns B and C?
(A) 21 (B) 22 (C) 23 (D) 24 (E) None of these

20. How many X's and O's in Row 3, Columns D and E?
(A) 49 (B) 50 (C) 51 (D) 52 (E) None of these

21. How many O's in Row 1, Column D?
(A) 13 (B) 14 (C) 15 (D) 16 (E) None of these

22. How many X's in Row 4, Column B?
(A) 15 (B) 16 (C) 18 (D) 19 (E) None of these

23. How many O's in Rows 2, 3 and 4, Column B?
(A) 30 (B) 31 (C) 32 (D) 33 (E) None of these

24. How many X's in Row 3, Columns C, D, and E?
(A) 39 (B) 40 (C) 42 (D) 43 (E) None of these

Answers To First Inspection Test

1. B	4. E	7. A	10. D	13. B	16. C	19. D	22. A
2. A	5. B	8. B	11. A	14. C	17. B	20. C	23. D
3. D	6. E	9. C	12. E	15. A	18. B	21. E	24. B

VIII. EXAMINING OBJECTS

Another test of speed and accuracy which also tests your ability to inspect, sort and examine objects of many kinds is here given to you for practice.

The diagram below at the left shows five bins into which pairs of parts are to be sorted.

Bin A is for pairs that are ALL RIGHT, and where both parts have the same number. One part is a square, the other round.

Bin B is for pairs that have a part that is BASHED IN. One part is square, the other round, and both have the same number.

Bin C is for a COMBINATION of two round or two square parts, both bearing the same number.

Bin D is for pairs in which the parts have different numbers. One part is round, the other square.

Bin E is for pairs in which the number spaces are empty. One part is round; the other square.

Look at each pair of parts below and decide which bin they go into. The letter of that bin should be recorded on the Answer Sheet.

The first six practice problems are answered correctly. When you understand these, go on and answer all the problems on these 3 pages.

Correct answers are shown after the last problem and you should use them to compare with your answers. After you have derived your answers — not before.

CODE FOR INSPECTION TEST

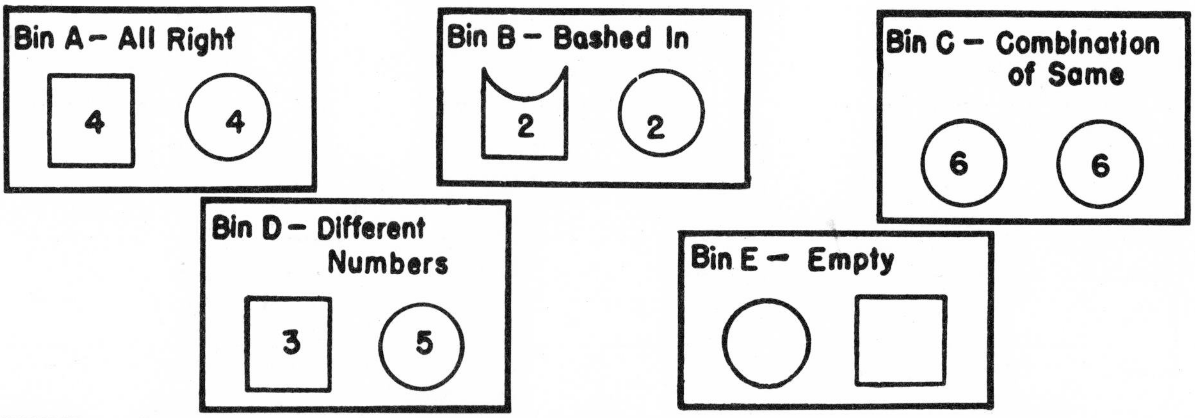

Bin A – All Right — 4 4

Bin B – Bashed In — 2 2

Bin C – Combination of Same — 6 6

Bin D – Different Numbers — 3 5

Bin E – Empty

9 9 C

5 5 ..... A

7 7 ..... B

S1290

..... E

3 3 ..... B

3 5 ..... D

1. 2 2 ....._
2. 3 3 ....._
3. 5 5 ....._
4. 3 7 ....._
5. 1 1 ....._
6. 4 4 ....._
7. 1 1 ....._
8. 7 7 ....._
9. 6 6 ....._
10. ....._
11. 3 3 ....._
12. 8 5 ....._
13. 6 6 ....._
14. 3 3 ....._
15. ....._
16. 5 5 ....._
17. 7 7 ....._
18. 4 4 ....._
19. ....._
20. 1 3 ....._
21. 8 8 ....._
22. 1 1 ....._
23. 2 2 ....._
24. 5 7 ....._
25. 8 8 ....._
26. 2 2 ....._
27. ....._
28. 4 4 ....._
29. 5 3 ....._
30. 7 7 ....._
31. 1 1 ....._
32. 2 2 ....._
33. ....._
34. 1 3 ....._
35. 6 6 ....._
36. 3 3 ....._

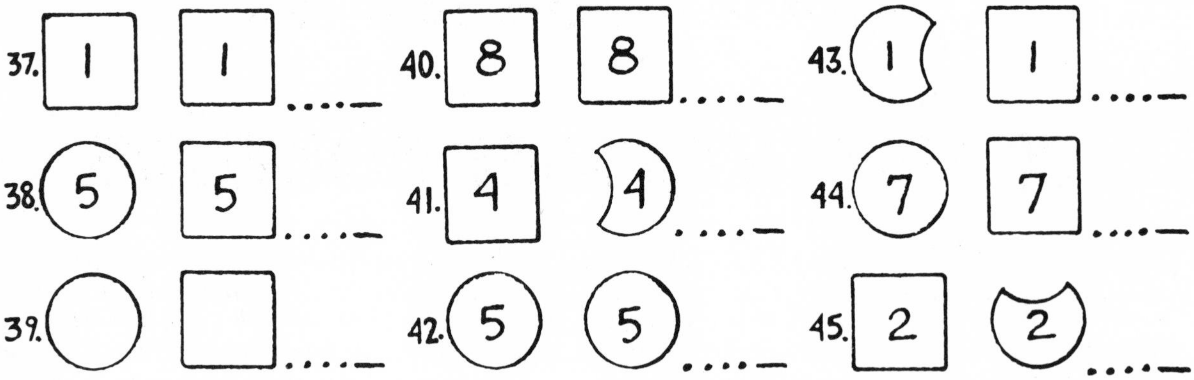

Correct Answers For The Foregoing Questions

(Please make every effort to answer the questions on your own before looking at these answers. You'll make faster progress by following this rule.)

1. B	7. B	13. B	19. E	25. A	31. B	37. C	43. B
2. C	8. B	14. C	20. D	26. B	32. C	38. A	44. A
3. C	9. C	15. E	21. A	27. E	33. E	39. E	45. B
4. D	10. E	16. C	22. C	28. C	34. D	40. C	
5. B	11. B	17. C	23. B	29. D	35. B	41. B	
6. C	12. D	18. B	24. D	30. C	36. B	42. C	

SCORE
%
NO. CORRECT ÷
NO. OF QUESTIONS ON THIS TEST

IX. NAME AND NUMBER COMPARISONS

CLERICAL SPEED. Name Comparisons and Number Comparisons are one of the most popular means of testing clerical aptitude. They emphasize your ability to quickly recognize similarities and differences. Although people differ greatly in this ability, it is possible for you to practice and to improve your skill in this type of question. Your score depends on both error and speed. Therefore you must work out for yourself a nice balance between the two. If you work too carefully you may obtain a low score because you are working too slowly in the hope of avoiding errors. On the other hand, if you work too quickly, you may complete a large number of items and, at the same time, incur penalties for a large number of errors. In your practice you must try different approaches to find out which one is best for you.

THESE questions may seem at first glance to be rather basic. As you read the instructions for answering them, however, you will find that they not only test your accuracy of observation and comparison, but also your accuracy in setting down the results of your observation, so that this method constitutes a two-fold test for aptitude. Working through the following practice questions carefully should help you to gain both accuracy and speed—two qualities essential to success.

The questions are broken down into short subtests. As you do each one, time yourself, and then check your answers with the key answers in the back. Set down the time it takes you to do each subtest, and the number of answers in each test that you answer correctly. By doing so, you can gauge your proficiency, and also your improvement as you progress from one test to the next.

A. COMPARING NAMES OR NUMBERS IN SETS OF THREE

Each of the following questions consists of three names or numbers which are much alike. For each question, compare the names or numbers, to decide which ones, if any, are exactly alike. If all three names or numbers are exactly alike, your answer will be (A); if only the first and second names or numbers are exactly alike, your answer will be (B); if only the first and third are exactly alike, (C); if only the second and third are exactly alike, (D); if all three names or numbers are different, your answer will be (E). Work each subtest out, and note the time you took, before checking the key answers.

SAMPLE TEST — WITH EXPLANATION

1. Davis Hazen
   David Hozen
   David Hazen
2. Lois Appel
   Lois Appel
   Lois Apfel
3. June Allen
   Jane Allan
   Jane Allan
4. Jno. M. Dea
   Jno. M. Dea
   Jno. M. Dea
5. Ann K. Dove
   Ann H. Dove
   Ann K. Dove
6. 21107
   21017
   21117
7. 34212
   34212
   34112
8. 10235
   10235
   10235
9. 32614
   32164
   32614
10. 23544
    25344
    25344

EXPLANATION AND ANSWERS: In question 1, all three names are different. Therefore the answer is E. In question 2 only the first and second names are the same. Therefore the answer is B. And in the third question only the second and third names are exactly alike. Therefore the answer is D. The other answers are 4-A; 5-C; 6-E; 7-B; 8-A; 9-C; 10-D. From your work with this Sample Test it should be obvious that you will be helped if you have in front of you a statement of the five choices A to E, and what they mean. That will save you the trouble of looking back to the original Directions.

TEST NO. 1

1. Lee Berlin
   Lea Berlin
   Les Berlin
2. Webster Cayne
   Webster Cayne
   Webster Cain
3. Charles Danis
   Charles Donis
   Charles Danis
4. Frank Collyer
   Frank Collyer
   Frank Collyer
5. Sylvia Gross
   Sylvia Grohs
   Sylvia Grohs
6. Thomas O'Neill
   Thomas O'Neil
   Thomas O'Neal
7. Jess M. Olsen
   Jess N. Olson
   Jess M. Olsen
8. Irene Crawford
   Irene Crowford
   Irene Crawford
9. Charles Duggan
   Charles Duggan
   Charles Dugan
10. Frank Dudley
    Frank Dudlee
    Frank Dudley

*Time:*_________ *No. Correct:*_________

TEST NO. 2

1. John Finn
   John Fin
   John Finn
2. Ray Finkelstein
   Ray Finklestein
   Ray Finkelstien
3. Sam Freedman
   Sam Friedman
   Sam Freedman
4. Harold Friedberg
   Harold Friedberg
   Harold Freedberg
5. Trude Friedl
   Trude Freidl
   Trude Freidl
6. Frank Gershaw
   Frank Gershaw
   Frank Gerchaw
7. Nancy Gerlach
   Nancy Gerlach
   Nancy Gerlach
8. Dorothy Goldberg
   Dorothy Goldburg
   Dorothy Goldberg
9. Philip Green
   Philip Greene
   Philip Greene
10. George Hampton
    George Hamton
    George Hamptun

*Time:*_________ *No. Correct:*_________

TEST NO. 3

1. Vincent Imperial
   Vincent Impirial
   Vincent Imperail
2. Robert Innes
   Robert Innes
   Robert Innes
3. Patrick Keane
   Patrick Keene
   Patrick Keen
4. Dora Krigsmann
   Dora Krigsman
   Dora Krigsman
5. Albert Lentz
   Albert Lentz
   Albet Lents
6. Seymour Lindell
   Seymour Lindel
   Seymour Lindell
7. Hugh Lunny
   Hugh Luny
   Hugh Lunny
8. Mal Mallin
   Mal Mallin
   Mal Malin
9. May Marshall
   May Marshall
   May Marshall
10. Walter Mattson
    Walter Mattson
    Walter Matson

*Time:*_________ *No. Correct:*_________

TEST NO. 4

1. Gloria Moore
   Gloria Moor
   Gloria Moore
2. Leo Musso
   Leo Muso
   Leo Muso
3. Morris Mutterperl
   Morris Muterperl
   Morris Mutterpurl
4. Helen Mutter
   Helen Mutter
   Helen Mutter
5. Jack Neiderman
   Jack Neiderman
   Jack Niederman
6. Donald Nearney
   Donald Nurney
   Donald Nurney
7. Adeline Neice
   Adeline Neice
   Adeline Niece
8. Ellis Nichols
   Ellis Nichols
   Ellis Nicols
9. Reed Newsom
   Reed Newsome
   Reed Newsom
10. Anna O'Brien
    Anna O'Brein
    Anna O'Brein

*Time:*_________ *No. Correct:*_________

TEST NO. 5

1. Chas. Nuzzolo
   Chas. Nuzzolo
   Chas. Nuzolo
2. John Nystrom
   John Niestrom
   John Nystrom
3. Wm. Oates
   Wm. Oates
   Wm. Oates
4. Grace O'Brien
   Grace O'Brien
   Grace O'Brein
5. Russell Nyborg
   Russel Nyborg
   Russel Nyborg
6. Emma Ornell
   Emma Ornell
   Emma Ornel
7. Geo. Ortega
   Geo. Ortega
   Geo. Ortaga
8. Henry Osmann
   Henry Osman
   Henry Osmann
9. Wm. Pannick
   Wm. Panick
   Wm. Panick
10. Edw. Pappone
    Edw. Papone
    Edw. Papone

*Time:*__________ *No. Correct:*__________

TEST NO. 6

1. Israel Pann
   Israel Pann
   Israel Pan
2. Sanda Perl
   Sanda Perl
   Sanda Pearl
3. Rose Penso
   Rose Penzo
   Rose Penso
4. Moe Pepperman
   Moe Peppermann
   Moe Peperman
5. Oscar Peretz
   Oscar Peretz
   Oscar Peretz
6. W. Pittman
   W. Pitman
   W. Pitman
7. John Pisculli
   John Piscully
   John Pisculi
8. Donald Pittelli
   Donald Pitelli
   Donald Pitelli
9. Edna Prescott
   Edna Prescott
   Edna Prescot
10. Sidney Pressler
    Sidney Presler
    Sidney Pressler

*Time:*__________ *No. Correct:*__________

TEST NO. 7

1. 78541
   78514
   75814
2. 36395
   36395
   36395
3. 89612
   86912
   89621
4. 78111
   71118
   71118
5. 97338
   93378
   98337
6. 37050
   35070
   37050
7. 62324
   62324
   62324
8. 25622
   26522
   22256
9. 55149
   55419
   55419
10. 22037
    22037
    22037

*Time:*__________
*No. Correct:*______

TEST NO. 8

1. 93476
   94376
   94376
2. 90731
   90731
   90731
3. 29522
   25922
   25922
4. 50090
   50090
   50900
5. 25816
   25816
   25816
6. 71555
   75111
   75155
7. 92889
   92889
   98289
8. 24892
   24892
   28492
9. 46648
   44648
   46648
10. 57048
    57084
    57084

*Time:*__________
*No. Correct:*______

TEST NO. 9

1. 74786
   77468
   74876
2. 73656
   73665
   75663
3. 44231
   44231
   44231
4. 85542
   84552
   82455
5. 41487
   44178
   48714
6. 92850
   92850
   98250
7. 63233
   63233
   62333
8. 23848
   28384
   23848
9. 56658
   55668
   55668
10. 41296
    41296
    41296

*Time:*__________
*No. Correct:*______

TEST NO. 10

1. 24526
   24526
   25426
2. 23004
   20043
   20043
3. 39401
   34091
   34091
4. 76374
   76374
   76374
5. 94440
   94404
   94404
6. 25227
   25227
   27225
7. 41185
   48511
   41185
8. 88090
   88090
   88090
9. 72659
   76529
   79256
10. 87995
    87995
    89795

*Time:*__________
*No. Correct:*______

TEST NO. 11

1. 27171
27171
21771

2. 65425
64525
64525

3. 85886
85688
85688

4. 23481
23481
23481

5. 70374
70374
73074

6. 38312
31283
31283

7. 90020
92000
90200

8. 94343
94343
94343

9. 83536
83536
85336

10. 96632
93266
93266

*Time:*_________ *No. Correct:*_________

TEST NO. 12

1. 63381
63381
63318

2. 81585
85185
85185

3. 90463
90426
90463

4. 22249
22249
22294

5. 57422
52742
57224

6. 36264
36264
36264

7. 20637
26037
26037

8. 56299
52699
52996

9. 22804
22804
22804

10. 33266
33266
36623

*Time:*_________ *No. Correct:*_________

Correct Answers For The Foregoing Questions

	TEST NO. 1	TEST NO. 2	TEST NO. 3	TEST NO. 4	TEST NO. 5	TEST NO. 6
1.	E	C	E	C	B	B
2.	B	E	A	D	C	B
3.	C	C	E	E	A	C
4.	A	B	D	A	B	E
5.	D	D	B	B	D	A
6.	E	B	C	D	B	D
7.	C	A	C	B	B	E
8.	C	C	B	B	C	D
9.	B	D	A	C	D	B
10.	C	E	B	D	D	C

	TEST NO. 7	TEST NO. 8	TEST NO. 9	TEST NO. 10	TEST NO. 11	TEST NO. 12
1.	E	D	E	B	B	B
2.	A	A	E	D	D	D
3.	E	D	A	D	D	C
4.	D	B	E	A	A	B
5.	E	A	E	D	B	E
6.	C	E	B	B	D	A
7.	A	B	B	C	E	D
8.	E	B	C	A	A	E
9.	D	C	D	E	B	A
10.	A	D	A	B	D	B

B. COMPARING PAIRED LISTS OF NAMES OR NUMBERS

This name and number comparison test differs slightly from Test A. Here, lists of five pairs of names or numbers are given, to be compared. You are to decide which of these pairs are exactly alike, and then count the number of identical pairs there are in each list of five. Your answers will be numbers, from one to five. The two sample lists given first have been answered correctly.

SAMPLE LIST

Adelphi College — Adelphi College
Braxton Corp. — Braxeton Corp
Wassaic State School — Wassaic State School
Central Islip State Hospital — Central Islup State Hospital
Greenwich House — Greenwich House

Answer: 3

SAMPLE LIST

78453694 — 78453684
784530 — 784530
533 — 534
67845 — 67845
2368745 — 2368755

Answer: 2

LIST 1

Diagnostic Clinic — Diagnostic Clinic
Yorkville Health — Yorkville Health
Meinhard Clinic — Meinhart Clinic
Tremont Diagnostic — Tremont Diagnostic
Griscom Infirmary-Griscom Infirmiry

LIST 2

73526 — 73526
7283627198 — 7283627198
627 — 637
728352617283 — 728352617282
6281 — 6281

LIST 3

Jefferson Clinic — Jeffersen Clinic
Mott Haven Center — Mott Haven Center
Bronx Hospital — Bronx Hospital
Montefiore Hospital — Montifeore Hospital
Beth Isreal Hospital — Beth Israel Hospital

LIST 4

936271826 — 936371826
5271 — 5291
82637192037 — 82637192037
726354256 — 72634356
527182 — 5271882

LIST 5

Trinity Hospital — Trinity Hospital
Central Harlem — Centrel Harlem
St. Luke's Hospital — St. Lukes' Hospital
N. Y. Dispensery — N. Y. Dispensary
Mt. Sinai Hospital — Mt. Sinia Hospital

LIST 6

725361552637 — 725361555637
7526378 — 7526377
6975 — 6975
82637481028 — 82637481028
3427 — 3429

LIST 7

Misericordia Hospital — Miseracordia Hospital
Lebonan Hospital — Lebanon Hospital
Gouverneur Hospital — Gouverner Hospital
German Polyclinic — German Policlinic
French Hospital — French Hospital

LIST 8

63728 — 63728
367281 — 367281
8277364933251 — 827364933351
62733846273 — 6273846293
62836 — 62836

LIST 9

King's County Hospital — Kings County Hospital
St. Johns Long Island — St. John's Long Island
Bellevue Hospital — Bellvue Hospital
Beth David Hospital — Beth David Hospital
Samaritan Hospital — Samaritan Hospital

LIST 10

62836454 — 62836435
42738267 — 42738367
573829 — 573829
738291627874 — 738291627874
725 — 735

LIST 11

Bloomingdal Clinc — Bloomingdale Clinic
Communitty Hospital — Community Hospital
Metropolitan Hospital — Metropoliton Hospital
Lenox Hill Hospital — Lenex Hill Hospital
Lincoln Hospital — Lincoln Hospital

LIST 12

638364728 — 6283648
627385 — 627383
54283902 — 54283602
63352 — 53554
7283562781 — 7283562781

LIST 13

Sydenham Hospital — Sydanham Hospital
Roosevalt Hospital — Roosevelt Hospital
Vanderbilt Clinic — Vanderbild Clinic
Women's Hospital — Woman's Hospital
Flushing Hospital — Flushing Hospital

LIST 14

62738 — 62738
727355542321 — 72735542321
263849332 — 263849332
262837 — 263837
47382919 — 47282912

LIST 15

Episcopal Hospital — Episcapal Hospital
Flower Hospital — Flouer Hospital
Stuyvesent Clinic — Stuyvesant Clinic
Jamaica Clinic — Jamaica Clinic
Ridgwood Clinic — Ridgewood Clinic

LIST 16

32123 — 32132
273893326783 — 27389326783
473829 — 473829
7382937 — 7383937
362890122332 — 36289012332

LIST 17

Arietta Crane Farm — Areitta Crane Farm
Bikur Cholim Home — Bikur Chilm Home
Burke Foundation — Burke Foundation
Blythedale Home — Blythdale Home
Campbell Cottages — Cambell Cottages

LIST 18

32123 — 32132
273893326783 — 27389326783
473829 — 473829
7382937 — 7383937
362890122332 — 36289012332

LIST 19

Caraline Rest — Caroline Rest
Loreto Rest — Loretto Rest
Edgewater Creche — Edgwater Creche
Haliday Farm — Holiday Farm
House of St. Giles — House of St. Gile

LIST 20

557286777 — 55728677
3678902 — 3678892
1567839 — 1567839
9927382 — 9927382
7865434712 — 7865344712

LIST 21

Isabella Home — Isabela Home
James A. Moore Home — James. A. More Home
The Robin's Nest — The Roben's Nest
Pelham Home — Pelam Home
St. Eleanora's Home — St. Elaenora's Home

LIST 22

273648293048 — 273648293049
334 — 334
7362536478 — 7362536478
7363 — 7362
7362819273 — 7362819273

LIST 23

St. Pheobe's Mission — St. Phebe's Mission
Seaside Home — Seaside Home
Speedwell Society — Speedwell Society
Valeria Home — Valerea Home
Wiltwyck — Wildwyck

LIST 24

63728 — 63738
63728192736 — 63728192739
428 — 458
62738291527 — 62738291529
63728192 — 63728192

LIST 25

McGaffin — McGafin
David Ardslee — David Ardslee
Axton Supply — Axeton Supply
Alice Russel — Alice Russell
Dobson Mfg. Co. — Dobsen Mfg. Co.

LIST 26

82637381028 — 82637281028
928 — 928
72937281028 — 72937281028
7362 — 7362
927382615 — 927382615

LIST 27

Albee Theatre — Albee Theatre
Lapland Lumber Co. — Laplund Lumber Co.
Jones & Son Inc. — Jones & Sons Inc.
Idelphi College — Adelphi College
S. W. Ponds Co. — S. W. Ponds Co.

LIST 28

85345 — 85345
895643278 — 895643277
726352 — 726353
632685 — 632685
7263524 — 7236524

LIST 29

Eagle Library — Eagle Library
Dodge Ltd. — Dodge Co.
Stomberg Carlson — Stomberg Carlsen
Clairice Ling — Clairice Linng
Mason Book Co. — Matson Book Co.

LIST 30

66273 — 66273
629 — 620
7382517283 — 7382517283
637281 — 739281
2738261 — 2728261

Correct Answers For The Foregoing Questions

(Please make every effort to answer the questions on your own before looking at these answers. You'll make faster progress by following this rule.)

1. 3
2. 3
3. 2
4. 1
5. 1
6. 2
7. 1
8. 3
9. 2
10. 2
11. 1
12. 1
13. 1
14. 2
15. 1
16. 1
17. 1
18. 1
19. 0
20. 2
21. 0
22. 3
23. 2
24. 1
25. 1
26. 4
27. 2
28. 2
29. 1
30. 2

X. TOOL RECOGNITION TESTS

This is one of the kinds of question you are likely to find on your test. Given sufficient time, any intelligent person should be able to answer these fairly simple questions. But on your test you probably won't be given sufficient time. Thus you'll be tempted to rush along faster than you should, making unnecessary errors. However, by practicing with the careful selection of questions in this chapter, you will noticeably increase your speed, your skill, and your accuracy in answering this kind of question. On your test you will find that you are familiar with these questions, and that they will offer you little difficulty.

Mechanical aptitude tests are used to measure many different abilities. And the results obtained are used for many different purposes.

Sometimes they measure your ability to use your hands or to manipulate materials. Other times they measure your dexterity; and also your ability to visualize shapes and forms; and to move them around in different patterns. Some people are better at these tasks than others, even without any training. It is believed that such people have better mechanical "aptitude."

But these ideas are not absolutely clear-cut, and frequently tests that are designed to measure mechanical aptitude draw upon the knowledge a person has in mechanical matters. The theory here is that those who are likely to do well in mechanical work have interested themselves in it and have absorbed more from what they have experienced than those who are not likely to do well in such work.

As a result we find that there is in use a wide variety of questions which draw upon a person's knowledge of tools, mechanical processes, movements and information. This type of mechanical test is frequently called an *achievement* test.

Mechanical aptitude and achievement tests come in a wide variety of forms. The questions may be entirely verbal. Or they may involve the use of diagrams and pictures. They may be given orally; or they may be printed and require written answers. And sometimes the candidate may be asked to work with his hands on special testing equipment while the examiner observes and times his effort. Another form of manual test consists of actual performance on a job, or in the production of *standardized worksamples.* In such tests the work set for the candidate is very much like the work required by the job. For economy and speed, worksamples are frequently presented on simulated or miniaturized equipment.

Since every craftsman should be familiar with the tools of his trade, and since familiarity with tools is an important measure of interest and motivation, tool recognition questions have become an important feature of many mechanical ability, aptitude and comprehension tests.

In order to familiarize you with this type of question we have assembled a large variety from many different examinations. As you go through the different tool recognition tests in this chapter you will understand better how to go about answering these questions. You'll also pick up a good deal of important information about tools and tool recognition.

As you will find in the following pages, all of these questions are of a practical nature. You are given the picture of a tool in most questions, and a situation is described. You must match the tool with the necessary operation. In other questions you are shown pictures of various tools and implements and must match those which are used together.

Some of the tools which you will encounter on these pages are basic to almost every mechanical trade and you should have little difficulty in answering questions about their use. Others may be unfamiliar to you, or may have some specialized use outside your own trade. In those cases, you must apply your knowledge of mechanics to figure out which tool would seem to fit the required operation.

In answering these questions, do not try to work by elimination. When you are given a group of tools and a long list of operations, the same tool may be used for more than one operation on the list, and often one or more of the tools shown may not be used in any of the operations.

Be honest with yourself in answering these questions. Do the best you can before looking at the key answers at the end of the chapter. Usually, if you are not sure of the answer, it will be to your advantage to guess. If the test is marked in such a way that wrong guesses penalize you more than "no answer," that will be indicated on the examination paper.

A SAMPLE QUESTION EXPLAINED

DIRECTIONS: Each question in this test consists of a numbered picture followed by four lettered illustrations marked A, B, C, & D. The problem is to determine which of the four lettered pictures goes best with the numbered tool or machine part. For each question blacken the space on your answer sheet corresponding to the letter of the best answer.

EXPLANATION OF A SAMPLE QUESTION: The illustration numbered "0" shows a valve used to turn water on and off. The picture that goes best with the valve is lettered "B," the piece of water pipe. Choices "C," "A," and "D" have little or nothing to do with the valve "0." Therefore, "B" is the correct answer, and the answer strip is blackened under B.

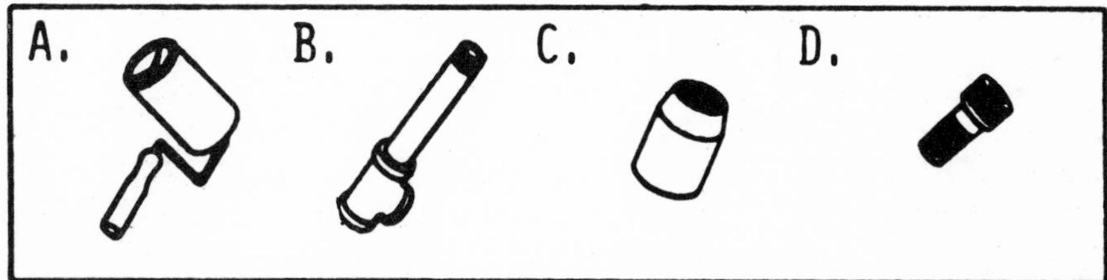

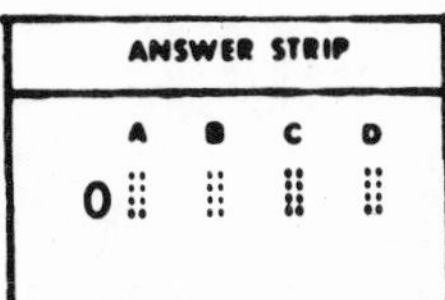

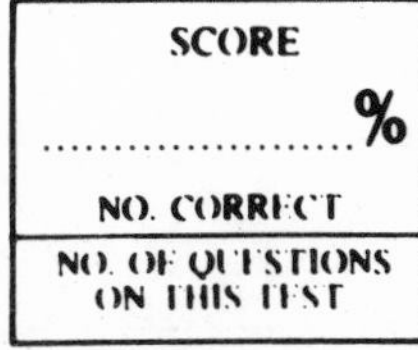

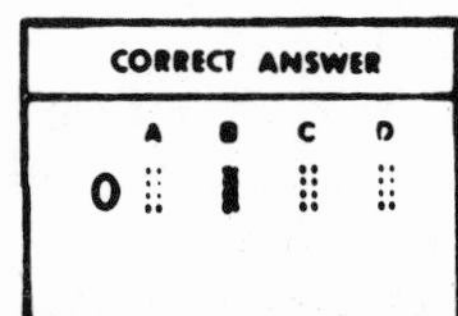

TOOL ANALOGY TEST I

TIME: 10 Minutes

DIRECTIONS: Each question in this test consists of a numbered picture followed by four lettered illustrations marked A, B, C, & D. The problem is to determine which of the four lettered pictures goes best with the numbered tool or machine part. For each question blacken the space on your answer sheet corresponding to the letter of the best answer.

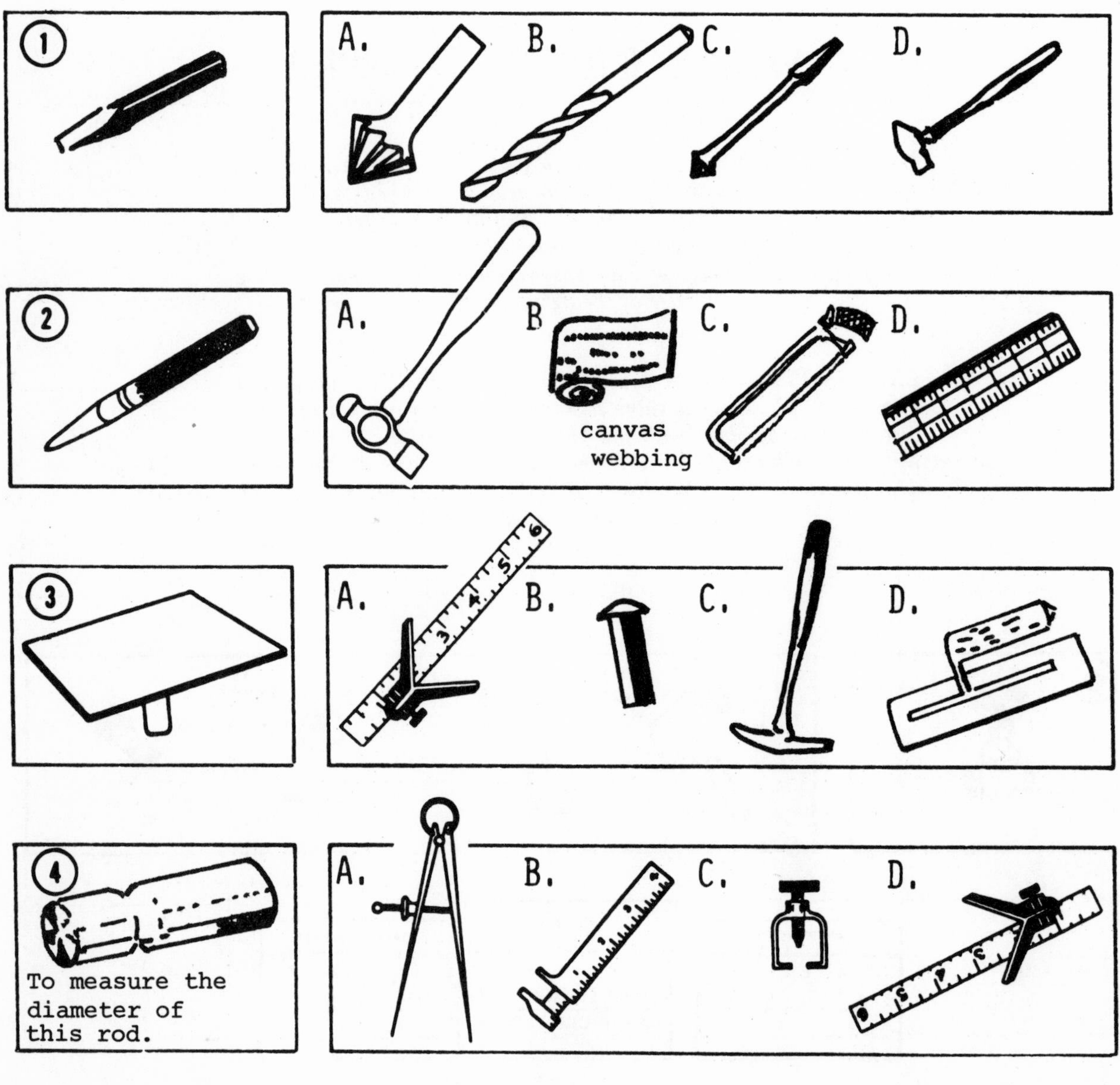

5

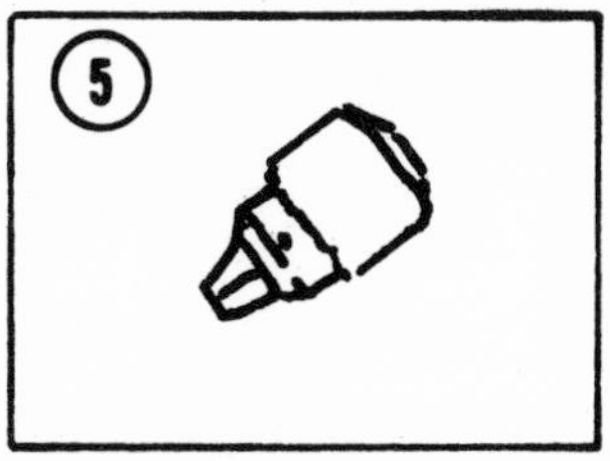

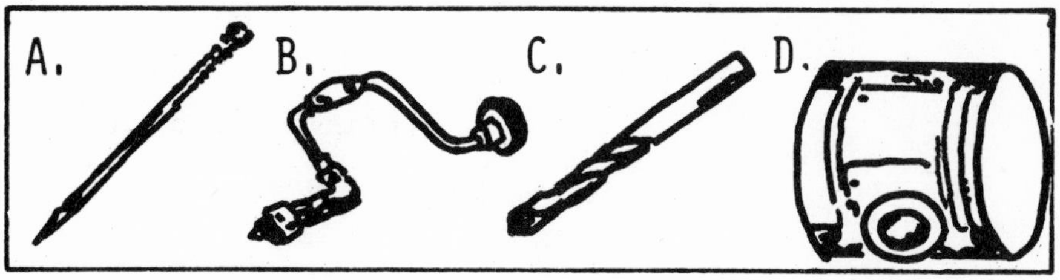

A.
B.
C.
D.

6

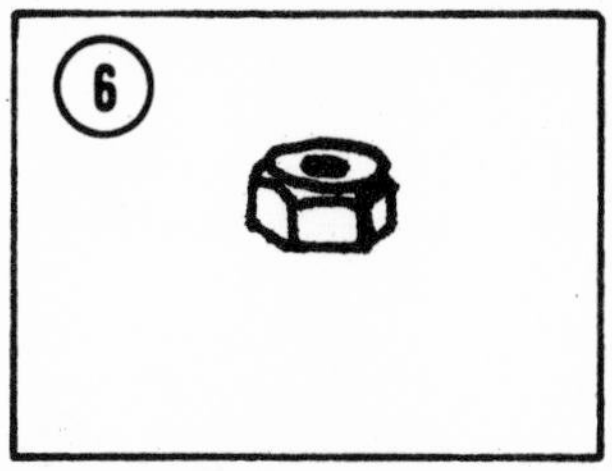

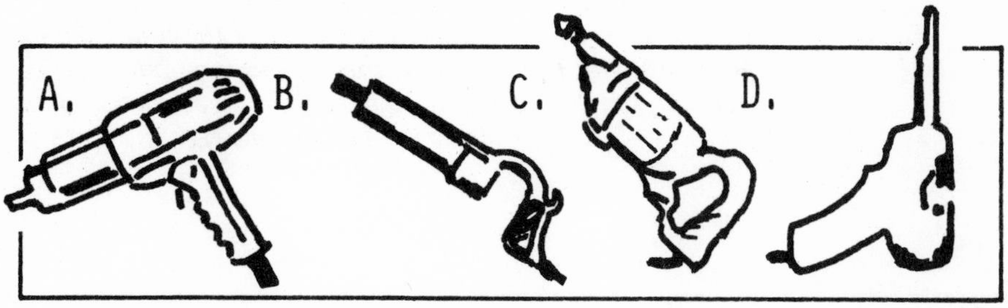

A.
B.
C.
D.

7

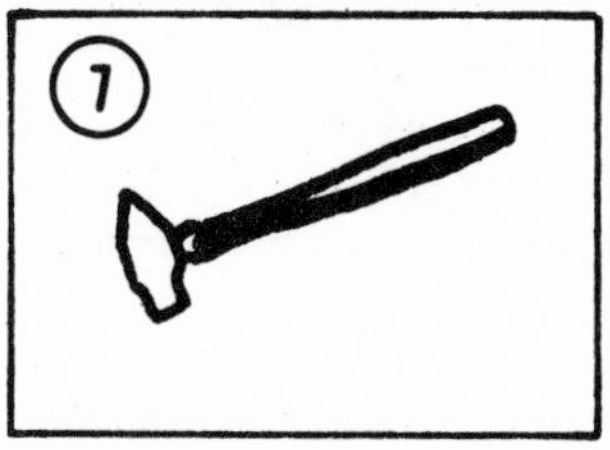

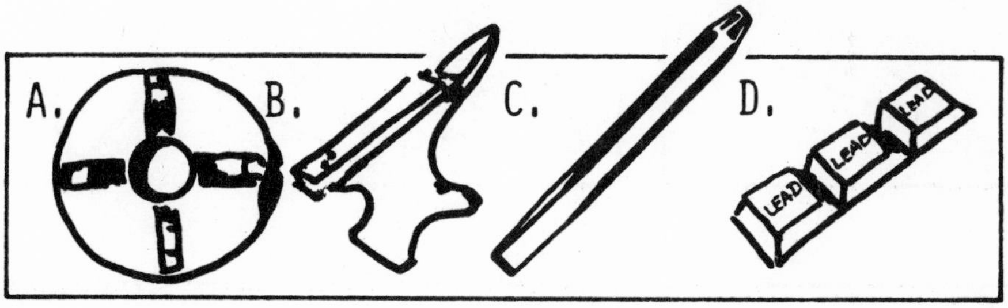

A.
B.
C.
D.
LEAD
LEAD
LEAD

8

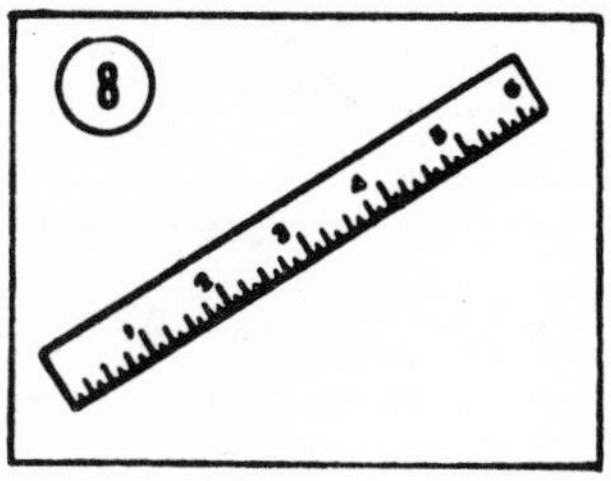

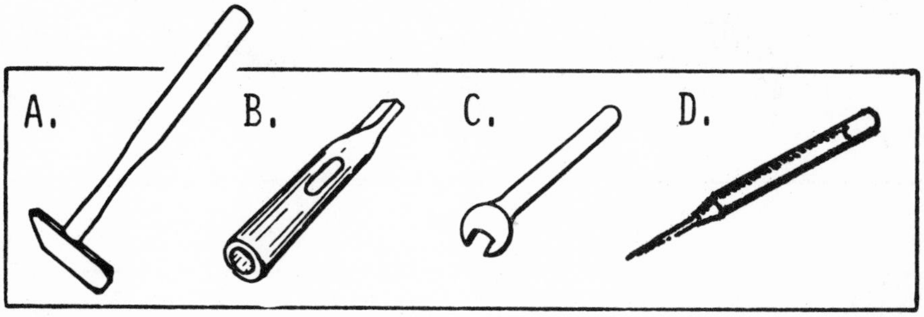

A.
B.
C.
D.

Correct Answers For The Foregoing Questions

ANSWER STRIP

	A	B	C	D
1				
2				
3				
4				

ANSWER STRIP

	A	B	C	D
5				
6				
7				
8				

SCORE

.... %

NO. CORRECT ÷

NO. OF QUESTIONS ON THIS TEST

CORRECT ANSWERS

	A	B	C	D
1				■
2	■			
3				■
4		■		

CORRECT ANSWERS

	A	B	C	D
5			■	
6	■			
7		■		
8				■

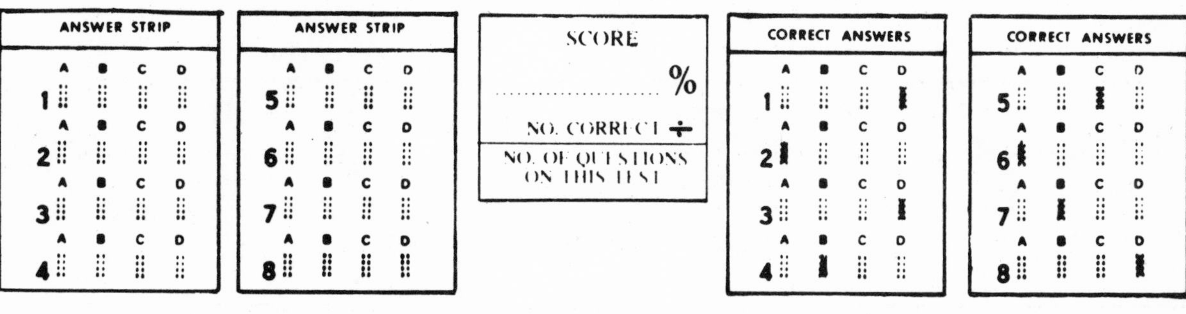

TOOL ANALOGY TEST II

TIME: 10 Minutes

DIRECTIONS: Each question in this test consists of a numbered picture followed by four lettered illustrations marked A, B, C, & D. The problem is to determine which of the four lettered pictures goes best with the numbered tool or machine part. For each question blacken the space on your answer sheet corresponding to the letter of the best answer.

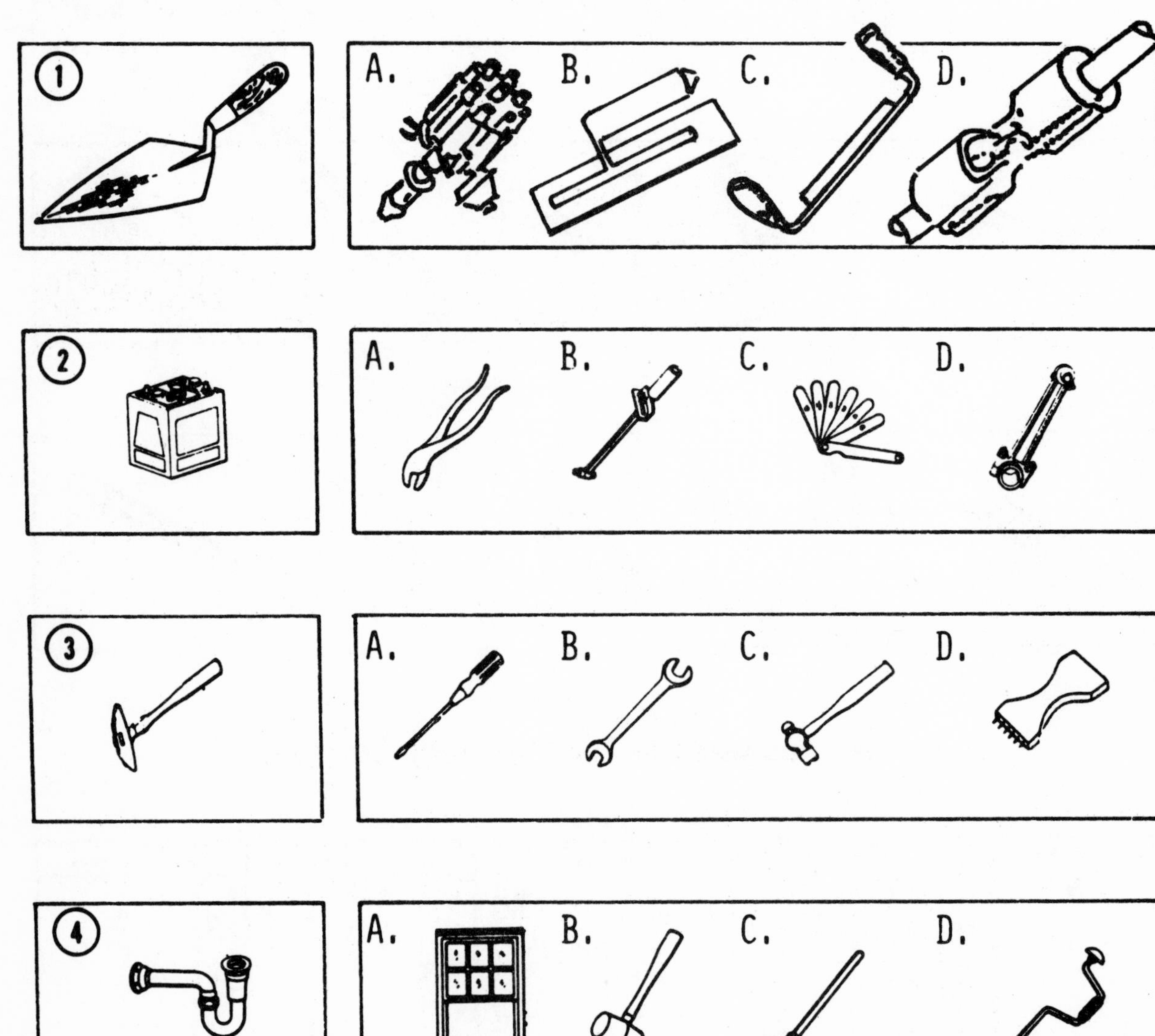

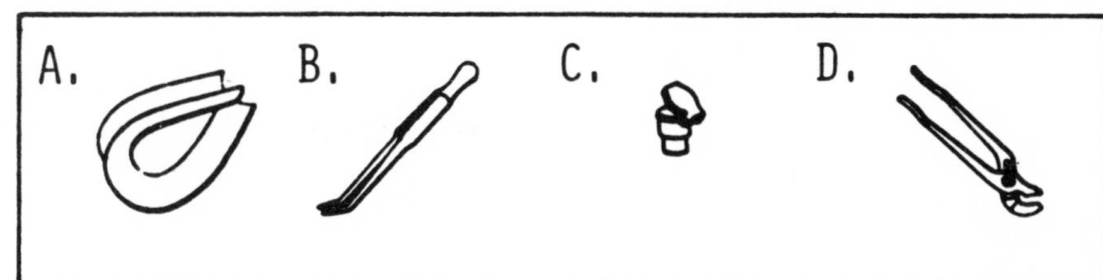

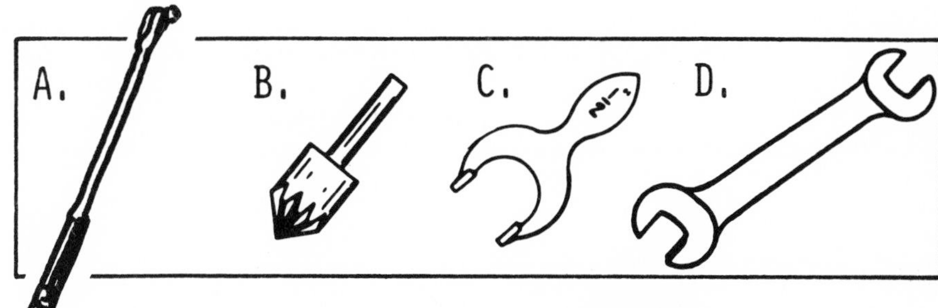

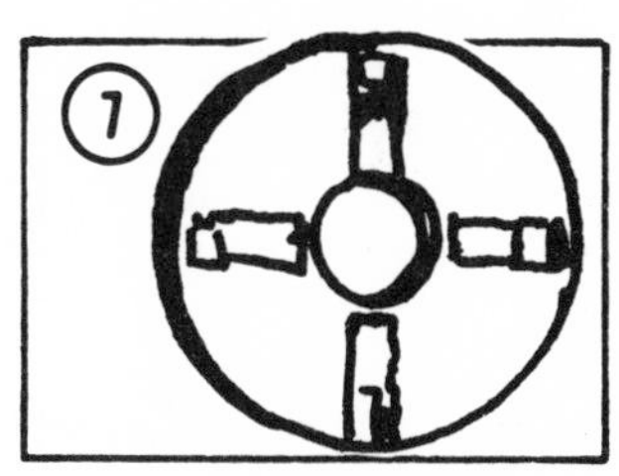

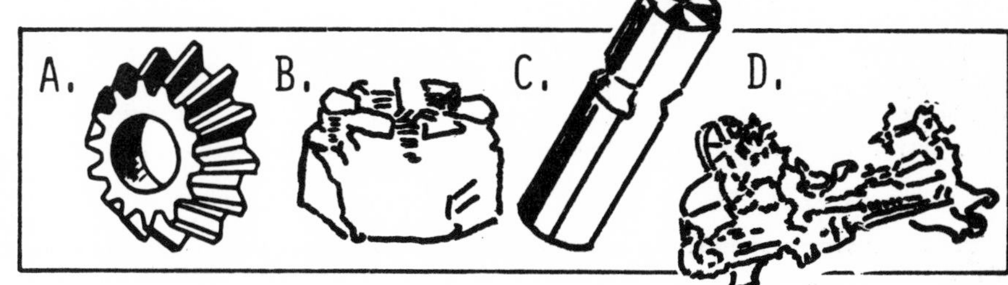

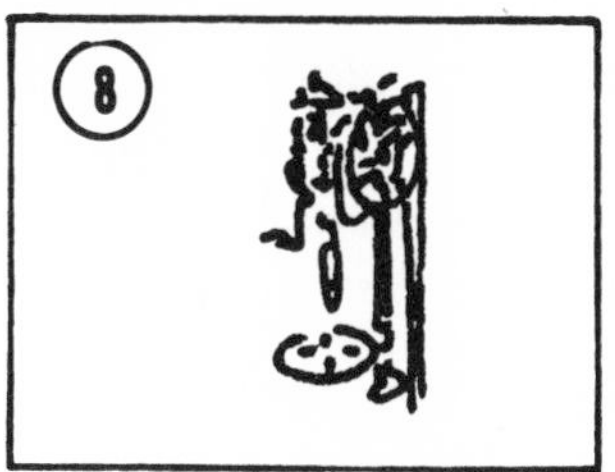

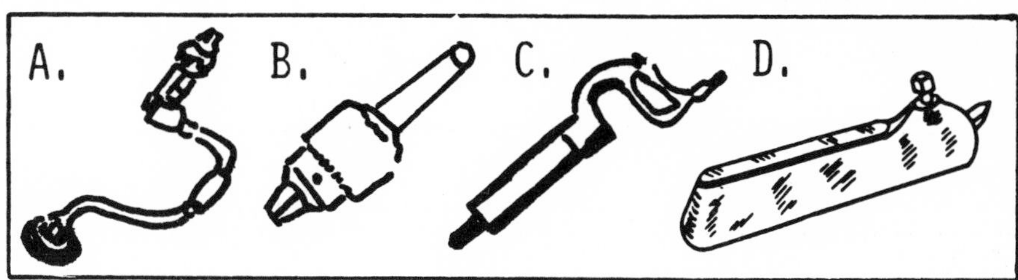

Correct Answers For The Foregoing Questions

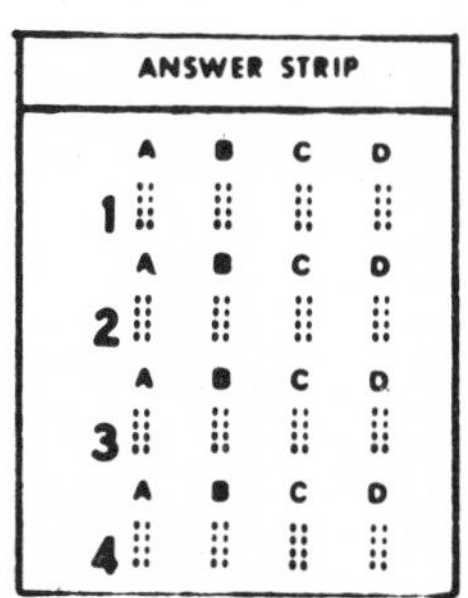

ANSWER STRIP

	A	B	C	D
1				
2				
3				
4				

ANSWER STRIP

	A	B	C	D
5				
6				
7				
8				

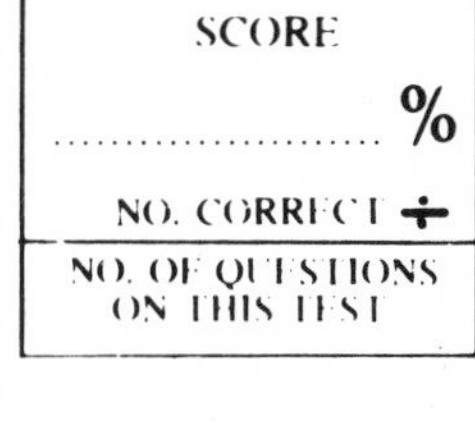

SCORE

.... %

NO. CORRECT ÷

NO. OF QUESTIONS ON THIS TEST

CORRECT ANSWERS

	A	B	C	D
1		▮		
2	▮			
3				▮
4			▮	

CORRECT ANSWERS

	A	B	C	D
5			▮	
6	▮			
7				▮
8		▮		

TOOL ANALOGY TEST III

TIME: 10 Minutes

DIRECTIONS: Each question in this test consists of a numbered picture followed by four lettered illustrations marked A, B, C, & D. The problem is to determine which of the four lettered pictures goes best with the numbered tool or machine part. For each question blacken the space on your answer sheet corresponding to the letter of the best answer.

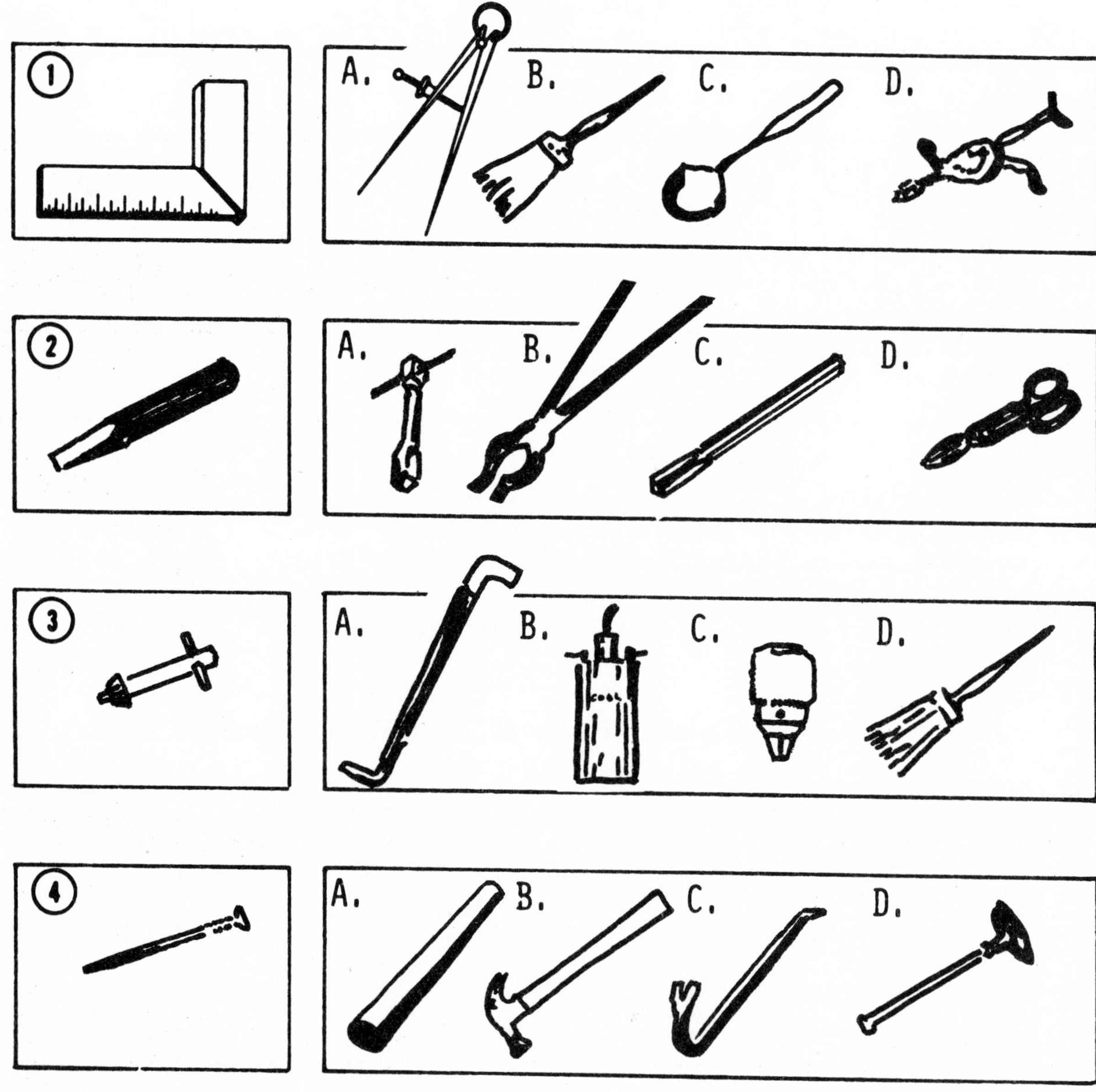

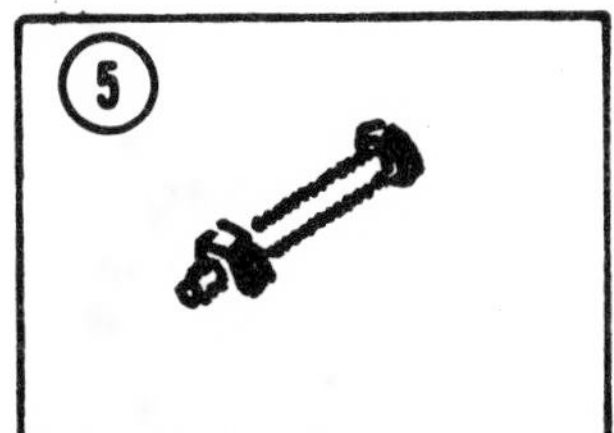

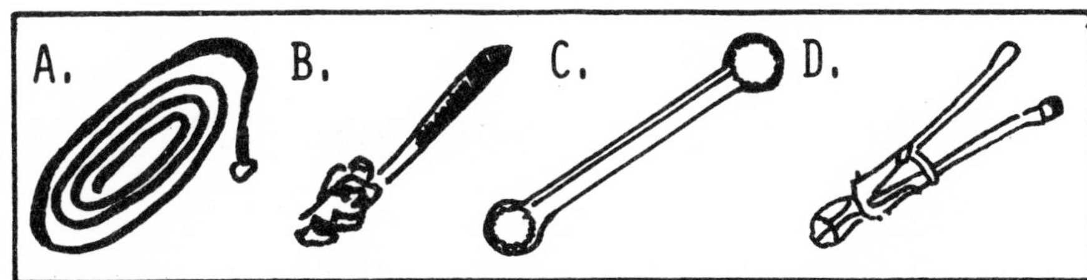

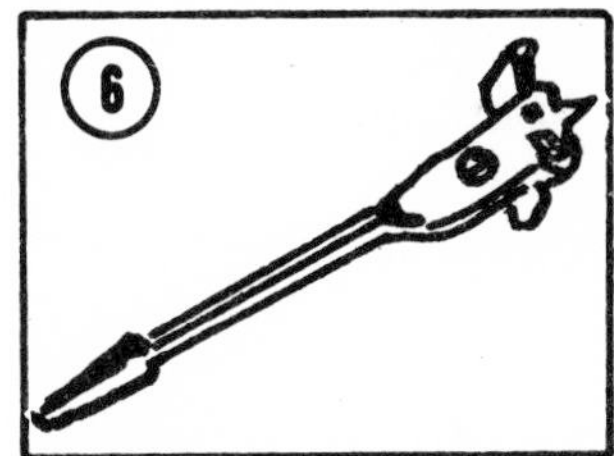

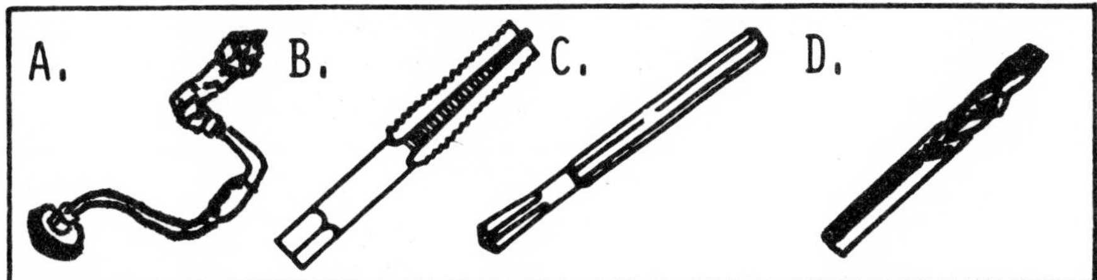

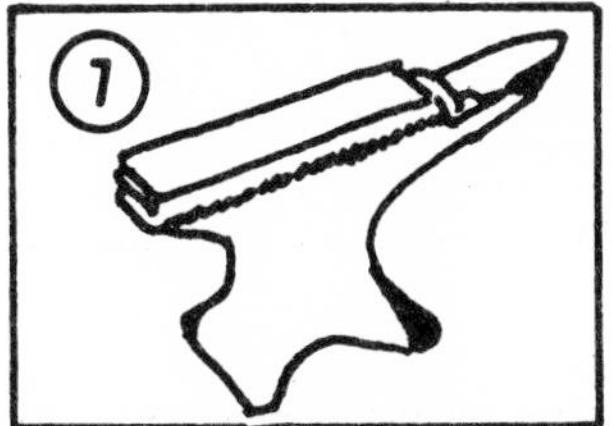

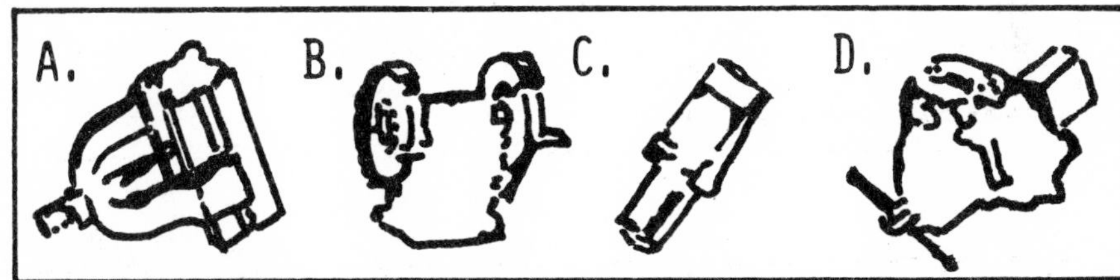

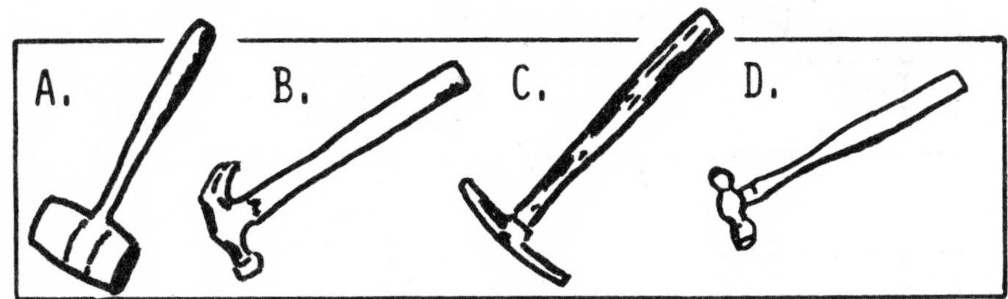

Correct Answers For The Foregoing Questions

ANSWER STRIP

	A	B	C	D
1				
2				
3				
4				

ANSWER STRIP

	A	B	C	D
5				
6				
7				
8				

SCORE

.... %

NO. CORRECT ÷

NO. OF QUESTIONS ON THIS TEST

CORRECT ANSWERS

	A	B	C	D
1	■			
2				■
3			■	
4		■		

CORRECT ANSWERS

	A	B	C	D
5				■
6	■			
7			■	
8				■

TOOL ANALOGY TEST IV

TIME: 10 Minutes

DIRECTIONS: Each question in this test consists of a numbered picture followed by four lettered illustrations marked A, B, C, & D. The problem is to determine which of the four lettered pictures goes best with the numbered tool or machine part. For each question blacken the space on your answer sheet corresponding to the letter of the best answer.

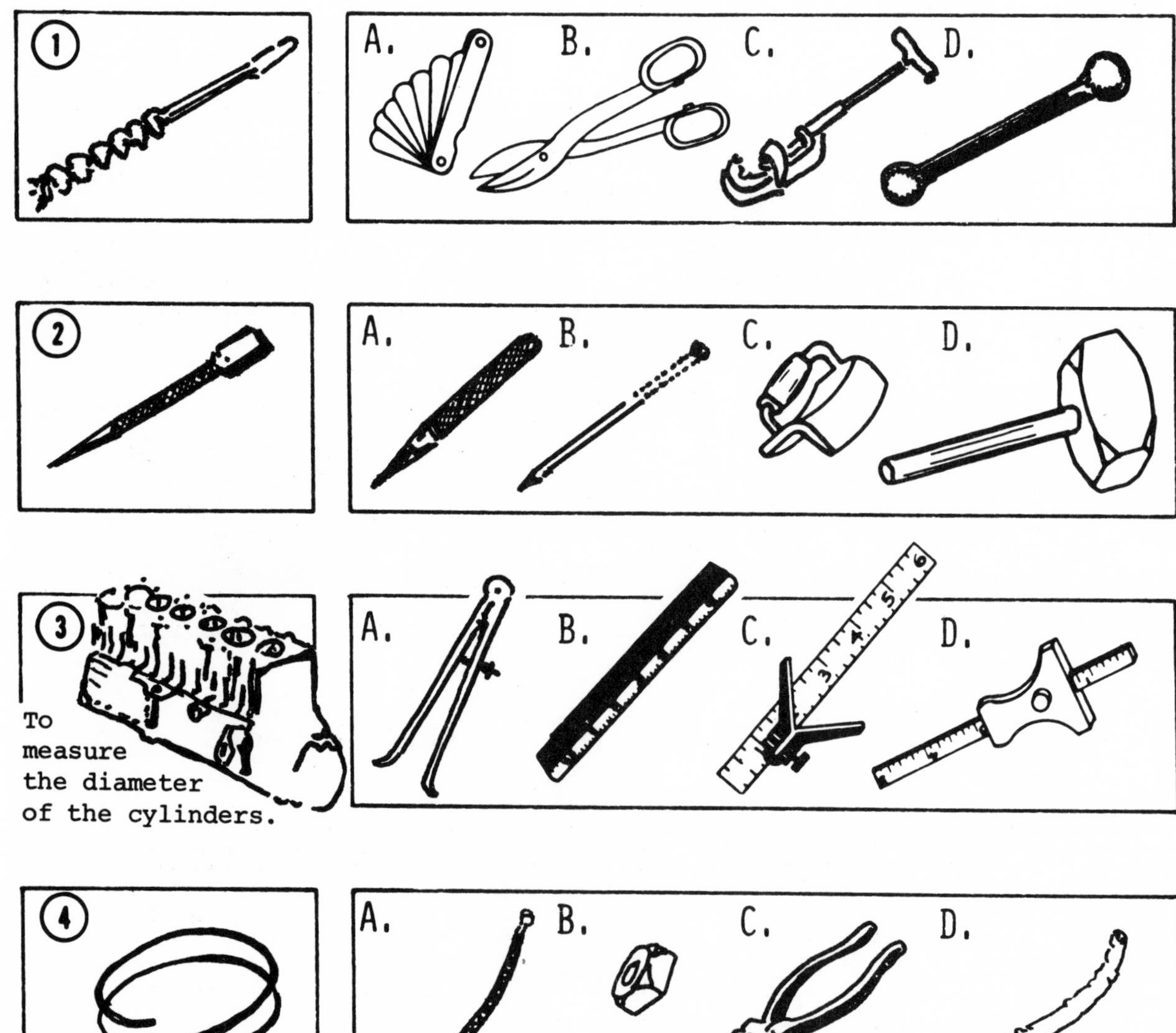

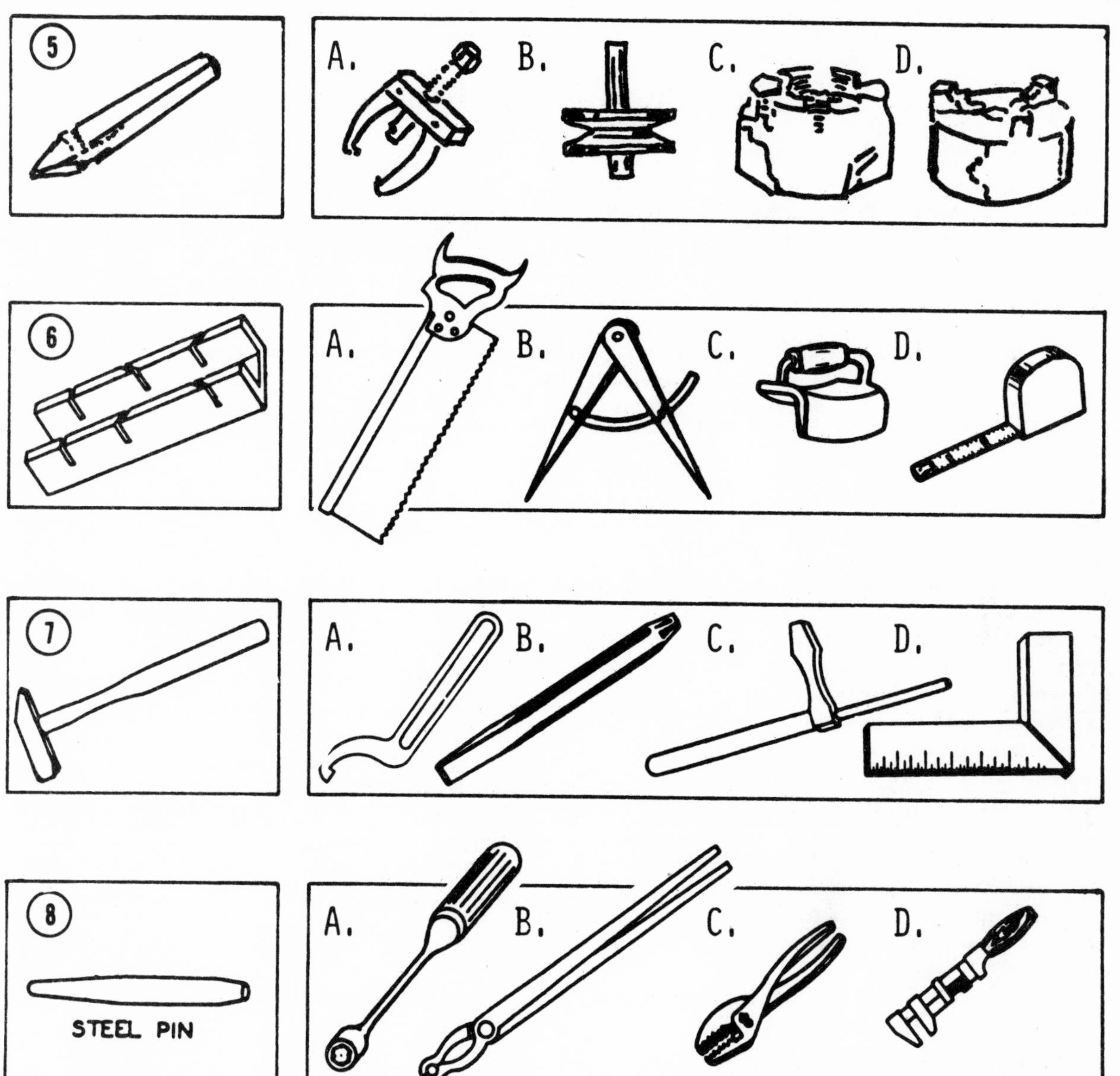

Correct Answers For The Foregoing Questions

ANSWER STRIP

1 A B C D
2 A B C D
3 A B C D
4 A B C D

ANSWER STRIP

5 A B C D
6 A B C D
7 A B C D
8 A B C D

CORRECT ANSWERS

1 A **B** C D
2 A **B** C D
3 **A** B C D
4 A B **C** D

CORRECT ANSWERS

5 A B C **D**
6 **A** B C D
7 A B **C** D
8 A **B** C D

XI. MECHANICAL INSIGHT TESTS

The following questions have been selected from various civil service and private industry tests. All are designed to gauge your mechanical aptitude and your inherent feeling for machinery. They all measure your mechanical ability. They will also help you determine whether or not you need to review basic arithmetic.

HUNDREDS of civil service jobs and many jobs in private industry require the ability known as "mechanical insight"; in other words, the ability to visualize the operations of a machine in motion, to see the relationships among the different parts of a machine, and the capacity to make the necessary computations which are part of the job of a man or woman whose work is around machinery.

Over many years, personnel experts and psychologists have been working together to provide a series of paper tests which will accurately predict the ability of a person to handle mechanical work. In practice it has been found that a person who does well on a pencil and paper test of this type will usually do well in the workshop.

Many questions on the following pages are designed to test the candidate's ability to think in terms of a third dimension. Others deal with hydraulics, the forces exerted by fluids in a closed system, and with the workings of valves. Some call for knowledge of the operations of pulley systems and levers. In others, it is necessary to analyze the motion of interlocking gear systems.

These questions also will enable you to discover your weak points before you take your examination. Do your best, and don't look at the answers until you have solved each problem yourself, or made your best effort to find the correct answer. You may find that the computations are difficult; that may call for brush-up in arithmetic. Or you may determine that a little review of basic physics may be what you need before you take the test.

You will find no "trick" or "catch" questions on a test of this type. The purpose of the examinations is to find the persons best qualified for work of a mechanical nature. If you have a background of mechanical experience or a natural aptitude for mechanical work, you should not find the questions too difficult.

DIRECTIONS FOR ANSWERING QUESTIONS

For each question read all the choices carefully. Then select that answer which you consider correct or most nearly correct. Write the letter preceding your best choice next to the question

Should you want to answer on the kind of answer sheet used on machine-scored examinations, we have provided several such facsimiles. Tear one out if you wish, and mark your answers on it . . . just as you would do on an actual exam.

In machine-scored examinations you should record all your answers on the answer sheet provided. Don't make the mistake of putting answers on the test booklet itself.

TEST I. MECHANICAL COMPREHENSION

TIME: 10 Minutes

DIRECTIONS: For each question read all the choices carefully. Then select that answer which you consider correct or most nearly correct. Blacken the answer space corresponding to your best choice, just as you would do on the actual examination.

1. Examine Figure 1 on the next page, and determine which of the following statements is true.
   (A) If the nut is held stationary and the head turned clockwise, the bolt will move up.
   (B) If the head of the bolt is held stationary and the nut is turned clockwise, the nut will move down.
   (C) If the head of the bolt is held stationary and the nut is turned clockwise, the nut will move up.
   (D) If the nut is held stationary and the bolt is turned counter-clockwise, the nut will move down.

2. Referring to Figure 2, which one of the following statements is true?
   (A) If the nut is held stationary and the head turned clockwise, the bolt will move down.
   (B) If the head of the bolt is held stationary and the nut is turned clockwise, the nut will move down.
   (C) If the head of the bolt is held stationary and the nut is turned clockwise, the nut will move up.
   (D) If the nut is held stationary and the head turned counter-clockwise, the bolt will move up.

3. Figure 3 shows a bolt and nut and five numbered pieces. If all of the pieces are long enough to go through the bolt, and if the circular hole extends through the bolt and through the other side of the nut, which piece must you use to fix the nut in a stationary position?
   (A) 1 (B) 2
   (C) 3 (D) 4
   (E) 5.

4. Examine the tenon and the numbered mortises in Figure 4. The tenon best fits into the mortise numbered
   (A) 1 (B) 2
   (C) 3 (D) 4
   (E) 5.

5. In making the tenon in figure 4, the best of the following tools to use is
   (A) hammer (B) knife
   (C) saw (D) drill
   (E) bit.

6. Study the gear wheels in Figure 5, then determine which of the following statements is true.
   (A) If you turn wheel M clockwise by means of the handle, wheel P will also turn clockwise.
   (B) It will take the same time for a tooth of wheel P to make a full turn as it will for a tooth of wheel M.
   (C) It will take less time for a tooth of wheel P to make a full turn than it will take a tooth of wheel M.
   (D) It will take more time for a tooth of wheel P to make a full turn than it will for a tooth of wheel M.
   (E) The faster wheel P is turned, the slower wheel M will turn.

7. If wheel M in Figure 5 makes 16 full turns, the number of full turns made by wheel P will be
   (A) 20 (B) 12
   (C) 10 (D) 18

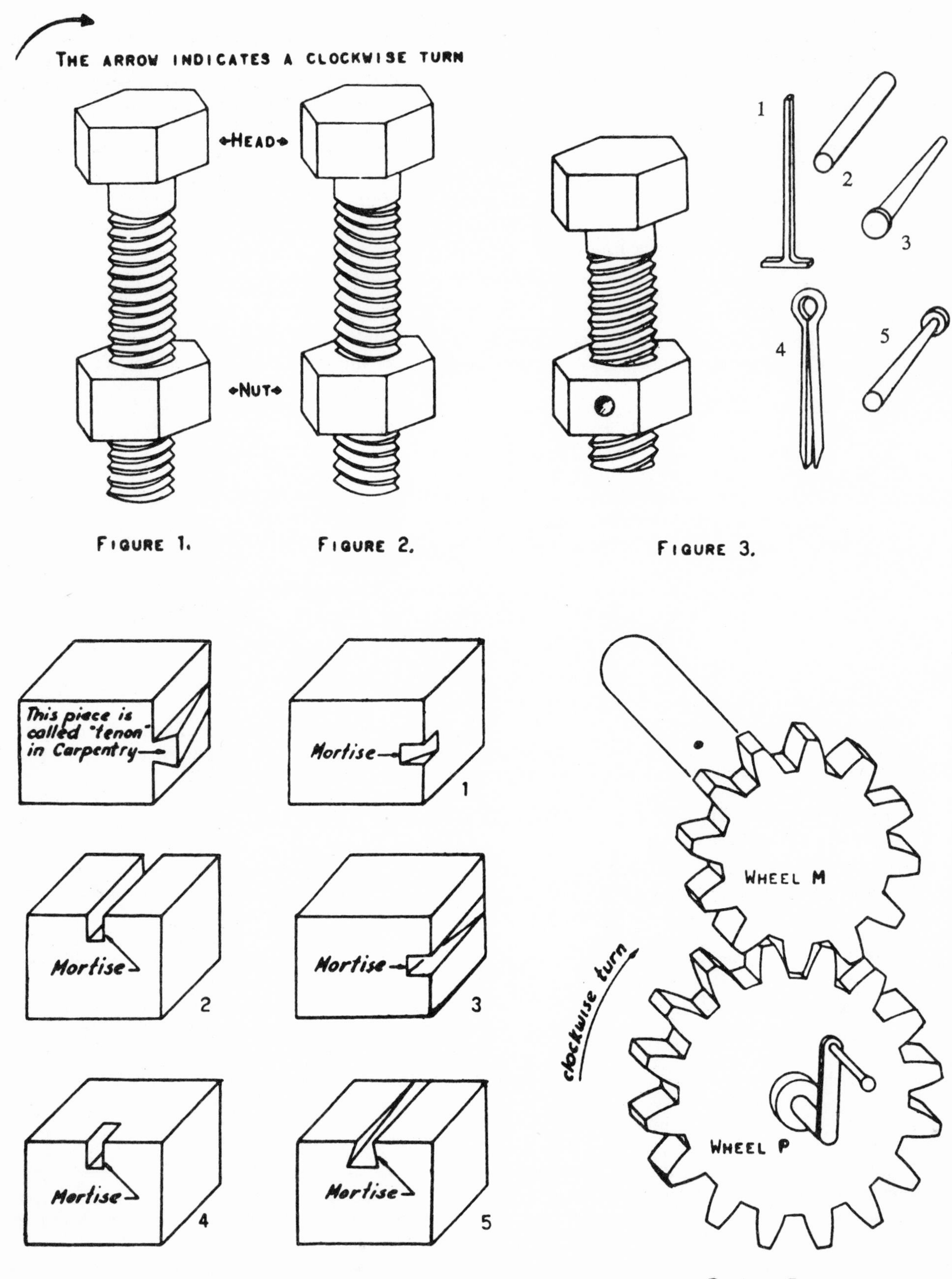

THE ARROW INDICATES A CLOCKWISE TURN
HEAD
NUT
1
2
3
4
5
FIGURE 1.
FIGURE 2.
FIGURE 3.
This piece is called "tenon" in Carpentry
Mortise
1
Mortise
2
Mortise
3
Mortise
4
Mortise
5
FIGURE 4.
WHEEL M
clockwise turn
WHEEL P
FIGURE 5.

8 Referring to Figure 5, the number of teeth shown on wheel M is
(A) 12 (B) 14
(C) 16 (D) 10
(E) 15.

9 Referring to Figure 5, the number of teeth shown on wheel P is
(A) 10 (B) 18
(C) 16 (D) 17
(E) 19.

10 A bar measuring exactly three inches in length is pivoted at one end and a movement of 0.120 inches is noted at the opposite end. The movement of a point on the bar exactly 7/8″ from the pivot end will be
(A) .015 inches (B) .105 inches
(C) .035 inches (D) .35 inches.

11

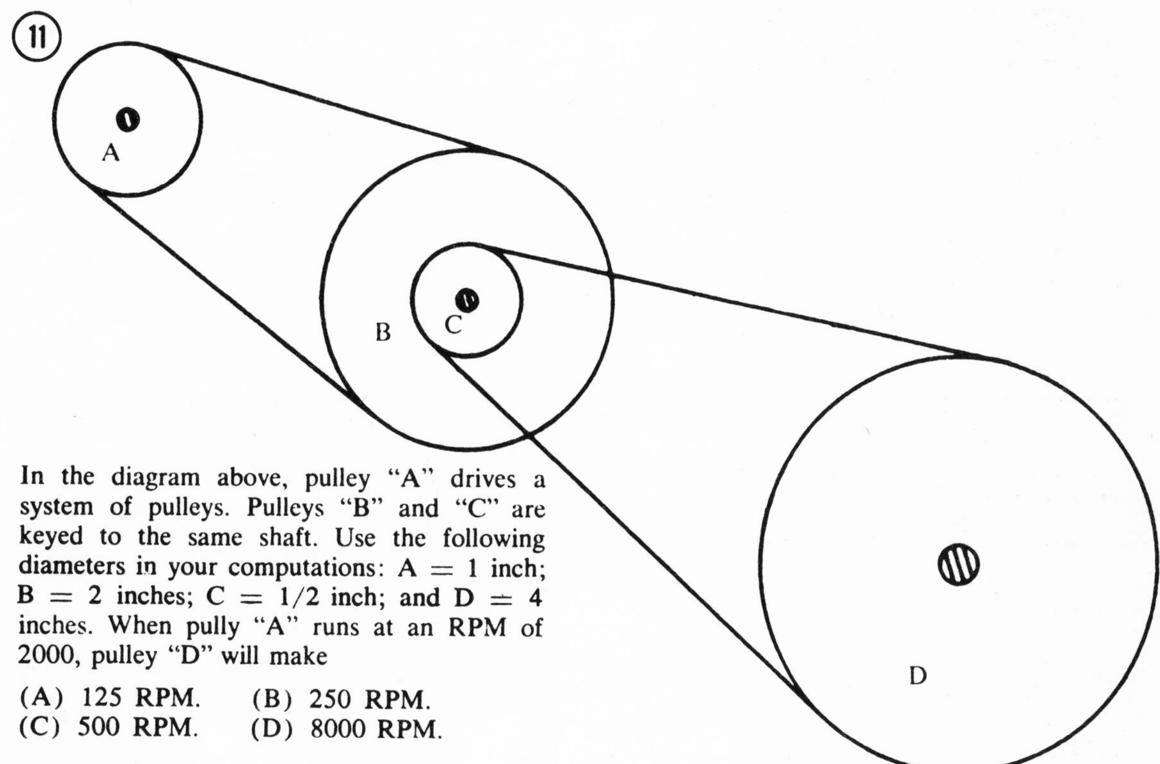

In the diagram above, pulley "A" drives a system of pulleys. Pulleys "B" and "C" are keyed to the same shaft. Use the following diameters in your computations: A = 1 inch; B = 2 inches; C = 1/2 inch; and D = 4 inches. When pully "A" runs at an RPM of 2000, pulley "D" will make
(A) 125 RPM. (B) 250 RPM.
(C) 500 RPM. (D) 8000 RPM.

(12)

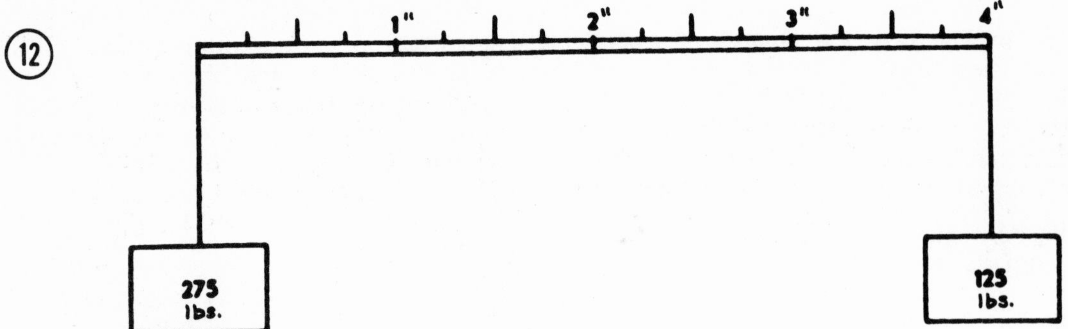

The bar above, which is exactly four inches in length, has a two hundred seventy-five pound weight hung on one end and a one hundred twenty-five pound weight on the opposite end. In order that the bar will just balance, the distance from the two hundred seventy-five pound weight to the fulcrum point should be (In your computation neglect the weight of the bar.)

(A) 1/2 inch (B) 3/4 inch
(C) 1 inch (D) 1 - 1/4 inches
(E) 1 - 1/2 inches.

(13)

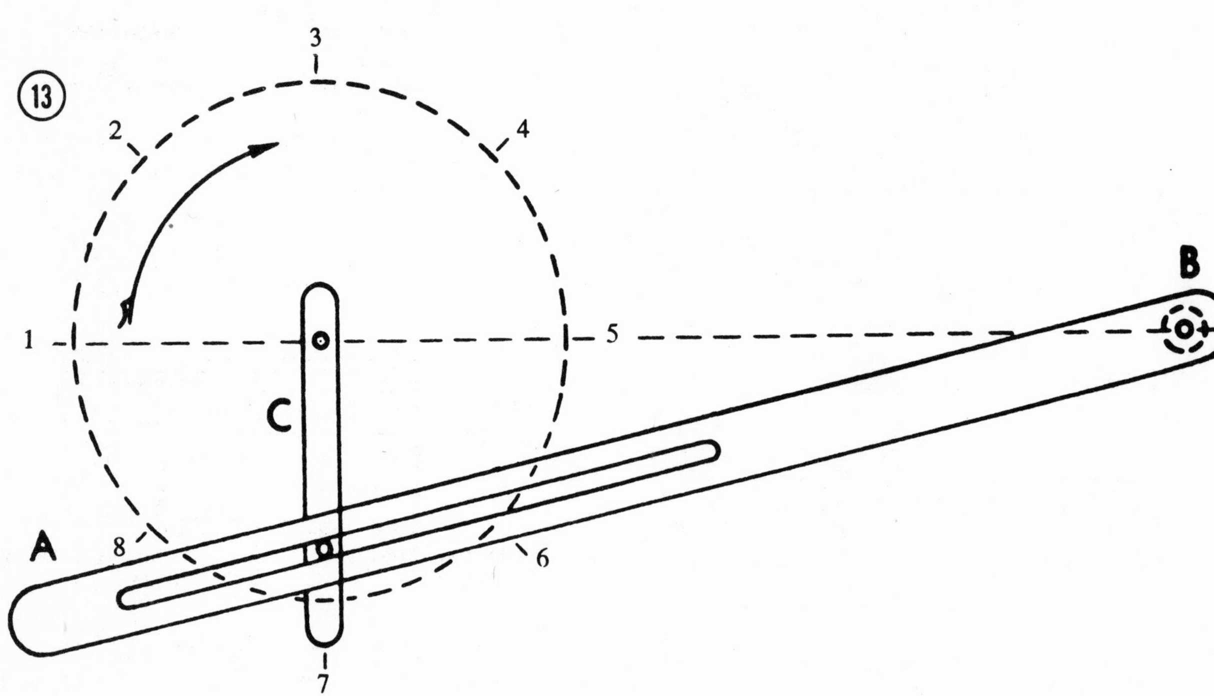

In the diagram above, crank arm "C" revolves at a constant speed of 400 RPM and drives the lever "AB". When lever "AB" is moving the fastest arm "C" will be in position

(A) 1 (B) 5
(C) 6 (D) 7.

(14) In the diagram shown, the axle eight inches in diameter has attached a handle 28 inches in diameter. If a force of 50 lb. is applied to the handle, the axle will lift a weight of

(A) 224 lb. (B) 200 lb.
(C) 175 lb. (D) 88 lb.
(E) 75 lb.

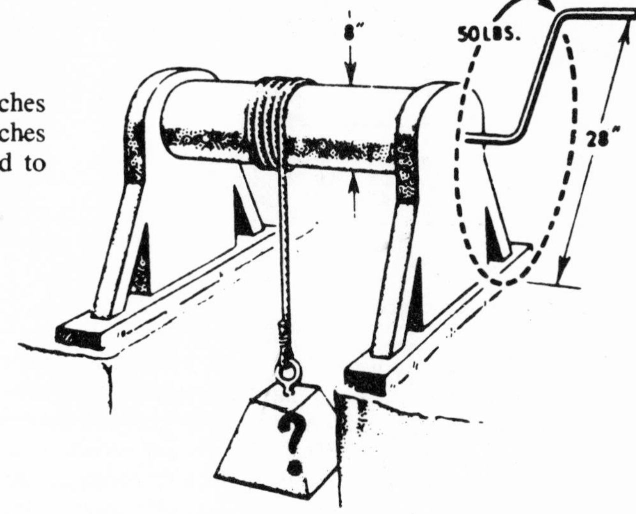

(15)

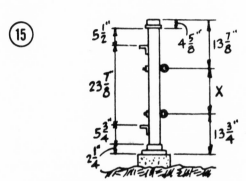

On the post, the dimension marked "X" is

(A) 9 3/4" (B) 10 3/4"
(C) 13 3/8" (D) 14 3/8"

(16)

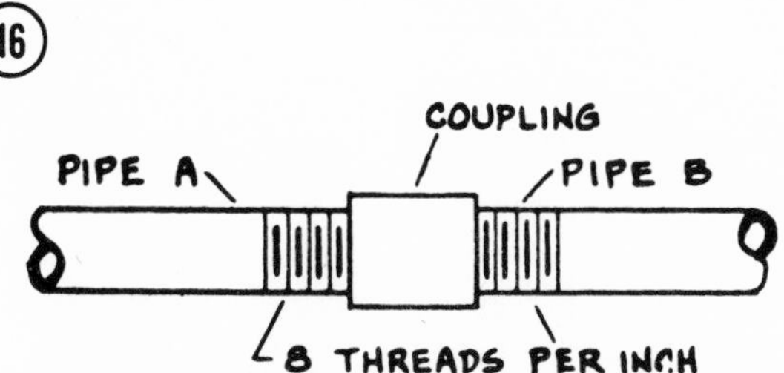

If pipe A is held in a vise and pipe B is turned ten revolutions with a wrench, the overall length of the pipes and coupling will decrease

(A) 5/8 inch (B) 1 1/4 inches
(C) 2 1/2 inches (D) 3 3/4 inches.

(17)

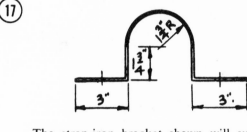

The strap-iron bracket shown will support a pipe. The required straight length of strap-iron to make the bracket is

(A) 20 1/2 inches (B) 17 inches
(C) 15 inches (D) 13 1/4 inches.

(18)

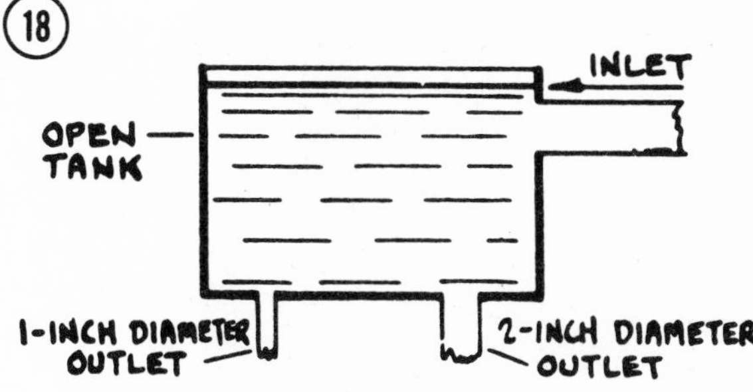

Eight gallons per minute of water flow at a given time from the one-inch outlet in the tank shown. What is the amount of water flowing at that time from the two-inch outlet?

(A) 64 gallons per minute
(B) 32 gallons per minute
(C) 16 gallons per minute
(D) 2 gallons per minute.

19

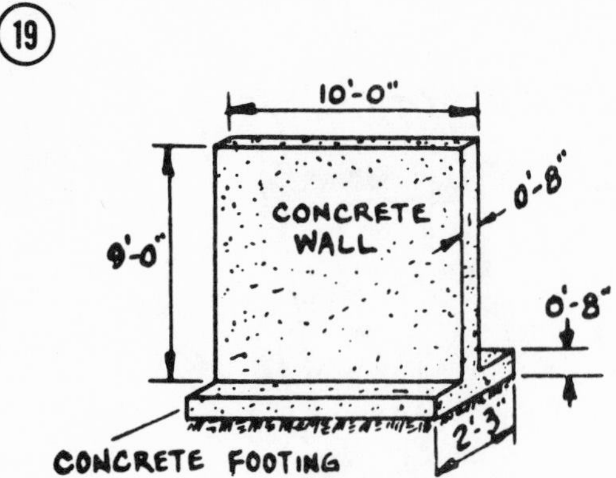

If the weight of concrete is 150 lbs. per cubic foot, the total weight of the wall and footing shown is

(A) 75 lbs. (B) 9000 lbs.
(C) 9667 lbs. (D) 11,250 lbs.

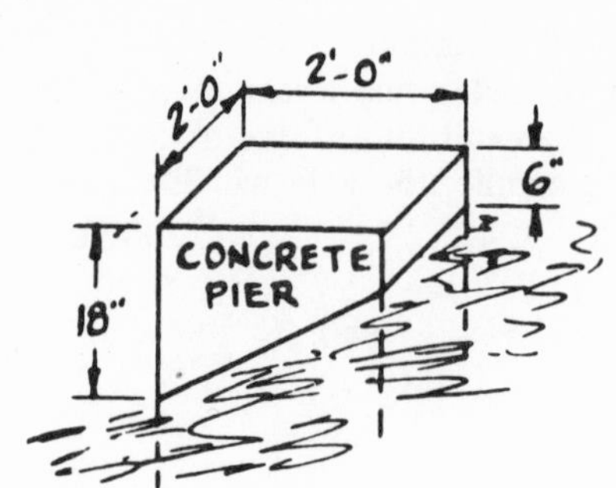

The number of cubic feet of concrete in the portion of the pier that is shown above the ground is

(A) 4 (B) 6
(C) 8 (D) 10.

CONSOLIDATE YOUR KEY ANSWERS HERE

1 A B C D E	2 A B C D E	3 A B C D E	4 A B C D E	5 A B C D E	6 A B C D E	7 A B C D E	8 A B C D E
9 A B C D E	10 A B C D E	11 A B C D E	12 A B C D E	13 A B C D E	14 A B C D E	15 A B C D E	16 A B C D E
17 A B C D E	18 A B C D E	19 A B C D E	20 A B C D E	21 A B C D E	22 A B C D E	23 A B C D E	24 A B C D E

Correct Answers For The Foregoing Questions

(Please make every effort to answer the questions on your own before looking at these answers. You'll make faster progress by following this rule.)

1.C	4.E	7.B	10.C	13.B	16.B	19.D
2.B	5.C	8.A	11.A	14.C	17.C	20.A
3.D	6.D	9.C	12.D	15.D	18.B	

TEST II. MECHANICAL COMPREHENSION

TIME: 15 Minutes

DIRECTIONS: For each question read all the choices carefully. Then select that answer which you consider correct or most nearly correct. Blacken the answer space corresponding to your best choice, just as you would do on the actual examination.

1

The dimension "X" on the piece shown is
(A) 2' - 3 2/3" (B) 2' - 4"
(C) 2' - 4 1/3" (D) 2' - 5 1/4".

2

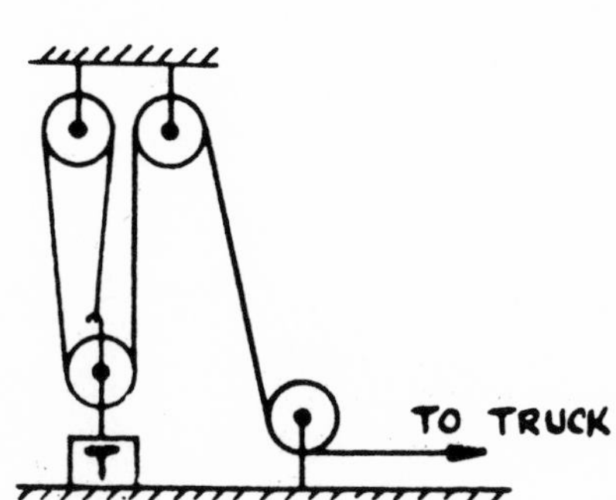

The tank "T" is to be raised as shown by attaching the pull rope to a truck. If the tank is to be raised ten feet, the truck will have to move
(A) 20 feet (B) 30 feet
(C) 40 feet (D) 50 feet.

3

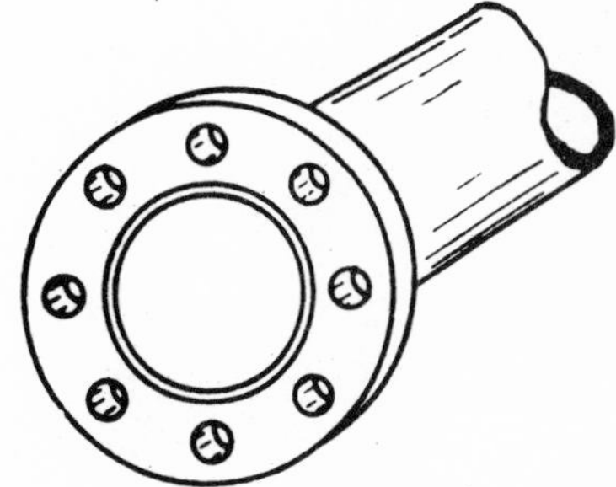

In the case of the standard flanged pipe shown, the maximum angle through which it would be necessary to rotate the pipe in order to line up the holes is
(A) 22.5 degrees (B) 30 degrees
(C) 45 degrees (D) 60 degrees.

4

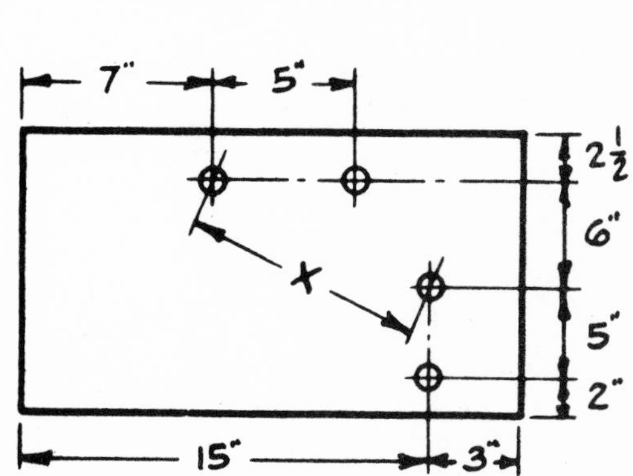

The distance "X" from center to center of the two holes is
(A) 10 inches (B) 9 inches
(C) 8 1/2 inches (D) 6 inches.

5

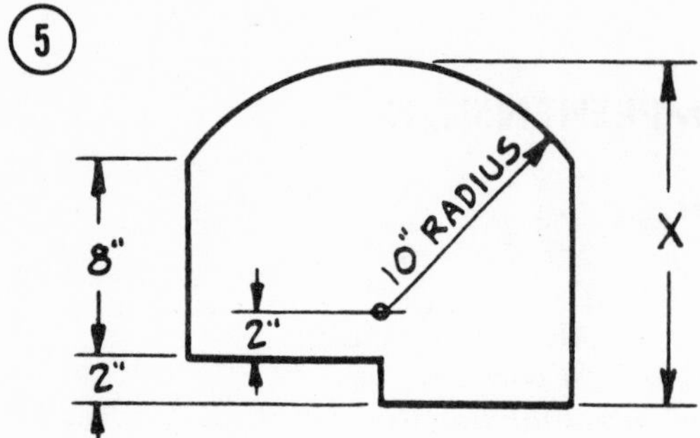

The distance "X" on the piece shown is
(A) 16 inches (B) 14 inches
(C) 12 inches (D) 10 inches.

6

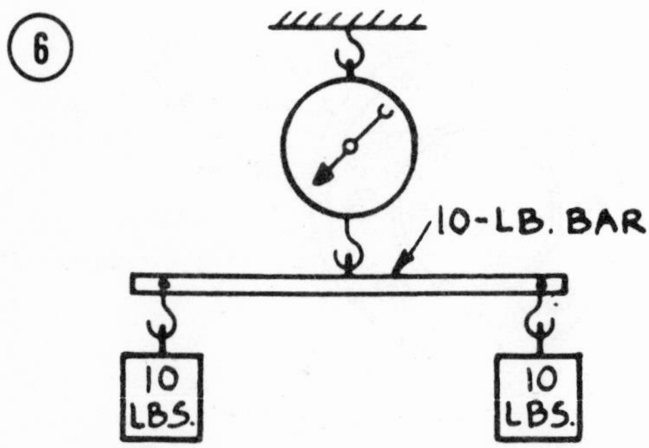

The reading on the weighing scale will be approximately
(A) zero (B) 10 lbs.
(C) 20 lbs. (D) 30 lbs.

7

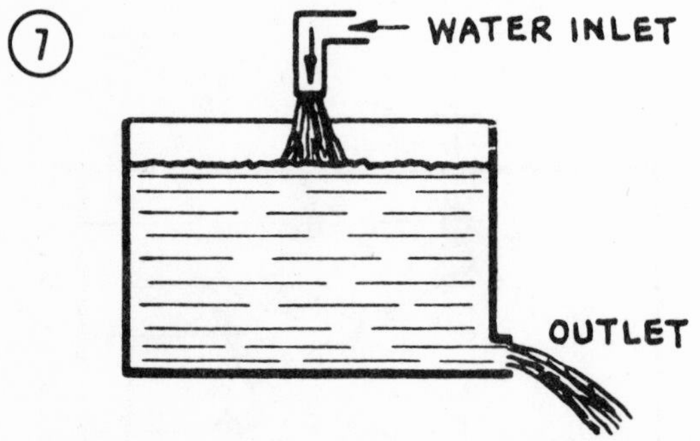

If water is flowing into the tank at the rate of 120 gallons per hour and flowing out of the tank at a constant rate of one gallon per minute, the water level in the tank will
(A) rise 1 gallon per minute
(B) rise 2 gallons per minute
(C) fall 2 gallons per minute
(D) fall 1 gallon per minute.

8

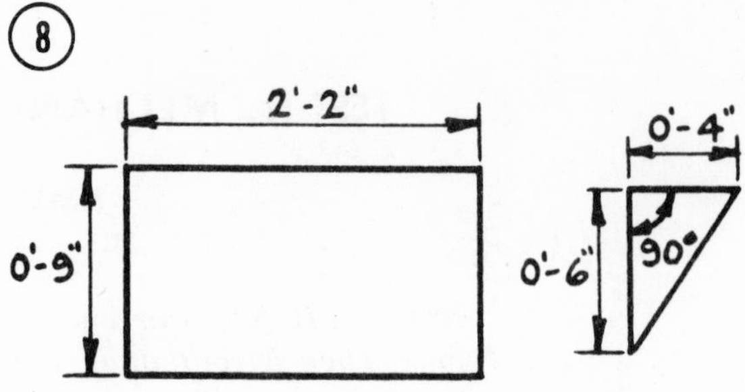

The maximum number of triangular pieces shown which can be cut from the piece of sheet metal shown is
(A) 12 (B) 16
(C) 20 (D) 25.

9

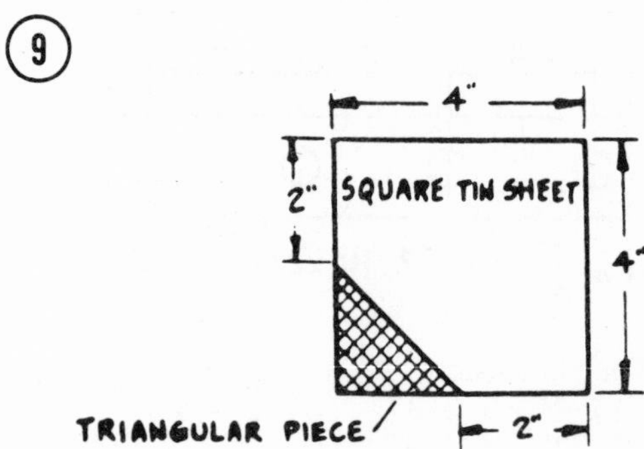

The maximum number of triangular pieces which can be cut from the tin sheet is
(A) 10 (B) 8
(C) 6 (D) 4.

10

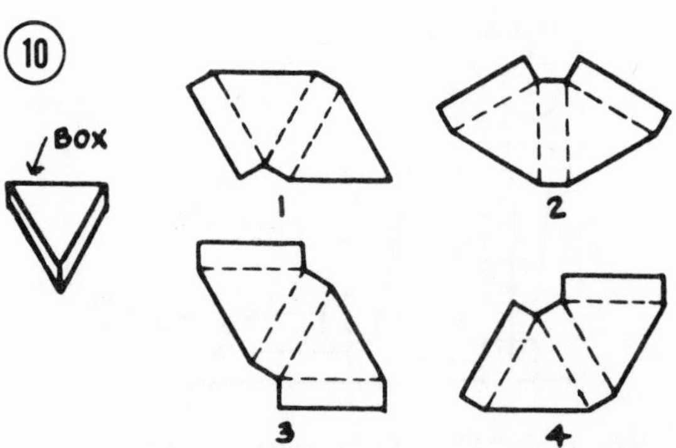

The flat sheet metal pattern which can be bent along the dotted lines to form the completely closed triangular box is
(A) 1 (B) 2
(C) 3 (D) 4.

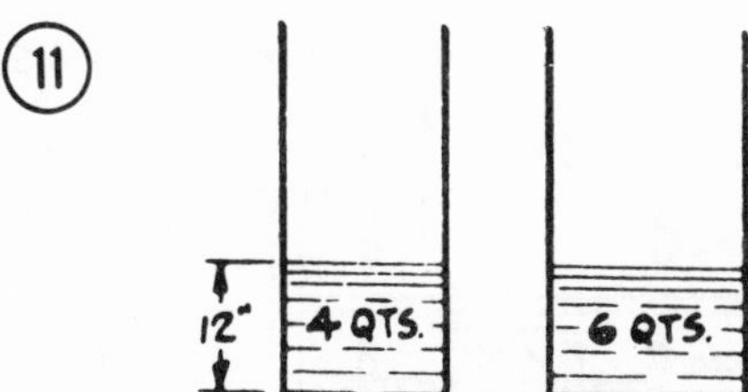

To bring the level of the water in the tanks to a height of 2 1/2 feet, the quantity of water to be added is

(A) 10 qts. (B) 15 qts.
(C) 20 qts. (D) 25 qts.

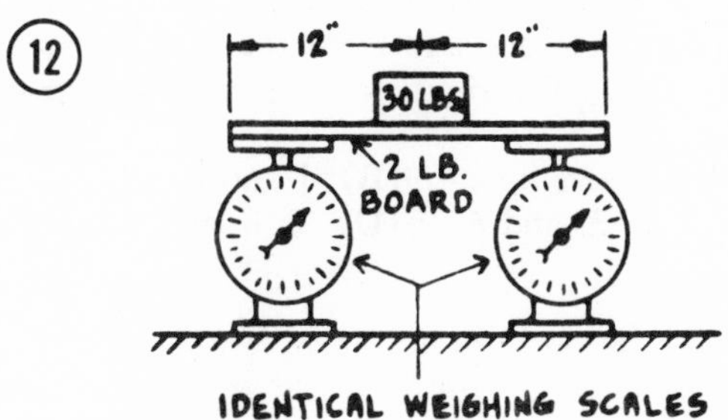

The weight held by the board and placed on the two identical scales will cause *each* scale to read

(A) 8 lbs. (B) 15 lbs.
(C) 16 lbs. (D) 32 lbs.

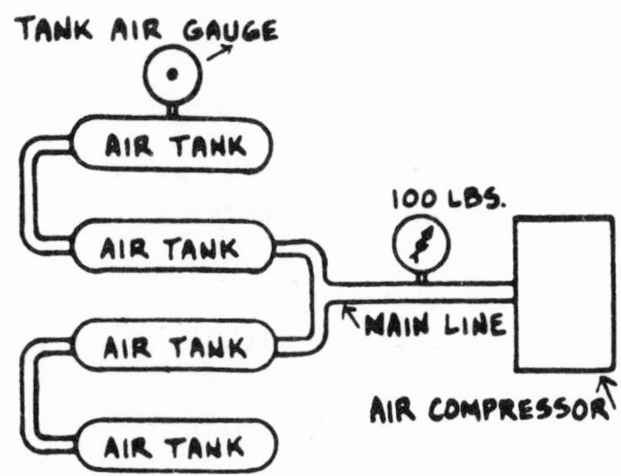

Four air reservoirs have been filled with air by the air compressor. If the main line air gauge reads 100 lbs. then the tank air gauge will read

(A) 25 lbs. (B) 50 lbs.
(C) 100 lbs. (D) 200 lbs.

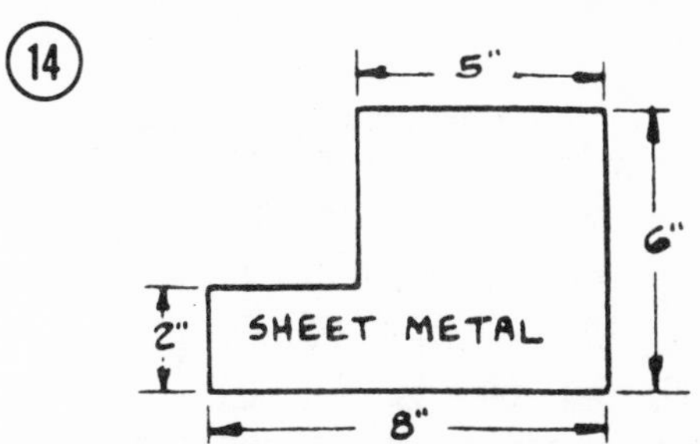

The area of the piece of sheet metal in square inches is

(A) 48 (B) 36
(C) 20 (D) 16.

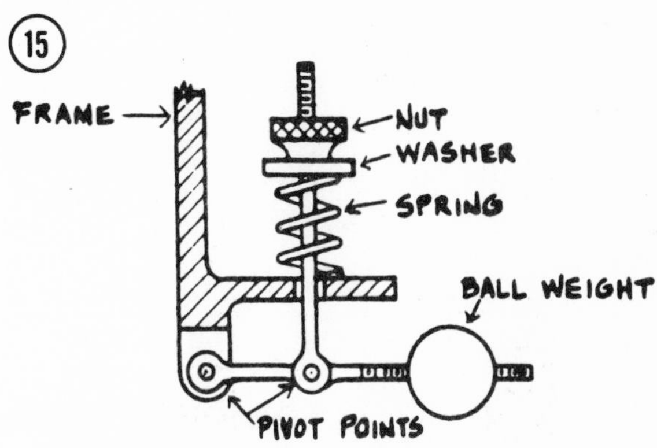

If the ball and spring mechanism are balanced in the position shown, the ball will move upward if

(A) the nut is loosened
(B) ball is moved away from the frame
(C) the nut is loosened and the ball moved away from the frame
(D) the nut is tightened.

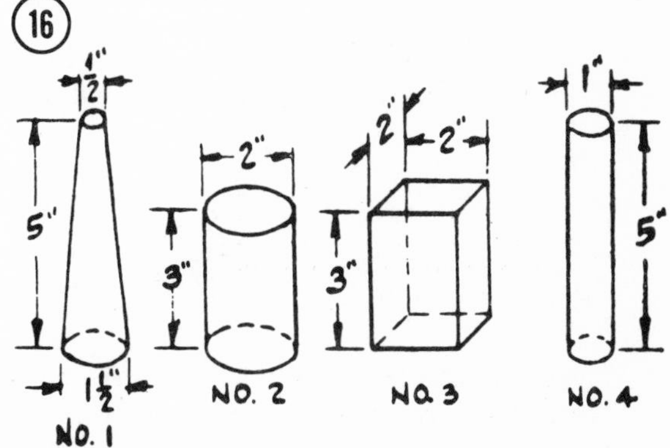

The container which will hold the most water is

(A) No. 1 (B) No. 2
(C) No. 3 (D) No. 4.

(17)

RIVETED SPLICE

In the structural steel splice the different types of rivets are shown by different symbols. The number of different types of rivets is

(A) 6 (B) 5
(C) 4 (D) 3.

(18)

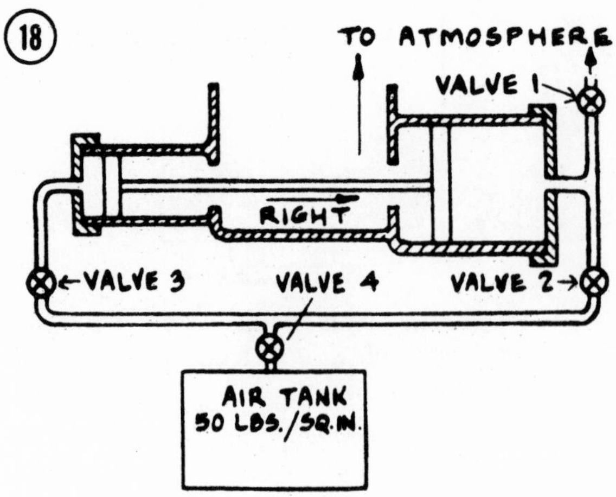

If all valves are closed at the start, in order to have air pressure from the tank move the pistons to the right, the valves to be opened are

(A) 2 and 4 (B) 1 and 2
(C) 2, 3, and 4 (D) 1, 3 and 4.

CONSOLIDATE YOUR KEY ANSWERS HERE

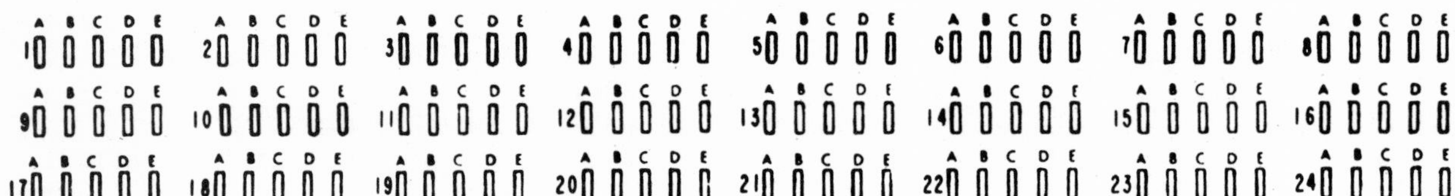

Correct Answers For The Foregoing Questions

(Please make every effort to answer the questions on your own before looking at these answers. You'll make faster progress by following this rule.)

1.B	4.A	7.A	10.C	13.C	16.C
2.B	5.B	8.B	11.B	14.B	17.C
3.A	6.D	9.B	12.C	15.D	18.D

XII. MATCHING LETTERS AND NUMBERS

DIRECTIONS: In this test of clerical ability, Column I consists of sets of numbered questions which you are to answer one at a time. Column II consists of possible answers to the set of questions in Column I. Select from Column II the one possible answer which contains only the numbers and letters, regardless of their order, which appear in the question in Column I. If none of the four possible answers is correct, mark "E" on your answer sheet.

A SAMPLE QUESTION EXPLAINED

COLUMN I: Set of Questions	*COLUMN II: Possible Answers*
1. 2-Q-P-5-T-G-4-7	(A) 5-G-8-P-4-Q
	(B) P-R-7-Q-4-2
	(C) Q-5-P-9-G-2
	(D) 4-2-5-P-7-Q
	(E) None of these.

The Correct Answer to the Sample Question is (D). How did we arrive at that solution? First, remember that the instructions tell you to select as your answer the choice that contains only the numbers and letters, regardless of their order, which appear in the question. The answer choice in Column II does not have to contain <u>all</u> of the letters and numbers that appear in the question. But the answer cannot contain a number or letter that does not appear in the question. Thus, begin by checking the numbers and letters that appear in Answer (A). You will note that while 5-G-P-4-Q all appear in the Sample Question, the number 8, which is included in Answer (A), does <u>not</u> appear in the question. Answer (A) is thus incorrect. Likewise, Answer (B) is incorrect as the letter R does not appear in the Sample Question; Answer (C) is incorrect as the number 9 does not appear in the question. In checking Answer (D), however, one notes that 4-2-5-P-7-Q all appear in the Sample Question. (D) is therefore the correct choice. Answer (E) is obviously eliminated.

Now proceed to answer the following test questions on the basis of the instructions given above.

TEST I. MATCHING LETTERS AND NUMBERS

TIME: 10 Minutes

The following are representative examination type questions. They should be carefully studied and completely understood.

DIRECTIONS: In this test of clerical ability, Column I consists of sets of numbered questions which you are to answer one at a time. Column II consists of possible answers to the set of questions in Column I. Select from Column II the one possible answer which contains only the numbers and letters, regardless of their order, which appear in the question in Column I. If none of the four possible answers is correct, mark "E" on your answer sheet.

Correct key answers to all these test questions will be found at the end of the test.

COLUMN I: Set of Questions	*COLUMN II: Possible Answers*
1. 6-4-T-G-9-K-N-8	(A) Z-8-K-G-9-7
2. K-3-L-6-Z-7-9-T	(B) 7-N-Z-T-9-8
3. N-8-9-3-K-G-7-Z	(C) L-3-Z-K-7-6
4. L-Z-G-6-4-9-K-3	(D) 4-K-T-G-8-6
5. 9-T-K-8-3-7-N-Z	(E) None of these.

Set of Questions	*Possible Answers*
6. 2-3-P-6-V-Z-4-L	(A) 3-6-G-P-7-N
7. T-7-4-3-P-Z-9-G	(B) 3-7-P-V-4-T
8. 6-N-G-Z-3-9-P-7	(C) 4-6-V-Z-2-L
9. 9-6-P-4-N-G-Z-2	(D) 4-7-G-Z-T-3
10. 4-9-7-T-L-P-3-V	(E) None of these.

COLUMN I: Set of Questions		*COLUMN II: Possible Answers*	
11.	Q-1-6-R-L-9-7-V	(A)	F-3-N-K-J-4
12.	8-W-2-Z-P-4-H-O	(B)	Q-H-4-O-5-M
13.	N-J-3-T-K-5-F-M	(C)	O-W-2-Z-4-8
14.	5-T-H-M-O-4-Q-J	(D)	R-9-V-1-Q-6
15.	4-Z-X-8-W-O-2-L	(E)	None of these.

Set of Questions		*Possible Answers*	
16.	S-2-L-8-U-Q-7-P	(A)	9-Q-T-K-2-7
17.	4-M-O-6-T-F-W-1	(B)	F-O-1-4-W-M
18.	J-M-4-X-W-Z-5-8	(C)	U-2-8-P-Q-S
19.	H-Q-2-9-T-I-K-7	(D)	Z-M-4-5-8-Q
20.	8-M-Z-V-4-P-5-Q	(E)	None of these.

CONSOLIDATE YOUR KEY ANSWERS HERE

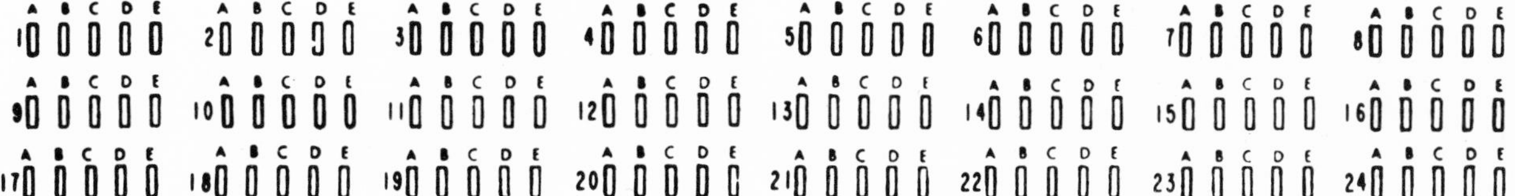

Correct Answers For The Foregoing Questions

(Please make every effort to answer the questions on your own before looking at these answers. You'll make faster progress by following this rule.)

SCORE 1
.... %
NO. CORRECT
NO. OF QUESTIONS ON THIS TEST

1.D	6.C	11.D	16.C
2.C	7.D	12.C	17.B
3.A	8.A	13.E	18.E
4.E	9.E	14.B	19.A
5.B	10.B	15.C	20.D

SCORE 2
.... %
NO. CORRECT
NO. OF QUESTIONS ON THIS TEST

TEST II. MATCHING LETTERS AND NUMBERS

TIME: 10 Minutes

The following are representative examination type questions. They should be carefully studied and completely understood.

DIRECTIONS: In this test of clerical ability, Column I consists of sets of numbered questions which you are to answer one at a time. Column II consists of possible answers to the set of questions in Column I. Select from Column II the one possible answer which contains only the numbers and letters, regardless of their order, which appear in the question in Column I. If none of the four possible answers is correct, mark "E" on your answer sheet.

Correct key answers to these sample questions are given at the conclusion of the test. Please don't peek at our key answers until you've answered all the questions on your own.

COLUMN I: *Set of Questions*	*COLUMN II:* *Possible Answers*
1. Z-5-3-L-7-K-4-G	(A) T-4-K-5-G-2
2. K-V-6-T-2-7-4-L	(B) 7-K-4-G-Z-5
3. G-T-V-9-L-4-5-3	(C) L-5-2-G-K-7
4. G-T-5-N-9-2-K-4	(D) T-2-7-L-6-V
5. K-4-5-T-G-2-6-P	(E) None of these.

Set of Questions	*Possible Answers*
6. V-K-Z-5-2-L-8-9	(A) N-K-8-3-5-7
7. N-Z-2-L-V-3-5-8	(B) V-N-5-8-2-L
8. N-P-3-9-V-5-6-Z	(C) 9-Z-3-V-P-6
9. Z-3-K-T-7-4-5-N	(D) K-5-Z-9-V-8
10. V-L-K-9-N-5-2-7	(E) None of these.

COLUMN I: Set of Questions	*COLUMN II: Possible Answers*
11. 7-8-L-5-Z-9-P-V	(A) 9-V-4-L-N-3
12. N-6-4-L-3-Z-G-9	(B) N-4-5-Z-3-9
13. V-9-3-4-K-N-5-L	(C) 8-5-Z-L-9-P
14. L-V-9-2-N-8-T-5	(D) N-9-8-V-L-T
15. 5-Z-L-9-P-V-2-8	(E) None of these.

Set of Questions	*Possible Answers*
16. L-2-4-8-V-P-7-N	(A) N-2-7-L-8-V
17. V-4-7-8-N-T-Z-6	(B) 2-V-T-8-G-7
18. T-L-5-N-6-8-7-V	(C) 8-6-T-L-N-4
19. L-6-N-T-2-G-8-4	(D) V-7-6-N-T-8
20. T-L-V-3-4-G-8-7	(E) None of these.

CONSOLIDATE YOUR KEY ANSWERS HERE

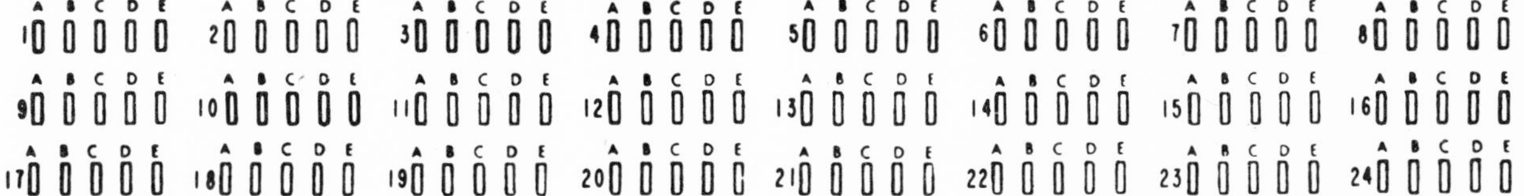

Correct Answers For The Foregoing Questions

To assist you in scoring yourself we have provided Correct Answers alongside your Answer Sheet. May we therefore suggest that while you are doing the test you cover the Correct Answers with a sheet of white paper.....to avoid temptation and to arrive at an accurate estimate of your ability and progress.

SCORE 1

.... %

NO. CORRECT

NO. OF QUESTIONS ON THIS TEST

1.B	6.D	11.C	16.A
2.D	7.B	12.E	17.D
3.E	8.C	13.A	18.D
4.A	9.E	14.D	19.C
5.A	10.E	15.C	20.E

SCORE 2

.... %

NO. CORRECT

NO. OF QUESTIONS ON THIS TEST

XIII. CODING ABILITY

DIRECTIONS: The codes given in Column I below begin and end with a capital letter and have an eight digit number in between. You are to arrange the codes in Column I according to the following rules.

1. *Arrange the codes in alphabetical order, according to the first letter.*
2. *When two or more codes have the same first letter, arrange the codes in alphabetical order according to the last letter.*
3. *When two or more of the codes have the same first and last letters, arrange the codes in numerical order, beginning with the lowest number.*

The codes in Column I are numbered (1) through (5). Column II gives you a selection of four possible answers. You are to choose from Column II the lettered choice which gives the correct listing of the codes in Column I arranged according to the above rules.

A SAMPLE QUESTION EXPLAINED

	COLUMN I: *Set of Codes*	*COLUMN II:* *Possible Answers*
1.	(1) E75044127B	(A) 4, 1, 3, 2, 5
	(2) B96399104A	(B) 4, 1, 2, 3, 5
	(3) B93939086A	(C) 4, 3, 2, 5, 1
	(4) B47064465H	(D) 3, 2, 5, 4, 1
	(5) B99040922A	

In the Sample question, the four codes starting with B should be placed before the code starting with E. The codes starting with B and ending with A should be placed before the code starting with B and ending with H. Then the codes starting with B and ending with A should be listed in numerical order, beginning with the lowest number. The correct way to arrange the codes therefore is:

(3) B93939086A
(2) B96399104A
(5) B99040922A
(4) B47064465H
(1) E75044127B

Since the order of arrangement is 3, 2, 5, 4, 1,---the answer to the Sample question is (D). Now proceed to answer the following test questions according to the above instructions.

S3013

CODING ABILITY TEST

TIME: 15 Minutes

The following are representative examination type questions. They should be carefully studied and completely understood.

DIRECTIONS: The codes given in Column I below begin and end with a capital letter and have an eight digit number in between. You are to arrange the codes in Column I according to the following rules.

1. *Arrange the codes in alphabetical order, according to the first letter.*
2. *When two or more codes have the same first letter, arrange the codes in alphabetical order according to the last letter.*
3. *When two or more of the codes have the same first* and *last letters, arrange the codes in numerical order, beginning with the lowest number.*

The codes in Column I are numbered (1) through (5). Column II gives you a selection of four possible answers. You are to choose from Column II the lettered choice which gives the correct listing of the codes in Column I arranged according to the above rules.

Correct key answers to all these test questions will be found at the end of the test.

	COLUMN I: Set of Codes	COLUMN II: Possible Answers
1.	(1) S55126179E	(A) 1, 5, 2, 3, 4
	(2) R55136177Q	(B) 3, 4, 1, 5, 2
	(3) P55126177R	(C) 3, 5, 2, 1, 4
	(4) S55126178R	(D) 4, 3, 1, 5, 2
	(5) R55126180P	
2.	(1) T64217813Q	(A) 4, 1, 3, 2, 5
	(2) I64217817O	(B) 2, 4, 3, 1, 5
	(3) T64217818O	(C) 4, 1, 5, 2, 3
	(4) I64217811Q	(D) 2, 3, 4, 1, 5
	(5) T64217816Q	
3.	(1) C83261824G	(A) 2, 4, 1, 5, 3
	(2) C78361833C	(B) 4, 2, 1, 3, 5
	(3) G83261732G	(C) 3, 1, 5, 2, 4
	(4) C88261823C	(D) 2, 3, 5, 1, 4
	(5) G83261743C	

		COLUMN I: Set of Codes	*COLUMN II: Possible Answers*	
4.	(1)	A11710107H	(A)	2, 1, 4, 3, 5
	(2)	H17110017A	(B)	3, 1, 5, 2, 4
	(3)	A11170707A	(C)	3, 4, 1, 5, 2
	(4)	H17170171H	(D)	3, 5, 1, 2, 4
	(5)	A11710177A		
5.	(1)	R26794821S	(A)	3, 2, 4, 1, 5
	(2)	O26794821T	(B)	3, 4, 2, 1, 5
	(3)	M26794827Z	(C)	4, 2, 1, 3, 5
	(4)	Q26794821R	(D)	5, 4, 1, 2, 3
	(5)	S26794821P		
6.	(1)	D89143888P	(A)	3, 5, 2, 1, 4
	(2)	D98143838B	(B)	3, 1, 4, 5, 2
	(3)	D89113883B	(C)	4, 2, 3, 1, 5
	(4)	D89148338P	(D)	4, 1, 3, 5, 2
	(5)	D89148388B		
7.	(1)	W62455599E	(A)	2, 4, 3, 1, 5
	(2)	W62455090F	(B)	3, 1, 5, 2, 4
	(3)	W62405099E	(C)	5, 3, 1, 4, 2
	(4)	V62455097F	(D)	5, 4, 3, 1, 2
	(5)	V62405979E		
8.	(1)	N74663826M	(A)	2, 4, 5, 3, 1
	(2)	M74633286M	(B)	2, 5, 4, 1, 3
	(3)	N76633228N	(C)	1, 2, 5, 3, 4
	(4)	M76483686N	(D)	2, 5, 1, 4, 3
	(5)	M74636688M		
9.	(1)	P97560324B	(A)	1, 5, 2, 3, 4
	(2)	R97663024B	(B)	3, 1, 4, 5, 2
	(3)	P97503024E	(C)	1, 5, 3, 2, 4
	(4)	R97563240E	(D)	1, 5, 2, 3, 4
	(5)	P97652304B		
10.	(1)	H92411165G	(A)	2, 5, 3, 4, 1
	(2)	A92141465G	(B)	3, 4, 2, 5, 1
	(3)	H92141165C	(C)	3, 2, 1, 5, 4
	(4)	H92444165C	(D)	3, 1, 2, 5, 4
	(5)	A92411465G		

COLUMN I: Set of Codes			COLUMN II: Possible Answers	
11.	(1)	X90637799S	(A)	4, 3, 5, 2, 1
	(2)	N90037696S	(B)	5, 4, 2, 1, 3
	(3)	Y90677369B	(C)	5, 2, 4, 1, 3
	(4)	X09677693B	(D)	5, 2, 3, 4, 1
	(5)	M09673699S		
12.	(1)	K78425174L	(A)	4, 2, 1, 3, 5
	(2)	K78452714C	(B)	2, 3, 5, 4, 1
	(3)	K78547214N	(C)	1, 4, 2, 3, 5
	(4)	K78442774C	(D)	4, 2, 1, 5, 3
	(5)	K78547724M		
13.	(1)	P18736652U	(A)	1, 3, 4, 5, 2
	(2)	P18766352V	(B)	1, 5, 2, 3, 4
	(3)	T17686532U	(C)	3, 4, 5, 1, 2
	(4)	T17865523U	(D)	5, 2, 1, 3, 4
	(5)	P18675332V		

CONSOLIDATE YOUR KEY ANSWERS HERE

Correct Answers For The Foregoing Questions

To assist you in scoring yourself we have provided Correct Answers alongside your Answer Sheet. May we therefore suggest that while you are doing the test you cover the Correct Answers with a sheet of white paper.....to avoid temptation and to arrive at an accurate estimate of your ability and progress.

SCORE 1

.... %

NO. CORRECT / NO. OF QUESTIONS ON THIS TEST

1.C	4.D	7.D	10.A
2.B	5.A	8.B	11.C
3.A	6.A	9.C	12.D
			13.B

SCORE 2

.... %

NO. CORRECT / NO. OF QUESTIONS ON THIS TEST

TEST II. CODING ABILITY

TIME: 15 Minutes

The following are representative examination type questions. They should be carefully studied and completely understood.

DIRECTIONS: *The codes given in Column I below begin and end with a capital letter and have an eight digit number in between. You are to arrange the codes in Column I according to the following rules.*

1. *Arrange the codes in alphabetical order, according to the first letter.*
2. *When two or more codes have the same first letter, arrange the codes in alphabetical order according to the last letter.*
3. *When two or more of the codes have the same first and last letters, arrange the codes in numerical order, beginning with the lowest number.*

The codes in Column I are numbered (1) through (5). Column II gives you a selection of four possible answers. You are to choose from Column II the lettered choice which gives the correct listing of the codes in Column I arranged according to the above rules.

Correct key answers to these sample questions are given at the conclusion of the test. Please don't peek at our key answers until you've answered all the questions on your own.

	COLUMN I: Set of Codes		COLUMN II: Possible Answers	
1.	(1)	L51138101K	(A)	1, 5, 3, 2, 4
	(2)	S51138001R	(B)	1, 3, 5, 2, 4
	(3)	S51188111K	(C)	1, 5, 2, 4, 3
	(4)	S51183110R	(D)	2, 5, 1, 4, 3
	(5)	L51188100R		
2.	(1)	J28475336D	(A)	5, 1, 2, 3, 4
	(2)	T28775363D	(B)	4, 3, 5, 1, 2
	(3)	J27843566P	(C)	1, 5, 2, 4, 3
	(4)	T27834563P	(D)	5, 1, 3, 2, 4
	(5)	J28435536D		
3.	(1)	G42786441J	(A)	2, 5, 4, 3, 1
	(2)	H45665413J	(B)	5, 4, 1, 3, 2
	(3)	G43117690J	(C)	4, 5, 1, 3, 2
	(4)	G43546698I	(D)	1, 3, 5, 4, 2
	(5)	G41679942I		

COLUMN I: Set of Codes			*COLUMN II: Possible Answers*	
4.	(1)	S44556178T	(A)	1, 3, 5, 2, 4
	(2)	T43457169T	(B)	4, 3, 5, 2, 1
	(3)	S53321176T	(C)	5, 3, 1, 2, 4
	(4)	T53317998S	(D)	5, 1, 3, 4, 2
	(5)	S67673942S		
5.	(1)	R63394217D	(A)	5, 4, 2, 3, 1
	(2)	R63931247D	(B)	1, 5, 3, 2, 4
	(3)	R53931247D	(C)	5, 3, 1, 2, 4
	(4)	R66874239D	(D)	5, 1, 2, 3, 4
	(5)	R46799366D		
6.	(1)	A35671968B	(A)	3, 2, 1, 4, 5
	(2)	A35421794C	(B)	2, 3, 1, 5, 4
	(3)	A35466987B	(C)	1, 3, 2, 4, 5
	(4)	C10435779A	(D)	3, 1, 2, 4, 5
	(5)	C00634779B		
7.	(1)	I997736426Q	(A)	2, 1, 3, 5, 4
	(2)	I10445311Q	(B)	5, 4, 2, 1, 3
	(3)	J63749877P	(C)	4, 5, 3, 2, 1
	(4)	J03421739Q	(D)	2, 1, 4, 5, 3
	(5)	J00765311Q		
8.	(1)	M33964217N	(A)	4, 1, 5, 2, 3
	(2)	N33942770N	(B)	5, 1, 4, 3, 2
	(3)	N06155881M	(C)	4, 1, 5, 3, 2
	(4)	M00433669M	(D)	1, 4, 5, 2, 3
	(5)	M79034577N		
9.	(1)	D77643905C	(A)	1, 2, 5, 3, 4
	(2)	D44106788C	(B)	5, 3, 2, 1, 4
	(3)	D13976022F	(C)	2, 1, 5, 3, 4
	(4)	D97655430E	(D)	2, 1, 4, 5, 3
	(5)	D00439776F		
10.	(1)	W22746920A	(A)	2, 1, 3, 4, 5
	(2)	W22743720A	(B)	2, 1, 5, 3, 4
	(3)	W32987655A	(C)	1, 2, 3, 4, 5
	(4)	W43298765A	(D)	1, 2, 5, 3, 4
	(5)	W30987433A		

		COLUMN I: Set of Codes		*COLUMN II: Possible Answers*
11.	(1)	P44343314Y	(A)	2, 3, 1, 4, 5
	(2)	P44141341S	(B)	1, 5, 3, 2, 4
	(3)	P44141431L	(C)	4, 2, 3, 5, 1
	(4)	P41143413W	(D)	5, 3, 2, 4, 1
	(5)	P44313433H		
12.	(1)	D89077275M	(A)	3, 2, 5, 4, 1
	(2)	D98073724N	(B)	1, 4, 3, 2, 5
	(3)	D90877274N	(C)	4, 1, 5, 2, 3
	(4)	D98877275M	(D)	1, 3, 2, 5, 4
	(5)	D98873725N		
13.	(1)	H32548137E	(A)	2, 4, 5, 1, 3
	(2)	H35243178A	(B)	1, 5, 2, 3, 4
	(3)	H35284378F	(C)	1, 5, 2, 4, 3
	(4)	H35288337A	(D)	2, 1, 5, 3, 4
	(5)	H32883173B		

CONSOLIDATE YOUR KEY ANSWERS HERE

Correct Answers For The Foregoing Questions

(Please try to answer the questions on your own before looking at our answers. You'll do much better on your test if you follow this rule.)

1.A	4.D	7.A	10.B
2.D	5.C	8.C	11.D
3.B	6.D	9.D	12.B
			13.A

SCORE 1 .... %
NO. CORRECT ÷
NO. OF QUESTIONS ON THIS TEST

SCORE 2 .... %
NO. CORRECT ÷
NO. OF QUESTIONS ON THIS TEST

XIV. TABLE CODING

DIRECTIONS: In this test of speed and accuracy you are given a three-line Code Table consisting of corresponding letters and numbers. In the first line you are given a Code Name. In the second line, the letters of the Code Word are given directly below the Code Name. In the third line, the Code Numbers are listed directly below the Code Word. For each question in this test you will use the CODE TABLE to determine if the Code Letters in Column II and the Code Numbers in Column III correspond to the Code Name, printed in capital letters in Column I. Study each question carefully, and mark your answer as follows:

(A) If there is an error in Column II only
(B) If there is an error in Column III only
(C) If there is an error in both Columns II and III
(D) If both Columns II and III are correct.

A SAMPLE QUESTION EXPLAINED

CODE TABLE

CODE NAME →	R	I	C	H	M	E	D	A	L
CODE WORD →	i	n	s	u	l	a	t	e	d
CODE TABLE →	0	1	2	3	4	5	6	7	8

	Column I: CODE NAME	*Column II: CODE WORD*	*Column III: CODE NUMBERS*
1.	MIRED	lniat	41058

In answering this Sample Question, your task is to determine if the letters given in Column II and the numbers listed in Column III are, according to the Code Table given above, the letters and numbers that appear directly below the Capital letters given in Column I. In the Sample Question, for example, do the letters "lniat" appear directly below the Capital letters "MIRED," according to the Code Table? And, likewise, do the numbers 41058 appear directly below the Capital letters "MIRED?" As you can see, the letters "lniat" in Column II are correctly coded to the Capital letters "MIRED." The numbers in Column III, however, are incorrectly coded: the numbers appearing directly below "MIRED" are 41056----not 41058. Since there is an error only in Column III, the Correct Answer to the Sample Question is (B).

Now proceed to answer the following test questions on the basis of the instructions given above.

TEST I. TABLE CODING

TIME: 15 Minutes

The following are representative examination type questions. They should be carefully studied and completely understood.

DIRECTIONS: In this test of speed and accuracy you are given a three-line Code Table consisting of corresponding letters and numbers. In the first line you are given a Code Name. In the second line, the letters of the Code Word are given directly below the Code Name. In the third line, the Code Numbers are listed directly below the Code Word. For each question in this test you will use the CODE TABLE to determine if the Code Letters in Column II and the Code Numbers in Column III correspond to the Code Name, printed in capital letters in Column I. Study each question carefully, and mark your answer as follows:

(A) If there is an error in Column II only
(B) If there is an error in Column III only
(C) If there is an error in both Columns II and III
(D) If both Columns II and III are correct.

Correct key answers to all these test questions will be found at the end of the test.

CODE TABLE

CODE NAME →	G	A	L	D	B	R	U	C	H
CODE WORD →	c	o	m	p	l	i	a	n	t
CODE NUMBERS →	1	2	3	4	5	6	7	8	9

	Column I: CODE NAME	*Column II: CODE WORD*	*Column III: CODE NUMBERS*
1.	BRALD	liomp	56234
2.	LAGUC	mocan	32168
3.	HURAD	taiop	97623
4.	CHUBA	ntali	89752
5.	DULGH	panct	47318

CODE TABLE

CODE NAME →	S	H	U	M	A	C	K	E	R
CODE WORD →	f	a	v	o	r	i	t	e	s
CODE NUMBERS →	0	1	2	3	4	5	6	7	8

Column I: CODE NAME		*Column II: CODE WORD*	*Column III: CODE NUMBERS*
6.	SUMAC	fvoai	02345
7.	MAKER	ortev	34658
8.	CRAMS	isrof	57430
9.	HARMS	arsof	14832
10.	UKRAH	vtsra	26841

CODE TABLE

CODE NAME →	S	I	M	O	N	D	A	L	E
CODE WORD →	e	d	u	c	a	t	i	o	n
CODE NUMBERS →	4	5	7	9	6	8	3	1	2

Column I: CODE NAME		*Column II: CODE WORD*	*Column III: CODE NUMBERS*
11.	MESON	uneca	72496
12.	DILES	tdoie	85124
13.	LEMON	onuct	12795
14.	OAESN	conea	93246
15.	IDMEA	dtuni	58923

CODE TABLE

CODE NAME →	C A R P E T K I N G
CODE WORD →	s p o r t i n g l y
CODE NUMBERS →	4 5 6 7 8 9 0 1 2 3

Column I: CODE NAME	Column II: CODE WORD	Column III: CODE NUMBERS
16. REGAP	otypr	68347
17. TIPEC	igrto	91874
18. KANRI	nplog	05261
19. AKGEC	pnyts	50384
20. PIKET	rglti	71089

CONSOLIDATE YOUR KEY ANSWERS HERE

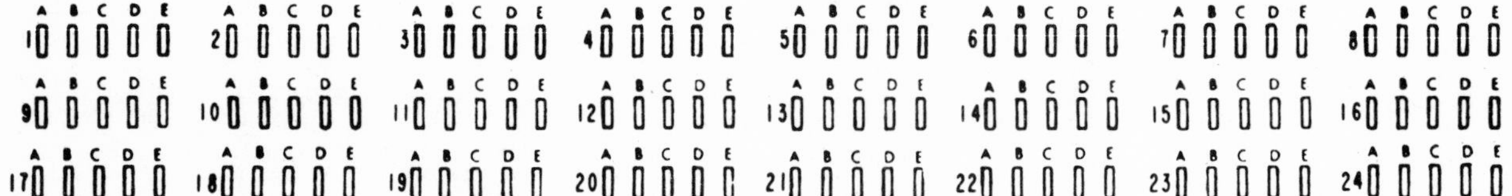

Correct Answers For The Foregoing Questions

To assist you in scoring yourself we have provided Correct Answers alongside your Answer Sheet. May we therefore suggest that while you are doing the test you cover the Correct Answers with a sheet of white paper.....to avoid temptation and to arrive at an accurate estimate of your ability and progress.

SCORE 1

.... %

NO. CORRECT

NO. OF QUESTIONS ON THIS TEST

1.D	6.A	11.D	16.B
2.B	7.C	12.A	17.C
3.B	8.B	13.C	18.D
4.A	9.B	14.A	19.D
5.C	10.D	15.B	20.A

SCORE 2

.... %

NO. CORRECT

NO. OF QUESTIONS ON THIS TEST

XV. CLASSIFICATION PRACTICE

DIRECTIONS: This test consists of a list of numbered words which you are to classify. For each word you are to mark your answer sheet as follows:

Mark "A" if the second letter is o, & the third letter is l;
Mark "B" if the second letter is o, & the third letter is i and the final letter is l;
Mark "C" if the second letter is o, & the third letter is anything but i, and the final letter is l;
Mark "D" if the second letter is not o, and the third letter is anything but i, & the fourth letter is anything but l;
Mark "E" if the word cannot be classified in any of these four categories.

SAMPLE QUESTIONS AND EXPLANATIONS

1. toil — A B C D E
2. sole — A B C D E
3. goal — A B C D E
4. trail — A B C D E

The Correct Answer for question #1 is B. The second letter of the word "toil" is "o," the third letter is "i" and the final letter is "l." For question #2, A is the Correct Answer. The second letter of "sole" is "o" and the third letter is "l." C is the answer for question #3; the second letter of the word goal is "o," the third letter is not "i," and the final letter is "l." Likewise, D is the Correct Answer for question #4; the second letter of the word "trail" is not "o," the third letter is not "i," and the fourth letter is not "l."

Now proceed to answer the following test questions according to these instructions. Correct answers appear at the end of each test.

CLASSIFICATION PRACTICE

TIME: 25 Minutes

DIRECTIONS: This test consists of a list of numbered words which you are to classify. For each word you are to mark your answer sheet as follows:

Mark "A" if the second letter is o, & the third letter is l;
Mark "B" if the second letter is o, & the third letter is i and the final letter is l;
Mark "C" if the second letter is o, & the third letter is anything but i, and the final letter is l;
Mark "D" if the second letter is not o, and the third letter is anything but i, & the fourth letter is anything but l;
Mark "E" if the word cannot be classified in any of these four categories.

Correct key answers to all these test questions will be found at the end of the test.

1. clay
2. spoilt
3. pole
4. broil
5. police
6. tepid
7. spring
8. volition
9. foul
10. spoof
11. tool
12. vicar
13. foliage
14. foible
15. violet
16. sale
17. dole
18. coastal
19. scowls
20. coil
21. molar
22. raise
23. moral
24. fools
25. foil
26. mallet
27. fervid
28. murals
29. mall
30. dorsal
31. soil
32. doldrum
33. poison
34. orals
35. boil
36. tonal
37. kiln
38. mollify
39. spools
40. solvent
41. cholera
42. portal
43. model
44. slope
45. devils

46. native
47. usual
48. hollow
49. farce
50. collar
51. sorrel
52. thermal
53. colic
54. verbiage
55. lion
56. howl
57. roller
58. focal
59. vole
60. holiness

CONSOLIDATE YOUR KEY ANSWERS HERE

1 A B C D E	2 A B C D E	3 A B C D E	4 A B C D E	5 A B C D E	6 A B C D E	7 A B C D E	8 A B C D E
9 A B C D E	10 A B C D E	11 A B C D E	12 A B C D E	13 A B C D E	14 A B C D E	15 A B C D E	16 A B C D E
17 A B C D E	18 A B C D E	19 A B C D E	20 A B C D E	21 A B C D E	22 A B C D E	23 A B C D E	24 A B C D E
25 A B C D E	26 A B C D E	27 A B C D E	28 A B C D E	29 A B C D E	30 A B C D E	31 A B C D E	32 A B C D E
33 A B C D E	34 A B C D E	35 A B C D E	36 A B C D E	37 A B C D E	38 A B C D E	39 A B C D E	40 A B C D E
41 A B C D E	42 A B C D E	43 A B C D E	44 A B C D E	45 A B C D E	46 A B C D E	47 A B C D E	48 A B C D E
49 A B C D E	50 A B C D E	51 A B C D E	52 A B C D E	53 A B C D E	54 A B C D E	55 A B C D E	56 A B C D E
57 A B C D E	58 A B C D E	59 A B C D E	60 A B C D E	61 A B C D E	62 A B C D E	63 A B C D E	64 A B C D E

Correct Answers For The Foregoing Questions

(Please make every effort to answer the questions on your own before looking at these answers. You'll make faster progress by following this rule.)

1.D	9.C	17.A	24.E	31.B	38.A	45.D	53.A
2.D	10.D	18.C	25.B	32.A	39.D	46.D	54.D
3.A	11.C	19.D	26.E	33.E	40.A	47.D	55.D
4.D	12.D	20.B	27.D	34.E	41.E	48.A	56.C
5.A	13.A	21.A	28.D	35.B	42.C	49.D	57.A
6.D	14.E	22.E	29.E	36.C	43.C	50.A	58.C
7.D	15.E	23.C	30.C	37.D	44.D	51.C	59.A
8.A	16.D					52.D	60.A

SCORE 1 .... %
NO. CORRECT ÷
NO. OF QUESTIONS ON THIS TEST

SCORE 2 .... %
NO. CORRECT ÷
NO. OF QUESTIONS ON THIS TEST

XVI. CODING PRACTICE

DIRECTIONS: In this test of speed and accuracy you are asked to make the kind of code changes that are required when Code Words and Numbers are changed. An office used the following to code cost prices secretly:

f i n d b y z e a l
1 2 3 4 5 6 7 8 9 0

The office then decides to switch the code to:

w r i t e s a b l y
1 2 3 4 5 6 7 8 9 0

This entails changing all the price tags. In Column I you are given a list of tag prices in the old code marks and you are asked to change them to the new code marks. In Column II you are to write the letters called for by the New Code.

SAMPLE QUESTIONS AND EXPLANATIONS

Column I: OLD CODE	*Column II: NEW CODE*
1. fzl........	____________
2. yen........	____________

In converting the Old Code letters to the letters required by the New Code, you must note carefully the numbers corresponding to each. For Question #1, the Old Code letters "fzl" correspond to the numbers 1, 7 and 0 respectively. The letters in the New Code corresponding to those same numbers are: w, a, and y. Therefore, the Correct Answer to Question #1 is: way. For Question #2, the letters "yen" of the Old Code correspond to the numbers 6, 8, and 3. The New Code letters corresponding to those same numbers are: sbi.

Now proceed to answer the following test questions on the basis of the instructions given above. The Correct Answers are included at the end of each test.

CODING PRACTICE

TIME: 10 Minutes

The following are representative examination type questions. They should be carefully studied and completely understood. The actual test questions will probably not be quite as difficult as these.

DIRECTIONS: In this test of speed and accuracy you are asked to make the kind of code changes that are required when Code Words and Numbers are changed. An office used the following to code cost prices secretly:

f i n d b y z e a l
1 2 3 4 5 6 7 8 9 0

The office then decides to switch the code to:

w r i t e s a b l y
1 2 3 4 5 6 7 8 9 0

This entails changing all the price tags. In Column I you are given a list of tag prices in the old code marks and you are asked to change them to the new code marks. In Column II you are to write the letters called for by the New Code.

Correct key answers to all these test questions will be found at the end of the test.

Column I: OLD CODE	*Column II: NEW CODE*	*Column I: OLD CODE*	*Column II: NEW CODE*
1. dnb........	________	9. ilza.......	________
2. nba........	________	10. blz........	________
3. blz........	________	11. fzi........	________
4. lzdy.......	________	12. dey........	________
5. ife........	________	13. nyid.......	________
6. fye........	________	14. lzey.......	________
7. alzd.......	________	15. dfl........	________
8. nel........	________	16. bea........	________

S3013

Column I: OLD CODE	Column II: NEW CODE	Column I: OLD CODE	Column II: NEW CODE
17. dnb........	____________	31. fly........	____________
18. zyd........	____________	32. ibad.......	____________
19. eidf.......	____________	33. lan........	____________
20. byi........	____________	34. iaf........	____________
21. fez........	____________	35. zany.......	____________
22. eay........	____________	36. dif........	____________
23. ayi........	____________	37. eaz........	____________
24. yif........	____________	38. fibl.......	____________
25. dfl........	____________	39. deaz.......	____________
26. faz........	____________	40. nay........	____________
27. eld........	____________	41. niz........	____________
28. inf........	____________	42. lea........	____________
29. bel........	____________	43. labz.......	____________
30. zyl........	____________	44. feil.......	____________

Correct Answers For The Foregoing Questions

(Please try to answer the questions on your own before looking at our answers. You'll do much better on your test if you follow this rule.)

1.TIE	12.TBS	23.LSR	34.RLW
2.IEL	13.ISRT	24.SRW	35.ALIS
3.EYA	14.YABS	25.TWY	36.TRW
4.YATS	15.TWY	26.WLA	37.BLA
5.RWB	16.EBL	27.BYT	38.WREY
6.WSB	17.TIE	28.RIW	39.TBLA
7.LYAT	18.AST	29.EBY	40.ILS
8.IBY	19.BRTW	30.ASY	41.IRA
9.RYAL	20.ESR	31.WYS	42.YBL
10.EYA	21.WBA	32.RELT	43.YLEA
11.WAR	22.BLS	33.YLI	44.WBRY

SCORE

.... %

NO. CORRECT ÷

NO. OF QUESTIONS ON THIS TEST

XVII. CLASSIFICATION-CODING ABILITY

DIRECTIONS: In this test of clerical speed and accuracy you are asked to classify each of the items in Column I according to the following code of classifications:

Column I: ITEMS	*Column II: CLASSIFICATIONS*
Cloth	*1*
Metal	*2*
Liquid	*3*
Fruit	*4*
Vegetable	*5*
Bird	*6*
Tree	*7*
Fish	*8*
Gas	*9*
Animal	*10*

In Column II you are to write the Numerical Classification for each Item in Column I.

SAMPLE QUESTIONS AND EXPLANATIONS

Column I: ITEMS	*Column II: CLASSIFICATIONS*
1. chickadee	______
2. balsam	______
3. copper	______
4. leek	______

The correct answer for question #1 is 6. A chickadee is in the bird family, and the corresponding numerical classification in Column II is 6. For question #2, the correct answer is 7. A balsam is in the tree family. The correct answers for questions #3 and 4 are 2 and 5 respectively. Copper is a metal and is coded as 2 in Column II. Likewise, a leek is a vegetable in the onion family, and is classified numerically as 5 in Column II.

Now proceed to answer the following test questions on the basis of the instructions given above. The Correct Answers appear at the end of each test.

CLASSIFICATION-CODING ABILITY TEST

TIME: 15 Minutes

DIRECTIONS: In this test of clerical speed and accuracy you are asked to classify each of the items in Column I according to the following code of classifications:

Column I: ITEMS	*Column II: CLASSIFICATIONS*
Cloth	*1*
Metal	*2*
Liquid	*3*
Fruit	*4*
Vegetable	*5*
Bird	*6*
Tree	*7*
Fish	*8*
Gas	*9*
Animal	*10*

In Column II you are to write the Numerical Classification for each Item in Column I.

	Column I: ITEMS	*Column II: CLASSIFICATIONS*		*Column I: ITEMS*	*Column II: CLASSIFICATIONS*
1.	lemur	________	11.	turnip	________
2.	hydrogen	________	12.	oak	________
3.	swallow	________	13.	hare	________
4.	radish	________	14.	bronze	________
5.	velvet	________	15.	pear	________
6.	apple	________	16.	nitrogen	________
7.	honey	________	17.	satin	________
8.	zinc	________	18.	robin	________
9.	poplar	________	19.	peroxide	________
10.	flounder	________	20.	perch	________

	Column I: ITEMS	*Column II: CLASSIFICATIONS*
21.	lemon	________
22.	lion	________
23.	oxygen	________
24.	tin	________
25.	cotton	________
26.	tuna	________
27.	spinach	________
28.	fir	________
29.	peacock	________
30.	lettuce	________
31.	crow	________
32.	methane	________
33.	starling	________
34.	zebra	________
35.	hickory	________
36.	vinegar	________
37.	peach	________
38.	fluke	________
39.	lead	________
40.	tweed	________
41.	calcium	________
42.	turtle	________
43.	persimmon	________
44.	hawk	________

	Column I: ITEMS	*Column II: CLASSIFICATIONS*
45.	shark	________
46.	madras	________
47.	pine	________
48.	spaniel	________
49.	carrot	________
50.	lark	________
51.	maple	________
52.	alcohol	________
53.	leopard	________
54.	antimony	________
55.	banana	________
56.	dacron	________
57.	sateen	________
58.	nickel	________
59.	benzene	________
60.	grapes	________
61.	okra	________
62.	gull	________
63.	fir	________
64.	carp	________
65.	chlorine	________
66.	otter	________
67.	gingham	________
68.	milk	________

Column I: ITEMS	Column II: CLASSIFICATIONS
69. orange	________
70. oriole	________
71. willow	________
72. scrod	________
73. argon	________
74. elk	________

Column I: ITEMS	Column II: CLASSIFICATIONS
75. felt	________
76. iron	________
77. molasses	________
78. currant	________
79. chard	________
80. turkey	________

Correct Answers For The Foregoing Questions

(Please try to answer the questions on your own before looking at our answers. You'll do much better on your test if you follow this rule.)

1.10	11.5	21.4	31.6	41.2	51.7	61.5	71.7
2.9	12.7	22.10	32.9	42.10	52.3	62.6	72.8
3.6	13.10	23.9	33.6	43.4	53.10	63.7	73.9
4.5	14.2	24.2	34.10	44.6	54.2	64.8	74.10
5.1	15.4	25.1	35.7	45.8	55.4	65.9	75.1
6.4	16.9	26.8	36.3	46.1	56.1	66.10	76.2
7.3	17.1	27.5	37.4	47.7	57.1	67.1	77.3
8.2	18.6	28.7	38.8	48.10	58.2	68.3	78.4
9.7	19.3	29.6	39.2	49.5	59.3	69.4	79.5
10.8	20.8	30.5	40.1	50.6	60.4	70.6	80.6

SCORE 1 .... %
NO. CORRECT ÷
NO. OF QUESTIONS ON THIS TEST

SCORE 2 .... %
NO. CORRECT ÷
NO. OF QUESTIONS ON THIS TEST

XVIII. DATA INTERPRETATION

These questions are all from actual, previous examinations. They have been carefully chosen to afford you the best possible practice for the questions you face on your test. They'll also give a good idea of what to expect. If you answer them carefully, you'll be well prepared for this type of question. Please notice that the tables and charts cover a variety of fields of work, and require of you no previous knowledge of the subject. Each set of questions is to be answered solely on the basis of the table or chart shown. Before answering each set of questions, look over the data given to you and get a good, general idea of what it means. Then, in answering the questions, refer back to the given data, and let who will be clever.

A SAMPLE QUESTION ANALYZED

CHART NO. I

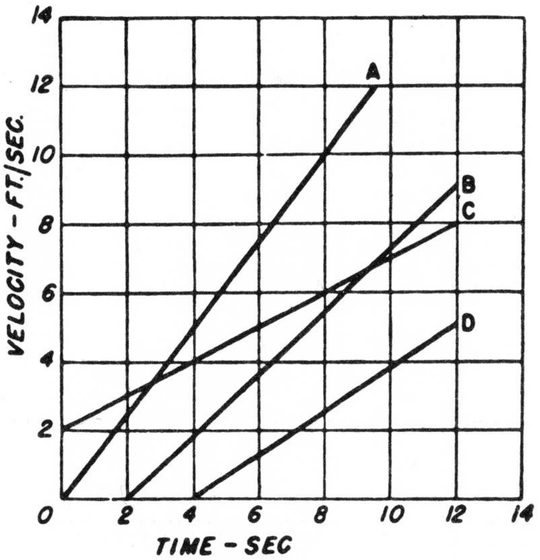

Look at the two columns of data below:

Time sec.	Velocity ft./sec.
0	2
2	3
4	4
6	5
8	6
10	7

// // // //
A B C D

Which one of the lines on the graph at the right most closely represents the data in these two columns?

VELOCITY - FT./SEC.
TIME - SEC

An examination of the graph shows that time values are indicated along the horizontal scale, and velocity values along the vertical scale. If we observe the velocity value at zero time, we see that the A line has a value of 0 velocity, and the C line a value of 2 ft./sec. No values are shown at 0 time for lines B and D. Hence line C is the only one which shows a velocity of 2 ft./sec. at 0 time.

Similarly at 2 sec. the velocity value for line B is 0, for line A is 2.5, and for line C, 3. Here again C is the only line which corresponds to the data in the table. At 4 sec. the velocity value for line D is 0, for line B is 1.9, for line C is 4, and for line A is 5. Here also line C is the only one that gives the value shown in the table. The same process can be repeated for time values 6, 8, and 10 sec., all of which show that line C is the only one corresponding to the values given in the table.

TEST I. DATA INTERPRETATION

TIME: 10 Minutes

The Data Interpretation questions take various forms: Charts, Tables, and Graphs. Also there are various types of each—for example, a graph may be the circle-type, the line-type, the bar-type, or a combination of these types. It is to be noted also that the subject matter which the test-makers draw on is very wide: cars, ships, schools, taxes, delinquency, etc.

DIRECTIONS:** **All the questions in this test refer to the following chart. Read each question carefully and answer it on the basis of the chart. Select the best case and mark the correct** letter **on the answer sheet.

Correct key answers to all these test questions will be found at the end of the test.

HOSPITAL CARE FOR PATIENTS

Case	Rent	Food	Shelter	Light	Fuel	Milk	Clothing	Household Supplies	Medical Care	Cod Liver Oil	Hospitalization	Fare	Cash Allowance
A	X	X	X		X		X				X		
B	X	X			X	X		X					
C		X		X		X		X	X	X			
D	X	X	X		X			X					
E			X	X			X		X			X	X
F			X		X		X		X				
G	X	X	X	X			X				X		
H	X		X				X					X	

Which case received:

1. Food, light, and hospitalization?
2. Medical service, shelter, clothing, and fuel?
3. Rent, food, shelter, fuel and household supplies?
4. Fuel, shelter, clothing, no hospitalization, but medical service?
5. Rent, shelter, no household supplies, no hospitalization, but fare?

6. **Food, milk, household supplies, no fuel, but medical service?**

7. **Shelter, clothing, light, no cod liver oil, but medical service?**

8. Shelter, clothing, no medical service, no cash allowance, but light?

9. Food, shelter, fuel, but no hospitalization?

10. Rent, fuel, milk, and household supplies?

CONSOLIDATE YOUR KEY ANSWERS HERE

1.________ 4.________ 7.________ 9.________

2.________ 5.________ 8.________ 10.________

3.________ 6.________

Correct Answers For The Foregoing Questions

To assist you in scoring yourself we have provided Correct Answers alongside your Answer Sheet. May we therefore suggest that while you are doing the test you cover the Correct Answers with a sheet of white paper.....to avoid temptation and to arrive at an accurate estimate of your ability and progress.

SCORE 1

.... %

NO. CORRECT ÷

NO. OF QUESTIONS ON THIS TEST

1. G
2. F
3. D
4. F
5. H
6. C
7. E
8. G
9. D
10. B

SCORE 2

.... %

NO. CORRECT ÷

NO. OF QUESTIONS ON THIS TEST

TEST II. DATA INTERPRETATION

TIME: 10 Minutes

The Data Interpretation questions take various forms: Charts, Tables, and Graphs. Also there are various types of each—for example, a graph may be the circle-type, the line-type, the bar-type, or a combination of these types. It is to be noted also that the subject matter which the test-makers draw on is very wide: cars, ships, schools, taxes, delinquency, etc.

DIRECTIONS: Read each question in this test carefully. ***Answer each one on the basis of the following table. Select the best answer and write it in the proper space on the answer sheet at the end of the test.***

Correct key answers to these sample questions are given at the conclusion of the test. ***Please don't peek at our key answers until you've answered all the questions on your own.***

Comparison of Petroleum Production in Four Different Countries for 1928-1932 (in thousands of barrels)

YEAR	U.S.	MEXICO	RUSSIA	PERSIA
1928	901,474	50,151	87,800	43,806
1929	1,007,323	44,689	103,000	42,489
1930	898,001	39,530	135,200	44,450
1931	851,081	33,039	162,800	40,638
1932	785,159	32,802	154,000	45,517

1. Which country led in the production of petroleum in 1932?

2. The smallest total amount of petroleum produced by any country in all years was produced by.

3. Which country shows the most consistent decline in the production of petroleum?

4. What per cent of the total production of petroleum in 1931 was produced by Russia?

5. During what year did all the countries combined produce the least amount of petroleum?

6. The amount of petroleum produced by Persia in 1930 was 7/34 of its total petroleum production between 1928-1932. Express this fraction as a decimal. Carry your answer to 2 decimal places only.

7. In which year was the average petroleum output of all countries nearest the total production of Persia for 1928 to 1932 inclusive?

8. Which group of countries produced the least amount of petroleum during 1930? (A) Russia and Persia (B) Mexico and Russia. Write either A or B for answer.

9. During which single year did both Mexico and Persia show the greatest per cent decrease over the previous year in the production of petroleum?

10. In which year did Mexico show the greatest numerical decrease (in thousands of barrels) in its production of petroleum?

11. Compute the per cent increase in production of petroleum for the United States from 1928 to 1929. Express as a decimal carrying your answer to two places. Do not use the word or sign "per cent" after your answer.

CONSOLIDATE YOUR ANSWERS HERE

1.__________	4.__________	7.__________	10.__________
2.__________	5.__________	8.__________	11.__________
3.__________	6.__________	9.__________	

Correct Answers For The Foregoing Questions

To assist you in scoring yourself we have provided Correct Answers alongside your Answer Sheet. May we therefore suggest that while you are doing the test you cover the Correct Answers with a sheet of white paper.....to avoid temptation and to arrive at an accurate estimate of your ability and progress.

1. U.S.	4. 15%	7. 1932	10. 1931
2. Mexico	5. 1932	8. B	11. .11
3. Mexico	6. .21	9. 1931	

SCORE 1	.... %
NO. CORRECT ÷	
NO. OF QUESTIONS ON THIS TEST	

TEST III. DATA INTERPRETATION

TIME: 10 Minutes

The Data Interpretation questions take various forms: Charts, Tables, and Graphs. Also there are various types of each—for example, a graph may be the circle-type, the line-type, the bar-type, or a combination of these types. It is to be noted also that the subject matter which the test-makers draw on is very wide: cars, ships, schools, taxes, delinquency, etc.

DIRECTIONS: Read each question in this test carefully. Answer each one on the basis of the following table. Select the best answer and write it in the proper space on the answer sheet at the end of the test.

Correct key answers to all these test questions will be found at the end of the test.

CHILDREN REMAINING AS PUBLIC CHARGES IN INSTITUTIONS, 1929-1935

End of year	Dependent or Neglected	Delinquent	Blind	Deaf	Total number of children remaining as public charges at end of year
1929	15,594	1,079	59	218	16,950
1930	18,042	1,109	57	192	19,400
1931	20,526	1,437	56	268	22,287
1932	21,515	1,335	53	311	23,314
1933	21,929	1,292	37	377	23,635
1934	20,992	1,236	37	394	22,659
1935	21,045	1,175	36	424	22,680

1. At the end of what year did the largest number of children remain public charges?

2. What percentage of the total number of children who were public charges at the end of 1929 were classed as dependent or neglected?

3. Of the total number of children remaining at the end of the year 1930, what percentage were not classed as dependent or neglected?

4. How many more deaf and blind children were cared for in 1934 than were cared for in those two groups in 1929?

5. Has the number of children in any one of the four groups shown a continuous and uninterrupted increase beginning with 1929 through 1935? Yes or No?

6. There is an arithmetical error in the Column "Total No. of Children remaining as Public Charges at the end of the Year." Write the year in which the error occurs.

7. The number of blind children cared for in 1935 is 9/14th of the number of blind children cared for in 1931. Express this fraction as a decimal. Carry your answer to three places only.

8. How many delinquent and blind children remained under care at the end of 1931?

9. Which showed the greater numerical increase in the total number of children cared for (A) 1930 over 1929 or (B) 1931 over 1930? Write A or B for the answer.

10. In which year was the number of children classified as delinquent nearest the average for the 7 year period?

11. Compute the total of the items listed under the column "Total Number of Children Remaining as Public Charges at the End of the Year."

CONSOLIDATE YOUR ANSWERS HERE

1.________	4.________	7.________	10.________
2.________	5.________	8.________	11.________
3.________	6.________	9.________	

Correct Answers For The Foregoing Questions

To assist you in scoring yourself we have provided Correct Answers alongside your Answer Sheet. May we therefore suggest that while you are doing the test you cover the Correct Answers with a sheet of white paper.....to avoid temptation and to arrive at an accurate estimate of your ability and progress.

SCORE 1

.... %

NO. CORRECT

NO. OF QUESTIONS ON THIS TEST

1. 1933	4. 154	7. 642, 643	10. 1934
2. 92%	5. no	8. 1493	11. 150925
3. 7%	6. 1932	9. B	

SCORE 2

.... %

NO. CORRECT

NO. OF QUESTIONS ON THIS TEST

TEST IV. DATA INTERPRETATION

TIME: 10 Minutes

DIRECTIONS: Read each question in this test carefully. Answer each one on the basis of the following table. Select the best answer among the given choices and blacken the proper space on the answer sheet at the end of the test.

Correct key answers to all these test questions will be found at the end of the test.

BUREAU X
WEEKLY PAYROLL RECORD *

Unit in Which Employed	Employee	Title	Gross Weekly Salary (Before Deductions)	Weekly Deductions From Gross Salary		
				Medical Insurance	Income Tax	Pension System
Accounting	Amoroso	Accountant	$95	$1.45	$12.50	$5.32
"	Knight	Bookkeeper	72	1.90	6.20	4.07
"	Rubin	Clerk	58	.65	8.20	3.31
"	Steurm	Typist	56	.65	7.90	3.53
"	Heller	Stenographer	61	1.45	6.40	3.78
Information	Reynolds	Clerk	56	1.30	5.60	4.22
"	Appel	Clerk	59	1.45	6.10	5.84
"	Wayne	Typist	58	1.30	5.90	6.26
"	Bustard	Stenographer	62	1.90	4.40	6.94
Mail	Horen	Clerk	66	1.30	7.40	5.54
"	Clift	Typist	54	.65	7.50	3.40
"	Maynard	Stenographer	58	1.90	3.60	3.71
Records	Balish	Clerk	64	.65	9.40	5.82
"	Meyers	Clerk	54	1.90	2.90	5.02
"	Warren	Typist	62	1.45	6.70	6.01
"	Stevens	Stenographer	69	.65	10.10	7.56

*NOTE: Gross weekly salary is the salary before deductions have been made; take-home pay is the amount remaining after all indicated weekly deductions have been made. In answering questions involving annual amounts, compute on the basis of 52 weeks per year.

1. Balish's annual take-home pay is most nearly
(A) $2500 (B) $2700
(C) $3100 (D) $3300.

2. The difference between Wayne's gross annual salary and his annual take-home pay is most nearly
(A) $300 (B) $500
(C) $700 (D) $900.

3. Of the following, the employee whose weekly take-home pay is closest to that of Rubin's is
(A) Steurm (B) Reynolds
(C) Appel (D) Wayne.

4. The average gross annual salary of the typists is
(A) less than $2750
(B) more than $2750 but less than $3000
(C) more than $3000 but less than $3250
(D) more than $3250.

5. The average gross weekly salary of the stenographers exceeds the average gross weekly salary of the clerks by
(A) $2 (B) $3
(C) $4 (D) $5.

6. Of the following employees in the Accounting Unit, the one who pays the highest percentage of his gross weekly salary for the Pension System is
(A) Knight (B) Rubin
(C) Steurm (D) Heller.

7. For all of the Accounting Unit employees, the total annual deductions for Medical Insurance are less than the total annual deductions for the Pension System by most nearly
(A) $600 (B) $700
(C) $800 (D) $900.

8. Of the following, the employee whose total weekly deductions are most nearly 27% of his gross weekly salary is
(A) Knight (B) Reynolds
(C) Meyers (D) Stevens.

9. The total amount of the gross weekly salaries of all the employees in the Records Unit is most nearly
(A) 95% of the total amount of the gross weekly salaries of all the employees in the Information Unit
(B) 10% greater than the total amount of the gross weekly salaries of all the employees in the Mail Unit
(C) 75% of the total amount of the gross weekly salaries of all the employees in the Accounting Unit
(D) four times as great as the total amount deducted weekly for income tax for all the employees in the Records Unit.

10. For the employees in the Information Unit, the average weekly deduction for Income Tax
(A) exceeds the average weekly deduction for Income Tax for the employees in the Records Unit
(B) is less than the average weekly deduction for the Pension System for the employees in the Mail Unit
(C) exceeds the average weekly deduction for Income Tax for the employees in the Accounting Unit
(D) is less than the average weekly deduction for the Pension System for the employees in the Records Unit.

CONSOLIDATE YOUR KEY ANSWERS HERE

Answer Sheet

	A	B	C	D	E
1					
2					
3					
4					
5					

Answer Sheet

	A	B	C	D	E
6					
7					
8					
9					
10					

Correct Answers

(You'll learn more by writing your own answers before comparing them with these.)

1. A	6. D
2. C	7. B
3. C	8. D
4. B	9. A
5. B	10. D

XIX. CODING SPEED

This is a test of clerical speed and accuracy. It involves matching code numbers to code words in accordance with a Code Identification Key. The idea is to complete as many questions as you can in the time allowed. Work as quickly and accurately as possible.

DIRECTIONS: The Code Identification Key contains a group of words with a Code Number beside each word. Each test question consists of one of the words from the Key followed by five possible Code Numbers arranged in columns labelled A, B, C, D and E. Choose the one Code Number for each word that corresponds to the number given in the Code Identification Key. On your answer sheet, blacken the letter of the column in which the correct Code Number appears.

SAMPLE QUESTIONS AND EXPLANATIONS

CODE IDENTIFICATION KEY

candy.........2067	letter........4895	car...........6239
bear..........8473	pencil........9723	basket........1546

QUESTIONS	A	B	C	D	E
1. candy	1546	8473	6239	9723	2067
2. bear	1546	8473	4895	9723	2067
3. car	1546	8473	6239	9723	4895
4. letter	1546	8473	6239	9723	4895
5. basket	1546	4895	6239	9723	2067
6. pencil	1546	4895	6239	9723	2067
7. letter	1546	4895	8473	9723	2067
8. bear	1546	4895	8473	9723	2067
9. candy	1546	6239	8473	9723	2067
10. car	1546	6239	8473	9723	2067

Notice that each of the questions is a word chosen from the Code Identification Key followed by five possible Code Numbers. The Code Word in question 1 is "candy." Looking at the Key, we can see that the code number for candy is 2067. Since 2067 is found in column E, the correct answer to the first sample question is "E."

CORRECT ANSWERS TO SAMPLE QUESTIONS

1. A	3. C	5. A	7. B	9. E
2. B	4. E	6. D	8. C	10. B

TEST I. CODING SPEED

TIME: 7 Minutes

DIRECTIONS: The Code Identification Key contains a group of words with a Code Number beside each word. Each test question consists of one of the words from the Key followed by five possible Code Numbers arranged in columns labelled A, B, C, D and E. Choose the one Code Number for each word that corresponds to the number given in the Code Identification Key. On your answer sheet, blacken the letter of the column in which the correct Code Number appears.

CODE IDENTIFICATION KEY

pear..........9572	table.........4163	silver........8569
beach.........8451	tree..........3490	door..........6301
house.........2015	boat..........7751	garden........4972
	tiger.........2508	

QUESTIONS	A	B	C	D	E
1. boat	8569	6301	2508	7751	9572
2. table	8569	7751	4163	2015	3490
3. door	8569	6301	4163	7751	3490
4. pear	8569	8451	4163	7751	9572
5. tree	4972	6301	2508	2015	3490
6. garden	4972	9572	2015	4163	6301
7. beach	4972	8451	4163	2508	6301
8. silver	8569	8451	4163	7751	9572
9. house	8569	8451	2508	2015	3490
10. tiger	8569	9572	2508	2015	6301
11. silver	4163	7751	4972	8569	6301
12. table	4163	8451	9572	2015	3490
13. boat	4163	8451	4972	7751	6301
14. beach	4163	8451	2508	7751	9572
15. tree	4972	3490	2508	8569	6301
16. tiger	4972	8451	2508	7751	3490
17. house	8451	8569	2508	4163	2015
18. pear	8569	7751	9572	2015	6301
19. garden	4972	7751	4163	2015	3490
20. door	4972	6301	4163	2508	3490

CODE IDENTIFICATION KEY

pear..........9572	table.........4163	silver........8569
beach.........8451	tree..........3490	door..........6301
house.........2015	boat..........7751	garden........4972
	tiger.........2508	

QUESTION	A	B	C	D	E
21. beach	8569	8451	9572	7751	2015
22. silver	4972	8569	9572	3490	2015
23. boat	4972	6301	9572	7751	3490
24. table	4163	6301	2508	7751	2015
25. garden	4972	8451	2508	4163	6301
26. tiger	4972	8569	2508	2015	3490
27. pear	8569	8451	4163	2015	9572
28. door	8569	6301	9572	2015	3490
29. house	4163	9572	2508	2015	3490
30. tree	8451	9572	4163	7751	3490
31. garden	4972	8451	9572	7751	6301
32. pear	4972	8451	4163	2015	9572
33. table	8569	6301	4163	2508	3490
34. boat	8451	9572	2508	7751	2015
35. beach	8451	8569	4163	3490	2508
36. tiger	4972	6301	2508	7751	2015
37. door	8569	6301	2015	7751	9572
38. silver	8569	6301	4972	2508	3490
39. house	8451	9572	2015	7751	2508
40. tree	4163	6031	4972	2508	3490
41. table	4972	9572	4163	7751	3490
42. beach	8451	8569	9572	2015	6301
43. pear	4972	9572	2508	7751	3490
44. tiger	8569	8451	4972	2508	9572
45. garden	4972	9572	4163	7751	3490
46. silver	8569	8451	2508	7751	6301
47. door	8569	8451	4972	3490	6301
48. tree	4163	8451	2015	2508	3490
49. house	8569	6301	9572	2015	3490
50. boat	8569	6301	4163	7751	3490

CODE IDENTIFICATION KEY

army..........4873	ocean.........7293	salad.........6591
chair.........8741	party.........5894	film..........8436
dress.........6720	window........3914	cash..........6209
	carpet........2395	

QUESTIONS	A	B	C	D	E
51. ocean	6209	8741	7293	5894	4873
52. dress	6720	6209	7293	6591	3914
53. salad	6720	8436	7293	6591	5894
54. army	3914	8741	7293	2395	4873
55. film	6209	8436	6591	3914	4873
56. cash	6209	8741	6591	3914	5894
57. window	6720	8436	3914	2395	5894
58. chair	6720	6209	6591	8741	4873
59. carpet	8436	2395	7293	3914	5894
60. party	6720	8741	7293	2395	5894
61. salad	6209	4873	6591	2395	5894
62. film	6209	8436	7293	6591	3914
63. chair	6720	8741	7293	2395	4873
64. window	3914	4873	6591	8741	5894
65. ocean	3914	2395	7293	6591	4873
66. army	6209	8741	8436	5894	4873
67. cash	6720	8436	7293	6209	3914
68. dress	6720	8741	6591	2395	4873
69. carpet	6209	2395	7293	5894	4873
70. party	3914	8741	7293	5894	4873
71. window	8436	6209	7293	2395	3914
72. ocean	6720	8741	7293	5894	4873
73. party	6209	8741	7293	2395	5894
74. chair	6209	8741	6591	2395	3914
75. salad	6720	8741	6591	7293	5894
76. carpet	6720	2395	8436	8741	5894
77. cash	6209	2395	6591	7293	4873
78. film	6209	8436	7293	2395	4873
79. army	6720	8741	8436	5894	4873
80. dress	6720	8741	6591	5894	3914

CODE IDENTIFICATION KEY

army..........4873	ocean.........7293	salad.........6591
chair.........8741	party.........5894	film..........8436
dress.........6720	window........3914	cash..........6209
	carpet........2395	

QUESTIONS	A	B	C	D	E
81. chair	8436	8741	6591	7293	3914
82. salad	6209	4873	6591	2395	3914
83. army	6209	8436	6591	5894	4873
84. window	6720	4873	8436	7293	3914
85. dress	6720	6209	7293	5894	3914
86. party	6209	8436	6591	5894	4873
87. cash	6720	8436	7293	6209	3914
88. carpet	6720	2395	6591	7293	3914
89. ocean	6209	8741	7293	8436	3914
90. film	8436	6209	6591	2395	4873
91. dress	6720	8741	7293	6591	5894
92. army	6720	2395	8436	7293	4873
93. cash	6720	4873	8436	6209	5894
94. salad	6209	4873	6591	8741	3914
95. chair	6720	8741	8436	6591	3914
96. ocean	6720	2395	7293	8741	3914
97. carpet	8436	2395	6591	8741	5894
98. film	8436	2395	5894	6209	3914
99. party	6720	6209	6591	8741	5894
100. window	6720	2395	8436	3914	4873

CONSOLIDATE YOUR KEY ANSWERS HERE

1 A B C D E	2 A B C D E	3 A B C D E	4 A B C D E	5 A B C D E	6 A B C D E	7 A B C D E	8 A B C D E
9 A B C D E	10 A B C D E	11 A B C D E	12 A B C D E	13 A B C D E	14 A B C D E	15 A B C D E	16 A B C D E
17 A B C D E	18 A B C D E	19 A B C D E	20 A B C D E	21 A B C D E	22 A B C D E	23 A B C D E	24 A B C D E
25 A B C D E	26 A B C D E	27 A B C D E	28 A B C D E	29 A B C D E	30 A B C D E	31 A B C D E	32 A B C D E
33 A B C D E	34 A B C D E	35 A B C D E	36 A B C D E	37 A B C D E	38 A B C D E	39 A B C D E	40 A B C D E
41 A B C D E	42 A B C D E	43 A B C D E	44 A B C D E	45 A B C D E	46 A B C D E	47 A B C D E	48 A B C D E
49 A B C D E	50 A B C D E	51 A B C D E	52 A B C D E	53 A B C D E	54 A B C D E	55 A B C D E	56 A B C D E
57 A B C D E	58 A B C D E	59 A B C D E	60 A B C D E	61 A B C D E	62 A B C D E	63 A B C D E	64 A B C D E
65 A B C D E	66 A B C D E	67 A B C D E	68 A B C D E	69 A B C D E	70 A B C D E	71 A B C D E	72 A B C D E
73 A B C D E	74 A B C D E	75 A B C D E	76 A B C D E	77 A B C D E	78 A B C D E	79 A B C D E	80 A B C D E
81 A B C D E	82 A B C D E	83 A B C D E	84 A B C D E	85 A B C D E	86 A B C D E	87 A B C D E	88 A B C D E
89 A B C D E	90 A B C D E	91 A B C D E	92 A B C D E	93 A B C D E	94 A B C D E	95 A B C D E	96 A B C D E
97 A B C D E	98 A B C D E	99 A B C D E	100 A B C D E	101 A B C D E	102 A B C D E	103 A B C D E	104 A B C D E

Correct Answers For The Foregoing Questions

To assist you in scoring yourself we have provided Correct Answers alongside your Answer Sheet. May we therefore suggest that while you are doing the test you cover the Correct Answers with a sheet of white paper.....to avoid temptation and to arrive at an accurate estimate of your ability and progress.

1. D
2. C
3. B
4. E
5. E
6. A
7. B
8. A
9. D
10. C
11. D
12. A
13. D
14. B
15. B
16. C
17. E
18. C
19. A
20. B
21. B
22. B
23. D
24. A
25. A
26. C
27. E
28. B
29. D
30. E
31. A
32. E
33. C
34. D
35. A
36. C
37. B
38. A
39. C
40. E
41. C
42. A
43. B
44. D
45. A
46. A
47. E
48. E
49. D
50. D
51. C
52. A
53. D
54. E
55. B
56. A
57. C
58. D
59. B
60. E
61. C
62. B
63. B
64. A
65. C
66. E
67. D
68. A
69. B
70. D
71. E
72. C
73. E
74. B
75. C
76. B
77. A
78. B
79. E
80. A
81. B
82. C
83. E
84. E
85. A
86. D
87. D
88. B
89. C
90. A
91. A
92. E
93. D
94. C
95. B
96. C
97. B
98. A
99. E
100. D

Practice Using Answer Sheets

Alter numbers to match the practice and drill questions in each part of the book.
Make only ONE mark for each answer. Additional and stray marks may be counted as mistakes.
In making corrections, erase errors COMPLETELY. Make glossy black marks.

1 A B C D E
2 A B C D E
3 A B C D E
4 A B C D E
5 A B C D E
6 A B C D E
7 A B C D E
8 A B C D E
9 A B C D E
0 A B C D E

1 A B C D E
2 A B C D E
3 A B C D E
4 A B C D E
5 A B C D E
6 A B C D E
7 A B C D E
8 A B C D E
9 A B C D E
0 A B C D E

1 A B C D E
2 A B C D E
3 A B C D E
4 A B C D E
5 A B C D E
6 A B C D E
7 A B C D E
8 A B C D E
9 A B C D E
0 A B C D E

1 A B C D E
2 A B C D E
3 A B C D E
4 A B C D E
5 A B C D E
6 A B C D E
7 A B C D E
8 A B C D E
9 A B C D E
0 A B C D E

1 A B C D E
2 A B C D E
3 A B C D E
4 A B C D E
5 A B C D E
6 A B C D E
7 A B C D E
8 A B C D E
9 A B C D E
0 A B C D E

1 A B C D E
2 A B C D E
3 A B C D E
4 A B C D E
5 A B C D E
6 A B C D E
7 A B C D E
8 A B C D E
9 A B C D E
0 A B C D E

1 A B C D E
2 A B C D E
3 A B C D E
4 A B C D E
5 A B C D E
6 A B C D E
7 A B C D E
8 A B C D E
9 A B C D E
0 A B C D E

1 A B C D E
2 A B C D E
3 A B C D E
4 A B C D E
5 A B C D E
6 A B C D E
7 A B C D E
8 A B C D E
9 A B C D E
0 A B C D E

1 A B C D E
2 A B C D E
3 A B C D E
4 A B C D E
5 A B C D E
6 A B C D E
7 A B C D E
8 A B C D E
9 A B C D E
0 A B C D E

1 A B C D E
2 A B C D E
3 A B C D E
4 A B C D E
5 A B C D E
6 A B C D E
7 A B C D E
8 A B C D E
9 A B C D E
0 A B C D E

1 A B C D E
2 A B C D E
3 A B C D E
4 A B C D E
5 A B C D E
6 A B C D E

7 A B C D E
8 A B C D E
9 A B C D E
10 A B C D E
11 A B C D E
12 A B C D E

13 A B C D E
14 A B C D E
15 A B C D E
16 A B C D E
17 A B C D E
18 A B C D E

19 A B C D E
20 A B C D E
21 A B C D E
22 A B C D E
23 A B C D E
24 A B C D E

25 A B C D E
26 A B C D E
27 A B C D E
28 A B C D E
29 A B C D E
30 A B C D E

TEAR OUT ALONG THIS LINE AND MARK YOUR ANSWERS AS INSTRUCTED IN THE TEXT

PART FIVE

Ability To Reason
And Perceive Spatial Relations
Final Advice

5

Practice Using Answer Sheets

Alter numbers to match the practice and drill questions in each part of the book.
Make only ONE mark for each answer. Additional and stray marks may be counted as mistakes.
In making corrections, erase errors COMPLETELY. Make glossy black marks.

	A	B	C	D	E
1					
2					
3					
4					
5					
6					
7					
8					
9					
0					

	A	B	C	D	E
1					
2					
3					
4					
5					
6					
7					
8					
9					
0					

	A	B	C	D	E
1					
2					
3					
4					
5					
6					
7					
8					
9					
0					

	A	B	C	D	E
1					
2					
3					
4					
5					
6					
7					
8					
9					
0					

	A	B	C	D	E
1					
2					
3					
4					
5					
6					
7					
8					
9					
0					

	A	B	C	D	E
1					
2					
3					
4					
5					
6					
7					
8					
9					
0					

	A	B	C	D	E
1					
2					
3					
4					
5					
6					
7					
8					
9					
0					

	A	B	C	D	E
1					
2					
3					
4					
5					
6					
7					
8					
9					
0					

	A	B	C	D	E
1					
2					
3					
4					
5					
6					
7					
8					
9					
0					

	A	B	C	D	E
1					
2					
3					
4					
5					
6					
7					
8					
9					
0					

	A	B	C	D	E
1					
2					
3					
4					
5					
6					
7					
8					
9					
10					
11					
12					
13					
14					
15					
16					
17					
18					
19					
20					
21					
22					
23					
24					
25					
26					
27					
28					
29					
30					

TEAR OUT ALONG THIS LINE AND MARK YOUR ANSWERS AS INSTRUCTED IN THE TEXT

I. HIDDEN FIGURES

This spatial relations test, sometimes called an "embedded figures test," presents a simple geometric pattern and requires the candidate to find it in a larger, more complete pattern which is sometimes a three-dimensional figure.

In some versions of the test the background is colored irregularly to increase confusion. We have not attempted here to increase your confusion.

In this Practice Chapter you are provided with a set of five simple figures labelled A, B, C, D and E. Then you will find a number of more complex figures which are numbered beginning with one. Next to each figure you are to write the letter of the simple figure which is found hidden or embedded in the more complex figure. There are three tests. Each one consists of facing pages, so that in answering questions the simple figures are constantly before you. Answers to all questions are on page *282*.

HIDDEN FIGURES TEST I

Simple Figures

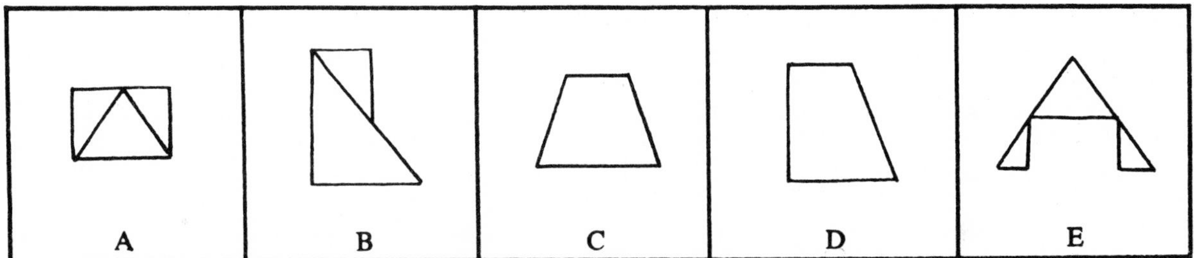

Find The Simple Figures Hidden In These More Complex Figures.

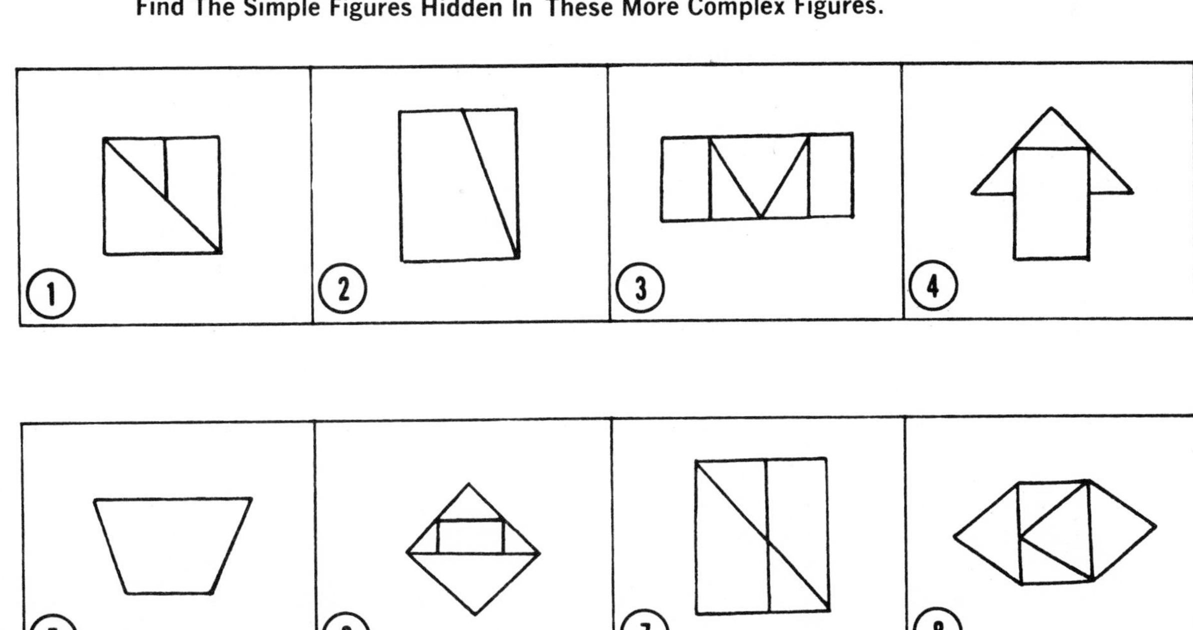

S890

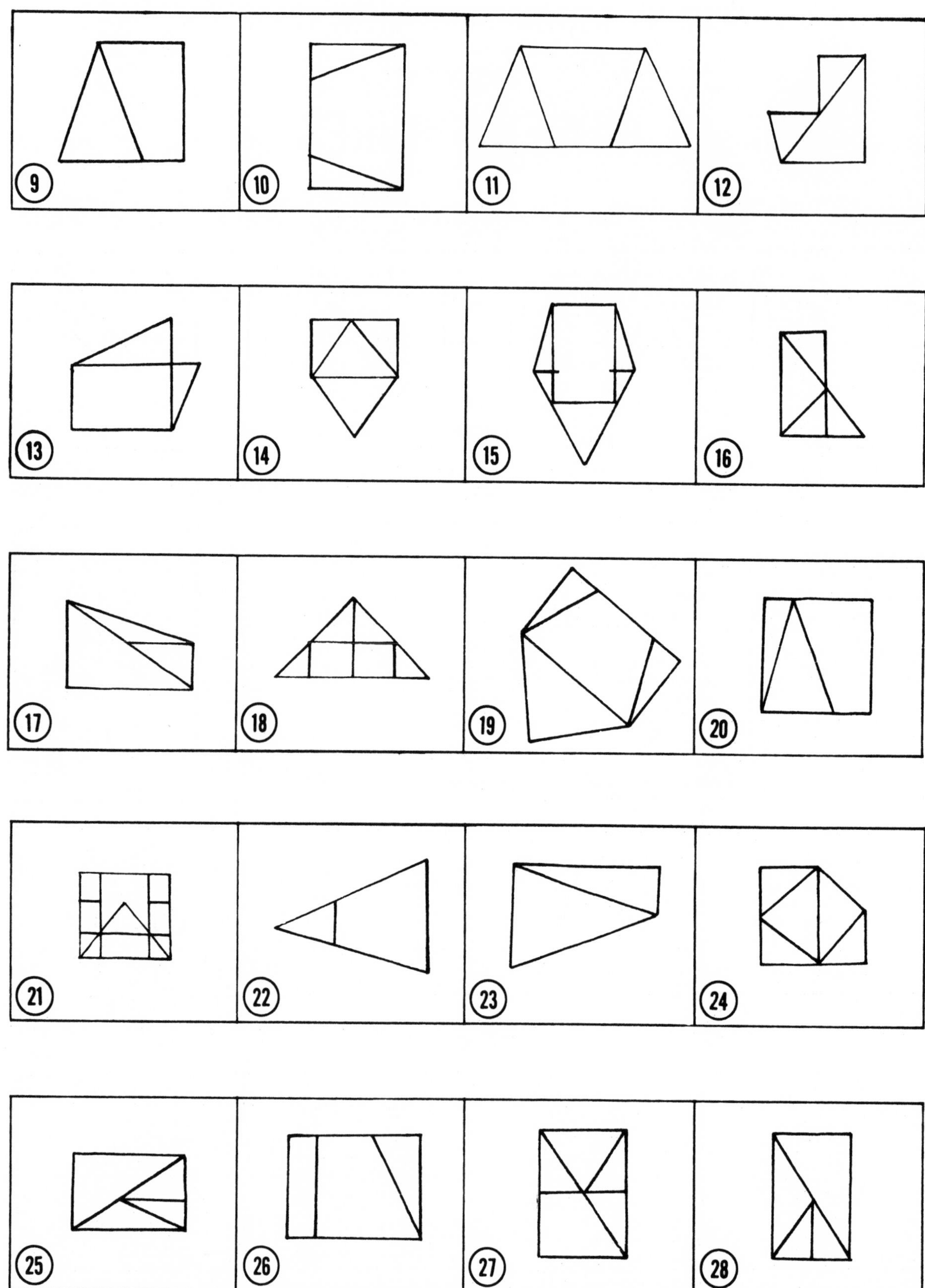

9
10
11
12
13
14
15
16
17
18
19
20
21
22
23
24
25
26
27
28

HIDDEN FIGURES TEST II

Simple Figures

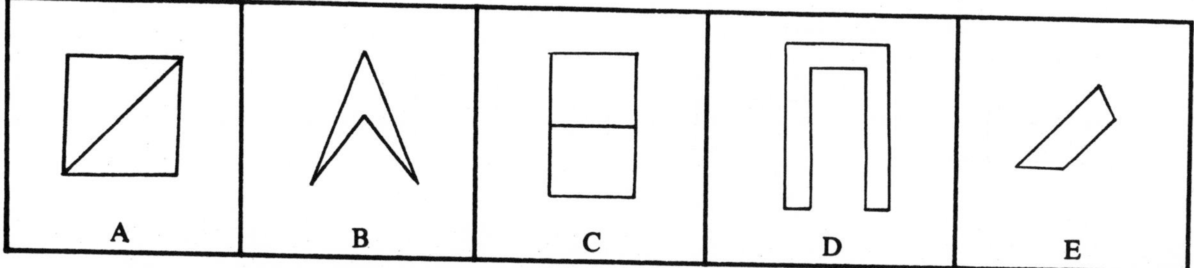

Find The Simple Figures Hidden In These More Complex Figures.

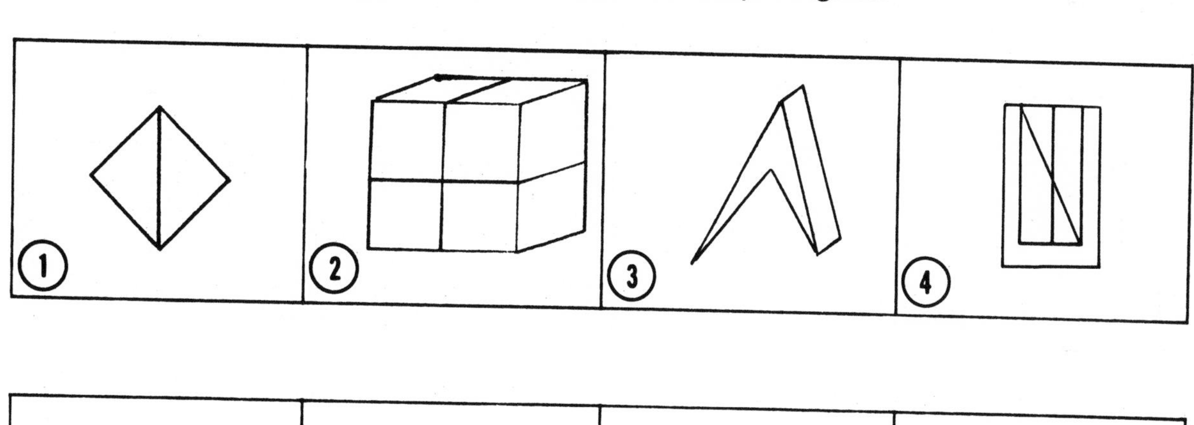

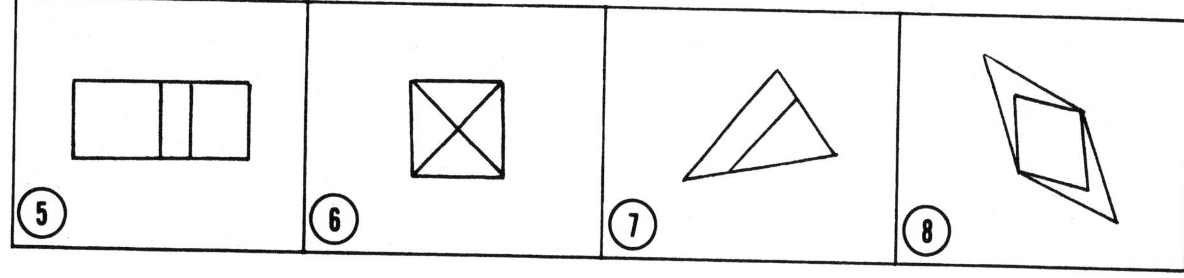

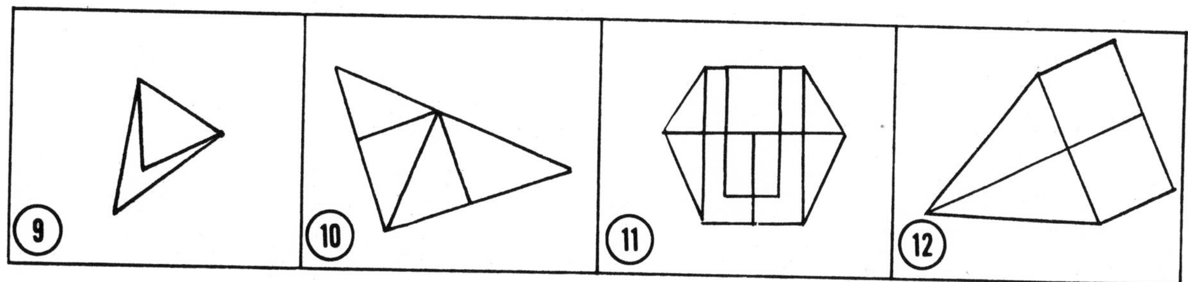

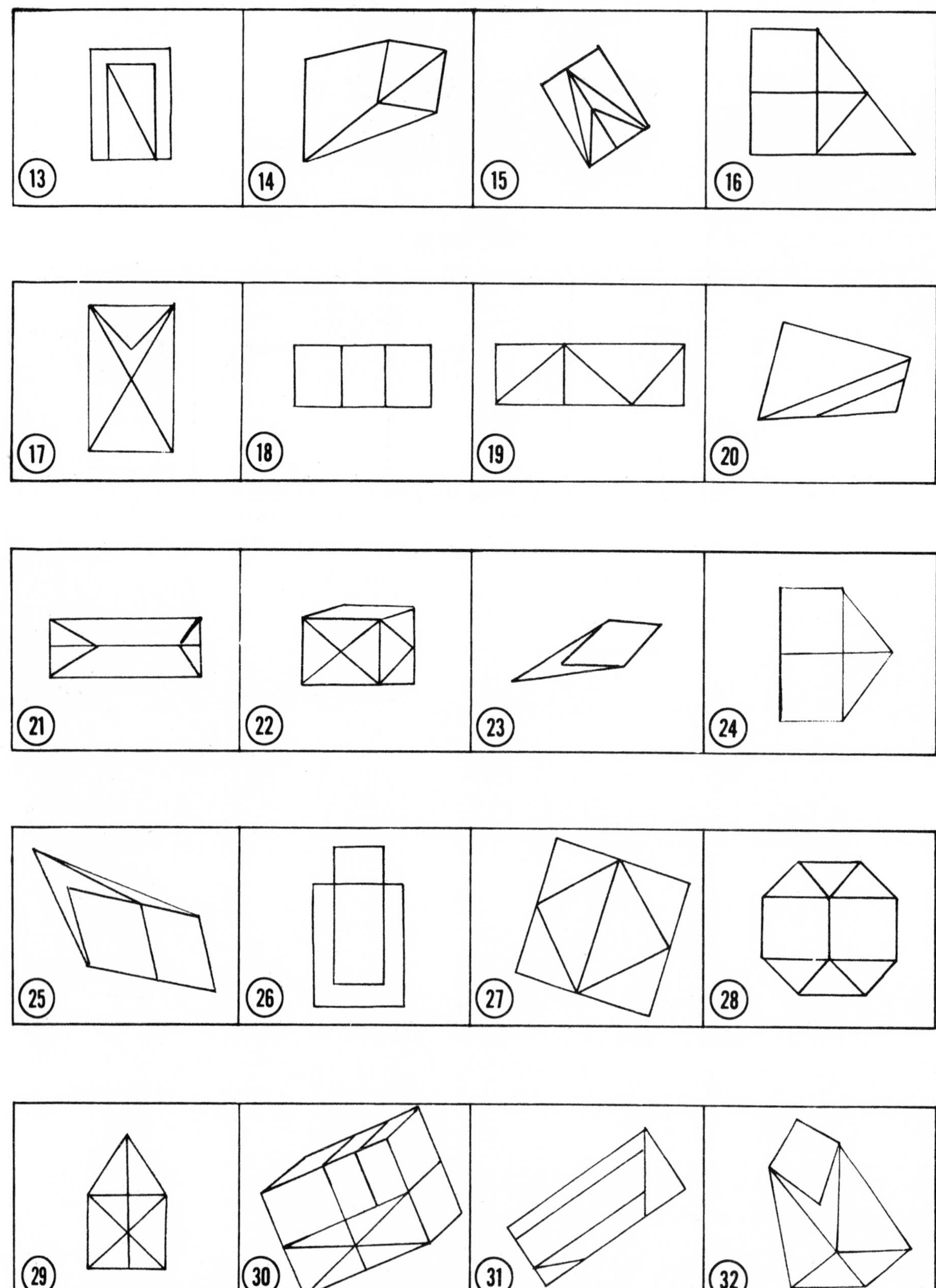
13
14
15
16
17
18
19
20
21
22
23
24
25
26
27
28
29
30
31
32

HIDDEN FIGURES TEST III

Simple Figures

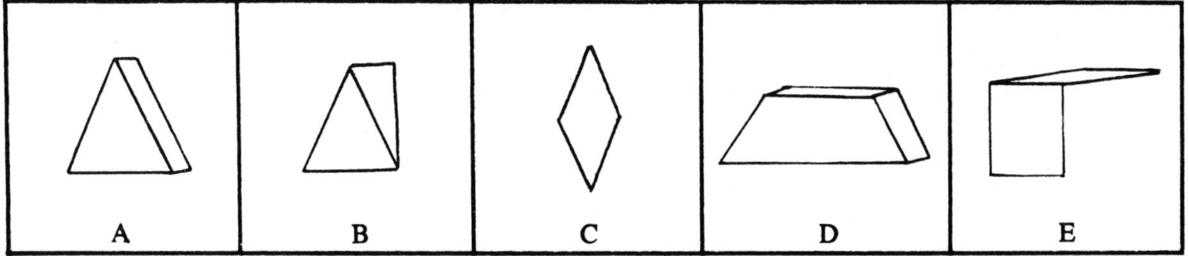

Find The Simple Figures Hidden In These More Complex Figures.

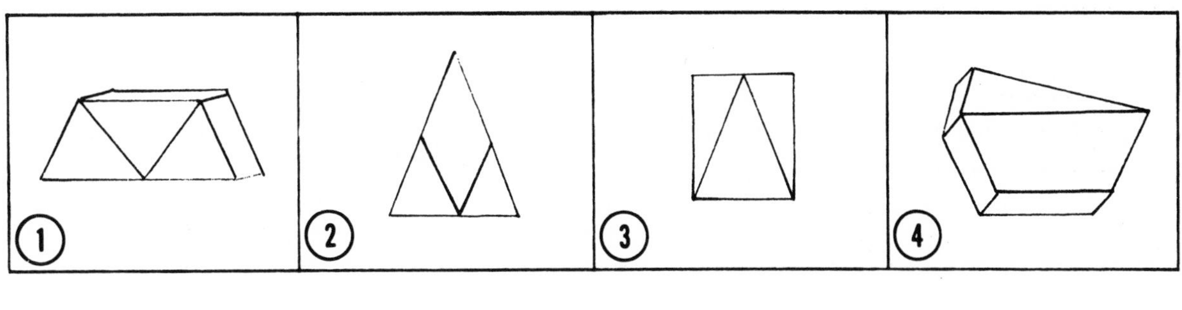

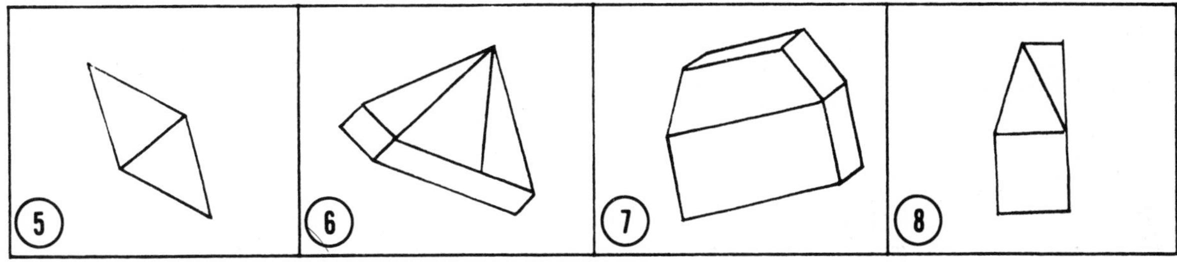

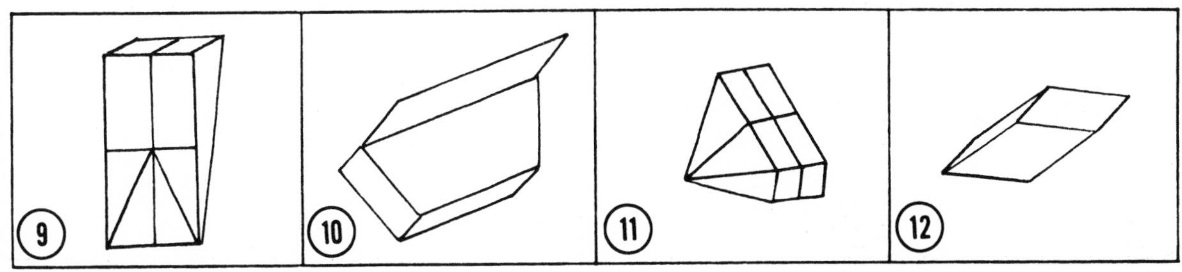

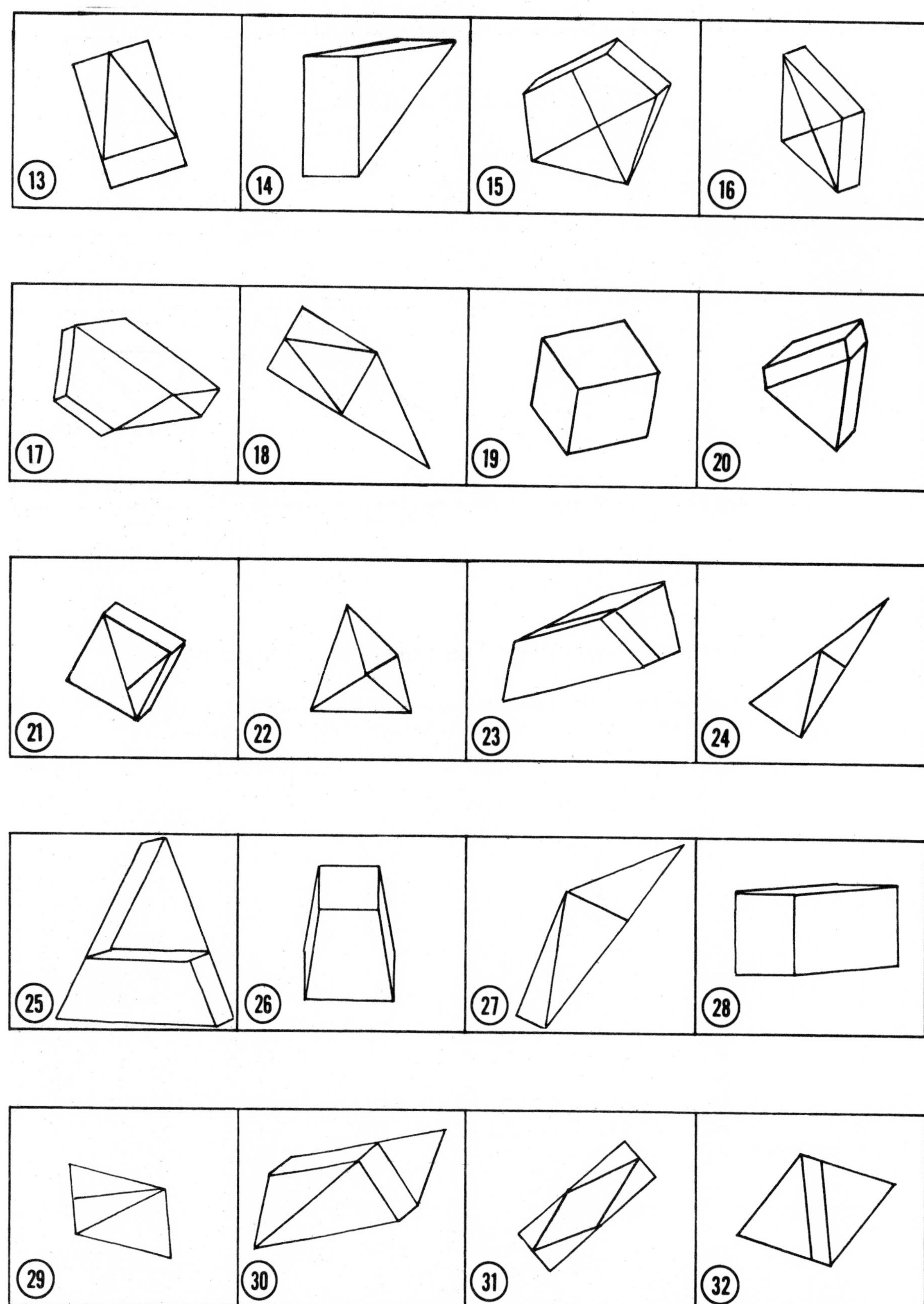
13
14
15
16
17
18
19
20
21
22
23
24
25
26
27
28
29
30
31
32

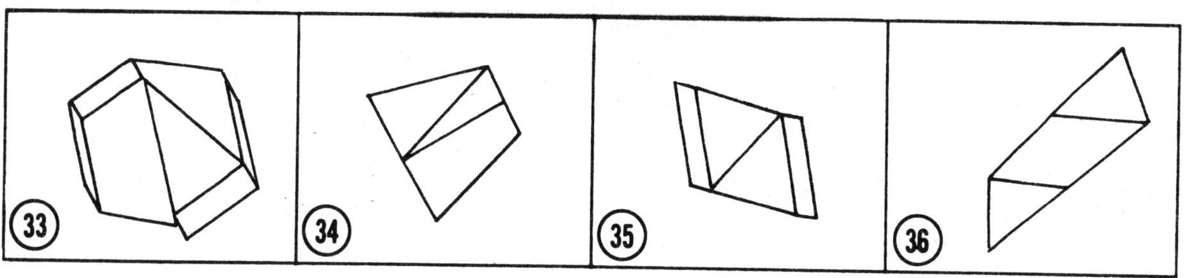

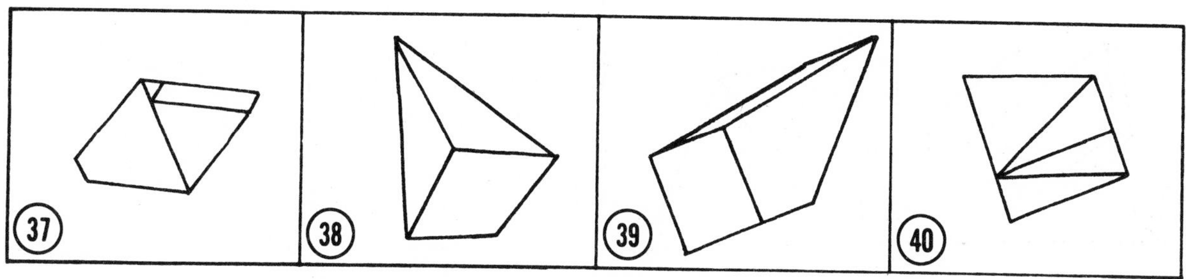

Correct Answers For The Foregoing Questions

(Please make every effort to answer the questions on your own before looking at these answers. You'll make faster progress by following this rule.)

TEST I

1. B
2. D
3. A
4. E
5. C
6. E
7. B
8. A
9. D
10. C
11. C
12. B
13. D
14. A
15. E
16. B
17. B
18. E
19. C
20. D
21. E
22. C
23. D
24. A
25. B
26. D
27. A
28. B

TEST II

1. A
2. C
3. B
4. D
5. C
6. A
7. E
8. B
9. B
10. A
11. D
12. C
13. D
14. A
15. B
16. C
17. B
18. C
19. A
20. E
21. E
22. A
23. B
24. C
25. B
26. D
27. A
28. C
29. A
30. C
31. E
32. B

TEST III

1. A
2. C
3. B
4. D
5. C
6. A
7. D
8. B
9. B
10. D
11. A
12. C
13. B
14. E
15. D
16. C
17. D
18. B
19. C
20. A
21. A
22. C
23. D
24. B
25. D
26. E
27. B
28. E
29. B
30. D
31. C
32. A
33. D
34. B
35. A
36. C
37. A
38. C
39. E
40. B

Practice Using Answer Sheets

DIRECTIONS: Read each question and its lettered answers. When you have decided which answer is correct, blacken the corresponding space on this sheet with a No. 2 pencil. Make your mark as long as the pair of lines, and completely fill the area between the pair of lines. If you change your mind, erase your first mark COMPLETELY. Make no stray marks; they may count against you.

SAMPLE

I. CHICAGO is

I - A a country
I - B a mountain
I - C an island
I - D a city
I - E a state

I A B C D E

SCORES

1 ______ 5 ______
2 ______ 6 ______
3 ______ 7 ______
4 ______ 8 ______

1	A B C D E	2	A B C D E	3	A B C D E	4	A B C D E
5	A B C D E	6	A B C D E	7	A B C D E	8	A B C D E
9	A B C D E	10	A B C D E	11	A B C D E	12	A B C D E
13	A B C D E	14	A B C D E	15	A B C D E	16	A B C D E
17	A B C D E	18	A B C D E	19	A B C D E	20	A B C D E
21	A B C D E	22	A B C D E	23	A B C D E	24	A B C D E
25	A B C D E	26	A B C D E	27	A B C D E	28	A B C D E
29	A B C D E	30	A B C D E	31	A B C D E	32	A B C D E
33	A B C D E	34	A B C D E	35	A B C D E	36	A B C D E
37	A B C D E	38	A B C D E	39	A B C D E	40	A B C D E
41	A B C D E	42	A B C D E	43	A B C D E	44	A B C D E
45	A B C D E	46	A B C D E	47	A B C D E	48	A B C D E
49	A B C D E	50	A B C D E	51	A B C D E	52	A B C D E
53	A B C D E	54	A B C D E	55	A B C D E	56	A B C D E
57	A B C D E	58	A B C D E	59	A B C D E	60	A B C D E
61	A B C D E	62	A B C D E	63	A B C D E	64	A B C D E
65	A B C D E	66	A B C D E	67	A B C D E	68	A B C D E
69	A B C D E	70	A B C D E	71	A B C D E	72	A B C D E
73	A B C D E	74	A B C D E	75	A B C D E	76	A B C D E
77	A B C D E	78	A B C D E	79	A B C D E	80	A B C D E
81	A B C D E	82	A B C D E	83	A B C D E	84	A B C D E
85	A B C D E	86	A B C D E	87	A B C D E	88	A B C D E
89	A B C D E	90	A B C D E	91	A B C D E	92	A B C D E
93	A B C D E	94	A B C D E	95	A B C D E	96	A B C D E
97	A B C D E	98	A B C D E	99	A B C D E	100	A B C D E
101	A B C D E	102	A B C D E	103	A B C D E	104	A B C D E
105	A B C D E	106	A B C D E	107	A B C D E	108	A B C D E
109	A B C D E	110	A B C D E	111	A B C D E	112	A B C D E
113	A B C D E	114	A B C D E	115	A B C D E	116	A B C D E
117	A B C D E	118	A B C D E	119	A B C D E	120	A B C D E
121	A B C D E	122	A B C D E	123	A B C D E	124	A B C D E
125	A B C D E	126	A B C D E	127	A B C D E	128	A B C D E
129	A B C D E	130	A B C D E	131	A B C D E	132	A B C D E
133	A B C D E	134	A B C D E	135	A B C D E	136	A B C D E
137	A B C D E	138	A B C D E	139	A B C D E	140	A B C D E
141	A B C D E	142	A B C D E	143	A B C D E	144	A B C D E
145	A B C D E	146	A B C D E	147	A B C D E	148	A B C D E
149	A B C D E	150	A B C D E				

II. ABSTRACT REASONING

Since this type of question may be stressed on your test, we have provided a large number of questions for your practice and learning. Read the instructions very carefully. Perhaps you will be helped if we tell you that all ten symbols are of one general class, and that each of the three in the first two boxes represent variants of that class.

In each of these questions, look at the symbols in the first two boxes. Something about the three symbols in the first box makes them alike; something about the two symbols in the other box with the question mark makes them alike. Look for some characteristic that is common to all symbols in the same box, yet makes them different from the symbols in the other box. Among the five answer choices, find the symbol that can best be substituted for the question mark, because it is *like* the symbols in the second box, and, *for the same reason,* different from those in the first box.

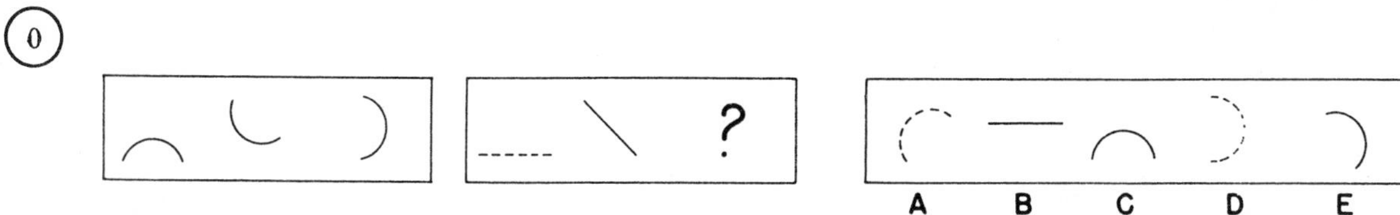

In same question 0, all the symbols in the first box are curved lines. The second box has two lines, one dotted and one solid. Their *likeness* to each other consists in their straightness; and this straightness makes them *different* from the curves in the other box. The answer must be the *only* one of the five lettered choices that is a straight line, either dotted or solid. Now do questions 11 and 12.

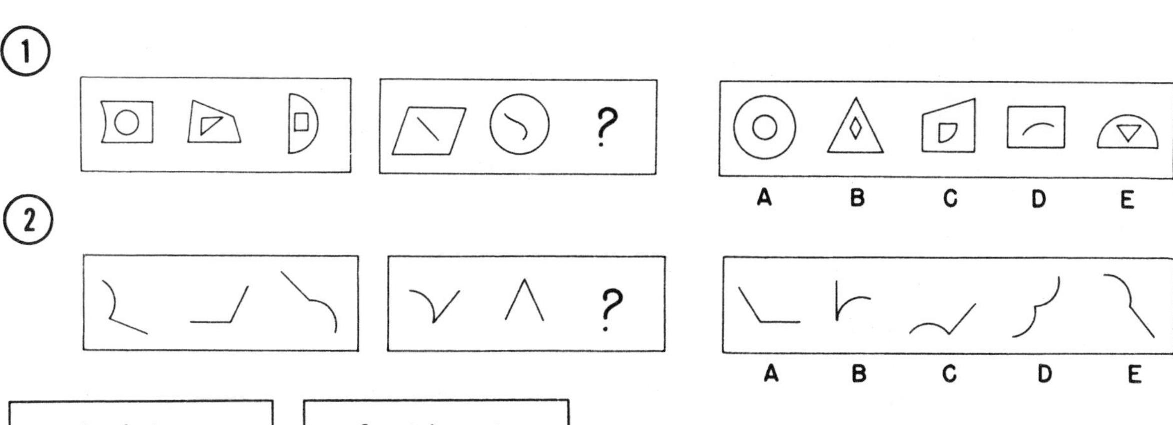

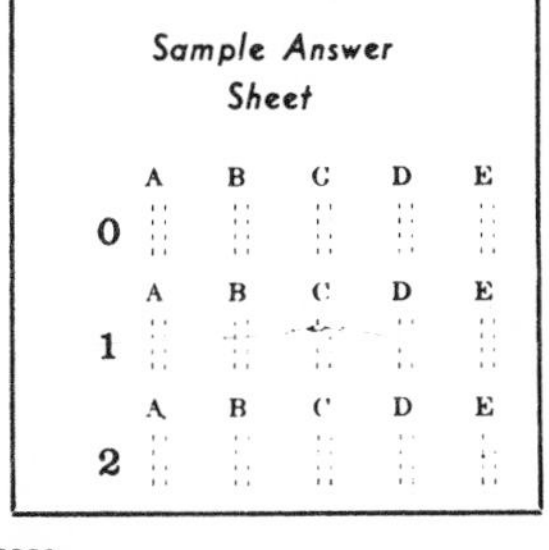

Correct Answers to Sample Questions

	A	B	C	D	E
0		▮			
1				▮	
2	▮				

NOTE.—There is not supposed to be a *series* or progression in these symbol questions. If you look for a progression in the first box and try to find the missing figure to fill out a similar progression in the second box, you will be wasting time. For example, look at question 0. A competitor who saw that both boxes had a horizontal figure followed by an oblique one might try to find a vertical figure to match the last one in the first box. If he chose D he would be missing the real point of tne question. Remember, look for a *likeness* within each box and a *difference* between the two boxes.

Practice Questions in Abstract Reasoning

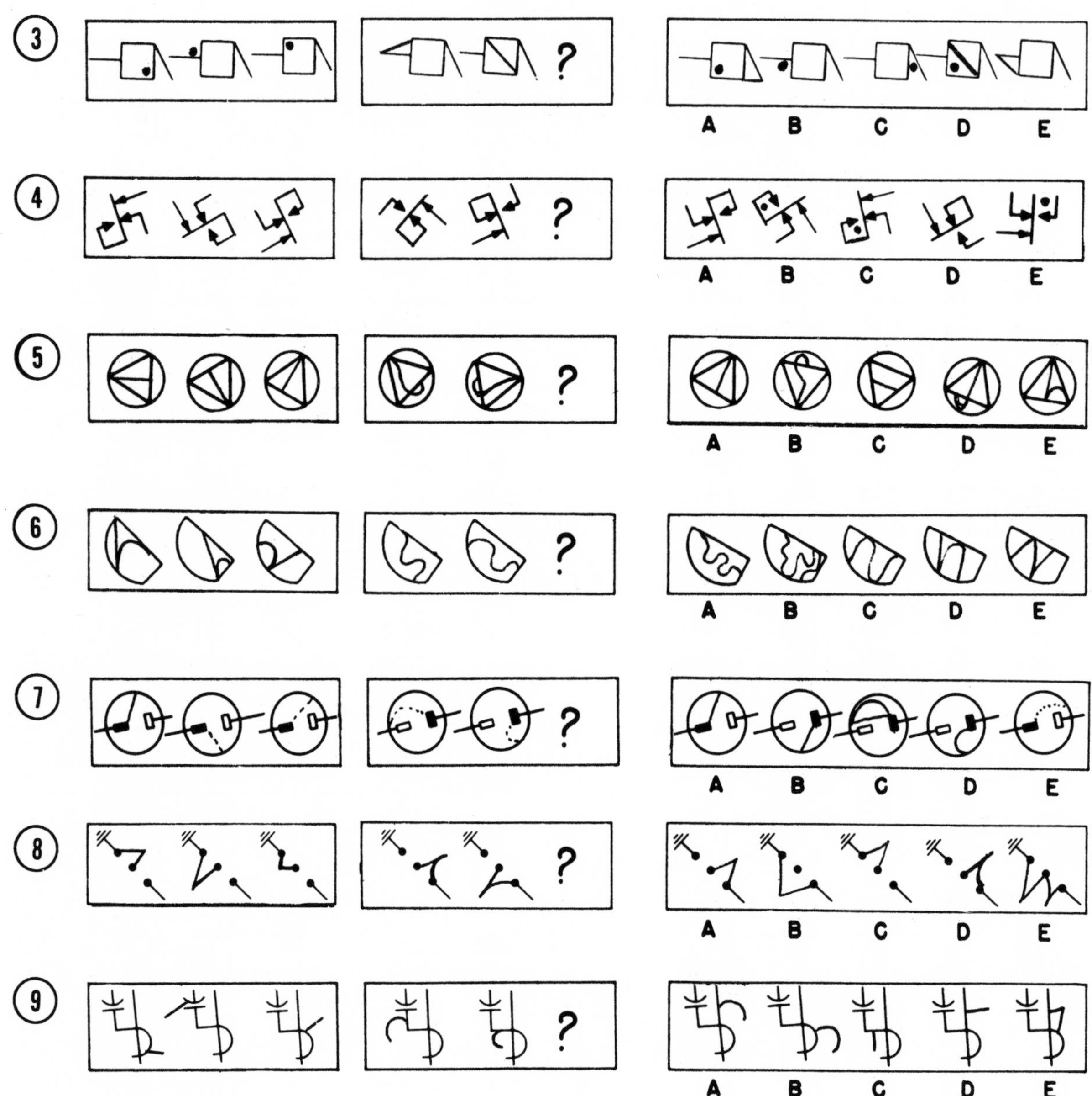

10
?
A B C D E
11
?
A B C D E
12
?
A B C D E
13
?
A B C D E
14
?
A B C D E
15
?
A B C D E
16
?
A B C D E
17
?
A B C D E
18
?
A B C D E
19
?
A B C D E

20 ?

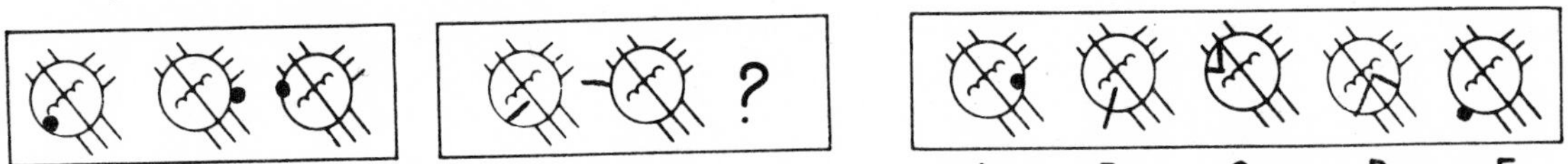

A B C D E

21 ?

A B C D E

22 ?

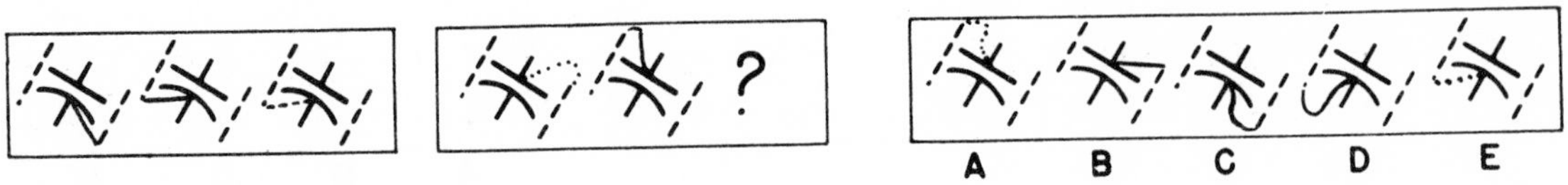

A B C D E

23 ?

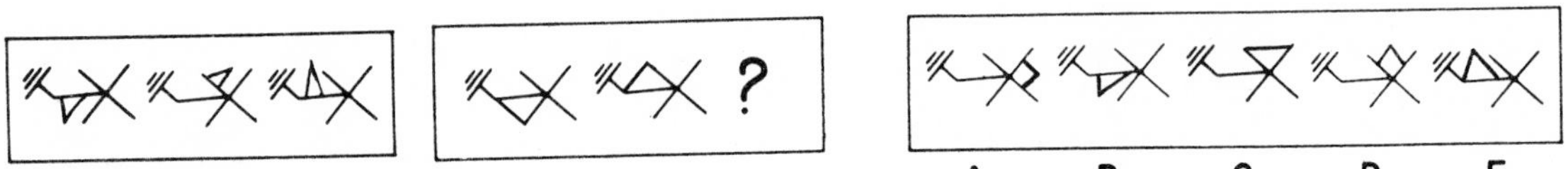

A B C D E

24 ?

A B C D E

25 ?

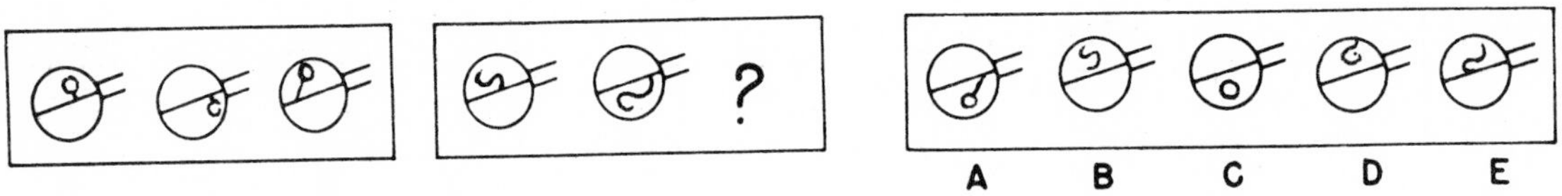

A B C D E

26 ?

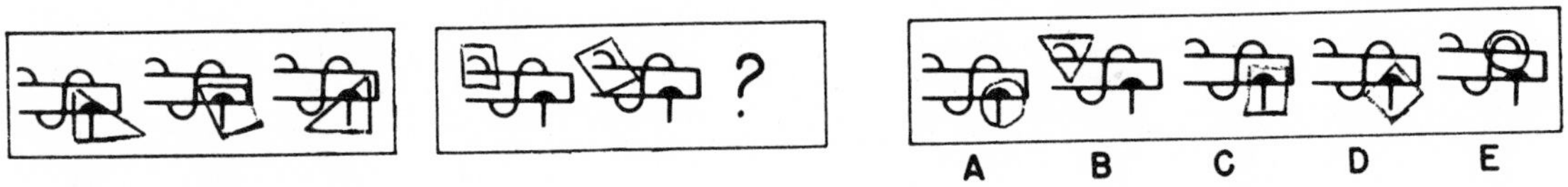

A B C D E

27 ?

A B C D E

28 ?

A B C D E

29

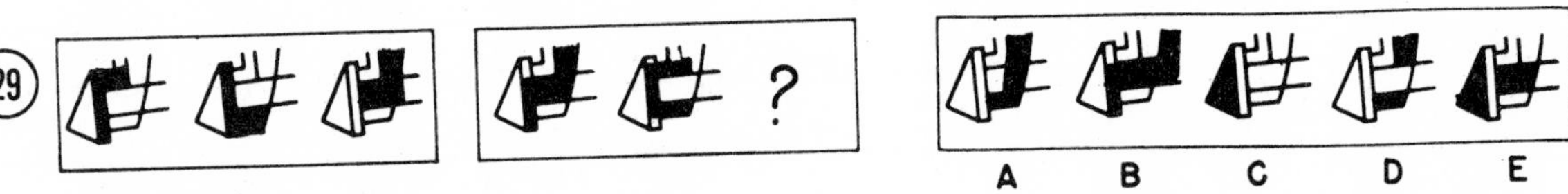

A B C D E

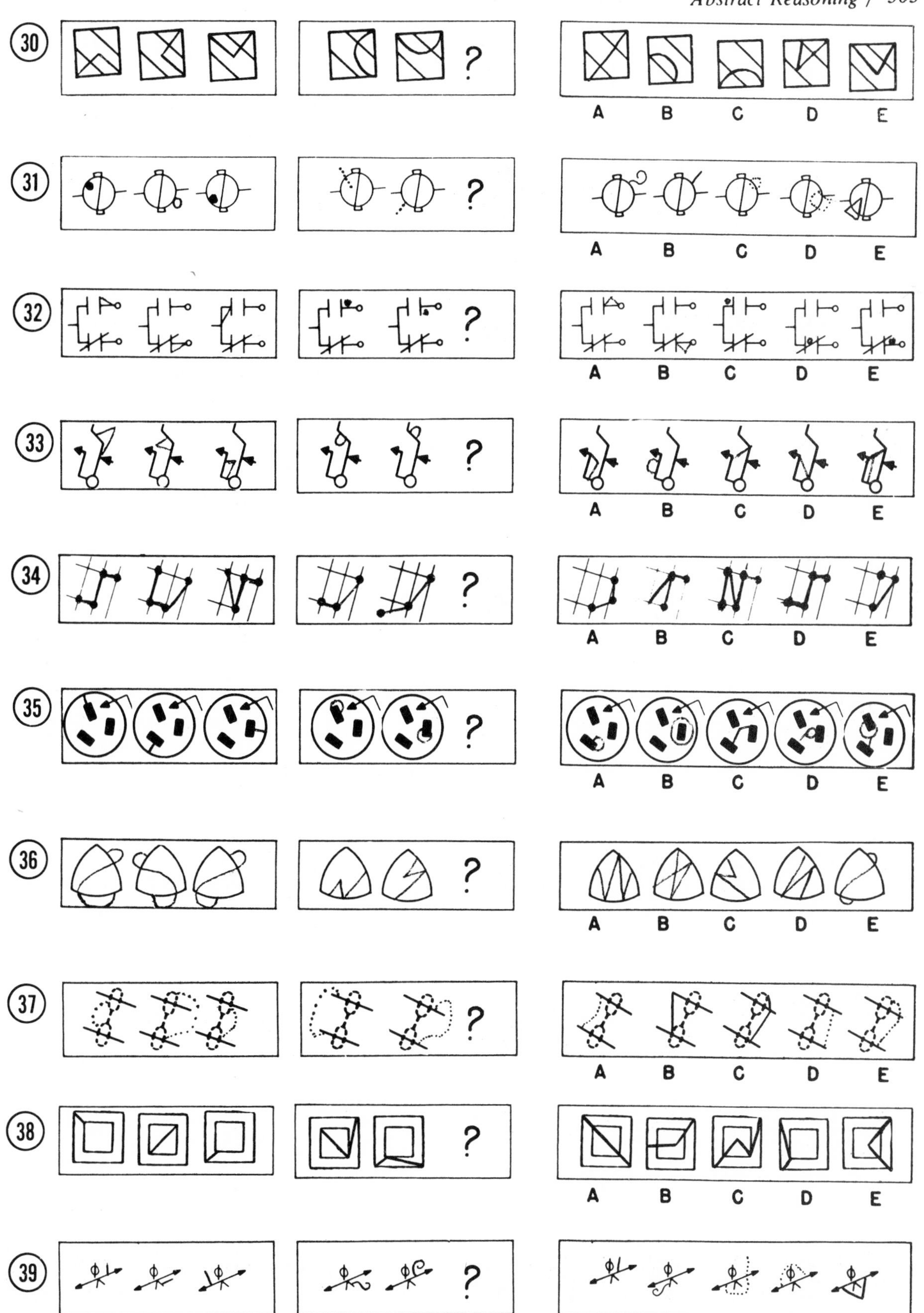
30
?
A B C D E
31
?
A B C D E
32
?
A B C D E
33
?
A B C D E
34
?
A B C D E
35
?
A B C D E
36
?
A B C D E
37
?
A B C D E
38
?
A B C D E
39
?
A B C D E

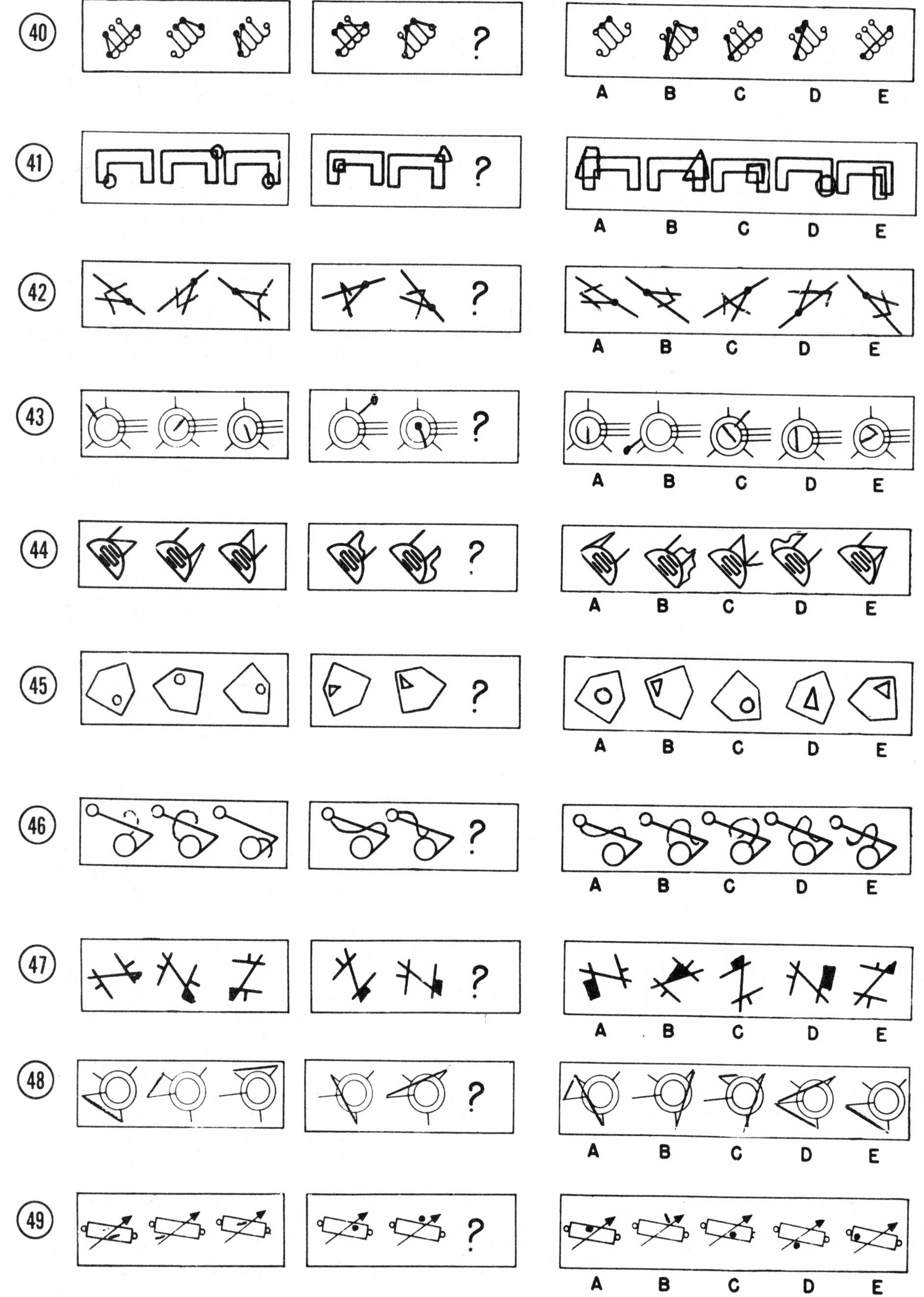
40
?
A
B
C
D
E
41
?
A
B
C
D
E
42
?
A
B
C
D
E
43
?
A
B
C
D
E
44
?
A
B
C
D
E
45
?
A
B
C
D
E
46
?
A
B
C
D
E
47
?
A
B
C
D
E
48
?
A
B
C
D
E
49
?
A
B
C
D
E

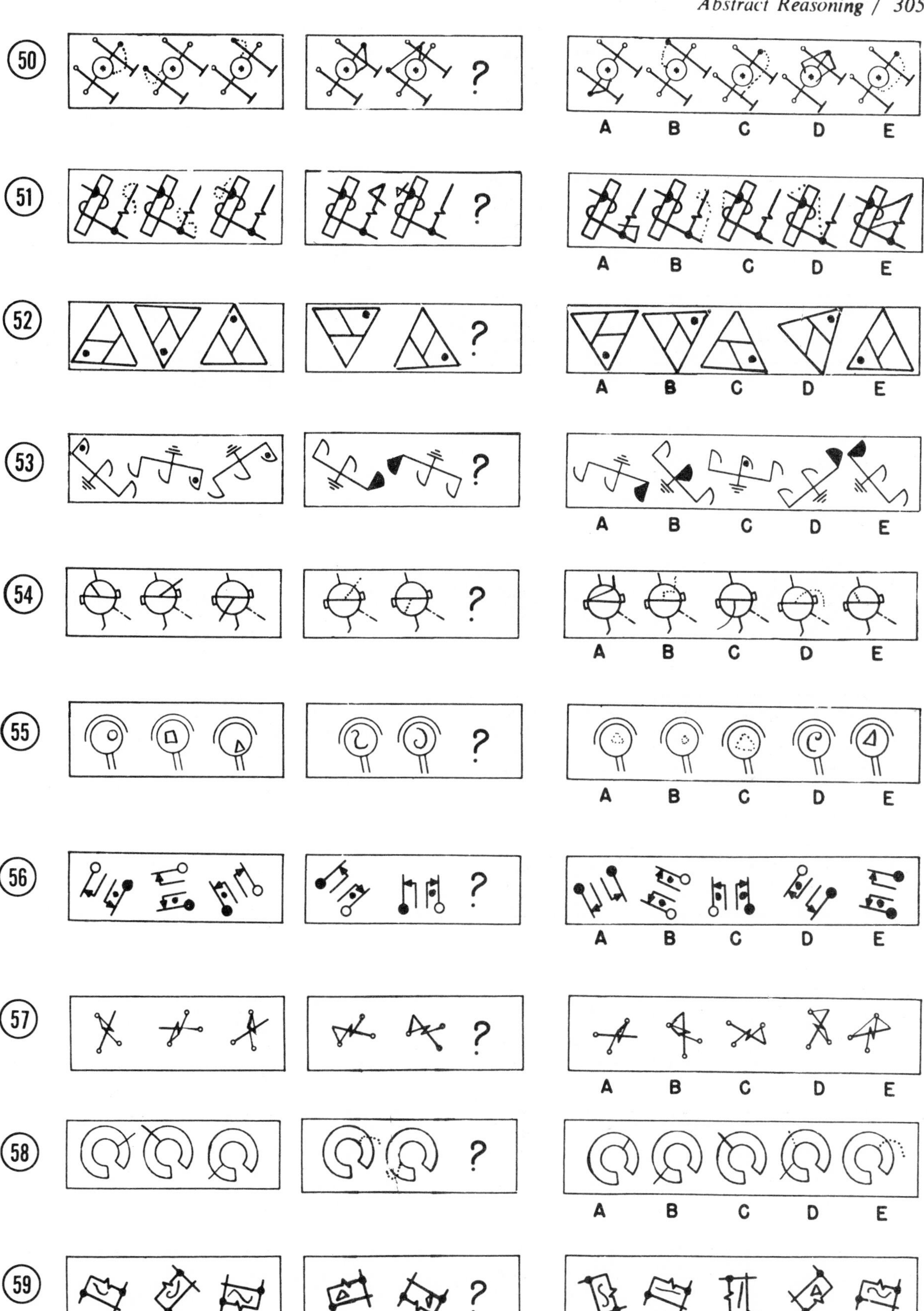
50
?
A B C D E
51
?
A B C D E
52
?
A B C D E
53
?
A B C D E
54
?
A B C D E
55
?
A B C D E
56
?
A B C D E
57
?
A B C D E
58
?
A B C D E
59
?
A B C D E

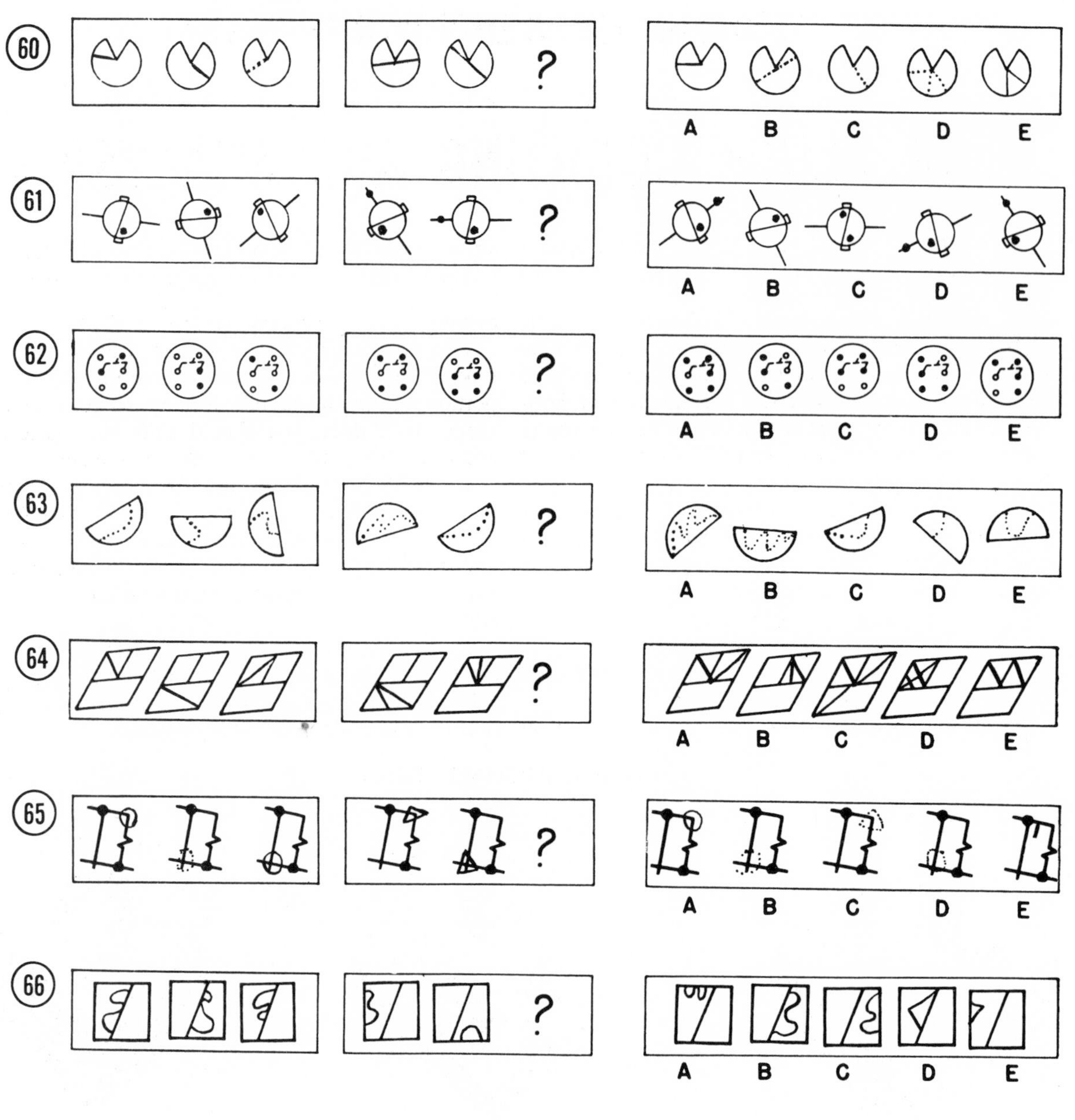

Correct Answers For The Foregoing Questions

(Please make every effort to answer the questions on your own before looking at these answers. You'll make faster progress by following this rule.)

0. B	9. A	18. B	27. D	36. C	45. B	54. E	63. A
1. D	10. C	19. D	28. A	37. A	46. A	55. D	64. B
2. B	11. A	20. B	29. B	38. D	47. C	56. D	65. C
3. E	12. D	21. D	30. C	39. B	48. B	57. C	66. C
4. D	13. A	22. A	31. B	40. B	49. D	58. E	
5. B	14. E	23. C	32. C	41. C	50. A	59. D	
6. A	15. C	24. B	33. B	42. C	51. A	60. B	
7. D	16. E	25. E	34. A	43. B	52. A	61. E	
8. D	17. B	26. B	35. A	44. D	53. D	62. C	

III. BLOCK COUNTING AND ANALYSIS

COUNTING, Turning, Visualizing and Analyzing them in different arrangements, positions and groupings. Variations on an important test theme in spatial relations and aptitude exams.

ABOUT this type of question there is little to be explained. In fact, the more we say, the more difficult will the task appear. You should examine each diagram critically, count the number of horizontal and vertical rows of blocks and be sure you're not leaving any out in figuring the total number of blocks in the pile.

Each pile of blocks will present a different problem and therefore should be attacked without any preconceptions. For instance, you might have a figure with four apparently identical parts. Under no circumstances should you count the number of blocks in one part and multiply by four to find the number of blocks in the whole figure. Count each part separately.

If you're hasty, you'll fall into a similar trap by counting the same column or row of blocks twice.

One other difficulty arises when dealing with this type of test question. If you stare too fixedly at one portion of the block pile it may seem to change shape. If it does, you should shift your gaze and approach the figure from a different angle.

In the 33 block-counting items that follow, blocks rest upon blocks immediately beneath them with the exception of the arches in items 4, 11 and 17, and with the exception of six upper blocks in item 13, which are presumably kept in place by a very strong cement.

The answer given for item 9 assumes there is no block in the northern corner. And for item 24 you will get the correct answer if you realize that there is at least one block in every column.

CUBE COUNTING ITEMS

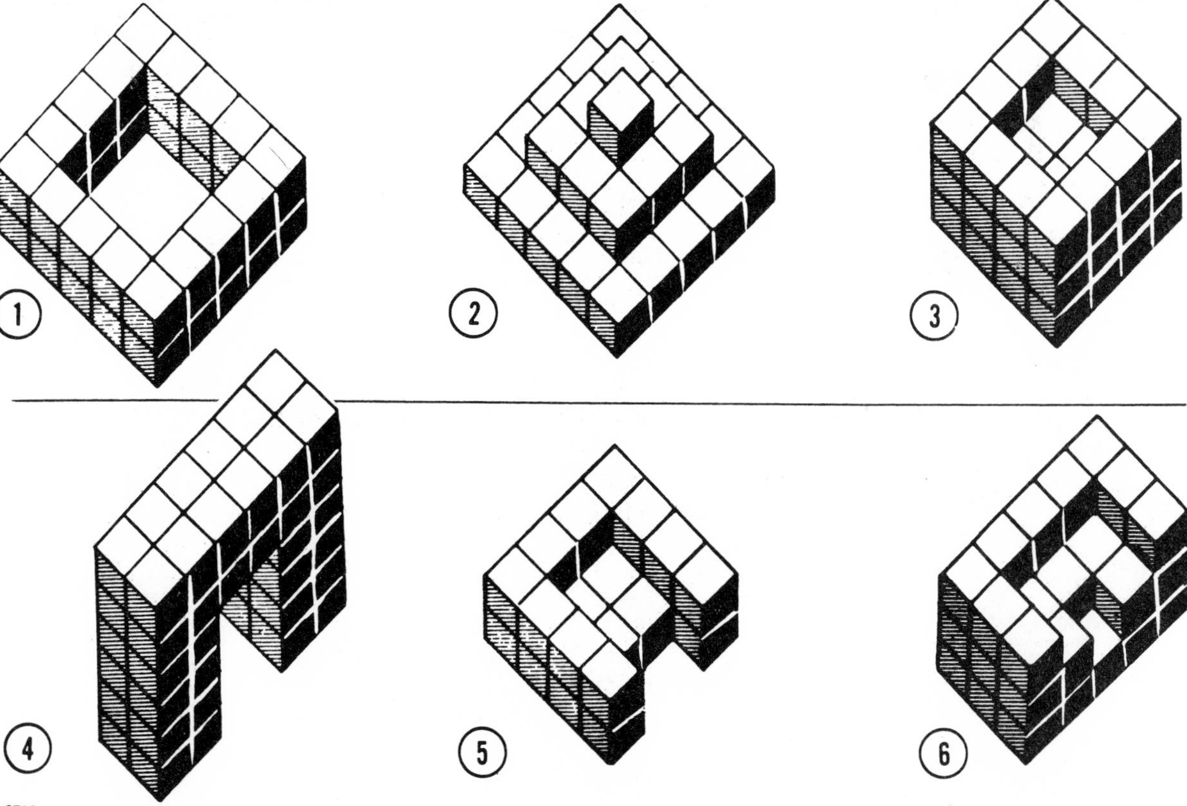

S718

7

8

9

10

11

12

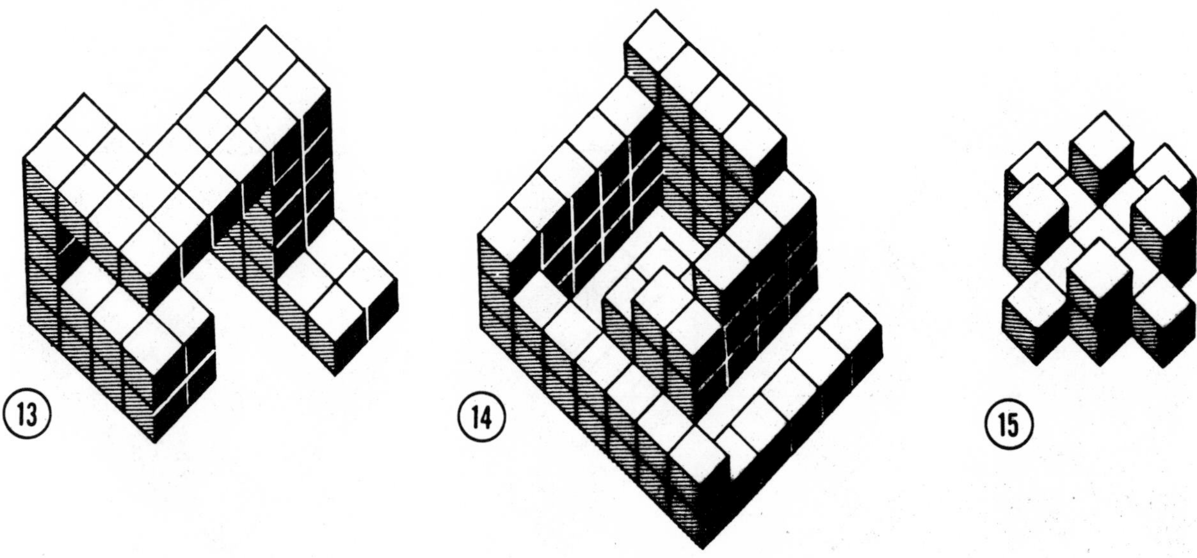

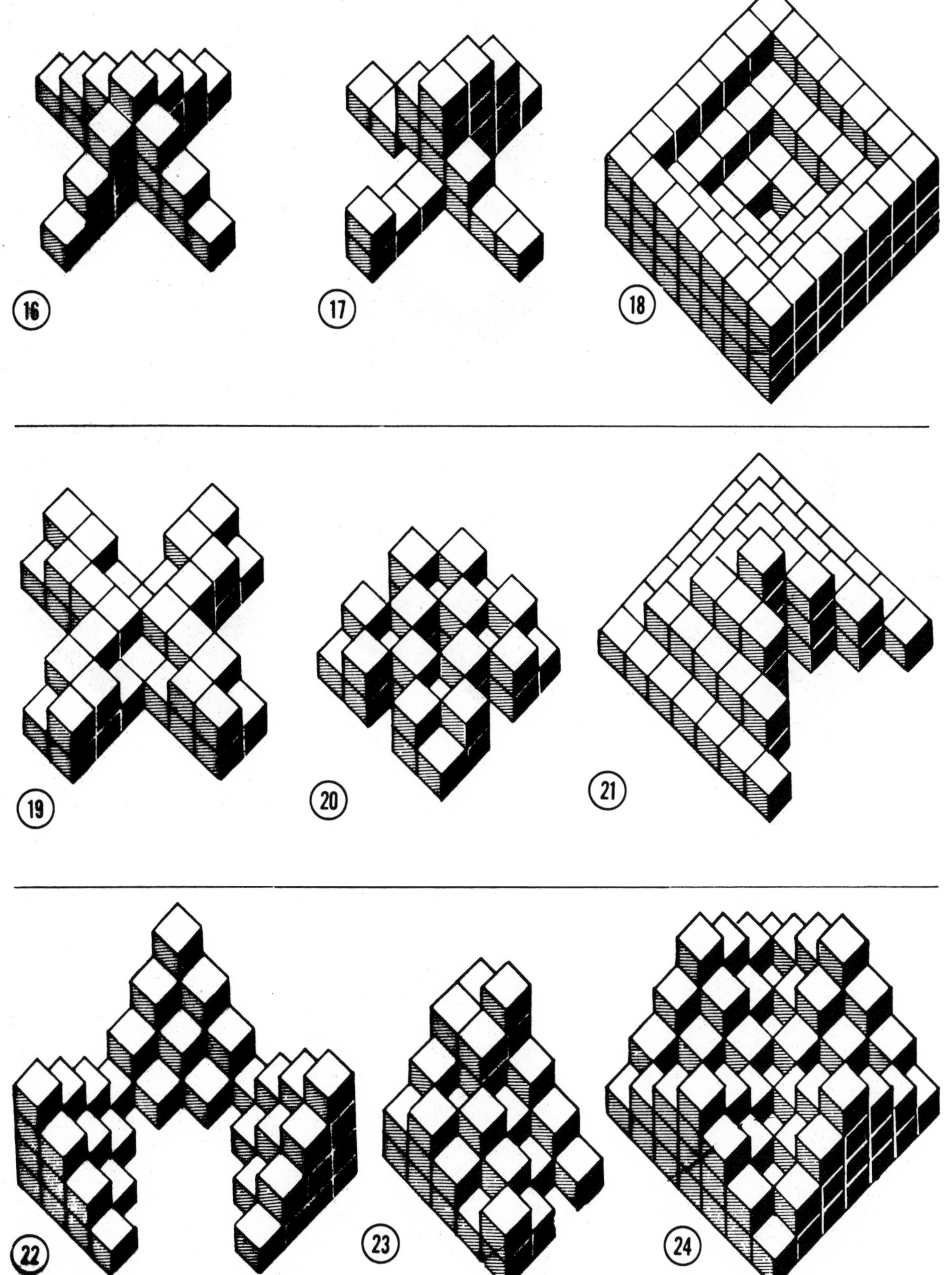
16
17
18
19
20
21
22
23
24

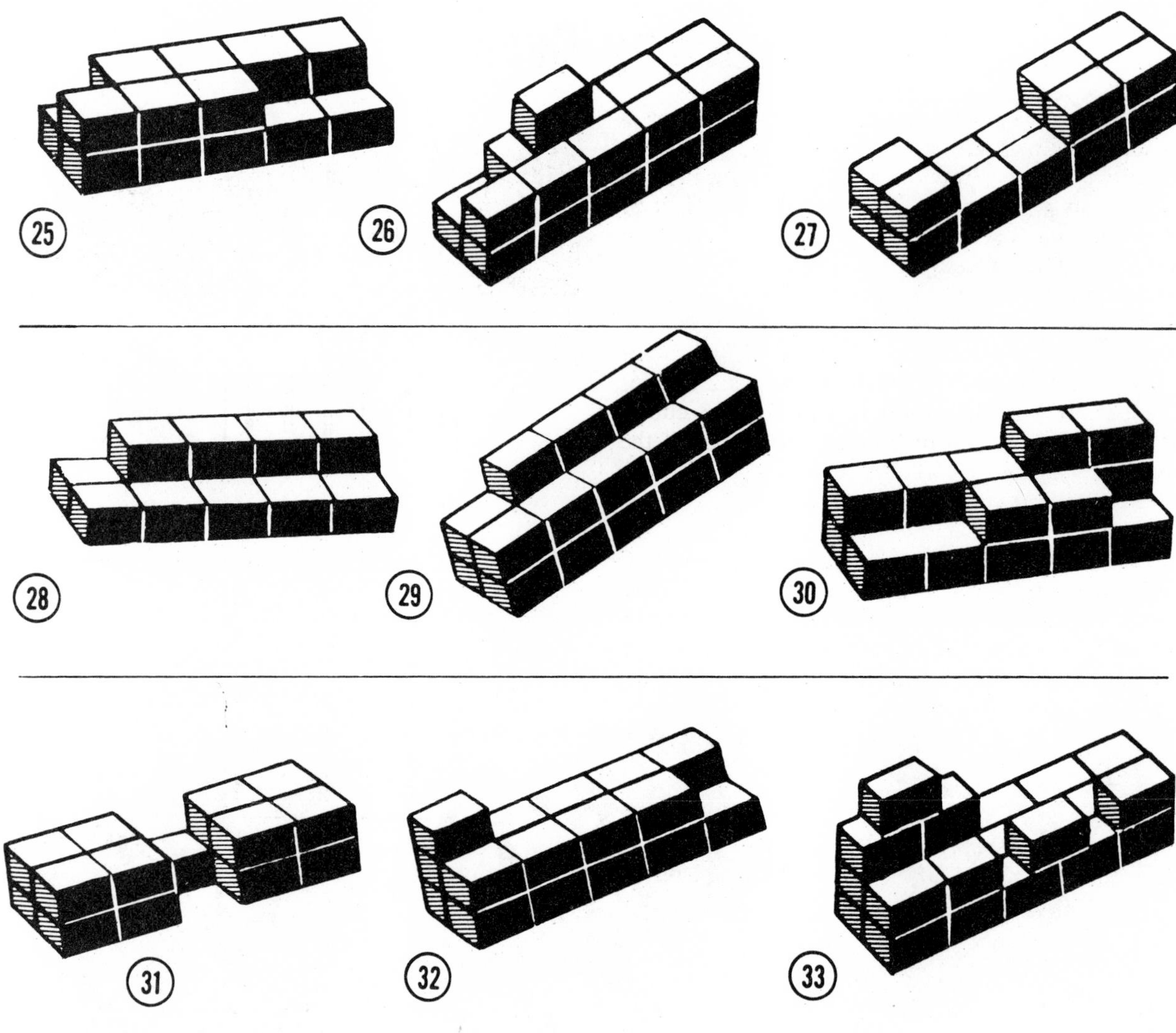

Correct Answers For The Foregoing Questions

(Please make every effort to answer the questions on your own before looking at these answers. You'll make faster progress by following this rule.)

1. 32	8. 48	15. 17	22. 58	29. 24
2. 35	9. 14	16. 28	23. 47	30. 19
3. 44	10. 59	17. 24	24. 105	31. 17
4. 56	11. 40	18. 112	25. 17	32. 20
5. 24	12. 95	19. 46	26. 20	33. 22
6. 38	13. 56	20. 32	27. 16	
7. 49	14. 63 or 64	21. 70	28. 14	

Touching Cubes

IN the questions presented below, all the cubes are exactly the same size; there are only enough hidden cubes to support the ones you can see. Each question number is on one cube in the group. You are to find how many cubes in that group touch the numbered cube. A cube is considered to touch the numbered cube if any part, even a corner, touches. Then mark your answer sheet to show how many cubes touch the numbered cube by (A) if the answer is 1 or 6 or 11 cubes; (B) if the answer is 2 or 7 or 12 cubes; (C) if the answer is 3 or 8 or 13 cubes; (D) if the answer is 4 or 9 or 14 cubes; (E) if the answer is 5 or 10 or 15 cubes. Questions 1 to 5 are based on one group of touching cubes, and questions 6 and 7 on another group.

In question 4, there are three cubes that touch the cube marked 4—the one right behind it which you cannot see, the one on top of that, and the one marked 5. Because the answer is three cubes, the space marked C should be blackened.

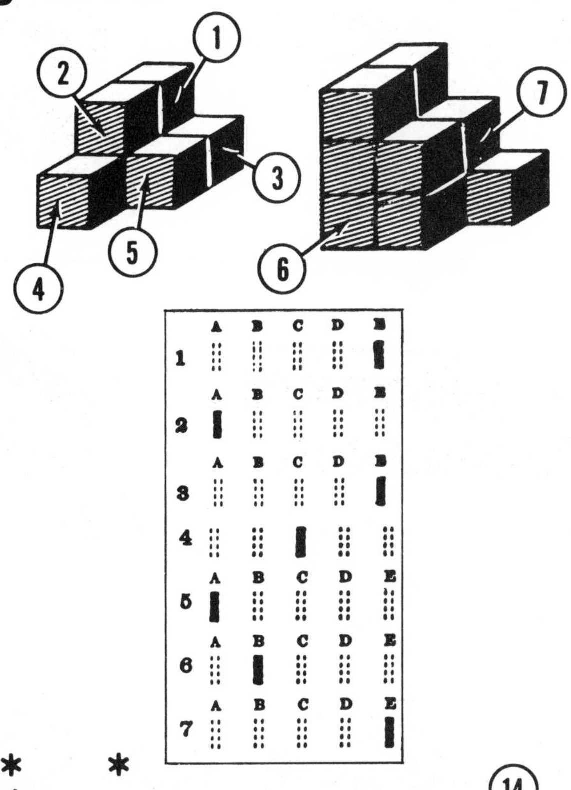

* * *

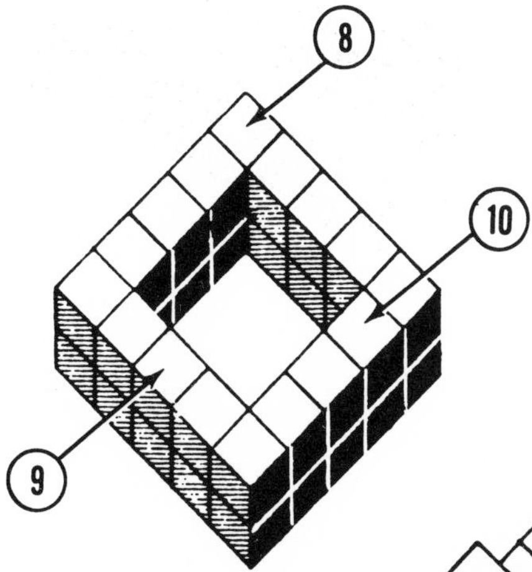

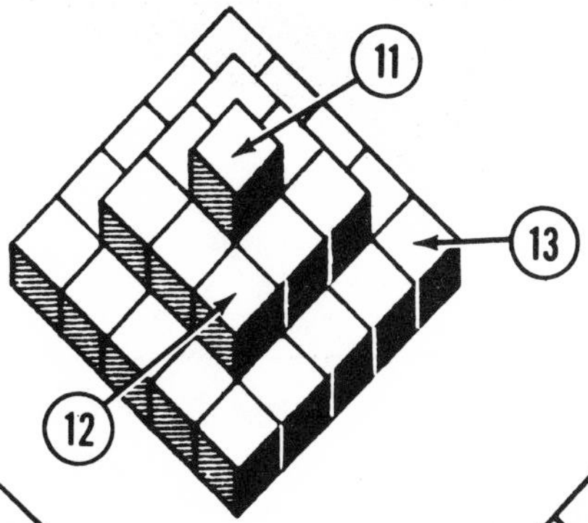

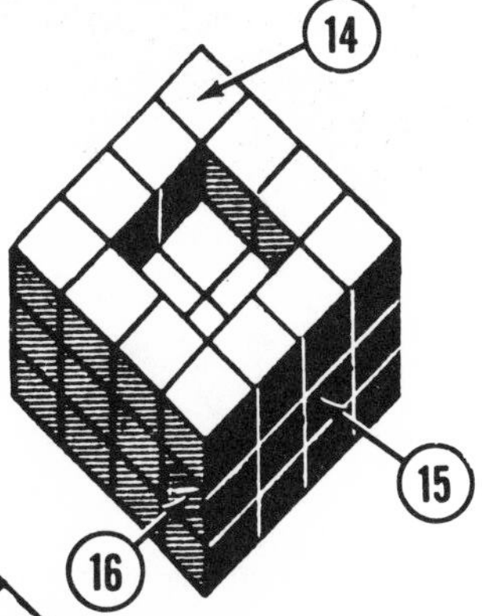

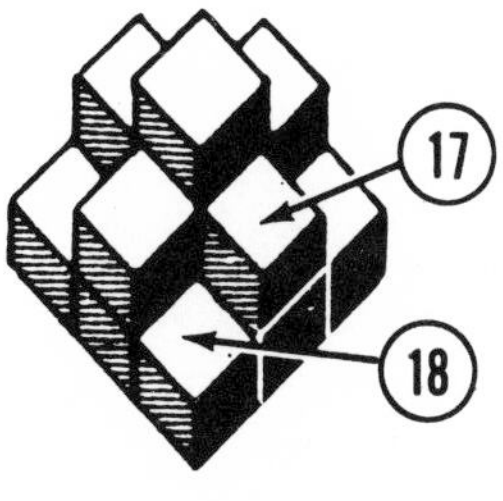

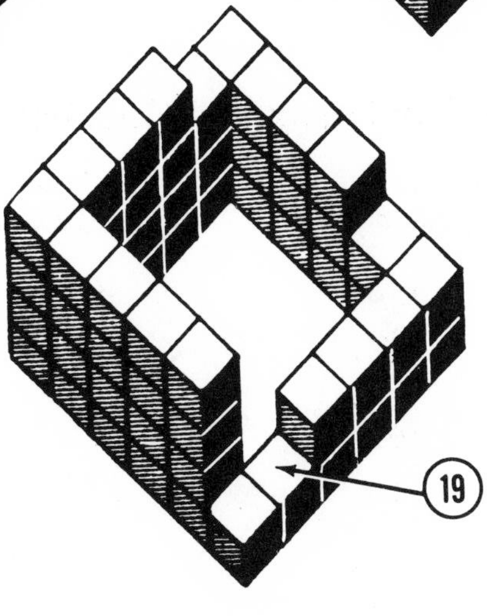

22
21
23
24
25
26
27
28
29
30
32
31
36
35
38
34
33
37
40
39
41
43
42
44
45

47
50
52
46
49
54
48
51
53
56
58
60
55
59
61
57
63
65
62
67
66
64
68
70
69

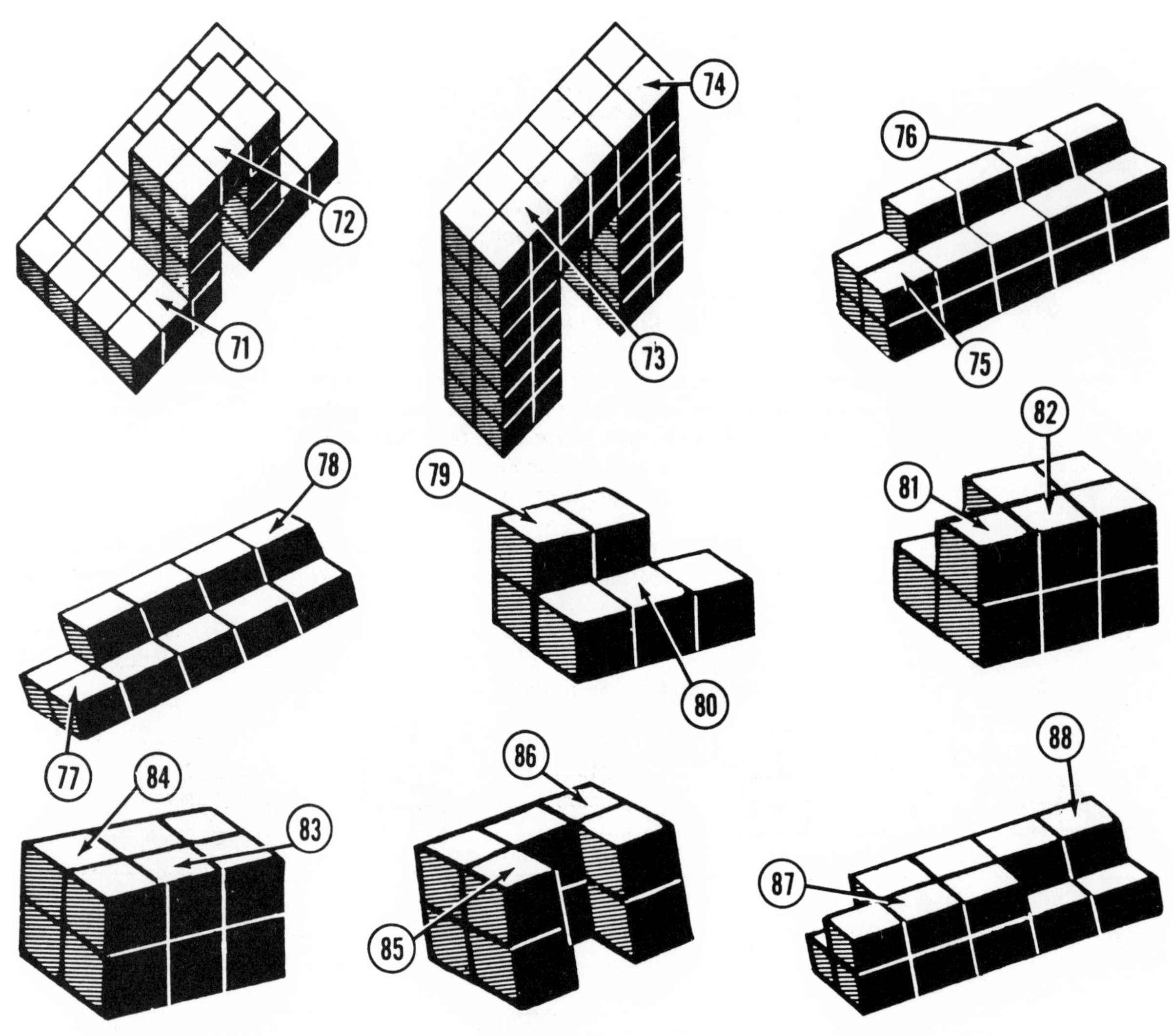

Correct Answers For The Foregoing Questions

8. E	25. A	42. A	59. C	76. C
9. E	26. D	43. D	60. B	77. D
10. B	27. D	44. B	61. D	78. E
11. D	28. B	45. C	62. E	79. E
12. C	29. D	46. A	63. D	80. A
13. D	30. A	47. B	64. A	81. A
14. A	31. E	48. D	65. A	82. E
15. E	32. A	49. D	66. E	83. A
16. E	33. D	50. C	67. A	84. B
17. E	34. E	51. C	68. D	85. E
18. A	35. C	52. A	69. A	86. E
19. E	36. B	53. E	70. D	87. E
20. D	37. A	54. A	71. B	88. E
21. D	38. E	55. A	72. D	
22. C	39. B	56. D	73. A	
23. E	40. D	57. C	74. B	
24. B	41. A	58. C	75. C	

Solid Figure Turning

Solid figure turning is one of a class of tests used to explore mechanical aptitude and knowledge. It is also employed to give an indication of your general intelligence, since there is no real separation between "general" and "mechanical" intelligence.

You cannot prepare thoroughly for this type of question since your ability will, to a large extent, determine the mark you get on such questions. However, familiarity with these questions and practice in answering them will erase any fear you might have and thus you will be enabied to answer them more quickly, and perhaps more accurately.

THE drawings in the following sample questions represent figures made up of cubes or other forms glued together. The problem is to find the *one* of the four figures lettered A, B, C, and D, which is the figure at the left turned in a different position. Some of the figures must be turned *over* to be correct, others must be turned *around*, and still others may have to be turned *both* over and around.

In sample question 1 you will notice that only (D) could be the figure at the left turned in a different position.

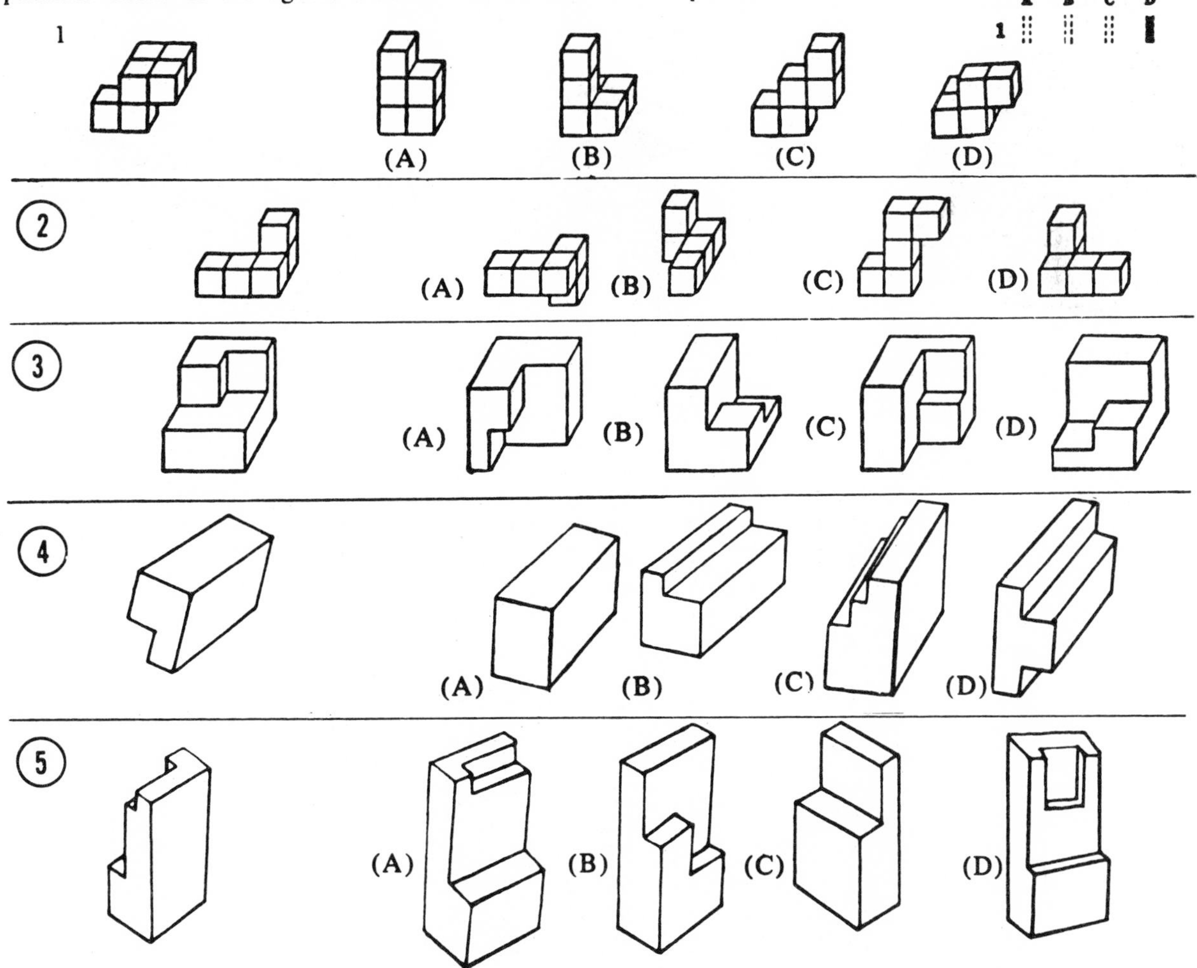

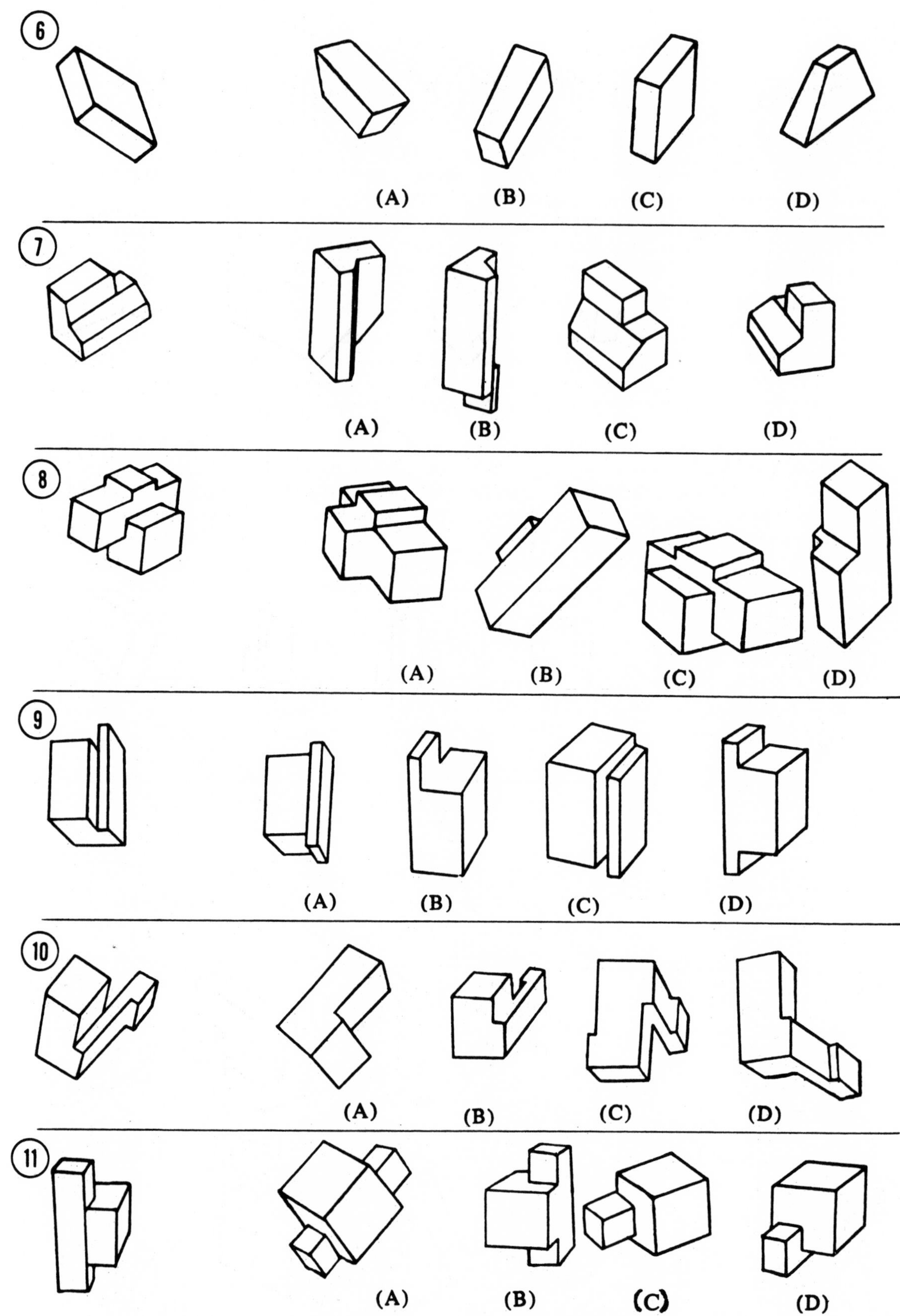
6
(A)
(B)
(C)
(D)
7
(A)
(B)
(C)
(D)
8
(A)
(B)
(C)
(D)
9
(A)
(B)
(C)
(D)
10
(A)
(B)
(C)
(D)
11
(A)
(B)
(C)
(D)

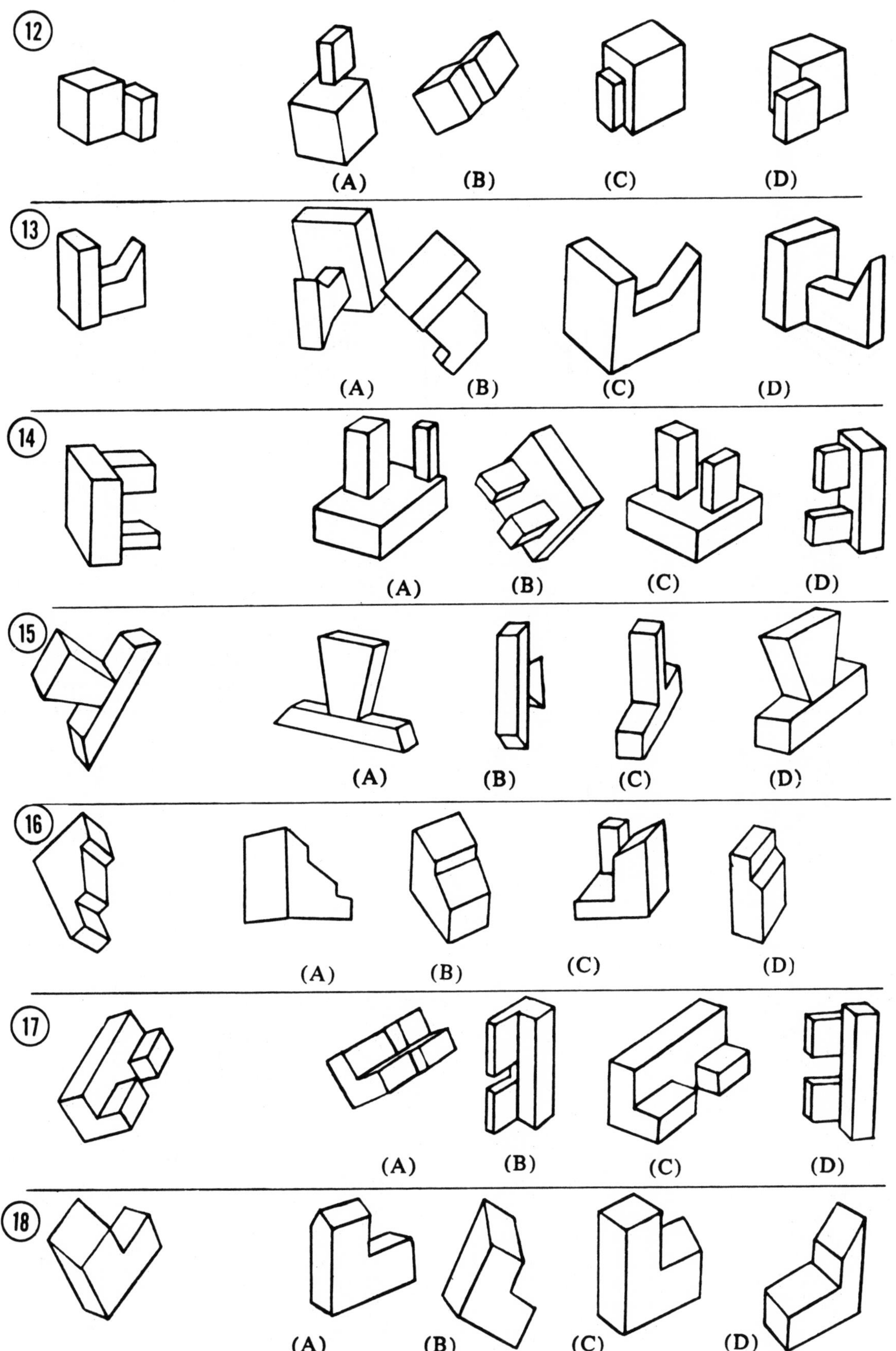
12
(A)
(B)
(C)
(D)
13
(A)
(B)
(C)
(D)
14
(A)
(B)
(C)
(D)
15
(A)
(B)
(C)
(D)
16
(A)
(B)
(C)
(D)
17
(A)
(B)
(C)
(D)
18
(A)
(B)
(C)
(D)

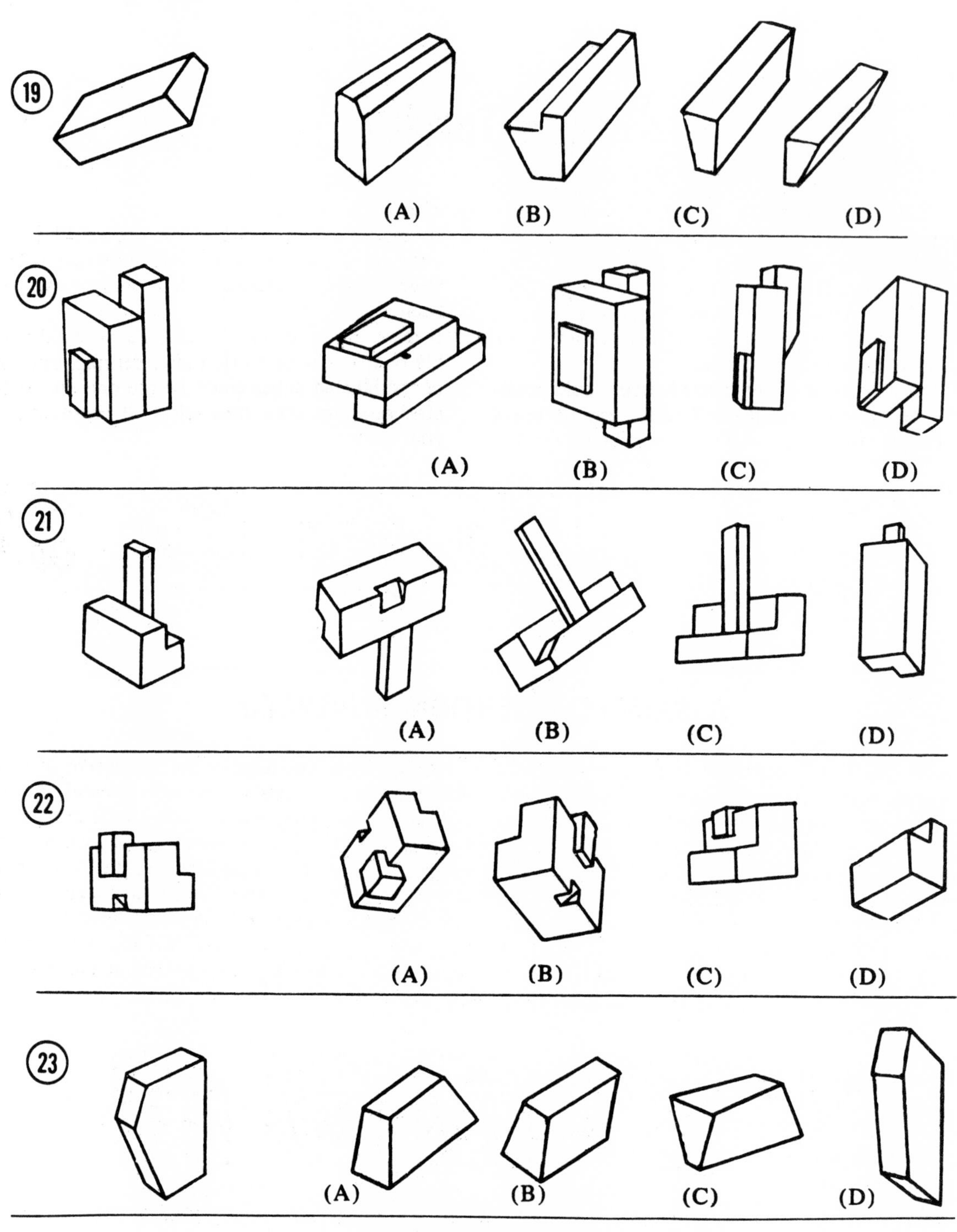

Correct Answers

(You'll learn more by writing your own answers before comparing them with these.)

1. D	6. C	11. B	16. A	21. C
2. B	7. C	12. D	17. C	22. B
3. D	8. C	13. D	18. B	23. D
4. B	9. B	14. C	19. C	
5. A	10. D	15. A	20. A	

Cube Turning

THE drawing at the left in each of the following questions represents a cube. There is a different design on each of the six faces of the cube. Four other drawings of cubes are labeled A, B, C, and D. After observing the cube on the left, you are asked to select one or more of the labeled cubes according to the following rules:

1. If more than one of the labeled cubes could possibly be the cube on the left after turning, select the cube (or cubes) which is the cube on the left after one turn only.
2. If only one of the labeled cubes could be the cube on the left after turning, then that cube is your answer, regardless of how many turns have been made.
3. If more than one of the labeled cubes could possibly be the cube on the left after turning, but none of the labeled cubes could be the one on the left after one turn only, then select all possibilities as your answer.

1.–S 

A B C D

A SAMPLE QUESTION ANALYZED

Sample Question 1 conforms to Rule 2 above: A is wrong because the triangle on top should point toward the cross, and not away from it. C is wrong, since the cube would have to be turned upside down to put the triangle on the right side of the cross, in which case the square would disappear. D is not the answer either, since the triangle should point toward the cross, and in D it points toward a circle. B is the correct answer; it is the original cube turned twice.

NOTE: You can simplify the answering of these cube turning questions if you will provide yourself with an actual cube; one of a pair of dice will do. Since each of the sides is numbered differently you will be able to arrive at and check your answers by actually turning it to various positions, in accordance with the requirements of the individual question. You may not be permitted to use this aid while taking your test, but it's well to be prepared just in case you are.

A B C D

---

2 

A B C D

3
A
B
C
D
4
A
B
C
D
5
A
B
C
D
6
A
B
C
D
7
A
B
C
D
8
A
B
C
D

A B C D

---

(10)

A B C D

---

(11)

A B C D

---

(12)

A B C D

---

(13)

A B C D

---

(14)

A B C D

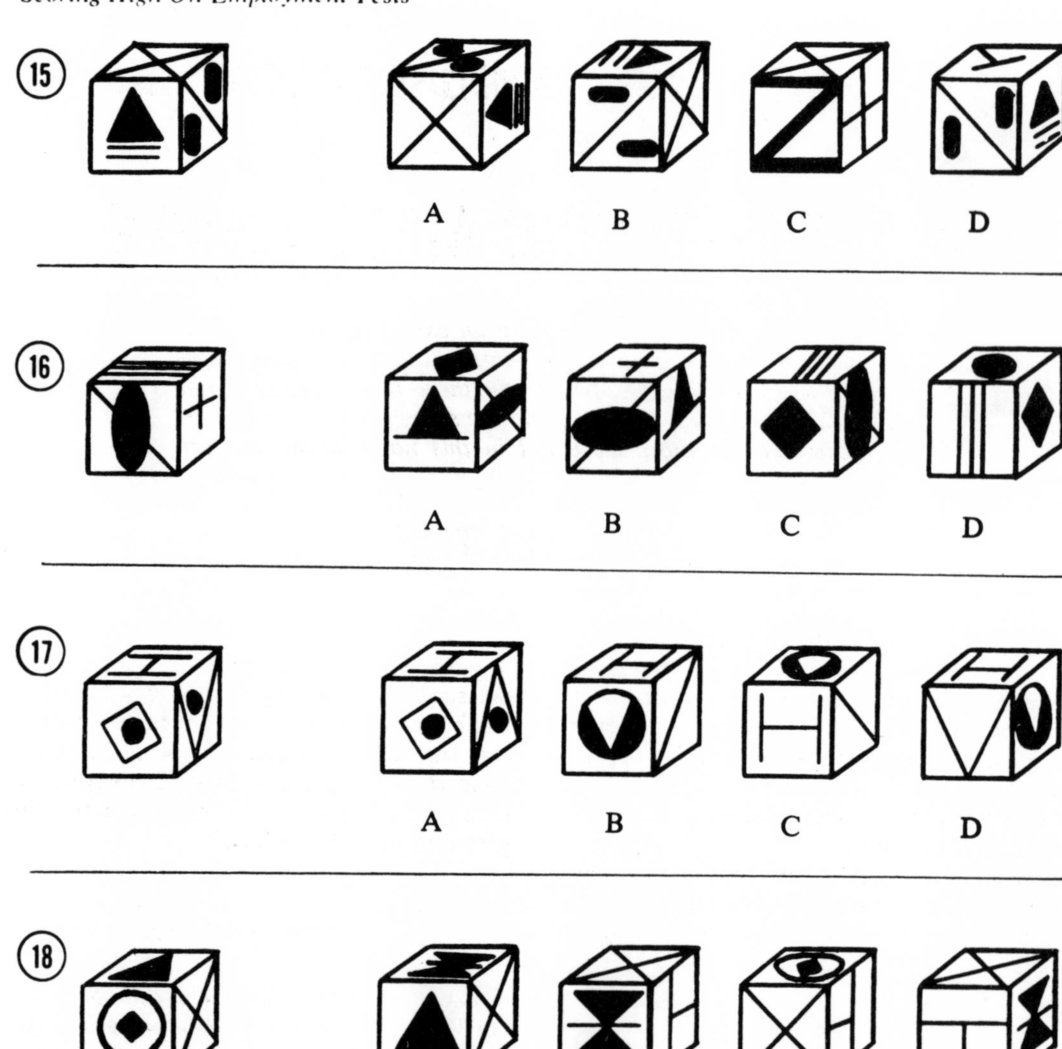

Correct Answers

(You'll learn more by writing your own answers before comparing them with these.)

1. C	7. A, C	13. A
2. A	8. B	14. D
3. B	9. C	15. B, C
4. D	10. B	16. B, C
5. B	11. D	17. C
6. B	12. A	18. A

IV. TEST—TAKING MADE SIMPLE

Having gotten this far, you're almost an expert test-taker because you have now mastered the subject matter of the test. Proper preparation is the real secret. The pointers on the next few pages will take you the rest of the way by giving you the strategy employed on tests by those who are most successful in this not-so-mysterious art.

BEFORE THE TEST

T-DAY MINUS SEVEN

You're going to pass this examination because you have received the best possible preparation for it. But, unlike many others, you're going to give the best possible account of yourself by acquiring the rare skill of effectively using your knowledge to answer the examination questions.

First off, get rid of any negative attitudes toward the test. You have a negative attitude when you view the test as a device to "trip you up" rather than an opportunity to show how effectively you have learned.

APPROACH THE TEST WITH SELF-CONFIDENCE. Plugging through this book was no mean job, and now that you've done it you're probably better prepared than 90% of the others. Self-confidence is one of the biggest strategic assets you can bring to the testing room.

Nobody likes tests, but some poor souls permit themselves to get upset or angry when they see what they think is an unfair test. The expert doesn't. He keeps calm and moves right ahead, knowing that everyone is taking the same test. Anger, resentment, fear . . . they all slow you down. "Grin and bear it!"

Besides, every test you take, including this one, is a valuable experience which improves your skill. Since you will undoubtedly be taking other tests in the years to come, it may help you to regard this one as training to perfect your skill.

Keep calm; there's no point in panic. If you've done your work there's no need for it; and if you haven't, a cool head is your very first requirement.

Why be the frightened kind of student who enters the examination chamber in a mental coma? A test taken under mental stress does not provide a fair measure of your ability. At the very least, this book has removed for you some of the fear and mystery that surrounds examinations. A certain amount of concern is normal and good, but excessive worry saps your strength and keenness. In other words, be prepared EMOTIONALLY.

Pre-Test Review

If you know any others who are taking this test, you'll probably find it helpful to review the book and your notes with them. The group should be small, certainly not more than four. Team study at this stage should seek to review the material in a different way than you learned it originally; should strive for an exchange of ideas between you and the other members of the group; should be selective in sticking to important ideas; should stress the vague and the unfamiliar rather than that which you all know well; should be businesslike and devoid of any nonsense; should end as soon as you get tired.

One of the *worst* strategies in test taking is to do *all* your preparation the night before the exam. As a reader of this book, you have scheduled and spaced your study properly so as not to suffer from the fatigue and emotional disturbance that comes from cramming the night before.

Cramming is a very good way to *guarantee poor test results.*

However, you would be wise to prepare yourself factually by *reviewing your notes* in the 48 hours preceding the exam. You shouldn't have to spend more than two or three hours in this way. Stick to salient points. The others will fall into place quickly.

Don't confuse cramming with a final, calm review which helps you focus on the significant areas of this book and further strengthens your confidence in your ability to handle the test questions. In other words, prepare yourself FACTUALLY.

Keep Fit

Mind and body work together. Poor physical condition will lower your mental efficiency. In preparing for an examination, observe the common-sense rules of health. Get sufficient sleep and rest, eat proper foods, plan recreation and exercise. In relation to health and examinations, two cautions are in order. Don't miss your meals prior to an examination in order to get extra time for study. Likewise, don't miss your regular sleep by sitting up late to "cram" for the examination. Cramming is an attempt to learn in a very short period of time what should have been learned through regular and consistent study. Not only are these two habits detrimental to health, but seldom do they pay off in terms of effective learning. It is likely that you will be *more confused* than better prepared on the day of the examination if you have broken into your daily routine by missing your meals or sleep.

On the night before the examination go to bed at your regular time and try to get a good night's sleep. Don't go to the movies. Don't date. In other words, prepare yourself PHYSICALLY.

T-HOUR MINUS ONE

After a very light, leisurely meal, get to the examination room ahead of time, perhaps ten minutes early . . . but not so early that you have time to get into an argument with others about what's going to be asked on the exam, etc. The reason for coming early is to help you get accustomed to the room. It will help you to a better start.

Bring all necessary equipment . . .

. . . pen, two sharpened pencils, watch, paper, eraser, ruler, and any other things you're instructed to bring.

Get settled . . .

. . . by finding your seat and staying in it. If no special seats have been assigned, take one in the front to facilitate the seating of others coming in after you.

The test will be given by a test supervisor who reads the directions and otherwise tells you what to do. The people who walk about passing out the test papers and assisting with the examination are test proctors. If you're not able to see or hear properly notify the supervisor or a proctor. If you have any other difficulties during the examination, like a defective test booklet, scoring pencil, answer sheet; or if it's too hot or cold or dark or drafty, let them know. You're entitled to favorable test conditions, and if you don't have them you won't be able to do your best. Don't be a crank, but don't be shy either. An important function of the proctor is to see to it that you have favorable test conditions.

Relax . . .

. . . and don't bring on unnecessary tenseness by worrying about the difficulty of the examination. If necessary wait a minute before beginning to write. If you're still tense, take a couple of deep breaths, look over your test equipment, or do something which will take your mind away from the examination for a moment.

If your collar or shoes are tight, loosen them.

Put away unnecessary materials so that you have a good, clear space on your desk to write freely.

You Must Have *TO GIVE YOUR* **Best Test** *PERFORMANCE*

(1) A GOOD TEST ENVIRONMENT

(2) A COMPLETE UNDERSTANDING OF DIRECTIONS

(3) A DESIRE TO DO YOUR BEST

WHEN THEY SAY "GO" — TAKE YOUR TIME!

Listen very carefully to the test supervisor. If you fail to hear something important that he says, you may not be able to read it in the written directions and may suffer accordingly.

If you don't understand the directions you have heard or read, raise your hand and inform the proctor. Read carefully the directions for *each* part of the test before beginning to work on that part. If you skip over such directions too hastily, you may miss a main idea and thus lose credit for an entire section.

Get an Overview of the Examination

After reading the directions carefully, look over the entire examination to get an over-view of the nature and scope of the test. The purpose of this over-view is to give you some idea of the nature, scope, and difficulty of the examination.

It has another advantage. An item might be so phrased that it sets in motion a chain of thought that might be helpful in answering other items on the examination.

Still another benefit to be derived from reading all the items before you answer any is that the few minutes involved in reading the items gives you an opportunity to relax before beginning the examination. This will make for better concentration. As you read over these items the first time, check those whose answers immediately come to you. These will be the ones you will answer first. Read each item carefully before answering. It is a good practice to read each item at least twice to be sure that you understand it.

Plan Ahead

In other words, you should know precisely where you are going before you start. You should know:

1. whether you have to answer all the questions or whether you can choose those that are easiest for you;
2. whether all the questions are easy; (there may be a pattern of difficult, easy, etc.)
3. The length of the test; the number of questions;
4. The kind of scoring method used;
5. Which questions, if any, carry extra weight;
6. What types of questions are on the test;
7. What directions apply to each part of the test;
8. Whether you must answer the questions consecutively.

Budget Your Time Strategically!

Quickly figure out how much of the allotted time you can give to each section and still finish ahead of time. Don't forget to figure on the time you're investing in the overview. Then alter your schedule so that you can spend more time on those parts that count most. Then, if you can, plan to spend less time on the easier questions, so that you can devote the time saved to the harder questions. Figuring roughly, you should finish half the questions when half the allotted time has gone by. If there are 100 questions and you have three hours, you should have finished 50 questions after one and one half hours. So bring along a watch whether the instructions call for one or not. Jot down your "exam budget" and stick to it INTELLIGENTLY.

EXAMINATION STRATEGY

Probably the most important single strategy you can learn is to do the easy questions first. The very hard questions should be read and temporarily postponed. Identify them with a dot and return to them later.

This strategy has several advantages for you:

1. You're sure to get credit for all the questions you're sure of. If time runs out, you'll have all the sure shots, losing out only on those which you might have missed anyway.
2. By reading and laying away the tough ones you give your subconscious a chance to work on them. You may be pleasantly surprised to find the answers to the puzzlers popping up for you as you deal with related questions.
3. You won't risk getting caught by the time limit just as you reach a question you know really well.

A Tested Tactic

It's inadvisable on some examinations to answer each question in the order presented. The reason for this is that some examiners design tests so as to extract as much mental energy from you as possible. They put the most difficult questions at the beginning, the easier questions last. Or they may vary difficult with easy questions in a fairly regular pattern right through the test. Your survey of the test should reveal the pattern and your strategy for dealing with it.

If difficult questions appear at the beginning, answer them until you feel yourself slowing down or getting tired. Then switch to an easier part of the examination. You will return to the difficult portion after you have rebuilt your confidence by answering a batch of easy questions. Knowing that you have a certain number of points "under your belt" will help you when you return to the more difficult questions. You'll answer them with a much clearer mind; and you'll be refreshed by the change of pace.

Time

Use your time wisely. It's an important element in your test and you must use every minute effectively, working as rapidly as you can without sacrificing accuracy. Your exam survey and budget will guide you in dispensing your time. Wherever you can, pick up seconds on the easy ones. Devote your savings to the hard ones. If possible, pick up time on the lower value questions and devote it to those which give you the most points.

Relax Occasionally and Avoid Fatigue

If the exam is long (two or more hours) give yourself short rest periods as you feel you need them. If you're not permitted to leave the room, relax in your seat, look up from your paper, rest your eyes, stretch your legs, shift your body. Break physical and mental tension. Take several deep breaths and get back to the job, refreshed. If you don't do this you run the risk of getting nervous and tightening up. Your thinking may be hampered and you may make a few unnecessary mistakes.

Do not become worried or discouraged if the examination seems difficult to you. The questions in the various fields are purposely made difficult and searching so that the examination will discriminate effectively even among superior students. No one is expected to get a perfect or near-perfect score.

Remember that if the examination seems difficult to you, it may be even more difficult for your neighbor.

Think!

This is not a joke because you're not an IBM machine. Nobody is able to write all the time and also to read and think through each question. You must plan each answer. Don't give hurried answers in an atmosphere of panic. Even though you see a lot of questions, remember that they are objective and not very time-consuming. Don't rush headlong through questions that must be thought through.

Edit, Check, Proofread . . .

. . . after completing all the questions. Invariably, you will find some foolish errors which you needn't have made, and which you can easily correct. Don't just sit back or leave the room ahead of time. Read over your answers and make sure you wrote exactly what you meant to write. And that you wrote the answers in the right place. You might even find that you have omitted some answers inadvertently. You have budgeted time for this job of proofreading. PROOFREAD and pick up points.

One caution, though. Don't count on making major changes. And don't go in for wholesale changing of answers. To arrive at your answers in the first place you have read carefully and thought correctly. Second-guessing at this stage is more likely to result in wrong answers. So don't make changes unless you are quite certain you were wrong in the first place.

FOLLOW DIRECTIONS CAREFULLY

In answering questions on the objective or short-form examination, it is most important to follow all instructions carefully. Unless you have marked the answers properly, you will not receive credit for them. In addition, even in the same examination, the instructions will not be consistent. In one section you may be urged to guess if you are not certain; in another you may be cautioned against guessing. Some questions will call for the best choice among four or five alternatives; others may ask you to select the one incorrect or the least probable answer.

On some tests you will be provided with worked out fore-exercises, complete with correct answers. However, avoid the temptation to skip the directions and begin working just from reading the model questions and answers. Even though you may be familiar with that particular type of question, the directions may be different from those which you had followed previously. If the type of question should be new to you, work through the model until you understand it perfectly. This may save you time, and earn you a higher rating on the examination.

If the directions for the examination are written, read them carefully, at least twice. If the directions are given orally, listen attentively and then follow them precisely. For example, if you are directed to use plus (+) and minus (−) to mark true—false items, then don't use "T" and "F". If you are instructed to "blacken" a space on machine-scored tests, do not use a check (✔) or an "X". Make all symbols legible, and be sure that they have been placed in the proper answer space. It is easy, for example, to place the answer for item 5 in the space reserved for item 6. If this is done, then all of your following answers may be wrong. It is also very important that you understand the method they will use in scoring the examination. Sometimes they tell you in the directions. The method of scoring may affect the amount of time you spend on an item, especially if some items count more than others. Likewise, the directions may indicate whether or not you should guess in case you are not sure of the answer. Some methods of scoring penalize you for guessing.

Cue Words. Pay special attention to qualifying words or phrases in the directions. Such words as *one, best reason, surest, means most nearly the same as, preferable, least correct,* etc., all indicate that *one* response is called for, and that you must select the response which best fits the qualifications in the question.

Time. Sometimes a time limit is set for each section of the examination. If that is the case, follow the time instructions carefully. Your *exam budget* and your watch can help you here. Even if you haven't finished a section when the time limit is up, pass on to the next section. The examination has been planned according to the time schedule.

If the examination paper bears the instruction "Do not turn over page until signal is given," or "Do not start until signal is given," follow the instruction. Otherwise, you may be disqualified.

Pay Close Attention. Be sure you understand what you're doing at all times. Especially in dealing with true-false or multiple-choice questions it's vital that you understand the meaning of every question. It is normal to be working under stress when taking an examination, and it is easy to skip a word or jump to a false conclusion, which may cost you points on the examination. In many multiple-choice and matching questions, the examiners deliberately insert plausible-appearing false answers in order to catch the candidate who is not alert.

Answer clearly. If the examiner who marks your paper cannot understand what you mean, you will not receive credit for your correct answer. On a True-False examination you will not receive any credit for a question which is marked both true and false. If you are asked to underline, be certain that your lines are under and not through the words and that they do not extend beyond them. When using the separate answer sheet it is important *when you decide to change an answer,* you erase the first answer completely. If you leave any graphite from the pencil on the wrong space it will cause the scoring machine to cancel the right answer for that question.

Watch Your "Weights." If the examination is "weighted" it means that some parts of the examination are considered more important than others and rated more highly. For instance, you may find that the instructions will indicate "Part I, Weight 50; Part II, Weight 25, Part III, Weight 25." In such a case, you would devote half of your time to the first part, and divide the second half of your time among Parts II and III.

A Funny Thing . . .

. . . happened to you on your way to the bottom of the totem pole. You *thought* the right answer but you marked the *wrong* one.

1. You *mixed answer symbols*! You decided (rightly) that Baltimore (Choice D) was correct. Then you marked *B* (for Baltimore) instead of *D*.
2. You *misread* a simple instruction! Asked to give the *latest* word in a scrambled sentence, you correctly arranged the sentence, and then marked the letter corresponding to the *earliest* word in that miserable sentence.
3. You *inverted digits!* Instead of the correct number, 96, you wrote (or read) 69.

Funny? Tragic! Stay away from accidents.

Record your answers on the answer sheet one by one as you answer the questions. Care should be taken that these answers are recorded next to the appropriate numbers on your answer sheet. It is poor practice to write your answers first on the test booklet and then to transfer them all at one time to the answer sheet. This procedure causes many errors. And then, how would you feel if you ran out of time before you had a chance to transfer all the answers.

When and How To Guess

Read the directions carefully to determine the scoring method that will be used. In some tests, the directions will indicate that guessing is advisable if you do not know the answer to a question. In such tests, only the right answers are counted in determining your score. If such is the case, don't omit any items. If you do not know the answer, or if you are not sure of your answer, then *guess.*

On the other hand, if the directions state that a scoring formula *will* be used in determining your score or that you are *not to guess,* then *omit* the question if you do not know the answer, or if you are not sure of the answer. When the scoring formula is used, a percentage of the *wrong* answers will be subtracted from the number of *right* answers as a correction for haphazard guessing. It is improbable, therefore, that mere guessing will improve your score significantly. *It may even lower your score.* Another disadvantage in guessing under such circumstances is that it consumes valuable time that you might profitably use in answering the questions you know.

If, however, you are uncertain of the correct answer but have *some* knowledge of the question and are able to eliminate one or more of the answer choices as wrong, your chance of getting the right answer is improved, and it will be to your advantage to *answer* such a question rather than *omit* it.

BEAT THE ANSWER SHEET

Even though you've had plenty of practice with the answer sheet used on machine-scored examinations, we must give you a few more, last-minute pointers.

The present popularity of tests requires the use of electrical test scoring machines. With these machines, scoring which would require the labor of several men for hours can be handled by one man in a fraction of the time.

The scoring machine is an amazingly intricate and helpful device, but the machine is not human. The machine cannot, for example, tell the difference between an intended answer and a stray pencil mark, and will count both indiscriminately. The machine cannot count a pencil mark, if the pencil mark is not brought in contact with the electrodes. For these reasons, specially printed answer sheets with response spaces properly located and properly filled in must be employed. Since not all pencil leads contain the necessary ingredients, a special pencil must be used and a heavy solid mark must be made to indicate answers.

(a) Each pencil mark must be heavy and black. Light marks should be retraced with the special pencil.

(b) Each mark must be in the space between the pair of dotted lines and entirely fill this space.

(c) All stray pencil marks on the paper, clearly not intended as answers, must be completely erased.

(d) Each question must have only one answer indicated. If multiple answers occur, all extraneous marks should be thoroughly erased. Otherwise, the machine will give you *no* credit for your correct answer.

Be sure to use the special electrographic pencil!

HERE'S HOW TO MARK YOUR ANSWERS ON MACHINE-SCORED ANSWER SHEETS:

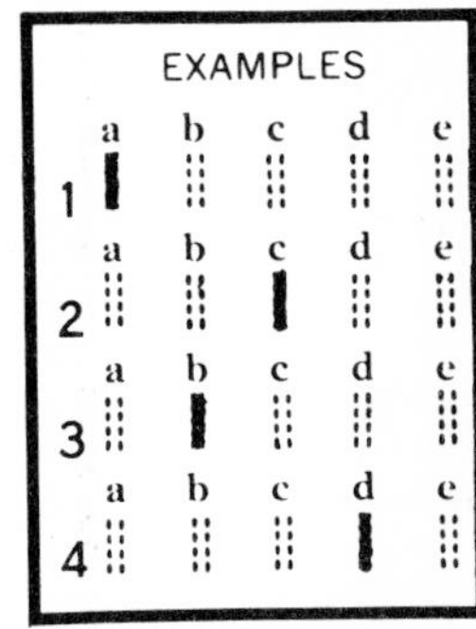

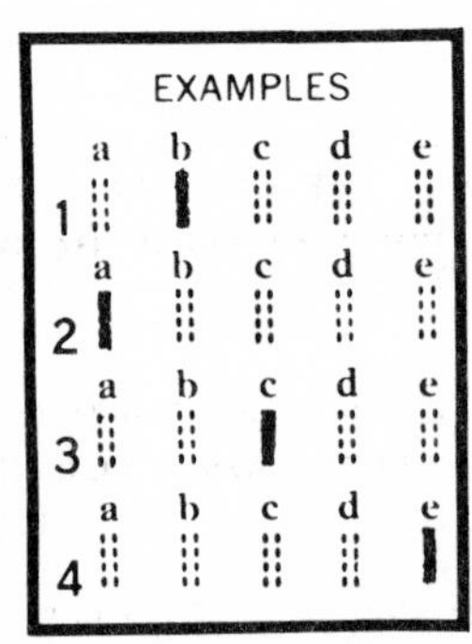

Make only ONE mark for each answer. Additional and stray marks may be counted as mistakes. In making corrections, erase errors COMPLETELY. Make glossy black marks.

Your answer sheet is the only one that reaches the office where papers are scored. For this reason it is important that the blanks at the top be filled in completely and correctly. The proctors will check this, but just in case they slip up, make certain yourself that your paper is complete.

Many exams caution competitors against making any marks on the test booklet itself. Obey that caution even though it goes against your grain to work neatly. If you work neatly and obediently with the test booklet you'll probably do the same with the answer sheet. And that pays off in high scores.

THE GIST OF TEST STRATEGY

- APPROACH THE TEST CONFIDENTLY. TAKE IT CALMLY.
- REMEMBER TO REVIEW, THE WEEK BEFORE THE TEST.
- DON'T "CRAM." BE CAREFUL OF YOUR DIET AND SLEEP . . . ESPECIALLY AS THE TEST DRAWS NIGH.
- ARRIVE ON TIME . . . AND READY.
- CHOOSE A GOOD SEAT. GET COMFORTABLE AND RELAX.
- BRING THE COMPLETE KIT OF "TOOLS" YOU'LL NEED.
- LISTEN CAREFULLY TO ALL DIRECTIONS.
- APPORTION YOUR TIME INTELLIGENTLY WITH AN "EXAM BUDGET."
- READ ALL DIRECTIONS CAREFULLY. TWICE IF NECESSARY. PAY PARTICULAR ATTENTION TO THE SCORING PLAN.
- LOOK OVER THE WHOLE TEST BEFORE ANSWERING ANY QUESTIONS.
- START RIGHT IN, IF POSSIBLE. STAY WITH IT. USE EVERY SECOND EFFECTIVELY.
- DO THE EASY QUESTIONS FIRST; POSTPONE HARDER QUESTIONS UNTIL LATER.
- DETERMINE THE PATTERN OF THE TEST QUESTIONS. IF IT'S HARD-EASY ETC., ANSWER ACCORDINGLY.
- READ EACH QUESTION CAREFULLY. MAKE SURE YOU UNDERSTAND EACH ONE BEFORE YOU ANSWER. RE-READ, IF NECESSARY.
- THINK! AVOID HURRIED ANSWERS. GUESS INTELLIGENTLY.
- WATCH YOUR WATCH AND "EXAM BUDGET," BUT DO A LITTLE BALANCING OF THE TIME YOU DEVOTE TO EACH QUESTION.
- GET ALL THE HELP YOU CAN FROM "CUE" WORDS.
- REPHRASE DIFFICULT QUESTIONS FOR YOURSELF. WATCH OUT FOR "SPOILERS."
- REFRESH YOURSELF WITH A FEW, WELL-CHOSEN REST PAUSES DURING THE TEST.
- USE CONTROLLED ASSOCIATION TO SEE THE RELATION OF ONE QUESTION TO ANOTHER AND WITH AS MANY IMPORTANT IDEAS AS YOU CAN DEVELOP.
- NOW THAT YOU'RE A "COOL" TEST-TAKER, STAY CALM AND CONFIDENT THROUGHOUT THE TEST. DON'T LET ANYTHING THROW YOU.
- EDIT, CHECK, PROOFREAD YOUR ANSWERS. BE A "BITTER ENDER." STAY WORKING UNTIL THEY MAKE YOU GO.

FOR FURTHER STUDY

ARCO BOOKS FOR MORE HELP

Now what? You've read and studied the whole book, and there's still time before you take the test. You're probably better prepared than most of your competitors, but you may feel insecure about one or more of the probable test subjects. If so, you can still do something about it. Glance over this comprehensive list of books written with a view to solving your problems. One of them may be just what you need at this time . . . for the extra help that will assure your success.

ARCO BOOKS FOR TESTS OF ALL TYPES

Countless attractive careers are open to test takers, as you will see from this selective listing of Arco Books. One or more of them can assure success in the test you are now taking. Perhaps you've discovered that you are weak in language, verbal ability or mathematics. You can brush up in the privacy of your own home with a specialized Arco Book. Why flounder and fail when help is so easily available? Perhaps even more important than doing your best on your present test is to consider other opportunities that are open to you. Look over the lists and make plans for your future. You might get a few ideas for other tests you can start to study for *now*. By taking job tests now you place yourself in the enviable position of picking and choosing the *ideal* job. You'll be able to select from several positions. You won't have to settle for the one (or none).

Each of the following books was created under the same expert editorial supervision that produced the excellent book you are now using.

So even though we only list titles and prices, you can be sure that each book performs a real service . . . saves floundering and failure.

Every Arco Book is guaranteed. Return it for full refund in 10 days if not completely satisfied.

Whatever your goal . . . CIVIL SERVICE . . . TRADE LICENSE . . . TEACHING . . . PROFESSIONAL LICENSE . . . SCHOLARSHIP . . . ENTRANCE TO THE SCHOOL OF *YOUR* CHOICE . . . you can achieve it through the PROVEN QUESTION AND ANSWER METHOD.

START YOUR CAREER BY MAILING THIS COUPON TODAY

ORDER NOW from your bookseller or direct from:

ARCO PUBLISHING COMPANY, INC. 219 Park Avenue South, New York, N.Y. 10003

Please Rush The Following Arco Books
(Order by Number or Title)

. . . .

. . . .

. . . .

. . . .

. . . .

. . . .

☐ I enclose check, cash or money order for $__________(price of books, plus 50¢ for first book and 10¢ for each additional book, packing and mailing charge). No C.O.D.'s accepted.

☐ Please tell me if you have an ARCO COURSE for the position of . . . .
(Write in name of position)

. . . .

☐ Please send me your free COMPLETE CATALOG

NAME____

STREET______________________________________

CITY________________**STATE**________________**ZIP #** __________

CIVIL SERVICE AND TEST PREPARATION—GENERAL

Title		Number	Price
Able Seaman, Deckhand, Scowman	______	01376-1	**5.00**
Accountant—Auditor	______	00001-5	**6.00**
Addiction Specialist, Senior, Supervising, Principal, Turner	______	03351-7	**8.00**
Administrative Assistant	______	00148-8	**6.00**
Air Traffic Controller, Turner	______	02088-1	**6.00**
American Foreign Service Officer	______	00081-3	**5.00**
Apprentice, Mechanical Trades	______	00571-8	**5.00**
Assistant Accountant—Junior Accountant—Account Clerk	______	00056-2	**6.00**
Assistant Station Supervisor, Turner	______	03736-9	**6.00**
Attorney, Assistant—Trainee	______	01084-3	**8.00**
Auto Machinist	______	00513-0	**6.00**
Auto Mechanic, Autoserviceman	______	00514-9	**6.00**
Bank Examiner—Trainee and Assistant	______	01642-6	**5.00**
Battalion and Deputy Chief, F.D.	______	00515-7	**6.00**
Beginning Office Worker	______	00173-9	**5.00**
Beverage Control Investigator	______	00150-X	**4.00**
Bookkeeper—Account Clerk, Turner	______	00035-X	**6.00**
Bridge and Tunnel Officer—Special Officer	______	00780-X	**5.00**
Bus Maintainer—Bus Mechanic	______	00111-9	**5.00**
Bus Operator Conductor	______	01553-5	**5.00**
Buyer (Purchase Inspector)	______	01366-4	**4.00**
Captain, Fire Department	______	00121-6	**8.00**
Captain, Police Department	______	00184-4	**8.00**
Carpenter	______	00135-6	**6.00**
Cashier, Housing Teller	______	00703-6	**4.00**
Cement Mason—Mason's Helper, Turner	______	03745-8	**6.00**
Chemist—Assistant Chemist	______	00116-X	**5.00**
City Planner	______	01364-8	**6.00**
Civil Engineer, Senior and Supervising, Turner	______	00146-1	**8.00**
Civil Service Arithmetic and Vocabulary	______	00003-1	**4.00**
Civil Service Handbook	______	00040-6	**1.50**
Claim Examiner—Law Investigator	______	00149-6	**5.00**
Clerk New York City—Clerk Income Maintenance	______	00045-7	**4.00**
Clerk—Steno Transcriber	______	00838-5	**5.00**
College Office Assistant	______	00181-X	**5.00**
Complete Guide to U.S. Civil Service Jobs	______	00537-8	**2.00**
Construction Foreman—Supervisor—Inspector	______	01085-1	**5.00**
Correction Captain—Deputy Warden	______	01358-3	**8.00**
Correction Officer	______	00186-0	**5.00**
Court Officer	______	00519-X	**6.00**
Criminal Law Quizzer, Salottolo	______	02399-6	**10.00**
Criminal Science Quizzer, Salottolo	______	02407-0	**5.00**
Detective Investigator, Turner	______	03738-5	**6.00**
Dietitian	______	00083-X	**5.00**
Draftsman, Civil and Mechanical Engineering (All Grades)	______	01225-0	**6.00**
Electrical Engineer	______	00137-2	**5.00**
Electrical Inspector	______	03350-9	**8.00**
Electrician	______	00084-8	**6.00**
Electronic Equipment Maintainer, Turner	______	01836-4	**6.00**
Elevator Operator	______	00051-1	**3.00**
Employment Interviewer	______	00008-2	**6.00**
Employment Security Clerk	______	00700-1	**5.00**
Engineering Technician (All Grades), Turner	______	01226-9	**6.00**
Exterminator Foreman—Foreman of Housing Exterminators	______	03740-7	**6.00**
Federal Service Entrance Examinations	______	00528-9	**5.00**
File Clerk	______	00962-4	**5.00**
Fire Administration and Technology	______	00604-8	**6.00**
Firefighting Hydraulics, Bonadio	______	00572-6	**7.50**
Fireman, F.D.	______	00010-4	**5.00**
Food Service Supervisor—School Lunch Manager	______	01378-8	**6.00**
Foreman of Auto Mechanics	______	01360-5	**4.00**
Foreman	______	00191-7	**5.00**
Foreman (Tracks) T.A., Turner	______	03739-3	**6.00**
Gardener, Assistant Gardener	______	01340-0	**4.00**
General Entrance Series, Arco Editorial Board	______	01961-1	**4.00**
General Test Practice for 92 U.S. Jobs	______	00011-2	**5.00**
Guard—Patrolman	______	00122-4	**5.00**
Heavy Equipment Operator (Portable Enginer)	______	01372-9	**5.00**
High School Civil Service Course	______	00702-8	**4.00**
Homestudy Course for Civil Service Jobs, Turner	______	01587-X	**5.00**
Hospital Attendant	______	00012-0	**4.00**
Hospital Care Investigator Trainee (Social Case Worker I)	______	01674-4	**5.00**
Hospital Clerk	______	01718-X	**3.00**
Housing Assistant	______	00054-6	**5.00**
Housing Caretaker	______	00504-1	**4.00**
Housing Inspector	______	00055-4	**5.00**
Housing Manager—Assistant Housing Manager	______	00813-X	**5.00**
Housing Patrolman	______	00192-5	**5.00**
Internal Revenue Agent	______	00093-7	**5.00**
Investigator—Inspector	______	01670-1	**5.00**
Janitor—Custodian	______	00013-9	**6.00**
Junior Administrator Development Examination (JADE)	______	01643-4	**5.00**
Junior and Assistant Civil Engineer	______	01228-5	**5.00**
Junior Federal Assistant	______	01729-5	**5.00**
Laboratory Aide, Arco Editorial Board	______	01121-1	**5.00**
Laborer—Federal, State and City Jobs	______	00566-1	**4.00**
Landscape Architect	______	01368-0	**5.00**
Laundry Worker	______	01834-8	**4.00**
Law and Court Stenographer	______	00783-4	**6.00**
Law Enforcement Positions	______	00500-9	**6.00**
Librarian	______	00060-0	**4.00**
Lieutenant, F.D.	______	00123-2	**8.00**
Lieutenant, P.D.	______	00190-9	**8.00**
Machinist—Machinist's Helper	______	01123-8	**6.00**
Mail Handler—U.S. Postal Service	______	00126-7	**5.00**
Maintainer's Helper, Group A and C—Transit Electrical Helper	______	00175-5	**6.00**
Maintenance Man	______	00113-5	**5.00**
Management and Administration Quizzer	______	01537-3	**6.00**
Mathematics, Simplified and Self-Taught	______	00567-X	**4.00**
Mechanical Apprentice (Maintainer's Helper B)	______	00176-3	**5.00**
Mechanical Aptitude and Spatial Relations Tests	______	00539-4	**5.00**
Mechanical Engineer—Junior, Assistant & Senior Grades	______	03314-2	**8.00**
Messenger	______	00017-1	**3.00**
Mortuary Caretaker	______	01354-0	**4.00**
Motor Vehicle License Examiner	______	00018-X	**5.00**
Motor Vehicle Operator	______	00576-9	**4.00**
Motorman (Subways)	______	00061-9	**6.00**
Nurse	______	00143-7	**6.00**
Office Assistant GS 1-4 Office Aide	______	00043-0	**5.00**
Office Machines Operator	______	00728-1	**4.00**
1540 Questions and Answers for Electricians	______	00754-0	**5.00**
1340 Questions and Answers for Firefighters, McGannon	______	00857-1	**4.00**
Operations and Maintenance Trainee	______	01241-2	**4.00**
Painter	______	01772-4	**5.00**
Parking Enforcement Agent	______	00701-X	**4.00**
Patrol Inspector	______	00101-1	**4.00**
Peace Corps Placement Exams, Turner	______	01641-8	**4.00**
Personnel Examiner, Junior Personnel Examiner	______	00648-X	**6.00**
Plumber—Plumber's Helper	______	00517-3	**6.00**
Police Administration and Criminal Investigation	______	00565-3	**6.00**
Police Administrative Aide, Turner	______	02345-7	**5.00**
Police Officer—Trainee P.D, Murray	______	00019-8	**5.00**
Police Science Advancement—Police Promotion Course	______	02636-7	**10.00**
Policewoman	______	00062-7	**5.00**
Post Office Clerk-Carrier	______	00021-X	**4.00**
Post Office Motor Vehicle Operator	______	01162-9	**4.00**
Postal Inspector	______	00194-1	**5.00**
Postal Promotion Foreman—Supervisor	______	00538-6	**6.00**
Postal Service Officer	______	01658-2	**5.00**
Postmaster	______	01522-5	**5.00**
Practice for Civil Service Promotion	______	00023-6	**6.00**
Practice for Clerical, Typing and Stenographic Tests	______	00005-8	**5.00**
Principal Clerk—Stenographer	______	01523-3	**5.00**

Title		Order No.	Price
Probation and Parole Officer	______	01542-X	6.00
Professional and Administrative Career Examination (PACE)	______	03653-2	6.00
Professional Career Tests	______	01543-8	5.00
Professional Trainee—Administrative Aide	______	01183-1	5.00
Public Health Sanitarian	______	00985-3	6.00
Railroad Clerk	______	00067-8	4.00
Railroad Porter	______	00128-3	4.00
Real Estate Assessor—Appraiser—Manager	______	00563-7	6.00
Resident Building Superintendent	______	00068-6	5.00
Road Car Inspector (T.A.), Turner	______	03743-1	6.00
Sanitation Foreman (Foreman & Asst. Foreman)	______	01958-1	5.00
Sanitation Man	______	00025-2	4.00
School Crossing Guard	______	00611-0	4.00
Securing and Protecting Your Rights in Civil Service, Resnicoff	______	02714-2	4.95
Senior Clerical Series	______	01173-4	5.00
Senior Clerk—Stenographer	______	01797-X	6.00
Senior File Clerk, Turner	______	00124-0	5.00
Senior and Supervising Parking Enforcement Agent, Turner	______	03737-7	6.00
Sergeant, P.D.	______	00026-0	7.00
Shop Clerk, Turner	______	03684-2	6.00
Social Case Worker, Turner	______	01528-4	6.00
Social Supervisor	______	00028-7	6.00
Staff Attendant	______	00828-8	4.00
Staff Positions: Senior Administrative Associate and Assistant	______	03490-4	6.00
State Trooper	______	00078-3	5.00
Statistician—Statistical Clerk	______	00058-9	5.00
Stenographer—Typist (Practical Preparation)	______	00147-X	4.00
Stenographer—U.S. Government Positions	______	00031-7	6.00
Storekeeper—Stockman	______	01691-4	5.00
Structural Apprentice, Turner	______	00177-1	5.00
Structure Maintainer Trainee, Groups A to E, Turner	______	03683-4	6.00
Supervising Clerk—Income Maintenance	______	02879-3	6.00
Supervising Clerk—Stenographer	______	01685-X	5.00
Supervision Course	______	01590-X	5.00
Surface Line Dispatcher	______	00140-2	6.00
Tabulating Machine Operator (IBM)	______	00781-8	4.00
Taking Tests and Scoring High, Honig	______	01347-8	3.00
Telephone Operator	______	00033-3	5.00
Telephone Maintainer, Turner	______	03742-3	6.00
Test Your Vocational Aptitude, Gladstone	______	03606-0	3.00
Towerman (Municipal Subway System)	______	00157-7	5.00
Trackman (Municipal Subways), Turner	______	00075-9	5.00
Traffic Control Agent	______	03421-1	5.00
Train Dispatcher	______	00158-5	5.00
Transit Patrolman	______	00092-9	5.00
Transit Sergeant—Lieutenant	______	00161-5	4.00
Treasury Enforcement Agent	______	00131-3	6.00
U.S. Professional Mid-Level Positions Grades GS-9 Through GS-12	______	02036-9	4.00
U.S. Summer Jobs, Turner	______	02480-1	4.00
Ventilation and Drainage Maintainer, Turner	______	03741-5	6.00
Vocabulary Builder and Guide to Verbal Tests	______	00535-1	4.00
Vocabulary, Spelling and Grammar	______	00077-5	4.00
Welder	______	01374-5	5.00
X-Ray Technician	______	0112%-X	3.00

MILITARY EXAMINATION SERIES

Title		Order No.	Price
Practice for the Army Qualification Battery	______	01301-X	5.00
Practice for the Armed Forces Tests	______	00063-5	5.00
Practice for the Navy's Basic Test Battery	______	01300-1	5.00
Practice for the Women's Placement Test	______	01303-6	4.00
Practice for Air Force Placement Tests	______	01302-8	5.00
Practice for Officer Candidate Tests	______	01304-4	5.00
U.S. Service Academy Admission Tests	______	01544-6	4.00